LEGAL FOUNDATIONS
OF THE WELFARE STATE

LAW IN CONTEXT

Editors: Robert Stevens (Haverford College, Pennsylvania), William Twining (University College, London) and Christopher McCrudden (Lincoln College, Oxford)

ALREADY PUBLISHED

Accidents, Compensation and the Law (Third Edition), P. S. Atiyah
Company Law and Capitalism (Second Edition), Tom Hadden
Karl Llewellyn and the Realist Movement, William Twining
Cases and Materials on the English Legal System (Fourth Edition),
  Michael Zander
Computers and the Law, Colin Tapper
Tribunals and Government, J. A. Farmer
Government and Law (Second Edition), T. C. Hartley and J. A. G.
  Griffith
Land, Law and Planning, Patrick McAuslan
Landlord and Tenant (Second Edition), Martin Partington
How to do Things with Rules (Second Edition), William Twining and
  David Miers
Evidence, Proof and Probability (Second Edition), Richard Eggleston
Family Law and Social Policy (Second Edition), John Eekelaar
Consumers and the Law (Second Edition), Ross Cranston
Law and Politics, Robert Stevens
Obscenity, Geoffrey Robertson
Labour Law (Second Edition), Paul Davies and Mark Freedland
Charities, Trusts and Social Welfare, Michael Chesterman
The Law-Making Process, Michael Zander
An Introduction to Law (Second Edition), Phil Harris
Sentencing and Penal Policy, Andrew Ashworth
Law and Administration, Carol Harlow and Richard Rawlings

Legal Foundations of the Welfare State

ROSS CRANSTON

WEIDENFELD AND NICOLSON
London

George Weidenfeld and Nicolson Ltd
91 Clapham High Street, London sw4 7ta

ISBN 0 297 78487 0 cased
ISBN 0 297 78534 6 paperback

Photoset by Deltatype, Ellesmere Port
Printed by Butler & Tanner Ltd
Frome and London

CONTENTS

Cases   vii
Statutes   xxv
Preface   xxxv

Chapter 1   Introduction   1

PART I   THE INDIVIDUAL AND THE LAW   11

Chapter 2   The Historical Background   13
             I   Civil Rights   16
             II Political Rights   26
             III Social Rights   29
             IV Conclusion   44

Chapter 3   The Individual and the Law   46
             I   The Administration of the Law   48
             II The Unequal Utilization of Legal Services   58
             III The Substance of the Law   65
             IV Publicly Funded Legal Services   81
             V   Conclusion   98

PART II   THE WELFARE STATE   101

Chapter 4   Social Welfare Regulation   103
             I   The Emergence of Social Welfare Regulation   105
             II The Legal Form of Social Welfare Regulation   120
             III Implementation   131
             IV The Role of the Courts   144
             V   The Impact of Social Welfare Regulation   152
             VI Conclusion   160

Chapter 5   Social Welfare Benefits   163
             I   The Juridical Nature of Social Welfare Legislation 165
             II Social Control Through Social Welfare
                 Legislation   191
             III The Social Context of Benefit Administration   209
             IV Conclusion   229

Chapter 6   The Provision of Public Services   232
              I   *The Paradox of Social Welfare Bureaucracies*   232
              II *Legal Control of Social Welfare Bureaucracies*   246
              III *Participation and Social Welfare Bureaucracies*   264
              IV *Universal Public Services*   269
              V   *Conclusion*   273

PART III SOCIAL CHANGE   275

Chapter 7   Social Change and the Legal System   277
              I   *Models of Social Change*   277
              II *The Role of the Legal System*   286
              III *Social Change Through the Courts*   301
              IV *The Record of Social Change*   310
              V   *Conclusion*   322

Chapter 8   Conclusion   324

              Notes   340
              References   396
              Index   449

CASES

A Common Soldier's Case (1752) 95 E.R. 646   349
Adriatic Terrazzo & Foundations Pty Ltd v. *Robinson, Owens and Australian Building & Construction Workers' Federation* (1972) 4 S.A.S.R. 294   391
Airey v. *Ireland* (1979) 2 E.H.R.R. 305   358
Alden v. *Gaglardi* (1973) 30 D.L.R. (3d) 760; (1971) 15 D.L.R. (3d) 380   392
Aldrington Garages Ltd v. *Fielder* (1979) 37 P. & C.R. 461; (1978) 247 E.G. 557   368
Allen v. *Jambo Holdings Ltd* [1980] 2 All E.R. 502; [1980] 1 W.L.R. 1252   351
American Cyanamid Co. v. *Ethicon Ltd* [1975] A.C. 396   53
Annison v. *District Auditor for St Pancras Borough Council* [1962] 1 Q.B. 489   385
Anns v. *Merton London Borough Council* [1978] A.C. 728   385
Argersinger v. *Hamlin* 407 U.S. 25 (1972)   358
Armory v. *Delamirie* (1722) 93 E.R. 664   19
Arrowsmith v. *Dickenson* (1888) 20 Q.B.D. 252   347
Artico v. *Italy* (1980) 3 E.H.R.R. 1   358
Asco Developments Ltd v. *Gordon* [1978] 248 E.G. 683   356
Asher v. *Lacey* [1973] 3 All E.R. 1008; [1973] 1 W.L.R. 1412   386
Asher v. *Secretary of State for the Environment* [1974] Ch. 208   386
Ashley v. *Ashley* [1968] P. 582   340
Attorney-General Canada v. *McCombe* [1978] 2 F.C. 746   371
Attorney-General of Canada v. *Mercier* [1977] 2 F.C. 389   377
Attorney-General v. *Bermondsey Guardians* (1924) 40 T.L.R. 512   379
Attorney-General v. *Birmingham C.C.* (1858) 70 E.R. 220   362
Attorney-General v. *Cockermouth Local Board* (1874) L.R. 18 Eq. 172   367
Attorney-General v. *Guardians of Poor of Union of Dorking* (1882) 20 Ch.D. 595   367
Attorney-General v. *Guardians of the Poor of the Merthyr Tydfil Union* [1900] 1 Ch. 516   206, 348, 378
Attorney-General v. *Guardians of the Poor Law Union of Tynemouth* [1930] 1 Ch. 616   348
Attorney-General v. *Leeds Corporation* (1870) 5 Ch.App. 583   367
Attorney-General v. *The Mayor, Aldermen and Corporation of Kingston-on-Thames* (1865) 12 L.T. 665; 34 L.J. Ch. 481   367
Attorney-General v. *Poplar Guardians* (1924) 40 T.L.R. 752   379
Attorney-General, ex rel. Tilley v. *Wandsworth London Borough Council* [1981] 1 All E.R. 1162; [1981] 1 W.L.R. 854   370, 386
Austin v. *The Vestry of the Parish of St Mary, Lambeth* (1858) 27 L.J. Ch. 388   366
Avon County Council v. *Howlett* [1983] 1 All E.R. 1073; [1983] 1 W.L.R. 605   382
Backhouse v. *Backhouse* [1978] 1 W.L.R. 243; [1978] 1 All E.R. 1158   341
Backhouse v. *Lambeth London Borough Council* (1972) 116 Sol.J. 802   386
Baker-Chaput v. *Cammett* 406 F.Supp. 1134 (1976)   370

Ballarat Trustees Executors and Agency Co. Ltd v. *Federal Commissioner of
   Taxation* (1950) 80 C.L.R. 350   341
Bannister and Legal Practitioners Ordinance, 1970–1975; ex parte Hartstein, Re
   (1975) 5 A.C.T.R. 100   359
Barnes v. *Commonwealth of Australia* (1937) 37 S.R.(N.S.W.) 511   386
Barnet Union v. *Tilbury* (1909) 73 J.P. 466; 7 L.G.R. 993   350
Barnett v. *Laskey* (1899) 68 L.J.Q.B. 55   366
Barns v. *Guardians of St Mary, Islington* (1912) 76 J.P. 11   345
Barrass v. *Reeve* [1980] 3 All E.R. 705; [1981] 1 W.L.R. 408   381
Barringer v. *The Council of the Municipality of Nyngan* (1953) 86 C.L.R. 495   363
Barrs v. *Bethell* [1982] Ch. 294   385
Basic Wage, Margins and Total Wage Cases of 1966 (1966) 115 C.A.R. 93   362
Batterton v. *Francis* 432 U.S. 416 (1977)   378, 379
Battle v. *Municipal Housing Authority for the City of Yonkers* 53 F.R.D. 423
   (1971)   384
Beach v. *Reed Corrugated Cases Ltd* [1956] 2 All E.R. 652; [1956] 1 W.L.R.
   807   374
Beames and Director-General of Social Services, Re (1981) 3 A.L.N. No.50   370
Becraft v. *Strobel* 10 N.E. 2d 560 (1937)   81
Belcher v. *Reading Corporation* [1950] Ch. 380   384
Bethel, Re (1971) 17 D.L.R. (3d) 652   341
Bevington v. *Crawford* (1974) 232 E.G. 191   368
Biddulph v. *The Vestry of St George's, Hanover Square* (1863) 8 L.T. 558   366
Bird v. *O'Neal* [1960] A.C. 907   391
Blackburn and Director-General of Social Services, Re (1982) 4 A.L.N.
   No. 46   370, 376
Blackpool Corporation v. *Locker* [1948] 1 K.B. 349   213
Bland v. *Chief Supplementary Benefit Officer* [1983] 1 All E.R. 537; [1983] 1
   W.L.R. 262   373
Bloomfield v. *Supplementary Benefits Commission* (1978) 123 Sol.J. 33   178
Boaks v. *Associated Newspapers Ltd* (1968) 118 N.L.J. 181; (1967) 111
   Sol.J. 703   224
Board of Social Welfare v. *Los Angeles County* 162 P.2d 630 (1945)   375
Boddie v. *State of Connecticut* 401 U.S. 371 (1971)   90
Booth v. *Woods* (1925) 41 Sh.Ct.Rep. 85   391
Borradale v. *Davenport* [1958] V.R. 470   357
Bowman v. *Frost* 158 S.W. 2d 945 (1942)   375
Brabenec and Director-General of Social Services, Re (1981) 3 A.L.N. No. 39   378
Bradbury v. *Enfield London Borough Council* [1967] 3 All E.R. 434; [1967] 1
   W.L.R. 1311   388
Brikom Investments Ltd v. *Seaford* [1981] 2 All E.R. 783; [1981] 1 W.L.R.
   863   356
Bristol City Council v. *Rawlins* (1977) 76 L.G.R. 166; (1977) 34 P.&.C.R.
   12   384, 385

Bristol District Council v. *Clark* [1975] 3 All E.R. 976 [1975] 1 W.L.R.
  1443   383, 384
British Anzani (Felixstowe) Ltd v. *International Marine Management (UK)*
  Ltd [1980] Q.B. 137   356
Broggi v. *Robins* (1898) 14 T.L.R. 439   355
Bromley London Borough Council v. *Greater London Council* [1982] 1 All E.R.
  129; [1982] 2 W.L.R. 62   385, 386
Brown v. *Board of Education of Topeka* 347 U.S. 483 (1954)   291, 307, 320
Brown v. *Southall Realty Company* 237 A. 2d 834 (1968)   365
Buhagiar and Director-General of Social Services, Re (1981) 4 A.L.D. 113   382
Burston Finance Ltd v. *Wilkins* (1975) 240 E.G. 375   391
Bushell v. *Secretary of State for the Environment* [1981] A.C. 75   368
Calder v. *Minister of Employment and Immigration* [1980] 1 F.C. 842   382
Califano v. *Westcott* 443 U.S. 76 (1979)   390
Califano v. *Yamasaki* 442 U.S. 682 (1979)   382
Callemeyn v. *Belgian State* [1974] E.C.R. 553, 561   369
Camden Nominees Ltd v. *Forcey* [1940] Ch. 352   79
Cameron v. *Holt* (1980) 54 A.L.J.R. 202; 28 A.L.R. 490   381
Canadian Pacific Ltd v. *Gill and Aujla* [1973] S.C.R. 654   180
Cannock Chase District Council v. *Kelly* [1978] 1 All E.R. 152; [1978] 1
  W.L.R. 1   384
Cantrell v. *The Guardians of the Poor of the Windsor Union* (1838) 132 E.R.
  822   386
Cardiff v. *Bismarck Public School District* 263 N.W. 2d 105 (1978)   388
*Cardinal and Director of Family Benefits Branch of Ministry of Community and
  Social Services, Re* (1981) 32 O.R. (2d) 65   372
Carlton Main Colliery Co. Ltd v. *Hemsworth Rural District Council* [1922] 1
  Ch. 521   367
Carson v. *Pickersgill & Sons* (1885) 14 Q.B.D. 859   358
Chambers and Director-General of Social Services, Re (1981) 1 S.S.R. 15   378
Chatsworth Properties Ltd v. *Effiom* [1971] 1 All E.R. 604; [1971] 1
  W.L.R. 144   393
Cheley v. *Burson* 324 F. Supp. 678 (1971)   377
Chester v. *Bateson* [1920] 1 K.B. 829   345
Chesterfield Football Club Ltd v. *Secretary of State for Social Services* [1973]
  Q.B. 583   371
Chorley Borough Council v. *Barratt Developments (North West) Ltd* [1979] 3
  All E.R. 634   341
City of Los Angeles, Department of Water and Power v. *Manhart* 435 U.S. 702
  (1978)   374
City of New York v. *Miln* 11 Pet. 102 (U.S. S.Ct. 1837)   80
Clark v. *Joslin* (1873) 27 L.T. 762   348
Clark v. *Universal Builders, Inc.* 501 F. 2d 324 (1974)   393
Clarke v. *Taff-Ely B.C. The Times,* 1 April 1980, p.3   384

Clear v. *Smith* [1981] 1 W.L.R. 399   381
Cocks v. *Thanet District Council* [1982] 3 All E.R. 1135; [1982] 3 W.L.R.
    1121   387
Cohen v. *Black* [1942] 2 All E.R. 299; 58 T.L.R. 306   354
Commercial Bank of Australia Ltd v. *Amadio* (1983) 46 A.L.R. 402   341
Commonwealth of Australia v. *Burns* [1971] V.R. 825   382
Commonwealth v. *Hunt* 38 Am.Dec. 346 (1842)   342
Cook v. *Imperial Tobacco Company* [1922] 2 K.B. 158   357
Cooper v. *Martin* (1803) 102 E.R. 759   347
Cooper v. *Wandsworth Board of Works* (1863) 143 E.R. 414   367
Costa v. *Belgian State* [1974] E.C.R. 1251, 1260–1   369
Coulson v. *Davidson* (1906) 96 L.T. 20   347
County of Contra Costa v. *Social Welfare Board* 40 Cal.Rptr. 605 (1964)   377
Coventry City Council v. *Cartwright* [1975] 2 All E.R. 99; [1975] 1 W.L.R.
    845   122
Coventry City Council v. *Doyle* [1981] 2 All E.R. 184; [1981] 1 W.L.R.
    1325   363
Cowart v. *Schweiker* 662 F. 2d 731 (1981)   371
Cowell v. *Taylor* (1886) 31 Ch.D. 34   357
Crake v. *Supplementary Benefits Commission* [1982] 1 All E.R. 498   372, 375
Cresswell v. *Potter* [1978] 1 W.L.R. 255   341
Crewe v. *Social Security Commissioner (Anderson)* [1982] 2 All E.R. 745;
    [1982] 1 W.L.R. 1209   378
Daish v. *Wauton* [1972] 2 Q.B. 262   373
Dallialian v. *Canada Employment and Immigration Commission* (1980) 33
    N.R. 118   380
Dandridge v. *Williams* 397 U.S. 471 (1970)   292, 392
Daniel v. *Belton* (1968) 12 F.L.R. 101   354
De Falco v. *Crawley Borough Council* [1980] Q.B. 460   387
Delahaye v. *Oswestry Borough Council, The Times,* 29 July 1980   387
De Lima and Minister of Community and Social Services, Re (1973) 35 D.L.R.
    (3d) 481; (1973) 2 O.R. 821   376
Demuren v. *Seal Estates Ltd* (1978) 249 E.G. 440; [1979] J.P.L. 462   151
DeWolf & Johnston v. *City of Halifax and Welfare Committee of City of
    Halifax* (1980) 37 N.S.R. (2d) 259   394
Dick v. *Deputy Attorney-General of Canada* (1980) 6 W.W.R. 431   383
Dimery v. *Department of Social Services of the State of Iowa* 320 F.Supp. 1125
    (1969); 398 U.S. 322 (1970)   377
Din v. *Wandsworth London Borough Council* [1981] 3 All E.R. 881; [1981] 3
    W.L.R. 918   387
Director-General of Social Security v. *Harris* (1982) 44 A.L.R. 645   382
Director-General of Social Services v. *Chaney* (1980) 31 A.L.R. 571   373
Director-General of Social Services v. *Hangan* (1982) 45 A.L.R. 23   382
Drane v. *Evangelou* [1978] 2 All E.R. 437; [1978] 1 W.L.R. 455   138, 356, 366

Dudley and District Benefit Building Society v. *Emerson* [1949] Ch. 707   393
Dunbar v. *Guardians of the Poor of the Ardee Union* [1897] 2 I.R. 76   345
Dunster v. *Hollis* [1918] 2 K.B. 795   355
Duport Steels Ltd v. *Sirs* [1980] 1 All E.R. 529; [1980] 1 W.L.R. 142   392
Dyer v. *London School Board* [1902] 2 Ch. 768   388
Dyson v. *Kerrier District Council* [1980] 3 All E.R. 313; [1980] 1 W.L.R.
1205   987
Eckersley v. *Secretary of State for the Environment* (1977) 76 L.G.R. 245;
(1977) 34 P.&C.R. 124   364
Edwards (Inspector of Taxes) v. *Bairstow* [1956] A.C. 14   373
Edwards v. *California* 314 U.S. 160 (1941)   26
Edwards v. *Habib* 397 F.2d 687 (1968)   365
Elliott v. *Southwark London Borough Council* [1976] 2 All E.R. 781; [1976]
1 W.L.R. 499   364, 368
Ellis and Ministry of Community and Social Services, Re (1980) 28 O.R. (2d)
385   372
Errington v. *Minister of Health* [1935] 1 K.B. 249   367
Escalera v. *New York City Housing Authority* 425 F.2d 853 (1970); 400 U.S.
853 (1970)   385
Etim v. *Hatfield* [1975] Crim.L.Rev. 234   381
Evans v. *Collins* [1965] 1 Q.B. 580   384
Ex parte Cornford; Re The Minister for Education (1962) 62 S.R.(N.S.W.)
220   388
Ex parte H.V. McKay (1907) 2 C.A.R. 1   362
Ex parte Martin (1826) 108 E.R. 382   348
Ex parte Whitchurch (1881) 6 Q.B.D. 545   366
F.F.F. Estates Ltd v. *Hackney London Borough Council* [1981] 1 Q.B. 503   363
Fairmount Investments Ltd v. *Secretary of State for the Environment* [1976] 2
All E.R. 856; [1976] 1 W.L.R. 1255   368
Farrell v. *Alexander* [1977] A.C. 59   364
Finlay v. *Director of Welfare (Winnipeg South/West)* (1978) 29 R.F.L. 395   382
Flemming v. *Nestor* 363 U.S. 603 (1960)   374
Ford Motor Co. Ltd v. *Amalgamated Union of Engineering and Foundry
Workers* [1969] 2 Q.B. 303   374
Forde v. *Skinner* (1830) 172 E.R. 687   345
Foxley v. *Olton* [1965] 2 Q.B. 306   370
Franklin v. *Minister of Town and Country Planning* [1948] A.C. 87   367
Fredman v. *Minister of Health* (1936) 154 L.T. 240   367
Freeman v. *Minister of Pensions and National Insurance* [1966] 2 All E.R. 40;
[1966] 1 W.L.R. 456   381
Frilli v. *Belgian State* [1972] E.C.R. 457   369
Frost (Inspector of Taxes) v. *Feltham* [1981] S.T.C. 115   372
Fry v. *Lane* (1889) 40 Ch.D. 312   341
Furmage v. *Social Security Commission* (1980) 2 N.Z.A.R. 75   375
Garland v. *British Rail Engineering Ltd* [1982] 1 C.M.L.R. 696   374

Garlick v. Knottingley Urban District Council (1904) 68 J.P. 494; 2 L.G.R.
  1345   361
Gateshead Union v. Durham County Council [1918] 1 Ch. 146   388
Gautreaux v. Chicago Housing Authority 296 F.Supp. 907 (1969)   390
Gideon v. Wainwright 372 U.S. 335 (1963)   303, 358
Glasgow Corporation v. Kelly [1951] 1 T.L.R. 345   381
Glossop v. Heston and Isleworth Local Board (1879) 12 Ch.D. 102   367
Goldberg v. Kelly 397 U.S. 254 (1970)   181, 220, 373, 390, 394
Gonzales v. C.P.A.M. Var [1976] 11 J.C.P. 18224   378
Gospavich v. Gospavich (1972) 5 R.F.L. 369   377
Gouriet v. Union of Post Office Workers [1978] A.C. 435   356, 365
Graham v. Baker (1961) 106 C.L.R. 340   374
Gray v. Scanlan (1924) 41 Sh.Ct.Rep. 3   391
Great Western Railway Company v. Bishop (1872) L.R. 7 Q.B. 550   361
Greater London Council v. Connolly [1970] 2 Q.B. 100   393
Green v. Daniels (1977) 13 A.L.R. 1; (1977) 51 A.L.J.R.
  463   322, 371, 380, 394
Guardians of Birkenhead Union v. Brookes (1906) 95 L.T. 359; 22 T.L.R.
  583   33
Guardians of Pontypridd Union v. Drew [1927] 1 K.B. 214   348
Guardians of the Poor of Fulham Parish v. Guardians of the Poor of Woolwich
  Union [1907] A.C. 255   346
Guardians of the Poor of Plymouth v. Gibbs [1903] 1 K.B. 177   348
Guardians of the Poor of the West Ham Union v. Ovens (1872) L.R. 8 Exch.
  37   33
Guardians of the Poor of the Wycombe Union v. Guardians of the Poor of the Eton
  Union (1857) 156 E.R. 1377   346, 349
Guarino v. Celebrezze 336 F.2d 336 (1964)   374
Guthrie v. Stewart [1926] S.C. 743   391
Hackney London Borough Council v. Ezedinma [1981] 3 All E.R. 438   363
Hameed v. Hussain (1977) 242 E.G. 1063   389
Hanlon v. The Law Society [1980] 2 All E.R. 199; [1980] 2 W.L.R. 756   358
Hargreaves v. Taylor (1863) 122 E.R. 230   367
Harris and Ministry of Community and Social Services, Re (1975) 8 O.R. (2d)
  721, 59 D.L.R. (3d) 169   382
Harris v. McRae 448 U.S. 297 (1980)   351
Harrison v. Hammersmith and Fulham London Borough Council [1981] 2 All
  E.R. 588; [1981] 1 W.L.R. 650   385
Hart v. Windsor (1843) 152 E.R. 1114   355
Hays v. Bryant (1789) 126 E.R. 147   347
Heidleberg v. Lynn 34 Am.Dec. 566 (1840)   342
Hesketh v. Birmingham Corporation [1924] 1 K.B. 260   367
Hewitt v. Rowlands (1924) 93 L.J.K.B. 1080   355
Hibbs v. Neighbourhood Organization to Rejuvenate Tenant Housing 252 A.2d
  622 (1969)   391

Hillbank Properties Ltd v. *Hackney London Borough Council* [1978]
    Q.B. 998   364, 368
Hines v. *Winters* 320 P.2d. 1114 (1937)   346
Holland v. *Peacock* [1912] 1 K.B. 154   344
Holmes v. *New York City Housing Authority* 398 F.2d. 262 (1968)   384
Hooper v. *Eaglestone* (1977) 34 P.& C.R. 311   356
Hopwood v. *Cannock Chase District Council* [1975] 1 All E.R. 796; [1975] 1
    W.L.R. 373   384
Horford Investments Ltd v. *Lambert* [1976] Ch. 39   368
Horn v. *Minister of Health* [1937] 1 K.B. 164   367
Housing Commission of N.S.W. v. *Allen* (1967) 69 S.R.(N.S.W.) 190   384
Hubbard v. *Pitt* [1976] Q.B. 142   298
Hulley v. *Thompson* [1981] 1 All E.R. 1128; [1981] 1 W.L.R. 159   377
Humphrey and Ontario Housing Corporation, Re (1979) 23 O.R. (2d) 583   384
In re C(L) (An Infant) [1965] 2 Q.B. 449   381
In re Campden Charities (1881) 18 Ch.D. 310   350
In re Decision of Walker [1944] K.B. 644   385
In re Marriage of Shore 139 Cal.Rptr. 349 (1977)   377
Islam v. *London Borough of Hillingdon* [on appeal from *R.* v. *Hillingdon
    London Borough Council, ex parte Islam (Tafazzul)*] [1981] 3 All E.R.
    901; [1981] 3 W.L.R. 942   387
Javins v. *First National Reality Corporation* 428 F.2d. 1071 (1970); 400
    U.S. 925 (1970)   357
Jay v. *United States Department of Agriculture* 308 F.Supp. 100 (1969); 441
    F.2d. 574 (1971)   394
Jefferson v. *Hackney* 406 U.S. 535 (1972)   390, 392
Jeune v. *Queens Cross Properties Ltd* [1974] Ch. 97   355
Kamara v. *Director of Public Prosecutions* [1974] A.C. 104   392
Keates v. *The Earl of Cadogan* (1851) 138 E.R. 234   355
Kenny v. *Preen* [1963] 1 Q.B. 499   356
Kerner v. *Flemming* 283 F.2d. 916 (1960)   371
Kerr v. *Bryde* [1923] A.C. 16   297, 391
King v. *Smith* 392 U.S. 309 (1968)   292, 376, 393
Krebs v. *Minister of National Revenue* [1978] 1 F.C. 205   372
Lambe v. *Director-General of Social Services* (1981) 38 A.L.R. 405   375
Lambert v. *Ealing London Borough Council* [1982] 1 W.L.R. 550; [1982] 2
    All E.R. 394   387
Lambeth London Borough Council v. *Secretary of State for Social Services* (1980)
    79 L.G.R. 61   386
Lambeth London Borough Council v. *Stubbs* (1980) 78 L.G.R. 650   363
Lambeth London Borough Council v. *Udechuka* (1980) 79 L.G.R. 1   384
Lassiter v. *Department of Social Services of Durham County, North Carolina*
    452 U.S. 18 (1981)   358

Le Blanc v. *Board of Education for City of Hamilton* (1962) 35 D.L.R. (2d)
  548   388
Le Clair v. *O'Neil* 307 F.Supp. 621 (1969)   380
Ledwith v. *Roberts* [1937] 1 K.B. 232   354
Lee v. *Department of Education and Science* (1967) 66 L.G.R. 211; (1967)
  111 Sol.J. 756   388
Lee v. *Enfield London Borough Council* (1967) 66 L.G.R. 195; (1967) 111
  Sol.J. 772   388
Lee-Parker v. *Izzet* [1971] 3 All E.R. 1099; [1971] 1 W.L.R. 1688   356
Legal Services Commission of New South Wales v. *Stephens* [1981] 2
  N.S.W.L.R. 697   357
Lemieux et al. v. *Unemployment Insurance Commission* [1977] 2 F.C. 246   383
Lewis v. *Martin* 397 U.S. 552 (1970)   376
Lillystone v. *Supplementary Benefits Commission, The Times*, 30 October 1981 371
Lincoln v. *Hayman* [1982] 1 W.L.R. 488   373
Liverpool City Council v. *Irwin* [1977] A.C. 239   239, 242, 295, 355, 384
Lloyds Bank Ltd v. *Bundy* [1975] 1 Q.B. 326   354
Local Government Board v. *Arlidge* [1915] A.C. 120   147, 367
Logsdon v. *Booth* [1900] 1 Q.B. 401   361
London Borough of Redbridge v. *Perry* (1976) 75 L.G.R. 90; (1976) 33 P.&
  C.R. 176   363
Luby v. *Newcastle-under-Lyme Corporation* [1965] 1 Q.B. 214   384
M.H.W. v. *Caines* (1973) C.C.H. 6167   371
Magarrill v. *The Overseers of the Townships of Whitehaven & Preston Quarter*
  (1885) 16 Q.B.D. 242   346
Maher v. *Roe* 432 U.S. 464 (1977)   351
Manigo v. *New York City Housing Authority* 273 N.Y.S. 2d. 1003 (1966);
  279 N.Y.S. 2d. 1014 (1967); 389 U.S. 1008 (1967)   384
Martins v. *Minister of National Health and Welfare* [1979] 1 F.C. 347; 92
  D.L.R. (3d) 767   373
Mason v. *Skilling* [1974] 3 All E.R. 977; [1974] 1 W.L.R. 1437   364
Master Builders' Association of N.S.W. v. *Australian Building Construction
  Employees and Builders' Labourers' Federation* (1974) 23 F.L.R. 356   391
Masters v. *Child* (1698) 91 E.R. 695   346
Mathews v. *Eldridge* 424 U.S. 319 (1976)   380, 390
McCall v. *Abelesz* [1976] Q.B. 585   134
M'Callum v. *Currie* (1924) 41 Sh.Ct.Rep. 6   391
McCarrick v. *Liverpool Corporation* [1947] A.C. 219   384
McDougall and the Corporation of the Township of Lobo, Re (1861) 21 U.C.R.
  80   342
McDougall v. *Secretary of State for Social Services* [1981] S.L.T. 259   370
McInnis v. *R.* (1979) 27 A.L.R. 449   358
M'Kellar v. *M'Master* [1926] S.C. 754   391
McKenna and Director-General of Social Services, Re (1981) 3 A.L.D. 219   378

McKenzie v. *McKenzie* (1970) 73 W.W.R. 206   342
McKinnon v. *Unemployment Insurance Commission* [1977] 2 F.C. 569   379
McPhail v. *Persons, Names Unknown* [1973] Ch. 447   308, 391
Maternity Leave Case (1979) 21 A.I.L.R. 88, 199   374
Meade v. *Haringey London Borough Council* [1979] 2 All E.R. 1016; [1979]
    1 W.L.R. 637   252
Mears v. *Safecar Security Ltd* [1982] 2 All E.R. 865; [1982] 3 W.L.R. 366   374
Measey and Director-General of Social Services, Re (1981) 1 S.S.R. 32   378
Megarity v. *D.J. Ryan & Sons Ltd (No.2)* [1981] 1 All E.R. 641; [1981] 2
    W.L.R. 335; [1980] 3 All E.R. 602   359
Metzger v. *Department of Health and Social Security* [1978] 3 All E.R. 753;
    [1978] 1 W.L.R. 1046   392
Mile End Guardians v. *Sims* [1905] 2 K.B. 200   344
Mint v. *Good* [1951] 1 K.B. 517   355
Mooney v. *Pickett* 483 P.2d. 1231 (1971)   378
Moore v. *Branton* [1974] Crim.L.Rev. 439; (1974) 118 Sol.J. 405   225
Morgan v. *Liverpool Corporation* [1927] 2 K.B. 131   363
Morris v. *Williams* 433 P.2d. 697 (1967)   394
Morton v. *Califano* 481 F.Supp. 908 (1978)   373
Murphy v. *Webbwood Mobile Home Estates Ltd* (1978) 19 O.R. (2d) 300   392
Nabi v. *British Leyland (UK) Ltd* [1980] 1 All E.R. 667; [1980] 1 W.L.R.
    529   373
National Coal Board v. *Galley* [1958] 1 All E.R. 91; [1958] 1 W.L.R. 16   374
National Coal Board v. *Thorne* [1976] 2 All E.R. 478; [1976] 1 W.L.R.
    543   123, 321
National Insurance Company of New Zealand Ltd v. *Espagne* (1961) 105
    C.L.R. 569   373
New York State Department of Social Services v. *Dublino* 413 U.S. 405 (1973)   378
New York Telephone Company v. *New York State Department of Labor*
    440 U.S. 519 (1979)   379
Newton v. *Stratford* 3 Conn. 600 (1821)   342
Nicholl v. *Epping Urban District Council* [1899] 1 Ch. 844   366, 367
9 Orpen Road, Stoke Newington, Re [1971] 1 All E.R. 944; [1971] 1 W.L.R.
    166   391
North Yorkshire County Council v. *Department of Education and Science* (1978)
    77 L.G.R. 457   388
Norwegian Case [1977] Rt. 1207; [1978] 6 European Law Digest 368   381
Nottingham City District Council v. *Newton* [1974] 2 All E.R. 760; [1974] 1
    W.L.R. 923   363, 365
Nottingham County Council v. *Middlesex County Council* (1936) 100 J.P. 1;
    (1935) 79 Sol.J. 922   345
O'Brien v. *Robinson* [1973] A.C. 912   355
O'Malley v. *Seymour* (1979) 250 E.G. 1083; [1979] J.P.L. 675   368
Ohio Bureau of Employment Services v. *Hodory* 431 U.S. 471 (1977)   379

Opinion of the Justices to the House of Representatives 333 N.E.2d. 388 (1975)   374
Opinion to the House 137 A.2d. 532 (1958)   346
Orman v. *Saville Sportswear Ltd* [1960] 1 W.L.R. 1055   374
Ortwein and Faubion v. *Schwab* 410 U.S. 656 (1973)   358
Osborne v. *Goddard* (1978) 21 A.L.R. 189   382
Pajelle Investments Ltd and Booth (No. 2), Re (1975) 7 O.R. (2d) 229   356
Pajelle Investments Ltd v. *Chisholm* (1974) 49 D.L.R. (3d) 21   357
Pajelle Investments Ltd v. *Herbold* (1976) 62 D.L.R. (3d) 749   357
Palser v. *Grinling* [1948] A.C. 291   362
Pampris v. *Thanos* [1968] 1 N.S.W.R. 56   355
Panke and Director-General of Social Services, Re (1981) 4 A.L.D. 179   371
Papachristou v. *City of Jacksonville* 405 U.S. 156 (1972)   354
Paramenter v. *Permanite Ltd, The Times,* 8 February 1980, p.2   377
Parrish v. *The Civil Service Commission of the County of Alameda,* 425 P.2d
    223 (1967)   376, 380
Parry v. *Cleaver* [1970] A.C. 1   374
Parsons v. *B.N.M. Laboratories Ltd* [1964] 1 Q.B. 95   373
Pasmore v. *The Oswaldtwistle Urban District Council* [1898] A.C. 387   367, 386
Paterson v. *Saville* [1934] J.C. 42   375
Pearce v. *Federal Commissioner of Taxation* (1979) 9 A.T.R. 740   373
People of the State of the New York v. *Berck* 300 N.E.2d. 411 (1973)   354
People's Refreshment House Association Ltd v. *Jones* [1954] 1 All E.R. 317;
    [1954] 1 W.L.R. 339   366
Perrot v. *Supplementary Benefits Commission* [1980] 3 All E.R. 110; [1980] 1
    W.L.R. 1153   378
Pickwell v. *Camden London Borough Council* [1983] 1 All E.R. 602; [1983] 2
    W.L.R. 583   385
Pierce v. *Society of the Sisters of the Holy Names of Jesus and Mary* 268 U.S.
    510 (1925)   388
Pigg v. *Caley* (1618) 74 E.R. 997   341
Pines v. *Perssion* 111 N.W.2d. 409 (1961)   357
Pirotte v. *Unemployment Insurance Commission* [1977] 1 F.C. 314   379
Plummer v. *P.W. Wilkins & Sons Ltd* [1981] 1 All E.R. 91; [1981] 1
    W.L.R. 831   373
Prescott v. *Birmingham Corporation* [1955] Ch. 210   248
Presho v. *Insurance Officer* [1984] 2 W.L.R. 29   379
Proc and Minister of Community and Social Services, Re (1975) 53 D.L.R.
    (3d) 512; (1975) 6 O.R. (2d) 624   195
Quan Yick v. *Hinds* (1905) 2 C.L.R. 345   342
R. Anthony Collett (1823) 107 E.R. 404   39, 349
R. v. *Bacon* [1977] 2 N.S.W.L.R. 507   392, 393
R. v. *Baddeley and other Justices, ex parte Moore* (1906) 70 J.P. 346; 50 Sol.J.
    377   344
R. v. *Barnet and Camden Rent Tribunal, ex parte Frey Investments Ltd* [1972] 2
    Q.B. 342   365

R. v. *Barnsley Supplementary Benefits Appeal Tribunal, ex parte Atkinson*
[1977] 3 All E.R. 1031; [1977] 1 W.L.R. 917   169, 322, 392
R. v. *Bartholomew Winship and William Grunwell* (1770) 98 E.R. 406;
(1770) Cald. 72, 76   31, 349
R v. *Bateman* [1981] Crim.L.Rev. 728   382
R. v. *Beacontree Justices, ex parte Mercer* [1970] Crim.L.Rev. 103; *The
Times,* 3 December 1969   391
R. v. *Beadle* (1979) 21 S.A.S.R. 67   358
R. v. *Booth* (1800) 168 E.R. 654   347
R. v. *Bramley* (1947) 11 J.Crim.L. 36   393
R. v. *Brennan & Brennan* [1979] 1 Cr.App.R.(S) 103; [1979] Crim.L.R.
603   366
R. v. *Bristol City Council, ex parte Brown* [1979] 3 All E.R. 344; [1979] 1
W.L.R. 1437   387
R. v. *Bristol Corporation, ex parte Hendy* [1974] 1 All E.R. 1047; [1974] 1
W.L.R. 498   363, 368, 384
R. v. *Bristol Supplementary Benefits Appeal Tribunal, ex parte Southwell*
(1977) 121 Sol.J. 663; *The Times,* 21 July 1977   322, 373, 392
R. v. *Busbey* (1731) 94 E.R. 374   346
R. v. *C. Laughton* (1814) 105 E.R. 402   347, 349
R. v. *Cambridge Crown Court, ex parte Hagi* 1979, unreported   358
R. v. *Cardiff City Council, ex parte Cross* [1981] J.P.L. 748   363
R. v. *Chief National Insurance Commissioner, ex parte Connor* [1981] Q.B.
758   381
R. v. *Chief National Insurance Commissioner, ex parte Dawber* Appendix to
R(U) 9/80   207
R. v. *Cockerton* [1901] 1 K.B. 726   388
R. v. *Colbeck* (1840) 113 E.R. 772   24
R. v. *Commissioner of Police of the Metropolis, ex parte Blackburn (No. 3)*
[1973] Q.B. 241   365
R. v. *Curtis* (1885) 15 Cox C.C. 746   348
R. v. *Davidson-Acres* [1980] Crim.L.Rev. 50   356
R. v. *Dunn* (1714) 88 E.R. 702   347
R. v. *Ealing London Borough, ex parte Sidhu, The Times,* 26 January 1982;
(1982) 80 L.G.R. 534   386
R. v. *Elswick* (1860) 121 E.R. 506   345
R. v. *Fearnley* (1786) 99 E.R. 1115   348
R. v. *Goldstraw* [1981] Crim.L.Rev. 728   382
R. v. *Grafton* (1979) 1 Cr.App.R.(S) 305   382
R. v. *Greater Birmingham Appeal Tribunal, ex parte Simper* [1974]
Q.B. 543   321, 370
R. v. *Greater Birmingham Supplementary Benefits Appeal Tribunal, ex parte
Khan* [1979] 3 All E.R. 759   378

R. v. *Guardians of Newtown* (1864) 28 J.P. 725   33, 350

R. v. *Guardians of the Poor of the Totnes Union* (1845) 115 E.R. 649   347, 350

R. v. *Guardians of the Poor of the Worcester Union* (1874) L.R. 9 Q.B. 340   346

R. v. *Haigh* (1790) 100 E.R. 776   349

R. v. *Hall* [1941] 2 W.W.R. 245   342

R. v. *Higworth* (1717) 93 E.R. 32   347

R. v. *Hillingdon London Borough council, ex parte Streeting* [1980] 3 All E.R. 413; [1980] 1 W.L.R. 1425   350

R. v. *Howes* [1964] 2 Q.B. 459   358

R. v. *Illingworth* (1714) 93 E.R. 19   348

R. v. *Industrial Injuries Commissioner, ex parte Cable* [1968] 1 Q.B. 729   381

R. v. *Inhabitants of Arundel* (1816) 105 E.R. 1045   344

R. v. *Inhabitants of Birmingham* (1811) 104 E.R. 597   346

R. v. *Inhabitants of Eastbourne* (1803) 102 E.R. 769, 770   347

R. v. *Inhabitants of Everdon* (1807) 103 E.R. 512   345

R. v. *Inhabitants of Harberton* (1786) 99 E.R. 1017   345

R. v. *Inhabitants of Hartfield* (1692) 90 E.R. 733   25

R. v. *Inhabitants of Manchester* (1714) 88 E.R. 702   347

R. v. *Inhabitants of North Shields* (1780) 99 E.R. 213   30, 349

R. v. *Inhabitants of St George, Exeter* (1835) 111 E.R. 455   344

R. v. *Inhabitants of St Mary Magdalen* (1853) 118 E.R. 970   344

R. v. *Inhabitants of Stowmarket* (1808) 103 E.R. 553   344

R. v. *Inhabitants of Tibbenham* (1808) 103 E.R. 620   346

R. v. *Inhabitants of Tolpuddle* (1792) 100 E.R. 1237   345

R. v. *Inhabitants of Woodsterton* (1732–3) 94 E.R. 452, 478, 504   347

R. v. *Inhabitants of the Parish of Ruyton of the Eleven Towns* (1861) 121 E.R. 813   345

R. v. *Inhabitants of the Parish of Sandwich* (1733) 94 E.R. 1072   345

R. v. *Inhabitants of the Township of Leeds* (1844) 114 E.R. 1493   346

R. v. *Justices of the North Riding of Yorkshire* (1823) 107 E.R. 390   39

R. v. *Kerrier District Council, ex parte Guppys (Bridport) Ltd* (1977) 75 L.G.R. 129; (1976) 32 P. & C.R. 411   364, 366

R. v. *Lalor* [1982] Crim.L.Rev. 60   382

R. v. *Littlejohn and Tirabasso* (1978) 41 C.C.C. (2d) 161   358

R. v. *Liverpool C.C., ex parte Windsor Securities Ltd* [1979] R.A. 159   7

R. v. *London Rent Assessment Panel, ex parte Braq Investments Ltd* [1969] 2 All E.R. 1012; [1969] 1 W.L.R. 970   365

R. v. *Manchester Supplementary Benefits Appeal Tribunal, ex parte Riley* [1979] 2 All E.R. 1; [1979] 1 W.L.R. 426   371

R. v. *Medical Appeal Tribunal, ex parte Gilmore* [1957] 1 Q.B. 574   373

R. v. *Medley* (1834) 172 E.R. 1246   361

R. v. *Meredith and Turner* (1803) 168 E.R. 676   31

R. v. *Merseyside County Council, ex parte Great Universal Stores Ltd, The Times*, 18 February 1982; (1982) 80 L.G.R. 639   385

R. v. *Miles* (1842) 6 Jur. 243   344
R. v. *Minister of Health, ex parte Davis* [1929] 1 K.B. 619   367
R. v. *Mountford* [1972] 1 Q.B. 28   391
R. v. *National Insurance Commissioner, ex parte Department of Health and
     Social Security* (1978) 122 Sol.J. 812   371
R. v. *National Insurance Commissioner, ex parte Insurance Officer* [1981]
     I.C.R. 90   381
R. v. *National Insurance Commissioner, ex parte Michael* [1977] 2 All E.R.
     420; [1977] 1 W.L.R. 109   373
R. v. *National Insurance Commissioner, ex parte Secretary of State for Social
     Services* [1981] 2 All E.R. 738; [1981] 1 W.L.R. 1017   373
R. v. *National Insurance Commissioner, ex parte Stratton* [1979] Q.B. 361   371, 373
R. v. *National Insurance Commissioner, ex parte Thompson* Appendix to
     R(U) 5/77 [1979] C.L.Y. 2559   208
R. v. *Paddington and St Marylebone Rent Tribunal, ex parte Bell, London &
     Provincial Properties Ltd* [1949] 1 K.B. 666   365
R. v. *Parnell* (1881) 14 Cox C.C. 508   393
R. v. *Pedly* (1834) 110 E.R. 1422   361
R. v. *Phekoo* [1981] 3 All E.R. 84; [1981] 1 W.L.R. 1117   356
R. v. *Poor Law Commissioners; In re Newport Union* (1837) 112 E.R. 20   390
R. v. *Poor Law Commissioners; In re The Parish of St Pancras* (1837) 112
     E.R. 1   390
R. v. *Poor Law Commissioners; In re Whitechapel Union* (1837) 112 E.R. 13   346
R. v. *Poplar Borough Council, ex parte The London County Council (No. 1)*
     [1922] 1 K.B. 72   346
R. v. *Poplar Borough Council, ex parte The London County Council (No. 2)*
     [1922] 1 K.B. 95   346
R. v. *Preston Supplementary Benefits Appeal Tribunal, ex parte Moore* [1975] 2
     All E.R. 807; [1975] 1 W.L.R. 624   350, 373
R. v. *Robinson* [1971] 1 Q.B. 156   391
R. v. *Secretary of State for Social Services, ex parte Hincks* (1979) 123 Sol.J.
     436   251
R. v. *Seward* (1834) 110 E.R. 1377   346
R. v. *Shepherd* (1980) 71 Cr.App.R. 120   356
R. v. *Slough Borough Council, ex parte Ealing London Borough Council* [1981]
     1 Q.B. 801   350, 387
R. v. *Solihull JJ., ex parte Johnson*, 1976, unreported   357
R. v. *South West London Appeal Tribunal, ex parte Barnett*, unreported,
     No. 315/72   375
R. v. *South West London Supplementary Benefits Appeal Tribunal, ex parte
     Bullen, The Times*, 11 May 1976   372
R. v. *St Margaret's, Lincoln* (1773) 1 Bott. (Const. ed.) 549   344
R. v. *Supplementary Benefits Commission, ex parte Lewis, The Times*, 5
     November 1981; [1982] 1 W.L.R. 420   371

R. v. *Supplementary Benefits Commission, ex parte Donlan, The Times,* 24 June
1977   218
R. v. *Wandsworth County Court, ex parte Wandsworth London Borough Council*
[1975] 3 All E.R. 390; [1975] 1 W.L.R. 1314   391
R. v. *West London Stipendiary Magistrate, ex parte Simeon* [1982] 3 W.L.R.
289   354
R. v. *West London Supplementary Benefits Appeal Tribunal, ex parte Clarke*
[1975] 3 All E.R. 513; [1975] 1 W.L.R. 1396   376
R. v. *West London Supplementary Benefits Appeal Tribunal, ex parte Taylor*
[1975] 2 All E.R. 790; [1975] 1 W.L.R. 1048   371
R. v. *Wetherill* (1784) Cald. 432   31, 259
R. v. *Wyre Borough Council, ex parte Parr, The Times,* 4 February 1982   387
R.C. and Director-General of Social Services, Re (1981) 3 A.L.D. 334   376
Redding v. *Lee* (1983) 47 A.L.R. 241   373
Regis Property Co. Ltd v. *Dudley* [1959] A.C. 370   355
Reiterbund v. *Reiterbund* [1974] 2 All E.R. 455; [1974] 1 W.L.R. 788; on
appeal at [1975] Fam. 99   223
Repatriation Commission v. *Law* (1981) 36 A.L.R. 411   379, 381
Reyes v. *Edmunds* 472 F.Supp. 1218 (1979)   376
Ricard v. *Unemployment Insurance Commission* [1976] 1 F.C. 228   378
Richardson v. *Belcher* 404 U.S. 78 (1971)   374
Rivera v. *Division of Industrial Welfare* 71 Cal.Rptr. 739 (1968)   393
Roberts v. *Dorset County Council, The Times,* 2 August 1976   321, 386
Roberts v. *Hopwood* [1925] A.C. 578   248
Robertson v. *Minister of Pensions* [1949] 1 K.B. 227   219
Robinson v. *Lowther* (1980) 10 Fam.Law 214   376
Robinson v. *The Mayor and Corporation of the Borough of Workington* [1897] 1
Q.B. 619   367
Robson v. *Secretary of State for Social Services,* unreported [1981]   375
Rootkin v. *Kent County Council* [1981] 2 All E.R. 227; [1981] 1 W.L.R.
1186   380
Rosado v. *Wyman* 397 U.S. 397 (1970)   392
Ross and North Carolina v. *Moffitt* 417 U.S. 600 (1974)   358
Rural Municipality of Storthoaks v. *Mobil Oil Canada Ltd* (1975) 55 D.L.R.
(3d) 1   382
Ryland v. *Commissioner of Taxation of the Commonwealth of Australia* (1973)
128 C.L.R. 404   341
Salford City Council v. *McNally* [1976] A.C. 379   363, 365, 383, 384, 393
Sampson v. *Supplementary Benefits Commission* (1979) 123 Sol.J. 284   218
San Antonio Independent School District v. *Rodriguez* 411 U.S. 1 (1973)   388
Saunders v. *Anglia Building Society (No. 2)* [1971] A.C. 1039   359
Saunders v. *Soper* [1975] A.C. 239   355
Savoury v. *Secretary of State for Wales* (1974) 119 Sol.J. 167; (1974) 31
P.&C.R. 344   238

Scott v. *State of Illinois* 440 U.S. 367 (1979)   358
Secretary of State for Education and Science v. *Tameside Metropolitan Borough
   Council* [1977] A.C. 1014   272, 388
Secretary of State for Social Services v. *Solly* [1974] 3 All E.R. 922   382
Seislowski v. *Secretary of Health, Education and Welfare* 477 F.Supp. 682
   (1979)   373
Sevenoaks District Council v. *Emmott* (1979) 78 L.G.R. 346; [1980] J.P.L.
   517   384
Shaddock (L) & Associates Pty Ltd v. *Parramatta City Council* (1981) 36
   A.L.R. 385   380
Shah v. *Barnet London Borough Council* [1983] 1 All E.R. 226; [1983] 2
   W.L.R. 16   371
Shah v. *Givert* (1980) 124 Sol.J. 513; *The Times*, 9 July 1980   391
Shallow v. *Shallow* [1979] Fam. 1   340, 376
Shapiro v. *Thompson* 394 U.S. 618 (1969)   292, 393
Shaw v. *Groom* [1970] 2 Q.B. 504   134
Shea v. *Vialpando* 416 U.S. 251 (1974)   377
Shepherd v. *Lerner* 6 Cal. Rptr. 433 (1960)   365
Simmons v. *Pizzey* [1979] A.C. 37   363, 389
Simon v. *Eastern Kentucky Welfare Rights Organization* 426 U.S. 26 (1976)   392
Sleafer v. *Lambeth Borough Council* [1960] 1 Q.B. 43   355
Sloan v. *Union Oil Company of Canada Ltd* [1955] 4 D.L.R. 664   374
Smedleys Ltd v. *Breed* [1974] A.C. 839   365
Smith v. *Board of Commissioners of the District of Columbia* 259 F.Supp. 423
   (1966); 380 F.2d 632 (1967)   373
Smith v. *Browne and Cooper* (1701) 90 E.R. 1172   341
Smith v. *Cardiff Corporation* [1954] 1 Q.B. 210   384
Smith v. *East Elloe Rural District Council* [1956] A.C. 736   367
Smith v. *Family Benefits Appeal Board* (1981) 42 N.S.R. (2d) 200   372
Smith v. *Hawkins* [1972] 1 All E.R. 910; [1972] 1 W.L.R. 141   381
Smith v. *Inner London Education Authority* [1978] 1 All E.R. 411   388
Smith v. *Marrable* (1843) 152 E.R. 693   355
Solicitor, Re a [1951] 2 All E.R. 108   60
Somma v. *Hazlehurst* [1978] 2 All E.R. 1011; [1978] 1 W.L.R. 1014   150
Southwark London Borough Council v. *Williams* [1971] Ch. 734   386, 392
Spain v. *Ocean Steamship Company Ltd* (1949) 83 Lloyd's L.R. 188   381
St Helen's Smelting Co. v. *William Tipping* (1865) 11 E.R. 1483   362
St James and St John Vestry Clerkenwell v. *Feary* (1890) 24 Q.B.D. 703   367
St Luke's Vestry v. *Lewis* (1862) 121 E.R. 934   144
St Pancras Borough Council v. *Frey* [1963] 2 Q.B. 586   384
Steel v. *Houghton et Uxor* (1788) 126 E.R. 32   20, 347
Stewart v. *Cohen* 309 F.Supp. 949 (1970)   371
Sturges v. *Bridgman* (1879) L.R. 11 Ch.D. 852   362
Summerfield v. *Hampstead Borough Council* [1957] 1 All E.R. 221; [1957] 1
   W.L.R. 167   384

Summers v. *Salford Corporation* [1943] A.C. 283   124, 384

Supplementary Benefits Commission v. *Jull* [1981] A.C. 1025   377, 382

Taff Vale Railway Company v. *The Amalgamated Society of Railway Servants*
   [1901] A.C. 426   288

Taormina v. *Cameron* (1980) 29 A.L.R. 151   382

Tate v. *Short* 401 U.S. 395 (1971)   351

Tawney's Case Bott 1793: V1, 269   31

Taylor v. *Munrow (District Auditor)* [1960] 1 All E.R. 455; [1960] 1
   W.L.R. 151   385

Te Velde and Director-General of Social Services, Re (1981) 3 A.L.N. No. 75   370

Textile Workers Union of America v. *Lincoln Mills of Alabama* 353 U.S. 448
   (1957)   374

Thomson and Director-General of Social Services, Re (1981) 3 A.L.N. No. 51   377

Thornhill v. *State of Alabama* 310 U.S. 88 (1940)   391

Thornton v. *Kirklees Metropolitan Borough Council* [1979] Q.B. 626   262, 387

Tinkler v. *Wandsworth District Board of Works* (1858) 44 E.R. 989   144

Tolfree v. *Florence* [1971] 1 All E.R. 125; [1971] 1 W.L.R. 141   381

Tomlinson v. *Bentall* (1826) 108 E.R. 274   346

Torrens v. *Walker* [1906] 2 Ch. 166   355

Tozeland v. *Guardians of the Poor of the West Ham Union* [1907] 1 K.B. 920   344

Tucker v. *Norwalk Housing Authority* (1972) C.C.H. Poverty Law
   Reporter § 2735.13   384

U.S. Department of Agriculture v. *Moreno* 413 U.S. 528 (1973)   390

Unipol SA v. *Vial* [1977] Dalloz Jur. 275   374

United States v. *Kras* 409 U.S. 434 (1973)   358

Vernon v. *Vestry of St James, Westminster* (1880) 16 Ch.D. 449   366

Vestry of Marylebone v. *Viret* (1865) 12 L.T. 673   366

W. and M. Roith Ltd, Re [1967] 1 All E.R. 427; [1967] 1 W.L.R. 432   374

Wakeman v. *Farrar* [1974] Crim.L.Rev. 136   381

War Amputations of Canada and Pension Review Board, Re (1980) 108
   D.L.R. (3d) 711   381

Ward v. *Williams* (1955) 92 C.L.R. 496   363

Warren v. *Keen* [1954] 1 Q.B. 15   355

Warth v. *Seldin* 422 U.S. 490 (1975)   302

Warwick and Minister of Community and Social Services, Re (1979) 21 O.R.
   (2d) 528   375

Waterford and Director-General of Social Services, Re (1980) 3 A.L.D. 63   376

Watson v. *Lee* (1979) 144 C.L.R. 374   379

Watt v. *Lord Advocate* [1979] S.L.T. 137   373, 379

Webb and Ontario Housing Corporation, Re (1979) 93 D.L.R. (3d) 187   384

Welsch v. *Likins* 550 F.2d 1122 (1977)   322

Westminster City Council v. *Chapman* [1975] 2 All E.R. 1103; [1975] 1
   W.L.R. 1112   391

Westminster City Council v. *Monahan* [1981] 1 All E.R. 1050; [1981] 1
 W.L.R. 698   391
Westminster City Council v. *Peart* (1968) 19 P.& C.R. 736   356
White v. *Roughton* 530 F.2d 750 (1976)   370
Wicks v. *Firth (Inspector of Taxes)* [1982] Ch. 355   372
Wilkes v. *Goodwin* [1923] 2 K.B. 86   362
Wilkie v. *O'Connor* 25 N.Y.S 2d 617 (1941)   375
Williams v. *Williams* [1974] Fam. 55   378
Wilson and Director-General of Social Services, Re (1981) 3 A.L.N. No. 76   379
Winkler v. *Cameron* (1981) 33 A.L.R. 663   382
Wise's Case (1670) 86 E.R. 48   349
Wood v. *Ealing London Borough Council* [1967] 1 Ch. 364   388
Wood v. *The Widnes Corporation* [1898] 1 Q.B. 463   366
Woodcock v. *South Western Electricity Board* [1975] 2 All E.R. 545; [1975] 1
 W.L.R. 983   297
Woodspring District Council v. *Taylor, The Times,* 15 May 1982   385
Woodward v. *Docherty* [1974] 2 All E.R. 844; [1974] 1 W.L.R. 966   362
Woolwich Corporation v. *Roberts* (1927) 96 L.J.K.B.(n.s.) 757   385
Worringham and Humphreys v. *Lloyds Bank Ltd* [1981] 2 All E.R. 434;
 [1981] 1 W.L.R. 950   374
Wyatt v. *Hillingdon London Borough Council* (1978) 76 L.G.R. 727; (1978)
 122 Sol.J. 349   250
Wyman v. *James* 400 U.S. 309 (1971)   380, 390
Yarmouth, Municipality of v. *Argyle, Municipality of* (1979) 33 N.S.R. (2d)
 598   342
Young v. *Geddie* (1978) 22 A.L.R. 232   351, 382
Young v. *Supplementary Benefits Commission, The Times,* 18 April 1980   382
Zanetti v. *Hill* (1962) 108 C.L.R. 433   354

STATUTES

United Kingdom
Apprentices and Servants Act 1851 (14 & 15 Vict., c.11)   18
Army Act 1881 (44 & 45 Vict., c.58)
   s.145   349
Artizans Dwellings Act 1882 (45 & 46 Vict., c.54)   112
Artizans and Labourers Dwellings Act 1868 (Torrens Act) (31 & 32
   Vict., c.130)   111
Artizans and Labourers Dwellings Improvement Act 1875 (38 & 39
   Vict., c.36)   111
Artizans and Labourers Dwellings Improvement Act 1879 (42 & 43
   Vict., c.63)   111
Attachment of Earnings Act 1971 (c.32)   351
Audit (Local Authorities) Act 1927 (17 & 18 Geo.V, c.31)   29
   s.2(6)   385
Boards of Guardians (Default) Act 1926 (16 & 17 Geo.V, c.20)   29
Child Benefit Act 1975 (c.61)
   s.19   377
Child Care Act 1980 (c.5)
   s.1   167
Chronically Sick and Disabled Persons Act 1970 (c.44)
   s.1   211   s.2   250
Common Lodging Houses Act 1851 (14 & 15 Vict., c.28)   110
Common Lodging Houses Act 1853 (16 & 17 Vict., c.41)   110
Companies Act 1948 (c.38)   127
Concealment of Birth of Bastards Act 1623 (21 Ja.I, c.27)   37
Costs Act 1531 (23 Hen.VIII, c.15)   84
Criminal Appeal Act 1907 (7 Edw.VII, c.23)
   s.10   357
Criminal Attempts Act 1981 (c.47)   68
   s.8   354
Criminal Justice Act 1972 (c.71)   27
Criminal Justice Act 1982 (c.48)
   s.70   354
Criminal Law Act 1977 (c.45)
   s.6–13   354   Part II   300
Defective Premises Act 1972 (c.35)   384
Disabled Persons (Employment) Acts 1944 and 1958 (7 & 8 Geo. VI,
   c.10, and 6 & 7 Eliz.II, c.33)   127
Education Act 1902 (2 Edw.VII, c.42)   271
Education Act 1944 (7 & 8 Geo.VI, c.31)   271, 289
   s.8   252   s.68   272
   s.13   272   s.99   252

Education Act 1979 (c.49)   273
Electric Lighting (Clauses) Act 1899 (62 & 63 Vict., c.34),
   Schedule, para.27(1)   297
Employers' Liability Act 1880 (43 & 44 Vict., c.42)   18
Employment Protection Act 1975 (c.71)
   s.111   379
Factory and Workshop Act 1891 (54 & 55 Vict., c.75)
   s.27   118
Factory and Workshop Act 1901 (1 Edw.VII, c.22)   119
   s.108   362   s.116(5)   362
Fair Trading Act 1973 (c.41)   313
Family Allowances and National Insurance Act 1961 (10 Eliz.II, c.6)
   s.4(2)   375
Family Income Supplements Act 1970 (c.55)   377
   s.1(1)(b)   375
Family Law Reform Act 1969 (c.46)   57
Fatal Accidents Act 1846 (9 & 10 Vict., c.93)   18
Finance Act 1970 (c.24)
   s.21(4)   371
Finance Act 1972 (c.41)
   s.75   371
Furnished Houses (Rent Control) Act 1946 (9 & 10 Geo.VI, c.34)   362
General Rate Act 1967 (c.9)
   s.17   387
Health and Safety at Work, etc. Act 1974 (c.37)   208
Health and Social Services and Social Security Adjudications Act 1983 (c.41)
   s.25, Schedule 8   372
Housing Act 1925 (15 & 16 Geo.V, c.14) Schedule 5, para.12(e)   341
Housing Act 1930 (20 & 21 Geo.V, c.39)   148
Housing Act 1957 (5 & 6 Eliz.II, c.56)
   s.4   363   s.42(1)   238
   s.6   73   s.48(1)   383
   s.9   139   s.77–8, Schedule 6 363
   s.9(1)   363   s.111(1), 113(1A)   384
   s.9(1A)   125   s.113   363
   s.9(1B)   363   s.113(2)   383
   s.16   139, 363 Part III   364
   s.22(4)   391   Third Schedule, para.2(1)(a)   387
Housing Act 1961 (9 & 10 Eliz.II, c.65)
   s.32   74   Part II   363
Housing Act 1964 (c.56), Part IV   363
Housing Act 1974 (c.44)   125, 267
   s.114–114A   364   s.125   355
Housing Act 1980 (c.51)   116, 139, 244, 269

s.42–3	388	s.64	364
s.44	241	Schedule 1, para.7A	351

Housing Finance Act 1972 (c.46)   116, 256
Housing (Homeless Persons) Act 1977 (c.48)
44, 53, 242, 250, 258, 263, 294, 300, 316, 321

s.2(1)–(2)	387	s.8	262
s.4	260	s.11	307
s.4(2)–(3)	387	s.12	262, 387
s.5	387	s.17	387
s.6	387		

Housing Rents and Subsidies Act 1975 (c.28)   362
Housing of the Working Classes Act 1885 (48 & 49 Vict., c.72)
s.12   73
Housing of the Working Classes Act 1890 (53 & 54 Vict., c.70)   112
Income and Corporation Taxes Act 1970 (c.10)
s.19   371
Increase of Rent and Mortgage Interest Restrictions Act 1923 (13 & 14 Geo.V, c.7)
s.10   362
Increase of Rent and Mortgage Interest (Restrictions) Act 1920 (10 & 11 Geo.V, c.17)   115, 297
Increase of Rent and Mortgate Interest (War Restrictions) Act 1915 (5 & 6 Geo.V, c.97)   114, 317
Infectious Diseases (Prevention) Act 1890 (53 & 54 Vict., c.34)   113
Juries Act 1825 (6 Geo.IV, c.50)
s.1   27
Juries Act 1974 (c.23)
s.1(1)   346
Justices Qualification Act 1744 (18 Geo.II, c.20)   27
Justices Qualification Act 1875 (38 & 39 Vict., c.54)   27
Justices of the Peace Act 1906 (6 Edw.VII, c.16)   27
Land Compensation Act 1973 (c.26)
s.39(1)   383
Landlord and Tenant Act 1962 (10 & 11 Eliz.II, c.50)
s.4   134
Landlord and Tenant (Rent Control) Act 1949 (12, 13 & 14 Geo.VI, c.40)   362
Law of Distress Amendment Act 1888 (51 & 52 Vict., c.21)
s.7   385
Law of Property Act 1925 (15 & 16 Geo.V, c.20)   367
Leasehold Reform Act 1967 (c.88)   51, 282
Legal Aid Act 1974 (c.4)
s.7(5)   359
Legal Aid and Advice Act 1949 (12, 13 & 14 Geo.VI, c.51)   57, 86

Local Authorities (Emergency Provisions) Act 1928 (18 & 19 Geo.V,
c.9)   29
Local Government Act 1929 (19 & 20 Geo.V, c.17)
s.1   346
Local Government Act 1933 (23 & 24 Geo.V, c.43)
s.59(1)(c)   346
Local Government Act 1972 (c.70)
s.102(3)   388
Local Government Finance Act 1982 (c.32)
Part III   386
Magistrates' Courts Act 1980 (c.43)
s.35   351   Schedule 4   351
Matrimonial Causes Act 1857 (20 & 21 Vict., c.85)   57
Matrimonial Causes Act 1878 (41 & 42 Vict., c.19)   57
Metropolitan Buildings Act 1844 (7 & 8 Vict., c.84)   361
Ministry of Social Security Act 1966 (c.20)
s.4(1)   370
National Assistance Act 1948 (11 & 12 Geo.VI, c.29)   262
s.4   370   s.36   250
s.21(1)(b)   386   Part III   259
s.29   250
National Health Service Act 1946 (9 & 10 Geo.VI, c.81)   289
National Health Service Act 1977 (c.49)   388
s.3   251
National Insurance Act 1911 (1 & 2 Geo.V, c.55)
s.87(1)   379
National Insurance Act 1965 (c.51)
s.22(1)   379
National Insurance (Industrial Injuries) Act 1946 (9 & 10 Geo.VI, c.62)
s.88(3)   375
National Insurance and Supplementary Benefit Act 1973 (c.42)
s.6   394   Schedule 4, para.4   394
Nuisances Removal Act 1855 (18 & 19 Vict.,
c.121)   109, 110, 112
Nuisances Removal and Diseases Prevention Act 1846 (9 & 10 Vict.,
c.96)   109
Old Age Pensions Act 1908 (8 Edw.VII, c.40)
s.3(1)(b)   44, 381 s.3(3)   381
s.3(2)   381
Parish Apprentices Act 1816 (56 Geo.III, c.139)   343
s.11   344
Parliamentary Commissioner Act 1967 (c.13)
s.5(2)   372

Poor Law Act 1575 (18 Eliz.I, c.3)   37
Poor Law Act 1930 (20 & 21 Geo.V, c.17) (repealed 1948)
  s.41, 42   386   s.163   341
Poor Law Amendment Act 1834 (4 & 5 Will. IV, c.76)   15, 21, 22, 31, 42
  s.15   342, 348   s.58   33
  s.27   347, 350   ss.69–70   37
  s.43   344   s 71   25
  s.52   350   s.98   344, 348
  s.54   347, 348   s.109   341
  s.57   347
Poor Amendment Act 1844 (7 & 8 Vict., c.101)   37
  s.12   344   s.26   349
Poor Law Amendment Act 1849 (12 & 13 Vict., c.103)
  s.16   33
Poor Law Amendment Act 1866 (29 & 30 Vict., c.113)
  s.15   350
Poor Law Board Act 1847 (10 & 11 Vict., c.109)
  s.20   344
Poor Prisoners' Defence Act 1903 (3 Edw. VII, c.38)   85
Poor Prisoners' Defence Act 1930 (20 & 21 Geo. V, c.32)   85
Poor Relief Act 1601 (43 Eliz. I, c.2) (repealed 1967)
                                       15, 30, 39, 40, 41, 341, 342
  s.1   15, 349   s.7   347
  s.4   343
Poor Relief Act 1662 (or Act of Settlement) (14 Car. II, c.12)   22
Poor Relief Act 1691 (3 Will. & Mar., c.11)
  s.7   350   s.11   347
  s.8   343
Poor Relief Act 1722 (9 Geo. I, c.7)
  s.1   347   s.5   345
  s.4   41
Poor Relief Act 1782 (Gilbert's Act) (22 Geo. III, c.83)   41, 349
Poor Relief Act 1795 (36 Geo. III, c.23)   349
Poor Relief Act 1814 (54 Geo. III, c.170)
  s.7   21
Poor Relief Act 1815 (55 Geo. III, c.137)   21
  s.5   344
Poor Relief Act 1819 (59 Geo. III, c.12)
  s.1   36
Poor Relief (Settlement) Act 1825 (6 Geo. IV, c.57)   23
Poor Removal Act 1795 (35 Geo. III, c.101)   22
  s.4   23   s.6   346
Poor Removal Act 1846 (9 & 10 Vict., c.66)
  s.1   346   s.4   346
  s.2   349

Powers of Criminal Courts Act 1973 (c.62)

s.31 (3A–C)	351	s.35	356, 363, 365

Protection from Eviction Act 1977 (c.43) — 138

s.1(2), (3)	76	s.5	356
ss.2, 3	356		

Public Health (London) Act 1891 (54 & 55 Vict., c.76) — 361

Public Health Act 1848 (11 & 12 Vict., c.63) — 110, 113, 361

Public Health Act 1875 (38 & 39 Vict., c.55) — 109, 112, 146, 386

ss.76–7, 80	361	s.308	113
s.299	367		

Public Health Act 1936 (26 Geo. V & 1 Edw. VIII, c.49) — 141, 316

s.92(1)	363	s.235	341
ss.93–4	139, 363	Part IX	361
s.99	113, 123, 124, 133, 135, 321, 325		

Public Health Acts Amendment Act 1907 (7 Edw. VII, c.53)

s.39(4) — 367

Public Order Act 1936 (26 Geo. V & 1 Edw. VIII, c.6)

s.5 — 354

Public Service Vehicles (Travel Concessions) Act 1955 (3 & 4 Eliz. II, c.26) — 385

Relief of Families of Militiamen Act 1803 (43 Geo. III, c.47)

ss.2, 6–7 — 349

Rent Act 1957 (5 & 6 Eliz. II, c.25) — 116

Rent Act 1965 (c.75) — 116, 362

Rent Act 1974 (c.51) — 116, 150, 154

Rent Act 1977 (c.42) — 128, 129, 130

s.1	364	s.70(1)	365
s.2	364	s.77	365
s.3(1)	364	s.77(1)	365
s.4	364	s.81	365
ss.7, 8, 9, 12, 13–16	364	s.98	364
s.14	384	ss.103–104, 106A	364
ss.19–21	364	ss.119–120	364
ss.27–33	364	ss.122, 123	364
ss.45–50	365	s.128(1) as amended	364
s.57	365	s.147	385
s.67	365	Part V	364
s.68	365	Schedule 15	364

Rent Restrictions (Notices of Increases) Act 1923 (13 & 14 Geo. V, c.13) — 391

Rent and Mortgage Interest Restrictions Act 1939 (2 & 3 Geo. VI, c.71) — 362

Representation of the People (Amendment) Act 1918 (8 & 9 Geo. V, c.50) — 27

Sanitary Act 1866 (29 & 30 Vict., c.90)   110
Colliers Act 1799 (39 Geo. III, c.56)   343
Silk Manufacturers Act 1772 (13 Geo. III, c.68)   362
Social Security Act 1975 (c.14)

ss.17(1)(a)(i)	378	s.44(3)(c)	375
s.18	377	s.46(2)	375
s.19(1)(a)	379	s.66(1)(d)	375
s.19(2)(b)	379	s.97(3)	373
s.20(1)(a)	378	s.101	373
s.20(1)(b)–(c)	378	s.119	382
s.20(1)(c)–(d)	377	s.119(2A)	382
s.20(1)(d)	378	Part I	381
s.24	381	Schedule 4	381

Social Security Act 1980 (c.30)   188, 216

s.12	373	s.14	373

Social Security Act (No. 2) 1980 (c.39)
    s.6   379
Social Security (Miscellaneous Provisions) Act 1977 (c.5)
    s.14(8)   370
Social Security Pensions Act 1975 (c.60)   183

ss.36, 38	374	ss.53–56	374

Social Security and Housing Benefits Act 1982 (c.24) Part I   374
Statute of Artificers and Apprentices 1562 (5 Eliz. I, c.4)   17, 117
Suing in Forma Pauperis Act 1495 (11 Hen. VII, c.12)   84
Supplementary Benefits Act 1966 (c.20)   117, 222
    Schedule 2, para. 5(2)   377
Supplementary Benefits Act 1976 (c.71)   188, 200

s.1(1)	370	ss.17–19	376
ss.3, 4, Sched. 1, para. 4(1)	370	s.18(3)	376
s.5	378	s.20(1)	382
ss.5, 6(1)	377	s.20(3)	382
s.6(1)(b)	371	s.21	381
s.8(1)	379	s.25	375
s.15(3)	372	s.27(1)	380
s.17(1)(c)	376	Sched. 4, para. 1 as amended	372

Taxation Act 1697 (9 Will. III, c.30)
    s.2   35
Theft Act 1968 (c.60)
    s.15   354
Towns Improvement Clauses Act 1847 (10 & 11 Vict., c.34)   109, 361
Trade Boards Act 1909 (9 Edw. VII, c.22)   106, 108, 119
Trade Union and Labour Relations Act 1974 (c.52)
    s.18   374
Unemployment Act 1934 (24 & 25 Geo. V, c.29)   29

Unfair Contract Terms Act 1977 (c.50)   70
Union Chargeability Act 1865 (28 & 29 Vict., c.79)
  s.8   346
Vaccination Act 1867 (30 & 31 Vict., c.84)   348
Vagabonds Act 1609 (7 Ja. I, c.4)   37
Vagrancy Act 1824 (5 Geo. IV, c.83)   206
  s.3   353   s.4   353
Vagrancy Act 1935 (25 & 26 Geo. V, c.20)
  s.1   354
Wages Council Act 1979 (c.12)   127
  s.16   364
Wages Councils Act 1945 (8 & 9 Geo. VI, c.17)   119
Wages etc. of Artificers etc. Act 1813 (53 Geo. III, c.40)   343
Workhouses Act 1790 (30 Geo. III, c.49)   22
  s.1   21
Workmen's Compensation Act 1897 (60 & 61 Vict., c.37)   18
Workmen's Compensation Act 1900 (63 & 64 Vict., c.22)   18
Workmen's Compensation Act 1906 (6 Edw. VII, c.58)   18

Australia
Administrative Appeals Tribunals Act 1975
  ss.6–7   373   s.44   373
Commonwealth Conciliation and Arbitration Act 1904   364
  Part IV   363   Part X   374
Commonwealth Franchise Act 1902   346
Freedom of Information Act 1982
  s.9   380
Income Tax Assessment Act 1936
  s.159R(1)   372   s.159T(1)–(3)   372
Invalid and Old-Age Pensions Act 1908
  s.17(c), (d)   381   s.52   381
  s.51   381
National Health Act 1953   388
Ombudsman Act 1976   322
  s.6(2)   372
Repatriation Act 1920
  s.101(1)   381
Social Security Act 1947   370
  s.15A   373   s.62(3)   377
  s.40(2)   370   s.69(2)   370
  s.43   375   s.72   375
  s.59(1)   375, 381   s.83AAA   381
  s.60(1)   375   s.83AAD   377
  s.62(1) (a)–(b)   375   s.83AAG   375

s.107(1)(c)	377	s.123(1)	370, 375
s.107(1)(c)(i)	379	s.124(1)(c)	168
s.107(3)	377	s.128	370
s.107(4)	379	s.140(1)	382
s.120	378	s.140(2)	382
s.120A	394		

New South Wales
Summary Offences (Repeal) Act 1979 — 354

Victoria
Housing Act 1958
  s.54AA — 386
Residential Tenancies Act 1980 — 356

s.63	365	ss.102–3	355
s.88	355	ss.146(b), 147	356
ss.97–8	355		

Social Welfare (Homeless Persons) Act 1977
  s.3(1) — 354
Vagrancy Act 1966
  s.5 — 354

Queensland
Vagrants, Gaming and Other Offences Act 1931–1978
  s.4(1)(i) — 354

South Australia
Handicapped Persons Equal Opportunity Act 1981 — 364
Residential Tenancies Act 1978–81 — 356

s.11(2)–(8)	356	s.47	356
ss.32–3	365	s.58	355
s.36	365	s.80	356
s.42(1)	355	s.86	365
s.43(b)	355	s.92(1)	354
s.46	74		

Tasmania
Maintenance Act 1967 — 376

Canada
Canada Labour Code 1970
  s.154 — 374
Pension Plan 1970

s.63(2)	375	s.86(1)	373
s.84(2)	372		

xxxiv   STATUTES

Unemployment Insurance Act 1971
  s.25   377   s.41   378
  ss.40–43   377   s.100   373

Ontario
Family Law Reform Act 1978 (R.S.O. 1980)
  ss.14–15   376
Landlord and Tenant Act (R.S.O. 1980)
  s.84(1)   364   s.121(4)   356
  s.96   355   s.122(1)   356
  s.121(1)   356

British Columbia
Family Relations Act 1978
  ss.1, 57   376
Residential Tenancy Act, R.S.B.C. 1979
  ss.69, 75   365   Part V   365

United States
Civil Rights Act 1964, Title VII   184
Economic Opportunity Act 1964   291
  s.2781(a)(4)   387   s.2811   387
  s.2791   387
Employee Retirement Income Security Act 1974   183
Model Uniform Residential Landlord and Tenant Act, paras.
  2.104, 3.101   355

PREFACE

All writers bring to their subject-matter values and goals. Even the writer of a law textbook has a conception of how the topic should be organized and the relative importance of its various aspects. In some cases writers set out competing perspectives, with an assessment of their merits and demerits. Others proceed from a particular perspective and consider the implications and solutions which are to be drawn from it. The latter is the approach adopted in this book; it works from premises such as the need to maximize the beneficial impact of existing social welfare legislation, and the desirability of social change to increase the wealth and political power of the poorer sections of society. Writers starting from other values and goals, such as those espoused by a Professor Hayek or Dr Marx, would no doubt emphasize competing considerations such as the cost of social welfare legislation, in the case of the former, and the support it gives to capitalism, in the case of the latter.

In preparing the book, I have benefited greatly from the advice and assistance of a number of people. Reuben Hasson, A. I. Ogus, Martin Partington, John Seymour, Michael Bryan and the Editors have read versions of the manuscript and made valuable comments and suggestions. Dan Coward, Wojciech Sadurski and Terry Halliday allowed me to read their unpublished work on the historical development of public health law, equality before the law and Max Weber respectively. My appreciation of the practical impact of the welfare state was furthered by Clive Grace, John Shutt and Robert Zara. At various points in the research, Virginia Buring, Libby Haigh, Carolyn McCusker and Anne Schick obtained or checked references. Early drafts of the manuscript were expertly typed by Glenda Johnson; more recently that task has been ably assumed by Pam Hart, Margrit Lublow, Liz Sullivan and Glenda Waddell.

1
Introduction

The emergence of the welfare state as a central feature of modern Western society has attracted considerable attention from historians and social scientists. Lawyers, too, have been concerned with the welfare state, and in recent years have produced scholarly accounts of its detailed rules. What has not yet been attempted is an analysis of the welfare state in terms of its legal foundations. How can the position of the individual in the law and the legal system of the welfare state be characterized? In what way are the regulatory and distributive techniques of the welfare state embodied in law, and do their emergence, form or implementation contribute to the failure of the welfare state to meet the expectations held of it? Can law and the legal system be used to effect social change in the welfare state, in particular by interest groups wishing to have the welfare state meet the promises it holds out or the expectations it generates? Let us briefly consider each of these issues in turn.

Traditional society often defined individual rights according to a person's status, and its legal system did not always contain protections against arbitrary action. By contrast the welfare state espouses legal values such as equality before the law and the rule of law.[1] Despite the advantages these legal values confer, they are not without their failings. For example, the notion of equality before the law is primarily formal in character, to do with the position of the individual in the administration of the law rather than in the substantive law. In other words, equality before the law is not generally understood to be concerned with the equal distribution of rights such as rights to wealth, power or other resources. In as much as it is limited in this way, equality before the law may legitimate the unequal distribution of rights. Certainly on some interpretations equality before the law demands that when the substantive law distributes rights equally, individuals have an equal capacity to utilize them.

The welfare state mitigates some of the inequalities which would otherwise exist in modern Western society, including inequalities in the distribution of rights. It does this by regulating private institutions, by the direct provision of benefits and services, and by limited economic and social planning. A very specific aspect of the welfare state is directed to overcoming inequalities in the utilization of legal rights by measures such as the public subsidization of legal services, the reform of procedural law, and the establishment of special tribunals and agencies. The major importance of law in the welfare state, however, lies in its regulatory and distributive roles.[2] The legal rules in this regard comprise an elaborate complex of statutes, regulations and procedural law.

In the main it is public policy, rather than the law itself, which determines the nature and extent of regulation and of the benefits and services distributed.[3] What the law does is first, to legitimate public policy; secondly, to detail the duties of the private institutions subject to regulation; and thirdly, to define the rights of individuals to state benefits and services or, to put it more accurately for many such benefits and services, the duties of state bureaucracies to provide these in specified circumstances. An ancillary role for law is to establish machinery for the implementation of the rights and duties created. In particular, the legal system acts to an extent to settle the disputes which arise over the ambit of regulatory and distributive rules.

In some cases, law legitimates, and gives concrete expression to, social change. The social change represented by the welfare state, and its embodiment in legislation, is an example. The legal system of the welfare state has only a limited potential, however, to act as an independent mechanism of social change. Among the barriers impeding change through the legal system are that courts typically deal with matters on an individual rather than a systematic basis, that court-created norms are relatively stable by contrast with the significant changes which can be achieved legislatively, and that reforms wrought in the courts might be reversed by political or administrative action.

This book, then, examines the legal foundations of the welfare state just alluded to – the position of the individual in relation to its law and legal system; the legal techniques for the regulation of private institutions and for the distribution of benefits and services; and the legal mechanisms for social change. It does this by marking off for special consideration areas of substantive and procedural law which are mainly relevant to the poorer sections of society. The position of the individual in relation to law and the legal system is tested for the poorer in society rather than, say, for racial minorities; the spotlight is on social welfare regulation and on social welfare benefits and services rather than, say, on the regulation of trade practices or on the subsidies and services provided to business; and social change is looked at from the perspective of social welfare interest (or pressure) groups rather than, say, of interest groups concerned with the environment or nuclear disarmament.

A difficulty with this focus on areas of substantive and procedural law which are mainly relevant to the poorer sections of society is where to draw the boundaries, for many branches of the law which are of concern to the poorer sections of society are also relevant to the rest of the community (as well as being well established academically). Labour law, criminal law, property law, tax law and family law are obvious examples, but even areas such as tort law have a bearing. Tort law, for example, enables many workers whose earning capacity is impaired by industrial accidents to obtain monetary compensation.

Although some reference is made to each of those areas of law, this book gives most attention to the law relating to rental housing (both public and private), social welfare benefits and legal services. Education is given occasional treatment, but there is only passing reference to transport and the personal social services. In addition to considering legal rules (the traditional paradigm for legal studies), this book also examines the social context of the rules (the paradigm which this series seeks to advance). The way the material is categorized and related has its roots in social phenomena rather than in the conceptual concerns of lawyers, and the discussion of particular topics draws on the relevant work of social investigators. Finally, the book proceeds comparatively, in that it looks at broad problems and principles and illustrates these with material from the common-law world of Britain, Australia, the United States and Canada. Looking at broad problems and principles has advantages because the specifics of the relevant substantive and procedural law are frequently autochthonous and generally change so rapidly that detailed references soon date.

Matters of definition

Before proceeding further, it is necessary to digress briefly to discuss two key concepts used throughout the book: 'the welfare state' and 'the poorer sections of society'.

In some interpretations the essence of the welfare state is government-protected minimum standards of income, nutrition, health, housing and education, assured to every citizen as a political right, not as charity. One of Titmuss's contributions was to identify additional aspects of the welfare state – that along with the social services are other forms of social welfare, fiscal welfare and occupational welfare.[4] Fiscal welfare refers to the benefits available through the tax system in the form of allowances for certain expenditure; while occupational welfare comprises work-related benefits such as sick pay, paid holidays and pension schemes, health and safety conditions, and subsidization (in cash or in kind) of housing, recreation, meals and education. In yet broader interpretations, the welfare state extends to cover matters such as management of the economy, regional policy, regulation of the physical environment, education, and spending on the arts, sport and recreation as well as on social welfare.[5] While this book accepts these broader interpretations, it concentrates on *social welfare*, since this is the most characteristic part of the welfare state. All modern Western societies have a form of welfare state, although it is obvious that they vary considerably in the details of the social welfare regulation imposed and the social welfare benefits and services provided.

Social welfare regulation is the legal regulation of private institutions such as property owners and employers in the interests, at least ostensibly, of those such as tenants and employees. In relation to social welfare benefits and services, the focus is mainly on direct statutory provisions, but there is some reference to fiscal and occupational welfare. Fiscal welfare is governed by tax law. Occupational welfare involves a variety of legal mechanisms, including private law (notably contract and trusts law), legal regulation (for example, mandating the provision of sick pay), tax law (deductions for employer/employee contributions), and public benefits (for example, subsidies for a business, which is not economically viable, so as to continue employment for its workers).[6] Both fiscal and occupational welfare tend to advantage the wealthier in the community: fiscal welfare advantages those paying higher marginal rates of taxation, while occupational welfare may operate to the benefit of higher-paid employees e.g. in occupational pension schemes where manual workers fare worse compared to white-collar workers in having to serve longer periods before qualifying and in obtaining less generous benefits, even when income differences during the working life are taken into account.[7] Moreover, occupational pension funds give to those who control the pattern of relevant investments considerable power over human welfare, for example over employment prospects, the environment and culture.[8] There is little legal regulation of these aspects of occupational welfare.

A distinction is sometimes drawn within statutory benefits and services between, on the one hand, those providing a minimum standard, for example social assistance and public housing, and, on the other hand, those such as social security and universal services like education. Among reasons for drawing the distinction are said to be that the former tend to be a matter of discretion, eligibility is unearned, and a means test is imposed, whereas the latter are more in the nature of rights and are more universal.[9] (On similar grounds a distinction has been drawn between early-twentieth-century measures, which are said to have constituted a 'social service state', providing only minimum standards, and the post-1945 measures of some Western societies, as a result of which benefits and services are provided to a relatively high standard for the whole population.[10]) Not only is this distinction less clear-cut than is sometimes suggested, but it may become less pronounced with the success in some countries of anti-collectivist political ideology and public expenditure restraints. Both types of statutory benefits and services are dealt with in this book.

The 'poorer sections of society' – the second concept used throughout the book – can be seen in economic, social or political terms, or, put another way, along the lines of class, status or power. Class position is normally taken to derive from the production system or to relate to a position in the economic hierarchy; status is concerned with social estimation and prestige, and is determined more by style of consumption; and power refers to the distribution of authority and does not always relate to class or status factors.[11] The economic dimension (and to a lesser extent the social dimension) has attracted most attention – for some because it is central to their theoretical understanding, but for others because it can be easily measured along certain lines. Attempts to measure the economic dimension usually regard low income as the hallmark of poverty, although other forms of wealth (or lack thereof) such as capital assets (including housing), occupational fringe benefits (including working conditions, hours, safety, and welfare benefits), public social benefits and private income in kind may be taken into account.[12] Low income (or wealth) is measured by social analysts in either absolute or relative terms. Absolute poverty is based on a calculation of minimum subsistence needs, derived from the opinions of experts, in particular nutritionists, as to what people need to maintain physical health.[13] The concept of relative poverty seeks to overcome the major criticism of absolute poverty, that it fails to take account of the standard of living in a particular society. Law has some role here, for one measure of relative poverty is based on the level of social welfare benefits set out in legislation, on the ground that this expresses the view of the state as to the standard below which none should fall.[14]

In this book legal phenomena are assumed to be relevant to the poorer sections of society on pragmatic grounds, because of their nature (e.g. much of the legislation on social welfare benefits and services) or because they impinge in particular on lower socio-economic groups. Mainly, but not always, the economic dimension of poverty is being envisaged.[15] In as much as the matter is implicit in the analysis, a relative definition of poverty is being used, but one which goes beyond income to cover other aspects of wealth (or its absence) such as housing and occupational welfare. There is some cause for a relatively imprecise approach given disagreements among social analysts. Not only are there differences over the matters already referred to, but there is a continuing debate over related issues such as the relationship between the poorer sections of society and the working class.[16] Moreover, the law itself has never been exact about the matter. Historically, the identification of who were the poor for the purposes of poor-law administration was very much a matter for the local poor-law authorities to determine.[17] The numbers actually receiving poor relief fluctuated according to economic circumstances, but at some places and in some periods in England might have been half the population.[18] Later the English poor-law legislation defined the poor to include those poor or indigent persons applying for or receiving relief – a circularity offering little, if any, assistance.[19] The matter was never subject to sustained examination by the higher courts. By the early twentieth century, however, administrators of the poor law had developed a test of destitution:

Destitution, when used to describe the condition of a person as a subject for relief, implies that he is, for the time being, without material resources (i) directly available and (ii) appropriate for satisfying his physical needs – (a) whether actually existing or (b) likely to arise immediately. By physical needs in this definition are meant such needs as must be satisfied (i) in order to maintain life or (ii) in order to obviate, mitigate, or remove causes endangering life, or likely to endanger life or impair health or bodily fitness for self-support.[20]

Other legislation has been similarly unhelpful. The statutes imposing the hearth tax in England contained exemptions for the poor, but the term was undefined.[21] Under the poor law, the magistrates could direct that a person be excused from paying the poor rate on proof of poverty, but there is an absence of authority on who was covered.[22] Rate relief is still possible in the event of poverty or hardship, but there is no definition in the relevant legislation.[23] In *R*. v. *Liverpool C.C. ex p. Windsor Securities Ltd,*[24] however, Cumming-Bruce L.J. said in relation to this provision: 'Though "poverty" is not a precise expression, it usually involves extreme financial stringency such that the applicant has some difficulty in meeting the conventional necessities of life.' By contrast, the courts have taken a relatively broad view of the meaning of poverty in the context of charitable trusts.[25] Poverty seems also to have been given a generous interpretation when the courts have considered the doctrine of setting aside unfair bargains for unconscionability on the grounds that they were entered by poor and ignorant persons without independent advice.[26]

The legal foundations of the welfare state: an outline

Generally speaking, the three Parts of the book coincide with the legal foundations of the welfare state already identified. The first part of the book explores the position of the individual in relation to law and the legal system, historically in Chapter 2 and at the present in Chapter 3. As Chapter 2 outlines, until relatively recently many sections of society were specifically excluded from exercising the civil and political rights enjoyed by others: for example, they could not vote or serve on a jury. Moreover, the law of settlement operating in some jurisdictions meant that many people could be uprooted from where they were living and removed to the area which, according to statutory and case law, was responsible for providing them with poor relief (sections I and II). The advent of the welfare state meant that these restrictions were formally removed. Section III of the chapter is a backcloth to the discussion in Chapter 5 of the juridical nature of modern social welfare benefits, but is most conveniently located in Chapter 2 with related historical material. Despite contemporary arguments, outlined in section III, it seems difficult to contend that the poor law in jurisdictions such as England gave a legal, as opposed to a moral, right to state support, since there was no effective way of enforcing its grant and since poor relief, when available, was often subject to onerous conditions.

Even at present, Chapter 3 contends, areas of substantive law still discriminate, albeit indirectly, against the poorer sections of society (section III). As the evidence referred to in section I of the chapter demonstrates, there seems to be some bias in the way the criminal law is administered. In addition, the legal system operates in such a way that the poorer sections of society face greater obstacles than others to advancing their legal claims and in obtaining legal assistance (sections I and II). The difficulty facing the poorer sections of society in exercising their legal rights was officially acknowledged when legal-aid schemes were founded, and later by public funding for developments such as law centres (section IV). Explanations for inadequacies in the public subsidization of legal services include the assumption that legal rights are capable of enjoyment so long as the state does not positively infringe them, ideological antipathy to the expansion of the welfare state, and the opposition of the legal profession.

The second part of the book examines the legal techniques of the welfare state by focusing on the types of social welfare legislation – the legislation regulating the behaviour of private capital; the legislation governing transfer payments; and the legislation providing for the operation of state services. In examining social welfare regulation, Chapter 4 uses as examples the legislation relating to rent control, housing standards and minimum wages. The historical outline in section I refers to the social forces behind the emergence of social welfare regulation. Section II concentrates on the current legislative form of social welfare regulation, which imposes obligations on those such as property owners and employers to behave in specific ways and, in the main, backs these with criminal sanctions. (There might also be secondary supports such as requirements to disclose information or to register with a social welfare bureaucracy.) One reason for the 'failure' of social welfare regulation is that the obligations it imposes are weak – compared with the ostensible benefits it is designed to achieve. In addition, agencies enforcing regulatory legislation might ossify or lack adequate resources to police those they are charged to regulate (section III). The courts have had a role in the enforcement of social welfare regulation; underlying their decisions are various policy considerations (section IV). The Chapter concludes by referring to some evidence relating to the social and economic impact of social welfare regulation (section V).

Chapter 5 begins with a discussion of the juridical nature of claims for social welfare benefits by reference to the degree of discretion entrusted to social welfare bureaucracies, the scope for disappointed claimants to obtain external review of decisions relating to them, and the similarity of such claims to traditional legal claims as in contract. Sections II and III of the chapter move to the wider context of such claims, such as the conditions imposed on claimants obtaining social welfare benefits (for example, the work test), and the passivity of social welfare bureaucracies. The result of the latter is an under-utilization of social welfare benefits.

The way social welfare bureaucracies develop a dynamic of their own, which does not necessarily coincide with the interests of their beneficiaries, is explored in Chapter 6. The focus of the chapter is the provision of public services. What is called the paradox of social welfare bureaucracies is illustrated in section I by reference to the legislation relating to slum clearance and public housing. The legal mechanisms for keeping social welfare bureaucracies to the mark are dealt with in section II, where reference is also made to some developments in administrative law. The material is followed by a case study of how the law in England controls the policies of local authorities in relation to homelessness. Then attention is given to the legal and other dimensions of participation by beneficiaries in social welfare bureaucracies – a popular solution to the paradox posed at the outset of the chapter (section III).

A theme running through the second part of the book is how social welfare legislation has been used in the welfare state as a means of social change – to bend the behaviour of capital to social ends and to create new rights to state benefits and services. The discussion of social change in the third part of the book concentrates on the perception which some groups have had, that law and the legal system of modern Western society can be used as a resource to advance the interests of different disadvantaged groups. Section I of Chapter 7 puts this strategy in the context of how change occurs in modern Western society, while sections II and III describe how test cases have been taken before courts and tribunals seeking favourable applications and interpretations of common and statutory law, and how legal assistance extended to groups of social welfare claimants, tenants and low-paid employees has been used to build up their political power and to act on their behalf in relation to state bureaucracies and capital. In certain respects this work parallels what the legal advisers to corporations, government departments and financial institutions do to advance the latter's interests – taking advantage of the law's provisions whenever possible and in some circumstances seeking to change them. Not all believe in pursuing social change through the legal system, and sections II and III also consider more radical strategies such as direct action. Given certain structural features, however, section IV considers to what extent change can be effected through these various strategies.

PART I
The individual and the law

2
The historical background

The transformation in legal values from traditional society is hinted at in Maine's celebrated, if frequently criticized, characterization 'that the movement of the progressive societies has hitherto been a movement *from Status to Contract*'.[1] Maine's dictum was employed in relation to the law of persons; the transformation for the law in general is possibly better captured by the notion of a movement from status to either equality before the law or the rule of the law.

This chapter discusses what the fundamental value of status meant for the poorer sections of society by examining its reflection in substantive and procedural law. In addition, it examines the erosion of status in this regard and the drift to the legal values of the welfare state, in particular equality before the law. Attention is given to three broad areas of substantive and procedural law – the law relating to civil rights, the law relating to political rights, and the law relating to social rights. Social rights is the term used to cover the rights to basic welfare and means the right to obtain relief under the system of the poor law. The examination of status and of its transformation lays the groundwork for the consideration in the following chapter of the position of the individual in relation to law and the legal system in the welfare state. In addition, it provides historical background for the subject-matter of Part II of the book – social rights in the welfare state. After some introductory remarks, then, the present chapter starts by giving attention to selected aspects of civil and political rights as these related to the poorer sections of society. It then turns to social rights, in particular the operation of social welfare benefits and services under the poor law.

Status in traditional society derived from membership of a class, group or locality; it was a relatively fixed and institutionalized condition determined by law rather than choice.[2] Little need be said about the status of the nobility, which was inextricably linked with their estates in land. For a time the bourgeoisie had a separate legal status; the charters of free cities conferred exemptions from feudal exactions, special rights of trade, commerce and manufacture, and entitlement to the protection of special courts administering the law merchant.[3] Serfdom in traditional society bound persons to serve on a certain lord's land or annexed them to the person of the lord himself.[4] Attributes of a serf's status were that he could not freely dispose of property or leave his lord without permission, although he was protected against being maimed or killed by him. Slavery was never an accepted status in England, although English law recognized it as the valid law of other jurisdictions.[5] In the United States, while slaves were treated as chattels, the courts held that they had certain minimal human rights so that, for example, their masters could in law be guilty of murdering them.[6] Until the twentieth century, women suffered disabilities in terms of civil and political rights, and also lost much of their capacity to deal with their property or to contract once they married because of the feudal doctrine of coverture, under which their separate legal existence was suspended in favour of their husbands.[7]

The status of the poor in traditional society differed somewhat from all these, primarily because as a matter of law it did not attach to particular individuals in a permanent manner. But the law subjected the poorer sections of society to a panoply of disabilities and controls: their civil rights were seriously curbed both in theory and practice; their political rights were minimal because, lacking property, they did not qualify to participate in government (by voting or standing for election) or in the legal system (as members of juries or as magistrates); and while they might have had a claim to support through the poor law, this was administered with considerable variation and arbitrariness. T. H. Marshall has argued that roughly speaking the formative period of civil rights was in the eighteenth century, of political rights in the nineteenth century, and of social rights in the twentieth century.[8] While this summation might be true in relation to the civil and political rights of other sections of society, it was much later that the poorer sections of society were endowed with civil and political rights. As will be seen, their civil rights continued to be infringed well into the nineteenth century, notably by the poor law, and even after the abandonment of property qualifications those obtaining relief under the poor law had important political rights abrogated. Social rights have still to be achieved if, as Marshall contends, these comprise the right to a basic standard of welfare and security, and the 'right to share to the full in the social heritage and life of a civilised being according to the standards prevailing in the society'.

The poor law – the body of legal rules governing those applying, and in some cases those likely to apply, for poor relief – was of central importance to the poor's enjoyment of civil, political and social rights. The Poor Relief Act 1601, the culmination of earlier Tudor legislation, provided the framework for the poor law for the next 350 years.[9] By Section 1 of the Poor Relief Act 1601 (43 Eliz. I, c.2) poor-law officials were responsible for

setting to work of the children of all such whose parents shall not . . . be thought able to keep and maintain their children; and also for setting to work all such persons, married or unmarried, having no means to maintain them, as use no ordinary and daily trade of life to get their living by;

and also for raising a poor rate

to set the poor to work; and . . . for and towards the necessary relief of the lame, impotent, old, blind, and such other among them, being poor, and not able to work, and also for the putting out of such children to be apprentices. . . .

Despite the continuity in the poor law between 1601 and 1948, there were important turning-points, perhaps the most important being the Poor Law Amendment Act 1834, which divides the Old poor law (1601–1834) from the New poor law (1834–1948). In brief, the 1834 statute and the orders made under it were designed to cut back on poor relief by tightening central government control, reducing the role of the magistrates, and imposing a strict work-test on able-bodied applicants (most significantly, by requiring them to enter a workhouse as a condition of obtaining relief).[10] One part of poor law was the law of settlement, the detailed rules which developed to determine what connection persons had to have with a locality before it was responsible for assisting them. An aspect of the law of settlement, important in relation to civil rights, was that poor persons could be compulsorily removed to the local area with the responsibility for assisting them. Institutionally, the poor law involved the appointment of local officials to administer poor relief, supervised by the magistrates. In the seventeenth and eighteenth centuries the idea was popular of restricting poor relief to those prepared to live in official institutions called poorhouses. The policy of institutionalizing the poor, and the deprivation of civil rights which that entailed, culminated in England in the workhouses of the nineteenth century. Although not finally repealed until 1948, the English poor law was gradually eroded in the twentieth century by specific measures such as old-age pensions, unemployment insurance, widows' benefits and pensions, and unemployment assistance.[11] The Beveridge Report (1942) laid the basis for modern social welfare benefits: it enunciated the need for comprehensive social insurance, supplemented by national assistance for those who were incapable of contributing to, or who fell through the meshes of, the social insurance scheme.

I CIVIL RIGHTS

In his *Commentaries on the Laws of England* (1765), Blackstone wrote that the first and primary end of law was to protect the absolute rights of individuals, which he reduced to three categories: the right of liberty, the right of personal security (which included freedom of movement), and the right of property.[12] Among the auxiliary rights of individuals to secure the protection of these primary rights, Blackstone identified the right of access to the courts. The civil rights described by Blackstone, however, were far removed from what many of the poorer sections of society experienced both at the time he was writing and subsequently. The ensuing discussion is illustrative only; it selects a few aspects of the civil rights of liberty, freedom of movement and access to the courts, and outlines their content and operation.

Freedom of contract: from servile status to free labourer

The maturation of civil rights such as habeas corpus, trial by jury, the freedom of the press, and the reform and then repeal of the Combination Acts had some relevance to the poorer sections of society. Another change for them was that from servile status to free labourer, represented in law by the advent of freedom of contract. Serfdom, while never formally abolished, fell into disuse, although it is well to note that legislation was necessary as late as 1799 to release Scottish colliers from bond servitude in which they were bound for life and could be transferred with their collieries.[13] Master and servant legislation continued until 1875 to subject lower-status labourers to the possibility of imprisonment for absenting themselves from service before their contract had expired or for misbehaviour in the course of employment.[14] As a result of freedom of contract, however, the average labourer's position was determined in law not by a fixed status acquired at birth as in traditional society, or by statutory provisions such as the Statute of Artificers 1562 (5 Eliz., c.4), but by the free contracts entered, the exercise of personal liberty.[15]

Whether the poorer sections of society gained on the whole under freedom of contract is, of course, a contentious issue.[16] Having freedom to contract certainly would have meant little to individuals who, because of need and the inequality of bargaining power, accepted the terms and conditions employers imposed. Indeed changes in the law consistent with freedom of contract reinforced employers' powers. When at the end of the eighteenth and in the early nineteenth centuries, for example, workers in England sought to raise their wages by having them fixed by the justices under a Tudor statute, Parliament repealed it on the basis that wage-fixing was inconsistent with free-market principles.[17] Moreover, because at that time collective action was inhibited by the Combination Acts, working people were consequently very much at the mercy of employers as to the wages they were paid.

What of the courts? At common law, employers seemed to have had a responsibility for their employees when they fell ill or were injured in their employment. But during the nineteenth century the courts relieved employers of that responsibility on the grounds that the employment contract automatically terminated or that there was an implied term giving the employer the right to terminate it.[18] The courts also reshaped liability rules. Vicarious liability provides an example. While the master-servant relationship was largely domestic, masters were liable for the acts of a servant and the latter had no independent liability. The masters' liability was thought to flow naturally from their position, for their servants were part of their household and they could be regarded as being responsible for the latter's conduct. This rule was too entrenched to be completely overturned, but in the nineteenth century it was modified in various respects. In the factory situation the argument was advanced that it was unfair for an owner to be responsible for the acts of an employee when the owner was not negligent. The obvious refutation was that since employees were without resources, there had to be someone capable of paying damages to the person injured. What the courts did was to limit the occasions on which employers were liable for loss suffered through injury caused by an employee to third parties, including other employees. First, the judges limited vicarious liability to the acts of employees committed 'within the scope of their employment'.[19] The second and more drastic limitation on employers' liability was the common employment rule, which prevented injured workers claiming against employers where their injuries were caused in an immediate sense by a fellow servant.[20] The upshot was that because workers responsible in law for causing accidents were unlikely to have any assets, the injured had no effective remedy.

Despite laissez-faire ideology and the doctrine of freedom of contract, there were many examples by the mid-nineteenth century where legislation regulated capital with the declared intention of mitigating its worst effects.[21] The plight of industrial workers had led to the Factory Acts, which purported to regulate freedom of contract in matters such as child labour and the hours and conditions of work. Compensation for injuries they suffered was improved by measures such as the Fatal Accidents Act 1846 (9 and 10 Vict., c.93), which enabled certain close relatives to obtain damages in the event of wrongful death, the Employers' Liability Act 1880 (43 and 44 Vict., c. 258), which limited the extent to which employers could invoke the defence of common employment, and the Workmen's Compensation Acts of 1897, 1900 and 1906, which established a system for compensating injured workers irrespective of whether an employer or fellow worker had been negligent. Legislative action was also taken in relation to the less obvious position of domestic servants after several well-publicized incidents, such as the prosecution of George Sloane, a special pleader living in Pump Court, and his wife, for assaulting and starving their servant, a pauper girl of eighteen.[22] The Apprentices and Servants Act of 1851 (14 and 15 Vict., c.11) made it a criminal offence for masters wilfully to refuse or to neglect to provide servants with food, clothing, lodging, or to assault them so as to endanger life or to cause permanent injury (s.1).

Access to the protections of the law

Protections offered by the law were under-utilized because most persons did not have the resources to proceed before the higher courts. The *in forma pauperis* procedure provided a rudimentary system of legal aid, but was quite inadequate. It seems that there was nothing comparable in England, for example, to what appears to have been the position in France before the Revolution when lawyers regularly represented peasants in their disputes with seigneurs over communal property.[23] Professor Atiyah refers to the famous case of *Armory* v. *Delamirie* in 1722,[24] where a chimney-sweep enforced his right to keep a jewel he had found against the goldsmith to whom he had taken it for valuation, but adds that 'such cases were, of course, rare'.[25] There were exceptional occasions when groups of poorer people resorted collectively to the assize judges or the Court of the King's Bench. For example, in 1808 the journeymen and some of the master weavers in Manchester and Glasgow applied to the King's Bench for a writ of mandamus to compel the magistrates to fix the rate of wages. Apparently this writ was delayed until legislation repealed the magistrates' capacity to fix wages.[26]

For some matters the justices proved reasonably accessible to ordinary people. The position in relation to applications for poor relief is referred to later in the chapter. In other areas ordinary people in seventeenth- and eighteenth-century England sometimes publicized their grievances by taking action before the justices, notably at Quarter Sessions, and in this way reached the ears of those in London.[27] So, too, in the magistrates' courts of nineteenth-century Australia individual workers took action against employers under the master and servant legislation for the summary recovery of wages.[28] Generally speaking, however, the poorer sections of society could only challenge threats to their standards of subsistence and their personal liberties by supplications, demonstrations and collective attacks on popular targets, since the courts and formal political processes were effectively closed to them.[29]

Even if poorer people had been able to invoke legal processes more easily, the law's substantive provisions were not especially solicitous of their plight. An example from criminal law is that while Bacon had believed that stealing food to satisfy present hunger did not constitute larceny, the views of Hale and later Blackstone, denying this, became generally accepted. The latter gave three reasons: that the poor were sufficiently provided for by charity and the poor law; that otherwise property would be threatened; and that the Crown could always pardon a poor person who was convicted. The first reason was far from always being true, the second was probably the real basis for the rule, and the last was spurious since it would have ruled out the whole defence of necessity in the criminal law. Glanville Williams believes that if the judges had recognized famine as an excuse for stealing in the troubled years following the Napoleonic wars, they might have helped to bring the government to a realization of the need for adequate public relief.[30]

The substantive law was overly concerned with the protection of property rights. A clear instance from statutory law were the game laws of eighteenth-century England, which restricted the right to kill wild game to landowners and imposed heavy penalties (including death) on unauthorized poaching. Most poachers were poor labourers, servants and artisans, many of whom poached through need, particularly in times of poor harvests.[31] A solicitude for property was also embodied in legal doctrine evolved by the courts. *Steel* v. *Houghton*[32] in 1788 is one example. There the plaintiff sued the defendant for trespass for gleaning done by his wife. The defendant pleaded as justification that the legally settled poor people in an area had a common-law right to glean. The court (Gould J. dissenting) rejected the contention as being inconsistent with property rights, a threat to law and order, an inducement to fraud and a threat to profitable farming. To the argument that the poor should share in the benefit of the harvest, Heath J. asserted the principles of political economy: 'They receive from the advanced price of labour, a recompense in proportion to their industry.' The judgment was consistent with the many contemporary private Acts for the enclosure of common lands and wastes, which were depriving people of the rights they had enjoyed to graze their animals, dig turf and catch fish.[33]

Apart from the favour with which the law continued to treat property, there were other ways in which it disadvantaged the poorer sections of society. In the main this was through statutory law. Vagrancy law is a good example: rather than operating against acts which anyone in society could commit, vagrancy offences had effect against persons because of their condition of not having financial resources. Early this century, legislation attempted to suppress working-class gambling but omitted to deal with the betting facilities of the wealthier.[34] Writing in 1914, Judge Parry noted the discrepancy between, on the one hand, the tight licensing control exercised over pubs, a major social centre for the poorer sections of society, and, on the other hand, the leniency operating with respect to the consumption of alcohol at the social functions of the wealthy.[35] In the main, substantive law along the lines of these examples, which disadvantaged the poorer sections of society fairly overtly, has been repealed. However, there are still instances, discussed in the following chapter, where the law acts indirectly to their disadvantage.

Restrictions on liberty: workhouses

It could hardly be said that the poorer sections of society enjoyed full civil rights so long as certain aspects of the poor law continued. One aspect examined later is how the able-bodied could be forced to do the most menial work as a condition of their receiving poor relief. Of children apprenticed under the poor law, Kahn-Freund refers to the ample evidence that the conditions under which they were apprenticed 'were in fact hardly distinguishable from the slave trade'.[36]

Perhaps those forced to enter the workhouses to obtain poor relief experienced the most apparent loss of personal freedom. Once inside they became subject to institutional control to which they had little chance of objecting. Under section 5 of the Poor Relief Act 1815 (55 Geo. III, c.137), a workhouse inmate could be convicted and committed to a sentence of twenty-one days' hard labour in an ordinary gaol or house of correction if he or she refused to work or misbehaved. The protection of the courts could only be invoked in extreme circumstances. For example, in a decision in 1780 Lord Mansfield C.J. indicated that workhouse officials would be indictable for treating inmates in an unacceptable manner.[37] Later the Workhouses Act 1790 (30 Geo. III, c.49) enabled justices, clergymen and doctors to examine and report upon the state of the poor in certain workhouses, whereupon poor-law officials could be summoned to answer a complaint at Quarter Sessions (s.1). The Poor Relief Act 1814 (54 Geo. III, c.170) provided that the masters of workhouses were not to inflict corporal punishment on adults or generally to confine them for more than twenty-four hours (s.7).

The New poor law, introduced by the Poor Law Amendment Act 1834, provided a legal regime of strict control of the inmates of workhouses. Married couples had generally to live apart, diet and conduct were controlled, and in return for relief a person could be temporarily detained.[38] Inmates might be obliged to perform a task such as breaking stones.[39] Under the General Consolidated Order of the Poor Law Commissioners 1847, workhouse inmates could be punished for misbehaviour by measures such as a restriction on their diet or confinement to a special room.[40] More serious misbehaviour could be prosecuted in the courts.[41] Magistrates still had power under the Workhouses Act 1790 to review the conditions in workhouses, and were given power by the Poor Law Amendment 1834 to oversee the implementation of rules made by the central authorities. The main responsibility for ensuring standards, however, lay with the latter.[42]

When the justices and the central authorities failed in their task of supervising the running of the workhouses, the newspapers and Parliament occasionally filled the gap.[43] The courts, however, had virtually no role at all. Workhouse officials could be prosecuted in the courts in the ordinary way for crimes such as assault and man-slaughter, but there were few instances where they were brought to account in this manner.[44] Indeed the courts created an immunity for poor-law officials in respect of an action for damages by recipients of poor relief for injury caused to them through the negligence of the former, for example while being set to work.[45] The legal justification was that poor-law officials were performing ministerial duties imposed by statute which only the central authorities, not the recipients of poor relief, could enforce. The upshot was that by virtue of applying for poor relief, persons relinquished an important civil right, that of access to the courts for the redress of a civil wrong.[46]

Freedom of movement: the law of settlement and removal

Writing in 1793, Thomas Ruggles argued that the law of settlement infringed personal liberties,[47] while in a well-known attack in *The Wealth of Nations* Adam Smith alleged: 'There is scarce a poor man in England of forty years of age . . . who has not in some part of his life felt himself most cruelly oppressed by this ill-contrived law of settlements.'[48] Both might well have added that the law of settlement also diverted attention and resources from the ostensible purpose of the poor law – assisting the poorer sections of the community.

Briefly, the law of settlement developed because the poor law placed the obligation on local areas to provide poor relief. The practice developed that a locality would relieve only those 'settled' there and might physically remove others if they applied for relief. The idea that an individual had a settlement in one area and could be removed there was placed on a statutory basis by the Poor Relief Act 1662 (14 Car. II, c.12), sometimes called the Act of Settlement. Until the enactment of the Poor Removal Act 1795 (35 Geo. III, c.101), persons could be removed not only if they applied for relief but also if it *appeared* that they *might* apply for relief. Every year some tens of thousands of removal orders were made under the poor law.[49] Once subject to a removal order, individuals had no right to go elsewhere, even if they would have been accepted, for the law only recognized their place of settlement.[50]

The law of settlement operated unequally. Methods of gaining a settlement included renting a tenement worth at least £10 per annum, having an estate in land, and paying the public taxes or levies of a town or parish. Clearly the wealthier could gain a settlement more easily in these ways, and thus avoid removal if their fortunes changed. To the courts the clear intention of settlement by renting was to enable those to gain a settlement who were unlikely to apply for relief because of their means.[51] Inflation eroded the value of the monetary limit so that gradually labourers, at least those in the larger towns, fell within it. Parliament took steps to counteract this, because labourers without a settlement in an area were thought to be 'in general the most industrious and the best conducted'.[52] The Poor Relief (Settlement) Act 1825 (6 Geo. IV, c.57) required the tenement to constitute a separate and distinct dwelling house. A court held that persons renting a flat with a common entrance to the street with other tenants – the type of accommodation which many poorer people would have occupied – did not qualify for settlement, since they did not have a separate and distinct tenement.[53] Weekly tenants – and poorer tenants were typically weekly tenants – could not qualify for a settlement by renting, since it was held that the requisite tenement had to be rented for at least a period of a year.[54] Settlement by estate was court-created rather than statutory, and reflected the high value the courts attached to property. 'This Court is tender of removing persons from their own property though ever so small', remarked the Chief Justice of the King's Bench in 1733.[55] The wide view which the courts took of settlement by estate was narrowed by Parliament, which prevented people from gaining a settlement by a small outlay on land.[56] Acquiring a settlement by payment of public taxes or levies was made more difficult by section 4 of the Poor Removal Act 1795, which provided that these had to have a value of £10 or more per annum – a clear impediment to the poorer section of the community.[57]

From the point of view of civil rights, one of the worst aspects of the law of settlement was that those affected by it had no effective say in its operation. Settlement disputes were between different poor-law authorities. By law a person could not be forcibly removed from a locality unless the poor-law authorities obtained a justices' order, but that rule was often ignored in practice. Chief Justice Holt expressed the view that it was desirable, but not absolutely necessary, that poor persons should be heard before they were removed.[58] *R. v. Hartfield*[59] established in 1692 that a poor person, and not simply a poor-law authority, was capable of appealing against a justices' removal order. In *R. v. Colbeck*[60] in 1840 Littledale J. remarked, with what seems to be considerable understatement:

It is reasonable that the pauper himself should have the power of appeal; for there may be inconvenience to him in being detained in a particular parish, or he may be aggrieved by being sent about from one to the other.

Nevertheless, the system operated on the basis that it was relatively unimportant to poor people whether, and where, they were removed. How could people appeal against a removal order when they lacked the knowledge, opportunity or resources? There are examples in the records of Quarter Sessions of persons appealing against a removal order, but it was very rare for matters to go beyond this stage.[61]

Serious hardship occurred through the break-up of families when different members had different settlements, although in theory this was not supposed to occur so as to separate husband and wife or where young children were involved.[62] Legislation in the nineteenth century was designed to limit the occasions where families were broken up.[63] But great cruelty occurred when poor-law officials attempted to prevent persons gaining a settlement in their area. The inhabitants of a locality were sometimes zealous in their actions to prevent a settlement and took the law into their own hands. Landowners pulled down their labourers' cottages so they would move to other areas and not gain a settlement.[64] Cases in the law reports illustrate how people were shunted back and forth between localities and subjected to threats (including, one must assume, violence) by poor-law officials with a view to avoiding a charge on the rates.[65] Officials sometimes sought to remove people by subterfuge so they would obtain a settlement elsewhere. A resolution of Sir Robert Heath, Chief Justice of the Circuits, in 1633, was against the illegal unsettling of people – but to no great effect.[66] Later the Court of the King's Bench held that it did not constitute conspiracy for officials to inveigle women to marry men settled in other areas or to apprentice poor children in another parish (where they would gain a settlement), provided that the means were lawful and they did not use threats, fraud or force.[67]

Under the Old poor law, an illegitimate child was settled in its place of birth (until it acquired a settlement of its own), since in law it was *filius nullius* and could not derive a settlement from its parents.[68] Examples appear in the law reports and local records of pregnant women being physically taken to another area (and in some cases dying as a direct result), with the intention that their illegitimate children would gain a settlement there.[69] The courts' restraints on this occurring were very weak. Where a pregnant woman was wrongly removed by fraud by poor-law officials, the courts accepted that the child did not gain a settlement in the place of birth, but not where this was done by others such as ratepayers.[70] Legislation facilitated the lawful removal of unmarried pregnant women to their place of settlement by providing that they were presumed to be chargeable to the poor rates where they were living even though they had not claimed poor relief.[71] The law operated unequally in this respect, since the courts held that wealthy women in this predicament rebutted the presumption.[72] The Poor Law Amendment Act 1834 finally enacted that the settlement of an illegitimate child was that of its mother until it attained the age of sixteen or acquired a settlement in its own right (s.71).

During the nineteenth century, several steps mitigated somewhat the harsh effects of the law of settlement. First, legislation developed the concept of irremoveability through residence, that a person could not be removed after residing in an area continuously for five years, later reduced to one year.[73] Hardship still occurred in a number of cases where working people temporarily left an area where they had lived for a substantial part of their lives, to seek work.[74] Secondly, persons were prevented from being removed if they suffered an accident or sickness while passing through a locality; consequently, they could receive medical attention on the spot instead of being removed in a dangerous state to their place of settlement.[75] Thirdly, although of doubtful legality, it became accepted that poor-law authorities could arrange for the payment of out-relief to persons settled in their area but residing elsewhere, so as to avoid their being removed.[76]

The law of settlement survived a century of attacks that it was not in keeping with modern conditions.[77] In fact its inhibiting effects on mobility became less with time and were counteracted by other factors such as the advent of modern means of transport.[78] Fewer and fewer people who were unable to maintain themselves needed to be removed from their place of residence as the geographical areas administered by poor-law authorities grew larger and their responsibilities fewer. Freedom of movement for poor people was inhibited in an additional respect in the United States. In *Edwards* v. *California*[79] in 1941 the Supreme Court struck down a Californian statute (apparently replicated elsewhere) which made it an offence to bring a non-resident into the state, knowing him to be a poor person. The motivation behind the legislation was to stem the large-scale movement of persons from other parts of the United States during the Great Depression – Steinbeck's *The Grapes of Wrath* tells the story of one such family – who were seeking employment in California. The Supreme Court held that the statute was an unconstitutional barrier to interstate commerce, and a majority went on to hold that a right of national citizenship of the United States was to enter any state, either temporarily or permanently.[80]

II POLITICAL RIGHTS

Participation in the political system

Political rights were gradually extended to the poorer sections of society during the nineteenth century, but it was well into this century before they were on the same footing as the rest of the population. The impediment with the most extensive effect was the existence of property prerequisites for the exercise of political rights. Property qualifications existed for election to the House of Commons until 1858, but longer for election at the local level. As late as 1936, property qualifications were imposed for the election of a town official in the United States.[81] Property qualifications stood in the way of full manhood suffrage in Britain until 1918, although other countries had already introduced the full franchise for men and women.[82]

Superimposed on these obstacles to the political rights of the poorer sections of society were the common-law and statutory disqualifications from election and voting, applying to the recipients of relief from the poor-law authorities.[83] In England the disqualifications were very wide, but they were gradually narrowed by statutory exceptions, for example for those vaccinated or for those entering a hospital run by the poor-law authorities. Some like Dicey resisted further reform – the recipients of such relief had failed to manage their own affairs, they argued, and therefore should not have a hand in managing those of others, or be in a position to elect their paymasters.[84] It was not until the Representation of the People (Amendment) Act 1918 that the disqualification on voting was removed in Britain, although recipients of poor relief were still prohibited from being elected to local government offices.[85] In the United States the disqualification on voting for paupers and those kept in poor-houses at public expense continued longer because it was enshrined in some state constitutions, although the courts narrowed down the meaning of the pertinent descriptions to exclude those such as old-age pensioners.[86]

Participation in the legal system

As with the political system, participation in the legal system was gradually extended to a larger section of the community. Section 1 of the Juries Act 1825 (6 Geo. IV, c.50) imposed property qualifications, albeit less stringent for a time than for most Parliamentary electors, which were only removed by the Criminal Justice Act 1972.[87] Property qualifications have been held to violate constitutional guarantees in some jurisdictions in the United States, while in others they have been expressly forbidden by constitutional provision.[88]

In England a substantial amount of justice in the lower courts has been and still is administered by part-time justices of the peace, rather than by stipendiary magistrates or judges as elsewhere. Until well into the nineteenth century the justices (magistrates) were predominantly local landowners resident in their counties, but amongst their numbers in fluctuating proportions were clergymen, businessmen and professionals, including lawyers.[89] The property qualifications laid down in the Justices Qualification Acts 1774 and 1875 (18 Geo. II, c.20; 38 and 39 Vict., c.54) were abolished by the Justices of the Peace Act 1906 (6 Edw. 7, c.16). However, even today there are few working-class justices because of the method of appointment and because many workers cannot take the necessary time off from their employment.[90]

Political repercussions

These various extensions of political rights had little direct relevance to the poorer sections of society, who were the last to benefit. The advent of the petty bourgeoisie in English local government in the nineteenth century often led to a parsimonious attitude regarding expenditure on public health, housing improvement and the poor law.[91] In a minority of areas where the working class had some electoral representation, or could exert political pressure on the council, their conditions were appreciably better.[92] The extension of the franchise in the second part of the nineteenth century meant that politicians had to court the poorer sections of society in national elections, in part an explanation for the development of the welfare state.

The extension of political rights enabled radical socialists to gain control of both the poor-law machinery and local government in a few areas in England in the early twentieth century. Before the First World War there are examples of district auditors surcharging such poor-law officials with poor-relief payments which the auditors decided were in excess of what was authorized by law.[93] In 1921 conflict came to a head in Poplar (East London), when a socialist council deliberately refused to levy a metropolitan rate, on the grounds that it was financially impossible to do so because of the poverty in the area. The London County Council applied for, and obtained, a writ of mandamus directing the Poplar Council to impose the rate, but the councillors still refused and raised procedural irregularities. The Court of Appeal rejected these and invoked the rule of law.[94] Lord Sterndale M. R. commented that the general issue was 'a political matter of great difficulty':

But that is a matter with which the Court had nothing to do. It is quite clear that the state of the country will not be improved if every subject takes it upon himself to decide whether or not he will obey the law. That would produce, as the Lord Chief Justice said, a state of anarchy. Therefore the law has to be enforced, as far as it can be.[95]

The defiant councillors were imprisoned when they refused to comply with the mandamus, but ultimately a compromise was reached at the political level.[96]

Despite government objections, several boards of guardians in the 1920s made generous payments of poor relief to the unemployed and refused to impose a labour test or modified workhouse test, using as legal justification the exception for special circumstances in the Relief Regulation Order 1911.[97] The government did little about the practice, but the defeat of the General Strike in 1926 emboldened it to reduce the cost of poor relief. Hitherto it had had to rely on the district auditors disallowing and surcharging the expenditure personally to those responsible, but under the Boards of Guardians (Default) Act 1926, the government could supersede locally elected poor-law officials by appointing others in their place, which it did in West Ham, Chester-le-Street and Bedwellty. In addition, central government officials conducted a campaign against poor relief being paid too generously to the unemployed. The Audit (Local Authorities) Act 1927 prohibited persons from serving on a local authority for five years if they had been surcharged more than £500, and the Local Authorities (Emergency Provisions) Act 1928 placed the administration of poor-law funds under greater control. Then in 1929 the functions of the poor law were transferred to the public assistance committees of the upper-tier local authorities.[98] Even then the government was obliged to replace the public assistance committees in Rotherham and Durham in 1932, when they refused to implement national policy on poor-law payments to the unemployed.[99] Finally, the Unemployment Act 1934 transferred responsibility to central government for assisting the able-bodied unemployed who were not covered by unemployment insurance.

III SOCIAL RIGHTS

Before the welfare state, the 'social rights' of the poorer sections of society consisted mainly of their claims to 'relief' (benefits and services) under the poor law. In the early nineteenth century there was a body of opinion which asserted that the Elizabethan poor law conferred an enforceable legal right to relief, but that this right was severely threatened by the proposals leading to the New poor law. If this legal right were ignored, argued William Cobbett M.P., then why should those legal rights be observed which protected the property and lives of the rich?[100] There were three possible sources of a legal right to poor relief under the Old poor law. First, there was the argument that it was grounded in natural law, which had some support in case-law.[101] Secondly, it was said that poor relief was based on the mutual obligations which members of society had to one another. In this vein Blackstone wrote:

For there is no man so indigent or wretched, but he may demand a supply sufficient for all the necessities of life from the more opulent part of the community, by means of the several statutes enacted for the relief of the poor. . . . A humane provision . . . dictated by the principles of society. . . . [102] A third argument for a legal right to relief could be found in the language of the Poor Relief Act 1601 itself. There were judicial remarks that the words meant that poor-law officials had a legal obligation to provide poor relief to the impotent poor without any need for a justice's order.[103] The value of these remarks is weakened, however, because there seems to have been no decision involving a direct claim by a poor person.

Whatever arguments there might have been in theory about a person's rights to poor relief, these seem to have been seriously undermined by the administrative practices of poor-law authorities: they might grant relief arbitrarily, approving it for some while refusing it to others in similar or more needy circumstances; and they could be rude and arrogant, and in some cases downright cruel, in the way they administered it. [104] (The way the administration of social welfare legislation in the welfare state undermines legal rights and duties is a recurrent theme in Part II of this book.)

A justice and ultimately the justices in Quarter Sessions were an alternative source of poor relief, and thus a means of redress, when poor-law officials refused to grant it.[105] In a number of cases, poor-law authorities appealed against what they thought was the generosity of the justices to the Court of the King's Bench.[106] Two of these decisions gave little comfort to the poor, for the King's Bench adopted a technical approach and quashed the justices' orders that relief be provided. Later *R.* v. *North Shields*[107] held that the poor-law authorities could not appeal from a justice's order to relieve, because 'the pauper might starve while the cause was in suspence'. But compared with the huge volume of disputes on settlement, there were relatively few instances where the Quarter Sessions heard appeals about poor relief.[108] Largely, this was because poor people refused relief would have had to take the initiative, whereas the disputants about settlement were almost invariably the poor-law authorities, who had the financial capacity to act.

The magistracy thus exercised a limited control over the daily administration of poor relief at the local level, although as part-time appointees they could not exercise constant review. Dr Burn was not alone in the eighteenth century in expressing the sentiment that the justices should have greater power to curb the abuses of poor-law officials.[109] However, regular criticism was levelled at the justices that they were too generous in ordering relief when poor law officials had refused it. In as much as this was true, it might have reflected the contrast between a paternalistic, upper/upper-middle-class magistracy, conscious of the need to preserve social order, and parsimonious local administrators, who bore the cost of poor relief through the poor rates.[110] The criticism led to the curtailment of the justices' power to order relief without poor-law officials first having refused it, including cases where poor-law officials were entitled to condition relief on a person's entering a poor-house and he or she refused.[111] Then under the Poor Law Amendment Act 1834 the justices were limited to ordering poor relief in cases where it was desirable that an old person receive it without having to reside in a workhouse and in situations of sudden or urgent necessity (e.g., accident).[112] As a result of this change it was difficult to say after 1834 that the poor had a right to relief, for their one legal avenue of redress against the adverse reaction of poor-law officials was effectively blocked.

On the criminal side, the superior courts did not have a large role in controlling the administration of the poor law. *Tawney's Case* in 1704[113] is some authority for the proposition that a poor-law official could be indicted if he failed in his duty to provide relief. Similarly, in *R.* v. *Wetherill* (1784) [114] the court seemed to think that officials could be indicted for lodging several poor persons in a cottage which was filthy and in such a state of disrepair as to expose them to the severity of the weather. But generally speaking, the superior courts seemed reluctant to permit prosecutions of poor-law officials in respect of their administration of relief. Writing in 1828, one textbook writer suggested that the court's attitude was because poor-law officials might be 'in low circumstances' so that a prosecution would cause them 'expense and inconvenience'![115] In *R.* v. *Meredith* (1803)[116] a majority of six judges to five were of the opinion that an official could not be indicted for failing to pay poor relief, unless specifically ordered to do so by the justices, except in the case of immediate emergency where there was not time to get such an order. In *R.* v. *Winship* (1770)[117] poor-law officials were indicted when they refused to obey an order of a Quarter Sessions to pay a 92-year-old woman a weekly allowance. The officials refused to relieve her unless she entered the poor-house. The court gave no opinion as to the merits of the prosecutions, but entered judgment for the officials on the ground that a Quarter Sessions did not have original power to award relief, a reason which, if correctly reported, seems to have been in direct conflict with the words of the relevant legislation.[118] There is also a line of decisions where the courts upheld technical objections to prosecutions for disobeying a justice's order to provide relief.[119]

So far we have been looking at the Old poor law. What of the New poor law? In theory the 1834 Act did not change the statutory duty of poor-law officials to afford relief.[120] Since in the nineteenth century many of the poorer sections of society were paying the poor rate, there would seem to have been a good political argument that as a corollary they had a strong right to relief. Indeed, various commentators retailed the rhetoric of a right to relief. In one of his textbooks William Lumley, a barrister and an official of the Poor Law Commission, wrote in 1842:

The law of England requires that every destitute person who is in want of any necessary of life, whether food, clothing, lodging, or medical or surgical assistance, shall receive immediate relief. . . . No distinction is made with reference to age, sex, country, character or condition.[121]

A writer in the *Solicitors' Journal* of 1865 said that the logical conclusion of this type of assertion was that the poor should have a claim akin to that which a creditor had to recover a debt.[122] No doubt the courts would have eschewed such a conclusion if the matter had been raised.

The reality of the New poor law was far removed from the idealized picture of a 'right to poor relief'[123], whatever may have been the position under the Old poor law. First, poor relief after 1834 was at the barest of standards because of the principle of less eligibility – that no one should be better off on poor relief than at work – and that relief might be conditioned upon a person entering a workhouse. Secondly, poor-law authorities had wide discretion under the legislation as to when and in what form they should provide relief.[124] Under the 1834 Act officials had to obey any rules, orders and regulations of the Poor Law Commission and could be prosecuted for failure to do so.[125] But except for a few cases the Commission's rules failed to amplify the legislation as to when relief was mandatory. Thus in a case in 1835,[126] smallpox broke out in an area and an agreement was made by a poor-law official with a doctor that paupers should be vaccinated. Shortly after, the official refused to allow this agreement to be carried into effect, and the poor in the area caught smallpox, including one who died. The court held that no criminal charge could be pressed against the official, for he was not under any legal duty to take the precautionary measure of vaccination. As if by way of excuse for this failure of the law, Littledale J. remarked that the paupers or the parents of the paupers might object to vaccination being effected. Legislation later remedied the effect of this decision.[127]

Thirdly, it has already been mentioned that there was only a limited appeal to the justices against the discretion of poor-law officials. Moreover, the higher courts were reluctant to interfere with the discretion of the poor-law authorities by use of the prerogative writs. In *R.* v. *Newton* (1864) [128] an application was made for a mandamus directing poor-law officials to administer medical and other relief to an elderly woman who was destitute. The court refused to grant mandamus, and in argument Cockburn C.J. commented: 'If we are to grant this rule, we may have all the paupers in the kingdom coming to this court.' There was the possibility of poor-law officials being prosecuted if they refused relief and the recipient suffered injury or death. But prosecutions were only instituted in extreme circumstances, and there was always the difficulty of securing a conviction.[129]

Finally, poor relief under the New poor law might have to be repaid, which detracted yet further from the notion of a right to relief. Section 58 of the Poor Law Amendment Act 1834 enabled the Poor Law Commission to issue rules that certain poor relief would be by way of loan. Coupled with this was section 16 of the Poor Law Amendment Act 1849 (12 and 13 Vict., c.103), empowering poor-law authorities to recover the cost of relief given on an outright basis in the previous twelve months if a poor person came into money or a security, or died leaving money or property. Both provisions were designed to reduce the cost of poor-law administration by deterring people from applying for relief.[130] The judges took up the provisions with gusto. Kelly B. remarked of the 1849 Act in *West Ham Union* v. *Ovens* (1872): [131] 'We ought to put a large and liberal construction on the Act, which was passed to prevent persons from looking to the parish for support, who have the means of supporting themselves.'

Repayment was clearly unjust when persons had to work as a condition of obtaining relief, for they were not paid for their labour. Apparently the practice developed that poor-law authorities recovered the cost of relief payments even when it was unclear whether or not they were given by way of loan. The courts confirmed this administrative perversion: the extraordinary claim upheld in *Birkenhead Union* v. *Brookes* (1906) [132] was for the cost of six years' maintenance in a workhouse. The *Birkenhead* decision was finally overruled in 1926, when the Court of Appeal held that there was no common-law right to recover poor relief unless it was clear at the outset that it had been given by way of loan.[133] Although an advance in legal theory, the latter decision did little to prevent poor-law authorities from recovering the cost of relief. All they had to do was to make plain that all relief was being granted by way of loan – as Bankes L. J. put it – 'by granting it upon the terms of a written form or of a paper stamped with a rubber stamp'.[134] During the miners' strike in 1926, some poor-law authorities advanced poor relief to the wives and families of miners and of other unemployed workers by way of loan. In Tynemouth the loans were being repaid, when in 1929 the poor-law authority decided to write them off after representations from the trade unions and the local Labour Party. A ratepayer in the area objected and sought a declaration in Chancery that the action was void. Eve J. held that the authority's action was *ultra vires* and void because it was not incidental or consequential to its statutory power.[135] Even assuming there was a general discretionary power to release the workers from further payment, Eve J. held, further, that it was not properly or reasonably exercised because it considered solely the interests of miners in that other steps might have been taken if some miners had been hard pressed by the repayments, and there were the interests of property-owners paying rates. Eve J.'s judgment merits close examination since the decision stands with *Roberts* v. *Hopwood* (1925)[136] – the only authority relied upon – as interference by the judiciary, on questionable grounds, with the decisions of a progressive local authority. It must have been regarded by the workers involved as one more act of retribution exacted for participating in the General Strike.

The poor law and morality

Under the poor law, the payment and receipt of poor relief were inextricably linked with notions of morality. Although it fluctuated in strength, the dominant philosophy was that poverty was the fault of the individual. Partly this attitude reflected local practice and custom.[137] Partly it was associated with the rise of capitalism and the expansion of the middle class, which reasoned that if it were possible for them to accumulate wealth others could do so as well, and that if people remained poor it was because of their own failings –

improvidence, idleness or intemperance.[138] Religion reinforced the dominant philosophy, for the Puritan ethic saw poverty as a condition attributable to the sin of not taking advantage of one's talents.[139] The dominant philosophy spawned several corollaries: for example, wealth was legitimated, for it was acquired by individual effort; and poor relief could easily go to undeserving cases without a deterrent administration which made its grant harsh and humiliating.

The Old poor law actually stigmatized the poor with moral delinquency in its statutory provisions. The leading example is the Act of 1697 (8 and 9 Will. III, c.30), which obliged all those receiving poor relief to wear the letter 'P' on the right shoulder of their uppermost garment (s.2). Badging the poor was applied at the local level and seems to have continued in some areas even after the legislation was repealed in 1810.[140] Critics such as Joseph Townsend argued that badging discouraged 'only the ingenuous, the immodest, and the meek. . . . The modest would sooner die than wear it'.[141]

There was a change in emphasis between the Old and New poor laws. Lingering under the Old poor law was the idea of a paternal ruling class which regarded the maintenance of the poor as part of their duty. The early nineteenth century saw the victory of the notion that individuals could only be cured of improvidence by throwing them onto their own resources and limiting them to the barest of poor relief. Thus the punitive nature of the New poor law was clear and deliberate. Towards the end of the nineteenth century a body of opinion emerged which argued that poverty was caused not only by personal weaknesses, but also by other factors such as accident (which might cause unemployment of a bread-winner), old age (associated with the loss of a capacity to earn) and economic recession (over which the individual had no control). Public policy gradually recognized this approach by measures such as workers' compensation, old-age pensions, national insurance, and state expenditure to generate employment. None the less, both majority and minority reports of the Royal Commission on the Poor Law (1909) agreed that the state must inculcate desirable habits in the poor, an attitude which survived the demise of the poor law.[142]

The diminution in status associated with the receipt of poor relief had a number of dimensions. Under the poor law, at least the Old poor law, recipients were obliged to accept controls over their general behaviour in the community. An illustration comes from the Warwick Quarter Sessions records of Easter 1641:

William Amarys of Salford – Whereas one William Amaris [*sic*] hath formerly by virtue of an order of this court had and received the sum of 12d. weekly for the space of one whole year last past and from the year next precedent 6d. weekly from the inhabitants of Salford in this county as a poor of that parish towards his relief, now forasmuch as it appeared to this court upon oath that the said Amaris is of ability to maintain himself and his family without any contribution at all, having now but one child at home with him, and whereas also it appeareth . . . that the said Amaris is of uncivil behaviour and very disorderly fellow and hath behaved himself very rudely and irreligiously in the church there, it is now ordered that the said Amaris shall from henceforth have only six pence weekly. . . . [143]

A direct control on behaviour under the poor law was that poor relief frequently took the form of in-kind benefits such as food, clothing and other necessities, rather than money. A justification was that this prevented misapplication by the recipients. Legislation enabled poor-law authorities to condition poor relief on a person entering a poor-house or workhouse. 'Visiting the poor' in their homes began in some areas in the early nineteenth century. Then the central government authorities put this on a formal footing in the second part of the nineteenth century by requiring relieving officers to pay frequent visits to those receiving relief out of the workhouse.[144] After the report of the Royal Commission on the Poor Law (1909), supervision was tightened to include regular home visits and verification of the wages of members of a recipient's household. One justification advanced for this policy in 1933 was 'the economies which are obtained . . . and the waste and demoralisation which arise from inadequate investigation'. [145]

All recipients of poor relief experienced a stigma, but some to a greater extent than others. Reflecting in part popular conceptions, the law placed persons into different categories. As we have seen, the Poor Relief Act 1601 divided the poor into the able-bodied, who only qualified to be set to work, and the lame, impotent, old, blind and similar persons, who qualified for poor relief. Later, the Poor Relief Act 1819 (59 Geo.III, c.12) allowed select vestries to 'distinguish, in the relief to be granted, between the deserving, and the idle, extravagant, or profligate poor' (s.1). In his book published in 1842, *The New Poor Law Amendment Act*, Archbold divided the poor into four classes – the honest, industrious, sober and moral; the aged and impotent; the vagrant, idle, drunken and vicious; and destitute children. And he set out the treatment appropriate to each – outdoor relief for the first and second categories, the workhouse for the third category, and eventual apprenticeship for the last.[146]

The stigma attached to illegitimacy was linked with the poverty of the parents of many illegitimate children, although it derived also from the belief that it threatened the integrity of marriage. At one level the link with poverty is clear by contrast – the illegitimate children of the upper classes seemed to escape the stigma and suffering of those born out of wedlock to poor parents.[147] The link between stigma, illegitimacy and poverty is also evident from the relevant provisions of the poor law. Under the Poor Law Act 1575 (18 Eliz. i, c.3), the parents of illegitimate children who applied or were likely to apply for poor relief could be punished, and under the Vagabonds Act 1609 (7 Ja. i, c.4) the mothers of illegitimate children who might be chargeable to the poor-law authorities could be incarcerated in a house of correction for a year, there to be punished and set to work. Local records show that whipping was used for a time as a punishment.[148] The infanticide to which these harsh punishments contributed led to the Concealment of Birth of Bastards Act 1623 (21 Ja.I, c.28), which made it an offence punishable as murder for a mother to conceal the death of an illegitimate child unless she could prove that the child was still-born.

From the middle of the seventeenth century these punishments were abandoned, and poor-law authorities turned to seeking reimbursement for the cost of any poor relief paid to illegitimate children. Early legislation provided that poor-law authorities could seek the cost, and putative fathers were imprisoned when they refused to pay.[149] Later legislation established procedures whereby a mother could charge a man in his absence with being the father of her illegitimate child, and if the justices were satisfied the man could be put under arrest until he agreed to make financial arrangements.[150] It seems that these powers were used by poor-law officials to force marriages, to negotiate corrupt deals with putative fathers, and to secure a maintenance order against men outside the parish.[151] As a result, the Poor Law Amendment Act 1834 repealed the penal provisions of the earlier legislation (ss. 69–70). However, the poor-law authorities retained the power to obtain a maintenance order against the father of an illegitimate child whom they supported, although the Act made the procedure more difficult. A major change of policy in the Poor Law Amendment Act 1844 (7 and 8 Vict., c. 101) was that a mother obtained the sole right to seek a maintenance order against the father of her illegitimate child and to retain the proceeds. The change was shortlived, however; legislation in 1872 re-established the right of poor-law authorities to seek an order against the father of an illegitimate child receiving poor relief for reimbursement of the cost.[152] Without support, and reluctant to turn to the poor law, many mothers who were poor abandoned their illegitimate babies, paid small amounts for them to be removed to a baby farm (where they were sometimes disposed of), or struggled to bring them up on very low incomes.[153]

Widows were a favoured category under the poor law and had a higher status than unmarried mothers. Under the New poor law, widows in the first six months of their widowhood or with legitimate dependent children could receive poor relief without having to enter a workhouse, although the Poor Law Commission cautioned that if given indiscriminately such relief could lead to improvident habits.[154] In addition, a widow with legitimate, dependent children who at the time of her husband's death was resident with him in some place other than her settlement, could obtain poor relief there, a significant privilege because it was an exception to the general rule that poor people could not receive relief other than in their place of settlement.[155] The moral judgement inherent in these exceptions is underlined by the fact that a widow was not allowed either privilege if she gave birth to an illegitimate child after her widowhood. Widows also acquired a privileged status of irremoveability under the settlement laws for the first twelve months of their widowhood.[156] Conditions for widows seemed to tighten towards the end of the nineteenth century in line with the general trend in the poor law.[157]

Members of the armed forces and their dependants seem also to have occupied a more favoured position, and to have been less stigmatized than others by the poor law. Service to country acted as a counterweight to the moral opprobrium associated with poverty. Under Elizabethan statutes, rates were levied to pay pensions to poor soldiers and sailors. Later, ex-servicemen and their immediate families could establish trades without restriction, and were exempt from the law of settlement while operating them.[158] While poor-law authorities might require persons to enter a workhouse if they wanted poor relief, the family of a militia man called out to service which was left unable to support itself could obtain an outdoor allowance, although not if he was demoted for misconduct.[159] Towards the end of the nineteenth century, conditions were tightened in relation to a serviceman's family, and a wife was expected to obtain work within a reasonable time after her husband's departure. While a member of the services could not be punished for deserting or neglecting to maintain his family, he remained liable to maintain them; execution could not issue against his person, pay or army equipment, but the army could make deductions from his pay.[160]

Work and poor relief

The relationship between work and the payment of poor relief obsessed poor-law policy-makers. The common morality, strengthened by the ethos of capitalism, was grounded in the belief that all could obtain work and success who wanted them. The unemployed were consequently classed as less deserving than the lame, impotent, aged and blind. The implication of the common morality was that the poor-law authorities should manipulate the poor-law system so as to force the poor to work. The workhouse and the labour tests of the New poor law embodied this idea in its most developed form.

The Poor Relief Act 1601 obliged poor-law authorities to set the able-bodied poor to work. As Best J. said in *R. v. Justices of the North Riding of Yorkshire* (1823): [161] 'According to the poor laws, he who is able to labour is to be maintained by labour only, and nothing is to be provided for him but a means of employment.' A justification for this approach was the rehabilitative effects it would have on the able-bodied poor. Abbott C. J. remarked in *R. v. Collett* (1823):[162]

It is the primary duty of the overseers to find employment for the poor, if possible . . . for the sake of the poor themselves, to whom no greater kindness can be done than by enabling them to earn their own living by labour, instead of suffering them to eat the bread of idleness, by which their habits and morals must soon be corrupted.

But although under the Poor Relief Act 1601 it seemed that individuals were to be denied poor relief if they were able-bodied – their only relief being to be set to work – it seems that they sometimes obtained it.[163] Perhaps this is not surprising. In commenting on the failure to set the poor to work, Blackstone noted the administrative difficulties facing local poor-law officials in organizing work on any scale.[164] There were also the initial costs of obtaining materials, which poor-law officials were reluctant to raise through the rates. Consequently, many poor-law officials found it easier to supplement the incomes of labourers when times were bad, especially in agricultural areas, where it suited landowners to have a ready supply of labour which could be laid off in the winter.

The system of subsidizing wages was placed on a more systematic basis in 1795 by the justices in Speenhamland, Berkshire. Their declaration stated that it was no longer expedient to regulate wages according to the statutes of Elizabeth, but that it was better that labourers should receive an income which kept pace with prices. Using the price of bread as a basis, they accordingly ordered officials to pay out-relief to workers to bring their income up to a prescribed level.[165] Justices in other areas emulated the Speenhamland decision. Historians have placed the Speenhamland system within the context of a last-ditch stand by the justices, representatives of established rural order, to maintain it in the face of the growing market economy.[166] Certainly the Speenhamland system extended the system of poor-law control since as a result many more persons received poor relief, however meagre. The alternative to the Speen-hamland system would have been to fix wages, but there were legal doubts about whether justices could set minimum (as opposed to maximum) wages. The Combination Acts meant that it was illegal for workers themselves to combine to raise their wages by collective bargaining. Legally, the Speenhamland system was partly confirmed by legislation in 1795, which provided that notwithstanding earlier legislation, certain industrious poor suffering illness or distress could receive out-relief (i.e. relief out of doors).[167]

A powerful attack developed against the Speenhamland system on the ground that it interfered with the law of supply and demand in the labour market by tying labourers to their rural parishes. Speenham-land was also criticized as benefiting landowners with cheap, subsidized labour at the expense of other rate-payers such as businessmen, although it now seems that allegations of its crippling cost advanced in the 1834 Poor Law Report were exaggerated.[168] In any event, as criticism of the cost of the Speenhamland system mounted in the early nineteenth century, legal arguments were invoked against it.[169] It was said that the 1795 statute simply removed the need to enter the workhouse in the case of emergency relief but did not create a new category of relief additional to those mentioned in the Poor Relief Act 1601; under that Act the un-employed could not receive pecuniary relief without being set to work. In 1819 justices in Hampshire held the practice to be illegal and ordered the authorities to discontinue it, and over the following decade justices in other areas followed suit.[170] When the issue was raised before the King's Bench in 1823 the court avoided a definite answer and sent the matter back to Quarter Sessions.[171] The Speenhamland system was eventually swept away by the New poor law. It had never been adopted throughout the whole country and had broken down in many areas before its legal demise.

Workhouses to set the poor to work were inspired by the writings of those like Sir Matthew Hale, who in the seventeenth century served as a judge of the Common Pleas, Exchequer and King's Bench. Hale wrote at a time when there was concern about the strength of Dutch commerce; in the poor he saw a supply of cheap labour to meet their competition.[172] There was no express power in the Poor Relief Act 1601 to pay wages, said Hale, but this was possible under the general clause in the statute enabling the authorities to execute all other things which seemed convenient. Hale proposed the erection of workhouses to employ the poor at equitable wages, coupled with imprisonment for those able-bodied who refused to work. Over the next century and a half, various attempts were made to establish self-supporting workhouses. But the labour was unskilled, unwilling, badly managed, and engaged in making products which were manufactured more economically in the mills. These workhouses deteriorated into institutions run as a deterrent to persons applying for relief, as refuges for the old and sick, or as penal establishments for the recalcitrant. The Poor Relief Act 1722 (36 Geo.III, c.23) enabled poor-law authorities to establish workhouses and to condition relief on entry to them (s.4). Gilbert's Act of 1782[173] was more elaborate, but was only adopted in a few areas. It provided that a union of parishes could establish a workhouse for the poor run by salaried officials and supervised by visitors of high social rank. The approbation with which the judges held workhouses was expressed in a judgment of Lord Mansfield in 1770.[174] In a later case Lord Ellenborough C.J. explicitly approved the element of compulsion involved in conditioning relief on entry to a workhouse: 'If it depended on the choice of the pauper, the poor-house would be useless.'[175] In the main the condition of the eighteenth-century workhouses was appalling and their administration rife with jobbery.[176]

The workhouse was planned as the lynchpin of the New poor law. Rather than being a source of profitable employment – the idea behind earlier workhouses – the Victorian workhouse was designed to be: a test of destitution (only the really desperate would apply to enter such an austere institution, where husband and wife were separated and behaviour was strictly controlled); a major medium for relief (for the able-bodied, relief was to be conditioned on a person entering a workhouse); and a form of social control (people cast on their own resources would work hard and save for times of need to avoid the workhouse). By 1870 workhouses were widespread, and most had been built since 1834.[177] In a letter to the Home Secretary in 1846, the Poor Law Commissioners wrote:

So long as industry and thrift lead to prosperity, and their opposites to poverty, it is natural that the least well-conducted portion of the poorer classes should find their way into the workhouse. The workhouse is likewise a receptacle for the sick, the aged, and bed-ridden, deserted children, and vagrants, as well as harmless idiots – classes of persons who need constant and careful supervision.[178]

When cases reached the superior courts, the judges were on the whole sympathetic to the new order. In one case justices had ordered the guardians to continue to pay relief to a labourer's widow, aged seventy-seven, without requiring her to reside in the workhouse. The Poor Law Amendment Act 1834 had enabled justices to make such orders, but the Queen's Bench held that although not mentioned in the legislation, justices could only do so after summoning the poor-law officials to give them an opportunity to object.[179] The judges' sympathy for the New poor law did not mean that it was accepted unquestioningly in legal circles. A strong editorial in *Justice of the Peace* in 1840 argued that it would be far better to spend money on improved housing for the poor rather than on workhouses, and an article in the *Solicitors' Journal* in 1862 pointed to the advantage of employing the poor on public works rather than sending them to workhouses.[180]

In practice the workhouses were less central to the New poor law than some of its stronger advocates intended. The 1834 Act permitted outdoor relief for the aged or infirm, and the Poor Law Commissioners and their successors later sanctioned outdoor relief for those who were sick, incapable of work, or unemployed.[181] Outdoor relief for the able-bodied was conditioned on a strict work-test in a labour yard – breaking rocks, picking oakum, or hard labour at a treadmill. The work was unremunerated (payment was given as relief not wages); tedious (it was a test of destitution, rather than to obtain a profitable return, for it was thought that the latter would have interfered with independent labour); and demoralizing (the rough work ruined the hands of some skilled workers which made them unfit to return to their trade). Refusal to perform a task of work by poor persons to whom or to whose family out-relief had been granted exposed them to proceedings under the vagrancy legislation as idle and disorderly persons.[182] From the inception of the New poor law, a considerable number obtained outdoor relief, although for several decades after 1870 there was a considerable tightening in its grant.[183] By the early twentieth century, outdoor relief was being granted as a matter of course. The Relief Regulation Order 1911, while purporting not to be a departure from previous orders, sanctioned outdoor relief in 'exceptional circumstances', subject to a work-test, provided that the guardians passed a special resolution and reported the matter to the central authorities.[184] Critics demanded that work in the labour yards be paid for in relief at so much per hour, and by World War I most yards had been closed.

The New poor law attempted to draw a sharp distinction between the working poor and recipients of poor relief by introducing the principle of less eligibility. It was a Benthamite idea, and demanded that relief should be less generous than what could be received in employment by the independent labourer of the lowest class, for otherwise 'the strongest incentive to industry and frugality will be destroyed. . . .'[185] It was thought that the principle would induce the able-bodied to work and would also implant in them the motivation to save for sickness and old age. The principle was justified in economic terms on the grounds that poor relief should not interfere with the labour market. Poor-law administrators congratulated themselves that the principle in operation stemmed 'the tide of pauperism' as workers affected by a heavy winter, an economic recession or a strike, refused 'the offer of the house'. The consequences were ignored or glossed over: the dispersal of a family's possessions to raise money to survive; the physical deterioration of its members; and perhaps its ultimate break-up when there was no option but to enter the workhouse. The principle of less eligibility was bound to fail in practice. By the time of the Royal Commission in the early twentieth century, some guardians were refusing to use the workhouse as a deterrent or to invoke the strict principle of less eligibility in circumstances of economic recession.

IV CONCLUSION

The twentieth century saw the maturation of formal equality in the enjoyment of civil and political rights. No more was property a formal prerequisite, or receipt of poor relief a formal bar, to participation in the political and legal processes. What this meant in practice is taken up in the following chapter. When modern social rights are examined later in the book many of the themes identified in the discussion of the poor law in this chapter recur – notably the legal character of social rights, the incorporation of morality in social welfare law and administration, and the centrality of work in social welfare policy. Partly, this is because of continuities in cultural attitudes and administrative practice when the poor law was abandoned.[186] Partly, there were legal continuities as legislation establishing new social rights incorporated poor-law principles.[187] For example, section 3(1)(b) of the Old Age Pensions Act 1908 disqualified those who had habitually failed to work.[188] In addition the wage-stop rule – intended to prevent recipients of unemployment assistance and later supplementary benefit from being better off than if they worked – was based directly on the 1834 principle of less eligibility.[189] But partly also, legal similarities reflect the fact that the poor law and the modern law of social welfare grapple with similar problems. When a social service is administered at local, provincial or state level, for instance, who should qualify for it in a particular case? The concept of 'local connection' in the Housing (Homeless Persons) Act 1977 is reminiscent of that of settlement under the poor law. Should the superior courts regularly review particular decisions about social welfare benefits and services? (It is interesting that Cockburn C. J. in 1864 and Lord Denning M.R., over a hundred years later, were hostile to the idea.[190])

Finally, the operation of the poor law casts light on decision-making by courts. This theme has not been dealt with systematically in this chapter, but it recurs throughout the book and we return to it in the concluding chapter. In many respects the poor law was sufficiently open-textured for the judges to introduce policy considerations into their decisions. This creative role was often disguised by the desire to avoid being seen making law, especially when the mechanical view of the judicial function (ensuring certainty by an adherence to precedent and statute) took hold during the nineteenth century. Clearly there are decisions which could have gone either way and can only be explained by judicial choice. Personal factors must have entered into some of these cases. For instance, in the early eighteenth century, Chief Justice Parker seems to have interpreted the law of settlement to benefit the poor, cutting across the attempt of the other judges to correct technical errors in order to uphold the validity of removal orders and to make it difficult to obtain a settlement.[191]

Moreover, there are examples of judge-made law explicitly founded on policy considerations. In many of these cases the judges simply accepted the dominant views about the poor and the operation of the poor law, but in several cases they had also been closely involved in the formulation of poor-law policy.[192] The notion of exceptive hiring is an example where the judges seem to have accepted that the poor law should be moulded to further economic development. In the first part of the eighteenth century the King's Bench had adopted a liberal approach to the statutory provision which conferred a settlement on an unmarried person without children, who entered a contract of employment for a year in a parish or town. In several cases the court held that servants gained a settlement under it despite their masters' attempts to find loopholes in the law.[193] By the nineteenth century, however, the courts seemed to reflect the dominant strand of opinion about political economy in developing the concept of an 'exceptive hiring' to apply to new forms of wage labour. Workers employed in the mines, in the mills and in foundries were thus held not to gain a settlement, even if employed for more than a year.[194] The effect was that local ratepayers could not object to the establishment of these industries on the basis that the workers employed there might later become a burden on them by applying for poor relief. Legal justification for the change seems to have been found in the changed relationship between employers and employees – wage labour having begun to replace the former notion of service.

3
The individual and the law

If we have to characterize the position of the individual in relation to the law and the legal system of the welfare state, a key idea is that of equality before the law. Equality before the law predates the welfare state; insistence on the equal application of laws was common to Rousseau, John Stuart Mill and Dicey. For Dicey, writing at the turn of the century, equality before the law was one element of the rule of law, the basis of the constitution. In the modern day, equality before the law is widely accepted as 'probably the most generally respected of all egalitarian ideals'.[1] It is enshrined in various written constitutions, notably that of the United States, and is regarded as fundamental in other modern Western societies. An obvious question, however, is what the idea of equality before the law entails?

One interpretation of equality before the law is *formal* in character; it requires impartiality (not permitting bias to influence decisions) and treating like cases alike (ensuring that people's rights are equally protected and their duties equally enforced).[2] In this interpretation, equality before the law does not touch the substance of the law. Certainly this standard of equality before the law is not to be lightly dismissed; it imposes checks on power and wealth, in as much as these subvert impartiality and prevent like cases being treated alike in the administration and enforcement of the law. For instance, it establishes a safeguard against the misuse of discretion by state bureaucracies, a concern touched on at various points in this book.

A second interpretation of equality before the law demands that in practice rights be equally the subject of protection and the duty of enforcement. As Williams points out, equality before the law means not the abstract existence of rights but the extent to which they govern what actually happens. 'If a fair trial or redress from the law can be secured in that society only by moneyed and educated persons, to insist that everyone *has* this right, though only these particular persons can *secure* it, rings hollow to the point of cynicism. . . .'[3] This *procedural* standard of equality before the law demands that steps be taken to ensure that rights are equally the subject of protection and the duty of enforcement. The public provision of legal services in the form of legal aid is well accepted as such a step.

There is a third, and more controversial, interpretation of equality before the law, which requires that the substance of the law treat people equally – not to disadvantage or to prefer – except where a departure from this can be justified.[4] Clearly in modern society there are frequent departures from this *substantive* standard; there is widespread classification and unequal treatment. The task is to determine whether particular instances of differentiated treatment are justified. Various attempts have been made to formulate tests to do this. One formulation is that those with similar backgrounds or in similar circumstances must generally be equally or similarly treated. A related approach is that law-makers must treat people equally if under prevailing community standards they are considered to be equal. A further formulation is that people must be accorded equal rights irrespective of original endowments for which they are not responsible, such as race, sex and possibly class. Finally it is said that distinctions in treatment are justified only if they are intelligible, relevant and reasonable.

None of these tests is especially clear in its application. There are boundary problems with the first approach, in agreeing on the criteria to identify those with similar backgrounds or in similar circumstances. What stands in the way, say, of the assumption of the nineteenth-century poor law, that the poor justify separate, punitive, treatment? In relation to the second approach there may be considerable disagreement over prevailing community standards, and even if these can be identified their implications for minorities may be adverse. Limits might be placed on the application of the third approach: if race and sex are included, what of poverty which, because of the structural features of society, is just as involuntary for the bulk of the population? In the application of the fourth test there are obvious difficulties in identifying intelligible, relevant and reasonable distinctions. It should be noted that this third, substantive, interpretation of equality before the law moves beyond legal, to moral, values, and may be antithetical to the formal and procedural interpretations of the idea.

This chapter examines some aspects of the position of those in the poorer sections of society in relation to law and the legal system. How the state enforces the law and how individuals invoke its provisions are sketched in the first part of the chapter. Then the second part of the chapter looks at a specific example, the unequal utilization of legal services. Reference is made to the reasons for this unequal utilization and to its consequences. The third part of the chapter considers certain inequalities in the substance of the law which bear unfairly on the poorer sections of society. The main distinction drawn is between provisions in the substance of the law which disadvantage such people rather directly, and those which favour certain categories such as landlords and employers over other categories such as tenants and employees. The chapter then has an analysis of publicly funded legal services, which are one mechanism to redress the imbalances facing the poorer section of society in the administration and the substance of the law. Since the public funding of legal services is an aspect of social welfare, the discussion acts as a useful bridge to the second part of the book where social welfare benefits and services are covered at length. Throughout the chapter an attempt is made to relate these matters to the foregoing discussion of equality before the law.

I THE ADMINISTRATION OF THE LAW

Broadly speaking, inequalities in the administration of the law are produced, if only indirectly, by economic and social inequalities. As Max Weber noted:

Formal justice guarantees the maximum freedom for the interested parties to represent their formal legal interests. But because of the unequal distribution of economic power, which the system of formal justice legalizes, this very freedom must time and again produce consequences which are contrary to the substantive postulates of religious ethics or of political expediency.[5]

Inequalities in the administration of the law take basically two forms. First, the way state officials administer the law sometimes disadvantages the poorer sections of the community. Distortion occurs because of biases on the one hand, and organizational and social pressures on the other. The result is that the formal standard of equality before the law is violated. The matter is best illustrated by reference to the criminal law.

Secondly, individuals do not have equal wealth and power and thus do not have equal capacity to exercise the rights which the law confers on them. The unequal capacity to exercise legal rights derives not simply from an inability to pay, but also from related factors such as confidence in the law. The differential capacity to exercise legal rights and liberties applies not simply to the civil law.[6] The second, procedural, standard of equality before the law is relevant in this regard.

State administration: the example of criminal justice

Commenting on the operation of the criminal law, Aubert says that it is almost as if it 'has succeeded in condemning poverty, homelessness, the lack of family and of stable work, without ever naming these characteristics as of any concern to the law. . . .'[7] A piece of evidence supporting Aubert's claim is that the lower social classes are over-represented in the official crime statistics compared with their numbers in the population as a whole.

There are three possible explanations for this. The first is that they commit more offences. Historically, writers identified a 'criminal underclass' and associated it mainly with vagrancy. Poverty came to be marked out as a principal cause of criminality, a theory which still has a certain currency, although these days the cause is couched more in terms of social conditions. So working-class youths are said to be on the whole less inhibited by cultural values from committing offences. Studies of juveniles in working-class areas emphasize the 'cultural normality' of certain kinds of delinquency, although other researchers interpret this more as a frustrated response to social conditions. There is also evidence that pronounced inequality in the distribution of resources causes the less well-off to decide that it is legitimate to engage in property crime.[8] As far as the statistical evidence is concerned, it seems that even allowing for the exaggeration in official records, those from lower socio-economic groups commit proportionately more offences than the middle class.[9] These findings must be qualified to an extent, because the research from which this conclusion is drawn has focused heavily on juveniles, suffers from difficulties in determining social class, and focuses on conventional crime.

The second explanation is that there is bias in the administration of criminal law. Studies have provided some evidence of this. For example, research into cautioning in England found that the police were reluctant to prosecute apprentices since they stood to lose their jobs, whereas manual workers could be prosecuted with little threat to their careers.[10] Analysis of cautioning done by a juvenile bureau in London found that working-class offenders were more likely to be sent to court, one factor being that working-class families were less able than middle-class families to impress police officers with the moral character of the juvenile in question.[11] West German research into shop-lifting concludes that stores and officials initiate formal sanctions selectively, with foreigners and blue-collar workers being over-represented.[12] There also may be some statistical evidence of bias in the way the courts sentence working-class offenders.[13] The processes by which these various groups are disadvantaged, and the varying extent to which it occurs, are largely unexplored. However, certain factors suggest themselves as explanations. For example, those enforcing the law, such as the police, have considerable discretion and must often take speedy decisions without adequate knowledge of the facts. Consequently, there is scope for their introducing perceptions that particular groups such as working-class youths are prone to wrongdoing.[14] Moreover, it would not be improbable – and Engels made the same point more than a century ago – if magistrates sometimes treated higher-class persons more leniently because they identified with those of a similar background or regarded their behaviour as not inherently criminal.[15] Another factor might be that higher-class persons have a greater access to legal assistance, which can have a favourable effect on outcome when persons come in contact with the criminal law.

A third explanation is that the poorer sections of society are more likely to be subjected to law-enforcement activity. One aspect is that relatively little attention is directed to offences which by their nature are committed by employers and property owners, such as consumer fraud and breach of pollution and health-and-safety-at-work laws. These offences tend to be hidden from the public so that they do not complain as much to enforcement agencies or demand that action be taken. There is also an ambivalence among the public about the criminality of such offences, an ambivalence which influences the approach of enforcement agencies. Even where proceedings are taken, convictions are often difficult to obtain and might simply attract a fine. Another aspect is the tendency for some police officers and some police departments to spend a disproportionate amount of time on the poorer sections of society. This occurs because although most police work involves responding to complaints, when taking the initiative the police might patrol inner-city areas and concentrate on those they regard as 'deviant' (such as groups of working-class youths). Such activity can be self-justifying, by producing the necessary arrest rates and criminal records. Moreover, the susceptibility of persons to police surveillance varies. For example, working-class youths might congregate in public places such as shopping precincts, whereas middle-class youths can afford more private forms of entertainment. Finally, working-class youths may be less capable of providing a favourable impression of themselves, or be less polite in their dealings with authority, which leads to their arrest.

The exercise of legal rights

Ability to pay affects whether a person can take advantage of what the law permits. Most private law, as well as large parts of the criminal law, function to facilitate private arrangements by individuals. If individuals wish, they can conclude contracts, acquire property, marry and so on, and the law imposes duties designed to make performance of these matters effective. Usually some expenditure is required for individuals to make these choices, even if there is no need to obtain legal assistance. Abortion is one such example where the poor may not be able to take advantage of what the law permits to the same extent as the rich. Those relying on public hospitals may be at a disadvantage over those who can afford the fees of private doctors and clinics. Even if a public hospital performs abortions, delay might mean that a pregnancy is too far advanced. Wealthier women can also shop around to obtain abortion on demand.[16]

Another situation where the poorer sections of society have not had the resources to take advantage of what the law provides is with leasehold enfranchisement, which has particular importance in some poorer, inner-city areas in Britain. Although 'owner-occupation' has increased in these areas in recent times, it has the grave disadvantage that many of the houses were built towards the end of the last century on 99-year leases. These leases will fall in over the coming decades, and in the ordinary course of events the property will revert to the freeholder.[17] The idea of the Leasehold Reform Act 1967 was supposedly to enable the occupants of these houses to obtain the freehold or a lease of fifty years. However, relatively few people have taken advantage of the Act. In addition to the direct cost of purchase, a leaseholder must pay the legal and valuation costs of the other side. Without assistance, the task for leaseholders is the daunting one of having to contact and negotiate with any intermediary leaseholders and the ultimate freeholder. Their identities might not be easy to uncover, and they might offer resistance and indicate that they will fight the question of valuation.[18] The negotiating process could be simplified if the Act adopted a standard formula for determining the freehold price.[19] A bolder move, which would recognize the obstacles to poor leaseholders, would be to recast the 1967 legislation so that leaseholders obtained their freehold automatically, subject to standard compensation.

How state officials administer the law may turn directly on the individual's ability to pay. A clear case is that the person who cannot raise bail remains in custody. It seems that in certain circumstances the police have fixed bail in the knowledge that those arrested cannot pay.[20] In particular circumstances the refusal of bail might be justified, but this ought to be done so that the basis is explicit (for example, because the person might abscond). In the United States bail bondsmen provide some assistance to those who cannot afford bail. Quite apart from the immediate incarceration suffered, poor people who do not obtain bail may ultimately have a harsher sentence imposed upon them. The available evidence indicates that a person in custody is more likely to plead guilty, more likely to be convicted despite a plea of not guilty, and more likely if convicted to be imprisoned.[21]

Fines weigh more heavily on the poor than on the affluent. One study of the social consequences of fines found that poorer people had to economize on necessities to pay them.[22] In some cases those fined may be imprisoned in default because they cannot pay. The problem of default is accentuated because defaulters spend a substantial period in prison in lieu of a relatively small fine.[23] The higher courts have said that it is wrong (and in the United States, unconstitutional) for a court to impose a fine which is beyond an offender's ability to pay, since this is likely to result in a sentence of imprisonment or the possibility of further offences to raise the money.[24] In practice, unless defendants take the initiative to draw attention to their means, it seems that lower courts often do not bother to investigate because of the delay and cost of doing so.[25] The Swedish 'day fine' system fixes the level of fines in statutes according to the gravity of the offence and then relates the fines imposed in particular cases directly to an individual's means.

In civil procedure, people may be at a disadvantage because of inability to pay. The most obvious example is that impecunious plaintiffs may be required to provide security for costs.[26] Another example is that it may be more difficult for them to obtain an interlocutory injunction because they cannot give an undertaking as to damages. The normal rule, established in 1975 in *American Cyanamid Co. v. Ethicon Ltd*,[27] is that an applicant ought to be granted an interlocutory injunction on the balance of convenience whenever there is a serious question to be tried. A factor to be taken into account in assessing the balance of convenience is whether the defendant would be adequately compensated by an undertaking by the applicant to pay damages for any loss sustained by reason of the injunction, should it later be decided at trial that the applicant does not have a case. However, in *De Falco v. Crawley B. C.* (1980),[28] a case involving the Housing (Homeless Persons) Act 1977, the Court of Appeal held that homeless persons should go beyond showing a balance of convenience and should establish a strong *prima facie* case. Reasons were that they could not give a worthwhile undertaking as to damages and that to order the local authority to house would interfere with its system of priorities. Even if this is a valid basis for distinguishing *American Cyanamid* – and that decision made plain that the undertaking as to damages was only one of the factors to be taken into account – the Court of Appeal omitted any comment on how their decision disadvantaged poorer persons. Yet in the same year the Court of Appeal had granted a Mareva injunction in a personal injury case to prevent assets being removed from the jurisdiction, without requiring the legally aided plaintiff to give an undertaking as to damages. 'I do not see why a poor plaintiff should be denied a Mareva injunction just because he is poor, whereas a rich plaintiff would get it', said Lord Denning M.R.[29] The decisions are difficult to reconcile on legal grounds.

The cost of litigation includes the expense of preparing the necessary documents, court fees, witness fees, and wages forgone to attend the hearing, quite apart from the expense of employing a lawyer. In 1834 James Stephen, the Colonial Undersecretary, remarked: 'These Irishmen are not the first, nor will they be the last, to make the discovery that a man may starve and yet have the best right of action a special pleader could wish for.'[30] A lack of means may affect the settlement process, as in motor-car accidents, since poorer persons may settle a legal claim to their disadvantage because of the cost of proceeding and the pressing need for compensation money. Unless strongly backed by a trade union or by legal aid, the poor plaintiff is especially vulnerable since large institutions do not always have an incentive to settle speedily.

For many years, debtors could be imprisoned for inability to meet a debt under a procedure begun in the later Middle Ages. The procedure was quite ineffective in inducing payment, for usually debtors could not pay. It was severely criticized for it meant that creditors had the extraordinary power to have a debtor imprisoned before any trial, and then later when the debt was established. The courts were largely passive – they did not attempt to ascertain a debtor's resources nor to impose a settlement – and the debtor's ultimate discharge normally lay in the hands of the creditor. Legislation formally abolished imprisonment for debt in the nineteenth century, but the courts could still commit a debtor to prison for culpable failure to pay a judgment debt. Many thousands continued to be imprisoned, mainly poor people.[31] In the United States, certain states abolished or restricted imprisonment for debt.[32] Ultimately in England imprisonment for debt was abolished and replaced by the attachment of earnings, which enables a regular part of a person's wages to be directed to the reduction of his or her debts.[33]

Wealth is usually associated with knowledge, skills, education and confidence, and all these influence whether individuals exercise their legal rights. One argument is that poorer people are less 'legally competent' – less knowledgeable, less skilled and less confident in relation to the law. Accordingly, it is said, they are more likely to become victims of injustice, but less likely to use the legal system to their advantage. The matter is explored below in relation to the unequal utilization of legal services. Another aspect is that the poorer sections of society may fail to take the initiative over matters capable of legal resolution because they are intimidated by what law is usually associated with (e.g., the police, the courts, and prison). As a result of their experience and the experience of others, they might feel – perhaps unjustifiably – that a matter will be brushed off by those in authority. There might also be the fear that if they take legal action their employer, their landlord or the social welfare department will retaliate. While the law tends to assume that granting rights to weaker parties neutralizes differences in power, many will regard acquiescence as a more rational response than the assertion of those rights. There also seems to be an attitude among some poorer people, especially among the elderly, that certain problems are 'private' and 'personal', and that they should find the solution within the network of family or friends. Finally, people might not conceptualize something as a legal problem about which anything can be done: rather, it is something that must be tolerated even though it makes life difficult. Certainly this was the response of residents in a deprived area of Cardiff:

> Environmental decay and the particular issues which arise do not suddenly occur, but develop over a period of time in such a way that they can become just a background part of living – something one deplores when in conversation with one's neighbour, but feels it futile to do anything about. . . . It is one thing to have one's determination to sort out a problem fuelled by the sense of injustice that arises when one feels singled out by the local authority, Supplementary Benefits Commission, or one's landlord. It is quite another to generate passion over an environmental problem which has developed over a number of years as an area decays, and which everybody 'has to put up with'.[34]

Asymmetry in civil-law matters

There are situations where the poorer sections of society have been active in instituting civil proceedings in the courts. With the assistance of legal aid, many have been able to obtain a divorce. Trade-union backing enables workers to bring personal injuries claims against employers for negligence, breach of statutory duty or breach of contract. Many motorists can claim against other drivers for personal injury or property damage because lawyers or motorists' organizations are prepared to support claims. But with other matters such as debt and mortgage default, ordinary people appear in the civil courts not as plaintiffs but as defendants, and in the great majority of cases do not defend the action.[35]

A consequence of ordinary people not using the civil courts to advance certain claims or to defend certain actions may be that the courts' decisions in these areas reflect the values of commercial, property or government interests. This need not be because the courts are biased, but because the arguments they hear are mainly from commercial, property and government interests. Moreover, these interests usually have strong cases because of expertise, advance planning, good record-keeping, and so on.[36] These interests cannot be unaware that in many cases they will obtain default judgments against individuals, and that in such circumstances their claims will receive little scrutiny from the courts. Indeed, there are always the unscrupulous who take advantage of the fact that a large number of individuals will not stand on their legal rights; they are similar to those described by Reginald H. Smith in his classic study, *Justice and the Poor*:

Because law is all-embracing, the denial of its protection means the destruction of homes through illegal foreclosures, the loss through trick or chicanery of lifetime savings, the taking away of children from their parents by fraudulent guardianship proceedings. . . . Denial of justice is not merely negative in effect; it actively encourages fraud and dishonesty. Unscrupulous employers, seeing the inability of wage-earners to enforce payments, have deliberately hired men without the slightest intention of paying them. There exist today businesses established, conducted, and flourishing on the principle that as against the poor the law can be violated with impunity because redress is beyond their reach.[37]

Public legal assistance, the legal regulation of transactions and so on are tools for 'keeping honest' those like employers, creditors, landlords and social welfare agencies. There is the more fundamental question, not tackled here, of whether the state should allow commercial, property and government interests to invoke its coercive power against individuals in cases where they rarely defend and where the courts do not have the resources to vet the claims.

The idea of a dual system of law – one law for the rich, one for the poor – occurs frequently in literature. Popular culture sometimes contrasts the lower courts, where ordinary people can be tried without legal assistance and imprisoned by low-status magistrates, with the higher courts, where the property and commercial interests of the wealthier are litigated, and the smallest case is tried by lawyers before professional judges. Tenbroek developed the idea of the dual system to highlight the inequality in Californian family law. Duality, he argued, was evident in the system of rules which the poor had to comply with to receive social welfare, compared with the civil family law which governed family relationships in the rest of society. One example he gave was that while common-law marriage was not recognized in family law, the income of a man cohabiting with a woman was considered by the state in determining her financial elegibility for social welfare benefits.[38]

The costs of court action were the most important factor in the development of an antinomy in English family law. Two separate jurisdictions, the High Court and the magistrates' courts, evolved side by side to deal with the same matrimonial problems, but according to different rules and by means of different remedies. In the nineteenth century it was very expensive to obtain a divorce by private Act of Parliament or by ecclesiastic decree, and that continued to be the case after the Matrimonial Causes Act 1857 (20 & 21 Vict., c.85). The poor had no recourse to legal process until 1878, when the Matrimonial Causes Act of that year (41 & 42 Vict., c.19) provided that the magistrates could grant a wife a separation order – but not a divorce – with maintenance and the custody of young children if her husband was convicted of aggravated assault on her. With time the magistrates' jurisdiction was extended. By 1910 the High Court was dealing with about 800 petitions a year for divorce and separation, whereas the magistrates handled some 15,000 applications a year. The Finer Report commented on the contrast between the 1857 reforms, which regarded legal intervention in family matters as so delicate and important that the jurisdiction was entrusted to professional judges of the highest rank, and the measures of 1878, considered adequate for the cruder requirements of the working classes, where remedies were administered by lay magistrates in courts closely associated with the police.[39]

In the twentieth century a limited number of poorer persons were able to obtain a divorce in the High Court under the poor persons' procedure, but assistance under it was grossly inadequate, and in 1935 there were still nearly five times as many complaints for magistrates' court orders as petitions for divorce. Even after the Legal Aid and Advice Act 1949, demand could not be satisfied, although most of the legal-aid funds were allocated to family matters. The magistrates' jurisdiction continued in importance. In 1971 at least one-third of the cases taken to the magistrates' courts ended at that point without divorce proceedings being taken. To explain the remarkable persistence of a dual family law, despite legal aid, the Finer committee referred to social and cultural factors: the poor were used to invoking magistrates' court jurisdiction; the social agencies they dealt with (principally social welfare officers) steered them in this direction; and the solicitors they instructed usually had a regular practice in the magistrates' courts. The magistrates' courts declined in popularity when the divorce Reform Act 1969 removed fault as an essential element for divorce.[40]

II THE UNEQUAL UTILIZATION OF LEGAL SERVICES

A particular aspect of inequality in the way the legal system operates is that the utilization of legal services within the community varies with social class.[41] The variation depends, however, on the type of matter. With property matters such as domestic conveyancing, the estates of deceased persons, and making or altering wills, a disproportionate number of users come from the higher social classes. With a second category of matters – mainly divorce, crime, and seeking compensation for injuries arising from motor-vehicle accidents – the incidence of use does not vary greatly with social class. Thirdly, with a few matters such as compensation for industrial injury, the lower social classes are obviously greater users of lawyers' services. In pursuing such claims, workers are assisted by trade unions.[42]

Virtually all commentators are misled by the finding that for a number of important matters (divorce, crime, motor-vehicle compensation) there appear to be few differences in lawyer-use along the lines of social class. This fact is partly responsible for the popular conclusion which rejects social class as a causal factor in lawyer-use. Yet the important (though neglected) point is that the pattern of lawyer-use in cases of divorce, crime and motor-vehicle compensation is the product of institutional arrangements benefiting the poorer sections of society. For some time, divorce work has been heavily subsidized by the state through legal aid; and those seeking compensation for motor-vehicle accidents obtain legal assistance from motoring organizations, or from lawyers because there is a good chance of compensation through insurance. In other words, a pattern which seems to undermine the association between lawyer-use and social class turns out, on further examination, to support it. Let us look first at the reasons for the pattern of utilization of legal services and then at the consequences.

Explaining utilization of legal services

Various explanations have been advanced as to the unequal utilization of legal services. The first emphasizes the immediate attributes of social class. There is some evidence that cost, or at least scepticism about the value of solicitors' services in relation to cost, is an important reason why people do not consult lawyers.[43] People might be deterred by cost, even if legal aid is available, because they do not know of its existence or think they are ineligible. The location of lawyers' offices might be another reason why those in the lower social classes seek legal advice less than others. Market forces produce an uneven geographic distribution of lawyers' services: lawyers' offices are concentrated in the central commercial districts (for closeness to institutions like banks, building societies, companies and the courts), and in the wealthier suburbs in some urban areas (where they are conveniently located for conveyancing work).[44] There is evidence that this affects whether people approach lawyers, because in surveys some people indicate that convenient location is the main reason for their choosing a particular lawyer. Of course if that lawyer had not been there these people may have persisted and found another. Other factors associated with social class may be that the disadvantaged do not own or have access to convenient transport to visit a lawyer; that lawyers' office hours are inconvenient (for example, workers might lose pay if they take time off work); and that people do not realize that they have a legal problem or that a lawyer might be able to assist them. Specifically, poorer people may not see the law as an instrument to assert legal claims in a positive manner. Their experience of law will often be as defendants, debtors, or social welfare claimants, in situations which are not of their own choosing. At the other end of the scale the wealthy may see law primarily as a preventive instrument, such as with tax and estate planning, to reap advantages which would otherwise not accrue.

The second explanation as to the use of lawyers turns on organizational factors. It contends that poorer people have fewer contacts with lawyers because a primary aim of the law, and the main activity of lawyers, is the protection and regulation of property interests.[45] Poorer persons experience other problems containing important legal elements, but the legal profession is not geared up for these because of the orientation of legal practice and training. So law firms routinely handle commercial work, conveyancing, estates, family matters, motor-vehicle accidents and crime, but may be hard pressed or unenthusiastic about dealing with matters brought by consumers, tenants (especially in public housing) and social welfare recipients.[46] Law courses, it might also be said, tend to be vocationally oriented in following and reinforcing traditional legal practice, and even though there has been a more pluralistic approach in recent times, courses are still confined by professional requirements. A further argument is that it is only recently that textbooks and manuals have been published in the social welfare area, which lawyers can consult if a client appears. All these factors have some part in moulding people's perceptions of what lawyers can do, so that those with a social welfare problem might not think of approaching them. By contrast, law centres cultivate areas of expertise such as welfare and housing law and become known as a source of assistance on such matters.

A particular aspect of professional organization, the rules of ethics, have inhibited the contacts that lawyers have with the poorer sections of society. The rules have traditionally prohibited touting and advertising. Lawyers who work part-time in law centres or legal advice centres might be prevented by these rules from adopting as clients those who first approach them at a centre when this is the most convenient arrangement. Because of the rules, lawyers who have chosen to practise in deprived areas might find it difficult to make their service known there, for example by sending circulars to, or holding meetings with, social workers or advisers. Fear of infringing the rules especially affects lawyers who might want to encourage a broader category of work like housing, or who might want to engage in a wider approach to legal practice such as group work.[47] Another rule inhibiting poverty practice has been that lawyers must not hold themselves out as being willing to cut fees to attract business. Thus the court in *Re a Solicitor*[48] upheld a disciplinary fine imposed on a solicitor who acted on a regular basis for a trade union, on the grounds that he was attracting business unfairly by cutting his fees. The justification for the rule is to prevent unfair competition, but the result is that lawyers cannot reduce fees to poorer people on a regular basis, although they may reduce them in isolated cases. These ethical rules are, however, under attack, and have been modified in some jurisdictions.

A third explanation focuses on the role of lay intermediaries in whether people take problems to lawyers. Various studies have shown that people who seek legal advice often discuss the matter with someone else beforehand, who recommends that it be sought. Personal intermediaries (relatives, friends, neighbours, fellow workers) seem to be more important than formal intermediaries (advice bureaux, estate agents, trade unions).[49] In as much as the disadvantaged do not have a similar network of knowledgeable and supportive relationships as other social classes, they are less likely to turn to the law.

Of these explanations the first, focusing on the immediate attributes of social class, is in considerable disfavour. The main grounds on which critics reject it seem to be, on the one hand, that all social classes underuse legal services where these might be of assistance, and, on the other hand, that some poorer persons use lawyers.[50] Yet this confuses two issues: the explanations for the use of legal services in general, and the explanations for the differences in use between social classes. The immediate attributes of social class are inappropriate to explain the first, but cannot be discounted as explanations for the second. An ancillary reason for rejecting the first explanation is said to be that those who feel the need to see a lawyer usually see one. However, 9 per cent of those in a survey conducted for the Royal Commission of Legal Services (England and Wales) felt the need to see a lawyer in 1977, but failed to see one. Even if we neglect the large number of people who never felt the need to see a lawyer – and this may include a large number who did not perceive that they had a legal problem – the number represented by this 9 per cent is more than one half the number in the survey (17 per cent) who actually saw a lawyer in that year. A considerable number of the 9 per cent gave cost as an explanation, which gives support to an argument for the centrality of social class.

Seen in one light the first explanation (turning on social class) subsumes the other explanations. The organization of legal services clearly affects their use, but is itself largely determined by wealth. If it became as profitable for lawyers in private practice to handle housing, employment and social welfare matters as to handle commercial and property matters, there is no doubt that the organization of legal services would change dramatically. The perception of whether lawyers were useful or appropriate would change, and (adopting the arguments of the organizational theorists) a wider section of society would seek legal assistance.[51] The explanation turning on the role of lay intermediaries is not necessarily inconsistent with the first explanation. It would seem that some poorer persons – for example, single parents living on social welfare benefits, old-age pensioners continuing to reside in neighbourhoods which have changed socially or economically – do not have the same network of supportive relationships as other classes in the community. Moreover, a common-sense hypothesis is that many of the lay intermediaries with whom poorer persons come in contact know few, if any, lawyers and are less inclined to value legal action than those with whom the middle and upper-middle classes come in contact.

What has been said is not to dismiss explanations which focus on organizational factors or lay intermediaries. The argument here, however, is that underlying these is the unequal distribution of wealth. The processes by which inequalities of wealth produce the differing use of legal services are complex, and it is in furthering our understanding of this complexity that these other explanations have a role. But their adherents suggest that they are something other than this – that in some way they are independent explanations. This downplaying of the importance of societal inequalities has a conservative bias. It leads to the conclusion that the focus of public policy should be on schemes which meet legal needs in general, because all social classes underuse lawyers. While the latter is true, to move the spotlight away from the greater underuse by the poorer sections of society is to neglect a clear inequality in the working of the legal system.

Unequal results

The upshot of the unequal utilization of legal services is that the poorer sections of society are disadvantaged in terms of outcomes. Although there is little evidence about the effectiveness of legal services in general,[52] it seems from various studies that there is a link between legal representation and success. Only 10 of the tenants but 123 of the landlords had legal representation in the 140 possession cases studied in two inner London County Courts in 1977. Possession orders were refused in the 10 cases, and it seems that the other tenants would have improved their chances if they had had professional legal advice and representation.[53] Twenty-three per cent of the some 63,000 persons appearing before Supplementary Benefits Appeals Tribunals on supplementary benefits matters in 1977 were represented by a third party – less than 1 per cent had legal representation, about 4 per cent had help from a trade union, claimants' union or other organization, 4 per cent had a social or welfare worker, and 15 per cent had a friend or relative. The percentage of favourable decisions was higher in cases where the claimant was represented (36 per cent as opposed to 14 per cent), although this varied according to the type of representation (37 per cent legal, 41 per cent trade union etc., 51 per cent social or welfare worker, 32 per cent friend or relative).[54] In a small United States study of disability hearings, there was a tendency for the represented to be at an advantage, but to a lesser extent in medical cases where there was already a considerable volume of information and knowledge.[55] The introduction of the Aboriginal Legal Service in Australia, and the representation it has provided for Aborigines before the courts, has been accompanied by lower penalties imposed for minor offences in the magistrates' courts, and reduced sentences on appeal.[56]

There may be a maximum success rate, however, beyond which representation has no influence on the overall result. Most of the studies are not adequately controlled for factors like the complexity of a matter, the strength of a case, and the quality of the representative. For example, those who are represented may have a higher chance of success in the first place – those more confident in their claim seek assistance, and lawyers etc. might sift out weaker cases – so that what appears to be a clear relationship between representation and outcome may be partly spurious. Variations in outcome depending on the type of representation need to be explored further. The figures quoted near the end of the previous paragraph suggest that supplementary benefit claimants were as well represented by lay advocates as lawyers. Moreover, there is a relationship between attendance and success, which may be at least as important as that between representation and success. The London County Court study shows that in 66 cases of rent arrears, tenants who attended had fewer possession orders made against those who did not. The percentage of favourable decisions from the SBAT study just mentioned were as follows:[57]

Representation by third party, appellant personally attending	37
Representation by third party, appellant not personally attending	34
Attendance by appellant without representation by third party	26
No representation or attendance in person by appellant	7

Clearly attendance by a person accompanied by a representative is most conducive to success. The effect of attendance on outcome may be because judges, registrars and tribunals assume that those who do not appear do not have a strong case. In fact, they may have good reasons for not attending court and tribunal hearings, such as illness, uncertainty and the difficulty of taking time off work. Where they do not think they have a strong case in law they may of course be mistaken.

Representation and outcome have been most thoroughly studied in the criminal courts. Traditionally, the majority of defendants tried summarily were unrepresented, even on serious charges, and even where custodial sentences were imposed. The position has improved somewhat because of duty-solicitor schemes and the extension of criminal legal aid. Various studies are used to draw the conclusion that defendants with legal representation do better than others in terms of obtaining bail, not pleading guilty when they are not guilty, being acquitted, and receiving a non-custodial sentence.[58] None of these studies is as conclusive as is sometimes claimed, and some are methodologically flawed because they assume that the only relevant difference is legal representation. Other factors besides legal representation affect decisions made about defendants, including the type of charge, the defendant's background and record, and the circumstances of an alleged offence.

Moreover, there are reasons for thinking that merely because a defendant is legally represented does not guarantee that the outcome will always be more favourable. Lawyers sometimes convince defendants to plead guilty against their own inclinations.[59] In many cases lawyers advise a guilty plea because they genuinely and correctly believe that their clients will be convicted anyhow and will be better off in terms of the sentence they receive. In other cases, the wider context leads to other inferences: for example, in magistrates' courts there might well be links between the police and regular lawyers – the police may acquiesce in their requests for remands or about the timing of cases, facilitate their access to the cells, and put business their way, provided that they in turn are not obstructive and straighten out 'messy cases' beforehand, such as ones with a 'confused plea'.[60] Plea bargaining occurs within a similar context and is not always what defendants want nor what is in their interests.[61]

III THE SUBSTANCE OF THE LAW

In his book *Justice and the Poor* published in 1926, F.C.G. Gurney-Champion argued that the law was unequal because of its administration rather than its substantive provisions. So far as England was concerned, he said, the substance of the law, with the exception of some trade-union law, was fair and equal to all classes and sections of the community. The problem was that although judges attempted to apply the law equally, it was quite impossible when parties were without proper legal assistance. Many have echoed Gurney-Champion's view that the problem facing the poor is in the administration of the law.[62] The aim of this part is to demonstrate that inequalities still exist in the substance of the law which disadvantage the poorer sections of society. If the third standard of equality before the law outlined at the outset of the chapter is accepted, then these areas of law are inconsistent with it, in that the disadvantages created by them cannot be justified.

Introduction

Inequality operates in at least three distinct ways in the substance of the law in relation to the poorer sections of society. First, there are provisions in the law which disadvantage them rather directly. The bulk of these have been repealed, but there are still a few examples in force, of which vagrancy legislation is the most important; it is examined below. Second, the law favours certain categories over other categories, and typically the poorer sections of society occupy the less-favoured categories. Historically, the law has tended to favour landlords over tenants, employers over employees, and producers over consumers. Landlords, employers and producers have tended to be wealthier than tenants, employees and consumers. Landlord and tenant law is the example which has been chosen for detailed discussion here.[63] Third, substantive and procedural law set the parameters within which the law is administered. To the extent that state bureaucracies are entrusted with wide discretion, they might apply the law in violation of the formal standard of equality before the law. Where this occurs it does so because non-legal influences shape the implementation of the law, but the relevant point here is that substantive and adjectival law itself can strengthen the tendency by the way it confers discretion. Aspects of this third point have already been touched on in this chapter and other aspects are raised in later chapters: for example, social welfare regulation might be cast in such a form that those who administer it develop enforcement philosophies inhibiting its effectiveness (see Chapter 4); and those administering social welfare legislation might be able to exercise their wide discretion in ways which are detrimental to the interests of its supposed beneficiaries (see Chapters 5 and 6).

Vagrancy legislation

Throughout most of its history, vagrancy law has disadvantaged the poor in an overt manner. However, its particular operation has varied considerably over the centuries although its substantive provisions have remained largely constant. The first vagrancy statutes in England were designed as part of a policy to force labourers to accept low-wage employment after the depopulation caused by the Black Death and the decline of serfdom. With the rise of commercialism in Tudor times, vagrancy law became more associated with the criminal law and was directed to maintaining social order, for example to prevent attacks on the increasing trade between commercial centres.[64] In later centuries, too, vagrancy law was used to deal with political discontent and social disturbance, although in England its main function was to deal with individual deviants. Punishment for vagrants was cruel by modern standards and whipping was practised for several centuries.[65] An Act of 1744 meant that vagrants could also be impressed into the armed services. However, local authorities did not always implement the more extreme punishments of mutilation, transportation, or death for repeating offenders. The vagrancy statutes were not supposed to be applied to those who fell under the poor law, but were commonly used against unemployed labourers.[66] This practice was facilitated because poverty was closely associated with crime in popular belief.[67] Similarly, special Tramp Acts were adopted in the United States in the late nineteenth century, in addition to vagrancy legislation, to control the hundreds of thousands of workers who as a result of economic depressions took to the road looking for work.[68]

Under the present vagrancy legislation in England, beggars are deemed to be idle and disorderly persons.[69] The Working Party on Vagrancy and Street Offences said in 1976 that begging should continue to be controlled because it could be a nuisance and because not all beggars were necessarily deprived.[70] It is a little surprising when an official body admits openly that persons should be subject to the criminal law because they are a nuisance to the respectable. The homeless can be prosecuted under the legislation as rogues and vagabonds if they sleep out and cannot give a good account of themselves.[71] The homeless might also be caught by that part of the legislation which deems a person found on enclosed premises for an unlawful purpose to be a rogue or a vagabond. The offences have little to recommend them when it is realized that they are mainly invoked against those such as derelict alcoholics, the single (and often young) homeless, and casual labourers.[72] Sleeping rough occurs because of the lack of cheap accommodation and the absence of sufficient treatment facilities in the case of derelict alcoholics. In the past some police forces have used the offences as justification for moving on those they have regarded as a social nuisance.[73] As the minority report of the Home Affairs Committee of the House of Commons argued in 1981, it is not a legitimate function of the criminal law 'to conceal from the squeamish the unpalatable nature of the hardship and degradation endured by these unfortunate people'.[74]

In the result the vagrancy legislation singles out poor people for discriminatory treatment and criminalizes what is really marginal and harmless behaviour. More serious behaviour of the same character is caught by other legislation.[75] Apart from the substantive offences, the procedure laid down in the legislation is unsatisfactory. Persons who commit offences under it are deemed to be idle and disorderly persons or rogues and vagabonds, and are liable to summary conviction. If they have a previous conviction for the offence or if they violently resist arrest as a rogue and vagabond, they might be deemed to be an incorrigible rogue and be liable for heavier penalties. Prison sentences have not been uncommon, but are unlikely to deter or rehabilitate. In 1982 imprisonment for begging and sleeping rough was abolished, although inability to pay a fine might still lead to imprisonment in default.[76]

Until recently there was a 'suspected person' provision in the vagrancy legislation. Known in common parlance as SUS, it covered every suspected person who loitered in streets or places adjacent to streets, with intent to commit an arrestable offence. Such persons were deemed rogues and vagabonds and could be arrested and sent to prison for up to three months. Judicial decision confirmed that the section had a wide ambit and could be used in a preventive way by the police, so long as they could give evidence of at least one suspicious act (not necessarily criminal) prior to and distinct from that which caused the person to be charged with the offence.[77] Immediately before its repeal there were some two and half to three and half thousand prosecutions a year for the offence. The arrest rates for blacks in some areas were greater than for whites, which did not seem to be an accurate indication of relative black and white involvement in crime. The section, together with other offences, was also used by some police forces to 'move on' groups of black youths from places like shopping streets, and to stop and search individual blacks on the streets late at night. The police denied racial bias and justified the use of SUS as a preventive measure against offences ranging from minor theft to more serious 'mugging'. Critics saw its use as part of an attempt to control poor and unemployed blacks, and to forestall wider social unrest.[78] As early as 1937, Scott L.J. had commented:

It seems to me wrong that these old phrases should still be made the occasion of arrest and prosecution, when in their historical meaning they are so utterly out of keeping with modern life in England. . . . Is it not time that our relevant statutes should be revised. . . . To retain such laws seems to me inconsistent with our national sense of personal liberty or our respect for the rule of law.[79]

In 1980 an all-party House of Commons Committee recommended that SUS be repealed, primarily because repeal would be of great symbolic importance for race relations but also because it was unsatisfactory in principle to penalize the forming of criminal intention.[80] The Criminal Attempts Act 1981 repealed SUS, but there are similar offences, some operating only in particular localities, which are still extant.[81] In the United States the courts have held that vagrancy laws which penalize loitering or loitering without apparent reason are unconstitutional on the due process grounds that they are so vague that potential offenders do not know what conduct is proscribed, and that arbitrary and discriminatory enforcement of the law is encouraged.[82]

Before 1935 the offences of sleeping rough and not being able to give a good account only applied to those who did 'not have any visible means of subsistence'. The requirement was repealed in that year because on its face it blatantly discriminated against the poor. Similar provisions continued in jurisdictions in the United States.[83] In Australian jurisdictions, 'not having any visible means of subsistence' has been an independent head of liability under vagrancy legislation. Queensland legislation provides that any person who 'having no visible lawful means of support or insufficient means, does not, on being charged before a court, give to its satisfaction a good account of his means of support', shall be deemed to be a vagrant.[84] This sort of offence is doubly objectionable. First, it diverges from the ordinary principles of criminal law by placing the onus on defendants to give a good account of their means, once the prosecution has raised a reasonable or probable presumption of the absence or insufficiency of lawful means of support. Persons charged with the offence have been precisely those ill-equipped to tackle this task. Second, in its application it penalizes poverty directly. The courts interpreted the offence narrowly to hold that it is not aimed at those who, although poor, derive their income from lawful sources. The sufficiency of a person's means, they have held, is to be judged according to the standard of living of the individual concerned.[85] In practice the police have applied the offence precisely to those who on this interpretation do not fall within its ambit.[86] New South Wales and Victoria repealed the offence in the late seventies, on the grounds that it operated in practice against the poorest and most vulnerable; that it gave the police and magistrates undesirably wide discretion; and that it fell within the category of 'victimless crimes'.[87]

Landlord and tenant law

There are three sources of inequality in the landlord and tenant relationship: first, despite legal regulation of matters like rent and housing standards, freedom of contract still determines important aspects of the landlord-tenant relationship; secondly, the substantive law of landlord and tenant, which operates in the absence of agreement between the parties, tends to favour landlords over tenants; and thirdly, tenants do not take advantage of the rights which common law and statutory law confer on them.

(a) Freedom of contract
The first source of inequality is relatively straightforward. The familiar problem of freedom of contract is that the interests of stronger parties generally prevail over those of the weaker. On the whole, landlords are in the stronger position and tenants in the weaker

because tenants tend to be poorer and more vulnerable,[88] and because of the shortage of privately rented accommodation. Moreover, the landlord's interests will be protected to a greater extent than the tenant's if the former uses a standard-form contract, because this will be prepared by lawyers or estate agents who, in relation to residential property, act more for landlords than for tenants.

The courts have developed a doctrine of unconscionability whereby contracts can be set aside because of unfairness resulting from a party's special disability. But it has been expressly stated that the doctrine does not apply to a homeless person who pays a high rent to obtain housing.[89] In the United States unconscionability is enshrined in the Uniform Commercial Code, and the courts have used this to strike down terms in leases.[90] In the future, tenants in Britain might obtain some benefit from the Unfair Contract Terms Act 1977. So too in jurisdictions such as South Australia, where the Residential Tenancies Tribunal may order, rescind or vary a term in a lease if satisfied that it is harsh or unconscionable.[91] All the barriers outlined above, however, stand in the way of tenants initiating the necessary legal action. Apart from such civil-law provisions, there is legislation which regulates particular aspects of the landlord-tenant relationship; this is considered below.

Freedom of contract means of course that landlords can allocate tenancies virtually to whom they wish. There are of course the limitations in anti-discrimination legislation, and there are other specific controls such as those over the operation of accommodation agencies.[92] But persons are differentially placed with respect to the means and criteria determining access to privately rented accommodation. For example, relatively poor tenants may be outbid for lettings by young workers or students who increase their rent-paying capacity by pooling their resources.[93] Landlords, estate agents and accommodation agencies may take advantage of the shortage of privately rented accommodation to discriminate against low-income families, especially if they have children.[94] While landlords might have a legitimate interest in minimizing the non-payment of rent, disturbance to other tenants or the damage to property, these results would not necessarily follow if low-income families were on an equal footing with other tenants. Rent allowances, for instance, can assist them to pay rent regularly. Legislatures in some jurisdictions in the United States and Australia have taken the view that it is unfair for landlords to discriminate against families with children; presumably they reason that children cause fewer disturbances or property damage than is commonly supposed, or that there are adequate mechanisms, such as the threat of eviction, to have parents control their children, or taking security bonds to compensate for any damage.[95]

(b) The substantive law

The second source of inequality in the landlord-tenant relationship has been the substance of the law. This is worth tracing historically. Relatively early, English law moved away from the notion that the landlord-tenant relationship was solely contractual to the idea that tenants had an interest in land. Tenants obtained considerable protection under this legal regime as to possession and the maintenance of the rent bargain. When after a general rise in prices in the sixteenth century landlords sought to obtain increased rents by wholesale evictions, the Court of Requests protected tenants' possession.[96] But despite such protection tenants were not on the same footing as freeholders. In particular they did not have the right to vote. Procedural and statutory changes in the nineteenth century attenuated the protection of tenants. Previous law had limited forfeiture in various ways, but in the nineteenth century equity rarely intervened, statute removed the need for landlords to reserve the right to re-enter in the case of non-payment of rent, the necessity for formal demand of rent was abandoned, and tenants' counterclaims were excluded in summary proceedings. Some of these changes reflected changes in contract law and in civil procedure, and were the outcome of nineteenth-century social and economic policy.[97] Lord Denning points to the judges' excessive concern in the nineteenth century with individual property rights and freedom of contract, and to how doctrines enunciated at that time carried over to modern landlord-tenant law as a result of *stare decisis*.[98] An example is that the judges held that, except in the case of an express warranty or deceit, a landlord was not bound to disclose to tenants the ruinous or unsafe state of a dwelling. The judges applied the principle *caveat emptor*, that people could protect themselves by inspecting and, presumably, paying a rent commensurate with the condition of a dwelling.[99] Added to the inequalities inherent in the rules of landlord and tenant law were those which occurred because the rules operated in social conditions different from when they evolved. Perhaps it was appropriate in an agricultural society for tenants to be legally responsible for providing amenities (e.g., water) or for keeping any building in repair, for they might have thought these optional, and would most likely have had the skills to effect repairs themselves. That was certainly not the case in an urban society, especially for tenants living in flats. In these circumstances it would have been more appropriate for landlords to have the obligation of repair, particularly when in most cases they were in the best position financially to assume the responsibility.[100]

Even today tenants are not greatly protected by the common law, although this is not the case in many jurisdictions in the United States where the courts have modified the common law so that it is more favourable to tenants. The common law imposes certain obligations on landlords, but these are limited in scope, and can be modified by 'agreement' between the parties to the further disadvantage of tenants. As we shall see, the shortcomings of the common law have led to legislation. Two concerns often facing tenants illustrate these points – the physical condition of rented premises, and interference with a tenant's occupation of premises.

There is an implied condition at common law that furnished premises are reasonably fit for habitation at the beginning of a tenancy, but this does not mean that the premises have to remain fit.[101] Only a limited number of defects are covered by the covenant such as infestation by bugs and defective drainage, but not the condition of appliances and furnishings. Apparently only tenants, and not their families or friends, can benefit, because the liability is contractual.[102] Moreover, landlords of unfurnished premises are under no duty to ensure that they are fit for human habitation.[103] Precedent did not require the rule about unfurnished premises, but it was in keeping with the social philosophy of the time and particularly the doctrine of *caveat emptor*. The rule was justified by reference to the adverse consequences which would follow if a warranty were implied in leases taken for building or agriculture – which quite ignored the problems facing poorer urban dwellers.[104] It is of interest that in nineteenth-century England the upper-middle and upper class rented *furnished* property when they visited places like London, Brighton or Bath. The courts in various jurisdictions in the United States have now overturned the common law and have held that there is an implied non-excludable warranty of habitability for all residential leases, both at their commencement and for their duration.[105]

At common law, landlords are generally not under any implied obligation regarding repair.[106] On the other hand, the common law imposes duties on tenants in relation to repair. Weekly tenants must use the premises in a tenant-like manner; and yearly tenants and tenants for a term of years must use the premises in a tenant-like manner and possibly also keep them wind and water-tight, fair wear and tear excepted.[107] Standard-form tenancy agreements frequently impose the additional obligation on tenants to keep and deliver up the premises in repair, fair wear and tear excepted. The courts have construed this to mean that tenants must keep the premises up to the condition they were in at the commencement of the term, replacing minor parts which can no longer be repaired. The injustice to tenants is apparent, for it could cause them heavy expenditure the benefit of which, in the case of short-term tenancies, would accrue mainly to the landlord. The courts have also held that despite the fair-wear-and-tear exception, tenants remain liable for consequential damage (e.g. interior damage where the roof develops a leak).[108]

In standard-form contracts landlords may agree to accept some responsibility for repairs, for instance external and structural repairs. But the courts have held that landlords cannot be liable under repairing covenants unless notified of the need for repair, even when disrepair should be apparent to them.[109] Tenants can obtain damages for breach of repairing covenants, but these might not cover the cost of repair. Damages are based on the diminution in the value of the tenancy, which will be very little in the case of weekly tenancies, although possibly not if they are protected by security of tenure legislation.[110] If the premises are uninhabitable, tenants can claim damages for inconvenience and for damage to their property or health but not, it seems, for the cost of alternative accommodation. It seems that tenants can obtain specific performance of a repairing covenant where there is a clear breach and it is plain what work is required.[111]

Parliament has stepped in, in England, to amend the common law on habitability and repair. Beginning with section 12 of the Housing of the Working Classes Act 1885 (48 & 49 Vict., c.72), landlords have had a statutory duty regarding fitness for habitation. The present law, section 6 of the Housing Act 1957, imposes a non-excludable obligation on landlords of low-rental housing to ensure that it is fit for habitation at the commencement of the tenancy and remains so for its duration. The statute provides that a house shall be deemed to be unfit if it is so far defective as regards repair, stability, damp, sanitary facilities, etc., that it is not reasonably suitable for occupation (s.4).

Section 32 of the Housing Act 1961 obliges the landlords of houses let for less than seven years to keep their structure and exterior in repair, and their water, gas, electricity and sanitary installations in repair and proper working order. Both provisions are limited in scope: because of inflation few tenancies now qualify for protection under section 6; and section 32 does not extend to internal structure, decoration and lighting, and does not set as high a standard for housing in poorer as compared with wealthier areas, since regard must be had to the age, character, locality and prospective life of a house in determining the standard of repair (s.32(3)).

Moreover, the courts have not always been favourably disposed to the provisions. For example, they have read down the statutory duty on landlords regarding fitness for habitation by holding that only the tenant (and not his family) can sue on it; that it does not extend to parts like common staircases in multi-occupied premises (a decision mitigated by statute); that the standard of fitness required is low; and that the covenant only applies in situations where the house is capable of being made fit at reasonable expense. The latter decision means that landlords actually have an incentive to ignore their obligations, for once a dwelling deteriorates beyond a certain point they cannot be obliged to take any action. With both provisions the courts have held that a tenant must give notice of a defect before the landlord can be liable, even with a latent defect.[112] The courts had little basis for reading down the legislation by importing this common-law requirement, since Parliament seems to have made the judgement that landlords were generally the best loss-bearers.

By contrast with England, other jurisdictions have proceeded down the path of a general, non-excludable obligation on landlords in relation to habitability and repair. So section 46 of the South Australian Residential Tenancies Act 1978–81 provides as a term of every residential tenancy agreement that the landlord shall provide the premises in a reasonable state of cleanliness; provide and maintain them in a reasonable state of repair; compensate the tenant for any reasonable expenses incurred where the state of disrepair has arisen otherwise than through a breach by the tenant; and comply with all buildings, health and safety requirements. The main duties cast on tenants are to keep the premises in a reasonable state of cleanliness, to notify the landlord of any damage to the premises, not intentionally or negligently to cause or permit damage to them, and not to cause or permit a nuisance.[113] The economic effects of regulation, such as that relating to habitability and repair, are considered in the following chapter.

A second example of the shortcomings of the common law relates to interference with a tenant's occupation of premises by harassment or unlawful eviction. Together with the torts of trespass, assault, nuisance, deceit, intimidation and so on, the covenants implied by the common law for quiet enjoyment and non-derogation from grant are of some relevance to harassment.[114] But the implied covenant for quiet enjoyment is confined to interruptions by the landlord or by those claiming through or under him, and lasts only while the landlord's estate is in existence. Accordingly it does not cover the acts of a superior landlord in the case of sub-tenants. Moreover, the covenant only extends to physical interruption with a tenant's possession or to a deliberate, persistent and prolonged course of intimidation – by no means the only forms of harassment.[115] Under the implied covenant for non-derogation, landlords who retain part of their property must not permit any activity there inconsistent with the lease. Legislation in some jurisdictions has improved those covenants from the point of view of tenants, for example extending the covenant for quiet enjoyment to interruption by those with superior title.[116]

At common law, fixed-term tenancies ordinarily terminate with the effluxion of time, but landlords must serve a valid notice to quit to bring periodic tenancies (weekly, monthly, yearly tenancies) to an end. Subject to contrary agreement, the common law required that to be valid a notice to quit should expire at the end of a completed period and should be at least of the same period as the tenancy (a month's notice for a monthly tenancy, etc., except that half a year's notice suffices for yearly tenancies). Since traditionally most poorer tenants have been weekly tenants, they have obtained little advantage from this rule. Statute now gives them protection: so in England a notice to quit must be in writing and be given not less than four weeks before the date on which it is to take effect.[117] The common-law rules about termination of a tenancy are drastically affected where rent control, and the security of tenure that goes with it, operate.

If tenants breach their lease, the landlord may be able to evict them. Landlords lose the right to evict if they waive the breach, either expressly or by implication. Waiver occurs, for example, if the landlord with knowledge of the breach demands or accepts rent falling due after its occurrence. The courts can grant tenants relief against forfeiture for non-payment of rent if they pay the rent and the landlord's expenses, and it is just and equitable to grant relief. Tenants can apply for an injunction to restrain landlords from evicting them in breach of these requirements or to reinstate them if they have already been evicted. In addition, tenants might also be able to sue for special damages (to cover expenses like hotel accommodation); general damages (for unspecified damage – the courts award standard rates for loss of occupancy); aggravated damages (to compensate for severe suffering or to express indignation at the way the tenant has been treated); and exemplary damages (to act as a deterrent to calculated wrongdoing).[118] There are now important criminal prohibitions on landlords effecting physical entry, peacefully or otherwise: they must proceed through the courts whenever they wish to recover the possession of premises in which a tenant or former tenant continues to reside.[119]

It is well documented that poorer tenants in inner-city areas have experienced harassment and unlawful eviction.[120] Gentrification has been an important cause, because property owners obviously need to obtain vacant possession to renovate and sell. Harassment and unlawful eviction also occur where landlords require a room for their own or a relative's use, where they are angered when a tenant applies to the authorities for his or her rent to be controlled, or where they object to a tenant's behaviour. In many cases landlords will not need to resort to these tactics, since tenants are usually ignorant of their rights and might relinquish security simply because the landlord requests it.[121]

In some jurisdictions harassment and unlawful eviction have been made criminal offences, and officials are appointed to enforce the law. The English Protection from Eviction Act 1977, section 1(2), makes it a criminal offence for a person unlawfully to deprive, or to attempt to deprive, a residential occupier of premises, unless the defendant establishes that he or she believed, and had reasonable cause to believe, that the occupier had ceased to reside in the premises.[122] Harassment is covered in section 1(3), which makes it an offence to commit acts calculated to interfere with the peace or comfort of residential occupiers or their households, or persistently to withdraw or withhold services reasonably required for occupation of the premises, with intent to cause them to give up occupation or to refrain from exercising any right or pursuing any remedy in respect of the premises. Banging on doors, removing fittings, or cutting off electricity or gas are acts which might constitute harassment, but it would seem that not all the acts covered by 'winkling' are included (i.e. sending around agents with inadequate offers to move, spreading rumours of imminent eviction, etc.). The courts have rejected the argument that the Act is social legislation, which should be construed liberally, and have applied instead the strict standards used with ordinary criminal offences.[123] The courts have also held that these provisions do not give rise to a civil cause of action for breach of statutory duty.[124] This makes it difficult for victims to obtain an injunction for breach of the provisions, because otherwise to restrain breach of the criminal law by injunction requires the approval of the Attorney-General or a showing of special damage.[125] However, tenants might be able to get compensation under legislation which allows this to be awarded against defendants after a conviction has been obtained.[126] Violent-entry provisions and the general criminal law of assault, criminal damage, and so on, might also cover acts of harassment and unlawful eviction.

(c) Enforcing legal rights

The third source of inequality in the landlord-tenant relationship – which relates to the discussion in the earlier parts of the chapter – is that, on the whole, poorer tenants do not assert their legal rights, no matter how favourable these might be. Either they do not know about their rights, or if they do, they face social, financial and legal obstacles to vindicating them. For example, they may fear eviction if they invoke repairing covenants. Some tenants fail to complain because they do not think a matter sufficiently serious, while others think a complaint would fall on deaf ears.[127] That tenants do not think disrepair sufficiently serious says little about its objective character, since poor tenants become accustomed to substandard conditions. Two studies of possession actions brought by landlords in county courts in London found that tenants were confused by the legal documents (many did not return the court form of admission or defence and those who did completed it incorrectly); few tenants received advice or assistance before the hearing, whereas most landlords had legal advice to draft their particulars of claim; many tenants did not appear and those who did tended not to have legal representation, by contrast with the bulk of the landlords; and those tenants who appeared and represented themselves were either incapable of presenting an adequate defence, or did not realize that with rent arrears a reasonable offer might lead to a suspended order.[128]

Revised legal procedures are a possible answer, and lie behind the idea of a separate housing tribunal. The assumption is that a new institution, set apart from the ordinary courts, and adopting a flexible and purposive approach to the implementation of legal rights, will promote access to its services. The New York Housing Court, for example, has wide jurisdiction over both civil and criminal matters; can make a variety of orders (possession, rent abatement, the appointment of receivers to effect repairs); has procedural advantages such as the capacity to consolidate pending actions concerning a particular building; and can cause public-housing inspectors to monitor compliance with an order.[129] Some Australian states have established residential tenancies tribunals with the aim of providing an informal, inexpensive, but expert forum in relation to matters such as disputes over the implied obligations of landlords and tenants, excessive rent, termination, security bonds, and landlord and tenant agreements.[130]

These housing tribunals have been less successful than originally claimed in making legal rights effective. Whether or not by design, the New York Housing Court undermined the gains that legal services lawyers in South Bronx had made on behalf of tenants using procedural and technical objections to prevent their eviction. The strategy had induced many landlords to settle in favour of tenants by increasing the cost and delay involved in eviction proceedings. Because procedure is simpler in the Housing Court, there has been less scope for this. 'Since trials were easier to obtain and less time-consuming in the Housing Court, landlords were somewhat more willing to take their chances before a hearing officer and therefore less generous in settling. Even more important, the Housing Court further disadvantaged the unrepresented tenant by reducing the case overload that had encouraged landlords to bargain.'[131] The Australian residential tenancies tribunals have been criticized for having the overriding aim of conciliation, when in particular cases arbitration would be of greater benefit to tenants. There has also been criticism of a conservative approach in decision-making.[132] Perhaps the major problem with these housing tribunals is that, like the ordinary courts, they are based on the fundamental premise that tenants must take the initiative to enforce or protect their rights. One procedural advance is that in South Australia the Commissioner of Consumer Affairs can institute or defend proceedings, or assume responsibility for any proceedings already begun, on behalf of tenants or necessitous landlords.[133] However, the Commissioner must still obtain the written consent of the party and of the Minister: the first requirement limits the possibility of class actions on behalf of unascertained tenants, and the second imposes an additional hurdle. A more fundamental reform would be to empower a public authority to take such action on behalf of groups of tenants, including those who are affected by, but have not complained about, a matter. A mass restitution procedure is no automatic panacea, however, for the public authority charged with its implementation might be relatively inactive.

Another prong of attack is to facilitate tenant self-help. Self-help avoids the expense and delay of formal legal procedures, reduces tenants' dependence on lawyers, and ultimately enhances tenants' capacity to control their own lives. The common law has not greatly favoured tenant self-help. At present the doctrine of independence of covenants in leases means that landlords can continue to enforce covenants against a tenant even if they are in breach of their own covenants. This contrasts with ordinary contract law, where important terms of a contract are usually interdependent. Therefore a tenant cannot simply cease to pay rent because a landlord is in breach of a repairing covenant, even if the premises are uninhabitable as a result.[134] However, the common law permits a tenant to do repairs which the landlord is obliged to effect, after the landlord is given notice and a reasonable time to act, and then to deduct the cost from future rent.[135] Moreover, where a landlord is obliged to repair, and fails to do so, equity may allow a tenant to set off the estimated cost of repairs as unliquidated damages against liability for rent arrears, if otherwise it would be manifestly unjust to the tenant (e.g., if the tenant cannot use the premises).[136]

These rules do not permit tenants to engage in a collective rent strike, i.e. to withhold rent as a bargaining lever to induce landlords to fulfil their repairing obligations. In *Camden Nominees Ltd* v. *Forcey*[137] Simonds J. granted an injunction against the chairman and secretary of a tenants' association engaged in a rent strike, on the basis that they were inducing or threatening to induce tenants to breach their contracts. Simonds J. held that there was no justification for the defendants' action, since the latter had a remedy in law by way of damages or in a proper case by way of specific performance, and added:

> It is a dangerous proposition that inequality in wealth or position justifies a
> course otherwise actionable, and that tenants may against their landlord
> adopt measures of self-help because in their judgment the law does not afford
> them adequate remedy for his default.[138]

Tenants on rent strike sued for rent or for possession might be
successful in raising the doctrines discussed in the previous paragraph. However, they might need legal assistance to do so and
therefore find themselves saddled with legal costs. The rights are also
limited in practice because the courts do not award generous damages
for disrepair, unless the premises are in bad condition or have caused
physical harm.[139] Moreover, repair and deduct does not seem a
realistic strategy for poorer tenants, for unless they have cash in hand
(an unlikely event), builders will be reluctant to undertake work on
the basis of small periodic payments which are withheld from each
rental payment. Further, tenants need considerable courage in
practice not to pay rent, since a landlord will probably threaten, or
institute, proceedings for possession.

Some American courts have held that a landlord's failure to
maintain a dwelling can go to the whole of the consideration to excuse
a tenant from further payment of the rent (but a reasonable rent is
payable). Others have recognized explicitly that the tenant's covenant to pay rent, and the landlord's covenant to provide a habitable
house, are mutually dependent.[140] A few American courts have
reached the same result with a doctrine of 'constructive eviction',
since the obligation to pay rent generally ends with eviction.
Constructive eviction occurs where the landlord's intentional act or
omission substantially interferes with the tenant's beneficial use and
enjoyment of the lease.

Several jurisdictions in the United States have legislation which
permits a tenant to withhold rent as a means of indirect pressure on
landlords to make repairs. The most sophisticated legislation has
three aspects: rent escrow (tenants must deposit withheld rent into a
fund); receivership (the courts can appoint an administrator for a
building until repairs are effected); and rent abatement (until the
defects are remedied).[141] The advantage of rent withholding over the
strategies authorized by English law is that it might be sufficiently
serious to force major repairs, which tenants could not finance out of
capital or cover with withheld rent. A difficulty with rent withholding

in practice is that it needs organizational skills to assemble a sufficient number of tenants – who might be afraid of retaliation – to have a real impact on a recalcitrant landlord. In some ghetto areas in the United States rent withholding has contributed to landlords abandoning buildings, but it is no means the sole cause, since abandonment in the United States is part of the problem of racial ghettos. In other countries abandonment is unlikely to occur, for there is a market for inner-city buildings, however substandard, either for immediate occupation, for gentrification, or for redevelopment. The economic consequences of social welfare regulation are addressed at greater length in the following chapter.

IV PUBLICLY FUNDED LEGAL SERVICES

Publicly funded legal services have a role in redressing the inequalities already examined in this chapter. One of the established arguments for legal aid has been to place the poorer sections of society on the same footing as others in the administration of the law. In recent times there has also been discussion about how legal services might go further to redress substantive inequalities. If the poor had a similar capacity to others to enforce and defend existing rights, it is said, substantive outcomes would favour them to a greater extent than at present. As we will see in Chapter 7 however, changes through the legal system face considerable obstacles.

After mention of the justifications for publicly funded legal services, we turn to their historical development and then to the actual manner in which they have been provided. There is a contrast between legal aid, which generally speaking subsidizes private practitioners who assist individual clients, and law centres, which employ salaried lawyers to assist both individuals and groups in deprived communities. The contrast is captured partly in the distinction drawn between legal services as a juridical right and legal services as a welfare right.[142] The former is the traditional approach, where legal services are available to poorer individuals for routine legal problems, through lawyers operating in the ordinary manner. The welfare rights' approach envisages salaried lawyers using legal processes to assist the poor, both individuals and groups, to pursue legal rights and social change.

Justifying the public subsidization of legal services

Public provision for legal services has been justified in terms of promoting equality before the law.[143] The argument is that equality before the law – mainly in its second, procedural sense – cannot exist without publicly subsidized legal services, for otherwise many cannot assert their rights. If, as defendants, they are before a court without adequate legal assistance, the integrity of the adversary process is threatened since it is based on the assumption that both parties can properly prove facts and present legal argument. In the criminal context it is a matter of enabling accused persons, who are in court not through choice, to meet the charges brought against them at the initiative of the state. In practice equality before the law has not always been an important touchstone for the provision of publicly funded legal services. The notion has featured in the United States, however, because of the protections in its constitution.

Meeting legal needs has been a more common justification for publicly funded legal services. Considerable research has been conducted to demonstrate that the legal needs of the poor are not met by existing institutions. Poor people have been interviewed about problems faced in the recent past (which are not revealed to the respondents as being necessarily legal problems), about what action they took, and more generally about the nature of services available in the community which provide legal assistance. The problems are chosen because in the expert judgement of the researchers they represent important legal issues. Usually the respondents are asked, or the researchers decide, if the problems experienced are serious. The finding of this research is that there is unmet legal need in the community, especially among the poor.[144]

There are difficulties with these studies in their claim to be measuring unmet legal need. What, for example, is a legal need? It cannot simply be a problem that is taken to lawyers, because a hypothesis of this method is that certain types of problems are not taken to lawyers. Neither can it be a problem which professional legal opinion defines as a legal need, because it seems accepted that many lawyers do not appreciate (or at least have not appreciated until quite recently) that there are complicated legal issues associated with matters like social welfare. On the other hand it cannot be said that a legal need arises wherever legal rules apply, since legal rules permeate everyday existence. Similarly, 'need' is a subjective matter and depends on a judgement about the desirability or usefulness of the end-result implied.[145] Phillips checked the problems received by social workers and found that they only occasionally thought that they encountered problems which could profitably be referred to a lawyer (mainly matrimonial matters); his judgement was that there were many serious legal problems over matters like evictions, accidents and social security. Social workers did not refer such cases to lawyers partly through ignorance of the law, legal aid and what lawyers did, but partly also because in their judgement lawyers fostered conflict, put profit first, and were generally unhelpful.[146] These latter considerations were part of their definition of legal need but would almost certainly not be part of lawyers'.

It has been not uncommon to justify publicly funded legal services on the necessity for citizens to be able to pursue and defend their legal rights. Underlying this additional justification is the notion that law is an integral part of society and that access to legal services is essential for individuals to function adequately. The rights argument sits comfortably with the traditional role of the lawyer who single-mindedly pursues the legal rights of individual clients, even though this conflicts with powerful individuals and institutions and perhaps with prevailing values in society.[147] Expanding this type of legal service, so the argument runs, furthers the public interest by enforcing legal rights which would otherwise go by default. Proponents of a 'national legal service' argue that the proper functioning of the modern state demands the protection of certain basic legal rights affecting liberty, housing, social welfare payments and employment. In their view this can only be achieved if – in addition to the effective operation of public enforcement agencies – legal services are available to all, irrespective of means, to enforce these basic legal rights.[148]

A fourth view is to justify publicly funded legal services because of what may be achieved through them in the way of improving the social and economic position of the poorer sections of society. A closely related argument is that certain laws designed to reduce social inequality, or to mitigate its effects (for example, social welfare laws), will not achieve their goals unless there are adequate legal services to guarantee their implementation. These arguments assume that legal services are more effective than other methods of social change – for example, enabling poorer communities to employ professional lobbyists who have access to the legislature and the executive.

The development of legal aid

'The general rule', said Lord Justice Bowen in 1885, 'is that poverty is no bar to a litigant, that, from time immemorial, has been the rule at common law, and also, I believe, in equity.'[149] In practice, of course, poverty effectively barred litigants from enforcing their common-law and statutory rights. There were, it is true, limited procedures under which it was theoretically possible for poor people to litigate. Statutes of 1495 (11 Hen. VII, c.12) and 1531 (23 Hen. VIII, c.15) established the *in forma pauperis* procedure, under which the poor did not have to pay for writs and could be assigned a lawyer free of charge in the common-law courts.[150] In the eighteenth century the formal requirements for suing *in forma pauperis* in the common-law courts became stricter. Only plaintiffs were covered, and poor litigants had to demonstrate the merits of a case beforehand by paying for counsel's opinion. Modifications were made in England in the late nineteenth century, and then in 1914 the poor persons' procedure was formalized.[151]

Despite the obvious inadequacies of the procedure, there was little pressure to change it – from the bar because it provided training for young barristers, from the Law Society because it did not interfere too greatly with the profession, and from the government because no great demands were made on public moneys. The poor persons' procedure was very limited: it did not apply to the county courts, did not cover out-of-court work, relied on honorary work by lawyers (there were many instances where cases favourably reported on could not be brought because there were no solicitors willing to take them), worked with a strict means test, and the poor still had to find the necessary out-of-pocket expenses.[152] Although the county courts established in 1846 were portrayed as the 'poor man's courts', in fact they benefited commercial interests, and from the outset the poor appeared in them as defendant debtors. Poor plaintiffs were almost unheard of, partly because the poor persons' procedure was not available, although some county court judges may have permitted it.[153] Despite overwhelming evidence, the profession continued to believe that poor people with meritorious claims could institute county court actions. That belief was perhaps only seriously challenged in 1970, when the Consumer Council study, *Justice Out of Reach*, demonstrated empirically that ordinary people hardly ever did so.

An apparent paradox in England was that there was nothing comparable to the poor persons' procedure in criminal proceedings. The slow development of criminal legal aid is not so surprising when it is realized that the criminal law had as a central role the defence of property interests. During the period up to the early nineteenth century the substantive criminal law grew considerably to cover what, until then, had been minor activities like poaching. Before 1836 those accused of felony were generally prohibited from having counsel, on the reasoning that judicial impartiality ensured a fair trial. It was only in the second part of the nineteenth century that the limits on accused persons giving evidence were removed. Criminal defendants were sometimes allowed to proceed *in forma pauperis*, and under the dock brief system a poor person appearing for trial at Assizes or Quarter Sessions could choose a barrister to represent him, from among those present in court at the time, on payment of a small sum. Both systems were quite inadequate in light of the demand.[154] The Poor Prisoners' Defence Acts of 1903 and 1930 provided that solicitors and counsel could be assigned to persons committed to stand trial for an indictable offence (initially only if they disclosed their defence), and there was a separate provision for the Court of Criminal Appeal.[155]

The present legal-aid scheme, part of the post-war Labour Government's welfare reforms, established a framework for civil legal aid in courts and tribunals, to be available to both the poor and those of moderate means (who were to pay a contribution proportionate to income). For the first time (apart from the dock brief system), lawyers were to be remunerated for work undertaken. A network of centres for legal advice was also to be established, staffed in part by salaried solicitors for those who appeared unable to afford it in the normal way. The courts were to continue to administer criminal legal aid, which was to be available in criminal cases where a person's means were insufficient and it was in the interests of justice. From the outset the legal-aid scheme was hit by financial stringency, and it was only gradually implemented.[156]

In understanding the development of legal aid, it helps to recall Max Weber's analysis of how the legal profession has been able to advance its material interests through its guild monopoly.[157] Some argue that legal aid was developed to give ideological justification to the legal system, by presenting the appearance of equal access to the law, with just sufficient advances to ensure that the myth could be sustained.[158] While legal aid might have performed this function, the explanation focusing on material interests seems closer to what moved the profession. An important element in the way lawyers have been able to advance their material interests is their pivotal role in the law-making process. Hughes' study of the passage of the Legal Aid and Advice Act 1949 shows that even if lawyers do not constitute a large percentage of a legislature, they can dominate the legal-aid debates on the basis of their 'expertise', channelling discussion in line with their perceptions of the problem and can display a remarkable professional solidarity across political lines in expounding values such as professional independence, and altruism, and in suggesting that lay people are largely ignorant of legal matters.[159]

It is relatively easy to list some of the material interests which the legal profession has had in the development of legal aid. For example, it has enabled a considerable number of young lawyers to acquire experience, reducing the need for elaborate professional training. (No doubt the results for clients of being defended by the young and inexperienced have not always been totally satisfactory.) Moreover, it has been an important source of work for the profession and has been especially valuable at times when there has been a shortage of work, or to put it another way, an over-supply of lawyers. Consequently, many traditional lawyers have supported legal aid and have argued for its extension to the middle class, despite the taint of public money.

It should not be thought a complete account of how the profession has acted can be provided by focusing on material interests. People sometimes mistake their material interests and are unsure as to what these require. Once a change to which they object is adopted, they might be able to bend it to their own interests. The profession has sometimes been divided, with different sections having conflicting material interests. In the early part of the twentieth century, for example, the Law Society in England wanted divorce transferred to the county court, which would have enabled these cases to be more easily handled, but the bar was against it because it threatened their monopoly of advocacy. Moreover lawyers, like other people, are motivated by factors which are not necessarily related to material interests. Weber himself laid heavy emphasis on how those in positions of power act to legitimate their authority. Perhaps the conventional wisdom of the legal profession about the need to avoid litigation can be seen in this light, since on its face it conflicts with self-interest.

A belief which has had an important role in the development of legal aid is that the profession must maintain its independence if the rule of law is to be preserved. The belief has been taken to mean that the profession must administer legal aid, rather than a government agency, and that legal aid should be provided mainly by private practitioners in their everyday practice, and not by state-employed lawyers. Interestingly, independence is not thought to be greatly affected by the receipt of public money. An ancillary belief has been that a state scheme of legal aid would destroy the valuable relationship between lawyers and clients. However, this overlooks the fact that the so-called valuable relationship in the case of many people is often lawyer-dominated. Entrusting the administration of legal aid to the legal profession produces the difficulty that it has the power to delay developments which it finds objectionable. Its recommendations are bound to be tinged with self-interest by the very nature of its existence as a body dedicated to the advancement of professional interests. Legislators, civil servants and government committees will often accept the recommendations of the legal profession because of the absence of any comparable counterweight on the other side, the task of pressing for fundamental changes necessary to overcome the unequal utilization of legal services being left to a small number of lawyers, academics and lay persons.

The English legal profession has successfully resisted the adoption of a public defender system, whereby salaried lawyers are employed to defend poor accused. Public defenders were already operating in the United States when bills to establish a comparable scheme were defeated in the House of Commons in 1919, 1920, 1921, and 1928.[160] The Widgery Committee in 1966 concluded that a public defender system would deprive accused persons of a choice of lawyers, and that accused persons would think that public defenders did not represent their interests but those of the Establishment.[161] Yet the first objection applies equally to the present English scheme, for there is no guarantee that an accused can freely choose his or her lawyer.[162] Moreover, we have already seen that a considerable number of criminal defendants see their barristers as acting against their interests by pressuring them to plead guilty. In jurisdictions in the United States, Australia and Canada, public defender schemes employing salaried lawyers provide criminal legal aid to those unable to afford private representation.[163] Despite high caseloads and a lack of continuity for clients in service, studies in the United States show that a public defender system is more efficient than private lawyers because of economies of scale, and just as effective in terms of outcome.[164]

Traditionally legal aid was charitable, and even under official schemes lawyers who participated were generally supposed to go unremunerated.[165] Professional bodies had to make frequent calls on lawyers to undertake honorary legal work for the poor. The response was less than enthusiastic among many, who did not feel under any moral obligation despite the important monopolies granted to the profession. Moreover, few lawyers assisted in the charitable legal-aid schemes which sprang up in the late nineteenth century in places such as England, the United States and West Germany.[166] The charitable basis of legal aid had a number of important consequences. First, lawyers retained control of it. Secondly, the profession could use it as a disciplinary tool against lawyers at the fringe of traditional practice. An example is that prior to the Great War the English Law Society managed to close down the 'legal aid societies', which enabled working people to bring personal injury claims on a contingency fee basis. The societies ran along the lines of the pre-paid legal insurance schemes operating in the United States today, with members paying a small, regular contribution, in return for which lawyers would conduct any legal business required. Eminently sensible though the societies were, and although they met a real need, the Law Society feared that they were used for touting – there was much talk of abuses like ambulance chasing – and deprived 'reputable' solicitors of business.[167] Thirdly, there was little chance of fundamentally questioning the adequacy of the system. Attacks from outside the profession could be rebutted as demonstrating a deep ingratitude for the services which lawyers freely gave. Critics within the profession, such as lawyers working for trade unions who came in contact with poorer individuals in their daily practice, were inhibited in their criticism because they might be identified with the 'disreputable' fringe of ambulance chasers. The charitable nature of what was done also led to considerable complacency in the profession.

Finally, the charitable basis of legal aid meant that the legal profession shared and reinforced the dominant perception that poorer people were largely responsible for their plight. A developed system of legal aid, and especially one in which the state was involved, would have been less consistent with this perception and the *laissez-faire* philosophy which underlay it. Closely related was the perception that the poor were less worthy of consideration than others. In 1925, the Poor Persons' Rules Committee (the Lawrence Committee) identified the distasteful character of divorce work for the poor as one reason for the dearth of solicitors willing to undertake it. The work was not simply distasteful *per se*, or for economic reasons, said the Committee, but also 'by reason of the fact that the persons concerned are often uneducated and ignorant'.[168] No doubt this view became embedded in professional consciousness. Other reasons today why lawyering for the poor is 'distasteful' are that it is less well remunerated than other categories of work, and that it is a class of work which some believe is less intellectually challenging. A final consequence of the charitable origins of legal aid has been that the idea of a right to it has been slow to evolve.

The courts have had an important role in the development of legal aid. There has been some hostility to legal aid amongst the judiciary: some judges have thought it has allowed individuals to bring unjustified claims, or to defend proceedings when there was virtually no hope, while others have objected that legal aid has been at the expense of the 'ordinary litigant' (presumably the middle class), that it has not been appreciated by its recipients, or that it has been too generous.[169] However, the majority seem to have realized that the courts operate more smoothly, at any rate in important criminal matters, if defendants are represented.[170] Consequently, the courts have moved to the position that it is desirable that legal aid should be provided in serious criminal cases where a sentence of imprisonment might be imposed.[171] But even today there is no absolute requirement that a poor person ought to be provided with legal representation in serious cases.[172]

In contrast to this approach, the right to counsel is regarded as a fundamental right in criminal proceedings in the United States. The Sixth Amendment to the Constitution provides that in all criminal proceedings 'the accused shall enjoy the right . . . to have the Assistance of Counsel for his defence'. Pursuant to this the Supreme Court has held that accused persons are guaranteed the right to an assigned lawyer in criminal proceedings if they are unable to afford one. The Court has expressed the right-to-counsel requirement as follows: 'No person may be imprisoned for any offense, whether classified as petty, misdemeanour, or felony, unless he was represented by counsel at his trial.'[173] Empirical studies have shown a gap between what the Supreme Court requires in this regard and what actually happens in practice.[174] The right to counsel does not cover discretionary appeals as opposed to appeals as of right or to applications for certiorari in the Supreme Court itself.[175] Civil proceedings are generally excluded.[176] In addition to the right to counsel, the Supreme Court established in *Boddie* v. *Connecticut*[177] that litigants could not be denied certain forms of civil relief (in that case a divorce) simply because they could not pay the court fees. But the Court has refused to apply this ruling to a person seeking a voluntary petition of bankruptcy and to a welfare recipient wanting to appeal against an administrative decision, on the grounds that these matters are not of sufficient constitutional significance. In the first case the Court was influenced by the fact that there are other methods besides bankruptcy for people to deal with their debts, and in the second case it pointed to the due process which the recipient had received before the welfare agency.[178]

The scope of legal aid

Like the legal system of which it is part, legal aid generally depends on individuals taking the initiative. One of the factors which deters people from doing this is that they may not realize that they qualify or they may think that legal aid operates in only limited areas like criminal law. Even if individuals apply for legal aid, they face a means test. Generally speaking, below certain levels of income and capital no contribution is required (the free limits); between the free limits and higher levels of income and capital (the eligibility limits), persons qualify but must make a contribution.[179] At times the means tests for legal aid have been so harsh that some people falling below the poverty line have not come within the free limits. In some cases those just outside the free limits have not been in a position to pay a contribution and thus have not obtained legal aid. As with other social welfare benefits, the means test has given rise to a certain stigma, and legally aided clients complain of the negative views which they feel those working in the courts display to them.[180] Administering the means test entails costs, which in some cases might barely cover the amount collected in contributions. The Swedish legal-aid scheme has always been generous, and both the middle class and poor have qualified under the financial eligibility limits.[181] Generous eligibility limits, coupled with contributions varying with means, probably attract public support for a legal-aid programme.[182]

Legal-aid authorities generally have wide discretion, but persons denied legal aid might be able to reapply or to appeal administratively or to the courts and be represented – at their own expense – by a lawyer or other person. A legal profession which, as in England, administers legal aid is in an exceptional position in the modern welfare state in the control it exercises over the administration of a state-funded benefit. The demand for accountability has led to the establishment in Australia and Canada of legal services commissions, with government and lay participation, to administer legal-aid schemes.[183]

There are various limitations on the scope of legal aid. First, it might not be available for certain civil proceedings. The justification is the possibility of abuse (e.g., the exclusion for defamation actions), but this is ill-founded since legal aid can be refused on the ground of abuse itself. Secondly, criminal legal aid might not cover fully the pre-trial stages of criminal proceedings, such as representation at a police station, appeals against a refusal of bail, or advice prior to the decision to plead. Thirdly, legal aid might not be widely available in the lower courts, even though these can impose suspended and immediate prison sentences. In England, where magistrates' courts have power to grant criminal legal aid, there have been considerable discrepancies in the refusal rates among them, reflecting differing social philosophies on the part of the magistrates and their clerks.[184] Other schemes (e.g., duty solicitors) go only part of the way to covering the gaps in the lower criminal courts. Thirdly, private prosecutions might also be excluded, although we will see that these have a role in improving housing standards. Finally, legal assistance might not be fully available in tribunal proceedings although in the modern welfare state tribunals play at least as important a role as the courts in the lives of tenants, social welfare claimants and employees.

Another formal limitation on legal aid is if an applicant has to demonstrate reasonable grounds for taking, defending or being a party to proceedings, or can be refused legal aid if proceedings appear unreasonable in the particular circumstances of the case.[185] The first part of this requirement is that a person has a good case in law and on the facts (the legal merits test), while the second part is concerned with wider considerations (the wider merits test). Legal-aid authorities seem to have adopted a conservative line with the legal merits test, if the high success rate of legally aided clients is any guide. Such an approach denies poorer persons a bargaining tool available to the wealthier, if the latter institute proceedings, not with any definite chance of success, but as a way of encouraging settlement by demonstrating that they 'mean business'.[186] Moreover, in areas where the case-law is relatively undeveloped, the poorer litigant is in a Catch–22 situation. It is unreasonable to take proceedings because the reaction of the courts is uncertain, yet unless proceedings are taken it will never be possible to ascertain what the law is.

In interpreting the wider merits test, one view is that legal-aid authorities should ask whether the comfortably off, yet not wealthy, person would take proceedings. On this test legal aid would be barred to many poorer persons, simply because of the small amount of money at stake, for it would not be reasonable for a middle-class person to risk court proceedings in this type of case. Consequently the test has been modified in England to take account of the value of the benefit to the particular applicant, bearing in mind the chances of success and the cost of achieving it.[187] None the less, this wider merits test still orientates legal aid to the individual problems of individual clients. Unless it is reasonable for the individual, aid cannot be granted to clarify the law or to pursue actions having a general community benefit such as test cases or legal proceedings on behalf of groups. Under the wider merits test it has also been said that it is not reasonable to fund a matter on legal aid if the group concerned (e.g., a tenants' union) could collectively defray the costs.[188] Yet instituting legal action, which only involves a small amount, may bring substantial benefits when other similar cases are added. A more appropriate benchmark is that legal aid should be granted to litigants where it is justified in the light of the potential gain to a large number of people in similar situations.

Because legal aid has not been widely used for test cases or cases with a group or community interest, it has had little role in legal change. In a few cases, reform has occurred indirectly where the availability of legal aid has led to an obvious waste of public expenditure. An important factor behind the abolition of appearances for uncontested divorces in England in 1977 was that considerable amounts of legal-aid money were funding unnecessary hearings. Other reforms associated with this change have been designed to make matrimonial proceedings clearer to ordinary people to enable them to take action without legal help.

The bulk of legal-aid expenditure has been on family and criminal matters, with little attention being given to others such as housing and employment.[189] We have already alluded to one explanation, that ordinary people regard the former as areas where legal services are appropriate. But individual demand is not the only factor, for as a result of government policy legal-aid money has not always been allocated in the most economic manner. For example, social welfare departments have encouraged women to seek maintenance orders in magistrates' courts, although in a great majority of cases they would not have been better off if successful. Reform of procedural law in family matters would obviate the need for a considerable amount of litigation. Legal-aid expenditure has also been heavily concentrated on court work, although there is a great deal of important legal work which never gets to court. Legal advice and assistance might be available to deal with some of this, although there is a substantial gap in matters of preventive law, such as community legal education.

Legal-aid work is concentrated in a relatively few lawyers' offices.[190] One reason is that some practices are not interested in legal-aid work because their commercial work is highly profitable and also more valued professionally. Another reason is economic, for to be profitable legal-aid work must be handled in volume. The firms interested in legal-aid work, and which have been successful in attracting it, might maintain their position through contacts in the courts, the police and so on, who are in a position to refer business. A repercussion of legal-aid work being handled in volume is that clients may not be given close personal attention because of the pressure of business. Matters may be delegated to clerks and staff, who may not elicit relevant information or prepare the strongest case. Legal-aid clients are already in a difficult position to obtain the maximum from their lawyers, and the economics of legal-aid practice compound the problem. Moreover, conditions are perpetuated whereby legal-aid work concerns mainly family and criminal matters. If a firm is not organized to handle matters such as consumer protection, housing, social welfare and employment in a routine manner, people who present such problems may be told that the firm cannot assist.

Law centres

First developed in the United States in the 1960s as part of the 'war on poverty', law centres have spread to other countries.[191] Initially, law centres faced opposition from the legal profession, which claimed that they would create social and professional divisions. For many local lawyers the fear was that they would lose business to law centres, although some also objected to what they thought was the political stance law centres adopted. In some places the profession was able to use the ethical rules of practice to advance these material and ideological arguments, for law centres had to obtain waivers for breach of certain of the rules such as those against touting and sharing fees with non-lawyers.[192] Political and legal action were also used.[193] The compromise eventually reached in England was that law centres would usually not engage in conveyancing, commercial matters, divorce and other matrimonial business, probate and the administration of estates, larger personal injury claims and criminal matters involving adults – all lucrative sources of income for the profession. The exclusion of conveyancing has meant that law centres cannot do the work involved in leasehold enfranchisement, although this is crucial to the residents of some deprived areas.

The justification for public subsidization of law centres is that they make legal services available to people who might not otherwise enjoy them through traditional legal aid. They do so by going beyond the narrow concerns of the latter to an interest in the wide range of decisions affecting ordinary people made by employers, businesses and government. The refusal of some law centres to do certain types of work (for example, for landlords) is justified on ideological and practical grounds. The counter-arguments are that to discriminate in this way might deny certain people legal assistance, and that a publicly funded organization should be open to all. The flaw in the latter point is that public funds are regularly allocated to special interests to use in the way they think fit. The exclusion of assistance to landlords can be justified because they can generally obtain assistance from ordinary lawyers. While the latter might be reluctant to represent tenants on legal aid because it is unprofitable, this is not necessarily the case with landlords where there is always the prospect of other profitable work such as probate and conveyancing. Many centres do not apply other than an informal means test, on the grounds that their location in deprived communities means that their clientele will be from the poorer sections of society, and that a formal means test would threaten their rapport with the community. Occasionally clients are asked to pay disbursements when outside costs are incurred.

In some jurisdictions governments have regarded law centres as too radical and have cut back their funding, causing some to close.[194] Particular umbrage has been taken to law centres instituting legal action against government authorities, although this is inevitable when the state is responsible for housing, education, planning, etc. – services which impinge directly on the poorer sections of society. For government to fund sources of potential opposition such as law centres is to recognize that local democracy demands the effective representation of all, in particular of minority interests. While according to traditional theory elected representatives do that, the reality is that even those legislators who devote themselves to the cause of the poorer sections of society are often no match for the coalition of elected representatives, government officers and private interests who make the crucial decisions.

A hallmark of some law centres is participation by the local community through management committees. Community participation is useful in strengthening the commitment of the community to a law centre; it makes a law centre more responsive to local wishes; it gives guidance to the staff on a community's problems and priorities; and it leads people to identify the centre as a realistic place to turn to with their problems. Community participation is a more accurate description than community control, because it is impossible for law centre staff not to influence decisions.[195] Through participating in the management of law centres members of the community acquire organizing skills and a knowledge of law and the legal system.

While engaging in casework, for which there is an obvious demand, many law centres also work with community groups (tenants, residents, social welfare claimants and employees). Casework and community work are intertwined, for the former can have implications for community work by identifying patterns of community concern.[196] However, too great an emphasis on casework can lead to a deluge of work, which exhausts staff and means an inferior service for clients.[197] Another problem with casework is that it can alienate support within a community, as where a law centre represents juveniles who are known and disliked by residents because of their criminal activities. A heavy caseload also runs the risk that underlying symptoms are ignored and that problems about which no one complains are neglected. Moreover, success in casework is sometimes ambiguous in that assisting particular individuals might be at the expense of other individuals, as where one client moves up the waiting list for public housing but in doing so displaces others. The problems of casework have led some law centres to move away from an 'open door' policy, to concentrate on 'community' or 'structural' work. These law centres may limit the advice they provide to off-the-street clients and be highly selective in the work they undertake.

Community work aims to strengthen organizations of tenants, residents, claimants and employees, by assisting them to take legal and political action. At a basic level this includes advising groups on the juridical form they might take, on their constitution, on how money should be held and meetings conducted, and on possible sources of funds. At another level it includes matters such as representing groups before planning enquiries and advising them on where and how to exert pressure on those in authority. The parallel here is with lawyers acting for government, commercial and property interests, who service individual legal problems but also engage in wider legal and political action. Community legal education can contribute to making individuals aware of their rights and how to enforce them. Law centres engaged in community work have been accused of unprofessional conduct by 'stirring up trouble', but the 'stirring' is often to have government, commercial and property interests comply with their legal obligations.

In the United States, test cases instituted by neighbourhood law offices have been a vehicle for social change through establishing novel points of law and having an impact beyond the interests of particular litigants. Law centres elsewhere have, however, devoted little attention to test cases because the nature of their legal systems differ. The courts in the United States have been well disposed to test cases. For example, the Supreme Court decided favourably a substantial percentage of the appeals taken to it by legal services lawyers.[198] American experience is that should a test case be unsuccessful it may attract useful publicity which highlights the need for legislative change. A danger of test cases is that they may draw effort away from more valuable community work.[199] Moreover, since the stakes are higher, a defeat is more calamitous.

Despite a general belief that limited social change can be effected, there are those in law centres who question whether anything of lasting value can be achieved. They argue that law centres channel conflict into the courts, defusing more effective forms of change; substitute their interests for the real interests of the poor; and result in lawyers dominating the poor. These critics believe that lawyers have only a limited role, primarily in assisting people to defend themselves against oppressive state action. This issue of whether it is possible to achieve social change through legal action is explored further in Chapter 7.

Other mechanisms

Publicly funded legal services are just one of the ways making for greater equality before the law. Other mechanisms include reforms to existing institutions (e.g. duty-solicitor schemes) and the establishment of new institutions (e.g., small claims courts, community justice centres). Changes such as these might be motivated, however, by a variety of factors. Take the duty-solicitor scheme in England and Wales, under which private lawyers are available at the courts to provide assistance to accused persons.[200] Ostensibly, the duty-solicitor scheme was promoted by the legal profession on a mainly voluntary basis to assist criminal defendants. In fact the scheme was adopted in some areas not so much because of a concern with social service, but because many solicitors saw it as a method of breaking the monopoly which a few solicitors' firms had obtained over criminal legal-aid work. Magistrates also welcomed the scheme because it reduced equivocal pleas and the number of remands, and magistrates' clerks because it deflected criticism about their allocation of legal-aid work.[201]

Furthermore, there is no guarantee that these mechanisms actually achieve what might be claimed for them. Procedural informality, as we saw with the New York Housing Court, may undermine the protections which were previously afforded. In some jurisdictions small claims courts attempt to equalize parties by depriving both of legal representation, the reasoning being that wealthier parties will be more likely to have lawyers so that a rule excluding them achieves greater balance. But there is still the problem that a company officer will be mismatched against an inarticulate individual, which might not be compensated for by the small claims judge taking an active role in assisting the less able party to present a case. Community justice centres are supposed to facilitate improved access to justice for the relatively poor and disadvantaged and to relieve existing courts and tribunals from the burden of dealing with some disputes. There is also the feeling that 'palm tree justice' might be more appropriate in continuing relationships such as between landlords and tenants and within families. However, the obvious dangers with these centres are that mediation can neglect an individual's rights in the search for compromise; they can overlook social change and the source of underlying conflict; and since appearances are purely voluntary, powerful businesses and state bureaucracies can ignore any settlement suggested because there is no legal backing.[202] On the whole the 'do it yourself' movement[203] seems of greater benefit to the middle class than to the poor, because it is more appropriate in areas where the law facilitates private transactions such as divorce and conveyancing, than where the function of law is to authorize government services and transfer payments, or to regulate the behaviour of commercial, property or government interests.

V CONCLUSION

Equality before the law is an important value of the welfare state. The argument of the first parts of this chapter was that 'equality before the law', in its formal and procedural senses, is contradicted by inequalities in the administration of the law and the way its provisions are invoked. The rights of the poorer sections of society are not equally the subject of protection or the duties owed to them of enforcement, the basic reason being that substantive equalities are subverted by social and economic inequalities. There are also inequalities in the substance of the law, as indicated in part III of the chapter. Overt inequalities are rare, but the substance of the law favours certain legal categories over others, such as landlords over tenants, and the poorer sections of society occupy the less-favoured categories. These areas of law violate the broader substantive interpretation of equality before the law.

None of this should lead to the conclusion, which some draw, that equality before the law is a worthless abstraction which legitimizes inequalities and militates against social change.[204] Merely because there are shortcomings in practice in equality before the law does not mean that the notion is incorrect or that competing notions are more desirable; equality before the law is worth striving for as a basic standard.[205] The prominent position which equality before the law occupies in the welfare state may be used as an argument to close the 'gaps' between the reality and the ideal. Public disquiet that equality before the law is denied in practice can be a powerful force which may be tapped to secure social change – to remedy the defects uncovered in the first three parts of the chapter. For example, we saw in part IV how equality before the law has been one justification for the public subsidization of legal services. A difficulty in using equality before the law as part of a strategy for social change, however, is that it seems that people generally have low expectations of, and not much contact with, the legal system, so that they do not see themselves as seriously disadvantaged by it.[206] The issue of social change in the welfare state is addressed later in the book.

PART II
The welfare state

4
Social welfare regulation

Regulation, and the provision of benefits and services, are central techniques of the welfare state. The second part of this book examines these techniques, with the particular focus on social welfare. Social welfare regulation – the subject of this chapter – mandates behaviour on the part of private institutions such as property owners and employers, with the declared purpose of advancing social welfare. The social welfare legislation governing the provision of benefits and services – discussed in Chapters 5 and 6 – delineates these, or at least it delineates the duties on social welfare bureaucracies to provide benefits and services to individuals in specified circumstances. Various issues are addressed relating to these regulatory and distributive techniques. Does their derivation, for example, explain their operation in practice? How are the techniques reflected in detailed legislative provisions? What social factors determine the pattern of their implementation? Although there are common themes throughout the discussion, the emphasis placed on each varies in the different chapters. For example, discretion is an issue in how social welfare regulation is enforced and appears in a different guise in the administration of social welfare benefits and services. In this account, however, discretion is given most prominence in the analysis of the social welfare legislation governing benefits. Another example is the phenomenon that state bureaucracies sometimes seem to be indifferent to those who should gain from their activities; this 'paradox' is dealt with at greatest length in the context of the provision of public services. Regulation is discussed in relation to both private institutions and social welfare bureaucracies; it is given most attention in this chapter.

The present chapter, then, examines social welfare regulation.

Examples are regulation which sets minimum standards for housing, controls rents and establishes security of tenure for tenants, obliges employers to pay minimum wages, establishes standards for health and safety at work, and mandates the provision of occupational welfare. Social welfare regulation purports to advance social welfare, but whether it does depends on a number of factors: on the forces behind its emergence and the legal form adopted, on its implementation by the agencies responsible for its administration and by the courts; on whether the private institutions purportedly regulated comply with its provisions; and on any side-effects of its implementation. These factors – the forces in the emergence of regulation, legislative form, the behaviour of regulatory agencies, the susceptibility of private institutions to legal regulation, and the side-effects of regulation – are recurrent themes in this chapter. On examining them it becomes apparent why regulation may be a weak tool in advancing social welfare.

An examination of the way regulation emerges shows that sometimes it is designed to reassure the community that measures are being taken, without much concern as to what their effects will be in practice. Even if the proponents of a measure intend it to be effective, the legislation which results may be defective because important economic and social interests force its modification. Regulation may also fall short of its goals because of its juridical form. Its provisions may be ambiguous, over-inclusive, conflicting, or simply not commensurate with its ostensible goals. These defects can occur because its provisions may reflect conflicts between different interests at the time of enactment; because those drafting the law did not foresee particular problems; or simply because not enough attention was given to drafting.

The enforcement of regulation by the agencies charged with the task might be inadequate, so that the institutions regulated can ignore the law with impunity. Financial and human resources are crucial to the enforcement of regulation, for they determine matters such as whether its implementation is adequately monitored and whether action is taken if a breach is detected. In turn, whether adequate resources are available to a regulatory agency turns on political factors; the absence of resources may indicate that nothing was really expected of regulation from the outset. However, it is well to recognize that certain types of regulation are inherently difficult to enforce even if relatively generous resources are allocated. As Lipsky writes of what

he calls street-level bureaucracies (the police, social welfare departments, legal service offices and so on):

Street-level bureaucrats work with a relatively high degree of uncertainty
because of the complexity of the subject matter (people) and the frequency or
rapidity with which decisions have to be made. Not only is reliable
information costly and difficult to obtain but for street-level bureaucrats high
case loads, episodic encounters, and the constant press of decisions force them
to act without even being able to consider whether an investment in searching
for more information would be profitable.[1]

Legislative sanctions are only one of the factors which determine
whether private institutions comply with regulatory requirements.
On the surface there are few economic incentives for property owners
to charge a controlled rent, because it will generally be below the
market rent. By the same token it might be good business for property
owners to meet statutory housing standards, so as to maintain the
value of their properties, or for employers to pay statutory minimum
wages, so as to further productivity and harmonious industrial
relations. The attempt to change the behaviour of private institutions
by regulation may be misconceived because it might be more effective
for the state to allocate financial resources to pay a social welfare
benefit (for example, a rent allowance) or to provide a service (for
example, adequate public housing).

As well as the direct effects of regulation if the private institutions at
which it is directed conform with its requirements, there are the
independent and unintended effects.[2] Independent effects are those
independent of any conforming behaviour, such as a change in
political support as a result of a measure. Unintended effects are those
which are not foreseen by the law-makers. These independent and
unintended effects may well be acceptable to the law-makers, even if
they do not admit this. In practice there is controversy about whether
particular effects can be causally linked to regulation. An example is
whether the drop in the amount of privately rented accommodation is
the result of rent control.

I THE EMERGENCE OF SOCIAL WELFARE REGULATION

The social welfare regulation which is considered here – public health
and housing law, rent control, and minimum-wage regulation – took
shape during the nineteenth century and the first part of the twentieth

century. The history of these measures is not one of an inexorable movement towards improvement. Along with advances were false starts, successful resistance to change, failures and reversals. Importantly, these measures were not always or even mostly the product of consensus. Their background was often a conflict between different interests, although in some cases the conflict was masked by an apparent consensus at the time a particular measure was enacted, or by the general approval given to a measure subsequent to its enactment.

Reformers who advocated social welfare regulation were motivated by ideals, but also by the desire to improve the productivity of the working class and to attract its support for particular political causes. The working class had little direct input into public health and housing reform, but with the growth of collective action, in particular through the trade unions, it made a more significant contribution to later regulation such as rent control and minimum-wage regulation. Opposition to the regulation considered here was to be expected from property owners and employers, since it intruded on their interests not only directly, but also indirectly through the additional taxation necessary to finance its implementation. However, it would be wrong to think that all property owners and employers were implacably opposed to it: some saw the economic advantages in having decently housed, reasonably paid workers; some supported limited regulation to forestall tighter control; and some recognized the advantages if their competitors were regulated. That the Trade Boards Act 1909 – which provided for minimum wages – passed through Parliament without serious opposition, for example, might well have reflected the fact that the politically influential, larger manufacturers had experienced undercutting from the sweated trades.

The forces behind social welfare regulation

The impetus for public health and housing reform in the nineteenth century came from social reformers, imbued with the Victorian zeal for improvement and economic efficiency, and from the intolerability of conditions, which gave rise to practical solutions to meet concrete day-to-day problems.[3] Often the cause of reform was assisted by the occurrence of cholera – no respecter of class – which galvanized Parliament into action. Nevertheless social reforms were justified by reference to the benefits they would bring social welfare. For example, public health reformers of the nineteenth century regarded their most important target as the poorer areas of the cities, where conditions were especially acute through overcrowding, inadequate water supplies, and a lack of sanitation and cleansing services. Statistical evidence was used – the advent of registration of births and deaths was important in this regard – to show that the highest rate of illness and death were in these areas. Important catalysts for public health reform were a series of official and unofficial reports, including the enquiries conducted for the Poor Law Commission in 1839 and 1840, and the report the Commission published in 1842, the *Report on the Sanitary Condition of the Labouring Population of Great Britain* by its secretary, Edwin Chadwick. Like most nineteenth-century reformers, however, Chadwick denied that poverty was the causal factor in the low standards of public health and housing experienced by the poor. Instead, poverty was thought to be the consequence of disease, and the high incidence of disease among the poor was attributed to ignorance, vice and intemperance. Moreover, the motivation of the reformers had an important base in economic considerations – the desire to eliminate the losses to the national product associated with disease, and the obstacles it set to the poor participating fully in the market place.[4]

The poorer sections of society do not seem to have clamoured for public health and housing reforms in the nineteenth century: their concerns were for better working conditions, the extension of the franchise, and the right to form trade unions.[5] Partly this was because the proponents of social welfare regulation were often the same persons who had perpetrated the poor law. There were also the side-effects of particular public health and housing measures – a point explored in greater detail below. Moreover in some areas there was an adequate supply of housing for the higher-paid, skilled workers, who might have given the lead to agitation. However, the growth of working-class strength with Chartism, and the possibility of economic breakdown in the 'hungry forties', may have exerted some pressure towards the official amelioration of living conditions.[6] Later, working-class influence was strengthened through the extension of the franchise and the enhanced legal position of trade unions. These circumstances were reflected in housing reform, where one motive was to win the electoral support of the aristocracy of labour. But it was really only with the collapse of private house-building at the turn of the century that the trade unions became interested in housing and began campaigning for its erection by public authorities.

The poorer sections of society seem to have had a greater involvement in the enactment of the Trade Boards Act 1909, which established machinery for setting minimum wages in low-paid industries. The low-paid workers themselves were in a weak position to combat exploitation because they were dispersed in small factories or working from their own homes and not organized into trade unions. For some time trade unionists had been trying unsuccessfully to organize sweated women workers, and on one occasion Mary Macarthur, a leader of the women's trade-union movement, marched through London at the head of a demonstration by low-paid women workers. Philanthropists, social reformers and the press took up the cause of sweated labourers. Severe unemployment in 1908 led to public demonstrations, organized mainly from the East End (significantly, an important location of the sweated trades), and to riots in Glasgow, which apparently spurred the Liberal government to action, to demonstrate to the working class that it had not misjudged by supporting it at the 1906 election.[7]

The working class becomes instrumental in the adoption of social welfare regulation with the introduction of rent control in 1915. With the war, house-building declined rapidly because of the shortage of labour and building materials. The housing position in cities such as Glasgow was exacerbated by the influx of munitions workers. Rents increased, and there was widespread discontent which took the form of a rent strike on the Clyde in 1915. The campaign was led by the Independent Labour Party and was initially concentrated around the shipyards, where it was supported by the largest employer. Similar action occurred in Birmingham, Birkenhead, Northampton and areas of London. These events culminated in a walk-out on the Clyde in six large factories and shipyards, whereupon the government saw the danger to the war effort and introduced nation-wide rent control.[8]

Those seeking social welfare regulation faced constant objections from, and were forced to concede ground to, those who denounced it as interference with private property, and as leading to the centralization of power and the infringement of liberty. These objections were at once both ideological and self-interested. Self-interest was plainly the case with builders and property owners, since their incomes might diminish if public health or housing legislation were adopted.[9] Opposition also came from those such as the private water companies whose profits were threatened by regulation, and from those engaged in the business of obtaining local Acts of Parliament (the traditional method of legislation for local areas), whose livelihood would disappear with the adoption of comprehensive, national enactments. Local authorities were in many cases mouthpieces for property and employer interests, but they also had independent, bureaucratic interests, leading to opposition.[10]

Public health and housing legislation

During the period of industrialization and urbanization in the late eighteenth and early nineteenth centuries, the law did not impose stringent standards regarding public health or housing. There were local ordinances dating from medieval times to maintain public health, and there was some attempt to control over-crowding.[11] These laws were not concerned with advancing the interests of the disadvantaged but with the threat posed to the general health, to property (over-building increased the chances of fire), and to social order (tenement housing was associated with vagrancy and crime).[12] Then, during the first part of the nineteenth century, some localities had Parliament pass local improvement Acts for their areas, empowering them to deal with cleansing, water supply and sewers. This patchwork was eventually supplanted by national legislation – the Towns Improvement Clauses Act 1847 (10 & 11 Vict., c.34) – which localities could simply adopt without the lengthy and costly procedure of obtaining a detailed local Act. Public Health Acts and Nuisances Removal Acts were consolidated in the Public Health Act 1875 (38 & 39 Vict., c.55).[13]

Nineteenth-century public health legislation contained important flaws, in large part a product of the forces opposed to its enactment, or at least of the general capitalist ethos of the time. These factors imposed definite limits as to how extensive and effective regulation could be. As a result of continued agitation by reformers and others, some of these flaws were reduced or eliminated. One flaw was that the procedures for applying public health law were cumbersome. For example, to lay a complaint that a dwelling-house was a public nuisance under the Nuisances Removal and Diseases Prevention Act 1846 (9 & 10 Vict., c.96), a local authority had first to obtain a certificate to that effect from two qualified medical practitioners. Only then could magistrates order the owner to improve. Later the Nuisances Removal Act 1855 (18 & 19 Vict., c.121) removed the need to obtain a certificate.

Another flaw was that local authorities were left with considerable discretion. For example, localities were generally free not to adopt the Public Health Act 1848 (11 & 12 Vict., c.63). Few localities did so because the 1848 Act threatened higher rates, and some larger localities incurred substantial expense to obtain a local Act to forestall its application. And even localities which adopted the Act failed to follow through by appointing inspectors to enforce it. However, the 1855 Act obliged local authorities to appoint a sanitary inspector, an important milestone in the establishment of the necessary administrative structure for the enforcement of public health law. Then the Sanitary Act 1866 (29 & 30 Vict., c.90) imposed duties on localities to inspect for nuisances and to enforce the legislation. Under the 1866 Act central government had default powers to enforce these duties. Despite this revolutionary principle, the Act was slow to be implemented. At the policy level the fundamental flaw of nineteenth-century public health law was that it focused on the health hazards consequent on slum conditions – the filth of the streets, the overflowing cesspools, the lack of drainage and the impure water – at the expense of the economic causes of slums. The poverty of slum inhabitants meant that they could not afford better housing and conditions.[14] Perhaps this focus is not surprising when slum dwelling was associated with a moral failing or a criminal leaning.

The regulation of housing conditions was unequal to the social problems facing the poorer sections of society. There was some provision for building and housing standards, and the use of cellars was also controlled.[15] The Common Lodging Houses Acts 1851 and 1853 (14 & 15 Vict., c.28; 16 & 17 Vict., c.41) governed the conditions of privately owned common lodging houses and required local authorities to license lodging-house keepers and lodging houses in the interest of sanitation.[16] But the simple prohibitions on overcrowding in the Nuisances Removal Act 1855 and the Sanitary Act 1866 were hardly likely to have an effect when there was no alternative housing available. There was no profit in builders erecting decent housing for the poor, who would not have been able to afford the rent, and for local authorities to build housing was antithetical to prevailing political philosophy. Overcrowding was accentuated by commercial development, railway building, and street and other municipal construction, since those responsible for these activities usually avoided the few legal obligations they had for finding alternative accommodation for those displaced.[17] In London some relief from overcrowding occurred in the 1880s when suburban trains and electric trams made working-class suburbs feasible.

The first real attempt to grapple with the housing situation was the Artizans and Labourers Dwellings Act 1868, known as the Torrens Act (31 & 32 Vict., c.130), which was designed to secure the adequate condition of individual houses. Under the Torrens Act, an officer of health could report that premises were unfit for habitation. The local authority could then require the owner to make the premises fit, or could issue a demolition order. Where the owner failed to do the work, the local authority could undertake it and take a first charge on the premises for the cost. Little was done under the Act, since many local authorities were reluctant to incur any expenditure from the rates. Compensation and rehousing clauses had been shorn from the original Bill, and there was no public-authority housing for those displaced. Consequently, some officers of health were reluctant to initiate action, since they could see that without new construction, demolition would simply intensify overcrowding. The Torrens Act was directed at individual houses. In the absence of local Acts, local authorities could only clear areas of slum housing under legislation concerned with street-widening or municipal construction. Early slum clearance was undertaken not simply with commercial, public health or municipal considerations in mind, but as a method of breaking up potential sources of crime and social unrest, and in some areas of reducing the payment of poor relief from the rates by forcing out the poor.

Then in 1875 the Artizans and Labourers Dwellings Improvement Act (38 & 39 Vict., c.36) gave local authorities specific power to deal with unfit housing on an area basis, and obliged them to provide for rehousing the persons displaced. One hope was that a 'filtering' process would occur if the slums were razed: a better class of person would move into the newly constructed housing and the poor would in turn replace them in their previous dwellings. A few local authorities such as Birmingham used the legislation for slum clearance. In other areas ratepayers objected to the cost, or local councillors hindered action because they owned slum property. Opponents persuaded Parliament to whittle down local-authority obligations. Amendments in 1879 watered down the rehousing obligation, which could not be effected other than in the immediate vicinity cleared.[18] In 1882 this was relaxed still further, in that rehousing had only to be provided for half those displaced.[19] Both strands of housing law – the concern with individual unfit housing and with slum clearance – were consolidated and amended in the Housing of the Working Classes Act 1890 (53 & 54 Vict., c.70). The Act was intended to strengthen the duty of local authorities to act and to facilitate their dealing with unfit housing.[20] None the less, it was not until the 1930s that slum clearance was practised on a large scale.[21]

Several points can be made in relation to the form taken by nineteenth-century public health and housing law. First, there is a close parallel in basic design between, on the one hand, the Public Health Act 1875 and the Housing etc. Act 1890 (themselves consolidating measures), and, on the other hand, the legislation currently in force. It might well be asked whether these nineteenth-century provisions, such as those relating to nuisance, are appropriate for present-day problems like substandard housing.[22] In the last decade, law centres and tenants' groups have had some success against substandard housing, on the basis that it is a nuisance under section 99 of the Public Health Act 1936, but they might well have achieved more with a modern housing code.

Secondly, the nineteenth-century legislation contained ambiguities and loopholes, not all of which have been resolved. For example, the Nuisances Removal Act 1855 defined a nuisance to include any premises in such a state as to be a nuisance or injurious to health. In 1872 the Court of the Queen's Bench interpreted this restrictively and held that because of its context in a public health statute, 'nuisance' did not include the many situations covered by common-law nuisance but was confined to those which had some effect on health.[23] As will be seen below, the meaning of statutory nuisance is still unclear.

Thirdly, public health and housing legislation relied heavily on the crude legislative technique of simply prohibiting undesirable activity. Prohibiting overcrowding or living in cellars had little impact, however, since the poorer sections of society did not have the economic capacity to pay higher rents and thus cause more adequate housing to be provided. Local authorities were also given the power to act in default of an owner remedying unfit housing, but were deterred from exercising it because of the cost. Slum clearance was made more difficult financially because owners used various devices to extract the maximum compensation when their property was resumed. Without greater state intervention – to build public housing, to control rents, to compel higher wages, or to provide social welfare benefits – the slums remained.

A fourth point is that the drafting of the legislation influenced its enforcement. Smith notes of the Public Health Act 1848 that 'local magistrates readily connived at resort to loopholes and imposed light penalties upon inescapable convictions'.[24] Many local authorities neglected to implement the legislation. Early legislation was permissive and many simply failed to adopt it. Even after the Public Health Act 1875 some local authorities were slow to appoint medical officers of health and public health inspectors, and were perfunctory in enforcing the law.[25] The position in relation to public health and housing legislation reflected the general inadequacy of governmental machinery. As the century progressed, state machinery expanded as the need for better enforcement procedures and more public servants was accepted. But even at mid-century, government was simply unable to cope with many social problems, not least because the enforcement machinery often reflected local commercial and industrial interests.

Fifthly, public health and housing legislation was not an unmitigated benefit for the poor. The very poor were hounded from one area to another by street clearance, commercial development, and public health reform. In some cases their hostility to sanitary interference resulted in violence.[26] The working class objected to the steps taken against their small workshops, slaughterhouses and domestic pigsties, were hostile to the way cholera corpses were buried communally, and resented the fact that the law made no provision for compensating them for articles destroyed or for dislocation caused by public health measures. Even after section 308 of the Public Health Act 1875 empowered local authorities to pay compensation for bedding and clothing seized during, say, a cholera outbreak, it does not seem to have been used frequently.[27] Until the Infectious Diseases (Prevention) Act 1890, local authorities did not have to provide shelter for those affected by disinfection, and even after the Act authorities were lethargic in complying.

Similarly, nineteenth-century slum clearance caused hardship for the poor, but on a larger scale and without, it seems, many compensating benefits.[28] Commercial development, railway building and street clearance displaced thousands of poor people without recompense or providing alternative housing. But if the pursuit of profit, municipal grandeur, or the social control of poor neighbourhoods were inherently likely to cause detriment to the poor, why should detriment also have occurred with measures ostensibly for the general benefit? First, the 'general benefit' was as much that of making the cities pleasanter and safer for the middle class as that of assisting the slum dweller. Secondly, local authorities did not have to arrange rehousing for everyone displaced by clearance – and even then they often avoided their limited obligations. Thirdly, the replacement housing they built was too expensive for those displaced and consequently was occupied mainly by artisans and the lower-middle class.[29]

The final point to make about the form of nineteenth-century public health and housing legislation is that reformers were under no illusions that the common law could provide solutions to social problems; they realized that legislation was necessary. Apparently there were a few judicial decisions granting relief to persons in urban areas affected by stinking rubbish, cesspools, etc., which were held to be common-law nuisances. The procedural obstacles to, and the expense of, seeking abatement through the assize of nuisance, led plaintiffs to bring actions on the case. The disadvantage of the latter was that the remedy was damages rather than abatement. Public nuisances were also indictable, but there seem to be few cases where legal proceedings were instituted.[30] Injunctions became more common as the nineteenth century progressed: for example, in 1858 an injunction was obtained against Birmingham Council at the instance of Sir Charles Adderley, Lord Bradford, Lord Leigh and Sir Robert Peel for polluting the River Tame with sewage.[31] However, the judges began to vary the standard for nuisance according to the type of neighbourhood – 'what would be a nuisance in Belgrave Square would not necessarily be one in Bermondsey'[32] – which would have made it almost impossible to obtain an injunction against industrial pollution in working-class neighbourhoods, despite its ill-effects on health and comfort.[33] Consequently, the nuisance action was of little use to the working class, even if they had had the financial resources of the knights and lords along the River Tame to undertake legal action.

Rent control

The Increase of Rent and Mortgage Interest (War Restrictions) Act 1915 restricted the right of landlords of dwelling-houses within defined values to increase the rent, except by the amount of any increase in rates or on account of expenditure incurred on improvements. Control was also imposed on the right of landlords to recover possession. Although a temporary measure, it soon became apparent that rent control could not be abolished with the war's end. Working people had new expectations as to just rents and as to the housing conditions they should enjoy (encapsulated in the political slogan 'homes fit for heroes'). Moreover, there was a heavy pressure on rents from the accumulated demand for housing and other building.[34] Consequently, rent control was extended by the Increase of Rent and Mortgage Interest (Restrictions) Act 1920, following the report of a committee under the chairmanship of the Marquess of Salisbury. However, the Act did not apply to new dwellings built after 1919 or to dwellings converted to flats after that date. Also excluded from control were dwelling-houses let at a rent which included payments in respect of board, attendance or more importantly, the use of furniture. The latter exception gave rise to 'lino tenancies' (linoleum on the floor and very little more), an early avoidance of rent control approved by the courts.[35]

Rent-control policy in the inter-war period was the product in the main of three forces: pressure by property owners for complete control; the Conservative Party belief that the Rent Acts were but a temporary measure to deal with a housing shortage; and the social reality that without the protection of the Acts many working-class people would suffer considerably. The upshot was limited decontrol in 1923 and 1933, primarily after landlords obtained vacant possession.[36] Despite rent control, renting was still reasonably profitable in the inter-war period, although a considerable number of rented houses were sold into owner-occupation. Shortly after the outbreak of World War II, rent control was imposed for all but a small number of high-grade houses.[37] There came into operation two streams of control – tenancies subject to the earlier Acts, and those brought into control by the 1939 Act. The picture was further complicated in 1946 when the Labour Government, drawing on the report of a committee under Viscount Ridley, established rent tribunals to fix rents in respect of tenancies where the rent included payment for furniture.[38] Some landlords abused the furnished/unfurnished distinction by installing the barest minimum of furniture to exclude a tenancy from full control.[39]

Substantial decontrol was a feature of Conservative rule in the

1950s, primarily through the Rent Act 1957. The aims of the Act were to resuscitate the private landlord, to induce landlords to improve their property by making renting more profitable, and to have privately rented accommodation continue as a viable alternative to council housing. None of these aims was achieved, for the real return on rental property fell considerably, and many landlords sold into owner-occupation. After the 1957 Act the proportion of homeless families admitted to temporary accommodation as a result of eviction or of a dwelling being sold, rose significantly. In the early sixties there was clear evidence that unscrupulous landlords were using harassment and unlawful eviction to obtain vacant possession, and the word 'Rachmanism' was introduced into the English language. The Labour Government, elected in 1964, reintroduced control for premises decontrolled under the 1957 Act, but through a new system of fair rents.[40] Tenancies still subject to control under the Rent Act 1957 were to continue as 'controlled tenancies', but the intention was that eventually they would be brought within the fair rents system. The Rent Act 1965 also contained prohibitions on harassment and unlawful eviction. The Conservatives' Housing Finance Act 1972 continued the conversion of controlled tenancies to the fair rents system. Rent allowances were introduced to mitigate the effects of consequent rent increases. Automatic conversion ceased when Labour returned to office in 1974.[41] Its Rent Act 1974 assimilated the position of furnished and unfurnished tenancies under the fair rents system but, to encourage owner-occupiers to let spare rooms, gave tenants with residential landlords only limited protection. A change brought about by the Conservative Government's Housing Act 1980 was to introduce shorthold tenancies, which can vary from one year to five years. On expiration of the period the landlord can obtain a mandatory order for possession on three months' notice. In addition, the Act abolished controlled tenancies, and also weakened the security of tenants with resident landlords.

This excursion into legislative developments provides a basis for understanding the legal form the Rent Acts have taken. Subsequent to its introduction in 1915, rent-control policy has been a product of the vicissitudes of party politics – except for the control introduced at the outbreak of World War II – although at various times the details of legislation have been mapped by 'expert' committees. The Labour Party has favoured relatively extensive rent control, although in many respects its legislation has concentrated on reversing Conservative government measures of decontrol, or closing 'gaps' in existing legislation or those exposed by judicial decision. Although the Conservatives have removed some property from rent control, they have had to concede to rent control a role, because of the opposition which would otherwise occur. Indeed rent control has a ratchet effect: it is difficult to abandon once introduced because of the political and social consequences of doing so, without significant public expenditure on rent subsidies or public housing. The political nature of rent control has introduced a complexity into statutory provisions which the courts have compounded by their interpretations. Consolidations have not assisted greatly, for they have been quickly followed by amendments. The accretion of provisions has caused adjacent tenants in similar dwellings to pay substantially different rents – a situation undesirable on grounds of equity. In addition the complexity of rent control has detracted from its ostensible purpose; since the system is difficult to understand, tenants have not taken maximum advantage of it.

Minimum wages

Early wage regulation, in the Statutes of Labourers, was designed to prevent workers taking advantage of the shortage of labour following the Black Death and of other social and economic changes. Numerous and detailed, these statutes provided for wages to be fixed, not absolutely, but in line with the cost of necessities, and made it unlawful for workers to refuse an offer of work or to leave their masters' service.[42] It seems that employers continued to invoke the statutes until the Tudor period, whenever labour shortages occurred, to prosecute those who refused work or who demanded high wages.[43] Legislation of the Tudor period, primarily the Statute of Artificers 1562 (5 Eliz. 1, c.4), updated the medieval law, but retained the principle that workers committed an offence if they refused to work. It entrusted to local justices the task of meeting yearly at the Easter sessions to set a schedule of wages after conferring with prominent persons in a locality and considering the state of the market.[44] An earlier Tudor statute made illegal combinations of workers to raise wages. The Statute of Artificers 1562 has been criticized as benefiting employers by enabling them to keep down wages, particularly since every justice would have been an employer of labour of some kind. Other writers have pointed out that the legislation was not completely one-sided: if workers could not refuse to work, employers could not dismiss them as they pleased. Moreover, the recital in the Statute of Artificers emphasized the need for justices to fix reasonable wages. R.H. Tawney also pointed out that many precariously surviving rural owner-occupiers were part-time wage-labourers, as well as occasional employers, so that the legislation did not necessarily benefit a privileged oligarchy of employers but also protected one class of workers against another.[45] Justices sometimes fixed what in effect were minimum rather than maximum wages.

By the end of the seventeenth century the fixing of wages under the Statute of Artificers 1562 seems to have become a formality.[46] Nonetheless, throughout the eighteenth century employers and workers continued to behave as if their legal privileges and disabilities continued. At the end of the eighteenth century there was a revival of interest in regulating wages, in particular in fixing minimum wages, to ameliorate the conditions of workers who were hard-pressed by the steep increase in the cost of living. But a Minimum Wage Bill was rejected when introduced in Parliament in 1795–6.[47] Major objections were that it would lead to the equality of wages, that it would produce unemployment, that it would interfere with the harmonious relations between employers and workers, and that it would force employers out of business. Workers had to look to the adoption in their area of the Speenhamland system, under which poor relief subsidized wages to subsistence levels.[48] Then in the early years of the nineteenth century the Statute of Artificers was employed, along with the Combination Acts and common-law conspiracy, to suppress trade unionism. Sometimes it was the preferred instrument because of difficulties of proceeding under the Combination Acts.[49] The authority of the justices to set wages was abolished in 1813, in keeping with market principles, but the offence of leaving work unfinished remained on the statute book. Talk of regulating wages subsided during the nineteenth century in keeping with the dominant philosophy of *laissez-faire*.

At the end of the nineteenth century, one strand of radical and progressive opinion was that as a matter of justice all citizens were entitled to a certain minimum income, along with minimum standards in hours and conditions of work.[50] In Britain the practical side of this concern was the campaign against sweated labour, both of workers in factories and home workers. Pursuant to section 27 of the Factory and Workshop Act 1891, certain factories were required to keep lists of home workers, and then the Factory and Workshop Act 1901 made provision for fining employers who employed home-workers working in dangerous or insanitary places, and enabled the Secretary of State to oblige employers to give home workers an accurate statement of their wage rates.[51] Neither measure was adequately enforced. Ultimately the Liberal Government enacted the Trade Boards Act 1909, which applied directly to four industries then notorious for sweating, and enabled wage-fixing machinery (trade boards) to be established in other trades where wages were 'exceptionally low'. The trade boards could fix minimum time rates, piece rates and, after 1918, overtime rates, and subsequent orders were enforceable through the criminal law. From 1909 to 1918 only eight trade boards operated over some 600,000 workers, but after World War I the system was put to wider use than the sweated trades and some fifty boards were added, so that by 1939 more than a million workers were covered. In the depression of the early twenties, the government tightened its control over the trade boards, and in a number of cases returned proposals to a board for reconsideration after a deputation of employers in the trade had made representations that the rates were too high.[52] The average wages fixed by the wages boards in the inter-war period, especially in agriculture, were low, and in some cases were not even as high as estimates of the amounts required for proper living standards. At the end of World War II, the Wages Councils Act 1945 provided that wages councils (the former trades boards) could be established generally, not just in specified trades, and empowered the councils to fix total remuneration (not just rates) as well as holidays.

Early wage regulation in England had an anti-worker complexion, although workers obtained benefits from it. It had wide coverage and its main aim was to set maximum wages. From the later eighteenth century, wage regulation had to contend with the economic wisdom that freedom of contract and the free market produced the greatest good. Indeed the Tudor statutes on wage regulation were repealed in 1813. After it was reintroduced in 1909, wage regulation had the narrow brief of setting minimum wages for the lowest paid. Writing in 1949, Kahn-Freund commented that the growth of the wages councils illustrated the 'trial and error' method of social policy 'that progresses from the particular to the general which is a proverbial characteristic of British statute making'.[53] He also referred to the antipathy of the trade unions to legal regulation – no doubt a reflection of their perception that the courts had an anti-trade-union bias.

The relative importance of social forces in wage regulation can be shown by way of comparison with Australia, which has similar traditions of law-making to Britain. Australia established centralized wage-fixing bodies around the turn of the century, after particularly bitter struggles between employers and workers in the 1890s.[54] The federal body (currently the Conciliation and Arbitration Commission) was originally proposed as a means of benefiting the community by settling industrial disputes through conciliation or, failing that, through compulsory arbitration. In fact just after it was established the Commission introduced the concept of the 'basic' wage (the minimum wage payable) and later introduced the idea of margins (the components added for particular workers, depending on wage relatives).[55] The wages set are enforceable at law and have tended to become the norm in the community, although they do not preclude further bargaining, individually or collectively.[56] The stark contrast with Britain, where official wage-fixing is comparatively limited, makes clear that legislative form is moulded by social context, of which a tradition of incremental law-making is but one factor.

II THE LEGAL FORM OF SOCIAL WELFARE REGULATION

Having explored the historical development of social welfare regulation, we are in a better position to appreciate current provisions. At one level the legal form these take is determined by social forces: we have outlined those relevant to the emergence of social welfare regulation in the nineteenth and the first part of the twentieth centuries. The product of social forces involved in law-making is crystallized in the words of a particular statute. Clearly the words are not immutable: some of those involved in the enactment of a statute may gain strength and be able to achieve its amendments; those involved in its administration may be successful in having it modified in the light of its enforcement and impact; or a different constellation of forces with different purposes may cause it to be altered, replaced or repealed.

At another level the legal form taken by social welfare regulation is shaped by specifically legal factors. One of these is the tradition in which legislation is drafted, which partly reflects the relationship between the legislature and the courts. In much of the common-law world, legislation is carefully drawn, taking into account previous judicial decisions on the meaning of particular words and phrases, since the courts have an important constitutional role and favour a rather literal approach to interpretation. Another factor is that just as institutions develop a momentum, so too does legislative form. Once a particular approach is adopted there are incentives for it to be continued, although it might be amended in the light of changing circumstances. On the one hand this may be the property of lethargy, a reluctance to think out new legal approaches, or of familiarity with the existing approach by its administrators, those whose behaviour is controlled, and possibly its beneficiaries. On the other hand more fundamental issues may be at stake, for a change in legislative form may extend to matters of substance. An example is that a move away from the legal concepts of statutory nuisance and fitness in the case of substandard housing to an integrated housing code might not only constitute a change of legislative technique but also represent more extensive regulation.

The general point which emerges from the following examination of the substance of the current social welfare regulation is that some of it does not measure up to the problems ostensibly addressed. Some is only partially successful, some is largely a failure, while some is worse than useless since it creates the illusion that effective action is being taken. The social forces behind social welfare regulation are a large part of the explanation, but legislative technique has a role, and it is to that that most attention is given in this part. Certain aspects of legislative technique become apparent. First, there are significant gaps in social welfare regulation, so that property owners and employers can avoid its effects. Secondly, there is the point referred to previously in relation to substandard housing, that some social welfare regulation is out of line with the present-day context of a particular problem. Rather than being rationally related to its ostensible goals, regulation comprises an accretion of provisions from different historical periods. A closely related point is that the legal approaches adopted are not always the most effective in achieving particular policy goals. For instance, simple criminal prohibitions are popular but are a relatively crude method of influencing behaviour compared with various types of administrative action. Finally, the focus on public health, housing and employment regulation should not lead to a limited view of the legal form which social welfare legislation can take. In addition to the quality standards and prior control which these aspects of social welfare regulation entail, there are other legal forms of promoting welfare objectives such as licensing subsidies and public ownership. Some of these are mentioned in the course of the present and following chapters.

Public health law

Much of the public health law outlined in the first part of the chapter still applies, although in modified form. While in the modern day, matters such as drainage, sewers and the water supply pose no special problem for the poorer sections of society, some aspects of environmental health do. Many deprived areas contain dangers on derelict land and from abandoned housing, have a general air of decay, and experience serious industrial and environmental pollution. These environmental problems often take a back seat in public policy. *Coventry C.C.* v. *Cartwright*[57] in 1975 is illustrative. The case was instituted by a community lawyer on behalf of a residents' association in the inner Coventry area, which complained that the accumulation of building materials, iron, and broken glass, etc., on vacant land owned by the local authority was a statutory nuisance. In the result the residents were unsuccessful, for the court held that the accumulation was not prejudicial to their health, on the basis that only if someone entered the land was there a danger. The court said that the decision would have gone the other way if the residents had established that there was a likelihood of disease emanating from the collection of materials on the land. The decision illustrates the limited nature of statutory nuisance as interpreted by the courts. As well as statutory nuisance there are other specific statutory provisions relevant to environmental health but they offer no assistance in a situation like that facing the residents in *Cartwright*'s case, where the public authority charged with enforcing them fails to take action.

As in the nineteenth century, the criminal law is an unsatisfactory method of dealing with overcrowding since poorer persons frequently have no choice but to overcrowd.[58] Either their income must be increased so that they can command better housing in the market, or public housing must be provided.[59] By contrast, the legislation relating to houses in multiple occupation is rather more adequate. In poorer areas these are mostly larger houses, which have been subdivided, and tend to be occupied by single people, couples who cannot afford to buy a house, and those who do not qualify for a public tenancy.[60] Initial legal control can be exercised when large houses are subdivided for multiple occupation, if this is a material change of use and the planning authority must give permission.[61] Once operating, houses in multiple occupation can be controlled with a view to improving their management and facilities.[62]

Housing standards

The statutory law relevant to housing standards is complex and cumbersome. Basically it comprises a number of nineteenth-century concepts, continued to the present day, together with an accretion of provisions designed to deal with particular difficulties. The condition of individual houses is governed, first, by the statutory nuisance provisions in public health law and, secondly, by specific provisions regarding fitness, amenities and repair. The courts have held that although these requirements may partially overlap, they constitute different standards.[63] Whereas the former requires only basic repairs ('patching up'), the latter can be used to effect a more substantial improvement in housing conditions.

As interpreted by the courts, the definition of statutory nuisance is unsatisfactory.[64] It is unclear whether the first limb – premises which are in such a state as to be prejudicial to health – includes mental or environmental health or social well-being. The second limb – premises which constitute a 'nuisance' – has been narrowed by judicial interpretation to mean common-law nuisance which affects public health.[65] Thus in 1976 in *National Coal Board* v. *Thorne*[66] the Divisional Court held that a house in a defective state of repair (windows, gutters, skirting boards) did not constitute a statutory nuisance, although it was an obvious interference with the personal comfort of the occupants, because these conditions were not a nuisance at common law, persons other than the occupiers not being affected. To succeed in that case the tenant would have had to show injury or likely injury to health, as required by the first limb.[67] The statutory nuisance provisions are usually enforced by issuing an abatement notice, and then seeking a nuisance order in the magistrates' court in the event of non-compliance.[68] The order can require the defendant to abate the nuisance or to execute any necessary works.[69] Persons aggrieved by a statutory nuisance can initiate action themselves under section 99 of the Act. On a fine being imposed – not just the making of a nuisance order – those aggrieved by the nuisance might also obtain compensation.[70] Despite the difficulties of establishing a statutory nuisance, community groups and law centres have had a good deal of success in using section 99 to have unsatisfactory housing conditions attended to, and to obtain monetary compensation where the local authority has failed to institute legal proceedings or has owned the property itself.[71]

At first glance the Housing Act's provision for unfit housing is more satisfactory than statutory nuisance. A house is unfit if it is not reasonably suitable for occupation having regard to specified matters such as repairs, damp, drainage, sanitary conveniences and facilities for preparing food.[72] The 1943 House of Lords decision, *Summers* v. *Salford Corporation*,[73] is usually cited as a leading authority; there it was held that a broken sash cord rendered the premises unfit. But the decision is not an indication that the courts will always be liberal, since it was a case where a tenant was suing for damages for personal injuries and there was an obvious desire on the court's part for her to succeed. Indeed the standard for fitness concentrates on structural matters and does not extend to amenities such as the presence of a bath, a hot and cold water supply or an internal water closet. Under the Act a local authority satisfied that a house is unfit must issue a repair notice to the owner requiring the execution of works to make it fit, provided that this is possible at reasonable expense.[74] The courts have interpreted 'reasonable expense' in a way favourable to owners – an inhibition on the use of the provision.[75] For an unfit house not repairable at reasonable expense, the local authority must take steps to obtain an undertaking that it will no longer be used for human habitation, that it will be repaired voluntarily, or that it will be used as short-life housing.[76] In the absence of a suitable undertaking to this effect, or in the event of a contravention of an undertaking, the local authority must make a demolition order or a closing order.[77] Alternatively, it can purchase the house and use it as temporary accommodation before demolition. As with section 99 of the Public Health Act 1936, individuals can initiate action in respect of unfit housing, but the procedure is more complicated and involves an application for judicial review.[78]

The enforcement of housing standards by demolition or closing order subtracts from the housing stock, and for this reason public policy has moved away from it in the last decade. The policy of conserving as much housing as possible is reflected in several legislative developments. For example, there is now a power inserted in the Housing Act 1957, section 9(1A), for a local authority to issue a 'repair notice' if it is satisfied that a house, whilst not unfit, requires substantial repairs to bring it up to a reasonable standard, having regard to its age, character and locality. Again the courts have interpreted this provision narrowly. Although there is no mention of it in the legislation, the Court of Appeal has held that the cost of repair and the impecuniosity of the owner may be taken into account.[79] In some deprived areas where there is no prospect of gentrification or redevelopment, owners can use this to argue that the cost of repair is unreasonable since it will usually exceed the increase in the market value and the return through increased rents. There is also a power in the Housing Act 1957 for a local authority to issue a repair notice where it is satisfied, after a representation from an occupying tenant, that a house, whilst not unfit, is in a condition which interferes materially with personal comfort. In addition, the Housing Act 1974 provides for the compulsory improvement of housing by way of the installation of amenities; loans must generally be available for the carrying out of this work. In 'general improvement areas' and in 'housing action areas', local authorities have compulsory improvement powers.[80] There are considerable delays built into these provisions which can thwart local improvement policy.

With area action the problem has been not so much one of inadequate provisions but of a failure of local authorities to use the powers they have in the most appropriate way. Under the Housing Act 1957, still in force, a local authority can declare a clearance area where the houses are unfit, or where by reason of bad arrangement they are dangerous or injurious to health, and demolition is the most satisfactory method of dealing with conditions in the area.[81] Once a clearance area is declared, the local authority must proceed to purchase the properties and arrange their clearance. Compulsory purchase orders must be approved by the Secretary of State, who has to arrange for a public local enquiry or other hearing if there are objections. Following the period in the fifties and sixties when slum clearance was popular, public policy swung back to rehabilitation and improvement. Reasons for this were that much slum housing had been cleared and the poor-quality housing remaining was not suitable for area clearance; that some working-class communities objected to further clearance; that clearance was thought to contribute to social problems by breaking up viable communities; and most importantly that rehabilitation was better tailored to the constraints on government expenditure. Consequently, local authorities were empowered to make rehabilitation orders for houses in clearance areas.[82] Initially at least they were slow to take advantage of this power for, having gone to the trouble of obtaining a compulsory purchase order, they were loath to reverse policy.[83]

The first criticism of the form of legislation governing substandard housing is that in certain respects it is either outdated in its conception or unduly complex in its application. The concept of statutory nuisance falls into the first category, although the procedure for its application is relatively straightforward and it has been successfully invoked by community groups and law centres. The standards in the Housing Acts are relatively clear-cut but the procedures for their enforcement are complex, time-consuming (particular periods must elapse so that owners can decide whether they will comply or sell to the authority), and invite obstruction by property owners (especially the way the courts have interpreted certain provisions, for example the 'reasonable expense' criterion).[84] Such defects in legislative form are separate from the financial impediments facing public authorities in implementing the Housing Acts.

A second criticism is the existence of two parallel 'codes' – one in public health law and the other in housing legislation. The incongruity is compounded in practice because the two tend to be administered by different bodies. Theoretically, the overlapping provisions have the advantage that if an authority runs into difficulty it can switch to a different head of power, but disputes within and between its agencies as to the best procedure can cause a paralysis of its capacity to act. There is considerable support for an integrated housing code – a single set of standards, procedures, and financial criteria for all schemes of voluntary and compulsory improvement.[85]

Advocates usually also argue for greater powers of compulsory improvement and repair. Among the justifications for compulsion are that the community has an overriding interest in the quality of the housing stock because housing is a national asset and because a dilapidated house can adversely affect a neighbourhood. Compulsion raises problems, however, which cannot simply be dismissed as the obscurantism of property owners. Many 'property owners' likely to be affected are poor, have just managed to purchase housing and so do not have the resources to make improvements unless they obtain full grants. Compulsory purchase has been suggested as the most effective method of securing an improvement in housing standards, but the costs are prohibitive. Moreover, many authorities have a record of unenlightened use of compulsory powers and of ignoring tenants' rights.[86]

Minimum wages

Minimum-wage laws are not uncommon in modern Western societies, but they suffer from various defects in legal form. For example, the Wages Council Act 1979 is relatively simple in design but despite its coverage – about three million workers in nearly half a million establishments – it does not extend to many industries with significant pockets of low-paid workers. In addition, confusion results because there is a proliferation of wages council rates for apparently similar jobs in the same industry and across industries. The complexity and incomprehensibility of wages regulation orders explains the difficulty in conducting publicity campaigns to inform low-paid workers of their rights. A Low Pay Unit report advocates that minimum rates be fixed across industries – they would be somewhat along the lines of the awards made by the Australian Conciliation and Arbitration Commission – with the result that orders would become simpler and self-enforcing.[87]

The disabled who can work receive low pay because their capacity to earn is reduced. In some jurisdictions they may be assisted to find employment by equal opportunities legislation.[88] The Disabled Persons (Employment) Acts of 1944 and 1958 go one step further and oblige larger employers to employ at least three per cent of registered disabled people. In addition, regulations under the Companies Act 1948 compel larger companies to include in their annual reports a statement in respect of the recruitment, training and career development of disabled persons – although whether this shames companies into greater activity remains to be seen.[89] Even if disabled persons are assisted to obtain employment as a result of provisions like this, their position is undercut by legislation permitting them to be employed at less than the minimum wage.[90]

Workers receiving low pay might be disadvantaged in other ways, for they might not benefit from other protective measures. For example, part-time workers might not qualify for benefits such as dismissal rights, maternity leave, redundancy payments, or notification of their terms of employment. Homeworkers may also be excluded from health and safety legislation on the grounds that they are self-employed rather than employees.[91]

Rent control[92]

It is the conventional legal wisdom that the English Rent Acts have been unnecessarily complex, patchwork and vague.[93] The fault is usually laid at the door of the legislature, and it is that aspect which is examined here, but as we see below an important part of the responsibility lies with the courts. Because of the historical accretion of provisions, there are a variety of residential categories relevant to the current Rent Act, with different legal rights and duties attaching to each. The key categories are fully protected tenant, tenant with restricted protection, shorthold tenant, and licensee with restricted protection.[94] Some of these are replete with difficulties, evidenced in the litigation arising in relation to them. A protected tenancy arises whenever a dwelling house (which may be a house or part of a house) is let as a separate dwelling, provided the house falls below specified rateable values.[95] The definition clearly excludes certain arrangements such as licences. The Act specifies various exceptions to full protection – tenancies let *bona fide* at a rent which includes payments in respect of board or attendance; student lettings; holiday lettings; tenancies where there is a resident landlord and the landlord's and tenant's dwellings are part of the same building (unless it is a purpose-built block of flats); and tenancies where the landlord's interest belongs to the Crown, a local authority, or a housing association or cooperative.[96] Where a protected tenancy terminates, the protected tenant becomes a 'statutory tenant'. In addition, certain persons such as the spouse of a tenant can become a statutory tenant when a protected tenant (or a statutory tenant by virtue of termination) dies. So long as a statutory tenant retains possession, that person must observe, but is entitled to the benefit of, all the terms and conditions of the original lease.[97] Protected and statutory tenancies are regulated tenancies for the purposes of the Act. Those who are not protected or statutory tenants, and some licensees, might attract restricted protection under the Rent Act, by virtue of which their rents can be fixed at a 'reasonable' level, and qualify for limited security.[98] The complexity obvious from this brief outline of the variety of categories controlled has led to recommendations for a simpler system.[99]

It has been said that regulation faces difficulties when it attempts to deal with polycentric problems, those comprising a large variety of diverse but independent factors. Is fixing the level of rent for rent-controlled premises an example, given that there are many affected premises in a variety of different situations? The rents of controlled tenancies had their rents fixed historically, with adjustments in limited circumstances.[100] The formula was too rigid, in as much as controlled rents became arbitrary compared with other rents as general economic conditions changed. The present law empowers rent officers (appeals can be taken to rent assessment committees) to fix 'fair rents' for protected and statutory tenancies in the light of all the circumstances (but not personal circumstances), in particular the age, character, locality and state of repair of a dwelling and the quantity, quality and condition of any furniture.[101] The scarcity value of a place, and hence the higher rent it would command in the open market, must be excluded from consideration, as must any defect or improvement caused by the tenant. The House of Lords has held that there is no obligation on a rent officer or rent assessment committee to follow any particular method of setting a fair rent, as long as the method used is reasonable and lawful.[102]

In practice rent officers do not face a polycentric problem because they have developed procedures which enable them to perform their task. The methods generally accepted to fix a fair rent involve examining the return on capital value or the registered rents of comparable dwellings. However, critics have argued that fair rents approximate to market rents too closely, and one reason is said to be that valuers and solicitors are preponderant on rent assessment committees. This has led to the suggestion that the committees be replaced by a Housing Court, or at least include representatives from tenants' associations. Another possible change would be to substitute a different formula, for example to fix rents on the basis of the value of accommodation, expressed in terms of its amenities (suitably weighted), structural condition and state of repair.[103]

Rent control would be undermined without security of tenure, for landlords could deter tenants from applying for rent control by evicting those who did. The Rent Act 1977 confers full security of tenure on protected and statutory tenants and a court can only make a possession order on specified grounds.[104] Critics argue that some of the grounds for possession are unnecessarily wide and that others are superfluous. For instance, possession might be obtained for rent arrears, but tenants might have withheld payment because of the landlord's failure to repair or tenants might not have obtained the rent allowances for which they were eligible. A major objection seems to be inconsistency in the administration of the law. On similar fact situations, county court judges vary as to whether they think it reasonable to grant possession. For example, in one court rent arrears of a certain amount might result in an outright order for possession, while in another arrears of the same amount might lead to a suspended order. By contrast with the strong security of tenure conferred on protected and statutory tenants, only limited security is given to those with restricted protection under the Rent Acts.[105] Clearly this facilitates retaliatory eviction by landlords who object, say, to an application for a reasonable rent or to complaints about disrepair.

The intent of rent control would also be defeated if tenants had to make additional payments to landlords other than rent. Accordingly, the Rent Act 1977 makes it illegal for any person to require or to receive a premium in addition to rent on the grant, renewal, continuance or assignment of a protected tenancy.[106] With a restricted contract, it is an offence for any person to require (but not to receive) a premium as a condition of the grant, etc. of rights under the contract, but only if there is a registered rent for the premises.[107] By contrast with some others, these provisions are broadly conceived and the courts seem to have given them a generous interpretation.[108]

The one area of doubt is in relation to deposits (sometimes called security deposits or bonds) against damage to the furniture or the dwelling or against rent arrears. Deposits are an obstacle to poorer tenants obtaining access to decent privately rented housing, and there is also the problem, not confined to poorer tenants, of disputes at the end of a tenancy as to whether a deposit should be forfeited. (Tenants have some scope for bargaining with an unreasonable landlord by omitting to pay the last few weeks' rent.) In practice security deposits have been widely required and now the Housing Act 1980 puts beyond doubt that certain deposits do not offend the restrictions against premiums.[109] In Canada, Ontario in effect prohibits security deposits, with the reasoning that they add an oppressive element to a relationship already containing a sufficient basis for conflict.[110] Other jurisdictions feel that a ban on deposits might lead landlords to discriminate against certain categories of tenant, such as parents with young children, and so only regulate their payment and return.[111]

III IMPLEMENTATION

Social welfare regulation on the statute books might appear to further social welfare goals, but its enforcement might be so incomplete as to make it virtually a dead letter. Partly the gap between the law in the books and the law in action can be attributed to the law itself, which might not really be intended to be effective but be conceived, for example, to stem public criticism. Regulation might also be deficient in design so that the law-enforcers, or those who are supposed to benefit from it, are not in a position to enforce it. These aspects have been examined in the earlier parts of this chapter.

This part looks at some legal problems affecting the enforcement of social welfare regulation but also gives attention to what actually happens in practice. One aspect is the importance of participation by ordinary people in the implementation of regulation: some regulation is actually premised on their taking the initiative to enforce it, while in other cases agencies rely on complaints from members of the public because they do not have the resources to detect much wrongdoing themselves. An important part of the inquiry is that agencies charged with enforcing social welfare regulation eschew legal proceedings. Attention is given to the law governing their discretion, its extent, and the reasons for its exercise.

Self-enforcement

Rent control is a good example of where, legally, an important part of the task of enforcing social welfare regulation is left to ordinary people. For example, for a rent to be registered a tenant or landlord must take the initiative and apply; otherwise the rent is generally speaking what the parties have agreed.[112] Moreover, as a general rule it is not a criminal offence for a landlord to charge a rent in excess of a registered rent.[113] Instead, a tenant can withhold the excess rent and sue the landlord for any excess paid. In other jurisdictions rent control only operates in the case of excessive rents: again tenants must take the initiative – in some cases they can only do this when the landlord notifies a rent increase – and apply to a public authority.[114]

Perhaps it is not surprising that tenants do not always take advantage of these provisions when it would be in their interests to do so. Ignorance, inertia, or apprehension that their landlord might retaliate and that other accommodation is hard to obtain, are factors which prevent tenants from taking the initiative. Various surveys of tenants have found that significant numbers have not heard of the rent-control machinery. Most who do know, but do not apply, say that they are 'satisfied', or that it would confirm the existing rent or result in an increase; but there are those who say that they fear eviction or unpleasantness from the landlord or that they feel morally obliged to stand by the rent agreed.[115] Even when tenants do apply, a not inconsiderable number ultimately withdraw their application, some because the landlord applies pressure to them after being informed of the application.[116] Tenants' unions and residents' associations may go some way to overcoming these inhibitions and pressures.[117]

There is a power under the Rent Acts for local authorities to apply for a rent to be registered to overcome the difficulty that many tenants are reluctant to do so themselves.[118] However, few local authorities make such applications. One reason is that they are short of the necessary human resources, and another is that it would open them to allegations of political partisanship. A Divisional Court decision in 1949 is also to blame for stultifying references by local authorities under the section. In that decision, the Divisional Court struck down an attempt by the Paddington Borough Council to refer 302 agreements to a rent tribunal to have their rents reviewed.[119] The Council had decided, as a matter of policy, that in any property in respect of which two or more reductions of rent had been made by the tribunal (which had occurred in this case) all other contracts of letting should be referred. The tribunal heard eight of the references and in each case reduced the rents. But the Court held that the Council had not exercised its powers in a *bona fide* and valid manner because some of the references were inaccurate and because the Council had not received complaints from the tenants or conducted an inquiry to determine whether there was a *prima facie* case. There are grave deficiencies in the court's reasoning. The inaccuracies may have caused some prejudice to the landlords, but this neglects the practical difficulties facing a local authority in obtaining accurate information, especially where landlords are obstructive. That tenants might not complain is the very reason for the provision. Finally, two previous reductions would seem a good indication that other rents might be reducible, without the need for an inquiry.

In 1972 the Court of Appeal adopted a more favourable approach to local authorities taking action. It upheld a decision of the Divisional Court, which had dismissed a landlord's application for prohibition against the reference of tenancy agreements to a rent tribunal.[120] A local housing group had put pressure on Camden Borough Council to make inquiry and refer agreements to the tribunal. Its officers investigated some twenty-two agreements and found that the rents were a little high. The landlords had prevented them from interviewing all the tenants, but following careful consideration and counsel's opinion the Council referred the twenty-two agreements. The evidence was that some tenants supported the reference, some were opposed, and some supporting it were not prepared to attend at the tribunal. The Court of Appeal held that the landlords had not shown that the Council was acting other than properly (for example, capriciously or vexatiously). The Court distinguished the earlier decision because here the Council had investigated each of the twenty-two tenancies, given careful consideration to the matter, and had taken the tenants' views into account.

Private enforcement

A scheme of social welfare regulation might facilitate direct private enforcement. Section 99 of the Public Health Act 1936 springs to mind; community groups and law centres have been reasonably successful in using it to improve substandard housing. Of course there is no legal obstacle to an individual launching a private prosecution, barring a statutory prohibition. If a conviction is obtained a court might be empowered to award compensation to the person.[121] Needless to say, private prosecutions are virtually unknown in the social welfare area – there is the cost involved, and in most cases there will be some delay before a prosecution can be heard, whereas individuals will generally want immediate relief. Moreover, an offender might regard any fine which can be imposed as an acceptable expense, and consequently might not be deterred by the threat of a private prosecution. Theoretically, it is possible for an individual to obtain an injunction against a breach, or threatened breach, of a criminal provision. In practice obstacles to this include the cost and the difficulty of establishing standing or obtaining the necessary consent of the Attorney-General.[122]

Apart from other factors, there are almost insuperable legal barriers to indirect methods of private enforcement. At common law, breach of a statutory provision may make a contract illegal and hence unenforceable. However, attempts to apply the doctrine in areas such as landlord and tenant have proved unsuccessful. In what is now the leading decision, *Shaw* v. *Groom*,[123] the tenant raised the doctrine in an action by the landlord for arrears of rent. She argued by way of defence that she had not been provided with a rent book in the form prescribed by section 4 of the Landlord and Tenant Act 1962. The Court of Appeal overturned the decision of the county court judge, and held that the landlord's breach did not bar his claim. In their interpretation of the legislation, Parliament had intended to punish a breach of the Act only by the imposition of a fine. The Court distinguished an earlier authority on the basis that the obligation to provide a rent book was collateral to the contract and did not operate as a term under it. However, there were strong public policy reasons underlying the decision. It is clear that Harman L.J. thought it unjust that a landlord should be barred from claiming rent arrears through failing to provide a rent book. Sachs L.J. was influenced by a similar consideration and also emphasized that the breach was a minor transgression, hardly warranting the forfeiture of rent arrears. He added that the tenant, being semi-literate, was far from being prejudiced by the breach! By contrast with the court's view of public policy, there are the policy arguments that rent books have a role in educating tenants about their rights, and that landlords would have had a greater incentive to comply with the relevant law to provide one if they were prevented from suing for arrears in the event of failing to do so.

There is difficulty in invoking the doctrine that a breach of statutory duty gives rise to a civil action for damages or an injunction. The courts have said that whether a civil cause of action can be implied is a question of legislative intention. Relevant considerations include whether a statutory duty is imposed for the benefit of persons such as the plaintiff and whether the beneficiaries of its performance would otherwise be without an effective remedy. In practice these tests produce inconsistent results. The Court of Appeal in *McCall* v. *Abelesz*[124] held that criminal prohibitions against unlawful eviction and harassment did not give rise to a civil action. Their reasoning was that the Act expressly preserves civil liability (for example, for trespass or for breach of the covenant for quiet enjoyment) and therefore could not have been intended to give rise to a civil action. In the result it is more difficult for victims to obtain damages for, or injunctions to prevent, unlawful eviction and harassment.

Enforcement agencies and their cases

Agencies enforcing social welfare regulation can obtain their cases by complaint or by taking the initiative themselves to discover non-compliance with the law. Complaints are a particularly important source in drawing an agency's attention to non-compliance, especially when it lacks the resources to engage in widespread detection work itself. Some non-compliance is such that without a complaint an agency would be hard pressed to know that it occurred, even if it engaged in systematic inspection. However, agencies cannot rely upon victims to complain when wrongdoing occurs. Those who in general have most cause for complaint might complain least, with the result that enforcement agencies are biased, even unconsciously, because they respond unduly to particular sections of the population.

To start with, even if people are knowledgeable about their legal rights or about the particular agencies charged with their implementation, they might lack the confidence or contacts to initiate and carry through a complaint. In 1976, for example, eleven community groups in London organized a concerted campaign to take out fifty summons on the same day in central London under section 99 of the Public Health Act 1936. In the result only seventeen were issued. One factor in the attrition was that tenants withdrew when the implications of legal action dawned. As one put it: 'Why should I stand up in court and tell everyone about my shame?'[125] A closely related point is that law-breaking is sometimes complex (e.g. breaches of minimum-wage orders), or diffused over time (e.g. non-repair by a landlord), so that people are not impelled to complain. Offences may involve relatively small sums of money in underpaid wages or excess rent, so that disproportionate effort seems involved, although cumulatively the amount might be extraordinarily significant.

Poorer tenants and low-paid workers are in a vulnerable position if they complain to enforcement agencies, for they might easily lose their housing or their job through vindictiveness. Low-paid workers tread a narrow path between employment and being out of work. Thus it is not surprising that significant numbers of workers refuse the arrears which the wages inspectorate finds on routine inspection to be owing to them.[126] Again, a survey of homeworkers found that they undertook what they frequently regarded as slave labour because it was the only chance of employment for them – they were trapped into working at home by family responsibilities or their geographic isolation.[127] While the law relating to security of tenure and unfair dismissal have some role in curbing victimization, they are by no means comprehensive. Contrast the American doctrine of retaliatory eviction, which protects from eviction tenants who complain to a public agency.[128] Inasmuch as there is a relatively high turnover of low-income tenants and low-paid workers, there is less chance of their complaining about breaches of legal requirements. Single working people who find housing conditions intolerable or their wages too low might simply move and never become involved in the issue of whether their landlord or employer is in breach of the law. There is not always an incentive to invoke the machinery of the law when potential complainants are faced with a *fait accompli*. Finally, enforcement agencies do not always seem to welcome complaints. Partly this is a failure to publicize their existence and to disseminate information about the enforcement work they undertake. For example, a survey of residents in Adamsdown (Cardiff) found that tenants rarely made the connection between housing disrepair and environmental health officers, perhaps because environmental health officers were employed by the local authority which was often the landlord responsible for disrepair.[129] Sometimes agency officials adopt a moralistic attitude: for example, they might regard tenants as being unconcerned with improving their living conditions, so that breaches of housing standards are overlooked, even where they can be sheeted home to the landlord.[130]

For the reasons outlined earlier, it is fatal if the agencies entrusted with implementing social welfare regulation rely solely on complaint: they need also to take the initiative and to engage in the systematic detection of wrongdoing. The enforcement agencies under examination all have a patchy record on inspection. For example, while local authorities inspect housing conditions for particular purposes, they are not infrequently in breach of the duties of inspection imposed on them by public health and housing legislation. Environmental health officers impose a fetter on their enforcement of housing standards when they decline to inspect public housing.[131] Justifications include that the managers of public housing adopt a reasonable attitude in the event of a statutory nuisance occurring, and that it is illogical for one arm of a local authority to enforce the law against another arm. The courts have held that housing standards do not cease to operate simply because a house is owned by a public authority.[132]

Perhaps the most publicized example of the failure of inspection has involved the wages inspectorate. The target set by the wages inspectorate from the mid-fifties was an inspection rate of 7½% per annum, with some variation between industries. On average, firms would only be inspected once every 13–14 years. In practice, with the constant turnover of establishments, and the absence of any legal obligation on establishments to register, the inspectorate did not even achieve this. Since the inspectorate took so long to visit firms, there was an inevitable turnover in the management of many. The inspectorate's policy in such cases was to regard the firm as having a clean record, even if offences had been committed previously.[133] A well-publicized inspection 'blitz' in 1976–7, which concentrated resources in particular geographic areas and on particular trades, demonstrated the inadequacy of inspection, for more than a quarter of the 2,973 employers visited were underpaying employees in wages and holiday pay.

Inadequate resources provide one explanation for the failure of inspection, but within this constraint a crucial factor is that employment agencies often seem to lack an aggressive attitude to monitor the implementation of social welfare regulation and to secure its enforcement. Moreover, many do not seem to have established a sense of priorities in which their limited resources are used in the most efficient manner. Bureaucratic structuring can incorporate detection and enforcement into the routine work of an agency. For example, agency officials can be required to give reasons why they do not recommend further legal proceedings when a breach of the law is detected, although a consequent danger is that officials in the field will overlook breaches so that they are never recorded in the first place. Another possibility is to establish specialist units which concentrate expertise and induce officials to demonstrate their activity. To set priorities, information needs to be accumulated on factors such as how seriously people view particular breaches, the harm they cause, the vulnerability of victims, and whether enforcement action is likely to have any impact. Complaints have a role here in identifying patterns of wrong-doing in relation to particular practices, institutions or laws.

Public enforcement: discretion in law and practice

The reality of social welfare regulation is that the agencies charged with its enforcement do not invoke the formal processes of law in many cases where breaches are found. For example, Hadden's study of five local authorities demonstrated that policy determined the way the compulsory repair and improvement powers of the Housing Acts were implemented: some local authorities had a strategy of securing action voluntarily, using compulsion as a last resort, while others pursued municipalization where private owners were unwilling or unable to act.[134] National statistics also demonstrate a failure to follow through with the enforcement of public health and housing standards. For example, the statistics for repair and improvement notices served in Housing Action Areas in England and Wales from January 1975 to March 1977 were as follows:[135]

Housing Act 1957 (Repair Notices)		Housing Act 1974 (Improvement Notices)	
Notices served	848	Notices served	539
Works completed	57(7%)	Works completed by owners	28(5%)
		Works completed by council in default	1(*%)
		Purchase notices served	34(6%)

While in some instances the attrition in these statistics would have been because compliance subsequently occurred, the evidence suggests that many breaches would not have been pursued. Many community workers and law centres have been disconcerted at the lack of prosecution of landlords engaging in harassment and unlawful eviction. Their concern found judicial support in *Drane* v. *Evangelou*,[136] a case of unlawful eviction following an application to a rent officer who had reduced the rent for the premises, where Lawton L.J. expressed surprise that there had not been a prosecution under what is now the Protection from Eviction Act 1977. The police are reluctant to become involved, and local authority harassment (tenancy relations) officers have few resources to investigate and prosecute offences. Coupled with the substantial problems of proving harassment, this leads harassment officers to conciliate when disputes occur. They argue that in many cases conciliation is more satisfactory than prosecution, which will simply exacerbate a dispute. The record of the wages inspectorate in prosecuting for under-payment of wages has been dismal. Over the ten years 1968–78, it undertook only 26 prosecutions, 21 of which were in the two years 1976–8. In the period 1968–76 it instituted only 30 civil proceedings to recover wages on behalf of workers.[137]

What is the explanation for this under-enforcement of social welfare regulation? Legislation does not enlighten us greatly about the exercise of discretion. On its face it rarely entrusts enforcement agencies with discretion. None the less, the courts have held that, in enforcing the law, enforcement agencies have a discretion, and should exercise it in the light of public policy.[138] In a few cases the statutory language is mandatory. For example, section 93 of the Public Health Act 1936 says that a local authority *shall* serve an abatement notice if satisfied that a statutory nuisance exists.[139] Under the Housing Act 1957, once a local authority accepts that a house is unfit for human habitation, it *shall* require that it be made fit if this can be done at reasonable cost, or if not it *shall* take other specified action (ss.9, 16). The Court of Appeal has held that the language in the latter sections creates mandatory duties, enforceable by the courts.[140] None of this assists greatly, and explaining under-enforcement leads to an examination of non-legal factors.

Historically, the relevant enforcement agencies have never been in a strong position to implement legal regulation and this, when rationalized in their 'advise and persuade' philosophy, has left its mark on their practices. Inspectors of nuisances, surveyors, and medical officers of health formed the basis for the nineteenth-century enforcement of public health and housing law. Yet resources were always tight – in some areas the office of inspector of nuisances was added to that of chief of police or combined with that of surveyor – and it was not until the end of the century that there was any demand for the training of inspectors.[141] Over the years, inspectors issued many orders to property owners regarding matters such as the abatement of defective drains, cesspools and privies. Few prosecutions ensued, however, partly because officials were corrupt (they were poorly paid) and because they were thwarted by political pressure and financial stringency. Local politicians were sometimes responsible for offences themselves, or had close links with those who were, and offenders may have gained ready sympathy by claiming that employment would be threatened by strict enforcement. Since formal enforcement was not a practical possibility given weak legislation and the dearth of resources, exhortation became the accepted way of proceeding. What was forced on inspectors by necessity, later became a means by which they could distinguish themselves from the police, and what they saw as the sordid and mechanical way of enforcing the law via the courts. However, some officials were motivated by more altruistic considerations. For example, some medical officers of health refrained from acting against unfit housing or overcrowding because this would simply have deprived the poor of their homes.[142] The wages inspectorate saw itself as having a role in transferring knowledge of more efficient methods of production to low-wage industries, as a means of raising wage levels. Given this attitude, it is not surprising that it eschewed prosecution.[143]

Inadequate resources are still an important factor in how social welfare regulation is implemented. A stark example of the shortage of human resources is provided by the wages inspectorate, with its many thousands of establishments to police. The inadequacy of human resources led R.H. Tawney to comment in 1914 that wage and factory inspectors were to workers what the police were to property owners, but that the former were deprived of the protection which was their right by law because of the parsimony of government.[144] In addition to adequate staff, an enforcement agency needs financial resources for particular enforcement activities. A housing authority might not prosecute for overcrowding if that gives rise to a duty to rehouse, but might wait until some occupiers move and then issue a directive prohibiting a further increase in numbers.[145] The capacity of public authorities to exercise their default powers against substandard housing and to do the necessary work themselves involves access to finance, which might never be recovered from the owner of the property. Existing resources would be used more efficiently with legislative changes, for example, obliging institutions covered by social welfare regulation to register with the relevant inspectorate.

Policy is a further factor explaining the implementation of social welfare regulation. Davies found that for the Rye Hill area of Newcastle in the sixties, which the Council intended eventually to redevelop, the environmental health inspectors

were asked to refrain from an over-lavish use of Closing Orders and Direction Orders lest they 'embarrass the CDA'. The 'embarrassment' of too great a rash of Orders would presumably lie, in part, in the difficulty of persuading a Ministry Inspector that the houses so adorned were in fact 'fit', and in part in the risk of dotting the various terraces with numbers of derelict and semi-derelict houses. . . . Yet one effect of the run-down of the normal 'policing' activities of the Public Inspectorate was to permit an increasingly irresponsible (and increasingly profitable) use of property. It also, of course, increased the misery of the tenants of those houses, either as continuing residents of them or as potential Council tenants.[146]

One reason that public authorities give for not using the full battery of legal provisions against substandard housing is that many property owners do not have the capacity to comply with them.[147] Grants to assist improvement and repair can overcome this difficulty to an extent. Some local authorities are reluctant to use the compulsory repair powers under the Public Health Act 1936 and the Housing Acts, because they believe that full standard improvement or conversion is the only sensible long-term policy. To this end they seek to have the owner sell to the local authority or a housing association.[148]

Enforcement agencies justify the absence of formal legal proceedings on the ground that they can better secure compliance with the law by advice and persuasion. A working party of the Ministry of Health put the argument this way when it considered sanitary inspectors – today's environmental health officers – in 1953:

Broadly, the function of a sanitary inspector is a regulatory one, that is, he is concerned to secure compliance on the part of the public with certain branches of the law designed to protect the health of the community. We say to 'secure compliance' rather than to 'enforce', because whilst enforcement by process of law is the ultimate remedy, compliance is in fact increasingly secured by advice, persuasion and education.[149]

Underlying the philosophy that advice and persuasion are more effective than legal proceedings in securing compliance with the law is the belief that most landlords, property owners and employers wish to comply but fail to do so because of factors such as misunderstanding or ignorance. That these groups are generally law-abiding may well be true, but even the law-abiding are encouraged to be lax when non-compliance does not attract punishment.[150] Moreover, many of those failing to comply with the law, for example minimum-wage laws, are not as ignorant or incompetent as the conventional wisdom suggests, but set out to maximize their profits without regard to whether they measure up to their legal obligations. The advise-and-persuade philosophy receives official support from government officials and legislators.[151] The judicial attitude is ambiguous: the general rule is that enforcement officials have a discretion to prosecute, but there are judicial *dicta* which recognize the desirability of prosecution in 'technical' cases or which disapprove under-enforcement.[152]

If advice and persuasion are the main tools of enforcement agencies, there are occasions when the formal processes of the law are invoked. The way the courts are likely to react is one factor in whether this occurs. If the courts are perceived to be lenient with non-compliers, then an enforcement agency will shy away from them.[153] To the extent that magistrates have links with property or employer interests they might be seen as sympathetic to these interests, even in an unconscious way, when proceedings are taken over matters such as housing standards, harassment of tenants or enforcement of minimum wages. It is not simply a matter of the courts' attitude, however, for the legislation might be deficient. Fines fixed by statute, for example, might be so low as to be derisory. On the other hand, the courts might impose fines well below the possible maximum. Enforcement agencies must share the blame if courts do not take seriously the legal proceedings instituted by them. If enforcement agencies rarely take proceedings, the courts can be misled into thinking that a legal provision is relatively unimportant, or that an offender has committed a single breach (whereas in fact he might have committed a series of breaches and only because of persistent wrongdoing be proceeded against). It would be wrong to think that the courts cannot change their attitude on a particular matter. For example, at one time the fines imposed for harassment and unlawful eviction were paltry, particularly if the defendant was a resident landlord. But in 1979 the Court of Criminal Appeal indicated how seriously it viewed the offences by holding that immediate imprisonment should be the usual penalty for using force or threats of force to evict.[154]

Enforcement agencies make no attempt to demonstrate that the 'advise-and-persuade' approach is more effective in accomplishing compliance with the law than the maximum enforcement which resources permit. This is not to say that stricter enforcement would produce a dramatic jump in law-abidingness, but there are good reasons for thinking that it would improve the performance of many landlords, property owners and employers. Unless enforcement agencies regularly invoke the law, it will not be taken seriously, and even the law-abiding will lack the incentive to adopt procedures which guarantee compliance with their legal obligations.[155] However, an enforcement orientation does not necessarily mean strict enforcement in all (or even most) instances of noncompliance; for example, the law would be brought into disrepute if formal legal proceedings were instituted for every trivial breach. The crucial point is that the law contemplates enforcement, yet this is subverted as enforcement agencies, with official approval, substitute under-enforcement. The wide discretion exercised by enforcement agencies is especially objectionable, because it is not open to public scrutiny and can conceal changing preferences, which diverge from the spirit of the law. In a sense, enforcement is part of the rule of law, for what legitimacy does a law have if it is never, or hardly ever, enforced? There is also the issue of equality before the law, for the discrepancies between the enforcement of different laws is plain for all to see. The contrast between the under-enforcement outlined above and, say, the attitude to prosecuting social security fraud is instructive. Both the rule of law and equality before the law demand that enforcement agencies apply the strict letter of the law unless there is justification, open to public scrutiny, for not doing so.

Can reform be effected to boost enforcement, especially at a time when finance is tight? Politicians are generally indifferent to the nuts and bolts of securing compliance with law and generally regard their responsibilities as complete once legislation is enacted. Those controlling law-enforcement agencies themselves are generally wedded to established practices, which they usually regard as effective in achieving lawful compliance. The poorer sections of society, for whose benefit social welfare regulation might operate, are sometimes ignorant of their legal rights and what can be done to enforce them. Political will and public pressure can modify enforcement. For example, collective action by groups such as tenants' unions, residents' associations, and trade unions can foster self-help, instil awareness about law, and stir law-enforcement agencies to action.[156] The capacity of ordinary people to enforce the law themselves or to complain to enforcement agencies can be enhanced, if only to a small extent, by imposing legal duties to inform on property owners and employers (such as the duties to display notices about minimum-wage orders and to provide rent books). With enlarged powers, the Ombudsman would be in a stronger position to examine the failure of agencies to enforce the law.

IV THE ROLE OF THE COURTS

Property owners and employers have used the courts as an avenue to resist social welfare regulation. Although they have not been able to do this in any major way, they have had minor victories. This part focuses on the reaction of the courts in areas of social welfare regulation referred to in other parts of the chapter.

Public health reform

Much nineteenth-century public health legislation involved public authorities infringing directly on property rights in the performance of their duties. In such circumstances the courts tended to favour property owners by demanding a clear, legislative mandate for each particular action; by requiring public authorities to examine the particular circumstances of each infringement of property rights and refusing to allow them to adopt a general policy for an area or problem; and by expecting strict compliance with legislative procedures and in some cases with court-created doctrines such as natural justice. It should not be thought that the judges were uniform in their attitudes, for some were more favourable to property rights and less disposed to sanitary ideals than others.[157] Public authorities could avoid the effect of these doctrines by careful planning.

  Tinkler v. *Wandsworth District Board of Works*[158] in 1858 is a leading decision. There the Board resolved as a general policy that privies and cesspools should be prohibited in the district, and that owners should instal water-closets. A landlord of thirty-nine cottages was served a notice to convert, but after he refused the Board entered his property and commenced the work itself. The Court of Appeal in Chancery affirmed the injunction granted him, on the basis that the Board had exceeded its powers. Bruce L.J. found some of the statutory powers 'remarkable' but in any event insufficient to justify the Board's actions. Turner L.J. was of a like mind and cautioned the defendants to 'keep strictly within [their] powers, and not be guided by any fancied view of the spirit of the Act which confers them'. He added that it was not open for the Board to adopt a general policy but that it should exercise its discretion in each particular case.[159] Once a public authority satisfied the various legal prerequisites, however, there was little the courts could do, without usurping the function of elected bodies. In *St Luke's Vestry* v. *Lewis*[160] in 1862, the local authority had converted privies to water-closets after the owner of a court in Islington had refused to comply with a notice to do this. The owner's counsel contended that the vestry had to establish that the privies were inadequate, and added that imposing the cost of water-closets on the owner of a small house 'would, in many cases, render it valueless; for the trifling rent that could be obtained for it would cease to be any compensation to the landlord'. In the result, the Court of Queen's Bench (Cockburn C.J., Wightman and Crompton JJ.) held that the local authority was entitled to do the work under the statute; the evidence – the chocked up filth is described in the report – no doubt proved persuasive. Subsequently, Parliament eased the way for public authorities by enacting that there was nothing unlawful in an authority embarking on a general scheme requiring conversion of privies to water-closets, provided the authority did not misuse its power.[161] Yet as late as 1922, a colliery company opposed the introduction of water-closets in its terraced housing, despite the fact that sewage was soaking through the walls of privies and oozing up through the ground in the backyards. P.O. Lawrence J. commented on the public health danger of the privies, and emphatically refused an injunction and declaration.[162]

The issue of property rights was not always clear-cut, however, because a finding in favour of property owners was not necessarily adverse to the interests of the poorer sections of society. For example, successful challenges by property owners and others to inadequate drainage and sewerage schemes benefited ordinary people, who were in no position themselves to institute litigation or exercise political pressure. The poorer sections of society were adversely affected by inadequate sewers, for sewage seeped into the yards of their tenements or courts or into their cellars, and in many areas they still needed water drawn directly from rivers and canals. An important legal basis to these successful challenges to offending sewerage schemes was that they constituted a nuisance, even though in at least one instance the scheme had operated for over a decade.[163] The background to the decisions was the growing public awareness of the pollution of rivers by sewage and, to a growing extent, industrial wastes, as reflected in various Royal Commissions.[164] The judges cannot have been but partly influenced by this popular concern. But the judges were also on firm legal ground, since in the particular circumstances the legislation specifically provided that outfall systems should not create a nuisance. At least some of the judges explicitly recognized in their decisions that while drainage and sewerage systems were essential for the public health of urban areas, they would have deleterious effects if operated improperly. Too often local authorities showed too little concern for their inhabitants in not adopting the methods already known for rendering drainage and sewage less harmful.

Yet in a series of cases in the late nineteenth and early twentieth centuries, the courts swung around and refused to interfere where public authorities were sued for failure to provide or maintain sewers or drains.[165] Initially the decisions were put on the basis that the public authorities were not themselves responsible for any nuisance, but were simply permitting inhabitants to continue to use the sewers and drains, admittedly at an increased rate with the growth of population. The earlier decisions were distinguished on the basis that they involved public authorities actively creating a nuisance when not authorized to do so by statute.[166] Later, the decisions were placed on the ground that the Public Health Act 1875 specifically enabled a person to complain of a breach of the Act to the Local Government Board.[167] Precedent had some role since there had been very broad statements, in other contexts, that where a duty was imposed by statute where none previously existed, and a remedy for breach of that duty was contained in the statute, that was the exclusive remedy. In addition, the well-established legal distinction between nonfeasance and misfeasance – that an individual could not maintain an action for neglect to perform certain duties, although he could sue in the event of improper performance (e.g. nuisance, negligence) – was sometimes applied directly to sewage and drainage authorities.[168]

Underlying whatever legal justifications were given for these decisions, however, were important considerations of public policy. Foremost amongst these was the financial cost to public authorities, and hence to the ratepayers, of complying with the full range of their statutory duties. A secondary consideration was the belief that to allow these actions would open the floodgates to litigation, since every owner of land in a district could sue in the event of not obtaining the statutory benefits.[169] Finally – and this is where policy considerations meshed with the legal justifications outlined – the judges put some weight on the desirability of having matters resolved in the political arena. Central government, not the courts, the argument ran, ought to take steps to ensure that a public authority fulfilled its statutory duty. Moreover, the judges objected, how could they direct a public authority to perform its statutory duties when this meant it carrying out a relatively large-scale scheme of drainage or sewerage, perhaps for a whole district?[170]

Housing, slum clearance and planning

With some exceptions, the judges tend to have a limited knowledge of social welfare legislation because of their background, training and professional life. The narrow scope of judicial notice, and the absence of the Brandeis brief used in American courts, have prevented evidence from being presented on the broad, social issues involved in such legislation. These factors, and the importance attached to private property, go part of the way to explaining the courts' handling of housing legislation.

Lord Bramwell gave an inking of the restrictive way some judges would treat the obligation on landlords to ensure that houses let at a low rent were fit for habitation when he described it in debate in the House of Lords in 1885 as contrary to the principle of *caveat emptor*, and argued that the best thing for working people 'was to teach them to look after themselves'.[171] Despite strong and continued legislative support for the provision and its successors, there were various decisions in which the courts restricted its effect. Reynolds explains these on the ground that the judges neglected the social dimensions of the legislation and therefore read it against the interests of tenants.[172] Action under the Housing Acts against individual unfit housing was occasionally challenged in court. The owner in a leading decision on natural justice, *Local Government Board* v. *Arlidge* (1915),[173] called into question the confirmation by the Local Government Board of a closing order made by a local authority against an unfit house. However, the House of Lords held that there was no requirement, under the doctrine of natural justice, that he be given the right to be heard orally by the Board (or its relevant officer) or to see the report made by the Board's inspector. At the level of policy the House of Lords was impressed that Parliament had established a procedure, which had been adhered to, whereby the owner could be heard at a local enquiry.

Property owners were active in political and legal forums regarding the slum clearance of the inter-war period. Where they could not prevent slum clearance, they sought to maximize the compensation payable for the destruction of their property. In some areas they were able to influence the decisions of local councils directly. In other areas they benefited from the fact that some Labour councillors opposed slum clearance because they regarded as anathema the flats which would replace the slums.[174] Given their record, it is no great surprise that the courts tended to side with property owners who objected to clearance and redevelopment plans. At this time many of the judges were taking great umbrage at the extension of state powers; Lord Justice Hewart's *The New Despotism* (1929) gave public expression to this attitude. No doubt the assumption of power by the Labour Party in 1929, and the enactment of its Housing Act 1930, compounded the reaction. The courts insisted on a strict compliance with procedure and made plain that this was because property rights were being infringed.[175] A decision in 1929 brought the whole slum-clearance programme to a halt until the Housing Act 1930 reversed its effect.[176] In his second reading speech on the Bill, the Minister of Health noted that the practice which the court had overturned had been followed for more than half a century and had received, so it was thought, legislative approval during that period.[177] Slum clearance subsequently went forward, but not without occasional interruptions and delays as property owners took action in the courts. The *Errington* decision in 1934[178] delayed slum clearance in Jarrow, a town which came to symbolize the misery of working people in the inter-war period. In a masterly analysis of the decisions affecting slum clearance published in 1936, Jennings castigated the courts for frustrating the legislative purpose.[179] Only one decision adopted a broad construction of the legislation, he argued, and in that case a broad construction favoured the property owner. Jennings concluded that because of their narrow background the judges ignored the social conditions which the legislation was intended to remedy.

In the period following Jennings' article, the courts adopted a somewhat more favourable attitude.[180] Partly this was because by the mid-thirties all the major political forces backed slum clearance. The trend continued immediately following World War II.[181] Underlying factors included the influence of wartime precedents and the desire not to hinder measures of social reform clearly approved by the electorate. The revival in the sixties of judicial activism in administrative law has had its repercussions in housing and planning matters. The court's actions cannot be understood simply in terms of the protection of property rights, although this is certainly an important aspect. When complainants have been deprived of property rights the courts have generally sided with them over a public authority.[182] But the courts' notion of the public interest – that they should facilitate the implementation of public policy on land use – has told against complainants who have raised an issue not of property rights but involving social or community values.[183] To an extent the courts are implementing the legislative intention in this regard, for although governments have given the impression that they take into account social factors such as public participation, in reality it makes few concessions along these lines.[184]

The Rent Acts

In run-of-the-mill decisions on landlord and tenant matters before the lower courts, there is no dispute about legal doctrine. Yet important protections afforded tenants are often rendered nugatory in practice because the judges overlook or ignore them.[185] That tenants appear without legal representation is one explanation – some judges may have the mistaken notion that even if unrepresented, tenants will adequately present any points of benefit to them. Others may conceive of the judicial function as deciding on the case presented to them, rather than entering into the arena by actively assisting one of the parties. The judicial perception might also be distorted because the overwhelming bulk of landlord and tenant work is originated by landlords. Comments about an American metropolitan court in 1973 are applicable elsewhere:

The court had years of experience as a vehicle for rent collection and eviction where no defences could be raised. The judges and clerks repeatedly hear about tenants who fail to pay rent or do damage to the premises, while they probably never have the opportunity to observe the actual conditions of the housing that the landlords are renting.[186]

Organizational pressures, time constraints and procedural formalities are other factors which militate against a proper consideration of the unrepresented tenant's case in the lower courts.

As for the superior courts, there is criticism of judges who 'have had too much exposure, socially and professionally, to the property owners' point of view'.[187] Certainly if a judge's professional practice included landlord and tenant work, it would most likely have been on behalf of landlords or commercial tenants, since few residential tenants obtain legal representation. Of course this does not mean that these judges will not be disinterested and dispassionate. Nonetheless it is fair to say that some judges have expressed hostility to the regulation of landlord-tenant matters. Sometimes they attribute their objections to the bad draftsmanship of the legislation, although a good deal of the legislative complexity derives from the need to close judicially approved loopholes. This criticism also takes a narrow view of the judicial function, when an alternative approach is to see the courts as working in partnership with the legislature to spell out any ambiguities or gaps in the statutory design. Moreover, the criticism often conceals an objection to the substance of regulation – that it subtracts from property rights and freedom to contract.[188]

The courts' reaction to an aspect of rent control is an illustration of these points. Following the Rent Act 1974, once it was no longer possible to use furnished tenancies to avoid the full protection of the Rent Acts, advisers to landlords developed the idea of the 'non-exclusive occupation agreement'. Under the Acts, a protected tenancy is a tenancy under which a dwelling house is let as a separate dwelling, and the use of the words 'tenancy' and 'let' means that licences are excluded. Since exclusive occupation is one of the indicia of a tenancy, the idea was that the non-exclusive occupation agreement would create a licence rather than a lease. Entrepreneurs advertising 'Landlords Lib' sold licence forms at 50p a time, and the legal profession organized day schools for property owners on how to use the new technique.[189] The agreements usually obliged the 'licensees', as they were called in the agreements, to share occupation with other persons the landlord might from time to time nominate, each to bear responsibility for part of the rent. The landlord could also terminate the arrangements at short notice.

Somma v. *Hazelhurst*[190] in 1978 was the first case in the Court of Appeal involving a non-exclusive occupation agreement. The court upheld the two agreements in the case and thus denied the defendants the protection of the Rent Acts. In his judgment for the court, Cumming-Bruce L.J. acknowledged that it was 'one more attempt by an owner of housing accommodation to provide it at a profit for those in great need of it without the restrictions imposed by Parliament', and he held that there were two questions which had to be answered. First, did the parties intend to be bound by the written agreement? In that respect, Cumming-Bruce L.J. pointed to the county court judge's finding that the defendants knew what they were letting themselves in for, and that both were educated and had signed the document.

Ignored was the first defendant's evidence that he did not take legal advice as it would have been too expensive, and that he preferred to have the accommodation on the terms offered rather than none at all. Secondly, asked Cumming-Bruce L.J., could it be said from the words of the agreements that they were intended to create a tenancy rather than a licence? Although certain clauses in the documents were more consistent with a tenancy than a licence, Cumming-Bruce L.J. thought that other clauses pointed to a licence. In his view, although there was no evidence that the landlady intended to impose an uncongenial sharer on the remaining occupier, the undesirable situation which could theoretically eventuate 'only illustrate[s] the risk inherent in the bargain that they made and are no grounds for invoking public policy to render unenforceable the right retained by the licensor'.

In *Somma*, the court said that the decision was 'peculiar to its own facts'. Nonetheless it was applied in a subsequent decision.[191] If widely accepted, the decision would have had serious implications, denying the full protection of the Rent Acts and opening the possibility of harassment through the use by landlords of sharing clauses. But then in *Demuren* v. *Seal Estates Ltd*[192] in 1978 a differently constituted Court of Appeal held that similar licence agreements were shams, that a joint tenancy resulted, and that the Rent Acts applied. The court thought that the agreement raised grave suspicions, but in the event felt able to distinguish the earlier decisions on the basis that there was a prior oral agreement in this case, which indicated a mutual, concurrent intention that the applicants should enjoy exclusive occupation of the whole flat. The upshot of these decisions is that the law is uncertain. Each case is decided on its own facts, although the burden is on the tenant to establish that in the circumstances the agreement really is a tenancy and not a licence. What can be said is that in some decisions the judges have stretched distinctions drawn by the common law to permit evasion of the Rent Acts. The difficulties ordinary people have in understanding agreements and the pressures facing them in obtaining accommodation have been accentuated.

While it is inherent in the nature of regulation that self-interested parties seek to adapt arrangements to lessen its impact, it is not the case that the courts must always give their imprimatur to such arrangements. The courts are not passive institutions; within limits they make law. There is a long tradition with rent control, as with taxation, of positively deciding to allow landlords to arrange their affairs to escape the clear intentions of the Rent Acts.[193] As mentioned previously, this is not to say that the courts always favour landlords (or property owners or taxpayers). In certain areas of rent control, judges have attempted to produce a workable system, taking into account the statutory aim of protecting tenants. For example, the House of Lords has found in favour of tenants more often than not, possibly because its members are just enough removed from everyday litigation 'that they do indeed bring to bear on their decisions a measure of objectivity and impartiality'.[194] Of course decisions favouring tenants do not necessarily favour poorer tenants. An example is the decision giving the right to sustain a statutory tenancy where a person has two homes; clearly only the better-off tenant would be in a position of having more than one home at a time.[195] The role of the courts is considered further in the concluding chapter.

V THE IMPACT OF SOCIAL WELFARE REGULATION

Who gains and who loses as a result of social welfare regulation? Does social welfare regulation have an impact on the behaviour of those property and commercial interests which on the surface stand opposed to its success? Does social welfare regulation actually improve the lot of the poor if that is its general purpose? And are there unintended and independent effects which, when taken into account, seriously detract from its success? Unfortunately there are few empirical studies which examine these questions in detail.

Social factors in impact

The nature of those regulated has an obvious effect on the impact of law. Independent and unintended consequences are a feature of social welfare regulation, but are accentuated if the variation in those affected is not taken into account. For example, it should not be surprising if small landlords, such as those who rent a spare room or who have inherited one or two properties, do not respond readily to changes in legal provisions or economic inducements. Small landlords with substandard property will not always have the financial capacity to repair or improve, even if they can subsequently raise the rent or if grants are available. Moreover, poorer tenants might object to repairs or improvements because of the consequent rent increases or the inconvenience.[196] Small landlords might be reluctant to raise the rent until a vacancy occurs, in an effort to retain a satisfactory tenant who assists in maintenance work. Likewise, where tenants have rented from the same landlord over a long period, and the two sides are compatible, the landlord might not want to charge the market rent, even in the absence of rent control. In addition, small landlords might not want to become embroiled in legal disputes because of the cost and time involved.[197] On the other hand, large landlords who see their property as a profitable investment are more likely to be influenced by legal and financial incentives, since their operations are more posited on rationality. If there is a reasonable turnover of tenants, these landlords can engage in profitable strategies within the law. Examples of skillfully manipulating rent control to maximize their returns are applying for a rent increase as regularly as the law permits; making improvements and repairs if the subsequent rent increase more than covers the cost; maximizing tax advantages; and possibly engaging in litigation which, if successful, will benefit them in relation to other dwellings.

The attitude of those being regulated also has implications for the implementation of the law. *A priori*, property owners and employers should generally oppose social welfare regulation because it inhibits their freedom of action. But in some cases the regulated do not have strong attitudes. While large landlords seem to have definite views about rent control, many smaller landlords are remarkably uninterested because they have not had sufficient experience of it.[198] Moreover, whatever their attitude to social welfare regulation, many landlords, property owners and employers comply with the law, and in some cases go beyond its requirements, because of inertia or social circumstances, because they believe that in general laws should be obeyed, or because they wish to avoid prosecution. Membership of professional associations, close connections with an area, or a high public profile tend to make property owners and employers reluctant to damage their reputation by engaging in unlawful or disreputable practices.

On the other hand some property owners and employers are indifferent to legal obligations or so inept that breaches occur. Others deliberately flout legal obligations. In legal terminology they go beyond avoidance, to evasion of the law. They do not see the objection to maximizing profits by using their own property as they please, and if prosecuted regard fines as a normal business expense, or as a risk attached to their way of doing business. A number of studies are illustrative. Gauldie gives various examples of evasion by landlords in the nineteenth century.[199] The picture Audrey Harvey painted in 1964 was of some landlords, including large property companies, evading the law and exploiting poorer tenants. Similarly, Harloe, Isaacharoff and Minns encountered various instances of deliberate evasion in their study of housing in London in the early seventies. For example, they found a landlord in Lambeth who used his contact on the council to avoid public health inspectors taking action against him. To get the market rent registered as the fair rent, a property company deceived new tenants into signing a 'joint' application to the rent office on a blank application form – the rent was filled in later.[200] A more recent example is the slum landlord who charged some nine times the registered rent, and who vigorously opposed tenants who applied to have fair rents fixed (which created expenses for the tenants even when they were successful).[201] Following the Rent Act 1974, rental accommodation was converted into 'bed and breakfast' accommodation as landlords, especially non-resident landlords, purported to use the exception to charge exorbitant rents.[202] The exception for holiday lettings in that Act gave rise to a situation where people desperate for accommodation were forced to take 'holidays' in some unsalubrious inner-city areas. In 1978 the Court of Appeal criticized the practice – not uncommon – of landlords allowing housing to become unfit for human habitation and using this fact to obtain vacant possession pursuant to the Rent Acts, so reaping a substantial profit on renovation or sale.[203]

The way that property owners and employers sometimes rationalize evasion of their legal obligations is indicated by the comments made by businessmen in one town in 1977, after a blitz by the wages inspectorate uncovered widespread breach of wages council orders. A spokesman for the chamber of trade said: 'I believe the so-called "guilty" shopkeepers hired help on an informal basis and had probably not taken the trouble to read the Government literature on pay'; one shopkeeper said that he was fed up with government forms and couldn't understand them; and another commented that if part-time assistants, mostly housewives 'earning pin money', were happy, what business was it of anyone else?[204] Such views express in part a feeling that the law is unfair because it unduly burdens small businesses, and in part the complaint that the law is too complex and incomprehensible. Similarly, an American study of the violation of rent-control law found that landlords in the more rigidly controlled properties admitted a higher proportion of violations of the law than others. Violations were not related to a landlord's opinion of rent control as a general policy, but the most rigidly controlled used what seemed to them unfair treatment to justify violation.[205] Property owners and employers may have few qualms about breaching the law because property and business are highly valued in our society. For example, small businesses paying low wages can justify their behaviour because they are constantly assured that on their success hangs the economic future of the nation. A closely related point is that property owners and employers may be hard-pressed in an economic sense. The Dutch criminologist, Bonger, thought that the contest between large manufacturing establishments and the small factories and workshops forced the latter 'to maintain the competitive struggle by incredibly long hours of labor, by an unlimited exploitation of the labor of women and children etc'.[206] The comment applies directly to breach of minimum-wage requirements, but if generalized applies to other instances of non-compliance with the law.

The evidence about impact

The absence of detailed studies means that it is difficult to make conclusive remarks about the impact of social welfare regulation. Assessing impact is necessarily vague and influenced, in part, by subjective values. Historians find it a hazardous business attributing the transformation of mortality and morbidity rates to particular public health measures. Moreover, public health measures such as slum clearance have had adverse side-effects such as overcrowding and the break-up of working-class communities. The current regulation of housing standards seems to have had only a minor impact. Although a few determined local authorities have made great strides, the change in the amount of unsatisfactory housing nationwide has not matched the rise in grant-aided improvement expenditure.[207] There is also evidence of adverse side-effects resulting from the regulation of housing standards. For instance, the possibility of compulsory improvement apparently deters people from buying in housing action areas, since they cannot afford the cost of improvement in addition to the cost of purchase.[208]

Rent control has been a definite gain for many poorer tenants, enabling them to obtain secure housing for a relatively low rent. The removal of rent control would adversely affect some of the poorest and most vulnerable persons in the community. Many tenants do not invoke its protection, while others fall outside its scope. As a result, rent control places tenants who fall within the system in a favoured position, in some cases at the expense of those in greater need. Moreover, a great deal of rent-controlled property is in substandard condition. Rent control itself has played some part in this, although another factor is that much of the housing subject to rent control is quite old.[209]

A common criticism of minimum-wage laws is that they have legitimized the payment of low pay rather than alleviated it. However, it is also said that without legal minimum wages, an unorganized minority of workers will be vulnerable to exploitation.[210] The wages councils seem to have done little to curb the sweating of women and migrant workers which mushrooms in times of recession. Indeed industries which have had wages councils for decades still have a significant number of low-paid workers. Wages councils orders are far from generous in absolute terms, and in the last decade have not improved the relative position of workers covered.[211] The rates fixed by wages councils often bear little relationship to those actually being paid by the more efficient and generally larger employers. In addition, the wages councils might have discouraged unionization, since there is less incentive to join a trade union if wages are fixed by law.[212] Of course there must be doubt whether certain low-paid workers will ever by unionized – the bulk are especially vulnerable to threats to their jobs. There are also the expenses and difficulties of recruiting union members in a large number of small establishments, especially if there is also a high turnover, and among those such as part-time workers and homeworkers.

Economic considerations

Many economists argue that government should not interfere greatly in the economy, and that given the chance the market can best handle most problems. They assume that if individuals want changes they will signal them through the market: for example, if they want better-quality housing they will make sacrifices in other areas of their budget and demand it. Consequently, these economists suggest that social welfare regulation should be modified, if not repealed. They argue that in general regulation is a failure, because its consequences are inefficient and often at variance with what is supposed to be intended, and that poorer persons actually suffer because they are least able to cope with the costs which regulation imposes. While conceding that the market will not make the poor richer (although individual poor people might enhance their position through participation in the market), they argue that this aim can be achieved more effectively by a straight-out transfer of income. Sometimes underlying these economic claims is an antipathy to government regulation on the ground that it infringes liberty. This section examines some aspects of this economic analysis as it relates to the three forms of social welfare regulation which have occupied us in this chapter – housing standards, rent control and statutory minimum wages.

An economic analysis of statutory housing standards contends that the maintenance costs and the uncertainty of the law's application induce some landlords to remove rental housing from the market, for example by selling into owner-occupation. Others are said to raise the rents of their tenancies. Landlords, goes the argument, would improve housing standards voluntarily if tenants were willing to pay higher rents, so that in effect the law compels tenants to allocate money to housing when they would prefer to spend it in other ways (in as far as the law allows rents to be raised to cover repair costs). Some tenants will move out as a result of rent increases, for example, doubling up with relatives and friends.[213]

The extent to which individual landlords and tenants are affected by statutory housing standards is more complex than this analysis suggests. For example, tenants may positively evaluate a new standard (or the enforcement of an old standard) and stay on, paying a higher rent to cover the landlord's costs. Where landlords cannot recoup the full cost of repair they may continue renting, either because they have been earning abnormal profits and still receive an attractive return, or because they hope eventually to reap capital gains. An empirical study of habitability laws in the United States failed to find a statistically significant association between their existence and rent levels, but hypothesized that its absence might be attributable to non-enforcement. However, the study found that receivership laws, which authorize local authorities to take control of substandard housing, had an effect, the increase in rent possibly outweighing the accruing benefits.[214]

Some economists argue that the free play of market forces through 'filtering' in housing markets substitutes for statutory housing standards. Filtering occurs as high-income groups move into new developments, vacating less desirable housing, which is then available for the next highest income group (and so on down the chain). But research into filtering indicates grave deficiencies in the theory. Those moving into vacated housing are unlikely to experience better-quality housing in the long run, because if owner-occupiers they will not be able to afford adequate maintenance, and if tenants they will face landlords who under-maintain to maximize profits. To ensure the demand for expensive dwellings, and thus to create sufficient vacancies, requires subsidies for the middle classes, because the rich are neither numerous nor mobile enough. For this reason, filtering is inequitable and inefficient, because it concentrates resources on those already better-off in society, and not on those who need them most. Filtering takes substantial time, and can be blocked by social factors such as immobility, or because a vacated dwelling is demolished, is converted to other uses, or is filled by a household which does not leave a vacancy behind (for example, a newly formed household).[215]

Rent control has long been a *bête noire* of a great many economists, who claim that it distorts housing markets by fixing rents below their market level. For example, they argue that rent control causes a housing shortage because tenants demand more housing than they would otherwise (e.g. young people move from their parents' homes into flats), and because landlords remove rental accommodation from the market since it is no longer profitable. Another effect is said to be the deterioration of the housing stock because landlords cannot afford to undertake the necessary maintenance, which in the long run leads to the heavy social cost of slums. Rent control is said also to result in housing being used inefficiently, because people remain in rent-controlled property although it is larger than what they need. Labour mobility is supposed to be discouraged, since tenants are reluctant to move if rent-controlled housing is not available elsewhere.[216]

Again the truth is far more complex than this picture suggests. Rent control has been only one factor in the long-term decline in privately rented housing in the twentieth century. The decline has also occurred because property owners have found other outlets for their capital (for example with the development of the stock exchange, unit trusts). Another important factor in the decline has been the widespread desire for home ownership. Redevelopment has also removed a great deal of privately rented housing from the market.

Moreover, particular measures of decontrol have not had an obviously lasting effect on the overall decline in privately rented accommodation. The Conservative Government claimed that its relaxation of rent restrictions in 1957 would encourage conversions, discourage sales and prolonged vacancies, and induce landlords to keep rented housing in good repair. But conversions and new construction were insignificant as dwellings continued to be lost from the privately rented sector by sale or demolition, and decontrol seemed to have no effect on encouraging landlords to repair.[217] Finally, it should be noted that rental housing is still a reasonably attractive proposition, despite rent control, because of the return from catering for particular groups, and because capital gains might be made through the appreciation in property values.[218]

The minimum wage is another example of legal regulation which many economists condemn. Friedman writes: 'In so far as minimum wage laws have any effect at all, their effect is clearly to increase poverty.'[219] The basis for this conclusion is that a minimum wage increases costs and thus causes employers to retrench their least productive workers. Those who obtain the minimum wage may benefit, but at the expense of other workers who are forced into unprotected employment or who are unemployed. There are statistical studies in the United States which show a relationship between minimum wages and unemployment, in particular the high rates of youth unemployment. However, these studies are far from clear about the magnitude, as opposed to the direction of the relationship, and they do not tackle the question of net benefits.[220] Moreover, there are obviously other factors besides minimum wages which cause unemployment. To understand, say, youth unemployment, account must be taken of matters such as demand shifts for this type of labour, demographic changes, and the overall level of economic activity in the community.

In summary, the empirical evidence does not give unequivocal support to the conclusions drawn by free-market economists about the effects of social welfare regulation. Conversely, the faith which this economic analysis has in markets is often misplaced, since markets are sometimes seriously impaired by transaction costs or externalities, or because people lack information or bargaining power. To use the example of housing standards, it seems naive to assume that tenants can dictate the quality of housing landlords provide by 'choosing between competing landlords' (i.e.moving) if they cannot pay a higher rent or if they are not really free to move because of employment or commitments.[221] Consequently, despite its drawbacks, social welfare regulation might be no less efficient than what would obtain under an improperly functioning market. As an example, it is reasonable to suppose that in many cases landlords are in a better position than tenants to make most repairs, so that the law is acting efficiently if it forces landlords to do this. Despite its limitations, however, economic analysis has a role in designing the scope and shape of social welfare regulation. It cannot be denied that there are instances where social welfare regulation, or at least the form it takes, is undesirable in the light of its social and economic costs and benefits. Where it is desirable to reduce social welfare regulation, however, transitional arrangements must be designed, since the distributional consequences of change adversely affect many people and undermine their justifiable expectations.

VI CONCLUSION

Social welfare regulation as a tool of social engineering has many deficiencies, and the reliance which reformers place on it is sometimes misplaced. On the one hand, social welfare regulation might fail because on its face it is characterized by ambiguities and gaps; on the other hand, its failure might only be evident when it is seen in context. At one level, failure might be a property of the way social welfare regulation emerges: it might not have had effectiveness or the interests of the poorer sections of society as its primary aim, as where its proponents are more concerned with its symbolic significance, with assuaging public opinion on a particular matter, or with furthering the interests of other sections of the community. Even if when first proposed it had been intended to bite on certain practices, social welfare regulation might have been edentated as a result of opposition from property and employer interests. At another level, failure of social welfare regulation might reflect defects of legislative form in the light of its aims, for example not using suitable language, retaining outdated concepts, or not foreseeing possible applications. The substantive provisions of social welfare regulation might be commensurate with its aims but – yet another level of regulatory failure – the enforcement machinery provided might be such as to subtract significantly from its impact.[222] A final level of regulatory failure occurs because undesirable independent and unintended effects swamp desirable direct and indirect effects. As we have seen in this chapter, these four levels of regulatory failure explain why public health measures, housing standards, rent control and minimum wage laws do not always measure up to expectations.

Now we are in a better position to evaluate the effectiveness of social welfare regulation. By contrast, say, with the neo-conservative condemnation that regulation is inherently or always defective, we have seen that its defects are because of specific features of its emergence, formulation or implementation. Against the criticism that the common law is a better avenue to improve matters such as housing conditions,[223] we have seen that social welfare regulation developed in the nineteenth century precisely because doctrines such as nuisance were inadequate to cope with the public health problems of an industrial and urban society. What was necessary in such cases was legislation to establish new legal rights and duties, and an administrative machinery to implement them. So too today, individuals are generally not in the position, for reasons outlined at various points in the book, to take the initiative to seek common-law remedies. Even if they do, the courts are not particularly creative in developing new applications of existing doctrines. Moreover, the courts do not operate institutionally to police compliance with their orders, let alone to make them effective in situations similar to those before the court.

Ultimately the efficacy of social welfare regulation comes down to the basic difficulty in our society of regulating property and business interests. Property rights and the right of businesses to engage in entrepreneurial activity with minimum hindrance are basic values. Laws which trespass on these values are at an immediate disadvantage, as are the agencies charged with their enforcement. Production is given added weight in times of economic recession; for example, housing and minimum-wage laws face the obstacle that they are perceived by many as conflicting with entrepreneurial activity. Ordinary people certainly realize that they can gain from the enforcement of social welfare regulation and regularly complain to regulatory agencies. But there is no great groundswell of public support for the regulation of matters such as housing standards, rent and minimum wages, or for existing regulation to be strictly implemented. These are low-visibility laws and only occasionally reach the surface of public consciousness by way of reports in the mass media. They will only be taken seriously if greater political support is mobilized in their favour.

5
Social welfare benefits

Legislation providing the framework for the payment of social welfare benefits and for the provision of services has usually entrusted social welfare bureaucracies with considerable discretion, on the ground that this enables the tailoring of benefits and services to individual need. In addition, the legislation has sometimes permitted significant controls to be imposed over the behaviour of claimants as a condition of their receiving benefits or services. These controls are imbedded in the fabric of society, touching fundamental values about family life and work, and have their origins partly in rehabilitative notions of channelling the habits of claimants in desirable directions and inculcating acceptable values.[1] Where there has been external review of the decisions of social welfare bureaucracies, this has generally been conducted in forums such as tribunals, which have differed from courts in relation to openness, independence, procedures, and reasoned decision-making. Basic principles of law such as natural justice, however, generally still obtain.

Over the last decade, law reformers have sought to advance 'welfare rights' by pruning the discretion of social welfare bureaucracies, reducing some controls over claimants' behaviour and moving external review closer to the model of courts – tribunals have been required to give reasons for their decisions, legally qualified persons have been appointed to chair them, their independence has been strengthened, and appellate bodies have been established over them consisting of judges or those with equivalent status. The replacement of discretion by definite and public rules, and the transformation of social welfare tribunals, can be regarded as bringing social welfare administration more into line with conventional formulations of the rule of law.[2] Although these formulations emphasize process rather than substantive values, some modern accounts contend that the rule of law does not countenance, say, attempts to buy behaviour.[3] Similarly, it can be argued that under the rule of law individual autonomy cannot be circumscribed too closely. Consequently, as long as social welfare legislation imposes significant social controls over its intended beneficiaries, it is arguable that it is inconsistent with an important legal value of modern society.

These various aspects of the role of law and the legal system are explored in relation to social welfare benefits in parts I and II of this chapter. (Their relevance to the provision of public services is explored in the next chapter.) Part I examines aspects of the juridical nature of social welfare legislation such as the discretion social welfare bureaucracies have under it and the mechanisms available to review decisions made pursuant to its provisions. Reference is also made to private welfare and to how this differs from state welfare. Part II highlights some of the substantive provisions of social welfare legislation, giving particular attention to the controls imposed over claimants. There is no doubt that these various legal dimensions, discussed in parts I and II, are important to the question of the existence of welfare rights. Whether a right exists, for example, cannot depend on the sole discretion of the person against whom it is asserted. It must have a relatively definite legal form and there must be some means of vindicating it, even if not through the ordinary legal system. From a legal perspective, content and purpose are relevant to the existence of a right.

But while these legal dimensions are important, they are not the whole story. Legal rights are not accomplished social facts. Whether they are, depends on factors such as the consciousness of individuals as to the existence of legal rights and their subjective feelings about, and behaviour in relation to, these rights. Individuals have to feel that they have a right, equal to others in the same position, and that they can assert that right. Further, those against whom a legal right is asserted must not only be under a legal obligation to grant it, but must facilitate and respect that right in practice.[4] So, for example, it is illusory to say that there is a 'right' to a social welfare benefit because it is recognized in law if that right is not palpable to eligible claimants, if they do not expect to receive it, and if the officials who administer it do not feel under any obligation to grant it.[5]

Some of the factors in whether legal rights to social welfare benefits are accomplished social facts are examined in part III of this chapter.

Of major importance is the mode of benefit administration, which can inhibit the effectiveness of social welfare legislation in achieving its ostensible goals. People have difficulty learning about, and then negotiating, the labyrinth of rules governing the many social welfare benefits and services. An important result is that there is a far from universal take-up of benefits and services by potential beneficiaries. In the past, benefit administration has been seen as a matter of dealing expertly and humanely with social welfare claimants, rather than as giving effect to their rights and duties. The two can, but do not necessarily, overlap. Because the state itself provides the rights to social welfare, it has tended to be assumed that there is no need for claimants to assert rights against it for it will ensure that they are given their due. Such attitudes continue to mould the collective consciousness of social welfare bureaucracies.

From the viewpoint of public policy, it follows that the legal recognition of welfare rights is only one side of the coin, and that what is also required is to institutionalize their implementation by steps such as structuring social welfare bureaucracies to facilitate their grant, and building up the capacity of individuals to assert them. Law and lawyers have some role in these institutional and social changes. Replacing discretion with rules, for example, might improve take-up by lessening the stigma attaching to, and encouraging applications for, social welfare benefits, because they are perceived more in the nature of rights, and entitlement is more obvious and publicized. By providing effective advice and advocacy services, community centres and law centres have had some success in assisting particular claimants and in acting as a focal point for the diffusion of knowledge about social welfare benefits in local communities.[6] Test cases have formed part of the strategy of some welfare rights' lawyers.

I THE JURIDICAL NATURE OF SOCIAL WELFARE LEGISLATION

The juridical nature of claimants' entitlement to social welfare benefits depends on three factors: first, the discretion in the relevant social welfare legislation; secondly, the provisions made for accountability through external review; and thirdly, the basis of the entitlement claimants have to benefit. The first factor is relatively straightforward and refers to whether the relevant law gives a social welfare bureaucracy a wide discretion to distribute a benefit on the one hand, or sets out in rules relatively objective standards of eligibility which obtain on the other hand. External review of the decisions of social welfare bureaucracies – the second factor – might be very underdeveloped at one end of the spectrum, while at the other end there might be a relatively sophisticated system with the possibility of an eventual appeal to the courts. The entitlement that claimants of state social welfare benefits have is statutory and its strength at law turns on the first two factors – the discretion the relevant legislation gives its administrators and the extent to which their decisions are subject to external review. However, it is useful to consider the basis of entitlement as a separate head because, by contrast with the statutory entitlement of state social welfare claimants, the beneficiaries of occupational welfare might have a contractual or equitable right to benefit which is enforceable in the courts in the ordinary way. These three aspects of legal structure – discretion, external review, and the basis of entitlement – are reviewed in this part. There is also a discussion of efforts to reform the juridical nature of social welfare benefits.[7]

The extent of discretion

The discretion available to state bureaucracies might be clear from the legislative language. Different types of discretion can be identified, falling along a continuum. In the first type a social welfare bureaucracy is entrusted to act as it 'thinks fit' or 'for any other reason'. Another type of discretion is where there are rules, but the rules empower the social welfare bureaucracy to depart from them in certain broadly defined circumstances, described in such terms as 'exceptional', 'unusual', or 'urgent'. Finally, there is the type of discretion which arises in most branches of the law because rules must be interpreted: this might be obvious on the face of legislation because the standards referred to are relatively open-textured (such as 'living together as husband and wife' or 'available for work', both considered later in this chapter), but this type of discretion can also arise where social welfare officials are under a 'duty' to, or 'shall', exercise their discretion in the light of specified, relatively objective, criteria. Open-textured standards might be embodied in legislation for a number of reasons, for example, because the nature of the subject-matter is such that law-makers cannot decide on situations likely to arise or cannot agree on the details on social policy. Even where there are specified, relatively objective, criteria, there can be disagreement on what these mean or on how certain facts are to be interpreted. A simple example of fact-indeterminacy is that the behaviour of a social welfare claimant suggests to one social welfare official an attempt to conceal the truth, to another anxiety leading to confusion.

These different types of legislation can be illustrated by reference to particular social welfare legislation.

(a) The absence of legislative standards[8]

An example of legislation giving social welfare bureaucracies a very wide substantive discretion is that empowering social workers to make cash grants. Section 1 of the Child Care Act 1980 provides:

> It shall be the duty of every local authority to make available such advice, guidance and assistance as may promote the welfare of children by diminishing the need to receive children into or keep them in care under this Act or to bring children before a juvenile court; and any provisions made by a local authority under this subsection may, if the local authority think fit, include provision for giving assistance in kind or, in exceptional circumstances, in cash.

There is no provision for appeals against decisions under this section.[9] The evidence is that there is considerable variation as to the way the provision is administered, which cannot be explained simply in terms of differences in needs. Some local authorities have evolved specific guidelines as to the circumstances in which payments may be made or whether they can be made by way of loan or grant. But with others the administration of the section is principally influenced by general policy, such as the attitude to public expenditure, or by social workers' own attitudes and values such as whether they think particular persons are deserving because they are trying to help themselves or are good managers.[10]

Even where there are no standards set out in legislation, argues Dworkin, that cannot mean that decisions can be made at large, nor does it exclude criticism about how decisions are made.[11] Certainly courts and court-like tribunals tend to regard wide discretion as anathema, and if they have the opportunity seek to fetter it, either by deriving standards from what they interpret to be the underlying purposes of the legislation, or from constitutional doctrines if these are available. One motivation for this is a view of the rule of law which demands that individuals should be subject to rules which are specific, public and clearly formulated so that they can make rational decisions about future conduct. In the social welfare context this means spelling out eligibility standards so that individuals can establish whether a claim is justified, and if so ensuring that they have the standing to vindicate this.

An example of this process of spelling out standards, even where the legislation fixes a wide discretion, has occurred with special benefit in Australia. This is a residual category of benefit designed for those who do not qualify for other pensions or benefits. Section 124(1) (c) of the Social Services Act 1947 empowers the Director-General of Social Security to pay special benefit 'in his discretion' to a person 'with respect to whom [he] is satisfied that, by reason of age, physical or mental disability or domestic circumstances, or for any other reason, that person is unable to earn a sufficient livelihood for himself and his dependants (if any)'. The Department of Social Security has published a list of those to whom it will normally pay special benefit. In several decisions the Administrative Appeals Tribunal has decided that individuals who do not fall within this list ought also to receive special benefit. But in addition, the AAT has enunciated several general propositions about when special benefit is payable. For example, in one decision it said that the phrase 'for any other reason' could not be read ignoring the preceding words, but was intended to embrace only reasons personal to a claimant which were capable of producing a consequential inability to earn a sufficient livelihood.[12] In another decision the Tribunal suggested that special benefit ought not to be paid where a claimant would qualify for another pension or benefit under the Act if only he or she satisfied one more requirement, for that would be to ignore that statutory requirement and to assume the power to repeal it.[13]

(b) Legislation conferring discretion

Supplementary benefits legislation between 1966 and 1980 provides an example of social welfare legislation setting out general criteria for the payment of social welfare benefits, but enabling the administering authorities to depart from them in certain defined circumstances.[14] The key section spoke of an entitlement to benefit and was side-noted 'Right to benefit'. 'Subject to the provisions of this Act, every person in Great Britain of or over the age of 16 whose resources are insufficient to meet his requirements shall be entitled to benefit as follows. . .' – a supplementary pension if a person had attained pensionable age, or a supplementary allowance otherwise.[15] The qualifying phrase 'Subject to the provisions of this Act' was all-important, for although the criteria in the section were clear-cut, the Supplementary Benefits Commission had discretion under other sections to depart from them. Thus where it appeared reasonable in all the circumstances, supplementary benefits could be paid to a person by way of a single payment to meet an exceptional need; supplementary benefits could be paid in urgent cases, notwithstanding the limitations normally obtaining; and in exceptional circumstances, supplementary benefits could be awarded at an amount exceeding that calculated in accordance with the provision set out in the Schedule, or a supplementary allowance could be reduced below the amount so calculated, or withheld altogether, as was appropriate to those circumstances.[16]

As with the absence of legislative standards, the preference of courts is to lay down guidelines as to how social welfare bureaucracies should exercise their discretion. Take the example of the courts' interpretation of the exceptional circumstances provision just outlined. In the first decision on the section,[17] the Divisional Court held that the Supplementary Benefits Commission should not automatically set off any exceptional circumstances payment against any long-term addition to which claimants were entitled – a discretion had to be exercised. In *R*. v. *Barnsley SBAT ex p. Atkinson*[18] the Court of Appeal held that it was not right for the discretion to be used against a whole category of persons such as students. 'Wide as the phrase "exceptional circumstances" may be, it must, in our judgment, have been used in reference to the particular circumstances of individual cases.' Following this decision, the legislation was amended to provide, retrospectively, that the circumstances of a case could be treated as exceptional if the case fell within a class of cases the circumstances of which were exceptional.[19] The amended provisions were considered by the House of Lords, which held that the higher cost of living in a particular area could never by itself amount to exceptional circumstances entitling claimants there to supplementary benefits at a higher rate than normal.[20] Exceptional circumstances, it held, meant circumstances indicating that the needs of a particular claimant were greater than the needs of the average claimant because of something special to him or her. While the amendment permitted a case to be treated as exceptional if it fell within a class of cases the circumstances of which were exceptional, it continued, the residents of a particular area could not be treated as a class because each would be affected in different ways by different prices.

(c) Discretion in interpretation

The interpretation of legislation occurs in various settings. For present purposes these can be divided into two broad categories: first, where the legislative standards or concepts are vague or difficult; and secondly, where they are relatively objective or straightforward.[21] Discretion is clearly present in interpreting the first category. However, standards which are relatively objective and straightforward cannot be applied by a process of syllogistic reasoning; discretion is present, even if of a mundane kind, because of the need to determine which legislation is appropriate to particular circumstances, what the language of the appropriate legislation means, which facts are relevant, and how the legislation applies to those facts. With both categories of interpretation, the reasoning process is often influenced by policy considerations.

An example of the first category is the fine line between income and capital, which raises its head in other branches of the law but is also relevant to the application of means tests in social welfare legislation. Is a lump sum recovered through the enforcement of a woman's maintenance arrears income, attributable to the period when it ought to have been received, or capital, so that a weekly amount is treated as deriving from it for the future?[22] If a claimant sells the house in which she is living for a price to be paid to her in monthly instalments over a period of years, is this income, or is she to be regarded as having capital to the present value of the outstanding instalments?[23] Is a lump-sum payment under a special government scheme for ex-servicemen who have been made redundant a 'payment in lieu of remuneration' to compensate them for loss of future income, or more a capital sum to enable them to set out on a new life?[24] Despite the certainty with which courts ultimately answered these questions, they were by no means pre-determined by the statutory language or by the purpose underlying the relevant social welfare legislation.[25]

Discretion can also enter in the interpretation of legislation which at first glance appears to involve relatively objective matters. An example is whether a person is 'incapable for work' for the purposes of disability, invalidity, sickness or similar benefits. On one interpretation, incapacity for work might be regarded as impairment, a purely medical condition in which there is physical or mental abnormality.[26] While the meaning of incapacity for work has an important medical component, many jurisdictions accept that reference must also be made to the broader context of how this affects a claimant's working life. Apart from the social justice of incorporating this broader context, it has some basis in statutory construction because the benefits mentioned are designed to mitigate the economic effects of incapacity for work and are not simply to compensate for medical disability. Accordingly, reference must be made to medical matters but also to a claimant's capacity for different types of work given his or her age, sex, education, skills, experience, etc., and the state of the labour market. Judgement is clearly necessary in interpreting these factors and disagreements occur. There is also the need to draw a boundary between what is often more generous disability etc. benefits and unemployment benefits and, in some jurisdictions, between different categories of disability etc. benefits.

In particular, there is no consensus as to how incapacity for work is to be interpreted in relation to the labour market. One interpretation[27] is that this only requires reference to the kinds of work available in the community, so that claimants might be held to be capable of work as a caretaker, gatekeeper, car-park attendant, or liftdriver, although in reality these jobs are not available where they live because employers discriminate against the disabled or because they prefer to employ younger or older persons. A more liberal interpretation is to have regard to whether particular claimants can actually obtain work in labour markets reasonably accessible to their current residence.[28] While a greater drain on public expenditure, this approach accords with the idea of social rights, and with the expectations nurtured by government that the disabled will not have to rely on the other, and usually less generous, forms of social welfare benefits alluded to.

No jurisdiction goes as far as accepting, except in the short term, that simply because claimants cannot follow their regular occupation they qualify for disability benefits etc. as being incapable of work.[29] This contrasts sharply with what a person might be entitled to under a private insurance policy for disability. The less generous approach of state welfare is explained partly by the desire to concentrate public resources on the most needy (those who can obtain employment, albeit at a low wage, are not thought to be in this category); partly by feelings of equity that a partially disabled person should not be treated any better than a person who has always worked in low-paid employment; and partly by the desire to avoid difficult administrative decisions about grades of disablement.[30]

(d) The example of fiscal welfare

'Fiscal welfare' is the term used to describe the benefits flowing to individuals as a result of tax concessions for expenditure on matters such as life-assurance premiums, contributions to private pension schemes, payments in relation to personal residences, and fees for private education.[31] The statutory language of the provisions relating to fiscal welfare tends to be that taxpayers who satisfy relatively objective requirements are 'entitled to' or 'shall' obtain the concessions.[32] But avoidance of the discretionary language of social welfare legislation does not mean that there is no room for disagreement over the interpretation of fiscal legislation. One reason that discretion might arise is the complexity of the provisions, a product of attempts by the authorities to curb the use of concessions for tax-avoidance purposes. Another reason is the open-textured nature of the concepts used. For example, whether a fringe benefit arises by reason of the taxpayer's employment, or whether an amount is 'necessarily incurred' for the purposes contemplated by a concession, will not unnaturally give rise to disputes between taxpayers and tax authorities,[33] as will the issue of whether a house is the 'only or main residence' of the taxpayer where this is a requirement for tax relief on mortgage interest payments.[34] As part of tax law, the provisions relating to fiscal welfare are generally interpreted so that if their language is ambiguous, the taxpayer is entitled to a generous interpretation. There is no well-accepted rule of construction, corresponding to this, for social welfare legislation.[35]

External review

The second factor in the juridical nature of social welfare legislation is the character of the machinery available for external review of primary decision-making. It may be said that it makes no difference whether there is machinery for external review, since officials are obliged to give effect to the law.[36] In practice, however, the strength of legal rights depends on the remedies available for their implementation. While the remedies shaping our notions of contractual, property, equitable or constitutional rights are judicial in character, in the social welfare area the rights are initially enforceable in tribunals rather than courts. There is no reason why this difference should affect the strength of social welfare entitlement. The justi-fication for social welfare tribunals is that they can decide matters quickly and in an informal manner, but at the same time bring a fresh view to a matter. Appeals might be taken from social welfare tribunals to an intermediate body, whose procedure is more formal and whose members are legally trained or might even be judges (possibly acting as *persona designata* rather than in a judicial capacity). Only then might claimants be able to resort to the courts. Despite the conscious effort to avoid the judicial model when social welfare tribunals were first established, it has loomed large in the law-reform efforts of the last decade. The underlying assumption has been that within limits the more court-like external review is, the better able it is to advance claimants' rights if not directly, at least through making primary decision-making more accountable. There can be no doubt that claimants are better placed with the development of external review.

In some jurisdictions Ombudsmen have dealt with complaints about matters such as delay, victimization or abuse of discretion by social welfare bureaucracies. However, their case-load in relation to social welfare benefits is comparatively small, and it is unlikely that they have had a major impact on the system.[37] A limitation may be that an Ombudsman is reluctant to investigate a matter in respect of which an individual has a right of appeal to a tribunal or court.[38]

(a) Social welfare tribunals

External review has not always existed for benefit administration, except for the costly and legally complex review which courts exercise over administrative action. Even after social welfare tribunals have been established, they have often operated as, or at least been perceived as operating as, part of the relevant social welfare bureaucracy.[39] Close links between social welfare tribunals and social welfare bureaucracies have taken various forms: for example, three-member tribunals have sometimes had as a member a direct representative of the relevant social welfare bureaucracy; tribunals have been serviced by the relevant social welfare bureaucracy rather than by independent officials; and the type of tribunal members appointed have felt bound to apply the official policy of the relevant social welfare bureaucracy, even where that has been in breach of the relevant legislation. It is clear that some, if not all, of these factors have lessened the chance of claimants succeeding in their appeals.[40] Other relevant factors have been that claimants have not been properly informed about appeal procedures; that there has been an unacceptable variation between tribunals; and that tribunal clerks have had too great an influence over decisions (for example, remaining when the tribunal considers its decision, interpreting official policy for members, writing the decision). Presenting officers have been criticized as not always acting in a dispassionate manner and as not being averse to making derogatory remarks about the claimants or raising irrelevant or prejudicial issues. Tribunal members have also been said to take decisions on extraneous and irrelevant grounds.[41]

Social welfare tribunals are intended to re-examine matters afresh and to substitute their own decision if they consider it necessary.[42] Their procedure is usually a matter for the tribunal to determine, but it seems that the principles of natural justice apply.[43] Claimants and their representatives can usually attend, be heard, call evidence, put questions and address the tribunal. In some jurisdictions, social welfare tribunals are more court-like in character in relation to some social welfare benefits compared with others. This parallels the different degrees of discretion social welfare legislation devolves onto social welfare bureaucracies.[44] In many jurisdictions, social welfare tribunals comprise three members, at least two of whom are independent members. One of the independent members might be a worker representative, on the basis that he or she will appreciate the claimant's plight, but also to give the tribunal a greater legitimacy and air of independence.[45] In practice, worker representatives have frequently been docile, heavily reliant on the chair, and generally unsupportive of claimants. Partly this is because they have imbibed societal notions of deserving and undeserving claimants and apply these to non-worker claimants; and partly because more militant workers might be deliberately excluded from panels.[46] The principles of natural justice oblige worker representatives to act without bias, although it is likely that this has little effect on their behaviour compared with the factors outlined. The social characteristics of other tribunal members differ markedly from those of the claimants appearing before them – they are older, have had more formal education, are of a higher social class, and tend to hold a number of similar positions.[47] Except where worker claims are involved (for example unemployment benefit), claimants themselves seem never to have direct representation on tribunals. In some jurisdictions, professionals who represent claimants (social workers, representatives from interested pressure groups) have been chosen as members, on the basis that they will be aware of a claimant's plight, even if they have not experienced it. For its review committees Canada has a system akin to arbitration whereby the claimant and the Department each nominate a member, with these two then co-opting a third person to act as chair.[48] Claimants nominate friends, doctors, politicians and so on, while the Department selects local dignitaries. All are supposed to act without bias and not as representatives of their nominators.[49]

Gradually – and the pace in this direction has quickened in the last decade – social welfare tribunals have become more court-like in character. Tribunals have become more independent of the executive, advocates have begun to appear on behalf of claimants, and written reasons have been given for decisions.[50] Reformers have also been keen to see the appointment of legally qualified persons to chair social welfare tribunals. The argument is that while lay-persons might have had a high commitment and goodwill, they have tended to regard the job as more straightforward than it is, so that proceedings have been unsystematic and over-influenced by sympathy or prejudice.[51] By contrast, legally qualified persons are thought to be better at evaluating evidence, at following statutory provisions and observing procedure, and at restraining prejudicial remarks. These developments have not occurred inexorably, for there has long been opposition to more elaborate external review from within social welfare bureaucracies. Like other bureaucrats, social welfare officials might oppose external review because it means a loss of control over a matter, possible criticism from an independent forum, and even adverse publicity. Certainly the possibility of external review exposes defects in primary decision-making, for the evidence is that in a substantial number of cases where an application for external review is lodged, social welfare bureaucracies alter their determination to a claimant's advantage.[52] In addition to self-interest, opponents of elaborate external review might also fear that inflexibility, delays and verbosity will be engendered, for these characteristics are widely thought to be associated with court-like bodies.[53] Proponents of the judicial model, however, have been able to point to the unsatisfactory decision-making resulting from existing arrangements, and to draw on dissatisfaction among claimants, as evidenced by the activities of claimants' unions and others. It is also said that otherwise social welfare claimants will be denied 'the rights which are being extended progressively to persons affected by decisions in other areas of government administration'.[54]

Representation before social welfare tribunals has been a major subject of debate in many jurisdictions because the great majority of claimants are unrepresented. Since representation has a positive effect on outcome from the point of view of claimants, there is an argument for public subsidization to further it. Reliance cannot be placed on the voluntary efforts of trade unions, social workers and welfare organizations; for example, many smaller trade unions do not have the finance or human resources to represent their members, and even where they do their officers will not have a sufficient volume of cases to build up expertise.[55] Whether lawyers should represent claimants before social welfare tribunals has been a vexed question. In some jurisdictions, lawyers are actually excluded, as before the Australian social security appeal tribunals.[56] Elsewhere the extension of legal aid to social welfare tribunals has been resisted on the practical ground of cost rather than because of more theoretical concerns that, for example, the sheer number of cases would quickly transform lawyers from advocates into jaded plea-bargainers; that lawyers schooled in the adversary process, with the judicial model of dispute-resolution uppermost, and subject to professional constraints, would not be the appropriate persons to represent claimants; and that the consequent formality would inhibit claimants.[57]

(b) Intermediate appellate bodies

Until recently, the only avenue to challenge the decisions of some social welfare tribunals was to seek judicial review from the courts. Not least for reasons of cost and delay, judicial review was unsatisfactory. In addition judges were regarded as being too far removed from the reality of social welfare benefits and thought to be inclined to a pedantry which would create undesirable complications. These reasons also meant that the introduction of appeals from social welfare tribunals direct to the courts was viewed with disfavour. What was favoured, therefore, was the establishment of independent appellate bodies to hear appeals from first-level social welfare tribunals. The appellate bodies would decide individual cases in an impartial and fair manner, according to statutory requirements, but at the same time would elaborate guidelines to structure decision-making by both social welfare bureaucracies and social welfare tribunals.

The intermediate appellate bodies which have been established have been structured in different ways. In Australia, for example, the task devolved on the Administrative Appeals Tribunal, a body presided over by a lawyer (in practice a Federal Court judge), and comprising lawyers and others with relevant qualifications, which reviews a range of decisions made under federal legislation.[58] The AAT exercises all the powers and discretions conferred on the primary decision-maker and so can affirm a decision, vary it, set it aside and substitute its own decision, or remit a matter with directions or recommendations. An idea floated at one time in Britain was that appeals from social welfare tribunals and other bodies should be taken to a newly established 'social court', but there were already in existence the social security commissioners who hear appeals from the national insurance local tribunals (and also from the Medical Appeal Tribunals and the Attendance Allowance Board). The commissioners, lawyers of at least ten years' standing, have the status of county court judges.[59] Their decisions are published and are regarded as precedent. Given that the commissioners already operated as an appeal body for social security, it was not surprising that appeals on supplementary benefits should also go to them.[60] The distinction seems motivated by the fear of a flood of appeals that would otherwise result from supplementary benefit appeals tribunals.

(c) The courts

Traditionally, the courts characterized social welfare benefits as discretionary rather than as a matter of right.[61] One result of this characterization was that it reinforced the courts' reluctance to review decision-making in the social welfare area.[62] Where social welfare legislation provided for dispute-resolution, we have seen that it entrusted the task to specialized tribunals on the basis that these would have the expert knowledge and would deal with matters in a speedy and inexpensive manner. Legislation often provided that the decisions of such bodies should be final, although the courts did not regard this as excluding judicial review.[63] However, the courts indicated that they would rarely exercise judicial review over the decisions of such tribunals because of the latter's expertise in social welfare matters. Lord Denning M.R. said in 1975:

It is plain that Parliament intended that the Supplementary Benefit Act 1966 should be administered with as little technicality as possible. It should not become the happy hunting-ground for lawyers. The courts should hesitate long before interfering by certiorari with the decisions of the appeal tribunals. . . . In short, the court should be ready to lay down the broad guidelines for tribunals, but no further. The courts should not be used as if there was an appeal to them. Individual cases of particular application must be left to the tribunals. And, of course, the courts will always be ready to interfere if the tribunals have exceeded their jurisdiction or acted contrary to natural justice. That goes without saying.[64]

The fear that the courts would be engulfed with cases was hardly plausible given the nature of potential litigants. There was also an inconsistency, for in other areas of law the judges were quite prepared to exercise judicial review. A useful comparison is the courts' approach to fiscal welfare – as we have seen, tax allowances sometimes perform a similar function to social welfare benefits. The floodgates argument was specifically rejected in a taxation case and, although the courts were warned to have a 'decent respect' for tribunal decisions, they were said to have a duty 'to say so without more ado' if they thought that the only reasonable conclusion on the facts found was inconsistent with a determination.[65] The courts' leniency in reviewing taxation decisions has been swayed by the considerable sums of money at stake and the numerous legal issues which have arisen in what, under the pressure of tax-avoiders, has become complex legislation.

The courts now characterize social welfare benefits as 'rights', rather than discretionary payments,[66] and are more disposed to entertaining challenges to the decisions of social welfare bodies. Moreover, in recent years the legislative position regarding appeals has become more clear-cut. In some jurisdictions there is now explicit provision that appeals can be taken to the courts on questions of law from the 'decisions' of social welfare tribunals.[67] However, just because the courts would have reached a different conclusion does not give them any warrant to overturn the decisions of social welfare bodies. And social welfare bodies have the last word on matters of fact. Thus in 1978 in *Bloomfield* v. *Supplementary Benefits Commission*[68] the court dismissed an appeal on the basis that the issues were ones of fact (whether the claimant was attending school and whether there were exceptional circumstances), that the supplementary benefits appeal tribunal had made enquiry, and that its decision was not perverse. The courts still profess a policy of caution with respect to interfering too readily with the decisions of social welfare bodies. For example, the declared policy of the courts in Britain is to defer to the expertise of the Social Security Commissioners, except where there are differences between the Commissioners or a point of general application is involved.[69] Clearly caution is justified where external review is undertaken by a two-tiered structure and the second tier comprises persons with considerable legal expertise, a high standing, and a constant involvement in the social welfare area. Even if legislation provides for an appeal to the courts, the legislative intention is that the vast majority of cases will be handled within the two-tiered structure. Consequently, the intermediate bodies are in a stronger position than the courts to develop a coherent body of legal principles.

There are sound policy reasons for an abnegatory attitude on the part of the courts. One is the need for judicial restraint when it comes to encroaching on the spheres of activity primarily entrusted to other areas of government. Another is that if the courts interfere too much, government will simply change the rules. There is also the overriding need to attain the relatively informal and speedy resolution of claims. Deane J. summed up the latter aspect well in an Australian decision in which the Federal Court dismissed an appeal by the Director-General of Social Security against interim orders of, and a preliminary ruling as to jurisdiction by, the Administrative Appeals Tribunal. The court held that these were not 'decisions' within the meaning of the appeal provision, for 'decision' meant a final decision or determination. Deane J. said:

It may be suggested that the proliferation of opportunities to appeal should be seen as a safeguard of the rights of the individual subject. Such a suggestion would, in my view, be misconceived. Indeed, if the view propounded on behalf of the Director-General in the present matter, namely, that an appeal lies as of right from every intermediate decision of a question of law in the course of the hearing by the Tribunal of an application to review, be accepted, the result would be that the individual subject who challenged a decision of the Executive before the Tribunal would not only have no assurance of an orderly and reasonably prompt resolution of his or her case by the Tribunal but that, in confronting the Executive, even if only to claim a widow's mite, he or she would be stepping into a maze in which the financial ruin of a myriad of possible appeals awaited at the whim of those who fund their enthusiasm for the fray, not from their own purses but from the long purse of Government.[70]

The basis of entitlement: state and private welfare

The entitlement to state social welfare benefits is grounded in statute, rather than in contractual, property, equitable or constitutional principles. Because state social welfare entitlement is often expressed as an interest which it is the duty of a social welfare bureaucracy to grant, rather than a right which claimants have directly, it might appear more akin to an interest protected by the criminal, rather than the civil, law.[71] Legally, however, the strength of the 'statutory right to benefit'[72] depends on the discretion the statute confers on the relevant social welfare bureaucracy – whether expressed as such or in terms of a right which social welfare claimants have – and the extent to which the bureaucracy's decisions are reviewable by tribunals or by the courts. There is no reason why a statutory entitlement to benefit cannot be as firmly based as a traditional claim in contract, say, so that a social welfare bureaucracy cannot override it for reasons such as public economy or administrative convenience or because a particular claimant is thought to be undeserving. Of course both a contractual right and a statutory entitlement to benefit can still be overturned by legislation.[73]

If state social welfare claimants make contributions towards social security other than through ordinary taxation, does this affect the legal character of their entitlement? In 1973 in *Canadian Pacific Ltd* v. *Gill,* Spence J., writing for the Supreme Court of Canada, said of the Canada Pension Plan:

The plan, therefore, is an exact substitute for a privately arranged insurance policy made between the deceased person and an insurance company with the benefits payable upon the death or disablement of the insured. . . . In so far as the word 'contract' is concerned, there is, in result, a contract between the contributor to the Canada Pension Plan and the Government which, by virtue of the statute, exacts from such contributor weekly deductions from his wages. . . . Pensions payable under the Canada Pension Plan are so much of the nature of contracts of employment. . . . [74]

There are less clear *obiter dicta* in other Commonwealth jurisdictions comparing social security with private insurance.[75] However, all these *dicta* have been uttered in collateral benefit cases, within the context of reasoning designed to demonstrate that since social security was of the same nature as a contract of insurance, it too should be excluded from consideration in assessing damages. The dominant trend of the authorities seems to be that although in some respects social security might be thought of as being akin to contracts of private insurance, the legal character of the two is different. As Lord Wilberforce pointed out in 1969 in a case involving a statutory pension scheme, mere use of the common word 'insurance' (such as in the descriptions social or national 'insurance') is not enough to produce a common principle.[76] The main difference between the two is that the entitlement of state social welfare claimants derives from the relevant statute and not from any contract, express or implied, between them and the state. Certainly to engraft onto the social security system the concept of accrued property rights would deprive it of its flexibility.[77]

Attempts in the United States to go beyond statutory entitlement, to establish a constitutional right to state social welfare benefits, have failed.[78] In a footnote to the *Goldberg* v. *Kelly*[79] opinion, the Supreme Court said in 1970: 'It may be realistic today to regard welfare entitlements as more like "property" than a "gratuity".' The footnote built on an attempt in the academic literature to assimilate state social welfare benefits with traditional notions of property. The argument for assimilating the two was that all property is 'state largesse' – realty, because ultimately title to it derives from the state, and personalty, because it cannot exist without the protection of the law. Consequently, it was said, the same protections ought to apply to social welfare benefits as to traditional categories of property such as realty and personalty.[80]

The obvious flaw in the argument was the vast difference between the legal basis of traditional property rights and of other 'state largesse' such as social welfare benefits. Although ultimately the state might determine the existence of private property, individuals are relatively free to deal with it as they please, and over the years the courts have developed a panoply of rules and remedies to give effect to their wishes. With social welfare benefits, however, statute fixes completely the terms on which they are available. If entitlements to them are directly enforceable it is mainly before specially established tribunals, which are not in a position to develop an elaborate common law. In the result, it is not surprising that on legal grounds alone the footnote in *Goldberg* v. *Kelly* has never been taken further.

By contrast with claimants of state social welfare, the beneficiaries of occupational welfare might have a contractual, or possibly an equitable, claim to benefits enforceable in the ordinary way in the courts. For example, sick pay might be a contractual right.[81] Where workers' rights to occupational welfare are recognized by their contract of employment, these can be enforced through the courts in the ordinary way. Apart from situations where it is dealt with explicitly in the contract of employment, there might be an implied right to occupational welfare. For example, in a few cases employers were held bound by an implied term to continue to pay remuneration while employees were away sick.[82] However, the relevant decisions involved persons in relatively high status employment, and when low status workers have sought to invoke the benefit of the implied term they have been unsuccessful.[83] At common law, provisions for occupational welfare contained in a collective agreement are presumed to be unenforceable in contract on the ground that collective labour agreements are not intended to create legal relations.[84] If the terms of a collective agreement are explicitly set out or incorporated in individual contracts of employment, they are, of course, binding.[85] In Britain the common-law rule has been enshrined in statute, to create a presumption against the legal enforceability of collective labour agreements unless the agreement is in writing and states specifically that the contrary is intended.[86] By contrast, legislation in other jurisdictions regards collective labour agreements as binding.[87]

As a result of legislatures attempting to impose minimum standards for all employees, the legal basis for occupational welfare lies in some instances in statute rather than in contract. A few examples suffice. Sick pay is a statutory obligation of employers in many European countries.[88] In many Western industrial countries there is legislation for paid annual holidays; in Britain, however, the matter is left to voluntary arrangements.[89] Maternity leave is governed by legislation in EEC countries and in other places such as Canada.[90] In Australia provisions for maternity leave have been incorporated into federal awards, enforceable in the courts, as a result of a test case brought by the Australian Council of Trade Unions.[91]

Perhaps the most elaborate statutory provisions in respect of occupational welfare relate to private pension schemes. Regulation in this regard has been motivated by the economic ramifications of private pension funds as well as by the desire to impose minimum standards to protect participants. In many ways the common-law protections for participants in private pension schemes are inadequate. Senior officers of companies will often have a firm contractual right to a pension – frequently an extremely generous pension. But sometimes they might find that their entitlement is insecure because it is not enshrined in their contract of employment or service agreement, or in a separate enforceable agreement, or because it has not been approved by the company in the requisite manner.[92]

Most employees are in the position that their contract of employment will simply refer to their right to become a member of their employer's scheme or to the requirement that they become a member.[93] While such a provision is enforceable, employees might not be able to establish entitlement to special benefits not covered in the ordinary scheme, but which they have been led to expect.

In addition to contractual rights, however, employees might have equitable rights in relation to private pension schemes because as a matter of practice these schemes are set up as a trust under a trust deed. Trust law imposes various duties on the trustees of these pension schemes, such as the duties to comply with the terms of the trust, not to profit from the trust, not to discriminate improperly between the beneficiaries, to keep proper records, and to produce all reasonable information to beneficiaries as to how the funds are being dealt with and invested.[94] However, trust law is far from satisfactory in protecting the beneficiaries of pension funds. Trustees are not obliged to give information on important matters such as their exercise of discretionary powers. Further, the level of benefits might be within the discretion of trustees so that beneficiaries cannot enforce their expectations under the scheme. Finally, trust law does not prevent schemes from depriving members of pension rights (except to require the return of their contributions) where, before retirement, they leave their job for other employment. Legislation has gone part of the way to overcoming such deficiencies. The lack of information facing beneficiaries has been remedied in the United States, where the Employee Retirement Income Security Act of 1974[95] requires pension funds to prepare and make available detailed annual reports, to send participants from time to time summary details of the relevant scheme, and when requested to furnish to participants a statement indicating the pension benefits which they have accrued, or the earliest date on which these will become non-forfeitable. Proposed legislation in Britain, which would have achieved access to information by giving trade unions fifty per cent representation in the management of pension schemes, has never been enacted.

Legislation has made some advances with respect to the entitlement of beneficiaries to private pensions. At a general level, many jurisdictions impose control over the way occupational pension funds are administered and over their solvency, so giving participants protections that do not obtain under trust law. The Social Security Pensions Act 1975 in Britain illustrates the more particular protections which have been imposed by statute.[96] Under that Act, beneficiaries of private pension schemes are guaranteed a pension for life, similar to that which they would receive under the state scheme. It consists of a guaranteed minimum pension equivalent to the state scheme basic pension and an earnings-related addition. The latter pension component is protected from the consequences of inflation by the state once pension payments are commenced. During the pensioner's working life, however, it is the responsibility of the occupational pension scheme to provide security against changes in the value of earnings. The guaranteed-minimum-pension provision results from the requirement that private schemes provide pensions of at least this level if there is to be contracting-out from the state scheme. In addition, to satisfy the contracting-out requirements, a private pension scheme must provide for widows' pensions in the event of an earner dying. Such provisions are less than the original pension but are also inflation-proofed. Further, pension rights must be preserved to a limited extent if participants transfer employment before retirement.[97] But there is nothing to prevent discrimination by category of employment, so that manual workers can be excluded from an occupational pension scheme or given lower entitlements. Men and women must be given equal entry to pension schemes as regards age and length of service for membership, and whether membership is voluntary or obligatory.[98] Since a private pension is in the nature of deferred pay,[99] discrimination in the provision of benefits would seem prohibited under Article 119 of the Treaty of Rome, which requires equal pay for equal work.[100] In the United States, the Supreme Court has gone as far as deciding that pension schemes violate Title VII of the Civil Rights Act of 1964 if they pay unequal annuity benefits or require unequal contributions, although as a generalization women as a class outlive men.[101] However, as long as it is lawful for schemes to discriminate by category of worker, women will continue to receive lower pension entitlements because they tend to occupy the lower-paid jobs.

Law reform

Efforts have been made to enhance the rights of social welfare claimants by replacing discretion with rules and by improving the external review of benefit administration. This focus quite rightly perceives that public-law concepts, rather than private-law concepts such as contract and property, are a better foundation for protecting the position of state social welfare claimants. But the dichotomy between law and discretion is less stark than is sometimes suggested. One reason is that discretion is inherent in the application of rules, a point made earlier in the discussion. The argument here is that it cannot be said *a priori* that rules are better than discretion in social welfare legislation: the crucial issue is to determine for the particular circumstances the right mix of rules and discretion, taking into account the costs and benefits of each.[102]

The trend in social welfare legislation from discretion to rules has not been uncontested. Advocates of discretion – usually non-lawyers – have argued that it allows for 'flexible responses to human needs and to an immense variety of complex individual circumstances'.[103] Decisions about need, it is said, cannot be made by reference to rules because rules require in their application like categories or classes. By contrast, cases of need are non-recurring in that the factors to be taken into account vary in every case, depending as they do on any particular claimant's history and present situation. Proponents of discretion also argue that legalization would lead to inflexibility, complexity and delays, would divert resources from the main task of social assistance, would make matters more esoteric for claimants, would lead to fragmentation as entitlement became itemized to embrace hundreds of articles and objects, and would cause claimants to see social welfare bureaucracies as arbitrary, ineffective and hostile. While conceding that discretion might sometimes lead to arbitrary decisions, its defenders have argued that because it best allows need to be met, to eliminate it would produce only the illusion of justice. To support their case they have also pointed to the considerable discretion in the formal legal system such as with juries, sentencing, parole and even judicial decision-making. As legal history demonstrates, they continue, discretion has always been necessary to mitigate the harshness of legalism – the mechanical application of rules without allowance for individual circumstances – the best example being the role of equity in respect to the common law. A further argument used in favour of discretion has been that it is conducive to the job satisfaction of officials, in that it enables them to exercise judgement, by contrast with the mechanical application of rules.

Legal rules, on the other hand, have been said to advantage social welfare claimants by giving them definite entitlements to benefits. Not only are social welfare officials prevented from making decisions arbitrarily, but claimants know in advance the grounds on which decisions will be made, are treated uniformly with others in the same situation, and are in a position to call the administration to account if they think it is in the wrong. In this view, then, legal rules are a step towards achieving the rule of law at a general level, and to giving the poor a resource at a more specific level. Even if discretion is exercised in accordance with internal rules, these might be secret; by contrast, legal rules must be published, and social welfare bureaucracies are said as a result to become more accountable to their particular clientele and to the public at large. From the point of view of social welfare bureaucracies, legal rules can be treated as giving guidance to the policy goals entrusted to them by the legislature. In making matters more definite, rules can have the secondary advantage of assisting social welfare bureaucracies to simplify decision-making and plan the allocation of scarce resources.

The world is not as simple as some of the stronger advocates of discretion or rules suggest. Many of the deficiencies of both have already been touched upon. As we have seen, the primary objection to discretion is the potential for officials to bend it to obtain outcomes which many would think undesirable. Another point is that while discretion might give officials job satisfaction, it also means that it is more difficult for them to present themselves as acting in a neutral manner without being personally involved one way or the other. Once claimants know that social welfare officials have discretion, they can concentrate their frustrations on particular officers when they are denied a payment.[104] As for rules, we have already seen that their application is a social rather than a logical process. Their insensitive handling can have unfortunate results if the circumstances of particular cases are ignored. Rules might also become ends in themselves because their underlying purpose is neglected. Moreover, there is the inevitable high degree of complexity of a rules-based system. One result may be that rules are not applied by those administering them because they are too voluminous or complex to be fully implemented in the light of the financial or human resources available. Indeed there is no guarantee that those entrusted with administering rules will not bend them or even flout them to achieve an end they desire. The modification of formal rules might be justified as achieving organizational goals, or at least as achieving one or some of them in a more efficient or congenial manner. Higher officials might tolerate the modification of formal rules because it is in the interest of employee morale, because of their relative powerlessness, or because it enhances their control since there is always the threat of withdrawing their approval. Various points can be made in relation to the substance of rules – they might be in conflict, confused or based on ignorance or error; they might be made without consulting those who are likely to be affected; and most importantly, their content might be disadvantageous to those affected by them.

The recent history of supplementary benefits legislation in Britain provides an example of the defects of law reform which concentrates on the issues of rules and discretion to the exclusion of other considerations. For most of its life, the Supplementary Benefits Commission welcomed the relatively wide discretion the relevant legislation gave it.[105] Various groups opposed to official policy contended that what was needed was a narrowing of the Commission's discretion. At one point the National Federation of Claimants' Unions demanded the abolition of all forms of discretionary power exercised by the Commission and the substitution of a guaranteed minimum income for all. Others in the welfare rights' movement were more circumspect; for example, the Child Poverty Action Group (CPAG) campaigned against what it said was an over-reliance on discretionary payments, on the grounds that these were an unfair method of distributing resources, acted as a rationing mechanism, had the stigma of a hand-out attached to them and placed too much power in the hands of individual officers. Along with other groups, CPAG also emphasized the paramount importance of increasing the rates for, and of reducing reliance on, supplementary benefits by improving social security.[106]

By the late seventies, official policy had also reached the conclusion that discretion must be reduced. The Supplementary Benefits Commission said that it was no longer appropriate that decisions vitally affecting millions of people should be undertaken by a body such as itself, not directly answerable to the electorate, and advocated instead that official policy should be incorporated in regulations or in regulations combined with a flexible code of practice. Of more immediate concern to the Commission was that the increasing use of discretionary payments had led to significant friction between claimants and staff because their distribution varied significantly from one group of claimants to another and from one office to another, and even between offices where similar patterns of need might have been expected to arise.[107] An official review of the supplementary benefits scheme, which reported in 1978, was especially concerned that administering discretionary payments involved costs which were quite disproportionate to the amounts involved and also gave rise to such a volume of appeals that the Supplementary Benefits Appeal Tribunals were being overloaded.[108]

These various pressures culminated in the Social Security Act 1980, which drastically amended the Supplementary Benefits Act 1976. According to the government, the new approach was to convert discretion into entitlement, but given the background above it was clearly also designed to make benefit administration more economical.[109] Legally, what happened was that the policies according to which discretion had been exercised, previously contained in confidential manuals but summarized in part in the Supplementary Benefits Handbooks, were given legal form in a series of detailed regulations made under the amended Act. In many cases these regulations have reduced or eliminated the discretion which had obtained, by defining precisely the way supplementary benefit is to be administered. But while the language is that of definite entitlements – a claimant 'shall' be paid or 'shall be entitled' if the criteria are met – there are still many examples where the administrators are explicitly entrusted with discretion, evidenced by language such as 'reasonable', 'unreasonable', 'normal', 'need', 'readily available' and 'in the opinion of'. Substantively much continues as before, although the official claim that existing policy has not changed at all is inaccurate.[110]

One criticism of the current supplementary benefits scheme is that the regulations are too detailed and complex, with the result that there is a poor knowledge of these among many benefit officers and a fortiori among claimants. Anomalies have also been identified, and attributed to the attempt to provide exhaustive drafting covering every possible situation. A popular reaction is to believe that the process of legislation has moved too far in the direction of rules – benefit administration is now so inflexible that it is productive of hardship, and the uncertainty of discretion has been replaced by the uncertainty of statutory interpretation.[111] A change in the supplementary benefits scheme had been supported by welfare rights groups and eventually by government, but for quite different reasons. Welfare rights groups thought rules would improve the position of social welfare claimants both in the way they were treated and also financially – they 'used the apparently legalistic argument for a shift from "discretion" to "rules" or "rights" to support their political case for an *expansion* of the substantive rights of the poor. . . .'[112] By contrast the government wanted to shift to rules because of the cost of a supplementary benefit scheme with wide discretion. Current criticisms stem as much from disillusionment with the financial stringency of the present scheme as from the legal form that the present supplementary benefits scheme takes. If the basic rates for supplementary benefits were more generous, there would be less need for additional payments, for example for exceptional needs and in urgent cases, and consequently less need for disputes about, or even the existence of, detailed regulations – but that is out of the question in the present political and economic climate.

The move towards more elaborate external review has been less controversial than replacing discretion with rules. External review is a widely accepted method of furthering rights, by providing dissatisfied claimants with an opportunity for putting their case afresh, often in person, to an independent decision-maker. The possibility of a further appeal, even if confined to a point of law, probably enhances public trust. In some of the more fanciful accounts there is the suggestion that external review provides an opportunity for claimants to participate in the decision-making process, although this does not seem to be taken to its logical conclusion that representatives of claimants should be appointed to bodies exercising external review.

The real issue in relation to external review has been what is the best machinery to be adopted. The traditional assumption was that under the rule of law the function had to be performed by the ordinary courts. However, it gradually became accepted that the courts are often inappropriate bodies to oversee primary decision-making, and that the task can be more effectively and efficiently handled by other institutions such as tribunals. Another intended feature of the tribunal system has been that it should be more inquisitorial and less adversarial than the traditional courts. The hope has also been that tribunals will not only provide redress for individuals by exploring the legal and factual dimensions of individual problems at greater length than is ordinarily possible, but that they will also improve the quality and legality of administration, as social welfare bureaucracies come to realize that their decisions can be reversed if they are amiss in their determinations. Claimants themselves seem to want external review by tribunals chaired by competent persons, balanced by active lay members, who together show a sympathetic understanding by listening and asking relevant questions and by assisting them to present their cases.[113]

Social welfare tribunals have been shown to have various deficiencies. For example, tribunals typically only concern themselves with those who appeal, and for reasons already mentioned few claimants take the initiative to do so. Further, claimants who do appeal often do not have the legal competence or do not obtain the assistance of a representative, or the tribunal does not adopt an inquisitorial approach and assist them to present their case in the best possible light. It is also said that the form taken by some tribunal hearings is unbalanced because claimants face experienced presenting officers who, however dispassionate, have a greater expertise in social welfare law and policy. Finally, there is the criticism that while the individual cases tribunals decide might have wide implications, social welfare bureaucracies can usually resist these if they wish. Among the institutional reforms suggested to overcome these deficiencies are preliminary mediation by independent officials who, if they cannot achieve a satisfactory outcome, will at least make a claimant more aware of his or her rights; making advocates available to those appearing before tribunals (but not necessarily, if ever, lawyers); and reducing the adversarial nature of hearings by using alternative mechanisms to increase the amount of relevant, reliable evidence before tribunals. Examples of the latter would be to require better notice to claimants of critical facts and issues, and the use of pre-hearings in the more complicated cases such as those involving disability.[114]

External review by bodies such as tribunals can be enhanced by reforms such as these, but there are still limits to what it can achieve in advancing the position of claimants. There are the points already made about bureaucratic obstruction and that external review is not greatly concerned with the substance of public policy. Further, external review individualizes disputes, which at one level might mean that claimants cannot support their case by adducing evidence to show, say, that a particular social welfare officer is less sympathetic to claimants than others. At a more general level it means that individual injustices are treated as isolated examples, the outcome of particular shortcomings, rather than the product of institutional policies affecting groups of people. It is for this reason that critics allege that external review converts social issues into individual disputes, diverts grievances into safe institutional structures, and neutralizes any movement for broader social change. To an extent, claimant groups and advocates working through community organizations and law centres might be able to aggregate individual grievances so as to advance group claims, shift the focus from immediate individual gains to long-term group gains, and pursue complementary remedies through the administrative and legislative processes.

II SOCIAL CONTROL THROUGH SOCIAL WELFARE LEGISLATION

An interpretation which features prominently in the literature is that the welfare state is a means of social control. For lawyers, this interpretation has significance because law is an important tool of social control. However, discussions of this interpretation are primarily historical, with little direct reference to legal provisions. Moreover, social control interpretations often degenerate into crude functionalism, lacking explanatory power. With imagination it is always possible to characterize a social welfare programme as a means of social control. Certainly, it is not always clear which meaning of social control is intended – direct social control (in which law would play an important part); making sufficient concessions to maintain social order; co-option by the rulers of those seeking radical reform; or timing and guiding reforms so that the interests of the rulers are maximized.[115] Acceptance of a social control interpretation also leads to an attitude which dismisses the welfare state as a confidence trick of the ruling class and ignores its benefits for ordinary people. In addition, crude social control interpretations ignore the historic complexity of particular developments.[116] Motives are often inferred from isolated statements and results, rather than elicited by detailed research. Take the argument that social welfare is manipulated to maintain social order. There are statements in which prominent politicians and others acknowledge a link between social welfare and social order. For example, in 1943 the then Quintin Hogg (now Lord Hailsham L.C.) commented in a Parliamentary debate on the Beveridge Report that 'if you do not give the people social reform, they are going to give you social revolution.'[117] Just prior to its demise, the Supplementary Benefits Commission opined that cuts in public expenditure and social welfare benefits could lead to social unrest.[118] While these comments might support the social control thesis, it seems more likely they were political rhetoric to win the support of more conservative interests for social welfare measures.

This part of the chapter is concerned with some examples of direct social control grounded in social welfare legislation. By direct social control is meant instances where persons are intended to behave in certain ways or to acquire certain values which they might otherwise choose not to do or have. Although it might appear at first glance simply to provide the framework for the payment of benefits, social welfare legislation contains many provisions which seek to affect direct social control in relation to claimants. One example is where social welfare benefits are payable in kind rather than in cash, which clearly determines the pattern of expenditure by claimants. In some cases, in-kind benefits are payable because a social welfare programme is designed to maximize political appeal or because of economic factors. In other cases in-kind benefits are made on the basis – to quote one precondition for in-kind supplementary benefit in Britain –that 'in the opinion of a benefit officer, the beneficiary is incapable of managing any payment of supplementary benefit in cash'.[119] For similar reasons, social welfare benefits might be compulsorily saved for a claimant or paid direct to some third party rather than to the claimant.[120] To continue with an example from supplementary benefit, if, in the opinion of a benefit officer, a claimant has failed to budget for housing and fuel requirements, the amounts can be paid in specific circumstances direct to the relevant landlord, mortgagee or fuel authority.[121] The most drastic social control in social welfare legislation is that claimants who refuse to support themselves might be prosecuted for the offence of failing to maintain themselves and/or their families.[122]

One justification for social control through social welfare legislation is that since public money is involved, the public, or at least its representatives, are entitled to try to influence claimants. As a New York court put it in 1941, a social welfare claimant has 'no right to defy the standards and conventions of civilized society while being supported at public expense'.[123] In some cases the hope has even been that controlling claimants would go towards solving the 'problem' that creates the need in the first place for social welfare benefits – for example, that unemployment would be reduced if the unemployed could be taught the work ethic; that single women would be less dependant on welfare if their sexual promiscuity were curbed; and so on. Another source of social control in social welfare legislation is the fear of 'abuse', that otherwise claimants would obtain benefits which they did not need or were not entitled to. Finally, some controls in social welfare legislation have an overt political character; for example, the nature of the trade (industrial) dispute disqualification varies between societies and over time depending in part on the political standing of the trade unions.

Clearly social welfare claimants are vulnerable to attempts at social control because of their dependence, their social characteristics and possibly also their ignorance of the system. Certainly they are not in a strong position to seek to have particular controls repealed or modified through the political process or to complain when social welfare bureaucracies use them in objectionable ways. Sometimes social welfare bureaucracies apply social controls inconsistently, favouring particular types of claimant, so that the principle of equality before the law is violated. Objection can also be taken to controls in social welfare legislation which encroach unduly upon the independence and autonomy which individuals supposedly have in our society. Women in particular are subject to controls in social welfare legislation – the cohabitation rule, for example, bears on them directly, but the implications for them of other controls are often overlooked. For example, women might find it more difficult to satisfy a work test for benefits while unemployed because they have children and it is assumed that they are not available for work or that they are unable to take appropriate steps to find work. (Conversely, for the purpose of sickness benefit, normal household work may be regarded as evidence of ability to work.) At a more general level there is the objection that social welfare claimants are subject to greater social control than other beneficiaries of government largesse such as businesses and farmers. Social welfare bureaucracies can be so obsessed with changing behaviour and inculcating values that their ostensible purpose of meeting need goes by the board.

Let us examine in greater detail some examples of direct social control which appear in social welfare legislation – the limits placed on women claimants as to the relationships they can form (through the cohabitation rule) and the steps they must take in respect of obtaining maintenance from their (ex)husbands or the fathers of their children; the obligation imposed on many social welfare claimants to seek work as a condition of continuing to receive social welfare benefits; and the constraints imposed on workers engaging in strike activity because of the trade (industrial) dispute disqualification for social welfare benefits. A major point pursued in the discussion is that the case for these particular social controls is frequently misconceived and inconsistent with modern conditions.

The cohabitation rule

In some cases, cohabitation – living together as husband and wife – qualifies a person for social welfare benefits, as in Australia where a cohabitee is entitled to a widow's pension if she has been maintained by a man and living as his wife for the three years immediately preceding his death.[124] Alternatively, the presence of a cohabitee might create a family unit which qualifies for social welfare benefits.[125] Moreover, with some social welfare benefits a higher rate is payable to a married or cohabiting couple than to a single person.[126] The social control aspect of cohabitation, however, is that it disqualifies persons, mainly women, from certain social welfare benefits either directly, or by requiring that the resources of the cohabitee be aggregated with those of the claimant.[127] Disqualification usually lasts for the duration of the cohabitation, although in some cases it has permanently extinguished a person's right to benefit.[128] Historically, the cohabitation rule has been associated with the moral judgements made about social welfare claimants. Until recently in the United States, for example, social welfare benefits were terminated if single women claimants had 'illicit' sexual relations, gave birth to illegitimate children or cohabited.[129] Elsewhere the association is demonstrated by the fact that for many years the disqualification lacked a specific statutory basis, but was incorporated into administrative practice under the rubric of statutory provisions such as those permitting benefits to be adjusted in the light of special circumstances,[130] or to be refused if a person was not of good character or deserving of a benefit.[131]

In the absence of legislative guidelines, the courts have spelt out some of the circumstances in which cohabitation disqualifies a person from receiving social welfare benefits. In a decision in 1934 a Scottish court considered that cohabitation was established, and so disqualified a woman from receiving a pension, because of the duration of the relationship (eight years) and the fact that the couple had had three children, even though she was not held out as the man's wife.[132]

A New Zealand decision in 1978 seems equally clear-cut – but this time against the existence of cohabitation – because the parties were not living under the same roof and so they could not be regarded as living together on a domestic basis as husband and wife.[133] A recent English decision seems relatively straightforward. The facts were that the claimant had sustained serious injuries in a car accident, and since her daughter-in-law was not available to assist her to cope, a Mr Jones agreed to do so out of feelings of loyalty, not because of any other bond between them. There was never any suggestion of a sexual relationship, and J had his own bedroom with a lock on the door. Woolf J. held that the tribunal had attached too much importance to the ground that there was one not two households under the same roof, and that J was performing similar duties and providing the same care and attention as a husband would give to his wife. He attached importance to the question of intent –why were they living together? In the circumstances there was an error of law because, given the facts, a tribunal, properly directed, was not entitled to come to the conclusion that the two were living together as husband and wife. [134] In an unreported decision in 1973, Lord Widgery C.J. said that if all that can be proved is that a man is living in the same household as a woman, that would fall short of cohabitation, for it could aptly cover a lodger.[135] A similar argument applies in relation to housekeepers.[136]

Despite its consistency with the underlying policy of social welfare legislation, it is unlikely that the oft-quoted Ontario decision of 1974, *Re Proc and Minister of Community and Social Services*,[137] will be widely accepted. There the court held that the phrase 'lives with that person as if they were husband and wife' had to be construed in the light of the underlying purpose of social welfare legislation – to provide benefits to those in need. Therefore the expression had to be applied by reference to the economic relationship of the persons living together – whether the man assumed any responsibility for supporting and maintaining the woman, the respective interests of the parties in any home, and the liability assumed by the man for the debts of the woman. Although an appeal from the decision was dismissed without written or recorded reason by the Ontario Court of Appeal, a subsequent decision of that court throws doubt on the authority of *Re Proc*. In the later case, the Court of Appeal held that the phrase 'living as husband and wife' involved a complex group of human relationships – conjugal, familial, social and economic.[138] The Full Court of

the Federal Court of Australia has rejected *Re Proc:* although the
Australian Social Services Act is designed to alleviate need, it has
held, it does this by making benefits available to those meeting
specific eligibility criteria and not to those who can show that for any
reason they are in need. To determine cohabitation, the court held, all
facets of the inter-personal relationship need to be taken into account,
only one of which is the financial support the man provides.[139]

Certainly tribunal decisions and administrative guidelines regard
cohabitation as a matter of fact revolving around considerations such
as the duration of the relationship, how the couple portray themselves
to the world, whether their commercial dealings are in joint names,
the sexual relationship between them, whether there is a child of the
relationship, and whether there is financial support or a pooling of
financial resources.[140] The danger of such an approach is that social
welfare officials and tribunals are given little guidance. For example,
there seems to be a tendency among some tribunals and courts to
expand the concept of cohabitation with the argument that modern
marriage encompasses a wide range of behaviour. By contrast, it is
possible to argue that in specific cases particular facts do not establish
cohabitation: for example, living under the same roof does not of itself
constitute cohabitation but may be a necessary arrangement because
of the parties' economic circumstances; a woman may use a man's
name for convenience since she might not otherwise obtain a lease or
services if there is discrimination against single women with children
or because she herself has bad debts; sexual relations might merely
indicate a casual liaison; and financial support might be given by a
lodger as rent or for housekeeping services or from a feeling of moral
obligation.

The social control features of the cohabitation disqualification have
been accentuated by its administration. In the first place, while social
welfare bureaucracies might claim that their administration has been
conducted sympathetically and discreetly, in practice it has often
been suffused with a concern for 'abuse' by claimants and has led to
extensive intrusions into their privacy (one of their few assets).[141]
Intrusions into claimants' privacy have taken various forms – detailed
questioning of claimants, surveillance of their homes, and the
questioning of landlords, neighbours and local shopkeepers. Secondly, in the administration of the disqualification, social welfare
bureaucracies have sometimes acted in a peremptory manner or on
the basis of slender evidence. 'Midnight raids' to determine cohabit-

ation were a feature of welfare administration in the United States, until limited by the courts.[142] At one time in Britain, investigators physically impounded the order books of claimants suspected of cohabitation.[143] Even the Supplementary Benefits Commission conceded that in some cases investigations were pursued for too long when there was little evidence of cohabitation.[144] Thirdly, claimants have sometimes had their benefits terminated without being given detailed reasons, other than a recitation of the statutory formula for cohabitation, a practice which places obstacles in the way of appeal. In the United States, claimants have a right to a hearing before social assistance benefits are terminated, but in other jurisdictions their only recourse is to appeal once that has occurred. In Australia the Administrative Appeals Tribunal might make an interim order for payment of benefits until it hears a matter.[145] In Britain, the suggestion that social welfare benefits not be terminated for cohabitation, without a hearing, has been rejected on the somewhat spurious grounds that this would lead to abuse 'because persons would appeal merely to obtain a few weeks' additional benefit'.[146] Fourthly, there seems to be discrimination in the application of the cohabitation disqualification. In Britain, proportionately fewer cases of cohabitation have been investigated or prosecuted in relation to social security benefits, compared with supplementary benefits, which might reflect the higher status widows have had compared with single, separated or divorced women, who only qualify for supplementary benefits.[147] In Australia, there is some evidence that black women, working-class women and students have been disproportionately disqualified under the rule compared with others.[148] Fifthly, in the administration of the rule there seems to have been an undue emphasis on whether a woman has had sexual relations with a man, although, as we have seen, the legal authorities recognize that this is only one of a number of factors in establishing cohabitation. Finally, decision-making by social welfare tribunals in relation to cohabitation has sometimes been inconsistent with statutory principles. In Britain in 1976 the Supplementary Benefits Commission conceded that in about a third of the cohabitation cases it examined, the evidence presented before supplementary benefits appeal tribunals left much to be desired.[149] An earlier survey of these tribunals concluded that there was a common belief among members that judging whether cohabitation existed was a question not of interpreting the law but of judging the honesty of claimants, who were regarded as having the onus of persuading them that they were telling the truth. Moreover, suspicion was often treated as fact, and evidence of a sexual relationship was frequently regarded as conclusive that a woman was cohabiting.[150]

The official view is that the cohabitation rule has nothing to do with enforcing a particular code of morality on claimants of social welfare. Rather the rule is defended on the basis that it would be unfair to treat an unmarried couple more favourably than a married couple. The difficulty with this argument is that in many ways the unmarried are not in the same position as the married. Women cohabitees, as we saw at the outset, do not always have the same rights to social welfare benefits as married women. Even defenders of the rule concede that its application can lead to hardship because some men do not accept a substantial financial responsibility for their cohabitees.[151] Indeed, in most jurisdictions men have no legal obligation to support cohabitees or children of whom they are not the parent.[152] Precisely because a man on a low wage cannot support a woman and her children, a couple might consciously choose cohabitation rather than marriage. While it is said that abandonment of the disqualification would cause public disquiet because people consider it to be equitable, application of the rule at present leads to social divisiveness, since it encourages members of the public to inform on suspected cohabitees. Rather than discouraging this, social welfare bureaucracies may rely heavily on informers to police the disqualification. Finally, the equity argument sits uneasily with the fact that claimants are generally not disqualified if they live in a homosexual relationship, with their family, or communally, even though they might be better off when compared with a married couple.

Although unhappy with the cohabitation rule, law reformers have almost universally supported it on equity grounds.[153] However, they have generally recommended that the disqualification would be fairer if legislation spelt out clearly the situations in which cohabitation would be considered to exist, and if the disqualification were administered with greater sensitivity. Unless one factor such as the duration of the relationship were regarded as determinative, however, any legislative definition could not go further than setting out the fairly well accepted ingredients already outlined. The recommendation about the administration of the disqualification has led to useful changes in some jurisdictions – ensuring that claimants are given more information as to what the rule entails; that only senior officers handle investigations; and that investigators are instructed that they do not have power to enter private premises, that even when invited to do so they should not enter or inspect bedrooms and that they should avoid enquiries about sexual matters. Further reforms in the administration of the disqualification might be to require that cohabitation be established beyond reasonable doubt, not just on the balance of probabilities; that there always be a tribunal hearing on whether cohabitation exists; and that investigations be conducted according to the standards contained in the Judges' Rules. A method of mitigating the harshness of the cohabitation rule, while not abandoning it, would be to provide that social welfare benefits should not cease immediately if cohabitation occurs. The rationale is to create a period in which the parties can adjust to the situation when they will have to depend on the man's income alone. If the relationship terminates because of this, the woman need not experience a period of financial insecurity between her benefit being discontinued and it beginning again. Another advantage of deferring cessation is that it gives a woman a chance to appeal against the decision.[154]

Great hardship has been caused by the cohabitation disqualification to substantial numbers of women who have had benefits withdrawn in situations where the man will not accept any substantial financial responsibility for supporting her or her children. In the past, the disqualification was administered in such a way that the moral behaviour of a social welfare claimant seemed of uppermost importance. Even now there can be little doubt that the disqualification influences behaviour, inhibiting the relationships which claimants engage in, or inducing subterfuge, for fear that social welfare benefits will be jeopardized. The consequence is that poor women are in a worse position socially, as well as economically, compared with wealthier women who do not need to rely on social welfare benefits. Titmuss makes the additional point that this different treatment can occur although both classes of women receive public assistance if maintenance is tax-deductable: 'while the decision to help the public assistance mother may involve judgments about moral behaviour, in the case of the taxpayer the decision is automatic and impersonal'.[155] A further objection to the cohabitation rule is that it reinforces women's dependancy on men, for once they are regarded as cohabiting, their independent source of income is withdrawn.[156] However, many married women are in the same position, so much so that if they obtain social welfare benefits because their husband leaves or dies they may be comparatively rich because their housekeeping allowance was so low.[157] Generous family allowance (child benefit) paid direct to women provides a partial solution in both cases.

Abolition of the cohabitation rule need not mean that a cohabiting claimant would be in an unduly preferred position compared with others. An income test could still be applied to the financial resources actually available to a woman, including those from her cohabitee. Defenders of the cohabitation disqualification argue that the necessary inquiries would need to be along similar lines to those presently undertaken, but this overlooks that by their nature financial inquiries are less intrusive than those relating to personal circumstances. A practical approach might be to adopt presumptions about a cohabiting man's contribution, for example to assume that it is equivalent to an equal share of housing payments and that it covers the maintenance of any children of the relationship. Focusing on the financial resources actually available, rather than on the fact of cohabitation, has been the approach of courts in the United States.[158]

Maintenance and social welfare benefits

A common policy is to enable social welfare bureaucracies to recoup some of the expenditure on social welfare benefits from those who have the legal obligation to maintain claimants.[159] Under the poor law, and more recently in the United States, a wide liability attached to persons to maintain their relations, but now the obligation is confined to (ex)spouses and children.[160] Underlying present policy is the principle that individuals must bear some of the cost of marriage breakdown or of parenting children. A consequence of the policy is that women – and it is they for whom it is mainly relevant – might be involved in legal action against their (ex)husbands or the fathers of their children when they would otherwise choose not to be.

There are three ways in which social welfare bureaucracies recoup some of the expenditure on social welfare benefits from those liable to pay maintenance in respect of claimants. First, legislation might impose obligations regarding maintenance and empower social welfare bureaucracies to enforce these directly. Enforcement occurs independently of claimants. This is the legal position in Britain. For the purposes of the Supplementary Benefits Act 1976, a man is liable to maintain his wife and children and a woman is liable to maintain her husband and children. The Act then empowers the social welfare authorities to proceed through the magistrates' courts to enforce these obligations and to receive directly the amounts involved.[161] In administering these provisions the social welfare authorities limit their claim to an amount so that a man is left with sufficient resources to meet his and his current dependants' requirements at supplementary benefits rates, with a margin for flexibility.[162] While this first course has advantages over the other approaches considered shortly, there is still the possibility that its administration might be demeaning to claimants. Social welfare bureaucracies might be given legal power, or simply assume the power, to terminate benefits on the ground that a woman has refused to render reasonable assistance in the enforcement of maintenance provisions, for example by not identifying the father of her child.[163]

A second way the social welfare authorities might recoup expenditure is by requiring a claimant to assign any right to maintenance to them so that they can then enforce it independently. This is an approach used in the United States and Canada.[164] As with the first method, maintenance payments flow to the state and claimants receive their income through social welfare benefits. The advantage is that claimants receive a guaranteed income, with the state bearing the risk of sporadic maintenance payments. Moreover, it avoids the problem that women might be reluctant to institute maintenance proceedings for fear of violence, because they do not wish to cause bother for the father of their child (who might have another family to support), because they hope, however unrealistically, for a reconciliation, because of the anticipated strain of legal proceedings, or because they associate the courts with criminality. However, there is still the problem that women might be penalized for not assisting the social welfare authorities to take action.

Finally, social welfare bureaucracies might have a discretion to require claimants to take reasonable steps to obtain maintenance as a condition of their receiving social welfare benefits.[165] Social welfare bureaucracies who administer a provision like this might not oblige a woman to seek maintenance in certain circumstances, such as if she justifiably fears violence. If maintenance is obtained, social welfare benefits will be reduced or not paid at all, depending on the amount and the relevant statutory provisions.[166] If a claimant's social welfare benefits have been adjusted on the assumption that maintenance will be paid, the hardship is obvious if payment is irregular, less than required, or not made at all. A claimant might be required to undertake the daunting task herself of initiating legal proceedings to remedy this. Even if a claimant's social welfare benefits are adjusted to take non-payment into account, there is still the strain of arranging this with the social welfare authorities. Recognizing the advantages to women of a regular income from social welfare benefits, registrars and judges in some jurisdictions pitch the level of maintenance on divorce so that a woman still qualifies for social welfare benefits, even though this relieves the man of a responsibility he would incur.[167] A claimant will gain no financial advantage from being required to institute proceedings, rather than claiming social welfare benefits, unless maintenance continues when she no longer qualifies for social welfare benefits (for example when she obtains employment), or unless the sum awarded for maintenance is higher than the social welfare benefits payable. In fact in many cases men cease paying maintenance after a relatively short period, and in the great majority of cases the value of maintenance is less than what would be payable by way of social welfare benefits.[168] The Australian Commission on Law and Poverty concluded that to remove the requirement that women take action to obtain maintenance would preserve their dignity and enhance the notion of benefits as rights.[169]

The employed, the unemployed and the work test

Generally speaking, social welfare legislation treats the unemployed worse than other claimants both in terms of the substantive benefits payable and the controls to which it subjects them. One factor is the assumption that otherwise the unemployed would choose not to work. Another is the feeling that equity must be maintained between the unemployed and the low-paid ('working poor').[170] Of course equity would be maintained by treating the unemployed generously, at the same time improving the position of the low-paid. At present the low-paid receive some protection through minimum-wage legislation. Social welfare benefits are generally not available to those in employment, except universal benefits such as family allowance (child benefit). In a few countries, the low-paid are eligible for a means-tested benefit, for example family income supplement in Britain.[171] The advantages of this type of benefit over the minimum wage are said to be that it is cheaper and economically more efficient, and that it spreads the burden of supporting the low-paid. However, the criticisms include that such a benefit perpetuates low-paid jobs when it would be better if they disappeared, that eligible persons do not always take them up, and that benefit levels can be cut back more readily by government.

One policy instrument to get the unemployed to work, which also maintains equity between them and the working poor, has been to depress the level of benefits so that claimants are no better off than they would be at work. On the one hand, this can be done directly: for example, at one time in Britain a 'wage stop' was written into supplementary benefits legislation so that the benefit payable, together with other payments such as part-time earnings, could not exceed what would be a claimant's net weekly earnings if he or she were engaged in full-time work in their normal occupation.[172] On the other hand, the general level of benefits might be pitched so that the great majority of claimants are no better off than at work. The upshot of the latter is that benefits are very low, indeed lower than what other social welfare claimants receive in similar circumstances. The underlying assumption that benefits need to be low to 'encourage' the poor to work overlooks the social, psychological and cultural incentives to work.[173]

The third policy instrument for getting the unemployed to work is the work test, which claimants must satisfy if they are to obtain social welfare benefits. While the work test might have an element of assistance to it, in practice its social control aspect is dominant.[174] Normally there are three legal requirements which constitute the work test: first, claimants must be unemployed; secondly, they must be capable of undertaking and available to undertake work; and thirdly, they must take the specific steps considered appropriate to obtain work.[175] The three requirements, especially the second and third, merge in law and practice. Basically availability for work is a general requirement, directed to a claimant's attitude, while taking reasonable steps is a specific requirement, concerned with a claimant's behaviour.

The first requirement is relatively straightforward; it is sufficient to note a few instances where the issue arises. For example, claimants who enrol in a full-time course are generally disqualified by the work test because they are regarded as being employed (or as being unavailable for work), even though they want a full-time job and have undertaken the course to acquire skills for the future or as stimulation from the drudgery of not having a job.[176] Claimants have been held to be employed even when operating an unprofitable business: the underlying policy considerations are, on the one hand, that those in this situation might still be in need, but on the other hand that they might eventually make a profit so that the receipt of social welfare benefits would provide 'a convenient, interest-free source of money to assist in building up a business. . . .'[177] Perhaps most importantly, those who involve themselves in voluntary community work, or who work in a cooperative with others without a job, might not be regarded as being unemployed to qualify for social welfare benefits.[178] Availability for work – the second requirement – means that the claimant must be prepared to accept offers of suitable employment.[179] Statements by a claimant might indicate a lack of willingness, or an outright refusal, to work.[180] A key issue is what employment claimants must be willing to accept without being disentitled to benefit: can they insist on holding out for jobs commensurate with their skills or must they take any job available, however menial?[181] Finally, claimants must take the specific steps considered appropriate to obtain work. At the least, claimants might have to register for work at the employment service (or its equivalent) and attend the job interviews it suggests. At the other extreme are the provisions which once deemed single, able-bodied men to be ineligible for social welfare benefits on the basis that they could always obtain employment – irrespective of the jobs actually available, their nature, their number and the practicality of partic- ular claimants obtaining them.[182] Along the spectrum, claimants might have to report regularly to the employment service, prove that they are taking an active and independent role in seeking employ- ment, move to areas where jobs are available, or adopt a style of presentation (appearance, attitude, dress) which is considered acceptable.[183]

The work test also has implications for those in employment, since persons can be disqualified from receiving social welfare benefits if they lose their job through misconduct or voluntarily leave without just cause.[184] Very significant numbers fall foul of these provisions every year; there does not seem to be any evidence about whether they affect the behaviour of those in employment.[185] Misconduct has been held to include unexplained loss of an employer's property; persistent absenteeism, even when an employee is trying to find a healthier job;

and refusal to obey an instruction, even if it conflicts with trade-union policy.[186] Whether workers have just cause for voluntarily leaving, arises where they wish to seek better opportunities and consider that it is more efficient to do this while unemployed. Generally speaking, claimants are required to look for alternative jobs before leaving current employment, although they will probably not need to do so if, say, their wages have been reduced, their employer fails to comply with the conditions of employment, or there are general grievances about working conditions which they have sought to redress through the proper channels.[187] A claimant who accepted voluntary redundancy involving a substantial financial benefit may not be able to demonstrate just cause in leaving employment.[188]

An official inquiry in Australia recommended that the work test be abandoned as a matter of routine and only applied where there is reason to suspect abuse of the system or where difficulty is experienced in filling a vacancy for which suitable persons are available. Its argument was that unless jobs are available, placing an unemployed person in the workforce simply displaces another.[189] There are other objections to the work test. First, it is misconceived in certain forms. If it is designed to test willingness to work, this is done better by determining the responses to suitable job offers compared with the answers to hypothetical questions. Moreover, to force the unemployed to accept an unsatisfactory job might be self-defeating by increasing the probability of successive spells of unemployment. Secondly, the work test can be humiliating in its application. Forcing claimants to accept any employment available, even if they find it unacceptable or not what they are accustomed to, is an obvious example. Again, it is an empty ritual in a period or area of high unemployment to require claimants to seek out and apply for jobs which they have little, or no, chance of obtaining. Indeed this very process could be counter-productive, for a claimant who is constantly rebuffed when approaching employers might become more incapable psychologically of taking advantage of job opportunities. Finally, the work test has undesirable economic and political ramifications. In forcing claimants to accept menial employment, it maintains a supply of cheap labour for underpaid, dirty jobs. Politically, its existence contributes to a climate in which the unemployed are blamed for their predicament and the task of appropriate economic management avoided.

Social welfare benefits and industrial disputes

In the leading decision of *Attorney-General* v. *Merthyr Tydfil* (1900)[190] the owners of a coal-mine objected to the poor-law authority paying poor relief to their striking workers. Their legal argument was that the strikers had no entitlement to benefit since they were able-bodied workers who could obtain work if they wanted it. The Court of Appeal pursued a middle way: the strikers themselves could not obtain poor relief, unless they became physically incapable of working through starvation. Indeed, the court remarked, the poor-law authority should consider prosecuting the strikers as idle and disorderly persons under the Vagrancy Act 1824. However, the court held, the wives and children of strikers were entitled to poor relief in the ordinary way. Of course there was nothing to prevent them sharing this with the strikers. Presumably the policy consideration behind this was that wives and children were not seen as responsible for their plight.[191]

The approach of the court in the *Merthyr Tydfil* decision has been incorporated into statutory law in the form of the industrial (or trade) dispute disqualification. It has been said to result in a 'neutral' policy in industrial disputes; while preventing strikers themselves from receiving social welfare benefits it has not disentitled their families if otherwise qualified. Neutrality is said to be underpinned by related aspects of social welfare legislation: it has not favoured strike-breaking by obliging claimants to fill vacancies left by strikers; it has not disadvantaged employers as fully as might occur if workers could strike in the knowledge that they would obtain full social welfare benefits; and finally, it has purported to stand aloof from the merits of particular strikes and lockouts. Certainly the merits of each industrial dispute would have to be examined if the industrial dispute dis-qualification were abandoned and it was necessary to determine whether a worker was guilty of misconduct or had voluntarily left employment. In this respect the policy of 'neutrality' makes a virtue of necessity, for it would be too controversial politically, as well as administratively difficult, for social welfare officials to tailor the payment of social welfare benefits to the merits of particular disputes.

It is arguable whether the policy of social welfare legislation in relation to strikes has ever been neutral. Certainly the 'neutrality' of existing policy is looking threadbare in the light of the popularity among conservative governments of the 'state subsidy' theory of strikes. As a result of this theory, social welfare legislation has been amended by some governments with the stated intention of preventing strikes and compelling strikers to return to work. The state subsidy theory postulates that paying social welfare benefits to those involved in strikes makes it easier for strikes to occur in the first place, turns short strikes into long strikes, and discourages the early settlement of strikes. Trade-union officials do not act as a moderating influence on strike activity, it contends, since there is no real drain on their resources if the state is the main support for strikers' families. Moreover, employers' resistance to the threat of a strike is said to be lowered if they know that it may become prolonged.

How does the industrial (trade) dispute disqualification apply? From the inception of the national insurance scheme in Britain workers have been disqualified from receiving unemployment benefit if, to use the current phraseology, they have lost employment because of a stoppage due to a trade dispute at their place of employment. *R.* v. *Chief National Insurance Commissioner ex p. Dawber*[192] held that a stoppage of work could still be due to a trade dispute, despite an intervening occurrence, if the former was the natural and probable consequence of the latter and was reasonably forseeable by the parties to it. On these grounds the claimants were unsuccessful in arguing that the stoppage was prolonged, not because of the trade dispute, but because a furnace was damaged. To the contention that the damage might not have resulted if the employer had shut down the furnace differently when the strike occurred, Forbes J. held that an error of judgement did not break the claim of causation. In R(U)15/80, however, the Chief Commissioner held that the stoppage of work due to a trade dispute was replaced by a stoppage due to a cessation of the company's operations when, during a strike, the company decided to cease trading because of developed financial pressures not themselves due to the strike. There is authority that a work to rule is not a stoppage; so workers who are stood down as a result of a go-slow by others can claim unemployment benefit.[193] In practice the possibility will not arise because employers will almost invariably discharge those working to rule and at that point a stoppage occurs.

A trade dispute is now defined as any dispute between an employer and employees, or between employees and employees, which is connected with the employment or non-employment, or the terms or conditions of employment of any persons, whether or not employees of the employer with whom the dispute arises.[194] In *R.* v. *National*

Insurance Commissioner ex p. Thompson,[195] the Divisional Court held that a dispute over who should pay for protective clothing on a site was not a trade dispute. There was merit in the claimant's argument, however, that the stoppage resulted not primarily from a trade dispute but from a breach by the employer of the Health and Safety at Work etc. Act 1974, which imposes a wide, general obligation on employers regarding the health and safety of their employees. Social Security Commissioners have held that workers thrown out of work because of picketing at their place of employment are caught by the trade-dispute disqualification because they are in that position by reason of the trade dispute between their employer and the pickets or between them and the pickets.[196] Picketed workers might be exempt from the disqualification, however, in that they do not 'participate' or are not directly interested in a trade dispute (see below).

How little connection must workers have with a strike to be caught by the disqualification? One approach is to disqualify only direct participants in a strike.[197] The argument used against this is that if only strikers are disqualified, industrial action might be organized so that only a few key persons who can cause widespread disruption go on strike. A second approach is to disqualify workers who have the same place of employment, who are in the same trade union, or who belong to the same category of workers as the strikers.[198] The Donovan Royal Commission objected to such provisions on the ground that they unfairly disqualify workers who have no interest in a dispute.[199] A third approach is the current legislation in Britain, which exempts workers from the disqualification if they can establish that they are not participating in or directly interested in a trade dispute.[200] Participation would seem to involve active support of industrial action. Workers do not necessarily participate if they omit to take active steps to prevent industrial action or if they attend a meeting which decides on industrial action.[201] To be directly interested, workers must stand to gain automatically in terms of remuneration or conditions.[202]

As mentioned, the families of workers affected by the trade-dispute disqualification have generally qualified for social welfare benefits. Influenced by the state subsidy theory of strikes, however, some governments have sought to limit this. For example, those disqualified from receiving unemployment benefit in Britain can obtain supplementary benefit for their family's requirements and for housing requirements.[203] But the law has been tightened in recent times; for example, a family's requirements are now automatically reduced by £15, on the basis that strike pay of this amount is available from the worker's trade union, whether or not this is in fact the case.[204] Therefore to maintain their members at the standard previously obtaining, trade unions have to pay at least £15 strike pay – a discouragement, it is said, to strikes.

Whatever the intention, it is not always the case that social welfare provisions based on the state subsidy theory of strikes have a significant effect on industrial action. It seems that social welfare benefits are paid in only a minority of strikes and then to only a minority of those involved. The most important sources of support for workers on strike seem to be pay in hand, personal savings and spouses' earnings.[205] An examination of particular strikes shows that workers and trade unions are sometimes confused about what social welfare benefits they are entitled to, which suggests that the possibility of obtaining them is not always a key consideration in industrial action.

III THE SOCIAL CONTEXT OF BENEFIT ADMINISTRATION

Examining the juridical nature of social welfare legislation and its substantive provisions provides only a partial understanding of the functioning of benefit administration. That does not mean that these different aspects are unrelated, for, as in other areas of the welfare state, legislative form and the structures for external review influence the law in action. Thus the extent of discretion in social welfare legislation determines the scope social welfare bureaucracies have to introduce extra-legal notions into the way benefits are administered. Again, the machinery available for external review of bureaucratic decision-making might be such that many claimants do not invoke its protections, and those who do might find that the personnel working it have goals which largely overlap those of the social welfare bureaucracy under review. Similarly, the control which social welfare bureaucracies exercise over claimants is governed not only by the provisions of the substantive law but also by the resources it has available, its official policy, the personal attitudes of its officers, and the stance adopted by their trade unions.

In this part, however, the focus is not on the juridical nature, or on the substantive provisions, of social welfare legislation, but on some of the salient social factors which influence how social welfare bureaucracies operate. In particular, three social factors are identified: the characteristics of social welfare claimants, the operating patterns of social welfare bureaucracies, and the perceptions of social welfare in society. The first of these is tackled indirectly through a discussion of the passivity of social welfare administration. The main point can be shortly stated, namely, that many of those eligible do not claim social welfare benefits because they lack the knowledge, capacity or motivation to do so (the 'take-up' problem), or because of the perceived disadvantages of doing so, such as fear of alienating social welfare officials. The operation of social welfare bureaucracies turns on factors such as their internal organization, the information they make available to the public, the routines they operate, and the adequacy of their financial and human resources. Societal perceptions of social welfare feed into the judgements which social welfare officials exercise at the point of delivery of social welfare benefits. Bureaucratic procedures and societal perceptions of social welfare mean that even if claimants 'take up' social welfare benefits, they might face obstacles in securing their entitlement – a dearth of information, unofficial rationing, or channelling at the point of intake or as their claims are being processed; or the apparent indifference, and in some cases hostility, of social welfare officials.

Law is relevant to each of these matters, although it is not always centre-stage as it was in the discussion in sections I and II of this chapter. Unfortunately, much of the legal debate has concentrated on the discretion in social welfare legislation and the mechanisms for external review, rather than on the processes of social welfare bureaucracies, although in practice the latter are often much more important in determining whether claimants obtain the social welfare benefits to which they are entitled. An obvious point, already alluded to, is that eligible claimants must apply for social welfare benefits before discretion and external review are directly relevant. In many ways it is irrelevant to whether eligible claimants apply that a system is oriented to rules rather than discretion, or that it has an elaborate structure for external review.

The passivity of benefit administration

The passivity of social welfare administration refers to the fact that social welfare claimants must themselves take the initiative and claim social welfare benefits. Social welfare bureaucracies are generally not obligated to uncover eligible claimants or to assist them to pursue their entitlements. The passivity of social welfare administration is based on the assumption that citizens are informed about their rights, are capable of seeking them if necessary, and are on an equal footing with government in pursuing them.[206] Social welfare bureaucracies vary in their 'passivity': some engage in more advertising than others and have a greater commitment to encouraging eligible claimants to apply. In exceptional cases the law might seek to determine the matter: for example, under section 1 of the Chronically Sick and Disabled Persons Act 1970, local authorities are under a duty to inform themselves of the number of persons in the area who are blind, deaf, dumb or handicapped and of the need to make arrangements for them; to publish information about the availability of these services (but only 'from time to time at such times and in such manner as they consider appropriate'); and to ensure that any person who uses these services is informed of other relevant services.

The passivity of social welfare administration manifests itself in the problem of take-up – that many of those who are eligible for social welfare benefits fail to claim them. Estimates of take-up rates must be treated with some caution because of the problem of calculating the numbers who are eligible.[207] Critics convert take-up rates into monetary amounts of unclaimed social welfare benefits, and compare these with the relatively smaller amounts lost through claimant fraud. While useful politically, this overlooks the fact that if take-up increased dramatically benefit levels would probably be reduced to confine the overall expenditure on social welfare benefits. Associated with the take-up problem is the phenomenon sometimes described as 'creaming the poor', that social welfare programmes benefit the better-off but leave the poorest relatively untouched.[208] Important causes of this are organizational policies and practices which put obstacles in the way of the poorest beneficiaries. For example, programmes are sometimes presented in a way which gives the impression that they are designed for the more 'respectable' claimant. The poorest applicants might also be discouraged by waiting lists, since typically they need immediate assistance. Creaming is more evident in the provision of services such as housing and education than of social welfare benefits.

Various factors explain how the passivity of social welfare administration operates to produce a gap in take-up. In relation to some social welfare benefits, ignorance and misconceptions on the part of eligible claimants are significant factors. Welfare rights groups have drawn attention to the lack of publicity for some benefits and to the fact that explanatory leaflets are frequently not on display or are unavailable. Social welfare officials might not draw the attention of claimants to other benefits to which they might be entitled – they might be hard pressed, they might lack skills and training, they might not want to raise expectations unnecessarily or they might wish to limit costs.[209] The complexity of social welfare benefits, compounded by administrative failings, might discourage claims. In 1976 the English National Consumer Council listed forty-five benefits, most with different means tests, administered at national and local level.[210] A particular complexity is that the receipt of some benefits is a disqualification for others, so that there needs to be careful calculation if a person is to be in the best position overall. Because of the specialization of functions, administrators of particular social welfare benefits often have little understanding of other benefits and might not be kept informed about changes to them. A particular administrative failing is that some explanatory leaflets and application forms are unnecessarily complicated. Unlike universal benefits, means-tested benefits involve a scrutiny of a claimant's affairs which some are reluctant to undergo. In addition, it cannot be neglected that a stigma attaches to the receipt of some social welfare benefits. Finally, the low potential gain which would come of applying, or the fear of being rebuffed, might deter some potential beneficiaries.

A common panacea for improving take-up rates is more publicity by means such as advertising and direct mailing. Apart from the cost – both of the publicity and of the increased benefits payable – social welfare bureaucracies are reluctant to undertake publicity on a large-scale basis on the ground that it would produce many abortive claims. Local campaigns in which potential beneficiaries have been personally canvassed have improved take-up, but they are relatively expensive and there is doubt whether they achieve long-term gains.[211] Take-up campaigns would seem to be most effective if targeted on particular groups, and if supported by social workers, health visitors, doctors and government officials already in touch with potential beneficiaries. The complexity of means tests has always been a strong argument in favour of benefits which are more universal in character, but moves along this line are unlikely when the political and economic climate favours selectivity. Bureaucratic solutions to low take-up include simplifying and consolidating means tests and application forms; 'passporting' to ensure that claimants for one type of benefit are automatically considered for other relevant benefits; and computerization to minimize the difficulties caused by the variety of benefits and means tests. Some social welfare bureaucracies have appointed welfare rights' officers to draw attention to possible entitlement, as well as to sensitize staff to the barriers to claiming.

The law has little to say about the passivity of social welfare administration. In 1947 in *Blackpool Corporation* v. *Locker*[212] Scott L.J. drew from the principle of the rule of law the conclusion that law should be accessible and that individuals should be able to ascertain their legal rights. The law has never given content to this principle, except in the very narrow sense that legislation and regulations must be published.[213] The legal system itself is based on the assumption that citizens must take the initiative to enforce their rights. If they fail to do so within the relevant period, their rights might become statute-barred or extinguished altogether. In the absence of a statutory obligation, social welfare bureaucracies are not under any legal duty to inform claimants of their entitlement.

However, the 'new administrative law' is modifying the law's traditional acquiescence in the passivity of social welfare administration. The Ombudsman in Britain seems to require that when a new social welfare benefit is launched, the relevant social welfare bureaucracy should take effective steps to publicize it to those intended to claim.[214] In addition, some tribunals charged with external review are indirectly encouraging social welfare bureaucracies to take reasonable steps to notify potential claimants of social welfare benefits, by ordering them to backdate late claims. They are doing this under statutory provisions which enable backdating where there is good (or 'reasonable' or 'sufficient') cause or there are special circumstances.[215]

Bureaucratic processes

As we saw in Chapter 3, dispassionate treatment is supposed to be the hallmark of state bureaucracies under equality before the law – citizens are to be treated according to established rules and procedures, applied in an impersonal and relatively fixed manner, rather than according to personal friendship, prejudice or arbitrariness. This official model of bureaucracy is modified somewhat for social welfare bureaucracies which have considerable discretion, constant contact with the public, and a clientele which is more deprived than the population as a whole.[216] The public pronouncements of social welfare bureaucracies regard claimants as having individual problems and may lead them to expect treatment tailored to their needs. However, social welfare bureaucracies diverge considerably from the ideal even when allowance is made for their special character.

A characteristic of social welfare bureaucracies, shared by certain other bureaucracies, is that relatively junior officers have the power to settle simple cases, and to make crucial decisions in the more complicated. For example, 'receptionists' – those officers with whom claimants first come in contact – might have a key role in social welfare bureaucracies and their behaviour might well result in the rationing of benefits available. As the first point of contact in a social welfare bureaucracy, receptionists can create an impression as to whether an application for benefits is welcome, determine whether a claimant obtains correct information as to eligibility, and influence the fate of an application by presenting it to superiors in a certain way.[217] Receptionists' behaviour in these respects can turn on factors such as their workload, the bureaucratic milieu and societal values. In some situations a social welfare bureaucracy might rely on receptionists to filter the total number of claims or to deter those likely to create special difficulty.

Social welfare officials can be expected to take an 'investigative stance', in which they do not accept an applicant's story at face value, but treat it as a collection of claims which have to be substantiated.[218] Facts for social welfare bureaucracies must be established in certain ways – a claimant's statements alone will often not suffice – such as through documentation (e.g. birth certificates, wage records), inquiries by officials (e.g. home visits, telephone calls to a previous employer), or expert evidence.[219] Whereas an applicant's claims are open to doubt, this sort of evidence is assumed to be reliable from the outset. Putting the onus on claimants raises obstacles to their success because they might not be able to substantiate a claim. For example, claimants might not regard it as important to keep certain documents or might lose documents because not having a permanent home they move from place to place. Without the resources to obtain their own expert evidence, they might find it impossible to counter that obtained by social welfare bureaucracies from doctors, health inspectors, valuers, planners, and so on.[220] In a very few cases, as with veterans' benefits, legislation mitigates these various difficulties by placing the burden of proof on the relevant social welfare bureaucracy to establish that a claimant is ineligible.[221]

Routines develop in bureaucracies as they construct conventional ways of interpreting rules and handling ordinary cases. Bureaucratic behaviour is of necessity determined by routine since the average officer cannot know all the rules and does not have the time to determine what course the rules set for every claim. In fact routinization is one of the virtues of bureaucracy for it contributes to reliability, continuity, efficiency and impartiality. Because of the large volume of rules which officers would otherwise have to assimilate, and because of the many claims which have to be handled, routinization is especially important in social welfare agencies. But to allow routine processing, bureaucracies must 'standardize' claims by fitting them into categories, and in doing this might ignore the complexity of particular cases.[222] Unless routinization is coupled with an adequate assessment procedure, relevant information might be disregarded and officials might overlook the consequences of their action for particular individuals. In the social welfare context this might lead to a failure to explore a claimant's full legal entitlements, for example whether they qualify for additional discretionary allowances.[223] Another consequence of routinization is that it might take some time for new developments (e.g. a judicial decision) to penetrate the daily practices of social welfare bureaucracies, because of the delay in incorporating them into manuals and other documentation. In itself routinization does not have to lead to the disadvantages of over-simplification and time-lags. Much depends on the human and financial resources available to social welfare bureaucracies and the way they are managed. These define the boundaries to the amount of search officers can engage in and the point at which they must decide that an answer is reasonably satisfactory, despite the fact that additional factors could be considered. At the time of writing, economic recession and political philosophy mean that in many countries social welfare bureaucracies are understaffed.

In recent times, law reformers have emphasized the importance of procedural rearrangements to improve primary decision-making.[224] Their argument is that it is more cost-effective for decisions to be made accurately in the first place rather than to support elaborate structures for external review. In general terms the thrust of proposed reforms is to routinize desirable behaviour (including that expounded in judicial decisions) by incorporating it into agency procedures. In other words, the aim is to make the routines of bureaucracies consistent with the rules and with overall policy. A closely related reform would be to increase the use of presumptions, so reducing the impact of the 'investigative stance', and possibly also to enlarge the number and kinds of situations in which claimants can offer supporting evidence after social welfare benefits have been granted. Moreover, self-declaration could be expanded to reduce intrusiveness, rather than having detailed investigations and home visits. The threat of prosecution would operate as the curb on claimants making false statements.

As with other bureaucracies, social welfare bureaucracies draw up manuals for everyday use by officials, summarizing legislative provisions and setting out agency policy. Manuals are especially important in social welfare bureaucracies to ensure uniform treatment, given the large volume of decision-making engaged in which is widely dispersed and frequently delegated to relatively junior officers. Another factor in the need for manuals in social welfare bureaucracies is the necessity to fill in the interstices of what is often vaguely worded legislation.[225] The upshot is that while the legislation indicates that social welfare officials have a wide discretion, this is greatly confined in practice by adherence to the manuals. In as much as social welfare officials apply manual provisions inflexibly, their decisions might be subject to judicial review for not considering the individual circumstances of each claim. In practice, however, manual provisions are applied automatically and decisions are not vitiated. It matters little that welfare manuals have no legal status except as evidence of bureaucratic practice, and that some of their provisions might be invalid because they are inconsistent with the relevant legislation.[226] It might be thought that the publication of the manuals used by social welfare and other bureaucracies would be a cardinal legal requirement, so that individuals can know their rights and whether they are being observed. Strong arguments can be mustered in favour of their publication, derived from the rule of law. However, there is no such requirement in the ordinary law, and the secrecy of manuals might even be preserved by official secrets or similar legislation. Following the Social Security Act 1980 in Britain, the provisions of supplementary benefits manuals have been incorporated into regulations, and apparently the only remaining secret provisions concern how officers should guard against fraud and abuse. Freedom of information legislation in the United States and Australia obliges the publication of social security manuals.[227]

There seems to be a significant amount of incorrect decision-making by social welfare bureaucracies attributable to factors such as staff shortages, the pressure of work and the complexity of social welfare law.[228] In some cases the errors are small and are corrected on routine review. The initiation of an appeal often has a salutary effect in correcting errors, because a decision is re-examined before it goes to external review. However, there is the obvious fact that many claimants do not appeal, so that no review is undertaken. There is evidence that the further a complaint proceeds up the hierarchy in a social welfare bureaucracy, the more likely that it will be revised in favour of a claimant.[229] This phenomenon is not unique to social welfare bureaucracies, and occurs because higher bureaucrats tend to see matters in a broader context, are possibly more aware of the cost of complaints, or take the view that it is better to resolve them than to lose control over matters to an external body. The Australian Department of Social Security has attempted to formalize internal review by appointing review officers, whose function it is to obviate appeals by providing a quick, relatively independent and cost-effective method of reviewing primary decision-making when claimants complain. The Administrative Review Council has suggested that the neutrality of review officers should be guaranteed by statutory provision, and that where a review officer does not decide in favour of a claimant the matter should automatically go to external review.[230]

Social welfare officers sometimes introduce notions into decision-making which are not contemplated by the relevant legislation or regulations. Their behaviour is mainly attributable to social factors rather than to individual deviance – it might reflect the bureaucratic culture or societal attitudes which are not sympathetic to certain types of claimants; it might be that officers are under political pressure to keep down public expenditure by curbing 'abuse'; it might stem from the control which officers have over clients simply because the latter are dependent on them for their subsistence; or it might be that, finding conflict unpleasant and stressful, officers attempt to reward cooperative rather than aggressive claimants.[231] In each case the result might be a judgmental attitude to particular claimants, an intrusion into their privacy, denying claimants information about programmes and how to qualify, or simply impeding claimants by 'mucking them around'.[232]

The law says little of assistance in controlling these and other undesirable practices. Compared with the substantive law of social welfare benefits, the procedural (adjectival) law is sparse. It is almost impossible to give specific content to statutory directions that social welfare bureaucracies should exercise their functions 'in such a manner as shall best promote the welfare of persons affected by the exercise of those functions'.[233] Specific measures are needed. One is that social welfare bureaucracies should give reasons for their decisions: this would further accountability, direct attention to the basis of decisions, and sensitize officials to decide according to law.[234] Another procedural reform, considered at greater length in the following chapter, is that representatives of claimants have a role in the operation of social welfare bureaucracies. The case for participation is that it would facilitate the distribution of information among eligible claimants, throw light on the problems they face, contribute to the formulation of policies and procedures, and exercise some control over the behaviour of social welfare officials.[235]

In theory the actions of social welfare officials might be called to account on one of the grounds the courts use to review administrative action. For example, a public authority entrusted with power to decide a matter must exercise independent judgement and should not abdicate its responsibility to another body which has not been legally delegated the power. Thus *Sampson* v. *Supplementary Benefits Commission*[236] in 1979 held that an officer of the Commission could not automatically adopt the view of the local education authority (as to the status of a course being undertaken by a claimant) which affected eligibility for benefit. The doctrine throws into doubt the procedure in some jurisdictions of social welfare bureaucracies simply adopting the decisions of the employment services as to whether claimants have satisfied the work test.[237]

Natural justice is another ground on which the courts review administrative action, but its development in the social welfare area is rudimentary. Take as an example the decision in *R.* v. *Supplementary Benefits Commission ex p. Donlan*.[238] The claimant there had applied for supplementary benefit and at his interview had been accompanied by a friend, who was a member of a claimant's union. The officer conducting the interview terminated it when the friend refused to leave. The appellant applied for an order of mandamus directed to the Supplementary Benefits Commission, requiring them to interview him in the presence of an adviser who would accompany him. The Divisional Court refused the order. Slynn J., with whom Lord Widgery C.J. and Melford Stevenson J. agreed, held that the legislation did not confer any right upon a claimant to have persons of their choice at an interview, nor did the rules of natural justice give any such absolute right. Slynn J. also rejected the appellant's contention that if he had no such right, there was still a discretion to allow him to have an adviser, and that the refusal to consider his claim as long as he was accompanied was an unreasonable exercise of that discretion. The Commission had offered to interview him on his own, Slynn J. said, so it had not acted unreasonably or arbitrarily, nor had it imposed a condition amounting to a refusal to exercise its discretion. While one can appreciate the court's reluctance to intrude onto an area entrusted to social welfare bureaucracies – 'It was clear that the interviewing was an administrative process', said Slynn J. – its interpretation of the content of natural justice and of what constitutes a reasonable exercise of discretion are arguable.

The courts do consider some claims for compensation against public authorities, although there is certainly no general right to compensation where a social welfare bureaucracy has acted so as to cause loss to a claimant, for example if it distributes misleading or erroneous information.[239] The courts have to tread warily in this area for fear of the enormity of claims which might be made and of intruding on what has been entrusted to the executive rather than to them. An exception is if the doctrine of estoppel applies. In the leading decision, *Robertson* v. *Minister of Pensions* (1949),[240] the War Office had written to an army officer that he qualified for a pension as having a disability attributable to military service. Consequently, he did not seek independent medical advice. In fact responsibility for the administration of such pensions had just passed to the Ministry of Pensions, which later decided that the officer's disability was not so attributable. Denning J. held that the Minister of Pensions was estopped from denying the statement of eligibility, since the War Office had ostensible authority to make it and both departments were agents of the Crown. The statement was intended to be binding and acted upon, and was in fact acted upon. The doctrine of estoppel, however, has its limitations. For example, it cannot operate to force a public authority to act in breach of its statutory duty.[241] Even more significantly, estoppel cannot be used to prevent a public authority from exercising its statutory discretion.[242]

Another exception is if negligence can be established in the operational, as contrasted with the planning, aspects of the work of a social welfare bureaucracy. For example, a court might award damages if a social welfare bureaucracy gives information or advice negligently about a claimant's eligibility for benefit, so long as it is given formally (for example in writing, rather than over the telephone) and without disclaimer.[243] However, loss caused through undue delay in the processing of an application caused, say, by staff shortages, would not be covered by this doctrine. Even though the social welfare bureaucracy might have foreseen such loss, it could not be said to have acted negligently, given its resources. It seems right that the courts should not enter into this type of inquiry because they do not have the expertise to adjudicate on such 'planning' aspects of administration.

The constitutional guarantees of individual rights in the United States have advantaged social welfare claimants – at least in theory. In 1967 the Californian Supreme Court held that the practice of social welfare bureaucracies of engaging in unannounced surprise visits during the night or early morning, to uncover evidence of cohabitation, violated the constitutional guarantee against unlawful search and seizure.[244] However, the Supreme Court has held that there is no constitutional barrier to home visits by caseworkers, because the state's interest in the efficient administration of social welfare, in particular the supposed rehabilitative effects of home visits, outweighs a claimant's right of privacy.[245] In 1970 in *Goldberg* v. *Kelly*[246] the Supreme Court held that the due-process clause of the constitution prevented social welfare bureaucracies from terminating AFDC (Aid to Families with Dependent Children) benefits without a prior hearing, for otherwise claimants would be deprived 'of the very means by which to live' while they appealed. In fact many social welfare authorities in the United States were slow to implement the decision because of the cost and inconvenience of pre-termination hearings and because they thought claimants would appeal, regardless of the merits, to obtain a continuation of benefits.[247]

Perceptions of social welfare

A social stigma attaches to social welfare claimants, although it varies with the type of benefit. At least two consequences flow from this: first, some of those who are eligible for social welfare benefits are deterred from applying; and secondly, it becomes easier for governments to adopt an ungenerous attitude to social welfare claimants, or at least to particular groups of claimants, as regards eligibility requirements, the level of benefits, or the way benefits are administered. The welfare state was in part designed to protect claimants from stigma by emphasizing entitlement to benefits and reducing the number of humiliating means tests. In recent times this has been undermined by the treatment of social welfare in some parts of the media, and by the resurgence of political ideas which laud the market and have as the other side of their coin the condemnation of welfare 'scroungers', 'chiselers' or 'bludgers'.

Underpinning community perceptions of social welfare are societal values such as competition, independence and success in the market place. Failure in the market place is disapproved by many and the result attributed to the worth of the individual involved, unless there are acceptable reasons such as old age, gross physical handicap, or possibly widowhood.[248] The historical background to this perception was referred to in Chapter 2. In a large survey in EEC countries in the mid-1970s, to the question why there were people in need, the two most common answers were laziness or lack of willpower on the part of individuals (25 per cent) and injustice in society (26 per cent).[249] Injustice was blamed a great deal in France and Italy, although in Britain individual laziness and lack of willpower were more commonly identified. The British approach coincides with that in the United States, where lack of effort is blamed more often than circumstances beyond a person's control.[250] Those who approach the state or charitable sources for relief from the consequences of unjustified failure in the market are doubly stigmatized, because they are also flouting the value of independence by not having saved or taken private insurance. Their stigma is further compounded because they are obliged to subject their personal affairs to official inspection to insure that they are truly in need and qualify for assistance. Largely because of their socialization, claimants themselves feel the stigma attaching to the receipt of certain social welfare benefits.[251]

Stigmatization is a matter of degree varying with the type of claim involved and the social and cultural factors operating in a particular society. Social assistance is generally said to involve more stigma than social security because the former involves the application of a means test and the consequent scrutiny of a claimant's affairs. In turn, the stigma attaching to social assistance is said to produce lower-than-average take-up rates since claimants do not wish to suffer the humiliation of claiming. In fact the difference between social security and social assistance is less clear-cut than is sometimes suggested, not only because there is a continuum between the two types of benefit but also because other factors are relevant to stigma such as the way particular benefits are administered. Perhaps community perceptions turn more on whether claimants are thought to 'deserve' particular benefits, whether because of age or physical handicap or because they have somehow worked for them, as contrasted with claimants who are thought to be the authors of their own misfortune or who do not seem to have earned them.[252] It seems that with the prolonged economic recession it has become less stigmatizing, at least in areas of persistent unemployment, to receive social welfare benefits when out of work, despite the stigmatizing effects as some governments redouble their attempts to uncover scroungers.[253] The ideology of some social welfare bureaucracies, which is at variance with market values, would seem also to have arrested some stigmatization.

Legislation has a role in the stigma attaching to social welfare benefits. On several occasions the legislature has acknowledged as much: for example, what became the Supplementary Benefits Act 1966 was introduced in Britain with the specific intention of breaking away from the stigma of the national assistance scheme by substituting more rights-oriented provisions. Historically, a prominent source of stigma was the 'good character' conditions attaching to the receipt of social welfare benefits. For example, under early legislation claimants could be denied a pension if they had a record of habitual failure to work, were guilty of a serious offence or serious drunkenness, were of bad character, or had deserted their family without just cause.[254] The conditions were intended to reward orthodox behaviour, but their existence could be said to testify to the official view that claimants were prone to deviancy. Even if the conditions were rarely invoked, they stood as symbols to mould with other factors the community perception of social welfare and its recipients. Gradually these 'good character' tests were repealed, on the basis that it was no longer appropriate to control the general behaviour of social welfare claimants or to penalize them unduly. Other controls attaching to benefits, such as the work test and the cohabitation rule, still give rise to stigma.

The statutory distinctions between the various social welfare benefits reflect, but also contribute to, the different stigma attaching to them. For example, widows have generally been regarded more favourably than divorced women and unmarried mothers, since widowhood is regarded as occurring without fault. The community perception has been reflected in separate, and often more generous, statutory provisions for widows;[255] in turn the existence of widows' pensions would seem to have reinforced community perceptions of the deserving widow. Perhaps the best example is the separate legislation for veterans' benefits, which is very generous when compared with other social welfare provisions in terms of eligibility, rates and coverage.[256] The community perception is important in explaining this – those who serve a nation in the armed services earn the entitlement to its generosity – although strong lobbying by ex-servicemen's organizations has ensured that this perception has taken legislative form. For example, veterans' legislation might place the burden on the authorities to establish that a person is ineligible. Moreover, eligibility sometimes arises if death or incapacity results from any occurrence which happened during active service.[257] Even a stricter test – that death or incapacity be due to service[258] – has taken a generous turn because of statutory presumptions and the liberal interpretation by tribunals and courts.[259]

Do courts have a role in fostering community perceptions of social welfare? In the higher courts there are general comments, often veiled, about social welfare and the welfare state. In many ways these are contradictory. For example, in the House of Lords in 1951 Lord Normand opined that 'the recent expansion of the social services must be set against the depreciation of the pound sterling',[260] and there are hints elsewhere that particular judges see a decline in personal liberties associated with the 'welfare state'.[261] Against these must be set positive remarks about the welfare state and about the value to individuals of the social welfare benefits it provides.[262] In particular, there is the passage in Finer J.'s judgment in 1974 in *Reiterbund* v. *Reiterbund*:[263]

The whole emphasis of the present law and its administration is to insist that supplementary benefits are the subject of rights and entitlement, and that no shame attaches to the receipt of them. I recognise, of course, that it takes more than a few years to eradicate an attitude bred over centuries, and that it is true that there are many who still regard it as a reflection on a man or woman to be in need of supplementary benefit. However, in my opinion a court responsive to the policy of the law has a duty to discourage rather than foster this attitude.

It is in the distinctions between benefits and claimants that courts can occasionally be seen to be reinforcing community perceptions. For example, in 1968 in *Boaks* v. *Associated Newspapers*,[264] the Court of Appeal held that it could be defamatory to say that a person was dependent on national assistance. Clearly the judges in this decision were not inclined to Finer J.'s view, in particular that the courts should discourage, rather than foster, the stigma of receiving social assistance. More recently, the Divisional Court has held on public policy grounds that a woman should be disentitled to a widow's allowance because she caused her husband's death by deliberate act, even though only a probation order had been imposed by the trial judge.[265] It seems strained to say that the legislature intended the rules of public policy to apply when there were provisions elsewhere in the statute setting out specific disqualifications.[266] The court seems to have reached its conclusion on the basis that the status of widow was the direct result of what the woman had done, although her reliance on supplementary benefits, for which she would qualify, could be described in the same terms. The result is to accentuate the distinctions between the two benefits – a blameworthy widow can obtain supplementary benefits but not social security.

Claimant fraud and over-payments

Any consideration of the stigma attaching to social welfare benefits demands that some attention be given to social welfare fraud, which has generated considerable publicity over the last decade.[267] At times the media, in particular the popular press, have reported instances of 'fraud' in what can only be described as a distorted manner.[268] On investigation, instances of 'fraud' have frequently proved to be nothing more than persons obtaining what they were entitled to, so that the criticism was really directed at the payment of social welfare itself in particular cases or at a particular level. It would be surprising if this type of media reporting did not have a cumulative effect in moulding popular perceptions of social welfare and social welfare claimants. Certainly one study in Scotland found that of the 230 respondents who felt that the government did not spend taxpayers' money wisely, 28 specifically mentioned social welfare fraud as an area of mismanagement.[269] This is not to deny that fraud occurs, although a wide range of behaviour is covered by this description: at the one extreme there might be an elaborate conspiracy to defraud, but at the other the offence might be contributed to by bureaucratic inefficiencies or legal complexity.

Offences of obtaining social welfare benefits by deception or conspiracy might be committed, but charges of this character under the general law are usually only invoked in serious cases.[270] The specific offences under social welfare legislation are making a false statement or representation in relation to social welfare benefits.[271] Statements or representations can be false under these provisions because of what they conceal, omit or suggest, and the offences of making a false statement or representation can be committed both on the application for and the receipt of benefits.[272] The crucial limitation to these offences is that they require *mens rea*, so that a person unaware of the falsity of a statement or representation cannot commit them. The High Court of Australia held in 1980 that, having regard to the subject-matter, the statutory language (e.g. the word 'false') and the substantial penalties, there is nothing to displace the general presumption that a guilty intent is necessary. The Court rejected the submission that in order to protect the revenue the legislature intended to create absolute liability, and it distinguished regulatory offences designed to protect public health and safety.[273]

However, there is still the issue of whether a claimant must have an intention to defraud, or whether it is sufficient for conviction that he or she know that a statement or representation is false. Claimants making a false statement not for the purpose of obtaining benefit but to deceive their employer so as to retain their job, or claimants making a false statement because they honestly believe that they have been underpaid in the past, might not fall into the category of having an intent to defraud. In 1974 in *Moore* v. *Branton*[274] the Divisional Court held that 'dishonesty in the true sense' was necessary, but two subsequent decisions of the Divisional Court have said that all that is necessary is that a claimant knowingly make a false statement or representation.[275] The legal justification given in the later cases was that the 'plain words' of the relevant section did not say something like 'with intent to obtain benefit', but the statutory language ('for the purpose of obtaining benefit') would seem to require precisely that. A policy justification for simply requiring knowledge that a statement or representation is false would be that it is in the public interest for benefit-application forms to be accurate, but this is more than counterbalanced by the need to construe criminal offences in favour of the subject if imprisonment might follow conviction. In practice the distinction will usually be immaterial, for the claimant who knowingly makes a false statement or representation does so to obtain benefit.

The number of prosecutions for breach of these statutory offences turns on the absolute number of offences, the resources allocated to uncovering and prosecuting them, and how the discretion to prosecute is exercised. As a practical matter, the absolute number of offences can probably never be known. Detection relies on information, often anonymous, from neighbours and the like, and on social welfare bureaucracies taking the initiative to check on claimants, for example those who appear to enjoy a higher standard of living than might be expected. Social welfare bureaucracies have wide powers under social welfare legislation to obtain information, powers which are relevant to investigatory work, but which can lead to further breaches of claimants' privacy.[276] In recent years, political pressure to detect fraud has led to a substantial increase in the number of fraud specialists in social welfare bureaucracies, but in some places these moves have been undermined by action by public-service trade unions. Information from neighbours and the like is mostly inaccurate,[277] but in some cases is publicly encouraged by politicians and the media, with the result that a less than savoury reputation of social welfare is fixed in the public mind. One obstacle to detecting welfare fraud is that employers paying low wages collude with, and employ, persons drawing benefits while the latter are supposedly unemployed or incapable of work.

As to prosecutorial discretion, in 1973 a committee under Sir Harry Fisher, a former judge, approved the policy of not proceeding in minor cases or those in which the health or infirmity of the claimant made it oppressive to do so.[278] There does not seem to be evidence on the extent to which social welfare bureaucracies plea-bargain or refrain from prosecuting. There is concern that investigators might sometimes intimidate claimants, about whom they have suspicions of fraud, into withdrawing a claim for benefit with the argument that that will be the end of any investigation. The concern is that this prejudges the issue of whether the suspicions have any foundation, and that claimants might be succumbing to the suggestion without receiving adequate advice on their rights. Nonetheless, it seems that a high proportion of the offences detected are prosecuted, compared with areas of social welfare regulation. *Prima facie*, this is a clear departure from the equality of treatment required by the rule of law. If its general deterrent effect is ignored, fraud investigation does not seem to be especially cost-effective, comparing its cost with the amount of money involved in the fraud uncovered. Certainly the number of claimants involved represent a small fraction of the total. Critics point out that the amounts involved in claimant fraud are many times less than the estimated amount of social welfare benefits which people are entitled to, but do not, claim, and the amount of money lost to the revenue through tax abuse. Moreover, the tax authorities may prosecute only a small proportion of those detected failing to comply with requirements, and instead merely impose a penalty on the amount of tax recoverable.

The great majority of persons prosecuted for social welfare offences are unrepresented, plead guilty and are convicted.[279] Penalties for social welfare offences are a fine or imprisonment, and restitution can also be ordered. Magistrates sometimes impose sentences which are quite excessive in the light of the offence: their frame of mind in doing this is indicated by comments about the serious nature of the offences, the prevalence of such offences in the community, and the drain on public funds involved. While at least one High Court judge in England has said, realistically, that abuse is always possible where money is concerned,[280] there have been occasions when superior court judges have retailed the exaggerations heard in magistrates' courts. In a decision in 1980, Lawton L.J. is reported to have said that claiming benefits while working was 'rife from one end of the British Isles to the other'. In his view, suspended sentences on probation were regarded as a 'let-off', while fines were inappropriate because the offenders claimed to have no money. He continued:

The time has come when we should say firmly that those who deliberately defraud the social security system should expect to go to prison, albeit that they are going there for the first offence. . . . The only possible way of dealing with this class of offence is the loss of liberty.[281]

The Divisional Court has given effect to such views by requiring imprisonment for those obtaining social welfare benefits by deception, even where relatively small amounts are involved and the claimants are of previous good character.[282] The only sign of hope for claimants is that they might not have to repay amounts wrongfully obtained, as well as serving a prison sentence, if they cannot do so within a reasonable period of release, on the basis that this would prevent them starting with a clean sheet.[283] By contrast the South Australian Supreme Court has adopted reasonably sophisticated and enlightened criteria for sentencing. That court has said that special intent to defraud has a close bearing on the question of penalty, although in each case there must be an examination of the particular circumstances.[284] Not only ought a non-custodial sentence be the norm for social welfare offences, the court has said, but fines should be pitched at a level which recognizes that social welfare claimants have few resources and that consequently a substantial fine is effectively a sentence of imprisonment. Restitution ought to be made, but otherwise a good-behaviour bond of a low amount, coupled with probation, is generally sufficient.[285]

Closely related to the fraud provisions of social welfare legislation is the power given to social welfare bureaucracies to recover over-paid benefits which have resulted from a misrepresentation or failure to disclose a material fact, whether or not fraudulent.[286] These statutory provisions enable recovery of the amount by legal process, but unless there is specific authority it seems doubtful that recovery effected by deduction from continuing benefit is lawful.[287] There is common-law authority that social welfare bureaucracies can recover benefits over-paid as a result of administrative error, on the basis that there is no lawful foundation for their payment and that they have been paid under mistake of fact.[288] Such an approach renders the statutory provisions redundant: the legal justification is that legislation must clearly indicate that it is removing a common-law remedy, but it can be argued that the existence of specific provisions for over-payment do this. In any event, it is possible to argue that recovery under this doctrine is prevented where a person has changed his or her position and it is inequitable for recovery to occur. Although mere spending of money has been held not to constitute change of position unless it is exceptional, irretrievable and detrimental,[289] a possible argument is that the innocent social welfare claimant who overspends satisfies these criteria because of the great hardship caused if he or she has later to repay.[290]

From the standpoint of legal policy it is important to distinguish different categories of over-payment, which are often confused in practice. The first category is straightforward, where a claimant has made a false statement or representation which constitutes an offence, but the social welfare bureaucracy simply seeks the amount over-paid because of a lack of evidence to prosecute. Then there are the over-

payments where a claimant has made a false statement or representation, but where no offence is committed because the claimant was
confused or badly informed. Confusion might arise because the
relevant forms are badly designed or demand a level of literacy
beyond what many claimants possess. Thirdly, there are instances of
administrative error such as the computer miscoding in a Canadian
case.[291] Whatever view is taken of the first category of over-payment,
there are strong arguments against unlimited recovery in the second
and third categories if claimants have acted honestly, especially if
hardship would result. It is not enough for social welfare administrators to have the discretion to write off the amounts in suitable cases,
for financial and other pressures push in the direction of their rarely
doing this.[292] At the very least, recovery ought to be prevented where
a claimant has exercised due care and diligence.[293] A stronger
protection is to prevent recovery unless claimants knew or should
have known that the over-payment or the information on which it was
based was incorrect, and if recovery would deprive claimants of the
income required for ordinary and necessary living expenses or if they
have changed their position for the worse.[294] In addition, deduction
from continuing benefit ought not to occur until a claimant has had an
opportunity to challenge the decision to recover or to make representations about the rate of deduction.[295]

IV CONCLUSION

In recent years, reform of benefit administration has been mainly in
the directions of rule-making and of developing mechanisms for
external review. While valuable, such changes have a procedural,
rather than a substantive, impact. To put it in its worst light, the rules
drawn up for social welfare benefits may be mean and oppressive, and
the only result for claimants of a sophisticated system of external
review may be delay (i.e. the same substantive decisions are made
when matters are sent back for reconsideration). Despite these
limitations, such changes may legitimate the social welfare system in
the eyes of many because it is then consistent with traditional notions
of the rule of law that persons ought to be governed by reasonably
definite rules which are publicly known, and that they ought to be
able to appeal to an independent body, such as a court or tribunal,
which will re-examine matters in an impartial manner.

It is possible to build on this view of the rule of law to strengthen

the position of social welfare claimants by justifying additional rights,
for example the right to be informed of their entitlement to social
welfare benefits and of what must be established for eligibility; the
right to present evidence before their claims are determined, to seek
independent advice, and to have a representative help them present
their claim; the right to be informed of evidence unfavourable to their
case, to challenge adverse witnesses and to produce additional
evidence before a decision is reached; the right to have their
application processed promptly; and the right to be given reasons for
all decisions affecting them.[296] Law has a role in incorporating these
rights into benefit administration – in obliging social welfare
bureaucracies to give wide publicity to social welfare benefits and
how to apply, in establishing new modes of operating within social
welfare bureaucracies, in opening decision-making to public scrutiny,
and in reducing stigma and social control. No amount of institutional
rearranging substitutes, however, for changes in the substantive rules
and for other, non-legal, measures such as adequate funding for the
social welfare system, competent and humane officials, and political
will.

   A criticism of the existing system of benefit administration is that it
prevents collective action by claimants, and so reduces their political
effectiveness, by individualizing claims and by fragmenting them into
the claimants of different classes of benefits and services.[297] The legal
position is that individuals, not groups, have rights to social welfare
benefits. Consequently, each claimant must establish individual
entitlement and there might be significant circumstances to distinguish one claim from another, even where on the surface they appear to
be the same. An ancillary factor is that unless officials have
permission, confidentiality normally precludes them discussing with
one claimant the circumstances of another. However, fragmentation
is not always the case and there are instances where community
groups and law centres have been able to put a group of claims of the
same nature to a social welfare bureaucracy. An example is the case of
claims for additional heating allowances for everyone on a housing
estate, based on the common lack of insulation of the buildings. There
are other examples where social welfare bureaucracies have unnecessarily refused to consider claims collectively, even though from
their point of view this would have been the more efficient and
effective way of dealing with them. Likewise, tribunals charged with
external review have created unnecessary difficulties for class actions

and test cases.[298] While there is a justifiable concern to ensure that the circumstances of each claimant's position are fully examined, tribunals were intended to operate more flexibly than courts.

Notwithstanding these legal and administrative obstacles, collective action in relation to social welfare benefits is by no means precluded. Social welfare claimants can band together, assisting each other with their particular claims. At a more general level they can exert the requisite political pressure for a more generously funded, less authoritarian and better administered benefit system. Law and lawyers have an indirect part to play in assisting claimants in these goals. We return to this in Chapter 7.

6
The provision of public services

The welfare state operates both universal public services, open to all, and specialized public services, directed to specific sections of society. Public education is an example of the first; public housing of the second. Both types involve the establishment of relatively large social welfare bureaucracies to administer them. An apparent paradox is that while supposedly administering the services in the interests of their intended beneficiaries, these bureaucracies frequently operate in a manner adverse to those interests. The aim of this chapter is to spell out the way in which legal procedures and legal principles affect the everyday activity of the social welfare bureaucracies providing services – specifically, how they relate to their clientele.

I THE PARADOX OF SOCIAL WELFARE BUREAUCRACIES

The paradox and its explanation

The paradox of social welfare bureaucracies is that although they might be ostensibly devoted to the wider public interest and to the interests of intended beneficiaries, frequently they appear to neglect these interests in what they do. In certain circumstances their behaviour is in even starker contrast with the assumptions which are said to be at their base, for they act in a manner which seems deliberately to trample on the interests, rights and liberties of their clientele. Consequently, a good deal of the effort of community groups, law centres and others is devoted to having social welfare bureaucracies measure up to the standards which are supposedly inherent in their operation. While these efforts have had success, in many cases they, too, have found social welfare bureaucracies to be remote, unresponsive and sometimes downright oppressive.

Social reformers do not seem to have imagined that social welfare bureaucracies would do other than good if endowed with sufficient legal capacity and adequate financial resources. For a long time they overlooked the paradox of social welfare bureaucracies: they were influenced by the model of the political system in which state bureaucracies faithfully implement the policy of elected officials, and it also seemed disloyal to attack the institutions established at their behest and the behest of earlier reformers. It was therefore not until the post-World War II period that the problem was recognized. Present-day social reformers acknowledge the institutional shortcomings but attribute much of the blame to the combination of high public expectations and the inadequate resources (including legal resources) to meet these. For example, they would argue that there would be fewer difficulties with public housing if the supply matched the demand and the criteria for allocating and operating it were more in the nature of legal rights.

Reformers are also more aware of other obstacles to achieving their goals. Social welfare bureaucracies are recognized as having various purposes, only one of which is to benefit the interests of their clientele. A popular view is that reform governments can be undermined by key bureaucrats who insulate their elected masters from their departments or agencies and from outside advice, espouse a conservative philosophy based on limited experience, and call for support on a grapevine of key contacts in the bureaucracy and elsewhere.[1] An explanation as to why this occurs might be that reform governments are relatively ignorant of the bureaucratic machinery and also attempt to bring to fruition policies which are far from being thought through when they come to power. At another level there is the view that reformers can have little influence over the key decision-makers compared with that exercised by commercial and property interests. In as much as specific complaints have to be taken seriously, these can be handled by social welfare bureaucracies exercising discretion without varying their fundamental policy.[2] For reformers, the answer (if there is an answer) would seem to be the more detailed formulation of policies (which would be expressed, amongst other ways, through proposals for tighter legal regulation), greater openness in administration, and more participation in the decision-making process by members of the public to counteract vested interests. The efficacy of these measures is touched on below.

There is an overlap here with an interpretation that state bureaucracies, including social welfare bureaucracies, are the means by which the powerful maintain their advantaged position *vis-à-vis* the working classes.[3] Bureaucratic rules and procedures, it is said, determine the unequal distribution of scarce resources such as housing, and of detriments such as environmental degradation.[4] Among the factors which are identified as being at the back of these mechanisms is the composition of the bureaucracy: the administrative class is said to be largely drawn from the middle and upper classes and have their elitist background reinforced by a privileged education. In addition, they are said to have a shared outlook sympathetic to property ownership and commercial enterprise, which is reinforced because the predominant pressures from outside the bureaucracy come from highly organized property and commercial interests.[5] A crude Marxist view of the paradox of social welfare bureaucracies is that their real purpose is 'capitalist reproduction' – assisting through public housing, education, the health services and social services to reproduce the labour force from one generation to the next and acting to maintain and develop capitalist relations. Other Marxists acknowledge that while serving capitalist interests, social welfare bureaucracies represent a gain for working-class interests, and that although not under working-class control they are subject to limited reform through political pressure.

Some conservatives see the paradox of social welfare bureaucracies as deriving from the failings of the welfare state, with the only cure being a significant reduction in its operation. The welfare state, they contend, is financially profligate, inefficient, and a threat to individual liberties, for it has gone beyond meeting the needs which individuals cannot satisfy themselves. Supporting this conservative view is a theoretical analysis of public bureaucracies which builds on the *a priori* assumption that government officials act to maximize rewards such as promotion or increased status. As a result, runs this analysis, bureaucrats pursue the survival and growth of their bureaucracy, even if to do this involves downgrading the public interest and the interest of supposed beneficiaries. Since economic considerations are not paramount, inefficiencies result, because there are no incentives to engage in efficient or socially useful behaviour or to pursue the optimal level of output.[6] While there is some truth in what these theorists describe as the unhappy operation of state bureaucracies, their account is marred by undue exaggeration and leads some to the fallacious conclusion that the maladies can only be cured by substantial amputation. The basic fallacy of the utility-maximizing approach to bureaucracy is to assume that because self-seeking operates in the economic sector, it operates everywhere. In fact, other forces, cultural and social, influence bureaucratic behaviour, and there is always the restraining effect of legal and administrative rules and sanctions to incorporate public-interest goals and efficiency.

Law and the paradox of social welfare bureaucracies

The model of bureaucracy derived from Weber is of a formal, rational process in which decision-making proceeds according to rules rather than personal predilections, with the consequent advantages of certainty and impartiality. Of these advantages, the equal application of rules – examined in Chapter 3 – is of great importance to legal thinking. Despite the ideal, Weber realized that in certain circumstances more particularistic modes of bureaucratic behaviour would emerge. Interestingly, he also saw that it was an advantage for the propertied, especially the capitalist class, if there was a dual system 'of formal adjudication of disputes within the upper class, combined with arbitrariness or *de facto* denegation of justice for the economically weak. . . .'[7] While Weber recognized that this dual system was not always possible, his observation is of direct relevance to the paradox of social welfare bureaucracies, since these are often endowed with wide discretion by their constitutive legislation. Partly, this is because social welfare bureaucracies are subject to conflicting or ambiguous expectations because they are not given a clear mandate. Partly also, it is a matter of policy, the justification for wide discretion being that because of the weakness and variety of their clientele, social welfare bureaucracies need a mode of action which can take individual needs into account. In practice, down-playing rules may have a directly opposite effect to making service to clients paramount, for wide discretion allows officials to introduce into decision-making their own prejudices or their own conceptions of what are the true needs of the public. Moreover, wide discretion can lead to a routinization in which bureaucratic action does not respond to people's needs, or it can encourage a bureaucracy to act more to preserve its power and prestige regardless of the interests of the public.

There is little countervailing force to these tendencies from the clientele of social welfare bureaucracies. Their social and economic deprivation inhibits political action, while the constitutive legislation of social welfare bureaucracies has little if any role for them or their representatives in formal decision-making.[8] A few attempts to incorporate greater client participation in social welfare bureaucracies are examined below. That their constitutive legislation encourages social welfare bureaucracies to think of their services as being tailored to individual needs and the lack of client participation might also explain why they are slow to examine fundamental questions such as their overall policy, the fairness of their relevant laws, rules and procedures, and the discretion entrusted to officials. Individualized services also underline clients' dependency: whether claimants receive a service and its quality may turn on the discretion of the bureaucracy rather than it being in the nature of a right. Alternatively, it may depend on a procedure such as queueing, which although fair in the particular circumstances means that individual competes against individual. What has been said is not to suggest that legalism provides the answer; the separate problems associated with it have been explored in the previous chapter.

A further factor in the response of social welfare bureaucracies may be that the issues are portrayed as technical ones which only they can understand. Clients are hindered in expressing their view because it seems necessary to penetrate professional language and technique. One particular professional language and technique is legal in character. For example, the difficulties for residents during the compulsory-purchase stage of slum clearance were exacerbated where public authorities invoked legal language and stressed legal correctness to protect their position from challenge.[9] The result of legal language and technique is that the relevant social welfare bureaucracies are distanced from their clientele. Decisions tend to be made not by reference to actual people but in terms of legal criteria.[10] Of course, distancing is compounded by non-legal factors; for example, social welfare bureaucracies are dealing with the poorer sections of society and there is clearly a social (and perhaps also racial) gap between the middle-class officials and their clients. In the main, the clientele of social welfare bureaucracies do not seek redress to activity which is clearly against their interests. Their fatalism is functional for a social welfare bureaucracy, because it means less resistance to its policies. Indeed bureaucratic activity might foster fatalism, for the latter might be the most appropriate response to the enormity and complexity of bureaucratic processes, especially if these disrupt daily life. For example, a decision about slum clearance leads to 'planning blight', which in turn contributes to feelings of helplessness and reinforces the view that clearance is the only solution. Democratic ideology assures the clientele of social welfare bureaucracies that they can be efficacious, but neither the political nor legal machinery is adequate if their voices are to be heard.

Mechanisms for legal redress have been improved in recent years; we explore some aspects below. Again non-legal factors have a bearing on the effectiveness of legal mechanisms. For example, in one survey of those respondents who believed they could do something about an unjust local government regulation if they wanted to, half as many in Britain as compared with the United States reported ever having attempted this.[11] It would seem that the emphasis on individual rights in the United States – an emphasis which the legal system has done much to foster – is a major cause of the difference.

Slum clearance

An example of the paradox of social welfare bureaucracies is provided by slum clearance (urban redevelopment). In many countries this was portrayed as advantaging slum dwellers, but its impact was often to benefit property and commercial interests to the detriment of the former. The explanations are not clear-cut or universally applicable. Although ostensibly to assist slum dwellers, clearance might well have had other goals such as commercial advance or civic improvement.[12] If it is assumed that the main goal of slum clearance was the benefit of the slum dwellers, however, the first explanation of its detriments for them would be their lack of control over, and knowledge about, the clearance process. In particular there was never any real consultation as to whether they wanted slum clearance, or if they did, as to how it should be implemented. Consultation became increasingly appropriate after World War II when substantial numbers of residents in new clearance areas opposed it, or at least the way it was implemented. One factor was that slum clearance destroyed community life and the mechanisms of mutual support in local areas.[13] Another was that the multi-storied flats often built to replace the slums acquired a reputation for social isolation and for physical defects such as damp. A further factor was that despite their scientific aura, clearance plans were sometimes revealed to be formulated on the basis of a very cursory examination of the quality of housing in an area. Even where residents wanted slum clearance, this was often because 'planning blight' (the decline of conditions in an area where slum clearance had been proposed) meant that existing housing was deplorable and could not be improved without massive expenditure.[14]

Savoury v. *Secretary of State for Wales* (1974)[15] illustrates the community opposition in some areas to slum clearance and the role of . the courts in controlling it. There a local community in Adamsdown, an area of Cardiff, objected to clearance, initially to the local authority, then before the inspector appointed to conduct a public local authority, and later through the courts. Their legal argument was that the compulsory purchase order should be quashed because section 42(1) of the Housing Act 1957 had not been complied with, in that it required the local authority to satisfy itself that suitable accommodation was available for those displaced by clearance, and that the accommodation proposed was unsuitable because it would not preserve the closely knit community with its strong community spirit. While rehousing on the site and preservation of a community were relevant factors to be taken into account, Cantley J. held that the legislation recognized that disruption would occur, 'suitable' was not the equivalent of ideal, and there was no evidence that the local authority had acted improperly. Ultimately, the campaign of which *Savoury's* case was part led the local authority to save one area from clearance and to rehouse more speedily the residents whose homes were destroyed.[16]

A second point is that in many cases slum clearance actually worsened the plight of slum dwellers, at least until clearance was effected and rehousing occurred. What often happened was that once an area was designated for slum clearance it began to suffer because landlords and owner-occupiers ceased to maintain their housing, since ultimately it would be cleared. So the fact that an area was designated for slum clearance actually led to its deterioration, thus justifying the initial decision of the need for clearance.[17] While a certain amount of planning blight was inevitable with slum clearance, it was unnecessarily increased by clearance plans made without an accurate knowledge of particular areas or because schemes projected too far into the future were delayed or in some instances never implemented at all.[18] The law provided little protection against planning blight for it gave wide discretion to bureaucracies to decide on clearance but then to postpone its implementation.[19] Theoretically the housing in clearance areas might still have been required to meet certain minimum standards,[20] and individuals might have been able to take legal action to obtain repairs or even to induce rehousing. As a practical matter, however, the residents of clearance areas remained exposed to the deterioration of their environment, despite the legal possibilities: many lacked access to legal services, and possibly some were also reluctant to alienate the clearance authority where it was the only realistic source of alternative accommodation. The residents' plight in clearance areas was often exacerbated by a lack of information as to what was occurring – the bureaucracies did not see their role as providing information, and information had to be gleaned from occasional contacts with officials such as those assessing the fitness of a dwelling, or later those determining the quality of public housing to which a person was entitled. Ideally legislation ought to have obliged clearance authorities to provide definite and early dates for rehousing.

Public housing

Public housing provides another illustration of the paradox of social welfare bureaucracies. In 1976 the National Consumer Council reported that in their tenancy agreements public-housing authorities in England and Wales took advantage of their bargaining power and exemption from ordinary landlord and tenant law to incorporate one-sided provisions, and a number even purported to exclude certain statutory obligations binding on them.[21] The NCC report found that while the tenancy agreements contained a great deal on what tenants could or could not do, and on the rights of public-housing authorities, most omitted to mention the authorities' obligations. Lord Wilberforce made the same point in relation to the public-housing tenancy agreement before him in 1976 in *Liverpool C.C.* v. *Irwin*:[22] 'On the landlords' side there is nothing, no signature, no demise, no covenant. . . .' Of the clauses pertaining to tenants' obligations, the NCC concluded that many were incomprehensible and that the pervasive mood was paternal at best and punitive at worst. For example, clauses prohibited tenants taking lodgers without consent, prohibited the keeping of animals, and gave authorities wide discretion to raise the rent and to evict. While the NCC acknowledged that in most cases authorities did not take advantage of their powers under these agreements, it thought it only proper that tenants be put on a more equal footing.

Historically it is possible to trace the legal subordination of public-housing tenants to the attitude of the housing charities of the nineteenth century, who believed that the working class could be 'improved' if they were tightly controlled in matters such as cleanliness and the regular payment of rent. Public-housing tenants have been in a worse position legally than tenants in the private sector because public-housing authorities have not always been bound by ordinary landlord and tenant law. Apart from this, the courts have generally been reluctant to interfere with the way public-housing authorities discharge their functions. In one decision Lawton L.J. justified this on the grounds that public-housing authorities had to face the electorate from time to time and the electors 'are in a far better position than this court ever could be to decide whether the powers have been exercised in a way which meets with general approval'.[23]

In certain cases, however, the facts have been so compelling, and the existing legal doctrines suitably malleable, that the courts have been prepared to assist public-housing tenants. In *Liverpool C.C. v. Irwin*, Lord Salmon said:

It has been argued that the council should not be taken to have accepted any legal obligations of any kind. After all, this was a distinguished city council which expected its tenants happily to rely on it to treat them reasonably without having the temerity to expect the council to undertake any legal obligations to do so. I confess that I find this argument and similar arguments which I have often heard advanced on behalf of other organisations singularly unconvincing.[24]

While that decision benefited public-housing tenants, by holding that public-housing authorities must take reasonable care to maintain the common areas of flats, it was to no avail to the particular tenants involved. The possession order obtained against them stood, because it was not established that the authority involved had failed to maintain.

Four aspects of public-housing law bear closer examination: that relating to allocation, to rent, to repairs and to security of tenure. With each, the legal position of tenants belies any claim that their position is paramount.

Schemes for the allocation of public housing have had to be developed because supply has never matched demand and because of the diversity in the housing stock. Any reduction in the amount of new building, or the sale of public housing, places additional pressure on allocation schemes. Within the boundaries set by available resources, public housing is allocated in accordance with bureaucratic procedures; a few of these have a basis in law. The procedures are said to permit housing authorities to deal flexibly with housing needs, but in fact they serve the needs of public housing authorities at least as much as those of applicants.[25] For example, 'respectable' applicants are allocated to the better housing because they are thought to deserve it, but also because they create fewer problems for housing managers. 'Problem families' and low income earners receive poorer housing – this means that the less desirable housing is filled, it reduces difficulties about rent arrears (since rents are lower), and it limits an authority's overall commitment for any applicable rent rebates. However, allocating these applicants to the less desirable housing confirms its reputation, perpetuates inequalities, and creates slum or 'sink' estates – such as the tower block in *Liverpool C.C.* v. *Irwin*[26] – despised both by those who live there and by the public at large.[27] To an extent, the allocation procedures project an image of order which functions to divert attention away from the fundamental inability of public-housing authorities to meet demand. The procedures also place applicants in competition with each other so that they are less likely to organize collectively to press for more and better housing.

Applicants for public housing are in a position of relative powerlessness. The first element in this is the lack of information. Housing authorities have tended not to publish their allocation schemes, although in Britain section 44 of the Housing Act 1980 now obliges them to do so. In addition, public-housing officials generally do not explain to individual applicants how the system will work in relation to them, and one author has described the bafflement, helplessness and resentment engendered.[28] To an extent, this is inevitable because the sheer volume of work combined with staff shortages mean enquirers have to be treated in a perfunctory manner. Resources are not the only factor, however, for the applicant's position is also moulded because housing authorities exercise their discretion against a background of social, political and economic realities. Many persons never register for public housing in the first place because they know that they might have years to wait or because they fear being sent to an unpleasant or distant estate or to a high rise flat, and many who register do not keep the housing authorities informed about their changed circumstances. Housing authorities have tended to favour families with children to the detriment of childless couples, one-parent families and single persons.

The second element in the powerlessness of applicants for public housing is that the law entrusts wide discretion to housing authorities regarding decisions about allocation. The justification is that it is better for housing authorities to be able to deal flexibly with the particular conditions of their areas. Once anti-discrimination provisions are put on one side, there are only minor statutory controls over allocation. For example, local authorities in Britain must give reasonable preference to those occupying insanitary or overcrowded houses, to those with large families, to those living in unsatisfactory housing conditions, and to those to whom it has a duty under the Housing (Homeless Persons) Act 1977.[29] In addition, local authorities must generally provide accommodation if they displace persons from their housing by action such as slum clearance, and suitable alternative accommodation is not otherwise available on reasonable terms.[30] Some authorities have refused to house those such as single persons with the argument, however inaccurate, that suitable alternative accommodation is always available to them in the private sector. Some authorities have regarded their duty to provide accommodation as discharged if a person displaced by slum clearance rejects an offer, however unsuitable.[31]

How do public authorities exercise their discretion regarding allocation?[32] Some insist that a person must satisfy residential requirements before being considered; some apply a means test; and some decide each year in advance how much housing they will allocate to particular categories such as ordinary applicants, priority categories (e.g. the sick), and the homeless. Within these limits there are a variety of systems: 'date order' systems, which are basically a first-come, first-served approach and therefore exclude considerations of individual need; 'merit' systems, which involve housing officials or politicians making what in many cases are moral judgements; and 'points' systems, in which applicants accrue points depending on their present housing conditions, the size and composition of their household, their length of residence, etc., and in which different-quality housing has different points thresholds. Many housing authorities use some variation of the points system and have applicants visited in their existing homes to check on the factors for which points accrue. In theory the points system means the individualized treatment of applicants rather than the legalistic application of rules, but there has been criticism that housing officials stereotype applicants in terms of their living conditions, personal cleanliness and demeanour, neglecting that people cannot always control these. Another is that the poorest are allocated the worst housing, since they are usually desperate for housing and do not have time to accrue the points necessary for the better housing. Applicants who refuse what are clearly unreasonable offers might find themselves struck off the waiting list.

Should applicants wish to challenge a decision on allocation they will probably find that the procedures, if they exist, are unclear, and that there is no provision for personal representations let alone representations by a lawyer acting on their behalf. Given the wide discretion entrusted to housing authorities, it is not surprising that the courts are reluctant to review decisions about allocation on grounds such that irrelevant considerations have been taken into account or relevant considerations disregarded.[33] By contrast, some courts in the United States have invoked constitutional tests of sufficient cause and equal protection to overturn decisions by public-housing authorities such as to exclude persons with poor housekeeping habits, single parents, or recipients of social welfare benefits.[34] Ombudsmen might give satisfaction to persons complaining about bias, delay or inefficiency in the allocation of council housing,[35] although it is another matter whether the housing authorities change their procedures in the light of Ombudsman investigations.

Public-housing authorities are usually not bound by any rent-control law.[36] Public-tenancy agreements might permit a variation in rent at any time, subject to reasonable notice. As with other aspects of public housing, the assumption is that the authorities will use their power fairly. Certainly they can often point to rent-rebate schemes for low-income tenants and to figures showing that the average un-rebated rents for public housing are lower than those in the private sector.[37] From the point of view of fairness, however, a contrast might exist between the procedures available in the two sectors for tenants dissatisfied about the rents they are paying. In Britain, for example, private-sector tenants can apply to a rent officer and then appeal to a rent-assessment committee. There is no such procedure in the public sector and tenants must seek judicial review in the courts, where the costs and other associated difficulties are obvious. The courts are hesitant to find that the rents charged by housing authorities are unreasonable, an underlying justification being that they are a matter of social policy rather than law.[38]

The law relating to the repair of public housing is that obtaining for the private sector, unless legislation provides otherwise.[39] First, the common-law obligations imposed on private landlords usually extend to public-housing authorities.[40] Public-housing authorities can exclude these responsibilities, however, as can other landlords, and it is not unknown for them to do so.[41] Similarly, just as private landlords vary their tenants' obligations through standard-form tenancy agreements, public authorities sometimes impose heavier obligations on their tenants. Paternalism might also be evident in the way housing authorities prevent or regulate tenants' engaging in matters such as external decoration or improvements. Secondly, general legislation imposing non-excludable obligations on landlords might also apply to public-housing authorities.[42] However, public-housing tenants might be inhibited from complaining about their breach because they did not have security of tenure. In addition, public authorities responsible for enforcing the standards might fail to do so, and where they and the housing authorities are both at the same level of government might not even inspect for non-compliance. Individuals might be able to enforce these statutory provisions directly but will generally not have sufficient incentive unless damages for personal injuries are at stake or unless they are supported as a test case by a law centre or by legal aid.[43]

Whatever the statutory protections available to private tenants, public-housing tenants have not generally enjoyed security of tenure but have been subject to eviction at any time.[44] Theoretically, public-housing tenants in this position might be able to challenge an eviction on the basis that the authority has acted in bad faith, not acted for a proper purpose etc., but in the few cases where these arguments have been raised tenants have had difficulty persuading courts.[45] In the United States, public-housing tenants whom it is proposed to evict must be adequately informed of the case against them and given an opportunity to rebut it.[46] To assimilate the rights of public- and private-sector tenants – 'desirable in the general interests of social equality and non-discrimination'[47] – the Housing Act 1980 in Britain gives public-housing tenants security of tenure.

Some public-housing authorities have freely evicted for rent arrears.[48] Some have automatically instituted eviction proceedings when tenants are a few weeks in arrears, although these might be by way of threat and not proceeded with if the arrears are paid.[49] Where a housing authority obtains a possession order, it might not agree to it being suspended unless the tenant makes suitable arrangements to pay a substantial amount of the arrears. Housing authorities justify their approach on the ground that otherwise rent arrears would spread in epidemic proportions.[50] Instances of deliberate refusal to pay rent are isolated, however, and public tenants in arrears are generally poor and have had difficulty meeting unexpected or large commitments arising, for example, through sickness, unemployment or marital discord, because of other pressing bills.[51] There is a variation in the rate of arrears between comparable areas. One explanation is inadequate management by housing authorities. Some do not ensure that tenants receive rent rebates where available, or that tenants receiving social welfare benefits have rent paid direct if this can be arranged. Some do not act quickly enough when it appears that arrears are beginning, by having tenants seek financial or other advice. Moreover, it is well to recognize that rent arrears sometimes occur because public tenants deliberately withhold rent as a form of protest because of the disrepair of their dwelling.

As an alternative to eviction, a number of housing authorities distrain against tenants in arrears. Distraint involves a housing authority seizing a tenant's goods which can eventually be sold if the arrears remain unpaid.[52] Housing authorities which use distraint claim a high success rate, with amounts being paid in full or agreements being made between tenants and bailiffs for regular payments so that goods need be seized in only a few cases. But this neglects the fact that such payments or agreements might be possible only because the tenants incur other debts to pay the arrears, and at the cost of imposing heavy burdens on social services departments who have to deal with the casualties of the policy.[53] A further objection to distraint is that the resale value of tenants' goods is so low that a tenant might still owe rent arrears after sale.[54] Finally, some housing authorities have used private bailiffs to carry out distraint, and there is less control over their activities and consequently a greater possibility of abuse.[55]

II LEGAL CONTROL OF SOCIAL WELFARE BUREAUCRACIES

Bureaucracies have a significant capacity to resist legal control. This feature was discussed in Chapter 4 in relation to the regulation of private bureaucracies – property companies and employers. It takes on a somewhat different complexion with respect to state bureaucracies because presumably as arms of the state the latter should be more disposed to obey the law. Putting to one side matters such as the need for a clear definition of legislative policy and for adequate resources for law enforcement, this part of the chapter is concerned with the extent to which law and the legal system can mould the behaviour of social welfare bureaucracies. Although the points that will be made relate generally to social welfare bureaucracies, the particular focus is on social welfare bureaucracies providing public services. Considered in turn are the role of the courts, of non-curial mechanisms for external review such as tribunals and the ombudsman, of regulation, and of internal bureaucratic procedures. There then follows a case-study of the legal responses to homelessness.

The role of the courts : institutional limits

The role of the courts in this area is limited for both constitutional and institutional reasons. At the constitutional level, there are limits to what the courts can do in a democratic society in impugning the actions of social welfare bureaucracies. While courts can bend legal doctrine, they do not have a completely free hand to ignore precedent or to develop new remedies in respect of administrative action. Even when acting within these parameters, however, there are institutional reasons why courts are not especially effective in controlling bureaucratic activity. The courts are reactive institutions and there needs to be someone with sufficient initiative, adequate resources and the requisite *locus standi* to invoke legal procedures. The litigant must then couch the claim in acceptable legal form. The grounds on which the courts interfere with administrative action are relatively wide.[56] But there are institutional limits to what a court can do if it does intervene. Litigation involving the relatively straightforward interpretation of a statutory provision is poles apart from that involving complicated issues of fact. The latter takes considerable time and effort and there is greater scope for distinguishing by later courts. In deciding on a particular interpretation of social legislation, a court might not fully appreciate the policies behind it. Judges are not always ideal for this task, if only because they tend not to specialize in particular types of litigation to build up a full picture of what social policy is. There are also limits to the courts' capacity to calculate costs and benefits in such matters, to decide the moral issues of preferring certain persons and groups over other persons and groups, and to engage in executive action themselves or to direct public expenditure in particular directions.

Even if a court grants a remedy, a successful litigant depends on the social welfare bureaucracy against which it is directed being willing to comply. Quite apart from subverting a court order indirectly, a social welfare bureaucracy might be able to convince the legislature to overturn it. Judicial remedies are relatively effective if they require a bureaucracy to perform (or to cease to perform) a single act, but in many situations the activities of a social welfare bureaucracy will only be redirected with continuous supervision over an extended period. This the courts, lacking the executive machinery, are less capable of undertaking. An illustration is the contrast between an injunction to prevent demolition of particular houses by a housing authority and an order that they be adequately renovated. None of this is to deny that litigation can have a useful political function: it might impose unacceptable delays on a social welfare bureaucracy, making it willing to compromise, or it might attract publicity to the behaviour of a particular social welfare bureaucracy, whether or not the case is won and whether if won it is a useful precedent for further claims. If sufficient discussion is generated around the issue involved in litigation, the political pressure on a social welfare bureaucracy might be such that it will vary its policy whatever the outcome of the litigation.

The role of the courts : doctrinal aspects

Many lawyers in the early part of the century did not take kindly to the growth of the welfare state. At least on the surface they did not object to the provision of public services *per se*, but rather to the growth of executive government and the arbitrary decision-making that was said to be associated with it. In fact, the remedy which those such as Dicey or Lord Chief Justice Hewart proposed to the growth of executive government seems to have included the repeal of much social legislation.

Roberts v. *Hopwood*[57] in 1925 epitomized this atttitude, for there the House of Lords upheld a decision of a district auditor to disallow and surcharge the members of the Poplar Borough Council for paying a minimum wage to its lowest grade of manual workers. The legislation enabled local authorities to pay their employees what they thought fit, and the council had maintained the minimum wage despite a fall in the cost of living. In spite of the contrary views of two distinguished judges in the Court of Appeal, Scrutton and Atkin L.JJ., the House of Lords held that the payment of the minimum wage was an unreasonable exercise of the discretion conferred on it. Parliament eventually remitted the surcharges.[58] Subsequently, the judges seem generally to have accepted similar measures. For example, in 1944 a court overturned a district auditor's order to disallow and surcharge Birmingham City councillors for paying children's allowances to council staff to help them meet increases in the cost of living. The court held that the amounts were not unreasonable and rejected claims that they were not genuinely wages and that the council had taken into account irrelevant considerations.[59] Then in 1982 the Divisional Court refused to interfere with a decision of a Labour council to make a local settlement with its striking manual workers, even though the terms of that settlement were more favourable to the workers than were those of a national settlement subsequently reached. The court held that there was no evidence that the authority had acted unreasonably, especially given that the strike had disrupted vital social services and was also causing hardship to commercial consumers.[60]

There have been occasional decisions, however, in line with the *Roberts* v. *Hopwood* decision, in relation to public services. Each of the decisions involved the courts overturning policies of local authorities. Although couched in terms of the legality of administrative action, the decisions contain competing notions of distributional equity and economic efficiency. In 1954 *Prescott* v. *Birmingham Corp.*[61] involved a local authority deciding to provide free travel for the elderly on its public transport. The legislation empowered the local authority to charge passengers what it thought fit, but a ratepayer succeeded in obtaining a declaration that the scheme was illegal. The Court of Appeal held that although the legislation gave the local authority a wide discretion, it was implicit that the undertaking was to be run substantially as a business rather than as a social service and that free travel constituted a gift to a particular section of the community in breach of the fiduciary duty to ratepayers. Following the decision, Parliament validated such travel concessions.[62] Similarly, in 1960 the Divisional Court held that a local authority was acting unreasonably in the rents it was charging for certain housing. The authority had wide discretion under the relevant legislation and purported to exercise it to shield its tenants from higher rents. Nonetheless, Parker L.C.J. (with whom the others agreed) held that the authority's decision was purely arbitrary, whether it was policy or politics, because it was inconsistent with the authority's duties to its ratepayers.[63] More recently, the House of Lords held, in the *G.L.C. case*, that the Greater London Council acted *ultra vires* and in breach of its fiduciary duty to ratepayers with regard to a reduction of fares by the London Transport Executive.[64] The G.L.C. was acting in accordance with its election manifesto of reducing fares. The House of Lords held that the L.T.E. was obliged to conduct its operations on ordinary business principles and therefore it and the G.L.C. were acting *ultra vires* in relation to the fare reduction. (Interestingly, Lord Diplock disagreed on this point.) The breach of fiduciary duty which the House of Lords discovered occurred because the loss of fares had to be made up from the rates and because the policy resulted in a loss of rate-support grant.

At the present there is some flux in administrative law, as judges seem increasingly prepared to stretch established doctrines to review certain types of administrative decision-making. In particular, there is a developing area of law in which social welfare bureaucracies may be liable to pay damages for loss caused through negligent administrative action. This includes the provision of services. The parameters of such liability are ill-defined, as the courts work out the balance between the need to compensate individuals who have suffered loss and the capacity of state bureaucracies to spread losses, on the one hand, and the desirability of not interfering with the exercise of administrative discretion at the policy level (especially given limited resources) and of avoiding a multiplicity of suits, on the other.[65]

Breach of statutory duty, irrespective of fault, may also enable a person suffering loss to sue a social welfare bureaucracy for damages. To succeed in such a case the courts have said that it must be established that the legislation intended to recognize such an action. Indicia used to infer this include whether the statute itself provides a separate remedy; whether the statute protects the public generally and not the class of persons of which the plaintiff is one; and whether the common law, independent of statute, contains an adequate remedy. In practice the search for legislative intention can be tortuous and the judges have considerable discretion. Sometimes they apply the test in a mechanistic way without investigating the underlying policy considerations. Claims for damages under the Housing (Homeless Persons) Act 1977 – discussed later in this chapter – are an example of this type of claim. *Wyatt* v. *Hillingdon L.B.C.* (1978)[66] is another example. A disabled person claimed damages from the local authority for negligence and/or breach of statutory duty in failing to meet her need for adequate home help or to provide practical assistance to her in her home. Under section 29 of the National Assistance Act 1948, a local authority had power to make arrangements for promoting the welfare of the disabled, and in relation to persons ordinarily resident in the area it 'shall, to such extent as the Minister may direct, be under a duty to exercise their powers under this section'. Section 2 of the Chronically Sick and Disabled Persons Act 1970 provided that it was the duty of a local authority to provide home help, meals, etc., where it was satisfied that this was necessary to meet the needs of a disabled person. The Court of Appeal held that the plaintiff did not have a cause of action because the National Assistance Act 1948 contained a specific provision for central government to take default action in the event of a local authority failing to perform its duty. In his judgment (with which Eveleigh L.J. agreed), Geoffrey Lane L.J. set out the policy considerations in stark terms:

It seems to me that a statute such as this which is dealing with the distribution of benefits – or, to put it perhaps more accurately, comforts to the sick and disabled – does not in its very nature give rise to an action by the disappointed sick person. It seems to me quite extraordinary that if the local authority, as is alleged here, provided, for example, two hours less home help than the sick person considered herself entitled to that that can amount to a breach of statutory duty which will permit the sick person to claim a sum of monetary damages by way of breach of statutory duty. It seems to me that eminently that is the sort of situation where precisely the remedy provided by section 36 of the Act of 1948 is appropriate and an action in damages is not appropriate.[67]

The *Wyatt* reasoning is in line with a long line of authority that the legislature intends to exclude judicial remedies when it makes an administrative or political remedy available.[68] There are defects to this reasoning: first, the legislature's intention is divined artificially for it depends simply on whether there is an alternative remedy; and secondly, an administrative or political remedy is not necessarily on all fours with a judicial remedy in that the former might not compensate individuals for loss suffered through past breaches. In terms of policy, however, compensation for administrative action is best dealt with by way of specific statutory provision rather than by judge-made remedies.

The political nature of the issue is sometimes justification for the courts refusing to act in relation to administrative action. In 1979 in *R. v. Secretary of State for Social Services, ex p. Hincks*[69] a consultant and four of his patients claimed that the Secretary of State, a regional health authority and an area health authority were all in breach of statutory duty by planning to use converted huts for a hospital. They sought a court order that the Secretary of State should reconsider tenders, taking into account the urgent need for hospital beds. Section 3 of the National Health Service Act 1977 imposed a duty on the Secretary of State, which could be delegated, to provide 'to such extent as he considers necessary to meet all reasonable requirements . . . hospital accommodation'. Wien J. rejected the plaintiffs' claim that they had a *prima facie* case for breach of statutory duty, since there were other channels provided in the 1977 Act for aggrieved persons to make complaint – through Community Health Councils and the Health Service Ombudsman. Wien J. gave two additional reasons: first, the allocation of funds to any particular area of social need was *prima facie* a political rather than judicial matter, since ultimately it was a question of how much taxation should be levied and how taxes should be spent; and secondly, it was impossible for the courts to define the duty to provide hospital facilities when science is constantly changing priorities.

The argument for judicial restraint is not, however, as clear-cut as Wien J. suggests; much depends on the nature of the issue. In *Hincks* itself what was at stake was not whether a new hospital should be built but whether the Secretary of State should reconsider tenders. Indeed in many situations a claim that a public authority has not complied with its statutory duty will not involve any significant public expenditure, for it will be a claim by an individual that a particular service ought to be provided to him or her – a claim by a disabled person for adequate homehelp, equipment, etc., by a homeless family for accommodation, and so on. Ultimately, significant public expenditure would be required if everyone in a similar position to the plaintiff made a successful claim. As we have seen at various points, however, there are very real social and economic barriers to individuals instituting litigation.

The justification for judicial restraint wears thin when judges are willing to intervene in some cases but not in others which seem comparable.[70] *Meade* v. *Haringey L.B.C.*,[71] also in 1979, is an interesting contrast with the *Hincks* case. There the local authority announced the closure of its schools because of a strike by caretakers and similar workers. A parent sought to compel the local authority to open the schools, on the basis that under section 8 of the Education Act 1944 it was under a duty to secure that there were sufficient schools available in the area for full-time education. The Secretary of State had already refused to make an order under section 99 of the Act for the authority to discharge its duty. In contradistinction to the established approach, the Court of Appeal held that the default power in section 99 did not exclude the courts from granting a remedy. The claim, it held, was not for failure to perform a statutory duty but for relief against positive and/or *ultra vires* activity. Both Lord Denning M.R. and Sir Stanley Rees thought that there was a case to answer that the local authority was acting *ultra vires* by working in collusion with, or at the behest of, the trade unions, or from improper motives of sympathy with the strikers. The fact is, however, that the approach of the judges was very influenced by the circumstances of the case. Ultimately Eveleigh L.J. and Sir Stanley Rees held by majority that the judge at first instance was right not to have granted an interlocutory mandatory injunction because the issue of whether the local authority had acted properly could only be determined at trial.

Non-curial external review

Creating non-curial mechanisms for the external review of decisions of social welfare bureaucracies has proceeded under various guises. The matter has been discussed in relation to social welfare benefits; it repays brief consideration in the present context. A great deal of attention has been directed to tribunals: granted that the courts are inappropriate, the argument runs, why not establish simpler bodies, although along roughly the same lines, which can respond to complaints cheaply, quickly, flexibly, and in an informal and inquisitorial manner? In *Justice in the Welfare State*, Street saw tribunals as the unique and valuable contribution of English law to the welfare state, at the same time pointing to needed improvements in their operation such as reduced delay.[72] There has been some argument for a general tribunal to which administrative matters can be appealed, along the lines of the French *Conseil d'Etat*. Australia has gone some way towards this at the federal level with the Administrative Appeals Tribunal.

A major breakthrough in relation to external review has been the adoption of the Ombudsman concept, in which an independent official can investigate fully and report upon complaints about government administration. The powers of some Ombudsmen are limited, however: for example, complaints might have to be routed through an MP; there are situations which the Ombudsman might not be able to investigate; the Ombudsman might not be able to release decisions to the press; and perhaps most importantly, the Ombudsman might only be able to act in cases of maladministration and not be able to question decisions on their merits or decisions made according to decided policy. In handling social welfare matters, Ombudsmen have found maladministration in cases involving delay, mislaid files, lost letters, errors in calculating benefit, misleading advice, misleading leaflets, failure to inform complainants about decisions, misdirection of letters, lack of liaison within a department, and disclosure of confidential information by mistake.[73] In addition, some Ombudsmen go beyond such breaches of conventional administrative practice to require social welfare bureaucracies to take the initiative to inform potential recipients of new or modified benefits or services. In the area of services, Ombudsmen have dealt with matters such as the failure of a public-housing authority to repair, the allocation of public housing, the refusal of accommodation to the homeless, and the failure to explain to local residents their rights to compensation in the event of slum clearance.[74]

There may be other procedures enabling external review. Small claims courts and community justice centres operate in some jurisdictions, and there are other comparatively recent developments such as public complaints boards and public advocacy services.[75] A well-established procedure in England is that the public can raise objections in the course of the audit of a local authority's accounts, which can ultimately lead to court action; a local government elector can also request the Audit Commission to order an extraordinary audit of an authority's accounts.[76] As we saw in the previous section, the audit method (or at least earlier variants) has been used in the past to oppose social welfare expenditure. However, public-interest groups have used the procedure, for example to challenge the demolition and gutting of resumed housing when it could have been used for short-life accommodation.[77] As with the courts, these non-curial mechanisms still rely on individuals taking the initiative, and a point made throughout this book is that many are inhibited in this respect.[78] That does not mean, however that the mechanisms are worthless – many invoke them and they may also have a deterrent effect on bureaucratic activity.

Regulation

While not denying the importance of external review, the regulatory approach sees as crucial the need for institutionalized control over bureaucratic behaviour. Institutionalized control ranges from the enactment of legislation, coupled with the anticipation that a social welfare bureaucracy will comply with it, through to the establishment of a separate bureaucracy to monitor a social welfare bureaucracy in the performance of its tasks. The effectiveness of legislation as a control mechanism turns on how much discretion is entrusted to a social welfare bureaucracy, whether the legislation is precise in its goals, whether it is easily understood by the officials implementing it, and whether there are sanctions supporting it. These factors are not necessarily compatible: for instance, detailed provisions to limit discretion might make matters so complex as to be self-defeating. For this and other reasons some discretion is necessary when social welfare bureaucracies administer services, just as it is when they administer benefits or enforce legal controls over private institutions. But too much discretion can lead social welfare bureaucracies to act on considerations other than those embodied in the legislation and to make decisions which are incorrect.

A more sophisticated method of controlling the activities of social welfare bureaucracies is through the establishment of inspectorates. These prod bureaucracies to meet the standards set by law as well as to adopt the best practices for doing so. Inspectorates may also have the legal power to apply sanctions against errant social welfare bureaucracies. One further step is that if people complain to them, they have the power to direct the relevant social welfare bureaucracy to act if satisfied that the complaint is well founded.[79] A particular type of inspectorate is that conducting audits of expenditure. As well as the cost, other objections to inspectorates are that they infringe the autonomy of social welfare bureaucracies, especially if these are at a different level of government, and that they do not have firsthand experience of the problems involved in providing services.

One dimension of the effectiveness of social legislation is the nature of the social welfare bureaucracy entrusted to administer it. *A priori*, a large social welfare bureaucracy, working mainly at field level, is not especially susceptible to control. However, it may be that lower-level decisions can be channelled by making the provision of services automatic on relatively simple criteria being satisfied. The problem of control is compounded to the extent that the service being administered is technically or legally complex, for it then becomes difficult to establish that it is not being properly administered. This is not to suggest that social welfare bureaucracies are monolithic: they comprise conflicting interests, and if some interests support legislation they might be able to ensure that it is implemented by using their authority if they are senior in the hierarchy, or by using their strategic position if they are down the line.

An important obstacle to the implementation of social welfare legislation is that often a central government acts not directly but by entrusting tasks to local, provincial or state governments. A popular view has been that whatever legal discretion such governments have under the central government statute, they are largely servants of the central government because of their financial dependence on it. But the differences in the services provided by different local, provincial and state governments belie the argument that each automatically implements central government policy. The differences can sometimes be attributed to party-political factors, with local, provincial and state governments controlled by left-wing parties extending services but right-wing governments keeping them to a minimum. Often the reality is not as clear-cut, for there are other factors such as the attitudes of key politicians which may be in conflict with the philosophy of their political party, the behaviour of local, provincial or state bureaucracies and their key officers, and the wealth of an area. Central domination is limited by the fact that local, provincial and state governments can call on political resources such as rhetoric ('central domination') and the support of locally based pressure groups. No matter how fictitious an electoral mandate might be, it can confer a legitimacy on what local, provincial and state governments do, even where this involves a failure to implement the law.[80]

Legally, even if local, provincial and state governments are bound to implement central legislation, its wording may be ambiguous, and in any event litigation to enforce it could be associated with considerable delay or with serious pitfalls.[81] As previously mentioned, central government might be able to use its control over finance to have local, provincial or state governments adopt its policies on social welfare matters.[82] Where finance is not determinative, however, the political and administrative costs of using forms of direct legal intervention, such as default powers, are high, and their use is relatively uncommon. An example was discussed in Chapter 2 – the imprisonment of the Poplar councillors in 1921 because of their failure to adopt central government policy on poor-law relief. A more recent case was when the Clay Cross local authority declined to implement the Housing Finance Act 1972, because it meant higher rents for council housing. The local authority justified its stand by claiming that it was elected on its housing policies. Its refusal was in keeping with its strong socialist approach to the provision of public services – it provided free milk for schoolchildren, free television licences to pensioners, had a policy of municipalizing privately rented housing, and so on. As a result of the Clay Cross action, the Secretary of State declared it to be in default, but instead of proceeding immediately to appoint a housing commissioner, directed that the district auditor conduct an extraordinary audit. The district auditor surcharged the councillors on the basis that the housing revenue account carried a loss through their negligence or misconduct in failing to bring the 1972 Act into operation. The legality of this action was upheld by the courts, which also gave short shrift to the councillors' argument that they were acting in accordance with their moral duties and severely castigated them for defying the Act.[83] As a result the councillors were disqualified from office and a housing commissioner was appointed. Nonetheless, the incident demonstrates the hurdles facing a central government when a local, provincial or state government sets out to defy its social welfare legislation. Even though central government finally succeeded, the upshot of the Clay Cross action was that 10,000 people avoided paying the increased rents for a year and a half. Moreover, it was really local government reorganization, rather than the disqualification of the councillors, which finally overcame the Clay Cross opposition.[84]

The procedural approach

The final approach to making a social welfare bureaucracy comply with its legal duties involves changing its procedures. In the context of services, the aims are to enhance the competence of its clientele to claim a service, to ensure that officials implement legislative policy, and to facilitate complaints by those who think they have been unfairly treated. The first aspect includes the familiar problems of maximizing take-up by publicizing services and advising people about rights and benefits. Law has some role here in imposing the obligation on a social welfare bureaucracy not simply to provide a service but to furnish persons with information about it. In addition, a certain amount can be done administratively by simplifying procedures and treating a service as a right. Many social welfare services fail on both counts, for example imposing a heavy burden on applicants to verify their means. There is a greater chance of legislative policy being implemented if it is integrated into the everyday practices of officials, to capitalize on their tendency to treat work as a set of procedures – as a number of stages in a process. Routinization in this manner requires senior officials to think through the steps necessary to implement legislative policy, to incorporate them in training programmes and standard operating procedures, and to revise these constantly in the light of experience. With regard to complaints, steps have been taken within some social welfare bureaucracies to establish easily accessible internal grievance machinery through which decisions can be challenged and entitlements to individual services pursued. While lacking the independence of external review, such grievance machinery has the advantages of cheapness and speed.

There are limits to the amount of bureaucratic structuring which can be undertaken to facilitate the provision of services. Legislation might not be sufficiently adequate in design to be operationalized in its bureaucratic context. The nature of the service being provided might impose boundaries to effectiveness: a simple illustration is that the take-up rate of rent subsidies in the private sector will never equal that in the public sector, for, in the case of the latter, public-housing authorities can link the payment of subsidies with the collection of rent.[85] The focus on procedures might mean that the substance of official action is neglected; in other words, a balance must be struck between procedures as ends and procedures as means to an end.

Further, it seems doubtful whether procedural reforms within social welfare bureaucracies can fully protect legal rights or guard against bureaucratic arbitrariness. Generally speaking, the beneficiaries of social welfare services are the least 'legally competent', so that information about a service might not reach them or they might not take advantage of grievance mechanisms. What is needed is for social welfare bureaucracies to act in an affirmative manner, encouraging the maximum response by affected groups and interests and attempting to raise their 'legal competence'.[86]

A case-study of homelessness

Each of the methods for controlling social welfare bureaucracies outlined – the courts, non-curial external review, regulation, and restructuring internal procedures – have limitations. Among these are that external review operates in a sporadic manner and assumes that individuals can take the initiative; that the regulation of social welfare bureaucracies often faces political and practical difficulties; and that the restructuring of internal procedures might not work if the relevant bureaucracy opposes it. The legal response in Britain to providing housing for the homeless illustrates some of these points. After some preliminary remarks, this section concentrates on the Housing (Homeless Persons) Act 1977. From a legal viewpoint this legislation is well in advance of that in other jurisdictions, where public authorities still have enormous discretion as to whether they will provide accommodation for those in need.[87]

The boundaries of homelessness can be drawn narrowly to cover those literally without shelter (or even those 'sleeping rough' within the terms of vagrancy legislation). The approach of some housing charities is to define all those in inadequate housing as homeless – inadequate in the legal sense of being unfit, overcrowded or a nuisance, or inadequate in the broader social sense because ordinary family life is impossible. The legal definition of homelessness in the Housing (Homeless Persons) Act 1977 is having no accommodation or having accommodation which one cannot secure entry to, occupation of which would probably lead to violence from someone residing in it, or which is such (e.g. a caravan) that there is no place to put it. Under the Act, being threatened with homelessness – defined as being likely to become homeless within twenty-eight days – is put on the same plane as homelessness itself. Thus, those in temporary accommodation can be homeless under the Act, such as women in refuges.[88] Clearly the number of applicants under the Act is no indication of the full extent of homelessness, because people might never apply but continue to live under intolerable strain (e.g. with relatives, or in short-life accommodation), or if they do apply might not be accepted by a particular local authority as being homeless. The main causes of officially recorded homelessness seem to be eviction by landlords, rent arrears (a common cause in public housing), mortgage default (in the case of owner-occupiers) and marital disputes.[89] Behind these immediate causes are more fundamental factors such as the decline in the amount of cheap rental accommodation, the shortage of public housing, the policies of public-housing authorities (on rent arrears or allocation priorities), and the general mismatch of housing needs and resources (alongside the homeless are those with second homes). A particular consequence of homelessness, raising legal issues, is that social welfare authorities sometimes take the children of homeless parents into care.[90]

Relief of homelessness under the Old poor law sometimes took the form of providing accommodation in cottages built specifically for this purpose. Cottages were also erected by parishes from bequests to the poor.[91] Legally, poor-law authorities had wide discretion as to how they would provide poor relief and did not have to be greatly concerned about the homeless. Needless to say there were few legal proceedings taken against poor-law authorities for failing in their duty, although in *R.* v. *Wetherill*[92] in 1784 two parish officers were indicted for lodging several poor persons in grossly inadequate accommodation. Under the New poor law of the nineteenth century, the homeless might be offered institutionalized accommodation in the harsh and deterrent environment of a workhouse.[93] Limited regulation came in the form of legislation, continued into the twentieth century, which obliged local authorities to provide such accommodation for the casual poor as the central authorities considered necessary.[94]

The turning point in relation to regulation came with the abolition of the poor law by the National Assistance Act 1948. Part III of that Act placed a duty on local authorities to provide temporary accommodation for those urgently in need of it owing to circumstances which they could not reasonably have foreseen, or in such other circumstances as the local authority determined in a particular case.[95] Under the Act, local authorities were to exercise the function of providing temporary accommodation under the general guidance of central government, which subsequently issued a number of circulars on the matter. Following an amendment to the Act in 1972, a court held that local authorities were entitled to establish their own criteria for homelessness, at variance with those established by central government.[96] Throughout the whole period many local authorities ignored their legal obligations or provided quite unsuitable accommodation.[97] They justified their obduracy on the grounds that it prevented queue-jumping for public housing; that it kept down rent arrears among public-housing tenants; that it discouraged problem families and outsiders trying to usurp the rights of local residents; and that a more generous policy was financially impracticable. More importantly, central government did virtually nothing to enforce the legal obligations of local authorities: successive governments abstained from using their default powers, and apparently the National Assistance Board used its statutory power only once to require a local authority to provide accommodation in a case of urgent need.[98]

The present obligation of housing authorities is set out in section 4 of the Housing (Homeless Persons) Act 1977:

If a housing authority are satisfied . . . that a person who has applied to them for accommodation or for assistance in obtaining accommodation is homeless or threatened with homelessness, they shall be subject to a duty towards him under this section . . . (5) Where – (a) they are satisfied – (i) that he is homeless, and (ii) that he has a priority need, but (b) they are not satisfied that he became homeless intentionally, their duty . . . is to secure that accommodation becomes available for his occupation.

Where persons do not have a priority need or are intentionally homeless, housing authorities need merely furnish 'advice and appropriate assistance'; if they are satisfied as to priority need, but are also satisfied that homelessness was intentional, they need provide accommodation only for a period which gives applicants a reasonable opportunity to find accommodation themselves.[99] Housing authorities, to whom application has been made, can transfer responsibility to another housing authority if the applicant and any person properly residing with him do not have a local connection with the area, they have a connection with the other area, and they do not run the risk of domestic violence in that area.[100] Moreover, housing authorities may perform their duty to secure that accommodation becomes available by making it available themselves, by securing that the applicants obtain it from another person, or by giving them such advice and assistance as will secure that they obtain it from some other person.[101] A Code of Guidance fills in many gaps in the Act: although the Act says that local authorities shall have regard to the Code in carrying out their functions, the Court of Appeal has held that it is not legally binding.[102]

What impact has the regime of regulation provided by the Act had on the behaviour of housing authorities? Overall, authorities have housed more homeless people following the Act. But while some authorities have implemented the Act, as confirming their own practices or as providing an opportunity to rationalize procedures, and a few have gone beyond it (e.g. by accepting the intentionally homeless), some have construed their obligations narrowly.[103] The latter have been able to do this for various reasons. First, the legislation itself creates opportunities for avoidance by using terms such as 'intentionally homeless' and 'local connection', and by omitting to mention matters such as the standard of accommodation to be provided. Consequently, some local authorities have accepted homeless people but have deliberately used low-standard accommodation as a deterrent.[104] These loopholes exist because the Act was a compromise between those who wanted a greater commitment to the homeless and others who feared that any measure was going too far. Secondly, community attitudes are not uniformly supportive of the sentiments underlying the Act. There is a strong view that many of the homeless are culpable and do not deserve help. Accusations have also been made that some people have become homeless to jump the queue for public housing – although this assumes that those qualifying under the Act are in competition for the same type of accommodation as ordinary applicants – and there is a fear of abuse by those not in genuine need. Assisting the homeless is seen as acting at the expense of those on a waiting list and of 'good tenants' in poor-quality public housing. To an extent these attitudes are reinforced by the Act, which introduces notions of blameworthiness in its provisions on priority need and intentional homelessness, and which creates several offences suggesting that applicants will commit abuses unless threatened with criminal prosecution.[105] Thirdly, the Act has not been associated with any increase in public finance to provide for the homeless. Instead of attempting to change behaviour by the inducement of financial aid, or the threat of aid being withdrawn, the Act relies on regulation to achieve its ends. Yet one finding of a study of 150 housing authorities in England and Wales was that the ability to respond to homelessness was as important as the willingness to implement the Act.[106] No doubt much can be done if authorities use existing resources more efficiently, such as short-life property, and invoke existing powers such as that to rate empty property, thereby giving owners an incentive to rent.[107] Finally, the Act does not contain a method by which central government could enforce it if it wanted. Local authorities must have regard under section 12 to any guidance given by central government, but this requirement cannot be enforced and there is nothing equivalent to the default powers in the National Assistance Act 1948.

Since central government has limited itself to using moral suasion, those wishing to see the Act implemented have had to take the initiative themselves. The courts have had a role in this regard, although groups such as SHELTER have used other devices such as media publicity and research reports. The Act does not create a direct appellate procedure when homeless persons are denied accommodation, but in certain cases it is possible to challenge adverse decisions in the courts on ordinary principles of administrative law. In this regard the Act gives some assistance since, under section 8, local authorities must state their reasons for denying accommodation under the Act. Before 1982, a popular method of challenging adverse decisions was by means of a homeless person seeking damages for breach of statutory duty. The leading decision, *Thornton* v. *Kirklees M.B.C.* (1979),[108] applied previous authority that where an Act imposes a duty on a public authority for the benefit of a specified category of persons, but prescribes no special remedy for its breach, a civil action for damages will normally lie. Despite the practical difficulties in establishing the existence and breach of statutory duty, since the Act leaves substantial discretion to housing authorities, a considerable number of claims for damages were successful, although admittedly only small sums were awarded.[109] The story was different as regards injunctions where authorities acted, or were about to act, in breach of their duties under the Act. The Court of Appeal held that interlocutory injunctions should not be granted ordering an authority to provide housing unless a *prima facie* case was made out; this was more onerous than the ordinary balance of convenience test for interlocutory injunctions.[110] Roskill L.J. also disapproved *ex parte* injunctions, even though homelessness is a case where urgent relief is regularly required.[111]

Then in 1982 the House of Lords held in effect that homelessness cases should proceed by judicial review in the High Court and not by claims, including claims for damages, in the county court.[112] The decision, *Cocks* case, was based on the dichotomy said to exist between the public-law and private-law functions of housing authorities under the Act. Supposedly the former are to decide the various matters outlined above (homelessness, priority need, whether intentionally homeless, etc.); the latter only arise if a housing authority decides that it has a duty to house. The House of Lords held that public-law duties can only be challenged on the grounds recognized by administrative law, by way of an application for judicial review in the High Court, not by way of an ordinary action. Among the justifications the House of Lords gave for this, was that the former procedure contains safeguards 'which protect from harassment public authorities on whom Parliament has imposed a duty to make public law decisions. . . .' Commentators have criticized this decision as narrowing the application of judicial review, and as reviving undesirable procedural rigidities to legal action.

Court proceedings have been successful in a number of cases in forcing local authorities to back down from refusing assistance under the Act.[113] But all the drawbacks associated with legal proceedings obtain with actions in relation to the Act. Delay is one – hardly appropriate where a person is homeless and needs immediate housing. Moreover, legal proceedings do not reach certain decisions taken under the Act. For example, separate procedures exist for resolving disputes between authorities over whether a person has a local connection with an area. The procedures call to mind the disputes about settlement under the poor law, since there is no express mention of applicants being able to present their side of the story. Finally, the upshot of the *Cocks* case is to add to the expense of legal action by channelling it into the High Court.

In summary, the Housing (Homeless Persons) Act 1977 establishes a regime of regulation – it purports to impose a duty on housing authorities regarding the homeless. But not all homeless people benefit under the Act, for its substantive provisions reflect the limits to which Parliament could go in the light of resistance by many authorities and of societal attitudes to the homeless. The Act does not establish any mechanism for reviewing the decisions of authorities made under it – whether an inspectorate or a review tribunal – except in the event of inter-authority disputes as to the local connection of applicants. Judicial review is possible on ordinary principles, although the courts have made this more difficult in practice. Possibly this is because of unease on their part as to the underlying social policy of the Act, because of what they see as a flood of cases under it, and because of a belief that housing authorities are making the best of a bad job in meeting the demand for housing. Given the absence of other mechanisms for policing compliance, the approach of the courts enhances yet further the ability of many housing authorities to limit the assistance they provide to the homeless. Some needed little encouragement; their disagreement with the Act's aims was obvious from the outset.

III PARTICIPATION AND SOCIAL WELFARE BUREAUCRACIES

So far the discussion of controlling social welfare bureaucracies to overcome the paradox outlined in part I of the chapter has revolved around relatively conventional measures – external review, regulation and internal procedures. Clearly there are associated steps to make social welfare bureaucracies more accountable. Obliging administrators to give reasons for their decisions – a popular tool of the law reformer – might have a salutary effect if a standard practice cannot be justified. Opening bureaucratic decision-making to greater public scrutiny through freedom-of-information legislation has the potential to foster a body of informed opinion which can critically evaluate administrative action. Creative use of planning, evaluation and research staffs within a social welfare bureaucracy, and making more information available to a bureaucracy's constituents, are other measures.

On its face, participation of the clientele of a social welfare bureaucracy in its operation is more radical than any of these since it might entail the transfer of power from officials to those in whose interests they supposedly act. Participation as a concept grows out of the perceived failure of the traditional political, bureaucratic and legal machinery to control decision-making and to provide ordinary people with influence over those decisions. Participation is discussed generally in this part, but with particular reference to social welfare bureaucracies providing services.

The concept of participation

Practical difficulties arise in designing participation for social welfare bureaucracies. Obvious difficulties concern the extent of participation, the manner in which it should take place, and the purpose for which it should exist. Clearly, mass participation in policy formulation is impractical and some method needs to be devised for representation of the public.

The most representative delegates would seem to be the most directly chosen – election would thus seem preferable to choice by existing decision-makers. Another factor is whether delegates need to be descriptively representative in terms of having the same characteristics as those being represented. Is it objectionable, for example, if community lawyers represent social welfare recipients, residents in a deprived neighbourhood or public-housing tenants? One of the main failings of participation in the Australian Assistance Plan was that the representatives were relatively mainstream, those already involved in voluntary organizations and civic activities, rather than persons who had experienced social welfare at first hand.[114] If representatives are to act in accord with their constituents' interests, do the latter need to know their interests or do these include objective needs which are not expressed or even known about? Then there are the issues of structure and level: should representatives participate in existing structures, exercise delegated power, or sit on specially established representative councils or review committees? Should participation be at the level of major policy-making or where discretion is daily exercised?

Equally important to the design of participation is whether the public has real control over decisions, mere influence, or simply the illusion of power.[115] Partly this is related to the purpose powerholders have in conceding participation: is participation genuine or is it merely token or manipulative, and if genuine, is it intended to reallocate power or simply to acquire information from the public? Participation has been taken up by some politicians and bureaucrats who conceive of it as a means of enhancing their legitimacy which they see threatened by social movements or by criticism that they exercise autonomous power and are not simply implementing the decisions of legislative bodies. Participation might also be a substitute for the allocation of financial resources, or the particular bureaucracy in which participation operates might lack control over the allocation of financial resources. For example, a social welfare bureaucracy at local, provincial or state level might allow participation but depend for its effectiveness on finance from central government or on favourable decisions by financial institutions or the corporate sector.

Participation might also fail because a bureaucracy's clientele lack the capacity to be effective. The problem seems especially acute within the social welfare context, for while there will be representatives with organizing and advocacy skills, to be effective they need ready access to information and to the 'hard' skills of the lawyer, planner, and environmental health officer.[116] For this reason, middle-class groups often reap the advantage of opportunities for participation since they have these skills, or at least access to them through social connections or financial power. Further, the effectiveness of participation might be impaired by the actions of politicians and bureaucrats, who object to incursions on their prerogatives and who adhere to the view that they are the 'representatives' or 'experts' whose role it is to make decisions for others. One strategy they might use is co-option, for the experience is that people can be seduced by the glamour and perquisites of power and thus lose touch with their communities. Arguments supporting opposition to participation are that it threatens the rationality and integrity of bureaucracies, and that it undermines the legitimacy of established institutions and procedures which enable people's voices to be heard in an orderly fashion.[117] Proponents of participation deny that the first is a paramount consideration and that the second is an accurate description of reality. Another objection to participation is that it threatens sound social policy because special interests lack the broader perspective of the public interest.[118] The counter-arguments are that existing procedures allow special interests to triumph, and that participation actually widens the range of interests able to make an input into decision-making.

Participation in practice

Participation has been prominent in the areas of planning (including slum clearance) where it has been the product of various forces, including the desire of some planning authorities to obtain more information to better formulate plans, and demands from some sections of the public to be able to influence the nature of their immediate environment. Legally the scope for public participation in planning decisions is less than what might be thought to exist in the light of the extensive discussions of the matter. In general terms it seems that participation in planning is more concerned with protecting individual property rights than with creating a role for the public at large, and, in as much as the public at large is involved, more with obtaining useful data from them or with informing them about tentative proposals than with enabling them to influence the formulation of plans.[119] As a matter of practice, planning authorities might allow the public to participate at inquiries, even if no legal right to do so exists. But if there is no legal right to participate, third parties are disadvantaged – they might only learn of a planning proposal by chance, and their submissions can be treated as irrelevant or superfluous.[120] Perhaps even more important in limiting participation is that there is generally no provision for third parties to receive assistance as regards its cost. The way participation is structured might also limit its effectiveness: it might occur after plans are formulated and decisions taken; it might only involve one large public meeting in an area; it might be disjointed, so that individuals do not see the connnection between the various stages; and if it covers a large geographic area it will probably not be of great interest to individuals, especially to those in deprived areas who are concerned with the immediate problems of decent housing and liveable conditions.[121]

Participation in planning has not been a great success, in particular for the poorer sections of society. Studies of slum clearance have consistently shown that residents did not know or were misinformed about the clearance process when obviously they would have benefited from constant contact with the authorities about the progress of a scheme.[122] Where there has been an influence it seems to have been more in relation to the timing and scope, rather than to the substance of, planning decisions.[123] The law is partly to blame. For example in Britain there is no obligation that tenants for a month, or less than a month, be notified of a compulsory purchase order.[124] Clearly this has reduced their chances of raising objections, yet they have comprised about three-quarters of the residents of some slum-clearance areas. Administrative practice also plays a part, as evidenced by the way the Housing Act 1974 was interpreted to facilitate a greater degree of public participation in respect of general improvement areas, where it was assumed that owner-occupiers predominated, compared with housing action areas, where the inhabitants were thought more likely to be 'problem' families and individuals.[125] There is also the fact that the poorer sections of society seem to have a limited conception of the efficacy of participation, at least where their interests are not directly at stake.[126] By contrast, property and commercial enterprises are more far-seeing, more motivated and have the financial capacity to participate effectively. Finally, much depends on the attitude of the relevant public authorities, for however generous they might be in allowing participation by the public, it cannot be effective if the crucial decisions are still being made in other forums.

Participation designed specifically for the poorer sections of society came to the fore in the 1960s with the war on poverty in the United States. 'Maximum feasible participation' of the poor in the programmes funded by the Office of Economic Opportunity was mandated by the legislation establishing it.[127] One assessment is that the O.E.O. programmes led to an increase in electoral participation by minorities, and so contributed to the pressure for civil rights' legislation and greater government (but not private) employment for them; another is that the O.E.O. legal services' programme was much more effective in advancing the interests of the poor than maximum feasible participation.[128] As with the American programmes, the Community Development Projects in Britain introduced local residents into their management. In turn the projects attempted to participate in local government decision-making by presenting ideas and attending officers' meetings when permitted. This was in line with their early aims of generating community leadership, promoting better co-ordination of government services, and making these services more responsive. Once the projects began operating, however, they came into conflict with councillors and officials. The projects came to see the concept of participation as an attempt by government to keep its pulse on poor communities and to limit problems such as vandalism and housing disrepair. The projects turned increasingly to working through trade unions and strengthening local community groups.[129]

Public housing has proved a fertile field for proposals for participation. On the one hand, there are those who believe that public-housing tenants should be able to control their own environment as of right, while on the other hand there is the pragmatic view that 'if tenants had a greater say in running an estate, this will often make them more aware of the problems, and at the same time make management more responsive to their needs'.[130] In some jurisdictions participation takes the form of an advisory committee of tenants.[131]

Apart from its lack of executive authority, tenants might not know of its existence or might be opposed to it as doing the housing authority's job or allowing other tenants to interfere in their lives.[132] Another approach is to allow tenant representation on public-authority housing committees.[133] The drawback is that tenants are almost invariably in the minority and without access to sufficient information to be effective. In Britain the Housing Act 1980 requires that housing authorities make arrangements, as they think appropriate, to inform and consult with tenants about housing management matters which will substantially affect them, although the obligation does not extend to consultation about rents and charges.[134] The statutory provision is so broad that consultative arrangements could vary from tenants simply being given access to, or membership of, a local authority advisory panel, to allowing tenants to assist at estate level in framing rules, allocating housing, and influencing expenditure on maintenance, improvements and communal activities. Under the Act, participation is confined to existing tenants, although there are others whose voice ought to be heard on certain matters, for example potential tenants on allocation policy. The most advanced form of participation is for public housing to be handed over to tenants acting through management co-operatives; in practice, this has only occurred to a limited extent.[135]

IV UNIVERSAL PUBLIC SERVICES

Public services fall along a continuum from the specialized to the universal, measured in broad terms by the degree of equality of access. Housing for the homeless is clearly specialized, while public schooling in many countries is universal. For particular services there is a variation between countries: for example, health services are towards the universal end of the continuum in Britain, but in countries such as the United States free health services are confined to specific groups such as the elderly and disadvantaged, with the rest of the population expected to meet the costs of their own health care through insurance.[136]

Equality of access to a public service in law does not mean that it exists in fact: the standard of universal services varies considerably between areas, and where the wealthier utilize a universal service they often use it more than others, frequently because they are more knowledgeable and persistent, but also because they appreciate its value. For example, the National Health Service in Britain fails to provide an adequate primary-care service in some declining urban areas and parts of London, and its existence has not overcome inequalities in health between social classes as measured by mortality and morbidity rates. Moreover, despite its universal and free character there is evidence that high-income groups make better use of it – for instance, even if the disadvantaged consult their medical practitioners more frequently than others, this is less than proportionate to their average degree of sickness.[137] Inequalities in universal services should not be a surprise, for it would be strange if they could be wholly isolated from the general inequalities of society. Inequalities in the level of services can sometimes be explained because the needs are so much greater in, say, inner-city areas. Moreover inequalities are not immutable, given political will and economic resources.[138] In addition, heavy use by the middle class of a universal service can have the desirable consequence of providing constant pressure for more public expenditure on it and for a higher standard in what is provided.

Law has generally not had a central role in making public services more universal. Once political decisions have been made about universality, however, these have been given expression in law. At this point, political, bureaucratic and social factors have undermined the universality enshrined in law.[139] Although the legal system has been used to further the universality required by law, it has also been invoked by conservative political forces opposed to universality. What follows is a brief examination by way of example of the role of law and the legal system in universal primary and secondary education.

The development of universal education

Lawson and Silver comment: 'Working-class and middle-class education in the nineteenth century had clear identities. They were separated by different curricula, length of school life, attendance rates and cultural and social objectives.'[140] Legislation in many societies has since provided for a system of free and compulsory primary schooling: corresponding to the statutory duty of education authorities to provide this, is the legal duty on parents to ensure school attendance.[141] Private education has generally been allowed to continue under such legislation.[142]

In the United States there has been a massive expansion of public secondary education: as Janowitz argues, public education has been the central component of the American notion of the welfare state, 'the idea that through public education both personal betterment and national, social and economic development would take place'.[143] Elsewhere, universal secondary education has been much slower to develop. For example in England a system of state secondary education was instituted under the Education Act 1902; test-case litigation was one factor behind it.[144] Until well into the twentieth century, however, it remained a middle-class preserve since attendence depended on financial capacity as well as ability. After the Education Act 1944 schooling at both primary and secondary stages became free and compulsory to the minimum school-leaving age. However, most local authorities continued to operate differentiated secondary schooling (grammar, secondary modern and technical), permissible under the 1944 Act. Comprehensive schooling – the pattern, in the main, in places such as the United States and Australia – was seen by reformers as one way of overcoming the class basis of education. Labour-controlled local authorities began to introduce it at their own initiative, and in 1965 the Labour Government invited local authorities which had not done so to draw up plans voluntarily for its adoption.

In the United States the courts have been centre-stage in attempts to expand equality of opportunity in education for blacks. Unfortunately that strategy has not been especially effective, for a number of reasons:

The contrast to Britain in the reform implementation efforts of the 1970s lies in the fact that the main burden of seeking to remedy school segregation was thrust on the courts and the judicial process. Limits to the efficiency of that strategy have become apparent. If federal courts decide to extend remedy, they lack the administrative machinery to effectively design and supervise mass desegregation plans. . . . Finally the veto power and terms of Supreme Court justices tend to make the anti-reform influence of a judge like Justice Rehnquist potentially much stronger than that of a short-term Conservative Education minister like Mrs Margaret Thatcher.[145]

The courts have had only a tangential influence in other jurisdictions. In Britain, parents opposed to comprehensive education have invoked their aid on a few occasions; in some cases they have been successful.[146] For example in 1967, the Court of Appeal granted an injunction against the conversion of eight schools to comprehensives in Enfield, London. The Court held that the changes showed an intention on the part of the authority to 'cease to maintain' existing schools and to 'establish new schools' in the terms of section 13 of the Education Act, and that accordingly the authority should have fulfilled a statutory requirement of giving notice as to the changes.[147] Enfield attempted to circumvent the decision in relation to one of the schools by simply resolving that all pupils who had completed a course of primary education had *ipso facto* attained a sufficient standard for admission, thereby avoiding the argument that it had ceased to maintain the school. An injunction again issued, on the grounds that the revised scheme for admission was in breach of one of the articles of government of the school.[148] Then a majority of governors of the school, in agreement with the authority's proposals, purported to vary the articles, but Donaldson J. issued a declaration that the time allowed for making representations about the change was too short and was thus in breach of the Act.[149] The articles were later amended, although the introduction of the comprehensives was delayed when the Conservatives won local elections.

The intervention of the courts in 1976 in the leading *Tameside* decision[150] was a significant interruption to the adoption of comprehensive education. There the Secretary of State had approved a plan submitted by the Tameside Council when it was controlled by the Labour Party to introduce comprehensive schooling. Following the success of the Conservative Party at local elections, the Tameside Council approved the plan but resolved to postpone the transformation of the existing schools. The Secretary of State directed the council to implement the whole plan on the basis that not to do so would cause disruption and uncertainty. The Secretary purported to act under section 68 of the Education Act 1944, which enabled him to give directions to a local authority when satisfied that it had acted unreasonably. The Divisional Court granted mandamus to enforce the Secretary's direction, but both the Court of Appeal and the House of Lords (which decided the issue just a week after the Court of Appeal) held that the Secretary's decision was unlawful. The legal basis for the decision was that under the Act the Secretary could not give a direction unless satisfied that no reasonable authority would act in the particular manner. Either the Secretary had misdirected himself on the correct question to determine the matter, or if he had applied the correct approach could not have been satisfied in the circumstances that the council was acting unreasonably. Underlying the decision was the importance the judges attached to the Conservative Party victory at the local elections, in which their attitude to comprehensive education was said to have played an important part. This overlooks the difficulty of giving any content to the concept of an electoral mandate when voters choose between parties espousing a plethora of policies The *Tameside* decision has been roundly criticized by many as being blatantly political. Others such as Lord Devlin generally supported the decision but thought that the House of Lords might have strayed too far into the realm of the administrator in the extent to which it interfered with the Minister's view of the facts.[151] Finally, in 1980, a Conservative Secretary of State approved the proposals of the by then Labour local authority to impose a wholly comprehensive system. Meanwhile, the Conservative Government had repealed the compulsion on local authorities to go comprehensive with its Education Act 1979.[152]

V CONCLUSION

Social welfare bureaucracies which are ostensibly to assist with the problems facing their clientele have become part of the problem – what I have called the paradox of social welfare bureaucracies. Thus, specialized public services, directed to those such as public-housing tenants, have acted on occasions in an unresponsive, even oppressive, manner. In addition, universal public services are not always universal in practice because they benefit the better-off more than the poorer sections of society.

These phenomena may be explained because the goals of a social welfare programme are not as they are publicly portrayed: for instance, a social welfare bureaucracy may be established to display that politicians are active and concerned, but its legal and financial resources may be grossly inadequate to perform the task it is supposed to address. Again the goals of a social welfare bureaucracy may be modified, or replaced, by the bureaucracy's own goals as it develops its own dynamics, or as it assumes that its expertise or professionalism gives it a better insight than others into what should be done about a matter. (A subsidiary aspect is that if the relevant legal provisions give the bureaucracy a wide discretion, this is one less obstacle to its adopting its own views.) Another explanation may be that the structures for accountability of a social welfare bureaucracy are underdeveloped. Finally, there is a social context in which social welfare bureaucracies operate – the background and attitudes of bureaucrats, the influence on them of special interests, and the social and economic deprivation of the clientele.

An accepted legal response to the paradox of social welfare bureaucracies has been to foster external review, both by traditional mechanisms (courts and tribunals) and by newer institutions such as the Ombudsman. But if external review along these lines can occasionally remedy injustice, its capacity to infuse social welfare bureaucracies with a new sense of purpose in relation to their total operation is generally limited. What is needed is tighter legal and bureaucratic control of their operations, and institutional changes such as in their patterns of recruitment, training programmes and operating procedures. Participation has been an increasingly popular solution to the paradox of social welfare bureaucracies, to give their clientele a voice in their operation. It is supposed to encourage social welfare bureaucracies to be more responsive, bring issues into the open, and make clients more skilful and knowledgeable about the exercise of power.[153] But even if participation in a social welfare bureaucracy gives the clientele a real influence, this may be only a minor avenue to the exercise of crucial political leverage. Participation in, even control over, a public-housing authority, for example, is of little use if the authority is starved of the resources to implement the repair strategy which tenants consider essential.

If social welfare bureaucracies are flawed, they are still vital for the poorer sections of society: their existence can ensure reasonably decent, if limited, public basic health care, housing and primary and secondary education. Social welfare bureaucracies are sometimes misinformed or misguided, but their inadequacies often reflect social and political failings, most notably, but not simply, that they are underfinanced in relation to the expectations held of them. Where inadequacies are explained in terms of bureaucratic or institutional mechanisms which are relatively independent of political and social forces, the lawyer can have an immediate role in suggesting reforms. In as much as reform involves the clientele of social welfare bureaucracies having greater political clout, the lawyer may have a role in building their strength and ensuring that more resources are channelled in their direction. It is to these issues of social change that we now turn.

PART III
Social change

7
Social change and the legal system

Despite the premise of equality before the law, inequalities still exist, as we saw in Chapter 3, in the administration and, if a broad interpretation be taken, in the substance of the law. Apart from the public subsidization of legal services, and related steps, are there legal mechanisms by which these and social inequalities can be reduced, and can any conclusions be drawn about their relative effectiveness? Part II of this book described how the welfare state works through regulating the practices of private institutions such as property owners and employers and through the provision of social welfare benefits and public services. Yet regulation is not always as adequate as publicly portrayed, either because of defective implementation or resistance by the institutions at which it is aimed, while social welfare benefits and public services are inadequate in their coverage and flawed in aspects of their administration.

Is it possible to overcome these defects through the legal system, in other words to ensure that the welfare state meets the standards apparently set for it, and to secure improvements? This chapter touches on these issues. It concentrates on the activities of those who do not have control of the state machinery. Moreover, it focuses on legal matters in its account of social change in the welfare state.

I MODELS OF SOCIAL CHANGE

For the purposes of the argument, it is useful to consider three models for effecting social change in the welfare state – the Fabian model, the community politics model and the direct action model. The Fabian model assumes that government responds when need is uncovered and the case for change is presented through reasoned argument, lobbying and publicity. The extent to which this occurs increases if the political party in power is ideologically committed to change. The community politics model is based on the belief that feasible proposals must be supported by developing the political strength of a community, mainly through organizing, to force change. The direct action model goes one step further, for it assumes that conflict is necessary to consolidate support and to demonstrate that people are determined to secure change. The models which are sketched are by no means exhaustive, but historically seem to be the most appropriate in considering change in social welfare provisions. If the concern was the general context of this change, the trade unions would have to feature prominently in the account, in as much as they have contributed to a general improvement in the living standards of ordinary people. The trade unions have in fact directed more attention to some aspects of social welfare such as old-age pensions than to the plight of other social welfare recipients, of public-housing tenants, or of the homeless.[1]

Generally speaking, particular tactics for effecting social change are associated with each model, although the relationship is by no means invariable: for example, the community politics model sometimes approximates to the direct action model in the tactics employed. In addition, it is not unknown for a group to espouse a particular model of social change yet to adopt tactics apparently inconsistent with it.[2] An example of how a particular movement may blend different tactics is the campaign which a tenants' organization used to win alterations in a rent-rebate scheme. The campaign involved both orthodox lobbying (the Fabian model), community politics and direct action in the form of a rent strike. A student of the campaign describes the combination of tactics and evaluates their efficacy thus:

The direct action advocated by the 'extreme left' opposition was not supported by a disciplined majority, or even a substantial minority, of the tenants. In these circumstances the rent strike became an inconvenience rather than a challenge to the council, and the mass lobbying of individual councillors was provocative rather than persuasive. The changes to the original scheme were secured by the indirect influence of the tenants both on the struggle within the Labour Party and on the election programme of the Conservatives. Many of the Labour councillors lived in council houses, or were closely associated either in their party or at work with council house tenants. They were under considerable social pressure to oppose a scheme that so many tenants rejected, and they were aware that re-nomination might not be forthcoming for those who continued their support.[3]

Organizations seeking social change do not always choose tactics which are appropriate to the circumstances. For example, a mass demonstration may not be viable if a community does not have sympathy for a particular issue. A small but well-publicized protest may be more effective in these circumstances if an issue is to become visible and thus capable of attracting wider support. Tradition, ideology or accident may determine how organizations use particular tactics, even though closer consideration would lead them to a more effective line of attack. The presence of lawyers in a particular group may orient the group towards legal tactics when there may be other appropriate strategies.

The Fabian model

Since established interest groups are observed achieving change, some social welfare interest groups believe that they can make similar advances by having a reputation for accurate information, by drawing up practicable proposals, and by lobbying politicians, government officials and the media. Until recently, government departments proposed social welfare legislation without the extensive consultation engaged in by other departments with relevant pressure groups. Once social welfare concerns are articulated in the corridors of power, the argument runs, decisions will be made taking them into account. Social welfare pressure groups will become accepted, so that social welfare bureaucracies will turn to them for advice and assistance. Educating the public at large about the issues, and attracting media support, are methods a pressure group can use to guarantee that it is listened to by those in authority. Politicians cannot ignore resource-poor groups, it is said, if they have the potential power to threaten a loss of political support.[4]

The so-called 'poverty lobby'[5] seems generally to represent the Fabian model of effecting social change – seeking to influence government policy by the soundness of its information and arguments and using the media in an attempt to create a groundswell of public opinion in favour of particular reforms. How successful has it been? In recent years, social welfare benefits and services like public housing have hardly improved and in some respects have become worse. In view of the record, it could be argued that the poverty lobby operates on fallacious assumptions of where power lies in society and how change occurs. It is delusion, the critics would contend, to think that social welfare groups can ever have the political clout of those representing powerful economic interests, which have an unequal share of political resources such as access to government research capacity, administrative experience and political skills. The poverty lobby can be and is ignored, they would say, because it eschews the only method of redressing the imbalance – organizing politically. Two points can be made in defence of the poverty lobby. First, it may be that in its absence the position of those such as social welfare recipients, the homeless and those in bad housing would have been worse. Secondly, the poverty lobby can definitely claim credit for certain changes which have benefited particular groups and for others which have ensured greater procedural justice.

Community politics

The community politics model of social change differs from Fabianism in its style of operation and underlying assumptions. While Fabians are usually a small group, operating directly on or through government, community activists work with a geographical community and seek change through organizing politically. If Fabians are *for* the disadvantaged, those seeking social change through community politics would claim to be *of* the disadvantaged. Although community activists tend to be an elite like the Fabians (in terms of their training if not their social origins) they believe that their action is firmly based in communities.[6] In terms of their assumptions, they believe that those with power and wealth will never concede benefits gracefully, and that they must be forced to make concessions through the exercise of political power. Patient organization at the community level is necessary to build up the power of community groups, to enable them in a pragmatic manner to bargain for and demand concessions.[7] Community groups are valued by some social theorists not simply for the benefits they may win but because through participation in such groups individuals may acquire a sense of political efficacy and social and political skills.[8] Public relations is vital both to mobilize support within a community and also to sensitize a wider audience to the claims being advanced. If something becomes 'an issue' in the local media, a local council, government department or company might be forced to give attention to it, especially if the cause attracts support from editorials, opposition parties or persons in the area with high social status. Another tool is intervention in a public manner in administrative or legal proceedings, such as an appearance by a residents' group before a planning inquiry. Clearly the model of the legal advocate has an important influence in this type of activity, but other experts such as planners and surveyors may be engaged to help prepare the case for a particular policy. In this and other ways, law centres have a role in the organization and operation of community groups.

The pessimists point to the practical difficulties of building community groups, for example the geographical community may not be the natural focus for dealing with a problem and there may not be sufficient patronage to retain dedicated organizers.[9] Individuals have divergent interests and are frequently difficult to weld into an effective community group. Once formed, a community group may be only semi-permanent, and therefore not acquire the acceptance of an established interest group. Whereas in some groups such as sporting clubs, benefits accrue only to members, in community groups the benefits obtained by a group are usually available to all, and it is more rational for the individual to become a 'free rider' than to incur the costs associated with supporting the group. Communities are not homogeneous, and there is the problem that a community group may come into conflict with other residents of an area about what is the desirable course of action.[10] People may also calculate that it is not worthwhile joining a community group because they have little chance of having an influence – a phenomenon sometimes identified as 'apathy'. This is not to say that community groups will never coalesce and have an influence. Groups of social welfare recipients, tenants and poor consumers have sprung up in the most inauspicious circumstances; their very existence testifies to their viability.[11] They may be comparatively small in relation to their potential clientele, have limited finance, be badly administered, lack cohesion, have a fluid membership, and need greater political skills. With a degree of success, however, a community group may become self-generating. A group will also be assisted if full-time organizers can be employed to administer it, for then the ordinary membership need make only nominal contributions and attend occasionally.[12]

Even if a community is organized, the critics continue, will it significantly influence decisions which vitally affect it but which are formulated in remote company boardrooms or government offices?[13] Many community activists are sceptical about community politics unless links are established with working-class organizations, notably trade unions.[14] One method of forging these alliances has been for community groups to become a source of information to trade unionists and to assist on matters where their work has led them to acquire special expertise. An example is that community workers have assisted trade unionists to obtain the maximum social welfare benefits payable where they were engaged in an industrial dispute or have been made redundant. There have also been attempts to raise the consciousness of communities about larger political questions, particularly the effects of reductions in public expenditure on health and welfare. At one level this has been done by pamphlets and political theatre, and at another has involved detailed research, to demonstrate matters such as patterns of property ownership by large institutions in particular localities, the way industries make and withdaw investments, and the manner in which the welfare state benefits the wealthy and industry.[15] It seems fair to say that, other things being equal, community groups will be more effective if they are linked to other similar groups or if they have the support of a broad cross-section of the body politic.[16] However, difficulties can occur when local community groups combine at a national level if the central office becomes isolated from its constituent bodies.

Proponents of community politics can point to achievements – just as critics can point to failures. The Mobilization for Youth Experience in New York in the early sixties reported 'drastic revision of the Welfare Abuses Law, changes in the administration of the local schools, and legislation easing and legalizing rent withholding in New York State'.[17] A housing rights project in North Islington (London) won substantial improvements in housing standards through the grassroots organizing of tenants and residents and the persistent lobbying of officials and politicians. The local council was induced to bring into public ownership and improve, on a systematic basis, a considerable amount of substandard, privately rented accommodation.[18] A Community Development Project (CDP) in Birmingham (Saltley) assisted in forming a residents' association, one aim of which was to assist leaseholders in the area to convert to freehold under the Leasehold Reform Act 1967. Progress was slow in the face of detailed negotiation by property owners and the indifference of central government to its suggestions that the Act needed amendments if conversion was to be facilitated. The CDP arranged for collective negotiation by one solicitor on behalf of all lessees and took a successful test-case to the Lands Tribunal on the amount payable to an intermediary leaseholder.[19]

Direct action

Direct action to achieve political ends eschews traditional political tactics such as lobbying, and instead uses organization, publicity and confrontation. A group may not consider traditional political tactics appropriate since it is not accorded the recognized position in decision-making of established pressure groups. Even if it is, it may find the leisurely pace of democratic politics inappropriate to the immediate change desired.[20]

The success of direct action turns on the extent to which it can exert pressure by arousing public support and threatening political consequences. *A priori*, certain issues seem more capable than others of forming the basis of direct action. For example, the rent and conditions on a public-housing estate are of immediate importance to a geographical community, but social welfare claimants are usually dispersed geographically and may be cut off from the support of others because of the negative stereotypes they bear. Organizers must be of the community or fit into it to enable them to communicate goals and to build up a group for what may be a lengthy and perhaps tedious campaign. Direct action requires a full-time commitment to keep up momentum and imagination to search out ways of building a group and deciding tactics. The crucial issue direct action organizers must face is, 'how do you convert this picket line into better education, employment and so forth?'[21] When carefully orchestrated, direct action can attract wider political support to the cause for change. In this respect the mass media plays a key role, for a handful of people might turn a matter into a public issue by direct confrontation with authority. However, time spent attracting media coverage can be at the expense of organizing, and there is a tension between generating dramatic copy and alienating the support of third parties because of physical conflict and law-breaking.

Direct action as a political tactic has an established role in Western societies in attempts by relatively poor and powerless groups to obtain a greater share of wealth and power.[22] Among the groups using direct action have been the trade unions in the nineteenth century, the suffragettes early this century, and the blacks in the United States in the mid-twentieth century. Many groups today do not accept the criticism that direct action is unconstitutional, unnecessary and the work of 'trouble-makers', for they see the existing system as unfair and not prepared to make fundamental changes in their favour.[23] That direct action has an established part in political history is not to say that it is always desirable or that it can always be approved. Nor is it to prejudge the issue in any particular historical context of who initiated any confrontation, and whether that confrontation was responsible for any eventual change or whether more fundamental forces were at work. A final point to make is that much of the direct action engaged in by groups today (e.g. rent strikes, picketing, squatting) is in a legally 'grey area' and is not necessarily or even mainly unlawful.

The more reflective proponents of direct action recognize that it entails careful building from the existing system, exposing its contradictions, organizing, generating a wide desire for change, and only after careful consideration challenging the system in its weak spots directly by confrontation – the boycott, sit-in, picket or demonstration. In other words, they see direct action as pragmatic, and acknowledge that people are imperfect, that there will be setbacks and that compromise will be necessary. 'If you start with nothing, demand 100 per cent, then compromise for 30 per cent you're 30 per cent ahead'.[24] However, direct action groups frequently become inward-looking and their political sense is warped as they become emotionally involved in a struggle and rule out compromise. That is not to say that a pragmatic direct action group will eschew confrontation because it is likely to be unsuccessful, for confrontation can build the self-esteem and cohesion of a group, radicalize its members for future struggle, and teach them organizing skills and lessons in how the political process operates.

Some commentators argue that although direct action may dramatize an issue, its effect on policy is marginal because it comes 'too late to change policy . . . [and] do[es] not offer reasoned alternatives which add to discussion'.[25] A similar conclusion from another point in the political spectrum is that direct action cannot achieve fundamental change – it cannot compensate for inadequate resources, and as soon as it appears as if it may achieve success it is suppressed.

But it is clear that direct action can achieve limited results. Homeless people have obtained a roof over their heads by squatting; tenants have managed to avoid full rent increases through rent strikes; and social welfare claimants have achieved benefits through the activities of claimants' unions. Direct action is generally local and achieves less at the national level, but by focusing attention on issues such as homelessness it has contributed towards long-term policy changes and the implementation of national policy at the local level. For example, squatting may not have built more homes, but it has played a part in ensuring that the existing housing stock is used more rationally.[26] The 'green bans' campaign in Australia is an example of a relatively successful direct action movement in which a few radical trade unionists joined hands with community groups to oppose the commercial redevelopment of areas of inner Sydney. The description derived from the bans which the union imposed in the interests of preserving the environment (hence 'green' rather than 'black' bans) if a community could show that it opposed redevelopment. Important aims in some areas were to press for the rehabilitation of housing occupied by low-income tenants and its retention for use by those tenants. While other factors influenced the course of events, such as the state of the property market, the 'green bans' had a role in preventing the destruction of a considerable amount of housing, although some has since been gentrified.[27]

Direct action has not always been successful. The response to direct action may be to buy off support by minor changes, to use resources to discredit or crush a direct action group, or intransigence until a direct action group disintegrates through lack of success or internal pressures.[28] When taken to extremes, direct action can alienate the support of obvious allies. For example, a former member of a claimants' union writes of one campaign: 'The saddest aspect was the virtual alienation of the local trade union organizations and the deep suspicion of the political parties that the Claimants Union was more concerned with headlines and short-term opportunism and was not prepared to work towards long-term social reform.'[29] Direct action can also become divorced from reality so that confrontation is valued for its own sake. Some squatting groups have been guilty of this, and the aim of assisting the homeless became secondary to what they saw as a method of violently confronting authority. Perhaps the most important qualification on direct action is that it is not a reliable weapon for long-term change if this depends on economic, social or political factors of considerable magnitude. But herein lies the rub: those lacking viable alternative to direct action, do not always have the resources to bring about fundamental change by building more enduring organizations or engaging in concerted lobbying or litigation.

II THE ROLE OF THE LEGAL SYSTEM

Social change may have to be legitimated and its full implications spelt out by a change in statute law. Many aspects of the welfare state discussed earlier in the book constituted important shifts in policy which were detailed in legislation. Apart from legitimating social change, law and lawyers have an independent role in the process of achieving it. It is wrong to over-emphasize this independent role, for in many cases the legal system is largely immaterial to the pursuit of social change by social welfare interest groups. A tenants' group seeking a change in law or practice may lobby legislators or administrators, collect petitions, and attract media coverage, activities which the law regulates only marginally. However, the legal system may loom larger if other tactics are chosen. For example, a tenants' group may become involved in a housing association or a housing co-operative, at which point legal assistance will be indispensable. It may litigate a test case in the hope that the courts will interpret a legal rule in a more favourable manner or will compel a landlord to comply with existing legal provisions. Even if litigation is unsuccessful, the group may have generated pressure for change (especially if there is considerable publicity), or maintained the commitment of its members while other tactics are used.[30] The legal system may also be used defensively against the actions of others, as where a tenants' group which engages in a rent strike, protest, picket or other form of direct action, is sued by a landlord, real estate agent or property company, or is prosecuted by the authorities. In this section there is a general discussion of social change through the legal system; we return to the concern with social change through the courts (one aspect of the legal system) in a more analytical fashion in section III of this chapter.

The historical context

The legal system was never especially important to the social reformers of the nineteenth and early twentieth century. Government was the pathway to a better society, and social change was seen as a matter of electing reforming political parties, of making representations through influential contacts and of generating a public awareness about issues. Involvement of the courts in social change was far from the minds of the nineteenth-century reformers, for they could see how ill-suited the courts were to matters such as factory, poor-law and lunacy reform. Magistrates were regarded as biased and the superior courts as moving slowly and taking a narrow, technical view.[31] Jeremy Bentham's view – 'amendment from the judgment seat is confusion' – was based on the belief that the judges were a conservative monopoly, that they lacked adequate information to engage in social reform, and that any reforms they introduced were partial in effect because of the nature of the judicial process.[32] Far better, argued Bentham, was to have a properly informed Parliament passing legislation with general effect. Bentham's disciple, Chadwick, tried to insulate the Poor Law Commission from ministerial control to prevent patronage, and from judicial review because of what he thought were the courts' inadequacies.[33] Finer summarizes Chadwick's view as follows:

The courts could clog administration by defeating Regulations on verbal or technical grounds. They were ill-informed on the public policy of the law. They were concerned with the individual plaintiff and not with 'large classes of cases and general and often remote effects, which cannot be brought to the knowledge of judges'.[34]

The social reformers of the late nineteenth and early twentieth centuries would have looked askance at suggestions for a judicial role in social reform. 'New liberals' such as Joseph Chamberlain demonstrated the efficacy of government reform.[35] Legislation and state action were also hallmarks of the approach of socialists to social change, and it was never considered that the courts should have anything to do with matters such as nationalization, municipalization, the redistribution of wealth, the regulation of the economy to stem unemployment, and the establishment of national minimum standards below which no person would be permitted to fall.[36] In the late nineteenth and early twentieth centuries, middle- and upper-middle-class persons established what were known as 'settlements' to achieve social change in areas such as the East End of London. Law does not seem to have been an important part of their strategy for social change and the 'poor man's lawyers' working there were engaged mainly in assisting working people with their individual problems.[37]

In any case, the actions of the courts in suppressing the incipient labour movement would have been fresh in many minds. The period of Liberal reform in early twentieth-century Britain coincided with a series of anti-trade-union decisions, notably the *Taff Vale* case of 1901.[38] In 1911 Winston Churchill, then Home Secretary, made his oft-quoted remark on the bias of judges:

Where class issues are involved . . . it is impossible to pretend that the courts command the same degree of general confidence. On the contrary, they do not, and a very large number of our population have been led to the opinion that they are, unconsciously, no doubt, biased.[39]

Around the turn of the century, Dicey was propounding the view, widely shared in the legal profession, that the courts should control the growth of the state which he saw as intruding on the liberties of the subject and undermining the rule of law. This view, echoed by many legal writers after Dicey,[40] must have confirmed social reformers in their belief that lawyers represented the forces of conservatism. Another reason that social reformers excluded the courts from consideration was the courts' purported demarcation between law and social policy, for this meant that they were hardly the most appropriate body to handle matters which could only be appreciated in their wider context. The emphasis on precedent and a strict approach to statutory construction ill-befitted a policy of social reform. Finally, it seemed difficult for the judges, perhaps less so for the lower-court judges, to deal sympathetically with matters involving working people, when their backgrounds, professional lives, and attitudes were so different. Illustrative of the latter is the view of Mr Justice Phillimore that social welfare conflicted with the law of nature that the fittest survived, by imposing a cost on the thrifty to benefit the failures of society.[41]

In the light of these factors, is it any wonder that the task of dealing with disputes involving social welfare legislation should be denied to the courts and entrusted to special tribunals?[42] Without the courts' disadvantages, tribunals were seen as having positive features such as flexibility, simplicity, cheapness, and susceptibility to government influence. When the Labour Party was in office in Britain following World War II, it recognized a possibility of judicial sabotage, and social reforms were insulated from the possibility of judicial review.[43] Appeals to the courts were prohibited both under the Education Act 1944 and the National Health Service Act 1946. In 1946 workmen's compensation was removed from the courts, where it had become needlessly expensive and technical, and replaced by a new national insurance industrial injuries scheme, in which disputes were handled by special tribunals. Aspects of rent control, which until then had been dealt with in the county courts, were also entrusted to newly established tribunals.[44] Partly as a result of the attitude of social reformers towards them, the judges were reluctant to interfere in the administration of the welfare state even when that was legally possible. To justify their approach, the judges said that the panoply of tribunals was sufficient to protect individual rights. When interference occurred, narrow social views were evident. Possibly a contributing factor was that the judges were cut off from a regular review of tribunal work, which might have led to a broader view.

The American example

Today the American courts have not simply a negative power to strike down legislation as unconstitutional, but a wide power to create policy either independently of or as a substitute for legislative policy. The establishment of the Supreme Court, as one of the three branches of government, with a mandate to interpret a widely drawn Constitution including a Bill of Rights, laid the basis for this far-reaching role for courts in American society. In the nineteenth century, de Tocqueville could write of the pervasiveness of legal language in the United States and of the extent to which the spirit of the law 'infiltrates through society right down to the lowest ranks'.[45] The rise of the prestigious law schools in the first part of the twentieth century, and their case-book method of teaching, reinforced the perception that courts were of prime importance in law-making. Roscoe Pound, a dominant voice in American legal education in the early part of this century, wrote of the advantages of judicial law-making over legislation:

It would seem that while legislation has proved an effective agency of ridding the law of particular institutions and precepts which have come down from the past and have not been adapted or were not adaptable to the needs of the time, it has not been able, in our legal system, except in rare instances, to do much of the constructive work of change in eras of growth . . . Judicial finding of law has a real advantage in competition with legislation in that it works with concrete cases and generalizes only after a long course of trial and error in the effort to work out a practicable principle.[46]

The courts' importance seemed heightened by the deficiencies of American legislatures. Federalism divided legislative power, corruption discredited it, and the *laissez-faire* ideology militated against its use. By contrast with other lawyers, American lawyers became advisers to corporations and governments over a wide range of matters, including how to effect favourable legal changes through the courts and the legislatures.

In the first part of the twentieth century, however, the mainstream of American reformers still had an attitude which did not differ fundamentally from the approach of English reformers, that the method of achieving reform was through government. An example was the agitation for workmen's compensation, in light of the failure of the common law to compensate workers for injuries suffered.[47] The progressive movement was dismayed at the attitude of the courts (especially the Supreme Court) towards measures regulating business and promoting social welfare, and consequently before World War I among its important demands was the power to recall judges and to recall judicial decisions.[48] (Until 1937, when Roosevelt appointees to the Supreme Court were able to institute a different trend, the New Dealers also faced obstacles from the Court similar to those experienced by the Progressives.[49]) From the time of World War I, however, there was a change in orientation among minority groups with unpopular causes and small constituencies who found the legislatures blocked to change in their favour. The National Association for the Advancement of Colored People turned to the courts when it became clear that the legislatures were relatively immune to black claims and that judges, at least those at the federal level, were not as amenable to the exercise of pressure by anti-black groups as were the legislators:

Despite large expenditures the NAACP gained little in lobbying Congress. The institution was insulated against Negro claims. The size and character of the Southern delegation, the committee system, seniority, and closure in the Senate doomed Negro efforts. In the 1920s Negroes failed to secure legislation making lynching a federal crime. Over and over again bills to prohibit the poll-tax failed. During World War II, many Negroes became convinced of the uselessness of pressure-group activities in Congress with the defeat of proposals to create a permanent Fair Employment Practices Commission.[50]

Strong support from prominent lawyers, initial successes, and the idea of using the courts as a forum for educating the population confirmed the court strategy that the NAACP adopted. The American Civil Liberties Union and similar groups also began using the courts in this period, not only in a defensive manner but also to assert existing rights and to establish new ones.[51] By the 1960s they were joined by those such as environmentalists and consumer advocates who contended that government departments and the regulatory agencies established during periods of reform, notably the New Deal, had been 'captured' by vested interests, and were impervious to influence from the ordinary citizens they were supposed to serve.[52]

With the background outlined it is easy to understand why some in the United States looked to the courts as a major avenue for tackling social welfare issues.[53] The courts are important centres of power and the indications in the desegregation cases were that they were prepared to use it in a progressive way for under-privileged minorities. Legislatures, on the other hand, were generally resistant to change: many had little interest in matters like social welfare, except to keep the cost as low as possible. In some instances legislatures were deliberately perpetuating the conditions the reformers were dedicated to overturn. Lawyers were prominent in reform movements – they had been spawned in considerable numbers by the centrality of law in American life – and it was natural that they should think of litigation as a method of social change.

The starting point is generally regarded to be *Brown* v. *Board of Education* (1954),[54] which held that segregated schooling was unconstitutional. *Brown* and the other desegregation cases also had repercussions for social welfare, since in the United States race is inextricably linked with poverty, and education is a crucial aspect of the American welfare state. These cases were followed by important Supreme Court decisions on civil rights, including those relating to the obligation of governments to provide legal representation for indigents charged with serious criminal offences.[55] Then in an influential article in 1964 Edgar and Jean Cahn argued that lawyers working in the neighbourhood law centres funded by the federal government under the Economic Opportunity Act 1964, as part of the 'war on poverty', should be concerned not only with individual legal problems but with seeking social change.[56] In this vein a number of cases were taken to the Supreme Court in the late sixties and early seventies, including several relating to the rights of social welfare recipients. For example, *King* v. *Smith*[57] held that a woman could not be denied benefits under the Aid to Families with Dependent Children (AFDC) programme simply because she was living with a man, unless he was legally obliged to contribute to the child's support. Interestingly, the Court reached its decision on the basis of its interpretation of the federal statute, with only Douglas J. deciding the case on constitutional grounds. In *Shapiro* v. *Thompson*[58] the Court held that the states could not impose residential requirements on the payment of social welfare benefits, since these violated the fundamental rights of unimpeded travel within the country. An assessment made about this time of the 'war on poverty' concluded that the legal services programme was its most valuable aspect in achieving institutional change.[59] Certainly legal services lawyers had various successes in the social welfare area, but not all decisions had the lasting quality of being based on constitutional grounds.

During the 1970s, however, lawyers found that the Supreme Court was not as sympathetic as previously in areas like social welfare. As a result, litigation before it was relegated to a lower priority in their strategy. An important reason was the changed political climate, which was reflected in the composition of the Supreme Court under Chief Justice Burger.[60] In addition, once most of the straightforward issues had been litigated the Court was required to depart more radically from accepted standards of judicial decision-making. Striking down residential requirements, for example, was in keeping with constitutional traditions, but it was more difficult when the Court was presented with arguments which were ultimately reducible to a constitutional objection to discrimination based on wealth.[61] The change was evident in several cases. Despite previous decisions placing a heavy emphasis on a person's right to privacy in the home, the Court held that there was no constitutional objection to requiring a beneficiary under the AFDC programme to accept periodic home visits by a caseworker.[62] In 1970 in *Dandridge* v. *Williams*[63] the Court held that there was nothing in the federal statute or the equal-protection clause of the Constitution to prevent a maximum amount of AFDC benefits being paid to larger families although this meant that many received less than their statutory 'needs'. The Court also held that the overall amount of AFDC benefits payable could be fixed at a lower level than for other social welfare benefits, despite statistical evidence that minority groups were disadvantaged by this.[64]

As a result of such decisions, there has been a greater emphasis in more recent times on lobbying legislatures and social welfare bureaucracies, and on litigating in the lower federal courts and the state courts where these are thought to be favourably disposed to social welfare claims. In a number of matters, the federal district courts have issued and overseen the implementation of affirmative decrees which have specified in detail what governments and government agencies must do to comply with the law.[65] To formulate the decrees the courts have relied heavily on expert evidence, on specially appointed masters, on the parties themselves, and on the standards inherent in the relevant legislation. The most important of these decrees have concerned busing and the conditions in mental hospitals and prisons. A decree relating to public housing in Chicago illustrates the potential of federal court action: in the relevant decision the Court held that the Chicago Housing Authority had violated the constitutional right of tenants of, and applicants for, public housing in Chicago by selecting sites for projects on racial grounds, and entered an order specifying in detail when, where and how future public housing should be constructed to conform with the equal-protection clause of the constitution.[66] Such decisions have significant ramifications for persons other than the immediate litigants, for they have a real effect on the allocation of resources. Thus a decision that a state must drastically improve the way it operates its prisons might necessitate considerable public expenditure.

The decisions have been the subject of controversy, for opponents argue that the allocation of resources is the prerogative of the legislatures or that the courts are defective as a means of implementing social policy because they lack the institutional resources to frame and police it.[67] Nevertheless, these far-reaching decisions have vigorous defenders, who assert that judicial intervention is necessary to secure the effective implementation of legal rights if government and government authorities would otherwise ignore them. They point out that the decrees are not simply the work of the courts but are the outcome either of settlements between the parties sanctioned by the courts or the work of court-appointed experts. Some add that the judiciary has institutional advantages in developing and applying social policy such as its insulation from narrow political pressures, its non-bureaucratic nature, and the fact that it must respond when presented with a claim.[68]

The American influence

Influenced in large part by the success of litigation in the United States, organizations elsewhere have turned to the courts in an attempt to challenge the operation of social welfare bureaucracies. Generally the litigation has been of a relatively mundane character, challenging the interpretations of legislation by social welfare bureaucracies or the failure of social welfare bureaucracies to carry out their statutory duties. A long-term aim has been to establish that certain social welfare and housing benefits are more a right than charity. Using test cases to effect reform has fallen most comfortably within the Fabian tradition, with the difference being that the focus of activity is the judiciary rather than Parliament, the executive, or local, state or provincial government. If social welfare groups had the capacity continually to mount test cases in court, the Fabian assumption runs, government departments and private institutions would modify their behaviour. Even adverse decisions might serve the purpose of highlighting a legal deficiency and the need for legislative change.

From about 1973, the Child Poverty Action Group's legal rights' office in London has been active in test-case litigation. It has researched areas of law (the cohabitation rule, etc.), encouraged mass appeals to tribunals, and brought test cases in the courts on matters affecting a number of social welfare claimants. The litigation has been designed to clarify the law, to obtain more benefits for particular claimants, 'to expose the myth' that social welfare is administered as a system of individualized justice (as has been claimed), and to test the legality of some of the administrative policies of social welfare bureaucracies. Despite these aims, CPAG recognized that litigation promised only partial success and that the time and cost might not justify it as a method of checking administrative malpractice.[69] In 1977, after five years' experience of test cases, CPAG's solicitor concluded that the institutional checks against bringing test cases were considerable, and that even if they reached court any success was threatened by legislative reversal.[70]

Community groups and law centres have also undertaken test-case litigation as a part of their strategy for social change. Some of the test cases have had only a local significance, as where the aim has been to change the objectionable practice of a landlord or employer. The Law

Centres Working Group, in their evidence to the Royal Commission
on Legal Services, explained that law centres could change landlords'
practices in an area

by constantly impressing upon landlords in one area that not only is it
expensive illegally to evict a tenant, but that, because of the speed with which
the Law Centre responds, they do not even have the satisfaction of seeing the
tenant out for a single night. . . . [71]

Then there are test cases such as *Liverpool C.C.* v. *Irwin*,[72] which was
brought on behalf of a group of public-housing tenants in a tower-
block in Liverpool, but which had important ramifications for the
general law of landlord and tenant. Despite such successes, however,
there is considerable scepticism among community groups and law
centres about the effectiveness of test-case litigation, unless it is but
part of a wider strategy. The arguments against test-case litigation
include the narrow scope for challenges because of substantive and
procedural obstacles, the possibility that legal proceedings will open
the door to delay and obstruction, and the fact that litigation might
deflect attention from more important issues.[73] The validity of those
objections is explored further in section III of the chapter.

Community activists and law centres use other aspects of the legal
system more than courts to place community groups on a firm
foundation and to strengthen their advocacy of social change.
Initially legal assistance takes the form of drafting a community
group's constitution and rules, helping with procedure at meetings,
and drawing up the documentation when a group buys, rents or hires
property. Once a community group is formed, legal work involves
advice on the implications of relevant legislation, administrative
decisions and case-law, and both formal and informal representations, as where a tenants' union takes up housing repairs with a
housing authority, a residents' association makes submissions about
the development of an area, or a claimants' group engages in a
campaign to maximize the social welfare benefits payable to its
members. Negotiations might be entered into with a housing
authority, for example, with a view to its changing its standard lease
or agreeing as to its future conduct. Legal advice and representation
are especially important if a community group takes on service
functions, as where a tenants' union founds a housing co-operative.[74]
Such legal activity is akin to the legal advice and assistance
commercial and government lawyers undertake for their clients, in

that there is sometimes a wider, possibly even a political, context to the work. However, a significant feature is that a good deal of the advice and representation can be and is done for community groups by non-lawyers, who have acquired their knowledge and skills on the job or through contact with lawyers.

Direct action and the legal system

Direct action groups become involved with the legal system more in a defensive than affirmative manner, either to protect themselves against unlawful action or to defend legal proceedings instituted against them. An example of the former would be squatters resisting forceful eviction without a court order, while the latter is illustrated by rent strikers defending eviction proceedings or pickets pleading not guilty to a prosecution. There is nothing to prevent direct action groups seeking change through such cases, for defending actions in legal proceedings initiated by others could be done in a systematic manner. Generally speaking, however, direct action groups do not see the legal system as having a positive role in achieving change, which they believe is better achieved in other ways. In their view, litigation simply delays matters, and law and the courts are biased against them, being designed to protect the power, order and property rights they are challenging. Cost is another factor deterring direct action groups from becoming involved with the legal system.[75] A key principle of direct action groups is participation by their members, so that the decision that outside experts such as lawyers should assume the burden of fighting a group's cause in a remote court is not taken lightly.[76] The underlying sentiment that involvement with lawyers can lead to a loss of direction and control over a course of action was summed up in a publication of rent strikers in East London in the late sixties, who had decided to defend possession orders sought by the landlord (the Greater London Council):

There is no doubt that since the introduction of legality, the Action Committee has lost its sense of direction. We have abandoned our original policy and strayed into legal thickets which few of us can understand. Maybe we had to fight this way. But it has certainly demoralised a lot of people.[77]

Another fear is that if a direct action group becomes involved with the law, its members may develop tunnel vision, so that success or failure is judged purely by the outcome of a court case, even though that may have only a partial bearing on the campaign. With a test-case, for instance, a direct action group may become unduly complacent if legal proceedings are successful, or unduly demoralized by a court defeat, although the legal issues relevant to different members, and therefore the applicability of the decision, may vary considerably. An illustration comes from the extended rent strike on the Clyde between 1921 and 1926. Clyde tenants defended actions for arrears for unpaid rent brought by their landlords, and were initially successful in a test case taken to the House of Lords in 1922, *Kerr* v. *Bryde*.[78] In summary, the House of Lords held that although the Increase of Rent and Mortgage Interest (Restrictions) Act 1920 permitted landlords to increase rent in limited circumstances, it still preserved the previous law that to increase rent a landlord had to serve a notice to quit on a tenant. Later decisions in the Dumbarton-shire Sheriff Court were also favourable, and notices of an increase of rent were held invalid because they contained mistakes such as incorrect addresses.[79] While the rent strikers took these decisions as endorsement of their action, Parliament had meanwhile enacted retrospective legislation to overturn the particular decision in *Kerr* v. *Bryde*, obviating the need for notices to quit if landlords wanted to increase the rent. Many tenants paid the increased rents demanded, which they were able to do because of increased prosperity in the shipbuilding industry.[80] Then in 1926 there were two crucial decisions of the Court of Sessions.[81] Whatever the merits of the decisions on the particular facts, both ignored that the spirit of the 1920 statute was intended to protect tenants, and that therefore there should be strict observance of the procedures relating to an increase in rent. The two decisions had a devastating effect on the morale of the remaining rent strikers, who believed that they were now liable for arrears accruing during the rent strike. In the result, the rent strike collapsed shortly after.

The aversion which many direct action groups have to the legal system is reinforced by instances where legal action in relation to a matter has proved unsuccessful, but political action has proved successful.[82] In 1975 in *Woodcock* v. *South West Electricity Board*[83] it was held that electricity boards were not legally obliged to connect squats. The Electric Lighting (Clauses) Act 1899, Schedule, para.27(1), stated that electricity authorities shall give and continue to give a supply upon request of the owner or occupier, but Dunn J. held that 'occupier' did not apply to persons such as squatters whose original entry was unlawful and forcible. Not only was there no evidence in the case that entry was forcible, but Dunn J. ignored authority that 'occupier' included those not having good legal title. By contrast, the *Squatters' Handbook*[84] tells of the tactics of one group of squatters when they faced difficulties in having gas and electricity services connected:

> Various types of action have been used to reconnect supplies. The occupation of an electricity board showroom in Notting Hill caused the GLC to lift their restrictions on LEB [London Electricity Board] right of entry into some homes in Maida Vale. Direct action is usually more successful and less expensive than using the courts.

Despite antipathy towards the law, direct action groups engaging in political action are frequently involved with it because of their tactics. Leaflets may be defamatory, picketing may constitute a nuisance or criminal offence, constant heckling at a political meeting may be unlawful, and demonstrators may commit various public-order offences. Another possibility is provided by the 'green bans' campaign in Australia, during which commercial developers whose plans were frustrated sued members of the trade union involved in tort for interfering with their business.[85]

An example of the problems direct action groups face is illustrated by *Hubbard* v. *Pitt* (1976).[86] A local tenants' group disapproved of the way property developers were involved in gentrifying an area, and began a peaceful picket outside the estate agents used by the developers, where they distributed leaflets explaining their case. The majority of the Court of Appeal held that the estate agents were entitled to an interlocutory injunction, preventing the group from continuing the picket, on the basis that there was a serious case to be tried that they were committing the tort of private nuisance by interfering with the enjoyment of the plaintiff's premises.[87] Lord Denning dissented, on the grounds that picketing was not a private nuisance in itself if it were directed to obtaining or to communicating information, or peacefully to persuading, so long as it was not associated with obstruction, threats or violence. In 1978 the estate agents withdrew their action so that it never came to trial, although they had achieved their objective of aborting the group's action. Judicial attitudes in the United States are more favourable to picketing, for the Supreme Court has held that it is a form of constitutionally protected free speech that cannot be enjoined if it is peaceful and orderly.[88] On this basis a court has upheld the picketing of the private residence of a slum landlord.[89]

The careful planning of tactics minimizes the chance that those engaged in direct action will be involved in legal proceedings.[90] Often direct action groups can exploit loopholes and technicalities in the law: for example, before the procedure was changed in England, squatters could avoid the effect of possession orders either by refusing to give their names or by substituting another family for the one against whom any order was directed.[91] Squatters have also avoided convictions for criminal offences such as burglary, criminal damage and theft of gas and electricity through a careful consideration of the legal issues. In addition to advising direct action groups on how to avoid unlawful acts, lawyers might also represent members when legal proceedings are commenced against them. Legal skills seem necessary if court proceedings are to be properly defended – if the relevant evidence is to be assembled and if a case is to be presented which takes full advantage of all the legal points available. A vigorous defence in a civil case might induce a plaintiff to conclude a favourable settlement. If a defence succeeds, there might be a strong incentive for an institution to modify its behaviour in the long term. An example from the United States is of a housing authority which, when a court held that its tenants' rent strike was justified, was forced to compromise with them because the decision placed it in the untenable position of operating the estate without rental income.[92] Despite these advantages of legal representation, a direct action group might want to convert any court proceedings into a political forum rather than to defend them in the ordinary way.

In a few instances, direct action groups have used the legal system to advantage in an affirmative manner. As a deterrent, squatters sought to prosecute bailiffs who violently ejected them and obtained mandamus against a magistrate who refused to entertain the case.[93] Eventually the bailiffs were convicted of causing an affray. Similarly, claimants' unions have encouraged members to appeal to social welfare tribunals as a matter of course against adverse decisions. 'Militant' representation of members before the tribunals has been designed to ensure claimants obtain full entitlement, to expose anomalies, to over-load the system and therefore to exert pressure for change, and to demonstrate that claimants have rights. Wide discretion in the administration of social welfare benefits has an advantage for claimants' unions, for it readily gives rise to arguments about its application in particular cases, but it also has a limiting effect on group campaigns for it means that claims are individualized.

Despite their activity at the tribunal level, claimants' unions have played virtually no role in the test cases taken to the courts on social welfare benefits. Rather their involvement with the law has been the outcome of direct action such as sit-ins in social welfare offices.

A campaign of direct action which attracts considerable public condemnation might well lead to repressive legal change. While in some respects squatting has had beneficial results, notably the enactment in Britain of the Housing (Homeless Persons) Act 1977, it has also led to adverse developments both in case-law and in statute law. When in the late 1960s squatting became widespread, the law in England did not prove a great barrier, for at that time trespass was only a civil wrong and not a crime. The Statutes of Forcible Entry, dating from the fourteenth century, could be avoided by squatters if they obtained entry to empty property without resorting to force. The Statutes actually benefited squatters once they were in possession, because under them it was an offence to use force to recover the premises. However, squatters could be prosecuted under the Statutes if they violently resisted or gave cause that they would, for they were then committing 'forcible detainer'.[94] The first change brought about by widespread squatting was a new procedure for the recovery of possession of land occupied by trespassers. Order 113 of the Rules of the Supreme Court[95] enabled owners to obtain a possession order against squatters five days from service of the summons, and required owners to take only reasonable steps to establish the squatters' identities. The courts seem to have interpreted the Rule in a manner favourable to property owners.[96] A decision of the House of Lords in 1973, which held that conspiracy to trespass could be a crime, was clearly a development in line with this trend and adverse to the interests of squatters.[97]

Meanwhile the Lord Chancellor (Hailsham) had asked the Law Commission to investigate the question of criminal trespass. The Commission's initial proposals were widely attacked as being too harsh to squatters and other trespassers; the controversy sparked was a salutary reminder that even reform of lawyers' law involves political choices. Eventually Part II of the Criminal Law Act 1977 was enacted on the basis of the Law Commission's modified proposals. The Act extends the criminal law against squatters, although it is less extensive than the original proposals or the law of other jurisdictions, where it is an offence to enter or remain on property without reasonable cause.[98]

III SOCIAL CHANGE THROUGH THE COURTS

As we have seen, there has been considerable success with test-case litigation in the United States on social welfare matters. Inspired by this, groups elsewhere have seen the courts as having a role, perhaps only limited, in ameliorating the conditions of the poorer sections of society. This part of the chapter outlines the marginal nature of that role in the common-law world outside the United States, by identifying procedural and institutional barriers to what the courts can do.

Procedural and evidentiary impediments

An obvious point is that courts are not self-activating; they depend upon the initiative of others before they can decide an issue. Despite the prevailing wisdom that individuals are sufficiently motivated to stand up for their rights and to press their legal claims, to assume that those with social problems will always seek redress is clearly fallacious. People may not be aware that there is a remedy for what is amiss or know which course to take. Even if they know that they have a claim, factors may inhibit them from pursuing it. Complaining may be unpleasant or troublesome, or a person may feel that it is not worth the time and trouble when compared with the anticipated outcome. Previous experience, the experience of others, or their general experience in life may inform potential complainants that they are unlikely to be successful.

Those mounting a test case may find a potential litigant, but he or she may be unwilling to become a test case. Social welfare recipients, for example, may be reluctant to engage in litigation challenging departmental policy for fear of risking official antagonism or because they find the prospect of appearing in court rather daunting. By contrast, test cases are less daunting for property owners, businesses or social welfare bureaucracies, especially if they engage in litigation as a matter of routine. At another level there is the ethical problem for lawyers, that the interests of the client might not always be consistent with law-reform activity. The former might best be served by a case being settled, whereas the interests of law reform might require that a case be persevered with so that it will establish a precedent.[99]

Bringing a test case is hedged with procedural restrictions. In most cases the doctrine of standing is not an obstacle, for there are social welfare claimants, tenants or consumers who can point to a direct interest which is affected. However, several cases from the United States illustrate how the doctrine can inhibit innovative litigation. In 1975 in *Warth* v. *Seldin*[100] various individuals and organizations resident in a particular area claimed that a local authority's zoning ordinance excluded persons of low and moderate income and thus contravened the constitution and civil rights' legislation. The Supreme Court held that they did not have standing to sue: the low-income plaintiffs could not show injury to themselves, while the organizations were not claiming (or could not show) that any of their members were being denied their rights, but only that the putative rights of third parties were affected. In another decision the Supreme Court held that a welfare rights' group, and a number of people who had suffered because of a hospital's policy of severely limiting free treatment to indigents, did not have standing to challenge the decision of the Internal Revenue, which had exempted the hospital from taxation as a charity.[101] The reasoning was that the plaintiffs could not show that the injury they asserted was a consequence of the defendant's decision, or that prospective relief would remove it, for the hospital's policy on free services to indigents might be determined by factors other than its tax status.

Court procedures might also hinder reform efforts if they can be used to delay a matter, even in cases in which the outcome is reasonably clear-cut and favourable. Vested interests have an obvious motive in delay: activity in violation of the law (for example, a landlord's breach of an obligation to repair) can be continued up to the trial, unless interlocutory relief can be obtained. Similarly, a person may be induced to abandon a claim, or a case may be weakened with time because witnesses are no longer available. The rules of evidence throw up barriers to establishing a test case. Ordinary people are apt to throw away documentation needed to support oral testimony. Statistical evidence is not admissible to demonstrate, say, that a local social welfare office is quite atypical in the way it administers benefits or services and is therefore exercising its discretion improperly.

Changes in the judicial process have been advocated to reduce the obstacles to instituting legal proceedings. In the United States a variety of mechanisms give greater scope for arguments to be put on behalf of minorities. The *amicus curiae* brief and the class action are two vehicles which have assisted in test-case litigation and which might also have been an incentive for the formation and consolidation of groups representing social welfare recipients, tenants and others. The *amicus curiae* brief enables a group to intervene in a case which it has not initiated. For example, various *amicus curiae* briefs were filed in *Gideon* v. *Wainwright* (1963),[102] in which the Supreme Court held that the state must supply lawyers to indigents charged with serious criminal offences. The *amicus curiae* brief reinforces the arguments of the party it is supporting, broadens the court's perspective by introducing other policy arguments, or puts something to the court which is too risky, unacceptable or emotional to be put by the principal party.

The class action enables a number of individuals to have similar matters determined at the one time instead of in separate proceedings. A small number of social welfare recipients, tenants, or consumers sue on behalf of others similarly placed, and if they are successful the judgment binds the defendant as regards all members of the class. The class action thus has an advantage over the single test case, for the latter may be ignored in relation to anyone other than the successful plaintiff. Class actions might also have advantages in terms of saving time and money as compared with individuals instituting separate proceedings. Moreover, class actions can attract useful publicity because of the significance and number of people involved and may also have a deterrent effect on those who find that their practices no longer pass unchallenged. Settling is a common method used by social welfare departments, landlords and businesses to avoid an adverse precedent,[103] but a class action limits the ability of a party to do this – settlement with one party does not terminate the action, and an overall settlement requires court approval. However, class actions do not overcome problems of proof or deficiencies in the substantive law and still require individuals to take the initiative. Their success in the United States is not necessarily a precedent for other jurisdictions, for in the United States the contingent-fee system provides an incentive to public-interest lawyers to instigate legal actions, law centres have been heavily subsidized, and groups and advocates are more established and familiar with test-case strategy.

There is the possibility of a representative action in other common-law countries if those involved have the same interest. The courts have interpreted the 'same interest' requirement narrowly. For example, a tenant cannot sue his landlord on behalf of himself and the landlord's other tenants in a matter of common interest, such as the state of repair of the building or the collection by the landlord of excessive amounts for electricity. The reasoning runs that the tenants have separate leases with the landlord and accordingly do not have a common interest. [104] A representative action may be possible where, say, a social welfare recipient claims a declaration on behalf of other recipients that the administration of a particular benefit is wrong, for there the class has a common interest in the correct interpretation of the law. In a Canadian case, a worker, who was locked out by his employer, was denied a social welfare benefit on the basis that the statutory language limited it to the incapacitated. Although the Supreme Court of Canada upheld the policy of the welfare agency in refusing the benefit, it accepted (but did not decide) that the worker could sue on behalf of all other persons in the province who were said to be eligible for the benefit. [105]

The major drive for reform in the judicial process has emphasized procedural justice – liberalizing access to the courts for disadvantaged groups in society. It is said that cheap and easy access to the courts is a basic human right, and that it is of paramount importance to achieving social reform for powerless groups and for their enjoyment of traditional social rights. Closely related is the argument that once individuals gain access to the courts they will be treated as if on an equal footing with other more powerful parties. Whereas the legislature and the executive may ignore a relatively powerless group advocating social reform, the courts must respond, even if unfavourably, when presented with suitably formulated legal arguments. Procedural rules such as discovery are said to assist equality further when a powerless group engages in litigation. There must be considerable doubt, however, whether social reform follows necessarily on procedural justice, since the courts may not be favourable to or capable of social reform. In fact there are good reasons for arguing that attempts to achieve procedural justice may actually inhibit social reform. First, they may divert effort and resources from more urgent problems; secondly, they may mislead reformers, who ultimately become disillusioned; and thirdly, they may present what are effectively symbolic changes as major achievements when, as far as substantive matters are concerned, the situation remains the same. It cannot be denied that there can be links between procedural justice and social reform. For instance, it may be that class actions improve the motivation of less powerful groups in the community or attract publicity which adds pressure for change. Certainly there seems to be evidence from the United States that when court procedures were liberalized, doctrinal reform occurred. However, it can be argued that both the doctrinal reforms and the procedural changes in American courts in the fifties, sixties and seventies derived from more fundamental societal factors. Moreover, the real issue is whether the position of less powerful groups in that country is any better than it was before these changes, for it would be fallacious to pursue procedural reform singlemindedly without giving close attention to outcome. This is not to suggest that procedural change should be ignored, but to underline that substantive reform should be the major consideration. The assessment of outcome is pursued at greater length below.

Institutional limits

Courts are primarily concerned with settling concrete disputes on a case-by-case basis rather than with the long-term social implications of their decisions. Judicial decision-making is incremental, and sometimes an overall policy must be derived inductively from a succession of separate decisions, each based on its own facts. The nature of a seminal case can influence the trend of the law, even though it may have been litigated precisely because the circumstances were atypical. The courts may not themselves be aware of the drift of change produced by their decisions because they are isolated from the context. The fact that judicial decisions are made in the context of particular cases can have a distorting effect when compared with the range of material to which legislators and public administrators have access – information on patterns of behaviour, statistical data, and historical and comparative documentation of a problem. The procedural and evidentiary limitations on courts make a full examination of the relevant facts impossible, while courts have no independent fact-finding machinery, and judicial notice only slightly expands the scope of an investigation. Courts must respond to the cases presented to them and judges have only a limited capacity to prod the parties to formulate a matter in a different way. As a matter of practice, courts do not try to obtain a positive representation of all interests relevant to an issue, the model of litigation still remaining that of individual parties in a particular case having their day in court without regard to others. For example, if the issue of social welfare benefits arises in litigation, a court will not invite social welfare pressure groups to make a submission, although they may have become involved with the party. By contrast, social welfare bureaucracies will often consult these groups when making a policy decision relating to benefits.

One line of jurisprudential thought is that social reform is beyond the limits of adjudication because the courts can only manage separable issues which can be isolated analytically. In this view the courts have neither the knowledge nor expertise to engage in social reform which involves 'polycentric' issues – cost-benefit analysis, for instance – where a litigant's argument relating to any matter varies depending on how the court reacts to any other issue.[106] Social reform is not necessarily polycentric, for all that a court might need to do is to enunciate relatively simple, but radical, standards. Moreover, it can be argued that judges are not incapable of investigating, understanding and evaluating complex evidence, and of balancing competing considerations, provided the judicial process is improved.

A constitutional limitation on common-law courts is that they cannot intrude too greatly into government functions unless permitted to do so by law. Courts are limited in the extent to which they can 'rework' legislative material even if they may be able to invalidate some parts and change the interpretation of others.[107] The contrast can be drawn with jurisdictions where constitutional provisions appear to give the courts a wider mandate to interfere. But common-law courts are neither as constrained, nor are courts working under a written constitution as unfettered, as is sometimes suggested. Take the popular thesis that common-law courts will not deal favourably with social welfare claims which, if successful, would force a government to spend large sums of money, since the appropriation and expenditure of money is not a judicial function.[108] The first point in qualification of the thesis is that there are cases where judicial review has meant considerable public expenditure. For example, estimates of the effect of two English Court of Appeal decisions in 1977 relating to supplementary benefits were that they would cost the government many extra millions of pounds a year.[109] Such decisions have been justified on the basis that the courts are simply implementing the legislative intention, which the executive has misinterpreted. Secondly, in so far as the thesis holds, it seems as valid in jurisdictions like the United States with a written constitution. In the United States, for example, there have been cases brought by social welfare recipients which commentators claim were unsuccessful because they would have obliged the government to expend considerable sums of money.[110] Thus despite constitutional provisions, the courts in the United States, as elsewhere, operate within limits set by convention as regards the measures they can take.

Public opinion and culture also have a role in defining how the judiciary operates. In general the causal links are imperceptible, but an example of their operation is how the attitude of the judiciary towards social welfare claims reflects the dominant morality of the community. Politicians have a range of ways in which they can actually seek to change public opinion – public speeches, press releases, and radio and television appearances. Unlike politicians, judges must rely largely on the acceptability of their judgments to professional and informed public opinion. Illustrative of the way public opinion affects judicial performance, if only indirectly, is the reaction to decisions of the Supreme Court of the United States during the fifties and sixties favouring minorities (including social welfare claimants). Large numbers of Americans thought that the Court was overstepping its powers, a view with support among most academic lawyers. That public reaction may have prevented more far-reaching decisions by the Court. Supreme Court justices are clearly aware that their influence rests on their prestige and public acceptability, since they obviously have no administrative or financial resources to implement their decisions independently of the executive. Certainly public reaction contributed towards an environment where politicians could appoint more conservative judges to the Supreme Court from the late sixties, and it is from this point that social welfare cases tended to be decided in an adverse manner.

Another boundary to judicial activism is the accepted way in which the courts reach decisions. The doctrine of precedent and the canons of statutory construction push judges in the direction of the *status quo* rather than of reform. Where there are precedents in the social welfare area (as with landlord and tenant matters), these have sometimes been forged in conditions which mean they are not always favourable to social welfare interests. Judges do not always follow previous cases strictly and may adopt a generous interpretation of legislation, but decision-making still occurs within a narrow framework. Even the United States Supreme Court built on precedent for most of its reform decisions, an example being *Brown* v. *Board of Education*,[111] which followed several other decisions striking down segregation. Indeed a criticism of the cases brought before the United States Supreme Court on social welfare matters, and an attempt to explain their failure after some initial successes, is that many were brought too precipitously and were based on the barest of principles.[112]

Completely novel arguments are likely to be unsuccessful before the courts, for great leaps in principle are eschewed. An early squatting case in 1971 seemed bound to fail, inasmuch as it required the judges to extend a common-law doctrine well beyond its ordinary realm.[113] In that case a squatting association had facilitated the entry of homeless families into unoccupied houses owned by the local council. In an action by the council for possession, one argument on behalf of the squatters was that their action was justified by the doctrine of necessity. It was said that the doctrine, which permits encroachment onto private property in cases of imminent danger to life, could be extended to cover the present facts. The Court of Appeal rejected the argument, and in so doing confined the doctrine to its traditionally narrow role. Similarly, a test case brought prematurely may establish an adverse precedent if it is unsuccessful. The *McPhail* case[114] in 1973 might be an example, for it gave Lord Denning M.R. the opportunity to suggest *obiter* that an owner of property had a limited right to use force against squatters. Until then it had been thought that an owner faced unacceptable risks in doing this and should proceed through the courts to regain possession.[115]

Social welfare law has not developed as a distinct body of principles. One reason is that it is largely statutory and there has not been much litigation in which the courts could develop principles. Taxation law is also statute-based but, because of the volume of litigation, distinct principles have developed, for example that the statutory language imposing a tax must be unambiguous. In the absence of comparable principles, the courts have relied on administrative-law doctrines and statutory interpretation when deciding social welfare cases. As regards the former, we have seen in other chapters that the judiciary often intervenes on the side of property rights, although it might otherwise give the executive a wide charter in the administration of social welfare benefits and provisions. The canons of statutory interpretation tend generally to cause social legislation to be applied narrowly.

Social reforms need constant adjustment in their implementation as feedback reveals areas of resistance and unforeseen consequences. The vagaries of litigation seem an inappropriate way to do this, for a court's decision stands at least until another challenge is made. Courts have only a limited capacity to interfere directly with the merits of administrative decisions, although they can do this indirectly by calling to account why these are made. So they can impugn a decision on the basis that natural justice was denied or that the decision was *ultra vires* or constituted jurisdictional error because of an improper purpose underlying it, because relevant considerations were ignored or irrelevant considerations taken into account, because no reasonable body would have made such a decision, because there was no evidence to justify its making, or because it resulted from an inflexible application of a policy or rule or was made under the dictation of another body not entrusted with power to make it. Compare the way governments can engage directly in limited experimentation with a scheme, making adjustments in the light of experience. The doctrine of precedent means that an earlier court decision is not easy (although not impossible) to modify, even if it is inappropriate. Of course, courts cannot decide to spend money themselves, even though this may be the only way that reform can be achieved. Similarly, courts cannot establish administrative programmes themselves, although they might order, by means of statutory interpretation, that the executive modify what has been done.[116]

A fundamental problem of the courts as an instrument of social reform is that their impact is interstitial rather than comprehensive. Judicial remedies operate only to a limited extent as a means of compelling a change in behaviour. Specific remedies are potentially powerful but they suffer certain inherent deficiencies. For example, the injunction is a blunt instrument – it may prevent completely an activity such as redevelopment in an inner-city area, whereas it might be more desirable to permit it to continue subject to detailed conditions. Injunctions also operate prospectively and cannot be used to compensate persons for past injustices (although it may be possible to link a claim for damages). Because courts have little machinery to implement their decisions, it is said that they may be more successful when their decisions are self-executing, i.e. when they confer rights on individuals who can enforce them themselves. However, there is the qualification that there are various obstacles in the way of people vindicating their legal rights. Decisions which are not self-executing but require bureaucratic action may never be implemented in practice. Community groups and law centres have an important role here in policing compliance with legal provisions, but their resources are limited.

IV THE RECORD OF SOCIAL CHANGE

Evaluating whether a particular legal measure has improved or will improve the position of its apparent beneficiaries is especially difficult. It might be said that activities of a social welfare interest group have effected a particular social change, whereas in fact this was caused by independent factors. So the withdrawal of plans for area clearance in the mid-seventies was attributable as much to cutbacks in public expenditure as to the activities of residents' associations.[117] On the surface there may not appear to have been any change as a result of a measure, although in fact there has been a transformation in attitudes. The goals behind a particular measure might be unclear, in conflict or varying, so that any social change cannot be measured against them as a standard.[118] Problems of interpretation occur because even if the goals are clear the change might be far removed from what was intended, yet still benefit those such as social welfare claimants. There is also a problem in interpreting social change if there are long-term repercussions or adverse side-effects which are difficult to measure or elusive to trace. Hall gives this example of the problems of balancing the costs and benefits of legal change: 'Urban renewal laws were intended to provide decent housing for poor people, but they have also enriched landowners and uprooted many poor persons without providing them with better housing. Were those laws effective?'[119]

An illustration of the difficulties of evaluating the costs and benefits of test-case litigation would be a decision which holds that a benefit provision should be construed more liberally than previously. The favourable, and common, interpretation would be that the decision improves that position of social welfare claimants since those previously denied the benefit now receive it. Justice is done for these individuals, and this improves the standing of the system as a whole. The case might also boost the self-confidence of the social welfare claimants (or at least some of them) in that they might feel more capable of achieving reform through their own actions. This interpretation might conclude that the decision is valuable in demonstrating that limited change is possible without a radical change in the system.

A less favourable interpretation might see the decision as achieving little for social welfare claimants, for although a particular group might now receive benefits or at least higher benefits, the amount of resources allocated for social welfare as a whole might not be increased. Consequently, other social welfare claimants will suffer, although possibly not to the same extent individually as the beneficiaries gain. When social welfare claimants realize there has been no improvement overall, they will become even more disillusioned with the system. Even if there is an overall benefit as a result of the decision, the less favourable view might suggest that the relevant agency will simply ignore it or that the government will take legislative or executive action to reverse its effect. The bottom line of this less favourable interpretation is probably that improvement can only occur if there is a fundamental change in political alignments, in the social structure or in the society's values, and that a single court victory will rarely, if ever, achieve any of these.

Procedural change encompasses matters such as greater openness in decision-making and respect for social welfare claimants and their rights. In some situations a change in procedure can ameliorate the conditions experienced by social welfare claimants even if it does not reduce their poverty in any way. An old person's move from unfit housing can be made smoother by the more considerate attitude of a housing authority, although there is absolutely no dent on existing legal provisions or social conditions.[120] In other situations, procedural change is worth little if there is no substantive change. By way of example, the only advantage a social welfare claimant would obtain as a result of being accorded natural justice is delay if a social welfare benefit is ultimately denied. Overall it seems that procedural change is not as vital for social welfare claimants as substantive change, although it cannot be dismissed out of hand, for the manner in which social welfare claimants are treated may be as important to them as whether they are materially benefited.

Procedural change improving the position of social welfare claimants falls possibly into three categories. First, there are those which result in social welfare claimants being treated with greater personal consideration. Changes in the law can do little directly in this sphere, although measures such as reducing the discretion available to social welfare bureaucracies may have an indirect impact. Another illustration of what can be done is provided by the law centre which convinced the local court that tenants of mortgagors should be notified after proceedings are commenced against their landlords by the mortgagees.[121] Often a mortgagee has not approved a tenancy and any power of the mortgagor to lease is forbidden in the mortgage document. Consequently the tenant can be evicted if the mortgagee forecloses or appoints a receiver.[122] Apparently the idea behind the notification was that although it would not affect the position of the tenant at law, he or she might be able to make representations to the mortgagee to be granted a new tenancy.[123]

The second type of procedural reform promotes greater consideration of an individual's needs. Relevant in this regard is the general principle of administrative law that a policy cannot be applied irrespective of the circumstances of individual claimants. Where social welfare bodies are required to give reasons for their decisions, this might result in more attention being given to individual needs.

Thirdly, a procedural reform may try to ensure that legal rights are given the emphasis in practice they have in theory. Widening the access of social welfare claimants to legal services and to courts and tribunals is one aspect of this. Another is the effort to improve the take-up of social welfare benefits and services – for example, to encourage persons to apply for the maximum to which they are entitled and to assist them to appeal against adverse decisions. Such steps might have a definite effect on the amount of social welfare benefits paid and services provided, at least in the short run. Funding for social welfare benefits and services is open-ended in the short run, in that those who establish a claim must be paid, although in the long run a government can compensate for increased claims in one area by cutting back elsewhere, possibly by failing to increase the level of benefits and services in line with inflation. The difficulty of separating procedural and substantive change is obvious from this example, for facilitating claims for social welfare benefits and services may produce substantive changes.

Substantive change does not necessarily involve increasing the social welfare benefits and services available. In particular situations it might be as important to build the political power of the poorer sections of society, enabling them to exercise greater control over their lives, by assisting in the formation of residents' associations, tenants' unions and workers' cooperatives. As well, a more efficient allocation of given resources can also bring about beneficial substantive change. For example, squatting and the litigation associated with it has made some housing authorities appreciate the foolishness of gutting perfectly usable housing when redevelopment would not take place for a considerable time.

The following sections attempt to assess the impact of various tactics in effecting social change, with the focus on those where law and lawyers have a prominent role. This account draws on diverse sources, but mainly on the experience of groups pursuing social change. The obvious deficiency in this approach is that it does not tap adequately information on the behaviour of institutions such as social welfare bureaucracies, property owners and employers, against whom reformers direct their activity.

Lawyers, law and social change

In addition to the achievements of test-case litigation, lawyers can point to their involvement in other activities which have resulted in social change. A good example at the community level is provided by the Contract Buyers' League, which obtained some redress for middle-aged blacks who had been over-charged in the purchase of housing in Chicago. Tactics included picketing the offices of real-estate agents, visiting their homes and neighbours, pamphleteering, withholding mortgage payments, attracting media coverage, and bringing test cases, one of which ultimately proved successful.[124] Without support from lawyers, the League would have been in a weaker bargaining position, but this was only one element in their success, and possibly less important than direct action, in particular the withholding of mortgage payments.[125] Similarly, lawyers have had a role at the national level. For example, a community lawyer and other community activists in Coventry had some success as part of a national campaign to discredit pyramid selling, in that clauses were inserted in the Fair Trading Act 1973 regulating the practice. But a national finance house was slow to assist those who had taken out second mortgages with it to finance their participation in pyramid selling schemes. Later the finance house made concessions when an action group of former participants undertook a sustained, national campaign of publicity and lobbying.[126]

Law centres can point to various successes as a result of their activity. Financially, they have obtained additional social welfare benefits through advice and advocacy and financial compensation in relation to housing (e.g. noise insulation, rehousing), and they have also assisted low-income-earners obtain the wages they are entitled to under minimum-wage laws. For many, law-centre activity has meant more secure or better accommodation because eviction has been prevented and landlords have been obliged to live up to their legal obligation to repair. Deprived communities have also benefited as a result of the work of law centres, as with planning decisions affecting particular areas.[127] Environmental improvements have also been achieved: for instance, law centres have taken up cases where residents have injured themselves by falling over on the broken and disrepaired pavements in an area and have been partially successful in persuading public authorities to carry out the necessary work.[128]

A frequent claim is that the mere fact that a law centre exists has brought about changes in the policies and procedures of property owners, government authorities and social welfare bureaucracies, if only because they have wanted to avoid the nuisance of having their decisions constantly questioned. For example: 'The Law Centre could assure clients of a speedy response from the Housing Department, once the clear threat of legal action had been established: though even this did not always prove the final answer, merely establishing a clear gap between statutory obligations and the ability of the service to respond.'[129] The volume of cases a law centre handles may be an important factor here, for unless challenges and monitoring are persistent there will be no incentive for institutions to change. Systematic studies are necessary to understand fully the impact of the activity of law centres, for example to determine whether landlords are more cognizant of the rights of tenants, or whether social welfare bureaucracies are more favourable to claimants in the exercise of their functions. A survey of American social welfare personnel indicated that their behaviour may have changed as a result of the presence of law centres: 'Possibly for the first time they have become aware of and concerned for the legal rights of their clients.'[130]

Law centres acknowledge that at times they have failed to achieve desired changes. Newham Rights Centre in London seems to have begun on an optimistic note, influenced by achievements in the United States, but in a short time seems to have become disillusioned. The Centre took some sixty housing-related test cases in 1976 as part of a campaign against the policy of the local authority regarding public housing, yet relations with the housing department continued to be 'appalling'.[131] The Centre became sceptical about the efficacy of achieving reform through law and turned more to community politics:

Often the victims of housing policy and government expenditure have no sufficient legal remedy. In such cases tenants' associations can win more for their members than a clever lawyer can squeeze out of the law or a judge. Furthermore, as we record below, the legal remedies available, when explored, can only be effective for a small number of tenants. For each case in which we succeed there are hundreds of people who never have the opportunity to succeed. And there are hundreds more with similar problems to whom the law offers no remedy. Inevitably the legal approach to a housing problem as an individual problem, remote from the same problem affecting the next door neighbour, obscures the issue . . .

So in cases of 'unfitness', whenever the Local Authority's Environmental Health Department disagrees that a property is unfit – we have as yet not had the resources to apply to the High Court for mandamus. A team of ten or a hundred lawyers would probably not achieve any detectable improvement in the overall housing situation. They might do more cases and help more clients but by reducing the theatre of argument to the Law Courts, they would merely define which lucky people qualified for legal redress. . . . All this leads to the conclusion that the law can never solve the basic problems of the community. At worst it is a cosmetic applied to the face of a society which is composed of rotten housing and widespread poverty. At its best it is an antiseptic cream to clear up the worst boils that appear before those boils develop into an untreatable outbreak – rebellion.[132]

The results of direct action

Squatting, rent strikes and the activities of claimants' unions demonstrate that direct action can sometimes reap social change. One suggestion is that direct action is more likely to have an impact when those engaged in it play a central role in an institution or programme, in which powerful groups also have a significant stake.[133] As already discussed, law and lawyers have some relevance to direct action.

Squatting in New York in the sixties and early seventies had mixed success: in some instances private owners accepted that squatters could remain as licencees or agreed to renovate squatted buildings with financial assistance from the City and to accept the squatters and remaining tenants at low rentals. The City itself agreed to the continued occupancy by squatters of property which was to be demolished as a part of the West Side Urban Renewal area and also to re-evaluate the plan. The squatters here conducted an intensive political campaign – they could draw on wide dissatisfaction with the plan, and they had the tacit threat of obtaining a court injunction against the plan on the basis that it failed to meet federal guidelines. But other squatters lost in their confrontation for possession of apartments owned by three hospitals: the hospitals seemed to be not as vulnerable to political or other pressure as private landlords (whose harassment had led to demonstrations and arrests) or the City, and there was no history of community activism in the areas surrounding the hospitals.[134]

Squatting in Britain occurred after the Great War, and gained prominence again after World War II when large numbers of ex-servicemen and their families occupied disused service camps. The government was in a weak position politically because there was general community support for ex-servicemen, the housing shortage was obvious, and the Labour Government had been elected on a platform of social reform. Eventually the government handed over former service camps to the squatters, but it drew the line and instituted prosecutions against squatters who turned to private housing in urban areas.[135] Public opinion was less favourable to the resurgence of squatting in the late sixties.[136] However, under pressure from squatters local councils were forced to use their empty housing more efficiently. Some simply tolerate squatting, but others attempt to regularize it by granting licences to squatters' organizations or by making squatters legal tenants. In fact squatters' organizations were valuable to local authorities since they took responsibility for the cost of repairs and administration, undertook to move their members when a building was finally needed, and also made it less likely that a council would be held to the statutory nuisance provisions of the Public Health Act 1936.[137] As well as providing housing for the homeless, squatting contributed to shifts in national policy – to the move away from large-scale redevelopment to financial assistance for the renovation of existing housing, and to the enactment of the Housing (Homeless Persons) Act 1977.

The most publicized squatting in Australia occurred in Victoria Street, Sydney, in 1973, when persons objecting to a large residential redevelopment proposed for the area moved in and squatted in the vacant buildings intended to be demolished. Together with the builders labourers' trade union (which imposed a 'green ban'), the squatters objected to the environmental impact of the development and the loss of low-cost accommodation in the inner city to which it would contribute. After some six months the squatters were removed *en masse* by the police; some were charged and convicted with entering and remaining on property without reasonable cause.[138] The upshot of the Victoria Street squatting was that as a condition of development approval, the developer undertook to restore some of the terraces. Ten years later terraces are vacant and have fallen into disrepair; part of the residential development has proceeded, other parts are still before the Land and Environment Court for approval, and what was a working-class area is now decidedly upper-middle class.

The 1915 rent strike by workers in Glasgow and other cities led directly to the introduction of rent control with the Increase of Rent and Mortgage Interest (War Restrictions) Act 1915. On the Clyde between 1921 and 1926 some 20,000 tenants in Glasgow, and some tens of thousands in West Scotland, engaged in a rent strike when landlords sought to increase rents. As a result the government appointed a Commission which in 1925 suggested simplified increases. Although in 1926 the strike petered out after adverse court decisions, the strikers apparently obtained savings overall in the rent which would otherwise have been payable. In the USA, a rent strike in public housing in St Louis in 1969 was ultimately successful. The housing authority was under pressure because of a deficit, because it was revealed that the rent schedule which had precipitated the strike had never been lawfully approved, and because mass evictions could not be contemplated for fear of race riots. After mediation by a prominent trade unionist – the only person accepted by both sides – a scheme of decentralized management was introduced, run by trained residents, with housing-authority assistance, enforcing community-developed standards (e.g. residents express preferences in relation to priorities in questionnaires), together with a social service programme including the appointment of social and youth directors.[139] By contrast with these successes, a rent strike by some 2,000 council tenants in St Pancras, London, in 1960 was defeated after ten months: five hundred eviction notices were issued and many tenants made private agreements to pay off arrears. The strike failed to attract wider support from the trade unions (the area was not heavily industrialized) or from the local Labour Party, which disassociated itself from the campaign when violence occurred.[140] Similarly, a rent strike in East London in 1968–70 over increased rents in council dwellings collapsed after the Court of Appeal upheld the legality of the increases.[141]

These and other rent strikes suggest that to be successful a rent strike needs certain ingredients.[142] First, rent-strikers must be clear about their aims, whether they object to all or only part of a rent increase or the extent of the repairs they expect to be made. Clearly if a rent increase is not effected as a result of a rent strike there is a gain for tenants, provided that it is not counteracted in other ways such as a failure to repair. Where a rent strike concerns repairs, a landlord may be provoked into carrying out emergency repairs to break the strike but fail to follow through with fundamental repairs.[143] The second point is that if a rent strike is to gain support and remain solid, tenants must be confident that they will not suffer from eviction or later reprisals.[144] It may be possible to delay matters and to encourage the landlord(s) to settle by defending eviction proceedings. Lawyers representing rent-strikers can usually find technical defences to hinder eviction proceedings, and if landlords proceed with the mass eviction of rent-strikers it may be possible to jam the courts by defending every case. However, landlords will usually seek to demoralize a campaign by proceeding selectively against the organizers. Finally, there must be organization, demonstrations, publicity and lobbying to gain wider support for a rent strike both among the tenants affected and in the wider community. Trade-union support was crucial in successes such as the Clydeside rent strikes, although it was easily mobilized there because many tenants belonged to the same shipbuilding unions and evictions clearly affected the well-being of union members.[145] Organization is necessary if it is decided to collect the rent withheld in a central fund for bargaining purposes or in the event of an unsatisfactory outcome, or if there is to be the co-ordinated defence of eviction proceedings.

Claimants' unions are a further example of direct action worth examining. Among the demands of claimants' unions have been that claimants should receive the maximum social welfare benefits to which they are entitled, that claimants should be fully informed about the administration of social welfare benefits, and that recipients should be treated in a more dignified manner by social welfare bureaucracies.[146] Tactics which have been used include sit-ins in social welfare offices and automatic appeals against adverse determinations. Claimants' unions usually comprise claimants and ex-claimants, and while a few members have gained publicity in the media the claimants' unions generally eschew tight organization or hierarchy. Another factor in the tactics of claimants' unions has been that membership is transitory: people join because of the promise of material gain, but usually withdraw when this is achieved.[147] Claimants' unions have clearly won social welfare payments which members would not have obtained, either because they did not have the knowledge of what to claim or how best to go about it.[148] It is also said that, as a result of successful claims, social welfare claimants have restored faith in themselves. Further, claimants' unions may have imparted organizing skills to members, which have been carried over to other issues. Some claimants' unions have organized co-operative shops and housing (via squatting). Valuable as these achievements have been, claimants' unions have failed to work for policy shifts at the national level.

The record of social change through the courts

In the United States, test-case litigation to improve the position of the disadvantaged has been on a larger scale and has extended over a longer period than in other countries. In the five years from 1967 to 1972, of the 219 cases involving social welfare issues brought to the Supreme Court, 136 were decided on the merits, and in 73 the outcome was favourable.[149] Few of the test cases elsewhere rival those in the United States in the breadth of the principles raised, the publicity generated, or the wider results which are said to have occurred.

But how effective was this test-case activity? The former director of the OEO legal services programme defends the achievements of its law-reform activity and identified different ways in which that activity increased the distribution of goods and services to poor people, such as through the enforcement and extension of minimum-wage laws.[150] He also points to how more people gained social welfare benefits because in test cases sponsored by the OEO legal services programme the Supreme Court struck down restrictive rules regarding cohabitation and state residency requirements:[151]

When the Supreme Court overturned these limitations in legal services lawsuits filed during 1968 and 1969, HEW [Department of Health, Education and Welfare] predicted a $300 million to $400 million increase in public assistance income. At the time of the Court decisions, that translated to a potential 3.5 percent to 5 percent increase in the welfare dollars distributed to the poor, a 2.5 to 3.6 percent reduction in the income gap, and a 1 percent increment in the total income received by the bottom fifth of the population.[152]

Moreover, a Californian legal services agency had the courts declare invalid Governor Reagan's action in reducing medical payments to the poor, thus restoring over $200 million in benefits,[153] while litigation compelled various states to implement the food stamps programme, leading to the payment of millions of dollars worth of food.[154] Totalling the benefits accruing as a result of these activities, and comparing them with the cost of the legal services programme, Johnson concludes 'that benefits to the poverty community outweighed the cost of the program by a ratio of approximately 7 to 1'.[155]

There are difficulties with this type of analysis and with extrapolating it into the future. Calculations of costs and benefits can only be estimates: for example, if a social welfare benefit becomes available as a result of a test case, there is no guarantee that it will reach potential beneficiaries – because of bureaucratic failure and the fact that not everyone who qualifies takes up social welfare entitlements.[156] More importantly, success in the past is no basis for saying that test-case litigation will always be successful. The situation in the United States in the sixties and early seventies was atypical. Today the courts work within a political and economic environment in which the real living standards of the poor are being squeezed. Even in the event of a court deciding a case which substantially benefits the disadvantaged, governments would most likely try to reverse the decision or cut back in another area of social welfare.[157]

The achievements of civil rights lawyers in test-case litigation concerning race outrank those of lawyers acting in social welfare matters. The reasons for the difference are important to an understanding of the limits to using the legal system as a means of social change. Civil rights lawyers were heavily involved in Supreme Court litigation from the 1930s onwards, whereas it was not until the mid-sixties that lawyers became active in social welfare matters. Social forces in the United States were conducive to the breakdown of racial discrimination – given expression by the courts in cases such as *Brown* v. *Board of Education*.[158] The need for black labour in urban areas meant that Southern segregation was no longer in keeping with market forces, while it became difficult after World War II for the United States to win international support when racial discrimination continued at home. By contrast there were few social forces pressing for any significant change in the relative position of those such as social welfare claimants, public-housing tenants and the homeless. In the light of such factors it is not surprising that the courts adopted a more circumspect stand in test cases involving social welfare issues.[159] Furthermore, apart from the symbolic value of decisions such as *Brown* v. *Board of Education*, court victories played only a supplementary role in the move towards greater racial equality. Indeed in housing and reverse discrimination cases, civil rights groups enjoyed only mixed success. More important were the direct action (civil disobedience) of blacks and their sympathizers and the legislative and executive actions of the federal government.[160]

While it is impossible to sum up precisely the experience of test-case litigation elsewhere – there are too few cases, they are not easy to categorize, and the long-term results of some are hard to identify – some points are worth making. Some of the supplementary benefits decisions instituted by the Child Poverty Action Group in Britain as part of its test-case strategy have been successful. The revival of section 99 of the Public Health Act 1936 by Shelter, the Public Health Advisory Service and community groups is of interest for it involved existing law being applied rather than changed. The narrow inter-pretation of the law in *National Coal Board* v. *Thorne*(1976)[161] is counterbalanced by the many successes which community groups have had with it in magistrates' courts. The experience with section 99 is especially interesting for, at the outset, those responsible for its revival were quite pessimistic about how the courts would respond.[162] If some test cases have had positive, albeit limited, benefits, others have had a less helpful effect. Obviously there are cases where a court has rejected the argument presented, although it should be reiterated that these might generate pressure for favourable legislative change. For instance, the failure of the plaintiff in *Roberts* v. *Dorset C.C.*(1976),[163] a case sponsored by Shelter, was one small part of the campaign which ultimately led to the Housing (Homeless Persons) Act 1977. But in addition, there are several examples where a test-case victory in the courts has been reversed by legislative or executive action. CPAG's first success, *R.* v. *Greater Birmingham Appeal Tribunal, ex p. Simper*(1973),[164] established that the Supplementary Benefits Commission should exercise a discretion and should not auto-matically set off against any long-term addition a benefit for exceptional circumstances. However, legislation was speedily enacted providing that officers should continue to offset against the long-term addition.[165] Lobbying by CPAG and other groups failed to have the bill amended during its passage through Parliament. Similarly, after CPAG and Shelter instituted a test case (which never came to court) on the duty of local authorities to provide temporary accommodation for persons in urgent need, an amendment substituted for the original duty a mere power of local authorities to provide such accommodation.[166] Legislation and regulations made under it were used to reverse claimants' victories in *R. v. Barnsley SBAT, ex p. Atkinson*[167] and *R. v. Bristol SBAT, ex p. Southwell*.[168]

Similar reversals of successful test cases have occurred in other jurisdictions.[169] In addition to reversals, there are instances of social welfare bureaucracies and of governments refusing to implement the outcome of successful cases. In a Canadian case, social welfare claimants eventually obtained an order for mandamus directing the social assistance committee of the city of Halifax to pay a particular social welfare benefit, after it refused to comply with an order of the provincial social assistance appeal board to do so.[170] Following the decision in 1977 in *Green* v. *Daniels*,[171] in which the Australian High Court granted a declaration to the effect that a school-leaver was entitled to unemployment benefits from the time she had left school, the Director-General of Social Security held that she was ineligible on other grounds and also refused to re-open the cases of other school-leavers who had been rejected on the grounds ruled to be unlawful. Investigations by the Commonwealth Ombudsman, protracted by the Director-General's obduracy, and an adverse report by him to the Prime Minister under the Ombudsman Act 1976, finally led to *ex gratia* payments being made to a few of the school-leavers affected. Meanwhile Parliament reversed the effect of the *Green* decision for the future.[172] In the United States, *Welsch* v. *Likins*[173] is an instance where a state government refused to incur the expenditure required by a court order, in that case on mental hospitals. Clearly these various instances illustrate that if test-case litigation is to be used to effect social change, it must go hand in hand with political action to prevent its effects being negated.

V CONCLUSION

In general terms, one avenue of social change in the welfare state cannot be said to be more effective than another. In particular circumstances, changes have been effected through Fabian tactics and community politics (lobbying, petitions, publicity, test cases in the courts, etc.), as well as through direct action. Along with the successes associated with these tactics, however, have been failures, stalemates where the status quo has been preserved from attack, and changes where the benefits and costs have cancelled each other out. As well as the tactics adopted, what a group is pursuing must also be considered. Outside the United States, the groups seeking social change through test cases in the courts cannot expect a great deal of success for the procedural, institutional and other reasons outlined. Relevant to institutional change are whether a group wants to compel or prevent a particular act, or to have an institution adopt a whole set of new practices on a permanent basis; whether one institution is involved (such as a social welfare bureaucracy) or a number (such as the landlords in a geographical area); and whether the immediate change requires only a single, high-level visible action, or a complex series of decisions within an institution with wide discretion hidden from public gaze.[174]

Finally social change, including social change through the legal system, cannot be isolated from the context of the economic and political power sought to be affected. A community group which comes up against a property company, finance house or social welfare bureaucracy may find that these bodies mobilize significant resources to protect their interests. Included amongst these are their contacts in government, the way they can portray the group, and the legitimacy of their opposition (for example, that a change threatens employment or requires considerable public expenditure).[175]

8
Conclusion

In this examination of the legal foundations of the welfare state, the focus has been on three interrelated features – (1) the relationship between the individual on the one hand and law and the legal system on the other; (2) the legislation creating social rights; and (3) the role of law and the legal system in social change. The framework provided by these features served to integrate the relevant, but disparate areas of substantive and procedural law considered, and to place these within their social, economic and political context. It remains to draw together some points which emerge from the study.

Prior to the advent of modern society, the legal rights and protections of individuals turned on their status – as lord, merchant, villein, poor person, and so on. Arbitrary action was often characteristic of the law. The hallmark of modern society is the move away from particularistic to universal norms, the legal rights and protections of which are open to all. The legal transformation is partly captured in Maine's well-known phrase about the movement from status to contract, although in the area of public law a key legal value of the new order is equality before the law. A formal interpretation of equality before the law requires impartiality in the administration of the law and that equals be treated equally. Power and wealth should be checked if they subvert these ends. Another interpretation of equality before the law demands that measures be taken so that in practice the law is administered impartially and equals are treated equally. In addition to these interpretations in relation to the administration of the law, a third interpretation of equality before the law looks to the substance of the law and asks whether departures from equality can be justified.

In the welfare state, equality before the law in the administration of the law is an ideal which is not always realized in practice. Economic and social inequalities, as Weber appreciated, subvert equality before the law by affecting how the state administers the law and how its provisions are invoked. Associated with both aspects are different patterns in the utilization of legal services in the community. In terms of the first aspect, state administration of the law, there is some evidence of bias in the way the criminal law is enforced. In particular, there is an imbalance in the resources allocated to enforcing the ordinary criminal law as compared, say, with social welfare regulation. The principle of equality before the law is modified in relation to the administration of social welfare benefits and services to enable these to be tailored to individual needs. Even so, social welfare bureaucracies sometimes act in a way which violates the standards of impartiality and the principle that equals be treated equally.

The second aspect, the differences in the way the rights and protections of the law are invoked, is a recurrent theme of the book. In relation to the civil law, a lack of wealth and its correlates (knowledge, skills, confidence and so on) lead to the non-assertion of rights by the poorer sections of society.[1] The combination of these factors is sometimes referred to as their lack of legal competence. Similarly, there is an under-utilization of social rights. For example, the beneficiaries of social welfare regulation fail to mobilize its protections either directly or by complaining to the relevant enforcement agencies. The take-up problem bedevils the provision of social welfare benefits and services. A factor in their non-assertion is the way they are administered. Social welfare bureaucracies are passive – they are generally under no legal obligation, and do not undertake, to assist beneficiaries to pursue their social rights. From the point of view of the beneficiaries' social rights, it may not be in their interests to claim, for fear, say, that their landlord, employer, or the social welfare bureaucracy administering their benefits will retaliate in some way.

There are law-related steps which have a part to play in mitigating the reluctance of individuals to assert rights. Examples from the administration of the law are procedural changes which may facilitate small civil-law claims (class actions, small claims courts, neighbourhood justice centres, and so on) and the enforcement of regulatory standards (along the lines, for example, of section 99 of the Public Health Act 1936). Public provision for, and the reorganization of, legal services have been mentioned at various points. In the substantive law, examples are doctrines which permit tenant self-help in the event of landlords failing to repair, and the doctrine of retaliatory eviction, which offers protection from eviction to tenants who complain to the relevant regulatory agency about a breach of housing standards. Various measures can be taken in relation to state bureaucracies. At a general level, requiring reasons for decisions (if requested), freedom of information legislation, and public participation may make state bureaucracies more accountable to potential beneficiaries. Another approach is to charge an agency with the task of pursuing rights on behalf of their beneficiaries, either individually or collectively. The principle underlying a 'poverty advocate' is not new; it is analogous to the procedure for public nuisance whereby the Attorney-General can seek an injunction on behalf of the public against an unlawful act or omission which interferes with the lives, safety or comfort of the public or a section of it. More specifically, regulatory agencies can be subject to mandatory duties to enforce the law, or at least to justify a failure to do so. Social welfare bureaucracies can be obliged, in both direct and indirect ways, to take reasonable steps to seek out potential beneficiaries. Finally, lawyers can assist and strengthen collective action in the form, say, of tenants' unions and claimants' unions. The former reduce the risk of retaliatory action, while the latter maximize claims for social welfare.

The under-utilization of the rights and protections of the law has immediate substantive effects. For example, because those such as workers and tenants under-utilize their rights, freedom of contract gives capital the advantage in standard-form contracts. The failure of claimants to 'take up' their social rights means greater personal hardship in the form of higher rents, lower-standard housing, less received in social welfare benefits, and so on. Apart from these immediate effects of the under-utilization of the rights and protections of the law, there are implications for the substantive law. If personal injury and family matters are put to one side, the courts have been exposed primarily to the arguments of commercial, property and government interests. That is one reason why, for example, the common law favours landlords over tenants. Areas of law like this violate the broad, substantive standard of equality before the law in that the preferences they create cannot be justified.

It is wrong to regard equality before the law as an empty shell which merely legitimates the existing distribution of rights in society. Equality before the law can be used as a standard to test the law and legal administration in relation to particular groups in society. The legitimacy of the welfare state would be undermined if equality before the law was obviously a sham. Therefore, a blatant disjuncture between equality before the law and reality can be used as part of a strategy to pursue measures of benefit to these groups and to defend gains already made. Clearly there are limits to this strategy if equality before the law is interpreted in a formal or procedural, rather than substantive manner. Moreover there may not be a strong public perception that equality before the law is being violated. Defenders of the status quo may claim that a particular divergence between equality before the law and reality is isolated and has not infected the system as a whole, may place a different but plausible interpretation on what equality before the law demands in particular circumstances, or may argue that given the lack of resources all possible is being done to observe the standard. Competing values such as freedom, security, efficiency and 'law and order' may blunt the impact of equality before the law.

The regulation of private capital and the provision of benefits and services are the primary techniques of the welfare state. These are reflected in a range of social welfare legislation which creates a variety of social rights. Factors relevant to the implementation of social welfare legislation are the background to its emergence, its form, the way it is administered, the response of those affected, and the side-effects it causes. First, there is the emergence of social welfare legislation. Specific measures of social welfare regulation, and specific social welfare benefits and public services, have been justified as mitigating some of the legal and social inequalities already mentioned – for example, the public provision of legal services, by addressing the concern that legal rights have not been equally enjoyed in practice by all sections of society; rent control and the regulation of housing standards, by overcoming the inequalities in the common law of landlord and tenant; and of course social welfare benefits and public services, by reducing economic inequalities. Reducing inequalities, or goals such as justice or compassion, are not the only motives behind social welfare legislation, for reformers may be concerned with rationalization or clarity, while professional and commercial groups may support change for self-interest or other reasons. The failure of social welfare legislation to achieve its goals may be evident in the way it emerges historically. It may have been designed for important symbolic reasons, without much attention as to whether it would be effective in practice. Another possibility is that although intended to be effective, the social welfare legislation which eventually emerges may be deficient because of opposition from political, economic or social interests. Once enacted, social welfare legislation may be undermined, or it may be turned to functions other than originally contemplated. Largely unexplored is whether these aspects are related to the use of primary or secondary legislation. To what extent, for example, are social rights set out in primary legislation subtracted from by their specification in secondary legislation?[2]

The force of social welfare legislation turns, secondly, on its form. Attention must obviously be given to the substance of any social right created and the nature of the underlying principles (e.g. sex equality, open government). Surprisingly, the point is sometimes overlooked by advocates of 'welfare rights'. One aspect is the extent of the advantage conferred. A second is the type of benefit, such as the dichotomy between welfare in money or in kind. Financial transfers of the first type may be said to preserve a relative freedom as compared with the latter which involves the provision of goods or services according to criteria as to what is thought appropriate. Another aspect is whether a social right is subject to onerous conditions, for, as with relief under the poor law, social welfare benefits are sometimes subject to conditions that claimants must behave in certain ways, or adopt (or at least appear to adopt) certain values, which they would not do freely. These conditions have their origins, at least in part, in morality (the cohabitation rule, the work test), economics (obliging claimants to institute maintenance actions) and politics (the industrial- or trade-dispute disqualification). The assumption is that the payment of public money gives the right to impose conditions. However, the conditions attached to some social welfare benefits adversely affect the dignity of individual claimants. Moreover, social welfare bureaucracies may concentrate to such an extent on enforcing these conditions that they overlook the underlying goals of the legislation. Specifically legal factors relating to the form of social rights are the legislative techniques and legal concepts employed. These may be inconsistent with the legislative goals, in conflict, inappropriate to the present-day context, or excessively complex, with the result that legislation does not measure up to the expectations held of it. Among the reasons for these defects are the circumstances surrounding the emergence of the legislation, inertia in reforming it, a lack of prescience on the part of those formulating it, and technical failings in drafting.

At a more general level, the juridical character of social welfare legislation may be inappropriate to its goals. The social rights it creates may be too indeterminate; in other words, the state bureaucracy or agency administering it may have too great a discretion because of the absence of legislative standards or the power to depart from those enunciated. Another possibility is that those administering social welfare legislation may lack accountability, either within the department or agency, or externally to bodies such as the courts, an ombudsman, a tribunal, or an inspectorate. Finally, the strength of the rights created by social welfare legislation may compare poorly with comparable rights in private law (for example, in relation to occupational welfare).[3] These features in the juridical character of social welfare legislation – discretion, accountability and the basis of entitlement – are complex but are nonetheless more relevant than traditional legal distinctions such as between primary and secondary legislation. Their complexity is illustrated by the first, the delineation of social rights. Discretion entrusted to an agency administering social welfare regulation may be used on the one hand to benefit capital, but on the other hand to insulate the powerless from draconian measures. Social welfare bureaucracies entrusted with considerable discretion can formulate policy which may either benefit or disadvantage claimants. A law centre may make significant gains in relation both to social rights subject to wide discretion, because of its knowledge of the system, and to social rights subject to narrow discretion, by taking advantage of technicalities and procedures.

However, these examples should not lead to an agnosticism about discretion. Certain combinations of rules and discretion are better than others, if beneficiaries are to be informed of their rights, treated with respect, and guaranteed that norms are applied equally to those in similar circumstances. The optimum combination varies with the circumstances – the social rights involved, the type of beneficiaries, the character of those entrusted with administration, the costs, whether any body charged with external review is in a position itself to develop standards, and so on. For example, wide discretion may be quite successful in cases where the issue is straightforward, finance is generous, beneficiaries are relatively well-informed, and the administration is imbued with integrity and a respect for beneficiaries. Some cases of one-off emergency relief for those affected by fire and flood are of this character. With most aspects of social welfare administration, wide discretion would generally seem to be undesirable and conducive to arbitrary decision-making – understanding among many types of beneficiaries is relatively low, not least because the legislative provisions are complex; many beneficiaries are vulnerable, socially, financially or both; and state bureaucracies are apt to assume that they know what is best for beneficiaries. However, at the other extreme the history of tax law demonstrates that a considerable body of rules can mean uncertainty because of legislative complexity and the multiplication of possibilities for disputed interpretation.

The third feature in understanding the implementation of social welfare legislation is the nature of its administration. There are a number of examples in previous chapters of how the importance of the type of administration manifests itself. The right which it was said persons had to relief under the poor law was belied by the way the local poor-law authorities administered it. A lack of financial and human resources detracts from the implementation of social welfare regulation, although internal procedures, agency priorities, and enforcement philosophy also determine whether breaches are uncovered and action taken. The reality of benefit administration in the welfare state is that social welfare bureaucracies are largely passive, relying on individuals to take the initiative, rather than seeking out eligible claimants. Claimants sometimes fail to obtain their full entitlements because of bureaucratic procedures associated with the point of reception, the investigative stance social welfare bureaucracies adopt towards claimants, and the way claims are routinely processed. The perceptions which beneficiaries have of social rights, and therefore their initiative in mobilizing them, is partly a product of the policies of social welfare bureaucracies, for example whether they communicate the existence of rights and minimize any stigma individuals feel in claiming. Local or provincial administration of public services may result in an undermining of the goals of the relevant social welfare legislation of the central government. Overall, social welfare bureaucracies sometimes act in a way which detracts from, and in some cases even negates, the social rights created by social welfare legislation. The causes of this include weaknesses in the relevant legislation, inadequate resources, the cult of expertise, and the tendency to focus on particular, measurable, ends to the detriment of the wider context. Part of the latter are the social characteristics and vulnerability of the typical beneficiary, and the isolation of beneficiaries of rights from those administering them.

Traditional legal principles such as natural justice have little if any relevance in understanding the reality of benefit administration. Making social rights effective, therefore, involves transforming social welfare bureaucracies as much as changes in, say, external review. Law has some relevance to this task. Modifying the discretion entrusted to social welfare bureaucracies, for example, may reduce the possibility of their introducing extra-legal notions into the administration of social rights. A language of rights in social welfare legislation, rather than of the duties of social welfare bureaucracies, may undercut conceptions which adversely affect the take-up of social rights.[4] There is scope for requiring social welfare bureaucracies to take the initiative in enforcing the law or to seek out eligible beneficiaries. Procedural law facilitating collective claims, such as provision for class actions, is another example. In addition to these legal measures, however, institutional changes are necessary. Internally, procedures need to be modified, manuals rewritten, staff trained, and beneficiaries involved. Externally, institutions such as Ombudsmen and inspectorates can encourage the institutionalization of desirable practices.

Implementation depends frequently on the extent to which the direct effects of social welfare legislation outweigh other effects. There are various problems in evaluating the direct effects of social welfare legislation. Even an important issue such as whether a particular social welfare benefit or service reduces inequality requires detailed calculations. Determining whether a particular measure of social welfare regulation has an impact on the institutions to which it is directed, or whether the conditions attached to social welfare benefits have moulded claimants' behaviour, is even more complicated because statistical evidence is not generally available. Consequently, it is often a matter of judgement whether a change has occurred, and whether the change is attributable to social welfare legislation. Social welfare legislation may give rise to evasion, or the wealthier or more calculating may obtain more benefit than intended. Examples of specific independent and unintended effects are the possibilty of compulsory improvement deterring house purchases in certain areas; if minimum-wage legislation adversely affects unionization; if rent control induces a decline in privately rented accommodation; and if clearance and redevelopment break up communities or benefit commercial or property interests.

At present the welfare state is under pressure in many Western societies. Its so called failure is explained in part by the legal factors just considered. In addition it seems necessary to refer briefly to some relevant social, economic and political factors. Socially, the welfare state has achieved a measure of security for many in need, but it has become apparent that significant numbers still live in poverty, including many qualifying for social welfare benefits and services, and many in low-paid employment supposedly protected by minimum-wage legislation.[5] In addition, the evidence has accumulated that the welfare state does not benefit all equally – the take-up of many social welfare benefits and public services is low, and public expenditure on the universal services frequently advantages the better-off rather than the poorer sections of society.[6] As a response, policies have been launched to increase the take-up of benefits, to improve the lot of the low-paid (for example, through universal child benefit or family allowance), and to ensure positive discrimination in favour of the poorer section of society (for example, urban aid programmes, housing improvement policies, and educational priority areas). None of these policies matches what for some seem to be the major causes of 'failure', that the welfare state has never been funded generously enough, or been designed to redistribute income, wealth and power in any significant way.

Rising unemployment, public expenditure limits and demographic changes (such as disproportionate increases in one-parent families and old people) are a second source of pressure on the welfare state. Many argue that economic growth is a prerequisite to maintaining the benefits and services of the welfare state.[7] Of course any addition to economic surplus may be directed to other purposes such as private consumption or defence, rather than to strengthening social welfare. Certainly economic growth enables the financial demands of the welfare state to be met more easily, obviating the political problems associated with increasing taxation or redistributing existing resources. Consequently, the economic recession in Western societies has made important inroads into the welfare state.

A third source of pressure on the welfare state is the resurgence of neo-conservative ideology. In the decades immediately following World War II the welfare state was thought to be an accepted feature of society, along with the mixed economy, both representing the middle way between *laissez faire* and collectivism. This picture has been upset by the neo-conservative attack on what are said to be the inefficiencies of the welfare state and the threats it poses to economic production and to liberty. Neo-conservatives regard much social welfare as having sapped independence and initiative, and weakened people's will to work and to make their own arrangements for contingencies such as sickness, unemployment and old age. Neo-conservative philosophy is premised on the assumption that individuals are generally the authors of their own plight. State social welfare should be available mainly for the really needy and for those who cannot care for themselves through physical or mental disability. In the neo-conservative view there should be a greater reliance on voluntary social services.[8] Exponents may concede that this is only viable with a degree of redistribution effected through means such as a negative income tax.

This is not the place for a detailed rebuttal of the neo-conservative case. A few points ought, however, to be made. Placing the blame on individuals neglects the fact that even if some people can better themselves, modern Western societies are structured in such a way that there are many who are disadvantaged. Neo-conservatives object that taxes penalize effort and divert investment from productive industry, yet many are prepared to support higher government expenditure on matters such as defence and public order. The threat to freedom which the welfare state is said to pose overlooks that freedom has different dimensions and that the welfare state enhances important aspects of freedom. Neo-conservatives often gloss over the state support given to fiscal and occupational welfare, and the fact that businesses and professions benefit from expenditure on social welfare. Given modern social arrangements, it is unrealistic to think that many of the functions social welfare bureaucracies perform can be transferred back to families or the community. The inefficiencies in the welfare state which neo-conservatives identify frequently derive from inadequate funding, rising expectations, and the preference given to fiscal and occupational welfare. Free services can encourage over-consumption, abuse and inefficiency, but not always by users, for some of the worst examples within the welfare state have been perpetrated by professionals who, for example, have taken advantage of their clients' ignorance to undertake unnecessary work. Legal and administrative controls may be as effective as user charges in curbing such practices.

Important social change has been effected by the social legislation of the welfare state. Law has legitimated, and spelt out the full implications of, social welfare regulation and the provision of social welfare benefits and public services. Those seeking to effect social change through social welfare legislation might therefore attempt to control the state directly or to influence those who have such control. Among the limitations to using social welfare legislation to effect social change, however, are that changes in legal norms are not necessarily reflected in changes in society and that the introduction of social welfare legislation might be accompanied by undesirable side-effects or might advantage one section of beneficiaries (low-paid, tenants) to the detriment of others (the unemployed, the homeless). There are also important forces and decisions shaping society beyond the influence of social welfare legislation. For example, social welfare regulation does not touch many crucial decisions about the quality of housing made by estate agents, property companies, financial institutions and government. Explaining these limits of social welfare legislation is beyond the scope of this book. Suffice it to say that the pursuit of social welfare goals may fail or be reversed, may be achieved only after a great struggle, or may be possible only because of dramatic developments such as the pressures produced by war. Relevant in these outcomes are the part played by party politics, the pivotal role of particular reformers, politicians and bureaucrats, the jockeying of vested interests who seek to delay change or to force concessions on particular points, and the pressure of the labour movement. If social welfare legislation is achieved, it may not have the legal or financial underpinning commensurate with its goals, or its impact may be blunted as a result of pressure from within the state machinery, from interests outside, or from a combination of the two. The beneficiaries of social welfare legislation are not in a strong position to counter these pressures. By definition they do not have much in the way of financial backing to exercise leverage, or the status or power which guarantees ready access to law-makers or the media. Collectively they have little meaningful impact except through a few pressure groups, perhaps the labour movement, and possibly sympathetic officials in some government departments. Their overall influence compares unfavourably with that of commercial interests, the media, and pressure groups espousing free-market ideology, all of which have profoundly shaped the modern welfare state.

What of the use of the legal system to effect social change? There seems no reason why social change which generally demands painstaking effort should be any easier when pursued through the legal system. Moreover, the idea diverges from the traditional conception of the legal system applying universal, neutral principles to vindicate individual rights and to resolve individual disputes. However, legal values such as equality before the law have been used as weapons in the reformers' armoury, enabling them to draw attention to the disjuncture between the hope these values represent and their reality. The 'access to justice' movement, based partly on this approach, advocates changes in the legal system such as the public subsidization of legal services, procedural reforms, and the creation of new institutions and agencies. The assumption is that greater 'access to justice' will lead to substantive changes, as claims are asserted which would otherwise be submerged. Concentrating on access to justice, however, may put the emphasis on procedural reform rather than on substantive results, and may deflect attention from the political prerequisites of social change. Any widening of access which occurs may benefit the wealthier and powerful more than the poorer section of society. Community lawyers and law centres have also worked through the legal system to effect social change. Legal advice to community groups, negotiation and representation on their behalf, and campaigns for legislative change are examples of how this is effected. All other things being equal, attempts at reform through the legal system have a better chance of success if they are part of a broader political strategy. Building effective community groups – a result of these activities – provides a political base to support reform activity.

The courts have a limited role in bringing about social change. A court decision may, for example, produce an advantage for certain beneficiaries of social welfare legislation, curb an arbitrary practice of a social welfare bureaucracy, or prove a catalyst for social welfare legislation. But courts are generally incapable of effecting far-reaching social change, even if they were willing to do so. Typically they deal with matters on an individual basis, so that a series of decisions on a matter will not necessarily be looked at systematically or in terms of their social or institutional background. It is fallacious to assume that social change will follow a favourable test case as a matter of course, since social change frequently depends on the distribution of resources. A favourable court ruling is not self-executing but needs the support of political power for its implementation. And government itself may ignore a test case or overturn it by legislation. Moreover, certain types of social change are beyond the reach of the legal system as they are beyond the reach of social welfare legislation. Indeed the courts have been at least as obstructive, as facilitative, of social change. While they have probably had only a minor effect on the overall implementation of social welfare legislation, in particular cases they have delayed or even frustrated particular measures. Because of their activity, certain areas of social welfare legislation have been removed to other bodies such as tribunals and Ombudsmen. Social welfare legislation has been read restrictively, and the courts have sometimes demonstrated a reluctance to grant remedies in the area of social welfare, even when in ordinary circumstances they would do so. This is not to say that all judicial decisions are in the same vein; there are decisions which have adopted a generous approach in handling social welfare legislation.

Are there factors which explain more systematically the courts' response to the social change represented by the welfare state? The background of judges is often mentioned as a factor. It can scarcely be expected that judges will view social welfare legislation or the claimants of social rights sympathetically, it has been argued, given their social and professional background. Certainly there are comments which lend weight to this interpretation, and decisions which seem to ignore the social dimension of social welfare legislation. There are also extra-curial statements by judges, of which Lord Justice Scrutton's oft-quoted remark to the University of Cambridge Law Society in 1920 is an example:

The habits you are trained in, the people with whom you mix, lead to you having a certain class of ideas of such a nature that, when you have to deal with other ideas, you do not give as sound and accurate judgement as you would wish.[9]

The 'class of ideas' of a judge may be Lord Devlin's 'accumulation of experience including tendencies, prejudices, and maybe bias. I do not mean a conscious bias'.[10] To quote Lord Devlin again, there is also an 'inherent probability that men and women of a certain age will be inclined by nature to favour the *status quo*'.[11] But social and professional background are only part of the explanation. Judges also reflect the dominant attitudes of society; in some cases these favour social reform. Not all judges share the same attitudes, in particular some have adopted a beneficent attitude to social welfare legislation and to the claimants of social rights. There has not always been a great deal of litigation regarding aspects of the welfare state, so that many judges have not been directly confronted by this dimension of life. Regular exposure to social rights may produce reasonably favourable perceptions. Finally, the nature of judicial decision-making minimizes, in many cases, the influence of a judge's personal attitudes.

Values are a second, if equally elusive, factor in judicial decision-making. Adherence to legal values is one aspect. For example, the clarity, certainty and coherence of legal principles are important considerations in judicial decision-making. There is also the reluctance to interfere in matters which attract public controversy. Equality before the law in its formal interpretation sometimes manifests itself. As we have seen, natural justice is sometimes incorporated into the administration of social welfare legislation. None of these legal values need necessarily undercut social rights. For example, natural justice has had the effect of fettering social welfare regulation, but would have a beneficial effect if incorporated into benefit administration (e.g. if a hearing were given before benefits were terminated under the cohabitation rule). As well as these legal values, courts are sometimes motivated by the threat posed to other values such as private property rights and public order. Hostility to interference with private property rights is obvious in the judicial reaction to social welfare regulation, which by its nature involves such interference. Closely related to the protection of private property rights has been the cosseting of ratepayers and taxpayers, which has sometimes had an inhibiting effect on social welfare expenditure. The reaction of the courts in these areas is encapsulated in the rules of statutory interpretation which demand clear language before private property rights and the interests of taxpayers and ratepayers can be adversely affected. The primacy which the courts give to public order is mainly relevant to those seeking social change by self-help or direct action, although it underlies the courts' reaction to radical governments which are conceived to be defying the law. Considerations of private property rights and public order coalesce in judicial decisions about squatting.

Clearly, social welfare legislation may be so clear-cut that private property rights must give way. Moreover, there are situations where the protection of private property rights achieves social welfare goals, just as the well-established principle that revenue legislation is construed to favour the taxpayer can enhance fiscal welfare. Perhaps most importantly, private property rights are typically not affected by social welfare legislation, which creates rights to state benefits and services. Although the courts have interfered with the decisions of social welfare bureaucracies regarding the application of social welfare legislation, their approach seems generally to have been to permit state officials wide discretion. To put it another way, the courts have failed to develop doctrines and remedies enabling social welfare claimants and the beneficiaries of public services to pursue their entitlements under social welfare legislation. Such claims must be couched in terms of the doctrines of administrative law, but much administrative law is concerned with public authorities exceeding or misusing their power.[12] By contrast, claims in the welfare state are often that public authorities have failed to exercise power – failed to pay benefits or to provide services to which individuals are entitled. A comparison can be drawn between the courts' attempt to protect traditional interests such as private property rights, and their reticence when the rights of social welfare claimants or the beneficiaries of public services are involved. Modern administrative-law doctrines may countenance review in cases where relevant considerations have been disregarded or irrelevant considerations taken into account; in cases of misunderstanding or ignorance on the part of decision-makers; and in cases in which there is no evidence supporting a finding. While in theory these grounds apply to social welfare matters, in practice they have had their main impact in the commercial, property and financial fields.

Apart from the social and professional background of judges, and the fundamental values which they tend to protect, the nature of judicial technique helps explain why the courts act as a brake on social change. The doctrine of precedent, and the canons of statutory construction, favour the status quo rather than social change. Doctrinal considerations are often the dominant factor in decisions, not mere camouflage for, or a rationalization of, other considerations. The corollary is that strictly legal reasoning sometimes results in a decision which benefits those claiming social rights. Judicial discretion is largely exhausted at the point where the meaning of social welfare legislation is quite plain, and the public authority administering it has complied strictly with its terms, has given those affected adequate opportunity to put their case, and has not misused its discretion. However, decisions can go either way in many instances because the authorities are in conflict or do not cover the case in point. While judicial decision-making is in many respects open-textured, in practice the courts tend to eschew reform. This is moulded, in part, by the other factors referred to – the social and professional background of the judges and the values underlying many legal doctrines. The absence of reform on the part of most courts is emphasized by the innovative approach of some United States courts, which have adapted common-law doctrines to modern social conditions.

But not all the blame can be attributed to the judges. The procedural and institutional processes of courts do not bring fully to light the broader aspects of problems. Relevant policy considerations, as contained in government documents and research reports, are generally excluded by the rules of evidence, and there is little likelihood that the judges will have acquired a feeling for the issues through other channels. The legislature is sometimes responsible, since it might attempt to avoid resolving an issue and delegate it to the courts without much guidance as to what ought to be decided.

The role of the courts is but one aspect of the legal foundations of the welfare state. Lawyers have a role in furthering understanding of these legal foundations, in addition to the exposition and analysis of the detailed rules of the welfare state. Lawyers can throw light on the reality of values such as equality before the law; on how the regulatory and distributive techniques of the welfare state take concrete form; and on the role of law and the legal system in social change. If the welfare state falls short of expectations, lawyers can contribute to an appreciation of the reasons by spelling out specifically legal factors in the emergence, form, implementation and impact of social welfare legislation. Much work remains to be done, especially at the level of social and legal theory. But the approach adopted here will provide a basis for these tasks as well as a starting point for the analysis of other aspects of law and society.

Notes

CHAPTER 1: Introduction

1 It can be argued that there has been a return to status as a basis of rights in the modern era, for example, as employees, tenants, consumers and so on.
2 Some writers add planning (e.g. Myrdal 1960) but this is not as central as regulation and distribution.
3 There is an argument in the United States that the Constitution imposes an obligation on government to provide the basic necessities of life (Michelman 1979). The argument is uniquely American and is far from accepted in the United States itself.
4 Titmuss 1968: 130.
5 For example, Robson 1976a: 47, 174–7; Sleeman 1979: 5–6.
6 See Rein 1981.
7 For example, Townsend 1979: 150–3, 807–11.
8 Minns 1980.
9 Friedman 1969: 220–47.
10 Briggs 1966: 11.
11 Runciman 1972: 43–9.
12 Townsend 1979: 78–9.
13 Williamson and Hyer 1975.
14 See also the use to which it is put as the subsistence level, below which a husband's income should not normally fall when a maintenance order is made (*Ashley* v. *Ashley* [1968] P.582, 590–1; *Shallow* v. *Shallow* [1979] P.1, 5–6). Note that the legislative standards for benefits are typically of absolute rather than relative poverty.
15 But see Chapter 7 on the political dimensions, and the discussion in section III of Chapter 5 on the social dimensions.
16 It seems that in the eighteenth century the terms 'labouring class' and 'poor' were synonymous, until the exigencies of the nineteenth-

century labour market divided the working class into skilled artisans and casual labourers. The present economic infrastructure is said to fragment the working class into categories turning on skill and whether they are compatible with the productivity plans of individual corporations and the economy as a whole (Giddens 1973: 219). Certainly many workers live in permanent danger of entering the ranks of the poor and share many of their social and economic disadvantages (Miliband 1974: 185). The welfare state has contributed to division by its separate treatment of the working poor, on the one hand, and the largely workless poor such as the aged, sick, disabled and single parents, on the other (see Townsend 1979: 410).

17 As will be seen in the next chapter, the Poor Relief Act 1601 distinguished only between the able-bodied and other poor.

18 Flinn 1976: 46. Some 10 per cent of the population were paupers in the 1840s, but between 1850 and 1880 the proportion was never higher than 6 per cent (Hobsbawm 1968b: 73, 134).

19 Poor Law Amendment Act 1834, 4 and 5 Will. IV,c. 76, s. 109; Poor Law Act 1930, s. 163.

20 Poor Laws and Relief of Distress (Royal Commission) 1909: 597. The test of the legal adviser to the Local Government Board.

21 Kennedy 1913: 56. In 1671 some 20 per cent of householders in one Essex village were excused from paying the hearth tax on the grounds of chronic poverty (Wrightson 1980: 40).

22 See Ashforth 1976: 142.

23 Similarly, poor persons is a term still extant in section 235 of the Public Health Act 1936, which deals with common lodging houses, but the Act gives no guidance as to its meaning. By contrast, the term 'working class' was defined in successive housing statutes, e.g., Housing Act 1925, Schedule 5, para. 12(e). See *Chorley B.C.* v. *Barratt Developments (North West) Ltd* [1979] 3 All E.R. 634 and the cases cited there.

24 [1979] R.A. 159.

25 See the cases cited in Chesterman 1979: 138. See also *Re Bethel* (1971) 17 D.L.R. (3d) 652; *Ballarat Trustees Executors and Agency Co. Ltd* v. *Federal Commissioner of Taxation* (1950) 80 C.L.R. 350; *Ryland* v. *Commissioner of Taxation* (1973) 128 C.L.R. 404.

26 *Fry* v. *Lane* (1888) 40 Ch. D. 312; *Cresswell* v. *Potter* [1978] 1 W.L.R. 255. Cf. *Backhouse* v. *Backhouse* [1978] 1 W.L.R. 243; [1978] 1 All E.R. 1158; *Commercial Bank of Australia Ltd* v. *Amadio* (1983) 46 A.L.R. 402.

CHAPTER 2: The historical background

1 Maine 1930: 182. See also Stein 1980: 101.

2 See Graveson 1953: 2.

3 Tigar and Levy 1977: 57, 81–5.

4 See *Pigg* v. *Caley* (1618) 74 E.R. 997.

5 *Smith* v. *Browne and Cooper* (1701) 90 E.R. 1172.

6 Genovese 1972: 28.
7 Kanowitz 1969: 35–6.
8 Marshall 1963: 76. See generally Coleman 1974; Stoljar 1973.
9 See de Schweinitz 1943. As late as 1936 in the second edition of his textbook, *The Poor Law Code*, W. Ivor Jennings could write: 'Upon that Act the modern Poor Law is based' (1936b:2).
10 From 1834, the Poor Law Commissioners (succeeded by the Poor Law Board 1847–71, the Local Government Board 1871–1919, and then the Ministry of Health 1919–48) could issue rules, orders and regulations on the administration of the poor law, although they could not interfere to order relief in particular cases (Poor Law Amendment Act 1834, s.15).
11 However, until 1948 poor relief remained an important, and in many cases the sole, source of benefit for many poor (see the figures in Steele 1949: 5). The poor law discussed in this chapter is the poor law of England. The poor laws of Scotland and of Ireland were along similar lines (see Banks 1872; Lamond 1892), as were those of the United States. The courts in several states of the United States held that English poor-law principles were part of their law (e.g., *Newton* v. *Stratford*, 3 Conn. 600 (1821)), but there is a decision to the contrary by Chief Justice Shaw of Massachusetts, who held that English poor-law principles were never appropriate to the circumstances of the American colonies (*Commonwealth* v. *Hunt*, 38 Am. Dec. 346 (1842). See generally Nelson 1975: 48). In any event English poor-law principles were introduced in several American states because their poor-law statutes assumed the English provisions (*Heidleberg* v. *Lynn*, 34 Am. Dec. 566 (1840)). With time, the volume of American case-law in relation to the poor law rivalled that of England, settlement being by far the most litigated area (e.g., 41 Am. Jur. 679–717. See generally Handler and Goodstein 1968; Trattner 1974). In Canada, the English Poor Relief Act 1601 was held applicable in British Columbia (*R.* v. *Hall* [1941] 2 W.W.R.245), but the decision was overruled in 1970 on the basis that the English poor-law statutes were inapplicable to the local circumstances, given colonial conditions and the absence of a system of government and of institutions comparable to those in England (*McKenzie* v. *McKenzie* (1970) 73 W.W.R.206). Local legislation introduced some of the principles of the English poor law into the Canadian provinces (e.g., *Re McDougall and Lobo* (1861) 21 U.C.R.80); indeed the concept of settlement has been continued in some provinces into the present (*Yarmouth* v. *Argyle* (1979) 33 N.S.R. (2d) 598). There seems never to have been any doubt that the English poor law had no application in Australia; legally, even if it had been suitable to the local conditions, the machinery for its enforcement did not exist (see *Quan Yick* v. *Hinds* (1905) 2 C.L.R. 345). There was resistance to adoption of the poor-law system partly because it constituted an admission that conditions were no better than in England, but mainly because the largely publicly funded charitable institutions meant the costs were borne elsewhere (by the British

government, rather than local rates, and by the unpaid charity workers) (Dickey 1980: 27).

12 1783, vol. 1: 121–45.
13 Colliers Act 1799, 39 Geo.III, c.56.
14 See Freedland 1970: 9–16.
15 Kahn-Freund 1977a.
16 See Hobsbawm 1968b: 64–104; Hartwell *et al.* 1972.
17 Wages etc. of Artificers etc. Act 1813, 53 Geo.III, c.40.
18 See the authorities cited in Schwarzer 1952: 36–7; Freedland 1976: 109. See generally Foster 1979.
19 See Fifoot 1959: 46.
20 The evidence is unclear whether the rule was adopted specifically to ease the financial burden enterprises would have experienced if they had been liable for the industrial injuries suffered by workers. See Friedman and Ladinsky 1967: 54; Schwartz 1981: 1770–2.
21 See Atiyah 1979: 506–68.
22 Burn 1964: 154–5.
23 Hammond 1913: 215.
24 (1722) 93 E.R. 664.
25 *Op.cit*: 15.
26 White 1979: 39. See also Hay 1975: 226–7; Thompson 1968: 303, 575–8.
27 See Atiyah 1979: 73–4; Walter 1980: 51–2.
28 Merritt 1981: 237, 395.
29 Malcolmson 1980: 125.
30 Williams 1961: 736. See also Mannheim 1946: 99.
31 See Hay 1977: 200–2, 211–12; Thompson 1975.
32 (1788) 126 E.R. 32.
33 See Atiyah 1979: 15, 88; Manchester 1980: 315–19.
34 See Dixon 1980.
35 Parry 1914: 252.
36 Kahn-Freund 1977a: 518. Under s.4 of the Poor Relief Act 1601, the children of poor parents could be compulsorily apprenticed until adulthood. To get rid of the responsibility, poor-law officials were tempted to apprentice poor children without much thought about their future or how the apprenticeship might be supervised. The temptation was even greater after 1691, because if apprenticed in another parish the children would gain a settlement there (Poor Relief Act 1691, 3 Will. and Mar., c.11, s.8). One of the blackest parts of poor-law history was the transfer of poor children to the mills and factories of industrial Lancashire and Yorkshire, supposedly under the provisions for poor apprentices (Romilly 1840: v. 2, 188. cf. Webb 1927: 200–4; Redford 1926: 22–30). The Parish Apprentices Act 1816 (56 Geo.III, c.139) tightened up procedures on binding and imposed restrictions on the distance at which a poor apprentice could be bound. The situation was slow to improve, and the use of poor apprentices in the factories drew to an end mainly because it became more economic for owners to employ other labour. Poor children also

faced harsh conditions when apprenticed other than in the mills and factories. The courts were reluctant to interfere with such apprenticeship agreements (*R.* v. *St Margaret's, Lincoln* (1773) 1 Bott. (Const. ed.) 549). The treatment of poor apprentices was not improved when the law provided that people could be compelled to take them (Dunlop and Denman 1912: 252). Until 1844, justices had to consent to the apprenticeship of poor children (Poor Law Amendment Act 1844, 7 and 8 Vict., c.101, s.12). In 1835 Lord Denman C.J. said that although it was unnecessary for a poor child to consent it could not be supposed that the justices would approve an arbitrary binding such as to a stranger against the will of a friend, relative or parent (*R.* v. *St George, Exeter* (1835) 111 E.R. 455). In fact the justices approved apprenticeships for poor children in a perfunctory manner. Moreover, it was not unknown for poor-law officials simply to allot poor children to particular inhabitants instead of going to the justices (*R.* v. *Stowmarket* (1808) 103 E.R. 553). In addition, the justices' jurisdiction was avoided by the poor-law authorities paying a premium for persons to take poor children as apprentices; legislation in 1816 attempted to prevent this (Lumley 1842: 72; *R.* v. *Arundel* (1816) 105 E.R. 1045; Parish Apprentices Act 1816, s.11). What benefits there were in the procedures established under the New poor law for binding apprentices would seem to have been undermined when the Queen's Bench held that they did not need to be complied with strictly (*R.* v. *St Mary Magdalen* (1853) 118 E.R. 970). In addition, the court held that the consent of apprentices (required by the rules if they were older than fourteen) could be assumed by their signature on the indenture. Under the General Consolidated Order of 24 July 1847, issued by the Poor Law Commissioners, children under nine or children who could not read or write their own name could not be apprenticed; only those with certain qualifications could receive a poor apprentice; part of any premium had to be given to the apprentice in the form of clothing (premiums could generally not be given for those over sixteen); and apprentices over fourteen had to give their consent (Articles 52–7 set out in MacMorran and Naldrett 1905: 82–91).

37 *R.* v. *Winship* (1770) Cald. 72, 76. Cf. (1770) 98 E.R. 406.
38 Halsbury 1912: v.22, 559–62.
39 *R.* v. *Baddeley ex p. Moore* (1906) 70 J.P. 346; 50 Sol.J. 377.
40 Articles 129–31.
41 Poor Relief Act 1815, s.5. See *Holland* v. *Peacock* [1912] 1 K.B. 154 (sexual intercourse between unrelated inmates). Cf. *Mile End* v. *Sims* [1905] 2 K.B. 200 (refusal to go to another workhouse).
42 Poor Law Amendment Act 1834, ss.43, 98. Cf. Poor Law Board Act 1847, 10 and 11 Vict., c.109, s.20.
43 For example, see the account in Anonymous 1865.
44 See *R.* v. *Miles* (1842) 6 Jur. 243.
45 *Tozeland* v. *West Ham Union* [1907] 1 K.B. 920. The Court of Appeal in *Tozeland* relied on earlier Irish decisions; the public policy

considerations used in these to justify the immunity were the burden
on the rates which would otherwise result and the possibility that
legal claims would undermine poor-law administration (*Dunbar* v.
Ardee Guardians [1897] 2 I.R. 76, 90). Immunity did not seem to
extend to non-ministerial acts – to an intentional tort, such as
assault by a master, or to an 'independent' tort, such as the illegal
sale and conversion of a poor person's goods (*Forde* v. *Skinner* (1830)
172 E.R. 687; *Barns* v. *Guardians of St Mary, Islington* (1912) 76 J.P.
11).
46 See, for example, the remarks in *Chester* v. *Bateson* [1920] 1 K.B. 829.
Interestingly, that case involved property rights.
47 Bk. 1: 126; Bk. 2: 86ff.
48 Smith 1776, v.1: 194.
49 See M.E. Rose 1976: 27.
50 See generally Holdsworth: v.10, 257–69; Halsbury 1937: v.25, 408–22.
51 *R.* v. *Tolpuddle* (1792) 100 E.R. 1237.
52 Parl. Deb. n.s., vol. 12, 1825, 1139.
53 *R.* v. *Elswick* (1860) 121 E.R. 506.
54 *Nottingham C.C.* v. *Middlesex C.C.* (1936) 100 J.P.1; 79 Sol.J. 922.
55 *R.* v. *Sandwich* (1733) 94 E.R. 1072, 1073.
56 See Poor Relief Act 1722, s.5.
57 See Styles 1963: 52.
58 Anonymous (1698) 90 E.R. 602. See also *R.* v. *Everdon* (1807) 103 E.R.
512.
59 (1692) 90 E.R. 733.
60 (1840) 113 E.R. 772.
61 For example, Styles 1963: 43–4. Although relatively few poor-law
cases before Quarter Sessions were appealed, there were still
thousands of decisions of the higher courts about the poor law in the
law reports. At one time a considerable number of appeals were dealt
with by the assize judges in decisions which are not reported. Most
litigation was about settlement. In the first volume of his *The State of
the Poor*, Sir F.M. Eden observed that the key aspect of settlement 'has
(perhaps) been more profitable to the profession of the Law, than any
other point in English jurisprudence' (1965: 176–7), while Lord
Mansfield called the expenditure on settlement litigation a disgrace to
the country (*R.* v. *Harberton* (1786) 99 E.R. 1017, 1018). Disputes
often dragged on interminably, some for up to a decade, and were
frequently appealed. Heavy involvement of lawyers promoted
excessive technicality in the law. For example, the courts developed a
concept of derivative settlement so that persons could be removed to
the place where their great-grandparents had been settled and where
they had never set foot (see *R.* v. *Ruyton* (1861) 121 E.R. 813). In the
nineteenth century, lawyers did not take the same active part in the
administration of the poor law, but there was still a considerable
volume of litigation. There are at least seven reported House of Lords
decisions on settlement between 1889 and 1935. Cases on settlement
had an air of unreality about them as the real issue – the fate of a

particular person – became submerged in a sea of technical reasoning.

62 See *R.* v. *Leeds* (1844) 114 E.R. 1493.
63 Discussed in *Fulham* v. *Woolwich Union* [1907] A.C. 255, 260.
64 Smith 1862.
65 For example, *R.* v. *Birmingham* (1811) 104 E.R. 597.
66 Dalton 1742: 174.
67 *R.* v. *Seward* (1834) 110 E.R. 1377.
68 Lumley 1842: 11–12.
69 *Masters* v. *Child* (1698) 91 E.R. 695; *R* v. *Busbey* (1731) 94 E.R. 374; Hampson 1934: 165; Goodman 1960: 337.
70 *R.* v. *Mattersey* (1832) 110 E.R. 435.
71 Poor Removal Act 1795, s.6.
72 *R.* v. *Tibbenham* (1808) 103 E.R. 620, 622.
73 Poor Removal Act 1846, 9 and 10 Vict., c.66, s.1; Union Chargeability Act 1865, 28 and 29 Vict., c.79, s.8.
74 For example, *R.* v. *Worcester Union* (1874) L.R. 9 Q.B. 340.
75 Poor Removal Act 1846, s.4. Cf. *Tomlinson* v. *Bentall* (1826) 108 E.R. 274.
76 *Wycombe Union* v. *Eton Union* (1857) 156 E.R. 1377.
77 E.g. Anonymous 1845; Polanyi 1957: 7, 88.
78 See Redford 1926: 79–83.
79 314 U.S. 160 (1941).
80 See esp. Douglas J. at p.181. *Contra City of New York* v. *Miln*, 11 Pet. 102 (U.S. S.Ct. 1837).
81 *Becraft* v. *Strobel*, 10 N.E. 2d 560 (1937).
82 For example, Commonwealth Franchises Act 1902 (Australia).
83 Anonymous 1906; Keith-Lucas 1952: 161–4; *Magarrill* v. *Whitehaven* (1885) 16 Q.B.D. 242.
84 E.g., Dicey 1962: Introduction, p. L. Dicey's arguments extended to excluding political representation of those entitled to old-age pensions, *ibid*: p. xxxv.
85 Local Government Act 1933, s.59(1) (*c*).
86 *Hines* v. *Winters*, 320 P.2d 1114 (1937); *Opinion to the House*, 137 A.2d 532 (1958). See Fraenkel 1937.
87 See now Juries Act 1974, s.1(1). See also Cornish 1968: 26–8.
88 47 American Jurisprudence 2d, 711–12 and Suppl.
89 Moir 1969: 84–5, 160–2.
90 See Burney 1979: 65, 224–5.
91 Henriques 1979: 147; Benwell C.P. 1978: 35.
92 Gauldie 1974: 125.
93 Webb 1929: 799.
94 *R.* v. *Poplar B.C., ex p. L.C.C. (Nos. 1 and 2)* [1922] 1 K.B. 72; 95.
95 *Ibid.*, at p.104.
96 Keith-Lucas 1962: 61–2; Ryan 1978.
97 S.I. 1911 No. 1295, r. 12.
98 Local Government Act 1929, s.1.
99 Ginsburg 1979: 65

100 Cobbett 1977: 2, 40, 43, 90; See also Parl. Deb., 3rd ser., v.23, 1834, 830 (Walter); Romilly 1840: v.1, 375. Note that under the poor law, an important part of the burden of supporting the poor was borne by the poor themselves, because section 7 of the Poor Relief Act 1601 imposed a duty on the children, parents and grandparents of poor persons to support them. The aim of the provision was to prevent poor persons becoming chargeable on the rates by enabling poor law authorities to have recourse against relatives for maintenance (*Arrowsmith* v. *Dickenson* (1888) 20 Q.B.D. 252, 256–7). Initially the courts interpreted the categories of liable relatives broadly, although ultimately it was held that only blood relatives and not step-parents or parents-in-law were covered (e.g., *Cooper* v. *Martin* (1803) 102 E.R. 759). However, the Poor Law Amendment Act 1834 extended the list of liable relatives to step-fathers, who had to maintain step-children until they were sixteen or the mother died (s.57). An order for maintenance under the section could be made by the justices at the instance of either a poor person or a poor-law authority, but if a poor person did not seek a justice's order – as few did – it was entirely at the discretion of poor-law authorities whether they proceeded against the relatives and how much they claimed (Report [on] the Poor Law 1834: 115). Some poor-law authorities were guided by common sense: what was the use of exacting payment from relatives who were less than affluent if this would place them in financial difficulties and oblige them to claim relief themselves? Legally, there was some justification for this stance since maintenance could only be ordered against those 'of sufficient ability' (*R.* v. *Dunn* (1714) 88 E.R. 702; *Coulson* v. *Davidson* (1906) 96 L.T. 20; *Freeman* 1911). For the history of provisions governing the liability of husbands for maintaining their wives, see Barton 1957; Neville Brown 1955.

101 *R* v. *Eastbourne* (1803) 102 E.R. 769, 770. See also Ruggles 1793: Bk.I, xiv, xv, 23; Bk.II, 60–1, 102.

102 Blackstone 1783: 131. Cf. *Steel* v. *Houghton* (1788) 126 E.R. 32 at 33, 35.

103 *Hays* v. *Bryant* (1789) 126 E.R. 147.

104 Anonymous 1832. Indeed in at least one reported decision a poor person died as a direct result of officials rejecting an application for relief: *R.* v. *Booth* (1803) 168 E.R. 676n.

105 Poor Relief Act 1691, 3 Will. and Mary, c.11, s.11.

106 *R* v. *Higworth* (1717) 93 E.R. 32; *R* v. *Manchester* (1714) 88 E.R. 702. Cf. *R.* v. *Woodsterton* (1732–3) 94 E.R. 452, 478, 504.

107 (1780) 99 E.R. 213.

108 Hampson 1934: 225n; Marshall 1926: 90; Forster 1973: 49.

109 Burn 1864: 211–12, 286–7.

110 See Anonymous 1833; Townsend 1971: 22, 24, 30, 32; Thompson 1968: 126, 129–31.

111 Poor Relief Act 1722, 9 Geo.I, c.7, s.1; *R.* v. *Laughton* (1814) 105 E.R. 402.

112 Ss. 27, 54. See *R.* v. *Totnes Union* (1845) 115 E.R. 649.

113 The case is reported in Bott 1793a: v.1, 296; Viner title Poor (A) 415.
114 (1784) Cald. 432.
115 Lewin 1828: 200n.
116 (1803) 168 E.R. 676.
117 (1770) 98 E.R. 406.
118 See 99 E.R. 214n.
119 See *R. v. Illingworth* (1714) 93 E.R. 19; *R. v. Moorhouse* (1785) 99 E.R. 936; *R. v. Fearnley* (1786) 99 E.R. 1115.
120 *Attorney-General* v. *Merthyr Tydfil Union* [1900] 1 Ch. 516, 542–3; *Pontypridd Union* v. *Drew* [1927] 1 K.B. 214, 216, 218.
121 Lumley 1842: 1.
122 Anonymous 1865.
123 Poynter 1969: 323; Edsall 1971: 18, 22.
124 Poor Law Amendment Act 1834, s.54.
125 Ss. 15, 98. See *Clark* v. *Joslin* (1873) 27 L.T. 762.
126 111 E.R. 524.
127 See the consolidating Vaccination Act 1867, 30 and 31 Vict., c.84.
128 (1864) 28 J.P. 725. The report is apparently incorrect as to the result: see [1900] 1 Ch. 516, 537n.
129 For example, *R. v. Curtis* (1885) 15 Cox C.C. 746.
130 Mackay 1899: 17, 21.
131 (1872) L.R. 8 Exch. 37, 38.
132 (1906) 95 L.T. 359; 22 T.L.R. 583.
133 *Pontypridd Union* v. *Drew* [1927] 1 K.B. 214.
134 *Ibid.*, at p.217.
135 *Attorney-General* v. *Tynemouth Union* [1930] 1 Ch. 616.
136 [1925] A.C. 578.
137 Cf. Wrightson 1980: 27, 32.
138 Checkland 1974: 13, 20; Woodward 1962: 288–300, 308–9.
139 Tawney 1938: 262–4.
140 Marshall 1926: 102; Hill 1966: 157; Ashby 1912: 66; Oxley 1974: 54, 129.
141 1971: 43–4.
142 Webb 1929: 545–6.
143 Warwick County Records: vol.2, 95. See also v.1, 141, 172; v. 2, 85; v. 3, 124–5.
144 Dumsday 1902: 33.
145 Moss 1938: 117.
146 Archbold 1842: viii.
147 McGregor *et al.* 1970: 168–9.
148 Bates 1907: v. 1, 211, 276; Gleason 1969: 12.
149 See Pinchbeck & Hewitt 1973: 207–19.
150 See *Ex parte Martin* (1826) 108 E.R. 382.
151 Ashby 1912: 85; Hampson 1934: 169–73; Report [on] the Poor Law 1834: 260ff.
152 See *Plymouth Guardians* v. *Gibbs* [1903] 1 K.B. 177. It seems that giving women the right to seek maintenance had little effect, since many were either unaware of the possibility or without the resources to

collect the evidence and then to institute proceedings: Henriques
1967: 119.
153 Wilson 1977: 45–6.
154 Archbold 1842: 3–4. See Thane 1978: 32, on the contrast with
unmarried mothers.
155 Poor Law Amendment Act 1844, s.26. See *Wycombe Union* v. *Eton Union* (1857) 156 E.R. 1377.
156 Poor Removal Act 1846 (9 and 10 Vict., c.66), s.2.
157 Moss 1938: 114–15; Stedman Jones 1971: 275.
158 Holdsworth: v.4, 399: v.13, 213. See also Ogus and Barendt 1982: 337–40.
159 Relief of Families of Militiamen Act 1803, 43 Geo.III, c.47, ss.2, 6–7.
160 *A Common Soldier's Case* (1752) 95 E.R. 646; Army Act 1881, 44 and 45 Vict., c.58, s.145.
161 (1823) 107 E.R. 390, 392.
162 (1823) 107 E.R. 404, 412.
163 For example, *Wise's Case* (1670) 86 E.R. 48. A legal justification for this was that the unemployed unable to maintain themselves fell within the description 'impotent' in s.1 of the Poor Relief Act 1601 and thus qualified for poor relief; the difficulty with this was that 'impotent' was *ejusdem generis* with lame, old and blind in the section. See *R.* v. *Collett* (1823) 107 E.R. 404, 405–6.
164 Blackstone 1783, vol.1: 361.
165 The Speenhamland decision is set out in Smith 1972: 74.
166 Hobsbawm 1968a: 104; Polanyi 1957. Cf. Galper 1970: 57.
167 Poor Relief Act 1795, 36 Geo. III, c.23.
168 Blaug 1974; Marshall 1968: 22ff.
169 Anonymous 1828. Cf. Reporter's Note (1823) 107 E.R. 409–12n.
170 Webb 1927: 184n, 188n.
171 *R.* v. *Collett* (1823) 107 E.R. 404.
172 Hale 1684.
173 Poor Relief Act 1782, 22 Geo. III, c.83.
174 *R.* v. *Winship* (1770) 98 E.R. 406.
175 *R.* v. *Laughton* (1814) 105 E.R. 402, 404. *R.* v. *North Shields* (1780) 99 E.R. 213 raised the question of whether a mother was obliged to enter a workhouse if she wanted relief for her child alone. The judges were divided and avoided deciding the issue, but the judgments reveal much about their views of the poor. Ashhurst J. answered that both mother and child must enter the workhouse because 'one object of the statute was to encourage her industry, by holding out the disgrace of going into a workhouse. . . .' Bullen J. was of the contrary view, on the ground that the Act could not be intended to make the workhouse support the whole family if only one needed relief. *R.* v. *Haigh* (1790) 100 E.R. 776 resolved the matter by holding that only the child was obliged to enter the workhouse. Lord Kenyon C.J. said that the alternative course of splitting the family 'would not only be repugnant to all ideas of mercy and humanity, but would also be prejudicial to the interest of the parish, who would in some measure be deprived of

the labour of such of the family who were able to work. . . .'
176 See Dowdell 1932: 45–52; Marshall 1926: 144; Holdsworth: v. 10, 176.
177 Williams 1981: 77, 81.
178 Quoted Nicholls 1898: v. 2, 379.
179 *R. v. Totnes Union* (1845) 115 E.R. 649. See also *In re Campden Charities* (1881) 18 Ch. D. 310, 317 *per* Jessel M.R.
180 Editorial 1840: 40; Smith 1862.
181 Ss.27, 52. See (1912) 22 *Halsbury's Laws of England* 563. Cf. *Barnet Union* v. *Tilbury* (1909) 73 J.P. 466; 7 L.G.R. 993.
182 Poor Law Amendment Act 1866, 29 and 30 Vict., c.113, s.15.
183 Fraser 1976: 5; Rose 1966; Williams 1981: 59, 64–5, 90–107.
184 S.I. 1911 No. 1295, rr. 9, 11.
185 Nicholls 1898: v. 2, 348.
186 Titmuss 1968: 190.
187 Poor-law case-law is rarely referred to by modern courts. But see *R. v. Slough B.C., ex p. Ealing L.B.C.* [1981] 1 Q.B. 801; *R. v. Hillingdon L.B.C., ex p. Streeting* [1980] 3 All E.R. 413; [1980] 1 W.L.R. 1425.
188 Dicey later doubted that the provision was enforced in practice (Dicey 1962: xxxiv).
189 Lynes 1979b: 11.
190 *R. v. Newton Union* (1864) 28 J.P. 725; *R. v. Preston SBAT* [1975] 2 All E.R. 807, 813; [1975] 1 W.L.R. 624, 631–2.
191 See the cases reported in Meadows 1742: 7, 11, 27, 31, 80.
192 For example, J. Scarlett (later Lord Abinger): Parl. Deb., N.S., v. 5, 1821, 573–82; Lord Brougham L.C., Parl. Deb., 3rd ser., v. 25, 1834, 211.
193 Poor Relief Act 1691, 3 Will. and Mary, c.11, s.7. See the decisions in Meadows 1742: 97, 107.
194 See the decisions in Nolan 1825: 377–8, 380–1.

CHAPTER 3: The individual and the law

1 Benn and Peters 1959: 122. From different points in the political spectrum see Hayek 1960: 85; Thompson 1975: 258–69.
2 Jennings 1959: 50; Pollock 1961: 20. See also Devlin 1979: 4, 85; Gold 1980: 371–3; Westen 1982: 545–51, 578n.
3 Williams 1971: 128–9. See also Benn and Peters 1959: 126–7.
4 See Marshall 1971: ch.7; Polyviou 1980: ch. 1; Sadurski 1981. Cf. Dworkin 1977: 227, 273.
5 Weber 1954: 228.
6 With ordinary criminal law it seems that those in working-class areas report as much crime to the police as others (e.g. Mawby 1979: 101–7). In relation to other types of criminal law, however, such as consumer law, there is some evidence that the higher social classes voice more complaints to public agencies (e.g. Cranston 1979b: 62; cf. McNeil *et al.* 1979).
7 Aubert 1970: 478.
8 Jacobs 1982.

9 See the careful review by Braithwaite 1979: 47 and *passim*.
10 Steer 1970: 43.
11 Bennett 1979.
12 Blankenburg 1976: 126.
13 Hopkins 1977; Snel 1978.
14 Rutter and Madge 1976: 163, 180. Cf. Dannefer and Schutt 1982.
15 Engels 1973: 280.
16 In the United States, Congress drastically limited public funding for abortions. The Supreme Court held that a poor woman does not have any statutory or constitutionally protected right to an abortion: *Maher* v. *Roe* 432 U.S. 464 (1977); *Harris* v. *McRae* 448 U.S. 297 (1980).
17 See Green and Stewart 1975; Essex and Gore 1979; Hague 1967.
18 See Birmingham Community Development Project 1979; Stewart 1981.
19 Following amendments by the Housing Act 1980, the 1967 Act does this for certain intermediary interests (Sch. 1, para. 7A).
20 Cox 1975: 67–9.
21 Bottoms and McClean 1976: 214–16; Armstrong 1977: 3–5.
22 Softley 1978: 27.
23 For example, Magistrates' Courts Act 1980, Sch. 4; Powers of Criminal Courts Act 1973, s. 31(3A–C).
24 Thomas 1979: 320; *Young* v. *Geddie* (1978) 22 A.L.R. 232; *Tate* v. *Short* 401 U.S. 395 (1971). See also Magistrates' Courts Act 1980, s.35.
25 NACRO Working Party 1981: 7, 11–14; Law Reform Commission (Australia) 1980: 233–5.
26 Generally, only on appeal.
27 [1975] A.C. 396.
28 [1980] Q.B. 460.
29 *Allen* v. *Jambo Holdings Ltd* [1980] 2 All E.R. 502, 505; [1980] 1 W.L.R. 1252, 1257.
30 Quoted MacDonagh 1980: 122.
31 See Kelly 1977:44–7, 65.
32 Ford 1926.
33 Attachment of Earnings Act 1971.
34 Adamsdown Community Trust 1978: 36. Cf. Reifner 1980: 38–9.
35 Evidence for this is fairly readily available in England from the *Civil Judicial Statistics*. Of the proceedings commenced in the Chancery division of the High Court, most concern property, trusts, wills, estates, revenue and commercial matters. The majority of the proceedings begun in the Queen's Bench division are debt-collecting claims and many of these are disposed of by summary judgment, i.e. they are not defended. Of the actions set down for trial, about three-quarters are for the recovery of damages for personal injuries. A perusal of reported cases shows that most of the litigation in the High Court going to judgment, excluding personal injury and family matters, and to an extent employment matters, involves commercial or property interests claiming against individuals or against each other, or challenging government decisions. The majority of

proceedings commenced in the county court are money plaints. From the nature of these plaints as outlined in the *Civil Judicial Statistics*, it can be inferred that most are brought by businesses. The bulk of these lead to judgments in default of defence or judgments on admission. 'Other proceedings', divorce and family matters, and commercial matters also feature prominently in proceedings commenced in the county court. Many of the 'other proceedings' commenced are claims for the recovery of residential premises, i.e. against individual tenants.

To summarize then: personal injuries and family matters to one side, the civil courts operate largely at the instigation of commercial and property interests. The same holds for the small claims procedure because this allows commercial parties to institute actions. Of course many individuals, not only poor persons, do not utilize the civil courts when they have meritorious claims. For example, a survey conducted by the Royal Commission on Civil Liability and Compensation for Personal Injury found that, of those who thought an injury which they had experienced was caused by something another person had done or failed to do, some two-thirds took no steps towards making a claim for tort compensation (1978: v.1, 62; v.2, 120–1).

36 Galanter 1974, 1975; Schuyt *et al.* 1977: 111–12.
37 Smith 1924: 8–12.
38 tenBroek 1964.
39 Committee on One-Parent Families 1974: v.1, 68–9.
40 See Gibson 1980: 623–4, on subsequent developments.
41 Confirmation of this is contained in various social surveys. For example, a survey conducted for the Royal Commission on Legal Services in England and Wales in 1978 showed clearly that the higher social classes used lawyers' services on personal matters disproportionately in relation to their numbers in the sample population in the year prior to the survey: vol.2, pp.188–91.
42 The Royal Commission survey found that the incidence of lawyer-use varied strongly with household tenure. Partly, the figure for owner-occupiers reflects the conveyancing monopoly; moreover, household tenure is linked to social class. The leading American study of lawyer-use found that a greater difference emerged taking educational background into account rather than social class or income; of course the three factors are related (Curran 1977). Compare the results of an Australian survey (Cass and Sackville 1975: 7): its finding that lawyer-contact did not differ markedly across income groups (except in property matters) is not surprising given that it asked about seeing a lawyer in the last *five years*. The authors concede that this says nothing about the frequency of use. As to knowledge, there is some survey evidence in the United States which shows that poorer persons do worse as regards knowledge of basic legal issues (Sarat 1977: 478–9).
43 For example, Royal Commission on Legal Services in Scotland 1980:

v.2, 74.

44 Foster 1973; Bridges *et al.* 1975: 19–20.
45 Mayhew and Reiss 1969.
46 See Macaulay 1979: 139–42; Fitzgerald 1977: 33–6.
47 Monopolies and Mergers Commission 1976: 19, 38.
48 [1951] 2 All E.R. 108.
49 For example, Royal Commission on Legal Services 1979: v.2, 207.
50 For example, Zander 1978: 288; Mayhew 1975: 411.
51 Parenthetically it might be noted that these changes would not
   necessarily put 'poverty practices' on an equal footing with those legal
   practices dealing with commercial and property interests, unless there
   were other changes in society. 'Poverty practices' might continue to be
   regarded as low-status because of the socio-economic background of
   the clientele, or because the nature of the work might not appear to be
   as crucial to society or as intellectually challenging as some
   commercial and property work.
52 In one study, however, experts examined the details of accident
   claims and concluded that those seeking legal advice were more likely
   to obtain compensation, and more likely to obtain a higher
   compensation, than others (Abel-Smith *et al.* 1973: 169–78).
53 Leevers *et al.* 1977:18ff. Few tenants considered obtaining a solicitor's
   advice because they did not realize that it might have been
   worthwhile, or because they were ignorant that legal aid might have
   been available and feared the expense.
54 Royal Commission on Legal Services 1979: v.2, 95–6.
55 Popkin 1977: 1027–8.
56 House of Representatives Standing Committee on Aboriginal Affairs
   1980: 47–8.
57 For similar but not identical results in Canada, see Issalys and
   Watkins 1978: 213.
58 For example, Bottoms and McClean 1976: 160; Wilkins 1975: ch. 3;
   Cashman 1981, 1982.
59 Baldwin and McConville 1977: 61–80.
60 Carlen 1976: 46–8.
61 See Blumberg 1973; McBarnet 1981: 78.
62 For an American exception, which concentrated on substantive
   procedural law, see Olshausen 1947.
63 On employees, see Simon 1954. The position of poorer consumers is
   referred to in Cranston 1984.
64 Chambliss 1964.
65 Dowdell 1932: 69–78.
66 Slack 1974.
67 Radzinowicz 1956: v.2, 2–3, 18–19; v.3, 282–3.
68 Harring 1977.
69 Vagrancy Act 1824, 5 Geo.IV, c.83, s.3.
70 Home Office 1976: 5.
71 Vagrancy Act 1824, s.4. Before they can be convicted, however, the
   prosecution must establish that they declined to use a reasonably

accessible place of free shelter or that in sleeping out they caused or were likely to cause damage to property or other offensive consequences. Vagrancy Act 1935, s.1.

72 See Cook 1979.
73 Archard 1979: 87–9. See, for the United States, Bittner 1967.
74 Home Affairs Committee 1981: xii.
75 See, for example, Public Order Act 1936, s.5 (abusive etc. begging); Theft Act 1968, s.15 (fraudulent begging); Criminal Law Act 1977, ss.6–13 (entering and remaining on property).
76 Criminal Justice Act 1982, s.70. See Secretary of State for the Home Department 1981: 3.
77 *Cohen* v. *Black* [1942] 2 All E.R. 299; 58 T.L.R. 306.
78 See Hall *et al.* 1978: 331; Rex 1979: 90.
79 *Ledwith* v. *Roberts* [1937] 1 K.B. 232, 276–7.
80 Home Affairs Committee 1980. Cf. *R.* v. *West London Stipendiary Magistrate, ex p. Simeon* [1982] 3 W.L.R. 289, 291.
81 Criminal Attempts Act 1981, s.8.
82 For example, *Papachristou* v. *City of Jacksonville* 405 U.S. 156 (1972); *People* v. *Berck* 300 N.E. 2d 411 (1973).
83 Foote 1956: 638–40.
84 Vagrants, Gaming, and Other Offences Act 1931–1978, s.4(1)(i). There is an express qualification that the subsection 'shall not extend to any person who is bona fide out of work and who is bona fide in search of employment'.
85 For example, *Daniel* v. *Belton* (1968) 12 F.L.R. 101; *Zanetti* v. *Hill* (1962) 108 C.L.R. 433.
86 Sackville and Forbes 1976: 27–8.
87 Summary Offences (Repeal) Act 1979 (New South Wales); Social Welfare (Homeless Persons) Act 1977 (Victoria), s.3(1), repealing Vagrancy Act 1966, s.5.
88 The income of private tenants is generally lower than that of others in the community, and disproportionate numbers are recipients of social welfare benefits. Landlords divide into various categories: resident landlords who rent spare rooms, or landlords who leave their accommodation for employment or other reasons; private landlords having one or two properties which they have probably inherited; commercial landlords, who see their tenancies as a long-term, profitable investment if they obtain the maximum rent increases allowable under any rent control and make necessary improvements to enhance the capital value; commercial landlords who purchase blocks or estates with a view to selling the individual dwellings to owner-occupiers; and landlords who provide housing for their employees (see Hillman 1980; Murie *et al.* 1976: 190–97; Department of Environment 1977a: 82, 86; 1977b: pt. 3, 72–4; Sackville 1975a: 57–8).
89 *Lloyd's Bank* v. *Bundy* [1975] 1 Q.B. 326, 336.
90 Bradbrook 1976a: 469.
91 Residential Tenancies Act 1978–81, s.92(1).

92 *Saunders* v. *Soper* [1975] A.C.239.
93 For example, McDowell 1978.
94 See Royal Commission on the Distribution of Income and Wealth
   1978b: 508; Harloe *et al.* 1974: 119–20.
95 MacCallum and Bradbrook 1978. See Residential Tenancies Act
   1978–81 (South Australia), s.58; Residential Tenancies Act 1980
   (Victoria), s.88.
96 Commons 1924: 221–2.
97 Siegel 1975: 669–70.
98 Denning 1949: 68–71.
99 *Keates* v. *Cadogan* (1851) 138 E.R. 234.
100 Feuerstein and Shestack 1950: 229–31. It appears that a custom of
    London required the landlord to repair: McGovern 1978: 666.
101 *Smith* v. *Marrable* (1843) 152 E.R. 693.
102 *Pampris* v. *Thanos* [1968] 1 N.S.W.R. 56.
103 *Hart* v. *Windsor* (1843) 152 E.R. 1114.
104 If the difference in treatment of furnished and unfurnished premises
    had been justified in policy terms, perhaps it would have been said,
    first, that furnished tenancies were usually for a short term and thus
    their fitness for immediate use was of some importance; and, secondly,
    that the very fact of leasing a furnished dwelling demonstrated that
    the tenant did not wish to be burdened with responsibility for the
    condition of the property.
105 Haar and Liebman 1977: 252–8; Tiplady 1981: 140–46. Nineteenth-
    century American law applied the rule about unfurnished premises to
    furnished premises as well (Jones 1906: 655–69).
106 There are two, possibly three, very limited exceptions. First, landlords
    must exercise reasonable care in providing safe access where this is by
    stairs not specifically demised to the tenant (*Dunster* v. *Hollis* [1918] 2
    K.B. 795). Secondly, they are obliged to take reasonable care to keep
    the stairs, lifts and rubbish chutes of multiple dwellings in reasonable
    repair and usability, and to take reasonable care to maintain adequate
    lighting of the communal parts (*Liverpool C.C.* v. *Irwin* [1977] A.C.
    239). Thirdly, there may be an implied obligation with weekly
    tenancies that landlords will do repairs (*Broggi* v. *Robins* (1898) 14
    T.L.R. 439; *Mint* v. *Good* [1951] 1 K.B. 517, 521–2. Cf. *Sleafer* v.
    Lambeth B.C. [1960] 1 Q.B. 43).
107 *Warren* v. *Keen* [1954] 1 Q.B. 15.
108 *Regis Property Co.* v. *Dudley* [1959] A.C. 370.
109 *Torrens* v. *Walker* [1906] 2 Ch. 166.
110 *Hewitt* v. *Rowlands* (1924) 93 L.J.K.B. 1080.
111 *Jeune* v. *Queens Cross Properties Ltd* [1974] 1 Ch. 97. Cf. Housing Act
    1974, s.125. See generally P.F. Smith 1980.
112 *O'Brien* v. *Robinson* [1973] A.C. 912.
113 Ss.42(1), 43(b). See also Model Uniform Residential Landlord and
    Tenant Act (U.S.), para. 2.104, 3.101; Residential Tenancies Act
    1980 (Victoria), ss. 97–8, 102–3; Landlord and Tenant Act, R.S.
    Ontario, Ch. 232, s.96; Rhodes 1973, 1980: 369–70.

114 See Arden and Partington 1980: 18–27.
115 *Kenny* v. *Preen* [1963] 1 Q.B. 499.
116 For example, Residential Tenancies Act 1978–81 (South Australia), s.47. While suggesting a similar step in England, the Law Commission did not think that the covenant should be extended to non-physical disturbances which might not constitute a breach under present law, with the rather dubious reasoning that there were signs that the courts themselves were moving in that direction (Law Commission 1975: 13, 17).
117 Protection from Eviction Act 1977, s.5.
118 *Drane* v. *Evangelou* [1978] 2 All E.R. 437; [1978] 1 W.L.R. 455. See Arden and Partington 1980: 31–5.
119 Protection from Eviction Act 1977, ss. 2, 3. See also Residential Tenancies Act 1978–81 (South Australia), s.80; Residential Tenancies Act 1980 (Victoria), ss. 146(*b*), 147; Landlord and Tenant Act, R.S. Ontario 1980, ss.121(1), 122(1).
120 For example, Murie *et al.* 1976: 183, 198.
121 See, for example, Lambert *et al.* 1978: 52.
122 For a detailed critique, see Ashworth 1979. Cf. Residential Tenancies Act 1978–81 (South Australia), s. 47(2); Landlord and Tenant Act, R.S. Ontario 1980, ss. 121(4), 122(1).
123 For example, *R.* v. *Phekoo* [1981] 3 All E.R. 84; [1981] 1 W.L.R. 1117; *R.* v. *Shepherd* (1980) 71 Cr. App. R. 120; *R.* v. *Davidson-Acres* [1980] Crim. L. R. 50. So, a landlord who fails to pay a gas or electricity bill, so that services are cut off, might not be convicted of harassment since the prosecution might not be able to establish the requisite intent (cf. *Westminster C.C.* v. *Peart* (1968) 19 P.&C.R. 736; *Hooper* v. *Eaglestone* (1977) 34 P.&C.R. 311).
124 *McCall* v. *Abelesz* [1976] Q.B. 585.
125 *Gouriet* v. *Union of Post Office Workers* [1978] A.C. 435.
126 For example, Powers of Criminal Courts Act 1973, s.35.
127 See the empirical studies cited by Partington 1980: 176.
128 Cutting 1976: 101; Leevers *et al.* 1977.
129 Johnson *et al.* 1978: 945–50. See also LAG 1977b: 13.
130 Residential Tenancies Act 1978–81 (South Australia); Residential Tenancies Act 1980 (Victoria).
131 Lazerson 1982: 154.
132 Stein 1982: 221.
133 Residential Tenancies Act 1978–81 (South Australia), s.11(2)-(8).
134 For example, *Re Pajelle Investments Ltd and Booth (No.2)* (1975) 7 O.R. (2d) 229.
135 *Lee-Parker* v. *Izzet* [1971] 3 All E.R. 1099; [1971] 1 W.L.R. 1688. See also Rank 1976. The theory is that the doctrine of independence of covenants is preserved, for the right to repair and deduct only gives the tenant a defence in the event of an action for non-payment of rent.
136 *British Anzani (Felixstowe) Ltd* v. *International Marine Management (UK) Ltd* [1980] Q.B. 137. See also *Brikom Investments Ltd* v. *Seaford* [1981] 2 All E.R. 783; [1981] 1 W.L.R. 863. Cf. *Asco Developments Ltd* v. *Gordon*

[1978] 248 E.G. 683.
137 [1940] Ch. 352.
138 At p.366. Cf. *Pajelle Investments Ltd* v. *Chisholm* (1974) 49 D.L.R. (3d)
      21.
139 Arden 1979c.
140 For example, *Javins* v. *First National Realty Co.*, 428 F. 2d 1071 (1970),
      cert. denied 400 U.S. 925 (1970); *Pines* v. *Perssion*, 111 N.W. 2d 409,
      413 (1961).
141 See Keating and Heskin 1972; Ventantonio 1976. For West German
      and Canadian provisions, see *Buergerliches Gesetzbuch*, paras. 536–9;
      Lipsky and Neumann 1969; *Pajelle Investments Ltd* v. *Herbold* (1976) 62
      D.L.R. (3d) 749.
142 Cappelletti *et al.* 1975: 85, 109. Cf. Hazard 1969: 700–1.
143 For example, Sackville 1975a: 9.
144 For example, Abel-Smith *et al.* 1973; Cass and Sackville 1975; Curran
      1977; Royal Commission on Legal Services 1979: vol. 2, 173–298.
145 Weale 1978: 68. See also Griffiths 1980: 30–4.
146 Phillips 1979. Cf. Fogelson and Freeman 1968.
147 Cf. White 1973: 37.
148 Society of Labour Lawyers 1978.
149 *Cowell* v. *Taylor* (1886) 31 Ch.D. 34, 38.
150 Lawyers did not receive remuneration for *in forma pauperis*
      proceedings, and, under the latter statute, litigants who lost had to
      pay the defendant's costs or could be punished (cf. Anon. (1697) 91
      E.R. 433; (1702) 87 E.R. 1132). For the *in forma pauperis* procedure in
      the Court of Chancery, see Jones 1967: 323–8, 382, 462. Note also the
      role of the Court of Requests.
151 R.S.C., O. 16, rr. 22–31. For developments of the procedure in the
      United States and Australia, see Maguire 1923: 281–90; Duniway
      1966; *Borradale* v. *Davenport* [1958] V.R. 470, 474–7.
152 See Abel-Smith and Stevens 1967: 142–9.
153 *Cook* v. *Imperial Tobacco Co.* [1922] 2 K.B. 158.
154 Barrister 1938: 190.
155 Criminal Appeal Act 1907, s.10.
156 The scheme is dealt with in Cottrell 1980; Royal Commission on
      Legal Services 1979: vol.1, 101–54; Zander 1978: 32–6.
157 Weber 1954: 202–3.
158 For example, Alcock 1976: 172.
159 S. Hughes 1976. Of course, in the case of courts, lawyers are the
      lawmakers.
160 Browne 1938: 253–9.
161 Home Office 1966: 77.
162 See *R.* v. *Solihull JJ. ex p. Johnson*, 1976, unreported, discussed in
      Harris 1976. *Legal Services Commission of New South Wales* v. *Stephens*
      [1981] 2 N.S.W.L.R. 697.
163 For example, Bohne 1977; Burns and Reid 1981; Sackville 1975b:
      88–98.
164 For example, NLADA 1976: 259, 460. There are, of course, defects,

e.g. the small scale of some of the studies.
165 For example, *Carson* v. *Pickersgill* (1885) 14 Q.B.D. 859.
166 Auerbach 1976: 53–62; Blankenburg and Reifner 1981: 228–37;
Brownell 1951; Leat 1975. Proponents of some of these schemes
justified them by the need to reduce class conflict.
167 Bentwich 1914: 561, 564.
168 Cited White 1975: 241.
169 See Abel-Smith and Stevens 1967: 308, 331–4.
170 For example, *R.* v. *Cambridge Crown Court, ex p. Hagi* 1979, unreported,
discussed [1979] LAG Bulletin: 238; *R.* v. *Howes* [1964] 2 Q.B. 459,
463.
171 See the authorities cited in Levenson 1977. See also *R.* v. *Beadle* (1979)
21 S.A.S.R. 67.
172 For example, *R.* v. *Howes* [1964] 2 Q.B. 459; *McInnis* v. *R.* (1979) 27
A.L.R. 449; *R.* v. *Littlejohn* (1978) 41 C.C.C. (2d) 161.
173 *Argersinger* v. *Hamlin,* 407 U.S. 25, 37 (1972). See also *Scott* v. *Illinois,*
440 U.S. 367 (1979); *Gideon* v. *Wainwright,* 372 U.S. 335 (1963).
   The European Court of Human Rights might be moving in this
direction. Article 6(3)(c) of the European Convention on Human
Rights provides that everyone charged with a criminal offence has a
minimum right to free legal assistance when the interests of justice so
require, if they do not have sufficient means to pay. The Court has
held that this guarantees practical and effective rights rather than
theoretical or illusory ones, that it guarantees the right to an effective
defence either in person or through a lawyer, and that breach of the
provision does not require proof of actual prejudice (*Artico* v. *Italy*
(1980) 3 E.H.R.R. 1). The Court has also indicated that Article 6(1) –
which provides that in the determination of his civil rights and
obligations or of any criminal charge against him, everyone is entitled
to a fair and public hearing within a reasonable time by an
independent and impartial tribunal – may require free civil legal aid
for those without means, where the procedure or the case is complex
(*Airey* v. *Ireland* (1979) 2 E.H.R.R. 305).
174 For example, NLADA 1976: 13–14.
175 *Ross* v. *Moffitt* 417 U.S. 600 (1974).
176 *Lassiter* v. *Department of Social Services of Durham County, North Carolina*
452 U.S. 18 (1981).
177 401 U.S. 371 (1971).
178 *United* v. *Kras* 409 U.S. 434 (1973); *Ortwein* v. *Schwab* 410 U.S. 656
(1973).
179 In addition to a contribution, successful legally assisted parties might
be liable for the costs incurred by the legal-aid scheme on their
account, by means of a statutory charge on any property recovered or
preserved through the proceedings or by settlement. See *Hanlon* v. *The
Law Society* [1980] 2 All E.R. 199; [1980] 2 W.L.R. 756, where the
injustices which can flow from such a provision were highlighted.
180 For example, Byles and Morris 1977: 49.
181 See generally Muther 1975.

182 Unassisted successful parties might be able to claim their costs from the legal-aid fund; e.g. *Megarity* v. *D.J. Ryan & Sons Ltd (No. 2)* [1981] 1 All E.R. 641; [1981] 2 W.L.R. 335; *Saunders* v. *Anglia Building Society (No.2)* [1971] A.C. 1039. But it is questionable whether large institutions should be able to do this to the detriment of the amount available for assisting poor people.

183 See Brooke 1977; Jones 1980. But in some jurisdictions these are still dominated by the profession. The Royal Commission on Legal Services for England and Wales rejected the idea of a legal services commission but accepted the need for lay participation at national and regional, but not local, levels: v.1, 61, 142.

184 Levenson 1982.

185 For example, Legal Aid Act 1974, s.7(5).

186 Of course once legal aid is granted, a person may be in a stronger bargaining position than a non-legally aided litigant, especially one who falls just outside the eligibility limits, if these are low.

187 Law Society 1981: 187.

188 Pollock 1975: 135–7. Cf. Adamsdown Legal Services Group 1976: 16–18.

189 Sackville 1975b: 147; Zander 1978: 32–4.

190 See 30th Legal Aid Annual Reports [1979–80]: 89.

191 Cooper 1983 and Garth 1980 cover the developments in various jurisdictions. Law centres are sometimes known as neighbourhood law firms or community centres.

192 For example, Monopolies and Mergers Commission 1976: 38.

193 See e.g. Johnson 1974: 91–2, for litigation in the US. See also *Re Bannister ex p. Hartstein* (1975) 5 A.C.T.R. 100.

194 Most dramatically in the United States under the Reagan administration.

195 Stephens 1980.

196 Merricks 1979: 237.

197 See Bellow 1977.

198 Johnson 1974: 189.

199 McCarthy 1974.

200 See Thomas and Mungham 1977; King 1976. Assistance under duty-lawyer schemes ranges from helping defendants apply for legal aid, to representation before a court on behalf of those applying for bail or an adjournment or pleading guilty. The duty solicitor has a long history in Scotland. The idea has been incorporated as part of the legal-aid schemes in jurisdictions such as Ontario and New South Wales (Osler 1974: 5–9; Cashman 1982).

201 See Bankowski and Mungham 1976: 50–64. Cf. Royal Commission on Legal Services 1979: v.1, 93, 96.

202 See Tomasic and Feeley 1981; Schwartzkoff and Morgan 1982.

203 Simplification of the substantive and procedural law governing divorce is an example (cf. Galanter 1976a; 1976b).

204 Cf. Balbus 1977.

205 See Unger 1976: 173, 195.

206 For example, a survey in Britain in 1979 asked over one thousand respondents whether they would receive the same treatment as anyone else if they had a problem with the police or with a government department (such as social security). Over eighty per cent expected equal treatment from both the police and the bureaucracy (Barker 1979; cf. Royal Commission on Legal Services 1979: v.2, 224–32). However, other surveys seem to have found that working-class people consider that equality before the law is illusory in practice (Morris *et al.* 1973a: 313; Byles and Morris 1977: 49). In the American Bar Association/American Bar Foundation survey of legal needs, some sixty per cent thought that the legal system favoured the rich and powerful over everyone else, with black/latinos and the poor expressing this view somewhat more strongly (Curran 1977: 253). Surveys in deprived areas of London and Sydney found that almost two-fifths and over one half of the respondents respectively agreed that the law favoured the rich over the poor (Abel-Smith *et al.* 1973: 249; Cass and Sackville 1975: 83).

CHAPTER 4: Social welfare regulation

1 Lipsky 1980: 29.
2 See Griffiths 1979: 351–5.
3 There is considerable conflict among historians as to the origins of nineteenth-century reform. See Hart 1974; MacDonagh 1958.
4 Midwinter 1969: 65.
5 See Gauldie 1974: 296.
6 See Hobsbawm 1977b: 255–7.
7 Halévy 1952: 244–53; Sells 1939: 15–22; Bayliss 1962: 1–12.
8 Schifferes 1976: 69. See also Gallacher 1949.
9 In the nineteenth century, the poorer sections of society rented accommodation. Some was owned by a few large employers, but most landlords were middle-class persons – small merchants, tradesmen and manufacturers, and professionals like doctors, solicitors and clergymen – who were drawn by the steady profit and the security which it would provide to their family on death (e.g. Butt 1971; North Tyneside CDP 1978, v.1: 10–12; Chalklin 1974: 57–60, 84–97).
10 There is the similar, if unchartered, role of the 'property lobby' in more recent times which has mobilized, with important success, against measures such as rent control. In general terms, banks, pension funds, insurance companies and other institutions have supported the 'property lobby' because of their investments in property companies and their involvement in property development (see Colenutt 1975).
11 In addition, nuisance law protected landholders from interference with the free use and enjoyment of their land. But most nuisance actions were in respect of mills, watercourses, dams and rivers, rather than in respect of threats to public health (see Barry and Fisher 1952: 1–2; Jaffe and Henderson 1956). At common law it was accepted that

it was a common nuisance to divide a house in a town for poor people to inhabit, 'by which it will be more dangerous in time of infection of the plague' (Viner: v.16, 23). In London, indictments for nuisance were supposed to be frequent, but it is reasonable to suppose that they made no greater dent on conditions. In the late eighteenth century some local authorities used covenants to enforce standards (Chalklin 1974: 104–5).

12 Developers could make enormous profits from building tenements, and many were willing to bear the relatively small losses from prosecutions – if these were ever instituted by the unpaid and unwilling officials (Barnes 1970).

13 Except for London which had to wait for the Public Health (London) Act 1891 (54 & 55 Vict., c.76). See Clarke 1949a: 128–9; Slater 1930: 126.

14 MacDonagh 1977: 133ff.

15 Metropolitan Buildings Act 1844 (7 & 8 Vict., c.84); Towns Improvement Clauses Act 1847; Public Health Act 1848. See Knowles and Pitt 1972.

16 See also Public Health Act 1875, ss.76–7, 80. Common lodging-houses provided a night's lodging for labourers and others and comprised large dormitory areas with common kitchens and dining rooms. These houses were notorious for their insanitary conditions and were said to act as a refuge for criminals. By 1853 there were 3,300 lodging-house keepers under inspection in London with something like 50,000 nightly lodgers. Because there was no definition in the Act – there had been one in the Towns Improvement Clauses Act 1847 – considerable litigation ensued. In *Logsdon* v. *Booth* [1900] 1 Q.B. 401, the court adopted the view of the law officers that 'a common lodging-house was that class of lodging-house in which persons of the poorer class are received for short periods, and, although strangers to one another, are allowed to inhabit one common room'. Controls are still extant (Public Health Act 1936, Part IX).

17 Dyos and Wolff 1973.

18 42 & 43 Vict., c.63.

19 45 & 46 Vict., c.54. See Sutcliffe 1974: 75, 102.

20 Parl. Deb., Commons, vol.345, 1890, 1822–6.

21 See Simon 1933.

22 See McAuslan 1975: 34, 44.

23 *Great Western Railway Co.* v. *Bishop* (1872) L.R. 7 Q.B. 550.

24 Smith 1979: 200–4.

25 Simon 1897: 440, 473.

26 See Stedman Jones 1971: 191.

27 *Garlick* v. *Knottingley U.D.C.* (1904) 68 J.P. 494; 2 L.G.R. 1345, was an unsuccessful action by a person whose bedding and clothing were destroyed.

28 For example, Wohl 1977: 137.

29 Hill 1883: 13.

30 See *R.* v. *Pedly* (1834) 110 E.R. 1422; *R.* v. *Medley* (1834) 172 E.R.

1246.

31 *Attorney General* v. *Birmingham B.C.* (1858) 70 E.R. 220. See Hennock 1973: 107; Lumley 1876: 25n.
32 *Sturges* v. *Bridgman* (1879) L.R. 11 Ch.D. 852, 865.
33 *St Helen's Smelting Co.* v. *Tipping* (1865) 11 E.R. 1483. See Brenner 1974.
34 Bowley 1947: 4–7.
35 For example, *Wilkes* v. *Goodwin* [1923] 2 K.B. 86. Reversed by Increase of Rent and Mortgage Interest Restrictions Act 1923, s.10.
36 See Evans 1974: 233–5.
37 Rent and Mortgage Interest Restrictions Act 1939.
38 Furnished Houses (Rent Control) Act 1946. The tribunals could also give these tenants limited security. In 1949 the jurisdiction of rent tribunals was extended to fix rents where tenants shared some accommodation with their landlord (Landlord and Tenant (Rent Control) Act 1949). As a means of preventing landlords avoiding rent limits, the Act also prohibited persons from requiring premiums.
39 *Palser* v. *Grinling* [1948] A.C. 291; *Woodward* v. *Docherty* [1974] 2 All E.R. 844; [1974] 1 W.L.R. 966.
40 Rent Act 1965. Fair rents were not to be fixed historically or tied to rateable value but were to have regard to the age, character and locality of a tenancy and its state of repair, discounting scarcity value.
41 Housing Rents and Subsidies Act 1975.
42 See Baker 1979: 277, 381.
43 Kimball 1955: v.1, 1; Williams 1956: v.1, lxxvi, 9.
44 Holdsworth: v.4, 380–2.
45 Tawney 1979.
46 For example, Hampson 1934: 56; Ashby 1912: 174.
47 The Silk Manufacturers Act 1772 (13 Geo. 3, c.68) which was enacted after pressure from silk workers, and which remained in force with modification for fifty years, had confirmed that silkweavers were entitled to a legal minimum wage.
48 Poynter 1969: 48–61.
49 Thompson 1968: 554.
50 Freeden 1978: 163–4.
51 Ss. 108, 116(5).
52 Sells 1939: 248.
53 Kahn-Freund 1949: 786.
54 For example, Merrifield 1980.
55 *Ex p. H.V. McKay* (1907) 2 C.A.R. 1. In 1966 the two elements were consolidated into a total wage, which includes a minimum wage – *Basic Wage, Margins and Total Wage Cases of 1966* (1966) 115 C.A.R. 93. The trade-union movement tends to support the reintroduction of the previous approach as a greater protection for the low-paid. The Commission has varied wages at least annually, after a hearing in which employers, the Australian Council of Trade Unions and the government present their views. The factors it takes into account include equity, movements in the cost of living and, more recently,

increases in productivity and the state of the economy.
56 Conciliation and Arbitration Act 1904, Part VI.
57 [1975] 2 All E.R. 99; [1975] 1 W.L.R. 845.
58 Housing Act 1957, ss.77–8, Schedule 6.
59 See Townsend 1979: 498–503. In allocating public housing, authorities must usually give preference to those living in overcrowded conditions, but they have no legal obligation to relieve overcrowding by making public housing available (e.g. Housing Act 1957, s.113).
60 Cf. *Simmons* v. *Pizzey* [1979] A.C. 37 – women's refuge.
61 *Redbridge L.B.C.* v. *Perry* (1976) 75 L.G.R. 90; (1976) 33 P. & C.R. 176.
62 Housing Act 1961, Part II; Housing Act 1964, Part IV. *Hackney L.B.C.* v. *Ezedinma* [1981] 3 All E.R. 438.
63 *Salford C.C.* v. *McNally* [1976] A.C. 379.
64 Public Health Act 1936, s.92(1).
65 See D.J. Hughes 1976.
66 [1976] 2 All E.R. 478; [1976] 1 W.L.R. 543.
67 The power of local authorities to issue repair notices where conditions interfere materially with the personal comfort of an occupying tenant – introduced in 1980 as section 9(1B) of the Housing Act 1957 – compensates partly for the damage done by the *Thorne* decision.
68 Public Health Act 1936, ss.93–4.
69 Despite the mandatory language, it has been held that the court had discretion to postpone the order. *Nottingham City D.C.* v. *Newton* [1974] 2 All E.R. 760; [1974] 1 W.L.R. 923. Cf. *Ward* v. *Williams* (1955) 92 C.L.R. 496.
70 Powers of Criminal Courts Act 1973, s.35.
71 See *Lambeth L.B.C.* v. *Stubbs* (1980) 78 L.G.R. 650; *Coventry C.C.* v. *Doyle* [1981] 2 All E.R. 184; [1981] 1 W.L.R. 1325.
72 Housing Act 1957, s.4. See *Morgan* v. *Liverpool Corp.* [1927] 2 K.B. 131, 145.
73 [1943] A.C. 283.
74 Housing Act 1957, s.9(1). It has been held that s.9 cannot be applied to an authority's own housing – unless someone else has an interest in it – because an authority would be serving notice on itself (*R.* v. *Cardiff C.C. ex p. Cross* [1981] J.P.L. 748). Quite apart from the questionability of this interpretation, the decision suffers from an uncritical acceptance of the fiction that corporate entities are indivisible.
75 See *F.F.F. Estates Ltd* v. *Hackney L.B.C.* [1981] 1 Q.B. 503. Cf. Hadden 1979b: App. J.
76 Housing Act 1957, s.16. Cf. *Barringer* v. *Nyngan M.C.* (1953) 86 C.L.R. 495.
77 A local authority then has the duty to rehouse the occupants, but a grave defect is that they have no immediate right to ordinary public housing and might be placed in temporary accommodation (*R.* v. *Bristol Corp. ex p. Hendy* [1974] 1 All E.R. 407; [1974] 1 W.L.R. 498).

78 *R.* v. *Kerrier D.C. ex p. Guppys (Bridport) Ltd* (1976) 75 L.G.R. 129; (1976) 32 P. & C.R. 411.
79 *Hillbank Properties Ltd* v. *Hackney L.B.C.* [1978] Q.B. 998.
80 See Hughes 1981: Ch.10.
81 Part III. An authority must be satisfied that there is suitable accommodation available for those displaced, that they have sufficient resources for the job, and that rehabilitation is not a viable alternative. *Eckersley* v. *Secretary of State for the Environment* (1977) 76 L.G.R. 245; (1977) 34 P. & C.R. 124.
82 Housing Act 1974, ss.114–114A.
83 See *Elliott* v. *Southwark L.B.C.* [1976] 2 All E.R. 781; [1976] 1 W.L.R. 499. See also Little 1976.
84 See Bradbrook 1975: 27, 30; Hadden 1978: 34–5.
85 For example, Law Centres' Working Group 1977: 48–63; Shelter 1977: 24–7; Hadden 1979b: 166–75. Cf. Bradbrook 1975: 38–40.
86 See Cutting 1977: 34; Wicks 1973; Society of Labour Lawyers 1973.
87 Jordan 1977: 56–7.
88 For example, Handicapped Persons Equal Opportunity Act 1981 (South Australia).
89 Company (Director's Report) (Employment of Disabled Persons) Regulations 1980, S.I. 1980 No.1160.
90 For example, Wages Council Act 1979, s.16; Conciliation and Arbitration Act 1904 (Australia), s.48.
91 See Crine 1981; Noble 1979.
92 For critiques of North American and Australian rent control, see Bradbrook 1975: 79–106; Law Reform Commission of British Columbia 1973: 47–55, 73–6; Ontario Law Reform Commission 1968: 63–72. See also Baar 1977.
93 Megarry 1967: v.1, xxvi.
94 See Arden 1978b.
95 Rent Act 1977, ss.1, 4.
96 Ss.7, 8, 9, 12, 13–16.
97 Ss.2, 3(1).
98 Ss.19–21, Part V.
99 For example, L.A.G. 1977b: 13–15.
100 See Rent Act 1977, ss.27–33. Controlled tenancies were abolished by Housing Act 1980, s.64.
101 Rent Act 1977, s.70(1).
102 *Mason* v. *Skilling* [1974] 3 All E.R. 977; [1974] 1 W.L.R. 1437.
103 See Law Centres Working Group 1977: 36; L.A.G. 1977b: 23; Shelter 1977: 18–20.
104 S.98, Schedule 15.
105 Ss.103–4, 106A.
106 Ss.119–20.
107 S.122. An excessive price for furniture is treated as a premium (s.123).
108 For example, *Farrell* v. *Alexander* [1977] A.C. 59.
109 See Rent Act 1977, s.128(1) as amended.
110 Landlord and Tenant Act, R.S.O. 1980, c.232, s.84(1).

Notes to pp. 130–139 365

111 For example, Residential Tenancies Act 1978–81 (South Australia), ss.32–3, 86; Cf. Residential Tenancy Act (British Columbia), R.S.B.C. 1979, Part V.
112 Rent Act 1977, ss.45–50, 67, 77.
113 S.57. Cf. s.81.
114 For example, Residential Tenancies Act 1978–1981 (South Australia), s.36; Residential Tenancies Act 1980 (Victoria), s.63; Residential Tenancy Act, R.S.B.C., ss.69, 75.
115 Committee on the Rent Act 1971: App. I, 306, 314; Zander 1968: 366; *Direct Action* Jan.-Feb. 1977: 35; Paley 1978: 18–19. In recent years in England, landlords have been the largest source of applications for a registered rent. It seems that one reason they apply is to take advantage of any upward trend in rents.
116 Cutting 1977: 26, 50.
117 Cf. *R.* v. *London Rent Assessment Panel, ex p. Braq Investments Ltd* [1969] 2 All E.R. 1012; [1969] 1 W.L.R. 970.
118 Ss.68, 77(1).
119 *R.* v. *Paddington and St Marylebone Rent Tribunal, ex p. Bell London & Provincial Properties Ltd* [1949] 1 K.B. 666.
120 *R.* v. *Barnet and Camden Rent Tribunal, ex p. Frey Investments Ltd* [1972] 2 Q.B. 342.
121 Powers of Criminal Courts Act 1973, s.35.
122 *Gouriet* v. *Union of Post Office Workers* [1978] A.C. 435.
123 [1970] 2 Q.B. 504. Contrast decisions in the United States on this point: *Brown* v. *Southall Realty Co.* 237 A.2d 834 (1968); *Shephard* v. *Lerner* 6 Cal. Rptr 433 (1960).
124 [1976] Q.B. 585.
125 Morris 1976: 499.
126 Winyard 1976: 19.
127 Brown 1974: 23.
128 Haar and Liebman 1977: 288–9; *Edwards* v. *Habib* 397 F.2d 687 (1968), cert. denied 393 U.S. 1016 (1969).
129 Adamsdown Community Trust 1978: 44.
130 Ermer 1972: 4–6, 11, 71.
131 For example, Environmental Health Officers' Association 1975: 40.
132 For example, *Salford C.C.* v. *McNally* [1976] A.C. 379.
133 Anon. 1977: 107. See also Anon. 1979.
134 Hadden 1978: 69, 76, 86–96. See also Robson 1977: 20, 24–6. Cf. Dickens 1970: 629–30.
135 Hadden 1979a: 728.
136 [1978] 2 All E.R. 437, 443; [1978] 1 W.L.R. 455, 461.
137 Beaumont 1979; Winyard 1976; Royal Commission on the Distribution of Income and Wealth 1978b: 125–6, 308–9, 531–4. On its under-enforcement of the disabled quota, see Jordan 1979.
138 For example, *Smedleys Ltd* v. *Breed* [1974] A.C. 839; *R.* v. *Commissioner of Police of the Metropolis ex p. Blackburn (No. 3)* [1973] Q.B. 241.
139 *Nottingham C.D.C.* v. *Newton* [1974] 2 All E.R. 760; [1974] 1 W.L.R. 923.

140 *R.* v. *Kerrier D.C., ex p. Guppys (Bridport) Ltd* (1976) 75 L.G.R. 129; (1976) 32 P.& C.R.411.
141 Henriques 1979: 143; Hennock 1973: 251; Gauldie 1974: 128; Midwinter 1969: 90–1.
142 Wohl 1977: 117–18; Butt 1971: 68–9.
143 See Sells 1939: 229–33, 236, 244, 326.
144 Tawney 1914: 126.
145 See Hadden 1978: 62.
146 Davies 1972: 148.
147 Fishman 1978: 553; Bradbrook 1977: 156.
148 Hadden 1978: 21, 31, 40.
149 Ministry of Health 1953: 47. See also Birtwistle 1972: 357; Wilcox 1972: 110; Lambert *et al.* 1978: 44.
150 Gross 1979: 9.
151 For example, Ministry of Health 1953: 47 (environmental health inspectors); Parl. Deb., Commons, vol.925, 1977, c.213 (Under-Secretary of State for Employment approving prosecution policy of wages inspectorate); Committee on the Rents Act 1971: 111 (harassment officers). Cf. Royal Commission on Criminal Procedure 1980: 139–40.
152 *Drane* v. *Evangelou* [1978] 2 All E.R. 437, 443; [1978] 1 W.L.R. 455, 461 (unlawful eviction); *People's Refreshment House Association Ltd* v. *Jones* [1954] 1 All E.R. 317, 322; [1954] 1 W.L.R. 339, 344 (minimum wages).
153 Cutting 1977: 24–5.
154 *R.* v. *Brennan & Brennan* [1979] 1 Cr. App. R.(S) 103; [1979] Crim.L.R. 603.
155 Pennock and Chapman 1974: 13.
156 Cf. Blumberg and Robbins 1976: 45–6; Abbott 1976; North Tyneside CDP 1978: v.3, 26–7; v.4, 35–6, 78. And see the example in Brent Community Law Centre 1976: 18–19.
157 For example, *Nicholl* v. *Epping U.D.C.* [1899] 1 Ch. 844, 851.
158 (1858) 44 E.R. 989.
159 That a local authority could not adopt a general policy of conversion was applied in subsequent challenges by landlords of working-class housing – an irritating, if not fatal, obstacle to any local authority intent on improving the public health of its area. See *Wood* v. *Widnes Corp.* [1898] 1 Q.B. 463; *Barnett* v. *Laskey* (1899) 68 L.J.Q.B. 55. Other examples of the courts siding with property owners, on the basis of such doctrines, involved privies (*Ex p. Whitchurch* (1881) 6 Q.B.D. 545; see also Anon. (1882); public urinals (*Vernon* v. *Vestry of St James, Westminster* (1880) 16 Ch.D. 449. Cf. *Biddulph* v. *Vestry of St George, Hanover Square* (1863) 8 L.T. 558); and drains and sewers (*Marylebone Vestry* v. *Viret* (1865) 12 L.T. 673; Jennings 1937). *Austin* v. *Vestry of St Mary, Lambeth* (1858) 27 L.J. Ch.388, which held that the local authority could prescribe the type of pipes for sewerage, is no exception to the trend of these decisions. The owner was not contesting interference with his property, and the case might have

gone the other way on appeal. It did not proceed because the litigation was tainted with maintenance (the plaintiff was backed by a pipe manufacturer).

160 (1862) 121 E.R. 934. See also *Hargreaves* v. *Taylor* (1863) 122 E.R. 230; *St James and St John Vestry, Clerkenwell* v. *Feary* (1890) 24 Q.B.D. 703; *Nicholl* v. *Epping Urban Council* [1899] 1 Ch.844.

161 Public Health Acts Amendment Act 1907, s.39(4).

162 *Carlton Main Colliery Co.* v. *Hemsworth R.D.C.* [1922] 1 Ch.521.

163 *Attorney-General* v. *Leeds Corp.* (1870) 5 Ch.App. 583. Lapse of time usually deprives a person of a remedy for nuisance. Cf. *Attorney-General* v. *Cockermouth Local Board* (1874) L.R. 18 Eq. 172; *Attorney-General* v. *Kingston-on-Thames* (1865) 12 L.T. 665; 34 L.J. Ch.481.

164 Sewage of Towns (1857–65), Pollution of Rivers (1866–74) and Water Supply (1868–69).

165 A similar turn-round occurred in other areas of administrative law. Compare, for example, *Cooper* v. *Wandsworth Board of Works* (1863) 143 E.R. 414 and *Local Government Board* v. *Arlidge* [1915] A.C. 120.

166 E.g. *Attorney-General* v. *Guardian of Poor of Union of Dorking* (1882) 20 Ch.D.595.

167 S.299; *Pasmore* v. *Oswaldtwistle U.D.C.* [1898] A.C. 387.

168 For example, *Robinson* v. *Workington Corp.* [1897] 1 Q.B.619.

169 For example, *Glossop* v. *Heston and Isleworth Local Board* (1879) 12 Ch.D. 102, 115.

170 There are subsequent decisions in the early part of the twentieth century where individual property owners succeeded against drainage and sewage authorities, mainly in actions for damages. But they were put on the basis that the plaintiff had been individually wronged, and that the action was not attempting to compel the public authority to fulfil its statutory duty for a whole district. See Robinson 1925: 163–9, 174–7. Cf. *Hesketh* v. *Birmingham Corp.* [1924] 1 K.B. 260.

171 Quoted Reynolds 1974: 381.

172 *Ibid.* Cf. Robinson 1976. The contrast can be drawn with the ease with which the Law of Property Act 1925 was implemented, because of the judges' long experience in handling property matters (Davies 1935: 528–9).

173 [1915] A.C. 120. Lord Haldane L.C. chose four Liberal law lords to hear the case, to remove the threat of judicial interference (Stevens 1979: 192, 197).

174 Schifferes 1976: 67.

175 For example, *R.* v. *Minister of Health ex p. Davis* [1929] 1 K.B. 619.

176 Kirby 1979: 79.

177 Griffith 1977: 111.

178 *Errington* v. *Minister of Health* [1935] 1 K.B. 249.

179 Jennings 1936a.

180 For example, *Horn* v. *Minister of Health* [1937] 1 K.B. 164; *Fredman* v. *Minister of Health* (1936) 154 L.T. 240.

181 For example, *Franklin* v. *Minister of Town and Country Planning* [1948] A.C. 87; *Smith* v. *East Elloe R.D.C.* [1956] A.C. 736.

182 For example, *Fairmount Investments Ltd* v. *Secretary of State for the
     Environment* [1976] 2 All E.R. 865; [1976] 1 W.L.R. 1255.
183 For example, *Elliott* v. *Southwark L.B.C.* [1976] 2 All E.R. 781, [1976]
     1 W.L.R. 499; *R.* v. *Bristol Corporation, ex p. Hendy* [1974] 1 All E.R.
     1047; [1974] 1 W.L.R. 498; *Bushell* v. *Secretary of State for the
     Environment* [1981] A.C. 75.
184 See McAuslan 1979: 33–5.
185 See the studies by Cutting 1976; Leevers *et al.* 1977: 32–7. See also
     L.A.G. 1977b: 15.1; Anon. 1980.
186 Mosier and Soble 1973: 63.
187 Editorial 1978a: 78.
188 Cf. *Horford Investments* v. *Lambert* [1976] Ch.39, 52.
189 Friend 1978: 7.
190 [1978] 2 All E.R. 1011; [1978] 1 W.L.R. 1014.
191 *Aldrington Garages* v. *Fielder* (1979) 37 P. & C.R. 461; (1978) 247 E.G.
     557.
192 (1979) 249 E.G. 440; [1979] J.P.L. 462.
193 Cf. Lawton L.J.'s comments in *O'Malley* v. *Seymour* (1979) 250 E.G.
     1083; [1979] J.P.L. 675.
194 Arden 1979a: 78.
195 *Bevington* v. *Crawford* (1974) 232 E.G. 191.
196 Harloe *et al.* 1974: 109–10.
197 Krohn and Tiller 1969; Paley 1978: 19, 21.
198 See Paley 1978: 20; Greve 1965: 35–6.
199 Gauldie 1974: 127.
200 Harloe *et al.* 1974: 111, 115.
201 *Direct Action*, Jan.-Feb. 1977: 24; *Guardian*, 20 Oct. 1976: 6.
202 Friend 1978: 10–12.
203 *Hillbank Properties Ltd* v. *Hackney L.B.C.* [1978] Q.B. 998.
204 *Daily Telegraph*, 18 Jan. 1977: 22.
205 Ball 1960.
206 Bonger 1967: 257.
207 Department of the Environment 1977a: 92; *ibid.* 1977b: 113.
208 Karn 1979: 184–6.
209 Bone and Mason 1980: 60.
210 See Crine 1980.
211 Royal Commission on the Distribution of Income and Wealth 1978a:
     141; 1978b: 472, 586.
212 Clegg 1976: 360; Royal Commission on Trade Unions and Employers'
     Associations 1968: 57–60, 65–8, 70–2.
213 See Ackerman 1971; Komesar 1973; Markovits 1976.
214 Hirsch *et al.* 1975. Cf. Meyers 1975; Schafer 1977.
215 Boddy and Gray 1979.
216 Hayek *et al.* 1975; Starr 1979.
217 Barnett 1969: 244–5.
218 See Bone and Mason 1980: 58–60; Elliott and McCrone 1975;
     Maclennan 1978; McCrone and Elliott 1979; Paley 1978: 30–42.
219 Friedman 1962: 180.

220 See Welch 1974; Leffler 1978.
221 With regard to externalities, the economic justification for legal regulation of housing standards is to force landlords to internalize the costs that substandard housing has on neighbours and on the environmental quality of an area (see Komesar 1978: 219–20).
222 Evidence from the United States is that there is a maldistribution in the enforcement of regulation of matters like housing standards. Explanations are that housing inspectors regard slum areas as physically dangerous, are discouraged because so little seems capable of achievement, and regard slum dwellers as undeserving. More evidence is needed before definite statements can be made about inequalities in regulatory enforcement.
223 For example Sax and Hiestand 1967.

CHAPTER 5: Social welfare benefits

1 Handler 1972: 3.
2 See Jones 1958: 145, 147, 155.
3 Campbell 1978: 66–7.
4 See Friedman 1971; Jowell 1975: 52–3; Vinogradoff 1928: 367–80.
5 See Mayhew 1975: 409; Scheingold 1974: 7.
6 Bond, 1975; Taylor-Gooby and Lakeman 1977.
7 In this chapter a distinction is drawn between social security (or insurance) and social (or public) assistance. The terminology varies between countries but the distinction is widely accepted between, on the one hand, social welfare benefits where persons have a strong entitlement, frequently underpinned by specific contributions (so that benefits are limited to those who have made their contributions), and, on the other hand, social welfare benefits where the discretionary element is stronger and payment is contingent on insufficient means (see Tussing 1974). The two kinds of benefit usually vary as to their rates, and while the public generally perceives the former to be 'legitimate', stigma might attach to receipt of the latter. Despite the distinction, the Court of Justice of the European Communities has said on various occasions that social welfare benefits often contain elements of both social security and social assistance – they defy general classification given the classes of persons to whom they apply, their objectives and the manner of their application (*Frilli* v. *Belgian State* [1972] E.C.R. 457, 465; *Callemeyn* v. *Belgian State* [1974] E.C.R. 553, 561; *Costa* v. *Belgian State* [1974] E.C.R. 1251, 1260–1).
Contribution is by no means essential for social security benefits (for example, there are no contributory social welfare benefits in Australia); even where social security is contributory, that has not prevented governments in places like Britain and the United States from reducing benefits in the interests of macro-economic policy; and social security rates might be quite low, so that its claimants have to draw social assistance (see, e.g., Martin 1979; Supplementary Benefits Commission 1979: 6–15). More importantly for present purposes, the

juridical character of the two types of benefit has merged over the years, largely because the legal structure for social assistance has been modelled on that for social security through a reduction in discretion and through the elaboration of mechanisms for external review.

8 There can be an absence of legislative standards both as to substantive and procedural matters. The focus of this section is on the substantive issue – the entitlement of claimants to social welfare benefits – but it is well to remember that a discretion of a social welfare bureaucracy to determine the manner of payment of benefit is of the same legal character (e.g., Social Security Act 1947 (Australia), ss. 40(2), 69(2), 123(1)).

9 Judicial review is possible: *Attorney-General ex rel. Tilley* v. *Wandsworth L.B.C.* [1981] 1 All E.R. 1162; [1981] 1 W.L.R. 854. The ombudsman might also investigate.

10 Freeman 1980; Hill 1979; Hill and Laing 1979: 38, 41; Lister and Emmett 1976: 10–12, 29.

11 Dworkin 1977: 32.

12 *Re Te Velde and Director-General of Social Services* (1981) 3 ALN No.75.

13 *Re Beames and Director-General of Social Services* (1981) 3 ALN No.50. Cf. *Re Blackburn and Director-General of Social Services* (1982) 4 ALN No.46. The *Beames* decision is debatable, because the very purpose of special benefit would seem to be to provide a flexible safety net in situations where a person does not qualify for a specific pension or benefit. In the United States the courts have used the constitutional guarantee of due process to compel social welfare bureaucracies to develop standards for the exercise of discretion (*White* v. *Roughton*, 530 F. 2d 750 (1976); *Baker-Chaput* v. *Cammett*, 406 F. Supp. 1134 (1976)).

14 The courts interpreted its precursor so that payments were regarded as being of a discretionary nature, 'the modern successor of poor law relief' (National Assistance Act 1948, s.4; *Foxley* v. *Olton* [1965] 2 Q.B. 306, 311–12).

15 Supplementary Benefits Act 1976, s.1(1), substantially re-enacting Ministry of Social Security Act 1966, s.4(1).

16 Supplementary Benefits Act 1976, ss.3, 4, Schedule I, para.4 (1).

17 *R.* v. *Greater Birmingham SBAT ex p. Simper* [1974] Q.B. 543.

18 [1977] 3 All E.R. 1031; [1977] 1 W.L.R. 917.

19 Social Security (Miscellaneous Provisions) Act 1977, s.14(8).

20 *McDougall* v. *Secretary of State for Social Services* [1981] S.L.T. 259.

21 Legislation sometimes confers on administrators the power to decide whether certain criteria are met, indicated by the presence of terms such as 'in the opinion of' or 'satisfied'. This aspect of discretion cuts across the two categories of discretion outlined and goes to the reviewability by the courts of the decisions made and not to the character of the distinction drawn. As Stephen J. said of a provision of this nature in the Australian Social Security Act 1947, where the relevant discretion reposed in the Director-General of Social Security: 'No general discretion is conferred upon him; instead specific criteria

are laid down in the Act and all that is left for him to do is to decide
whether or not he attains a state of satisfaction that the
circumstances exist to which each of these criteria refer' (*Green* v.
Daniels (1977) 13 A.L.R. 1, 9).
22 *R.* v. *West London SBAT ex p. Taylor* [1975] 2 All E.R. 790; [1975] 1
W.L.R. 1048. See now Supplementary Benefits (Resources)
Regulations 1981, SI 1980 No. 1526, rr. 3(2)(b), 13.
23 *Lillystone* v. *Supplementary Benefits Commission, The Times*, 30 October
1981. See now *ibid.*, r. 3(2)(c). Cf. Supplementary Benefits Act 1976,
s.6(1)(b).
24 *R.* v. *National Insurance Commissioner ex p. Stratton* [1979] Q.B. 361.
25 Other examples include 'remunerative full-time work' – *R.* v.
Supplementary Benefits Commission ex p. Lewis, The Times, 5 November
1981 (see Family Income Supplements (General) Regulations
1980, SI 1980 No. 1437, r.5); 'resources' – *R.* v. *Manchester SBAT
ex p. Riley* [1979] 2 All E.R. 1; [1979] 1 W.L.R. 426 (see
Supplementary Benefit (Resources) Regulations 1980, SI 1980 No.
1300, as amended, r.10); 'ordinarily resident' – *R.* v. *Barnet LBC ex p.
Shah* [1983] 1 All E.R. 226; [1983] 2 W.L.R. 16; 'attention in
connection with bodily functions' – *R.* v. *National Insurance Commissioner
ex p. Secretary of State for Social Services* [1981] 2 All E.R. 738; [1981] 1
W.L.R. 1017; and 'earnings' – *Attorney General of Canada* v. *McCombe*
[1978] 2 FC 746.
26 Of course there is scope for disagreement between medical
practitioners as to the facts or how they should be interpreted. The
possibility of medical disagreement is reduced where legislation deems
certain conditions such as blindness or the loss of a pair of arms or
legs to be disablement.
27 Assumed but not argued in *R.* v. *National Insurance Commissioner ex p.
DHSS* (1978) 122 Sol. J. 812; Appendix to R(S) 1/79. See CS 13/80,
noted at [1982] J.S.W.L. 49; R(S) 2/78; R(S) 24/51. Cf. R(S) 17/51.
In the United States this approach is written into legislation (42
U.S.C., para.423(d)(2)(A), *Kerner* v. *Flemming* 283 F. 2d 916 (1960)).
See, too, *Cowart* v. *Schweiker* 662 F. 2d 731, 736n (1981). For Canada,
MHW v. *Caines* (1973) C.C.H. 6167, cited Issalys 1979: 131, 136,
335n.
28 For example, *Re Panke and Director-General of Social Services* (1981) 4
A.L.D. 179, 182 per Davies J.
29 For example, R(S) 2/78; *Stewart* v. *Cohen* 309 F. Supp. 949, 955
(1970). Cf. *Chesterfield Football Club* v. *Secretary of State for Social Services*
[1973] Q.B. 583, decided, however, in a different context.
30 Liebman 1976: 847–9, 855n.
31 Rate concessions are another form of fiscal welfare – for instance,
private schools might be exempt as charities – but are outside the
scope of this discussion. The graduated tax rates are themselves a
crude form of fiscal welfare.
32 For example, Income and Corporation Taxes Act 1970, s.19; Finance
Act 1970, s.21(4); Finance Act 1972, s.75; Income Tax Assessment

Act 1936 (Australia), ss.159 R(1), 159 T(1)-(3), 159 V(1).

33 For example, *Wicks* v. *Firth* [1982] Ch.355; *Pearce* v. *Federal Commissioner of Taxation* (1979) 9 A.T.R. 740.

34 *Frost (Inspector of Taxes)* v. *Feltham* [1981] S.T.C. 115.

35 Cf. *Morton* v. *Califano*, 481 F. Supp. 908 (1978); *Seislowski* v. *Secretary of Health, Education and Welfare*, 477 F. Supp. 682 (1979).

36 See Dworkin 1977: 32–4.

37 Bradley 1980: 313.

38 Parliamentary Commissioner Act 1967, s.5(2); Ombudsman Act 1976 (Australia), s.6(2).

39 See, for example, Report of the Committee on Administrative Tribunals and Enquiries 1957: 42.

40 See Mossman 1977a: 76.

41 For example, Fulbrook 1978; N. Lewis 1973; Lister 1974a.

42 For example, Supplementary Benefits Act 1976, s.15(3); R(SB) 9/81; *Re Cardinal and Ministry of Community and Social Services* (1981) 32 O.R. (2d) 65.

43 *R.* v. *South West London SBAT ex p. Bullen, The Times,* 11 May 1976 (breach of natural justice because of a refusal to adjourn a hearing which the claimant did not attend because of a job interview). But in R(SB) 9/81, breach of natural justice was rejected: the grounds were said to be flimsy (the woman chairing the tribunal was said to have raised her eyebrows and sighed during the proceedings) and the notes of evidence showed that all points put forward were properly recorded and considered. See also *Krebs* v. *Minister of National Revenue* [1978] 1 F.C. 205; *Re Ellis and Ministry of Community and Social Services* (1980) 28 O.R. (2d) 385; *Smith* v. *Family Benefits Appeal Board* (1981) 42 N.S.R. (2d) 200.

44 Compare the supplementary benefits appeal tribunals and the national insurance local tribunals in Britain (Bradley 1976: 113). These are to be replaced by social security appeal tribunals: Health and Social Services and Social Security Adjudications Act 1983, s.25, Schedule 8.

45 For example, Supplementary Benefits Act 1976, Schedule 4, para.1 as amended.

46 Cf. Fulbrook 1978: 235; Lister 1977: 62.

47 For example, Bell *et al.* 1974: 310–12; Frost and Howard 1977: 22–3, 40–43.

48 Canada Pension Plan, RSC 1970, Chap. C.5, s.84(2).

49 See Issalys 1979: 126, 128.

50 On written reasons, see Supplementary Benefit and Family Income Supplements (Appeals) Rules 1980, SI 1980 No.1605, r.7(2). *Crake* v. *Supplementary Benefits Commission* [1982] 1 All E.R. 498, 506–8; R(SB) 5/81. Cf. R(SB) 6/81, where failure to give adequate reasons seems automatically to have been regarded as wrong in law. See also R(U) 2/81.

51 Bell 1975: 6.

52 For example, Lynes 1982: 145.

53 For example, Committee on Administrative Discretions 1973: 12–13.
54 Administrative Review Council 1981: 15.
55 Lawrence 1978.
56 Mossman 1979: 228.
57 See Abel-Smith and Stevens 1968: 249; Moore 1978b.
58 Administrative Appeals Tribunal Act 1975, ss.6–7; Social Security Act 1947, s.15A. For other jurisdictions: Skoler and Weixel 1981.
59 Social Security Act 1975, s.97(3); Social Security Act 1980, s.12.
60 See Social Security Act 1975, s.101; Supplementary Benefit and Family Income Supplements (Appeals) Rules 1980, SI 1980 No.1605, r.8(1). See also *Bland* v. *Chief Supplementary Benefit Officer* [1983] 1 All E.R. 537; [1983] 1 W.L.R. 262.
61 For example, *National Insurance Company of New Zealand Ltd* v. *Espange* (1961) 105 C.L.R. 569, 574, 585.
62 An extreme view was expressed in *Smith* v. *Board of Commissioners of the District of Columbia*, 259 F. Supp. 423, 424 (1966), affirmed on other grounds 380 F. 2d 632 (1967).
63 *R.* v. *Medical Appeal Tribunal ex p.* *Gilmore* [1957] 1 Q.B. 574.
64 *R.* v. *Preston SBAT ex p.* *Moore* [1975] 2 All E.R. 807, 813; [1975] 1 W.L.R. 624, 631–2.
65 *Edwards (Inspector of Taxes)* v. *Bairstow* [1956] A.C. 14.
66 For example, *Lincoln* v. *Hayman* [1982] 1 W.L.R. 488, 490; *Plummer* v. *P.W. Wilkins and Sons Ltd* [1981] 1 All E.R. 91, 93; [1981] 1 W.L.R. 831, 834.
67 Social Security Act 1980, s.14; Administrative Appeals Tribunal Act 1975, s.44. Cf. Canada Pension Plan, RSC 1970, Chap. C-5, s.86(1) ('final and conclusive'); Unemployment Insurance Act 1971, s.100 ('final'). See also *Martins* v. *Minister of National Health and Welfare* [1979] 1 F.C. 347, 92 D.L.R. (3d) 767.
68 (1979) 123 Sol. J. 33.
69 *R.* v. *National Insurance Commissioner, ex p.* *Secretary of State for Social Services* [1981] 1 W.L.R. 1017, 1022, 1024; *R.* v. *National Insurance Commissioner ex p.* *Stratton* [1979] Q.B. 361, 368–9; *R.* v. *National Insurance Commissioner ex p.* *Michael* [1977] 2 All E.R. 420, 422, 424–6; [1977] 1 W.L.R. 112, 115–16.
70 *Director-General of Social Services* v. *Chaney* (1980) 31 A.L.R. 571, 593.
71 See MacCormick 1977: 203–4.
72 *Watt* v. *Lord Advocate* [1979] S.L.T. 137, 145; *Redding* v. *Lee* (1983) 47 ALR 241; *Goldberg* v. *Kelly* 397 U.S. 254, 262, 265.
73 For example, *R.* v. *Bristol SBAT ex p.* *Southwell* (1977) 121 Sol. J. 663.
74 [1973] S.C.R. 654, 669–70.
75 For example, *Nabi* v. *British Leyland (UK) Ltd* [1980] 1 All E.R. 667, 670; [1980] 1 W.L.R. 529, 531 (but there was no suggestion, as there is in *Gill*'s case, that social security is contractual); *Daish* v. *Wauton* [1972] 2 Q.B. 262, 272 (Stephenson L.J. goes on in this passage explicitly to recognize that social security benefits are 'uncovenanted'). *Contra*: *Parsons* v. *BNM Laboratories Ltd* [1964] 1 Q.B. 95, 120, 130, 144, which explicitly rejects the analogy.

76 *Parry* v. *Cleaver* [1970] A.C. 1, 42.
77 *Flemming* v. *Nestor* 363 U.S. 603 (1960). See also *Richardson* v. *Belcher* 404 U.S. 78, 80–1 (1971); *Guarino* v. *Celebrezze* 336 F. 2d 336 (1964).
78 See *Opinion of the Justices to the House of Representatives* 333 N.E. 2d 388 (1975). Cf. Michelman 1979.
79 397 U.S. 254, 262 (1970).
80 Reich 1964.
81 Cf. *Graham* v. *Baker* (1961) 106 C.L.R. 340. See generally Atiyah 1979: 426–9.
82 For example, *Orman* v. *Saville Sportswear Ltd* [1960] 1 W.L.R. 1055.
83 See Freedland 1976: 111; *Mears* v. *Safecar Security Ltd* [1982] 2 All E.R. 865; [1982] 3 W.L.R. 366. *Mears* specifically disapproved the statement of principle in *Orman*.
84 *Ford Motor Co. Ltd* v. *A.U.E.F.W.* [1969] 2 Q.B. 303. Cf. *Sloan* v. *Union Oil of Canada Ltd* [1955] 4 D.L.R. 664.
85 *National Coal Board* v. *Galley* [1958] 1 All E.R. 91; [1958] 1 W.L.R. 16.
86 Trade Union and Labour Relations Act 1974, s.18.
87 For example, Conciliation and Arbitration Act 1904 (Australia), Part X; Canada Labour Code, RSC 1970, Chap. L-1, s.154; *Textile Workers Union* v. *Lincoln Mills of Alabama* 353 U.S. 448 (1957).
88 For example, Social Security and Housing Benefits Act 1982, Part 1.
89 See Davies and Freedland 1979: 283–6.
90 See Upex and Morris 1981: 222.
91 *The Maternity Leave Case* (1979) 21 A.I.L.R. 88, 199.
92 *Beach* v. *Reed Corrugated Cases Ltd* [1956] 2 All E.R. 652, 659; [1956] 1 W.L.R. 807, 815; *Re W. and M. Roith* [1967] 1 All E.R. 427; [1967] 1 W.L.R. 432. See also *Unipol SA* v. *Vial* [1977] Dalloz Jur. 275.
93 Ellison 1979: 29.
94 See *ibid.* 66–78.
95 29 USC, paras. 1023–5.
96 See Mesher 1976.
97 Ss. 36, 38.
98 Ss. 53–6.
99 *Parry* v. *Cleaver* [1970] A.C. 1, 16, 32, 36, 42, 51.
100 Cf. *Worringham and Humphreys* v. *Lloyds Bank Ltd* [1981] 2 All E.R. 434; [1981] 1 W.L.R. 950; *Garland* v. *British Rail Engineering Ltd* [1982] 1 C.M.L.R. 696.
101 *City of Los Angeles, Department of Water and Power* v. *Manhart* 435 US 702 (1978).
102 See Adler and Asquith 1981; Jowell 1975.
103 Titmuss 1971: 127.
104 See Supplementary Benefits Commission *Notes and News No. 7*, April 1977.
105 For example, Supplementary Benefits Commission 1977: 1.
106 For example, Bull 1980: 75–6; Lister 1979: 639.
107 Supplementary Benefits Commission 1979: 1, 23–5, 37.
108 Department of Health and Social Security 1978.
109 Parliamentary Debates, Commons, Vol. 989, 28 July 1980, 1064.

110 There are accounts of the scheme in Lister 1981; Ogus and Barendt
    1982; Lustgarten 1981. See also Partington 1981.
111 For example, Harlow 1981: 551.
112 Partington 1980c: 629. See also Adler and Asquith 1981: 12–13;
    Prosser 1981: 165–8.
113 Bell 1975: 18. Cf. Fulbrook 1978: 132–3, 137.
114 See Hammer and Hartley 1978: 223–32.
115 Higgins 1980: 15.
116 Cf. Gilbert 1970; Piven and Cloward 1973.
117 Parl. Debates, Commons, 1943, v.386, 1818.
118 Supplementary Benefits Commission 1980: 7.
119 Supplementary Benefit (Claims and Payments) Regulations 1981, SI
    1981 No. 1525, r.12(a).
120 Under the system of housing benefit in Britain, council tenants on
    supplementary benefit have their rent paid direct.
121 Rr. 3–6. Cf. Social Security Act 1947 (Australia), ss. 43, 72, 83
    AAG, 123 (1), 128.
122 For example, Supplementary Benefits Act 1976, s.25.
123 *Wilkie* v. *O'Connor* 25 N.Y.S. 2d 617, 619 (1941). Cf. *Bowman* v. *Frost*
    158 S.W. 2d 945 (1942); *Board of Social Welfare* v. *Los Angeles County*
    162 P. 2d 630 (1945).
124 Social Security Act 1947, ss.59(1), 60(1). See also Canada Pension
    Plan, RSC 1970, Chap. C-5, s.63(2).
125 For example, Family Income Supplements Act 1970, s.1(1)(b).
126 For example, Social Security Act 1975, ss.44(3)(c), 46(2), 66(1)(d) as
    amended. For earlier provisions, see Ogus and Barendt 1978: 388–9;
    Parker 1981: 22–6.
127 The following discussion is confined to the position of women.
128 For example, a widow's benefit under the National Insurance
    (Industrial Injuries) Act 1946, s.88(3), repealed by Family
    Allowances and National Insurance Act 1961, s.4(2).
129 Chilton 1970.
130 As in Britain between 1948 and 1966: National Assistance
    (Determination of Need) Regulations 1948, SI 1948 No. 1334, r.3.
131 As with widows' pensions in Australia between 1942 and 1976: see
    Social Services Act 1947, ss.62(1)(a)-(b).
132 *Paterson* v. *Saville* [1934] J.C.42.
133 *Furmage* v. *Social Security Commission* (1980) 2 N.Z.A.R. 75.
134 *Crake* v. *Supplementary Benefits Commission* [1982] 1 All E.R. 498. *Robson*
    v. *Secretary of State for Social Services*, unreported, noted [1981] LAG
    Bull. 238.
135 *R.* v. *South West London Appeal Tribunal, ex p. Barnett*, unreported, No.
    315/72.
136 *Crake* v. *Supplementary Benefits Commission* [1982] 1 All E.R. 498.
137 (1974) 53 D.L.R. (3d) 521; 6 O.R. (2d) 624.
138 *Re Warwick and Minister of Community and Social Services* (1979) 21 O.R.
    (2d) 528.
139 *Lambe* v. *Director-General of Social Services* (1981) 38 A.L.R. 405.

140 See R(G) 2/72; R(G) 1/79; R(SB) 17/81; *Re R.C. and Director-General of Social Services* (1981) 3 A.L.D. 334; *Re Waterford and Director-General of Social Services* (1980) 3 A.L.D. 63; Kerr 1978.

141 See Lister 1974a: 14–18; Sackville 1977: 83–4.

142 Reich 1963; *Parrish* v. *Civil Service Commission of Alameda County* 425 P. 2d 223 (1967). Cf. *Reyes* v. *Edmunds* 472 F. Supp. 1218 (1979).

143 Supplementary Benefits Commission 1976b: 1.

144 *Ibid*: 9.

145 See *Chaney* v. *Director-General of Social Services* (1980) 31 A.L.R. 571.

146 Supplementary Benefits Commission 1976b: 22.

147 Committee on Abuse of Social Security Benefits 1973: 140–1.

148 Royal Commission on Human Relationships 1977: 86.

149 Supplementary Benefits Commission 1976b: 10.

150 Lister 1974b: 41.

151 See Lister 1974a: 8.

152 Exceptions imposing support obligation with respect to cohabitees include the Maintenance Act 1967, s.16 (Tasmania); Family Law Reform Act 1978, ss. 14–15 (Ontario); Family Relations Act 1978, ss. 1, 57 (British Columbia).

153 Committee on One-Parent Families 1974: 340; Sackville 1975a: 89. See also Field 1981: 192.

154 See Supplementary Benefit (Aggregation) Regulations 1981, SI 1981 No. 1524, r.7.

155 Titmuss 1968: 195.

156 Cf. Wilson 1977: 81, 153.

157 Rose 1981: 500.

158 See *King* v. *Smith* 392 U.S. 309 (1968); *Lewis* v. *Martin* 397 U.S. 552 (1970).

159 For example, Altman 1976; Muller-Fembeck and Ogus 1976; Singer 1974.

160 Chambers 1979: 273, 356. Note also that relatives such as children and children-in-law might be obliged to enter into a maintenance guarantee with the immigration authorities as a condition of a person being allowed entry to a country. This might not be legally binding because it is non-contractual or has no statutory basis (cf. Supplementary Benefits Act 1976, s. 17(1)(c)). In any event, it might not prevent the person from obtaining social welfare benefits (*R.* v. *West London SBAT ex p. Clarke* [1975] 3 All E.R. 513; [1975] 1 W.L.R. 1397; *Re De Lima and Minister of Community and Social Services* (1973) 35 D.L.R. (3d) 481; (1973) 2 O.R. 821; *Re Blackburn and Director-General of Social Services* (1982) 4 A.L.N. No.46).

161 See ss.17–19; *Robinson* v. *Lowther* (1980) 10 Fam. Law 214; Calvert 1978: 430–7.

162 See s.18(3); *Shallow* v. *Shallow* [1979] Fam. 1; Hayes 1978–9. Imprisonment for maintenance default is still possible in some jurisdictions and is defended because of the difficulty of enforcement against the resentful and mobile. But in cases where default occurs through economic necessity, imprisonment seems largely futile,

especially since it is likely to result in two families rather than one relying on social welfare benefits.

163 Cf. *County of Contra Costa* v. *Social Welfare Board* 40 Cal. Rptr 605 (1964) – no need to undergo a lie-detector test to determine the truth of the information she had supplied.

164 For example, *In re Marriage of Shore* 139 Cal. Rptr 349 (1977); Ryan 1976.

165 Social Security Act 1947 (Australia), ss.62(3), 83 AAD. Cf. *Gospavich* v. *Gospavich* (1972) 5 R.F.L. 369. At one time social welfare authorities in Britain 'encouraged' women to seek maintenance, although they had no legal power to do this (Streather and Weir 1974: 14–15; Supplementary Benefits Commission 1977: 149–58).

166 See, e.g., *Supplementary Benefits Commission* v. *Jull* [1981] A.C. 1025.

167 Barrington Baker *et al.* 1977: 13–14; Buchanan 1981. Cf. *Hulley* v. *Thompson* [1981] 1 All E.R. 1128; [1981] 1 W.L.R. 159.

168 Committee on One-Parent Families 1974: 102, 104.

169 Sackville 1975a: 188.

170 Cantley J. gave expression to this feeling in a case where an injured worker was claiming damages: it was unlikely the worker would be spurred to getting a job, Cantley J. remarked, when the social welfare benefits he was receiving for doing nothing were more than soldiers obtained for risking their lives in Northern Ireland (*Paramenter* v. *Permanite Ltd, The Times*, 8 February, 1980, p.2 (news report)). An American court has remarked: 'By way of commentary on the welfare state, it is an unexplicable anomaly that those who work are denied benefits even when their income is less than the sums nonworking recipients receive with AFDC. . . . any national or state policy of encouraging persons to work is substantially denigrated by such a system' (*Cheley* v. *Burson* 324 F. Supp. 678, 681 (1971); appeal dismissed, 404 U.S. 878 (1971). See also *Dimery* v. *Department of Social Services of the State of Iowa* 320 F. Supp. 1125 (1969), vacated and remanded, 398 U.S. 322 (1970)).

171 Family Income Supplements Act 1970.

172 Supplementary Benefits Act 1966, Sch. 2, para. 5(2), repealed by Child Benefit Act 1975, s. 19. Apparently the wage stop was applied in practice without explanation to the claimants involved, and wages were stopped at levels which were quite unrealistic (Elks 1974).

173 For example, Goodwin 1972; Robert *et al.* 1981: 20–4.

174 See Social Security Act 1947 (Australia), s.107(3); *Shea* v. *Vialpando* 416 U.S. 251, 264 (1974).

175 For example, Social Security Act 1975, ss.18, 20(1)(c)-(d); Social Security Act 1947 (Australia), s.107(1)(c); Unemployment Insurance Act 1971 (Canada), ss.25, 40–3. Cf. Supplementary Benefits Act 1976, ss.5, 6(1) (as amended).

176 *Re Thomson and Director-General of Social Services* (1981) 3 A.L.N. No. 51 (but on the peculiar facts it was held that the claimant was unemployed); *Attorney-General of Canada* v. *Mercier* [1977] 2 F.C. 389. Cf. Supplementary Benefit (Conditions of Entitlement) Regulations

1981, SI 1981 No. 1526, rr.7(2), 8(1)(a).

177 *Perrot* v. *Supplementary Benefits Commission* [1980] 3 All E.R. 110, 117; [1980] 1 W.L.R. 1153, 1162. Cf. R(U) 12/55; *Re Brabenec and Director-General of Social Services* (1981) 3 A.L.N. No. 39.

178 *Re McKenna and Director-General of Social Services* (1981) 3 A.L.D. 219 (but the determining factors there seemed to be that the claimant did not regard himself as 'unemployed' and that the co-operative was eventually intended to be profitable). See also Social Services (Unemployment, Sickness and Invalidity Benefit) Regulations 1975, SI 1975 No. 564, r.7(1)(h). Cf. R(U) 34/53; CU 25/72 cited in Mesher 1976: 40.

179 The requirement about being capable for work is directed to situations where sickness etc. benefit is appropriate.

180 R(U) 15/58; *McKenna's case*. Cf. *Gonzales* v. *CPAM* Var [1976] 11 JCP 18224 (French Cassation, soc., 12, 12 June 1974).

181 Social Security Act 1975, ss.17(1)(a)(i), 20(1)(b)-(c); Social Security (Unemployment, Sickness and Invalidity Benefit) Regulations 1975, SI 1975 No. 574, r.7(1)(a); Supplementary Benefit (Conditions of Entitlement) Regulations 1981, SI 1981 No. 1526, r.7.

182 *Mooney* v. *Pickett* 483 P. 2d 1231 (1971). Similarly the 'four week' rule, which once operated in Britain, and under which single males under forty-five were only granted supplementary benefit four weeks at a time.

183 Social Security Act 1975, s.20(1)(d); Supplementary Benefits Act 1976, s.5; Supplementary Benefit (Conditions of Entitlement) Regulations 1981, SI 1981 No. 1526, rr.5, 8. Cf. *Williams* v. *Williams* [1974] Fam. 55, 59–60. See also *Re Chambers and Director-General of Social Services* (1981) 1 S.S.R. 15; *Ricard* v. *Unemployment Insurance Commission* [1976] 1 F.C. 228, 231. Cf. the provisions discussed in *New York State Department of Social Services* v. *Dublino* 413 U.S. 405 (1973).

184 Social Security Act 1975, s.20(1)(a); Supplementary Benefit (Requirements) Regulations 1980 SI No. 1299, r.8; R(SB) 18/81. Cf. *R.* v. *Greater Birmingham SBAT ex p. Khan* [1979] 3 All E.R. 759 (decided under earlier provisions). See also Unemployment Insurance Act 1971 (Canada), s.41; Social Security Act 1947 (Australia), s.120; *Batterton* v. *Francis*, 432 U.S. 416 (1977).

185 See Fenn 1980.

186 R(U) 17/64; R(U) 11/59; R(U) 41/53.

187 See the decisions mentioned in Ogus and Barendt 1982: 112; Mesher 1976: 69–71. See also *Re Measey and Director-General of Social Services* (1981) 1 S.S.R. 32.

188 *Crewe* v. *Social Security Commissioner* [1981] 2 All E.R. 745; [1982] 1 W.L.R. 1209.

189 Myers 1977: 15–16.

190 [1900] 1 Ch. 516.

191 In practice, some poor-law authorities paid out-relief to strikers, often by way of loan, and partly in kind (Gennard 1977: 80–3). The *Merthyr Tydfil* case was followed in subsequent decisions (e.g. *Attorney-General*

v. *Bermondsey Union* (1924) 40 T.L.R. 512; *Attorney-General* v. *Poplar Union* (1924) 40 T.L.R. 752. See also Jennings 1930).
192 Appendix to R(U)9/80.
193 Cited Calvert 1978: 150.
194 Social Security Act 1975, s.19(2)(b).
195 Appendix to R(U)5/77; [1979] C.L.Y. 2559.
196 For example, R(U)2/53; R(U)1/74.
197 For example, Social Security Act 1947 (Australia), s.107(1)(c)(i). Accepted as workers who participated in the decision by their trade union and at their workplace to go on strike. In 1979 the eligibility requirements for unemployment benefit were tightened.
198 National Insurance Act 1911, s.87(1); National Insurance Act 1965, s.22(1). For elsewhere, see Social Security Act 1947 (Australia), s.107(4) as amended in 1979; *McKinnon* v. *Unemployment Insurance Commission* [1977] 2 F.C. 569; *New York Telephone Company* v. *New York State Department of Labor* 440 U.S. 519 (1979); *Ohio Bureau of Employment Services* v. *Hodory* 431 U.S. 471 (1977); *Batterton* v. *Francis* 432 U.S. 416 (1977).
199 Royal Commission on Trade Unions and Employers' Associations 1968: 250, 253–4.
200 Social Security Act 1975, s.19(1)(a), as amended by Employment Protection Act 1975, s.111.
201 R(U)5/66.
202 *Watt* v. *Lord Advocate* [1979] S.L.T. 137; *Presho* v. *Insurance Officer* [1984] 2 W.L.R. 29.
203 Supplementary Benefits Act 1976, s.8(1).
204 Social Security Act (No. 2) 1980, s.6.
205 Gennard 1977, 1979. See also Durcan and McCarthy 1974.
206 See Leibfried 1979: 180–3; Ringeling 1981: 300–3.
207 Townsend 1979: 824–47.
208 Miller *et al.* 1970: 38.
209 Fulbrook 1978: 59; Handler and Hollingworth 1970a: 1179.
210 National Consumer Council 1976a: 85ff.
211 Hetzel *et al.* 1978: 251.
212 [1948] 1 K.B. 349, 361.
213 See *Watson* v. *Lee* (1979) 144 C.L.R. 374.
214 Bradley 1980: 311.
215 For example, in *Re Wilson and Director-General of Social Services* (1981) 3 A.L.N. No. 76. See also Partington 1978a: 78–85; C.G. 1/78; C.G. 3/80. Cf. *Pirotte* v. *Unemployment Insurance Commission* [1977] 1 F.C. 314.
216 Stevenson 1973: 173.
217 See A.S. Hall 1974: 124; Cunningham 1977.
218 See generally Zimmerman 1974.
219 Cf. Supplementary Benefit (Claims and Payments) Regulations 1981, SI 1981 No. 1525, r.4.
220 See Street 1981: 304.
221 For example, *Repatriation Commission* v. *Law* (1981) 36 A.L.R. 411.
222 Brown 1975: 81; Prottas 1979: 3–5. Cf. Francis and Stone 1956: 41.

223 See the evidence in Supplementary Benefits Commission 1980: 109.
224 For example, Administrative Review Council 1981: 30–5; Handler 1979: 103, 128; Issalys and Watkins 1978: 17–93.
225 But manuals are used even with detailed legislation, e.g. in the tax area.
226 See *Green* v. *Daniels* (1977) 13 A.L.R. 1, 9, 11.
227 5 USC, §552(a)(1)(D), (a)(2)(C); Freedom of Information Act 1982 (Australia), s.9.
228 See the survey evidence in Supplementary Benefits Commission 1980: 137.
229 Coleman 1971: 6–9.
230 Administrative Review Council 1981: 34.
231 Among other factors are said to be the differences between social welfare officers and claimants in terms of class, status and educational background. In fact, social welfare benefits are typically administered by persons who are on relatively low grades. However, friction might still be engendered because officers resent administering benefits to those not much worse off (if at all) than they are. For the only study which seems to relate officers' backgrounds to benefit administration, see Levitan *et al.* 1972: 13.
232 For example, Fulbrook 1978: 59–62, 70; Hill 1969: 82; Moore 1980.
233 Supplementary Benefits Act 1976, s.27(1).
234 Cf. Supplementary Benefit (Determination of Questions) Regulations 1980 SI 1980 No. 1643, r.3.
235 See Richardson 1978a.
236 (1979) 123 Sol. J. 284.
237 But see the specific provisions in Supplementary Benefit (Determination of Questions) Regulations 1980, SI 1980 No. 1643, r.5(1)(c)(2).
238 *The Times*, 24 June 1977. See also *Le Clair* v. *O'Neil*, 307 F. Supp. 621, affirmed 401 U.S. 37 (1969).
239 The statutory provisions for backdating claims, already referred to, might operate in such cases.
240 [1949] 1 K.B. 227.
241 Cf. *Dallialian* v. *Canada Employment and Immigration Commission* (1980) 33 N.R. 118, 140–2.
242 An illustration in the social welfare area is *Rootkin* v. *Kent C.C.* [1981] 2 All E.R. 227; [1981] 1 W.L.R. 1186.
243 See *L. Shaddock & Associates Pty Ltd* v. *Parramatta C.C.* (1981) 36 A.L.R. 385.
244 *Parrish* v. *Civil Service Commission of Alameda County* 424 P. 2d 223 (1967).
245 *Wyman* v. *James* 400 U.S. 309 (1971).
246 397 U.S. (1970). Cf. *Mathews* v. *Eldridge* 424 U.S. 319 (1976).
247 See Baum 1974; Berney *et al.* 1975: 854.
248 See generally Goffman 1963; Matza 1967.
249 Other reasons were unluckiness, 16 per cent; and 'an inevitable part of modern progress', 14 per cent (Commission of European

Communities 1977: 71). See also Golding and Middleton 1982:
157–201.

250 *Ibid*: 100. For Australia, see Bryson and Eastop 1980.
251 See the survey results in Ritchie and Wilson 1979: 23. See also Briggs
and Rees 1980: 60; Handler and Hollingsworth 1969: 5.
252 For example, Wilensky 1975: 37.
253 Roberts *et al.* 1981: 29–30.
254 For example, Old Age Pensions Act 1908 (8 Edw. 7, c. 40), s. 3(1)(b),
(2), (3); Invalid and Old-Age Pensions Act 1908 (Australia), ss.
17(c),(d), 51–2.
255 For example, Social Security Act 1975, s.24, Schedule 4, Pt. I; Social
Security Act 1947 (Australia), ss. 59(1), 83 AAA.
256 But there can still be defects: see Starr 1973.
257 For example, Repatriation Act 1920 (Australia), s.101(1).
258 For example, Naval, Military and Air Forces etc. (Disabled and
Death) Service Pensions Order 1978, SI 1978 No. 1525, r.3.
259 For example, *Freeman* v. *Minister of Pensions* [1966] 2 All E.R. 40;
[1966] 1 W.L.R. 456; *Repatriation Commission* v. *Law* (1981) 36 A.L.R.
411. *Re War Amputations and Pension Review Board* (1980) 108 D.L.R.
(3d) 711.
260 *Glasgow Corp.* v. *Kelly* [1951] 1 T.L.R. 345, 347.
261 *In re C(L) (An Infant)* [1965] 2 Q.B. 449, 470.
262 For example, *Spain* v. *Ocean Steamship Company Ltd* (1949) 83 Lloyd's
L.R. 188, 190; *R.* v. *Industrial Injuries Commissioner ex p. Cable* [1968] 1
Q.B. 729, 737. See also Lord Denning in Neligan 1979: Foreword.
263 [1974] 2 All E.R. 455, 463; [1974] 1 W.L.R. 788, 797, on appeal at
[1975] Fam. 99.
264 *The Times*, 14 February 1968; (1968) 118 N.L.J. 181, affirming *The
Times*, 14 June 1967, (1967) 111 Sol. J. 703.
265 *R.* v. *National Insurance Commissioner, ex p. Connor* [1981] Q.B. 758.
266 For example, where a person is undergoing imprisonment: s.82(5)(b).
Cf. *R.* v. *National Insurance Commissioner ex p. Insurance Officer* [1981]
I.C.R. 90. See the interesting Norwegian case: Supreme Court, 3
December 1977, [1977] Rt 1207; [1978] 6 European Law Digest 368.
267 For the role of pressure groups in fostering this see, e.g., Chippindale
and Walker 1976.
268 Golding and Middleton 1982: 59–111; Windschuttle 1979: 155–79.
269 Dean *et al.* 1980: 37–40.
270 For example, *Etim* v. *Hatfield* [1975] Crim. L.R. 234; *Wakeman* v. *Farrar*
[1974] Crim. L.R. 136.
271 For example, Supplementary Benefits Act 1976, s.21.
272 *Tolfree* v. *Florence* [1971] 1 All E.R. 125; [1971] 1 W.L.R. 141.
273 *Cameron* v. *Holt* (1980) 54 A.L.J.R. 202; 28 A.L.R. 490.
274 [1974] Crim. L.R. 439; (1974) 118 Sol. J. 405.
275 *Clear* v. *Smith* [1981] 1 W.L.R. 399; *Barrass* v. *Reeve* [1980] 3 All E.R.
705; [1981] 1 W.L.R. 408.
276 Cf. *Smith* v. *Hawkins* [1972] 1 All E.R. 910; [1972] 1 W.L.R. 141.
277 For example, Parl. Deb., Commons, v. 926, 1977, 303–6; Meacher

382 *Notes to pp. 226–231*

278 Committee on Abuse of Social Security Benefits 1973: 205–6.
279 See Lidstone *et al.* 1980: 39–41.
280 *Young* v. *Supplementary Benefits Commission, The Times,* 18 April 1980, on appeal as *Supplementary Benefits Commission* v. *Jull* [1981] A.C. 1025.
281 *The Times,* 26 February 1980. See also *Secretary of State for Social Services* v. *Solly* [1974] 3 All E.R. 922, 925 *per* Lord Denning M.R.
282 *R.* v. *Goldstraw* [1981] Crim L.R. 728; *R.* v. *Bateman* [1981] Crim. L.R. 728; *R.* v. *Lalor* [1982] Crim.L.R. 60.
283 *R.* v. *Grafton* (1979) Cr.App.R. (S) 305.
284 *Taormina* v. *Cameron* (1980) 29 A.L.R. 151.
285 *Young* v. *Geddie* (1978) 22 A.L.R. 232; *Winkler* v. *Cameron* (1981) 33 A.L.R. 663. See *Osborne* v. *Goddard* (1978) 21 A.L.R. 189, when the court accepted defences of duress and marital coercion from a woman who presented a false document to obtain benefit, after beatings and threats from her husband.
286 Supplementary Benefits Act 1976, s.20(1); Social Security Act 1975, s.119(2A); Social Security Act 1947 (Australia), s.140(1); R(SB) 3/81 – course of conduct with authorities belied failure to disclose; *Re Harris and Ministry of Community and Social Services* (1975) 8 O.R. (2d) 721; 59 D.L.R. (3d) 169.
287 *Finlay* v. *Director of Welfare (Winnipeg South/West)* (1978) 29 R.F.L. 395. Cf. Supplementary Benefit (Duplication and Overpayment) Regulations 1980, S.I. 1980 No. 1580, rr.6–7; Social Security Act 1947 (Australia), s.140(2).
288 *Commonwealth* v. *Burns* [1971] V.R. 825. Cf. R(S)3/81.
289 *Rural Municipality of Storthoaks* v. *Mobil Oil Canada Ltd* (1975) 55 D.L.R. (3d) 1.
290 Alternatively, it might be possible to argue estoppel: while *Burns* specifically rejected estoppel, the justification it gave, that 'a party cannot be assumed by the doctrine of estoppel to have lawfully done that which the law says that he shall not do' (at p. 830), seems inaccurate; the law did not specifically prevent over-payment, but simply did not authorize it. See *Avon County Council* v. *Howlett* [1983] 1 All E.R. 1073; [1983] 1 W.L.R. 605.
291 *Calder* v. *Minister of Employment and Immigration* [1980] 1 F.C. 842. See also the remarks in *Re Buhagiar and Director-General of Social Services* (1981) 4 A.L.D. 113.
292 For example, *Director-General of Social Security* v. *Harris* (1982) 44 A.L.R. 645; *Director-General of Social Services* v. *Hangan* (1982) 45 A.L.R. 23.
293 As in Social Security Act 1975, s.119. However, the Social Security Commissioners have interpreted this restrictively – R(A)1/79; R(G)1/79.
294 Cf. *Califano* v. *Yamasaki* 442 U.S. 682, 685 (1979).
295 *Contra* Supplementary Benefits Act 1976, s.20(3).
296 See Mossman 1977a; Sparer 1969: 3–5.
297 Alcock and Harris 1982: 52.

298 For example, R(U)7/71 (a case could not be treated as a test case except with the consent of all concerned and with the approval of the statutory authorities, and the issues had to be common in each of the cases). Cf. *Lemieux et al.* v. *Unemployment Insurance Commission* (1977) 2 F.C. 246. See also *Dick* v. *Deputy Attorney-General of Canada* (1980) 6 W.W.R. 431.

CHAPTER 6: The provision of public services

1 Popularized in Crossman 1975.
2 Lambert *et al.* 1978: 163.
3 For example, Sjoberg *et al.* 1966.
4 See Pahl 1970; Castells 1978.
5 For example, Community Action, No. 29, Jan.-Feb. 1977.
6 See, for example, Niskanen 1975.
7 Weber 1954: 230.
8 See Merton *et al.* 1952.
9 English *et al.* 1976: 69.
10 See Davies 1972; Ermer 1972: 4–6, 11, 71.
11 Almond and Verba 1963: 144. See also Heidenheimer *et al.* 1975: 105–7.
12 See especially Friedman 1968; Mayne 1983; Spearrit 1974. See also pp.111–114 above.
13 These did not appear to re-grow on the new housing estates (e.g. Young and Willmott 1957).
14 English *et al.* 1976: 15; Paris and Blackaby 1979: 75–7; Stein 1974: 187, 192.
15 (1974) 119 Sol. J. 167; (1974) 31 P. & C.R. 344.
16 Adamsdown Community Trust 1978: 66–8.
17 Dennis 1970: 351.
18 Dennis 1972: 103, 160.
19 For example, Housing Act 1957, s.48(1).
20 For example, *Salford C.C.* v. *McNally* [1976] A.C. 379.
21 National Consumer Council 1976b.
22 [1977] A.C. 239, at 253.
23 *Bristol D.C.* v. *Clark* [1975] 3 All E.R. 976, 981; [1975] 1 W.L.R. 1443, 1449.
24 At p.261.
25 Decisions about allocation need also to be made in relation to existing tenants who want a transfer. The following discussion concentrates on new applicants, although many of the remarks appertain to both types of decision.
26 [1977] A.C. 239.
27 Corina 1976; Damer 1976.
28 Niner 1978: 29.
29 Housing Act 1957, s.113(2).
30 Land Compensation Act 1973, s.39(1).
31 For example, Gee 1974: 10; Jacobs 1976: 126–7, 146–50.
32 See Butcher *et al.* 1979: 77–8; Cullingworth Committee 1969; English

1976, 1979; Gray 1976; Hatch *et al.* 1977: 46–52, 216–39; Lewis 1976; Lewis and Livock 1979; Morton 1979; Winyard 1978. See also Bradbrook 1975: 117–24.

33 *R.* v. *Bristol Corp. ex p. Hendy* [1974] 1 All E.R. 1047; [1974] 1 W.L.R. 498.

34 *Tucker* v. *Norwalk Housing Authority* (1972) C.C.H. Poverty Law Reporter, §2735.13; *Battle* v. *Municipal Housing Authority for the City of Yonkers* 53 F.R.D. 423 (1971). Cf. *Manigo* v. *New York City Housing Authority* 273 N.Y.S. 2d 1003 (1966), affirmed 279 N.Y.S. 2d 1014, cert. denied 389 U.S. 1008 (1967). See also *Holmes* v. *New York City Housing Authority* 398 F. 2d 262 (1968), where it was established that due process requires reasonable and ascertainable criteria for the allocation of public housing.

35 Hughes and Jones 1979.

36 For example, Rent Act 1977, s.14; Housing Act 1957, ss.111(1), 113(1A).

37 For example, Department of Environment 1977c: App. 3.

38 *Evans* v. *Collins* [1965] 1 Q.B. 580; *Smith* v. *Cardiff Corp.* [1954] 1 Q.B. 210; *Belcher* v. *Reading Corp.* [1950] Ch. 380; *Summerfield* v. *Hampstead B.C.* [1957] 1 All E.R. 221; [1957] 1 W.L.R. 167; *Luby* v. *Newcastle-under-Lyme Corp.* [1965] 1 Q.B. 214.

39 Repairs to public housing have to be seen in the wider social and economic context. A great deal of public housing was built to very low standard in the first place, and even where the housing was initially of reasonable standard the style of caretaking and the absence of facilities and environmental planning have been contributing factors in vandalism and deterioration. Moreover, some housing authorities have under-maintained their estates because of financial stringencies.

40 *Liverpool C.C.* v. *Irwin* [1977] A.C. 239.

41 For example, National Consumer Council 1976b: 12, 15.

42 See *Salford C.C.* v. *McNally* [1976] A.C. 379; *Hopwood* v. *Cannock Chase D.C.* [1975] 1 All E.R. 796; [1975] 1 W.L.R. 373; *Summers* v. *Salford Corp.* [1943] A.C. 283; *McCarrick* v. *Liverpool Corp.* [1947] A.C. 219.

43 Cf. *Clarke* v. *Taff-Ely B.C.*, *The Times*, 1 April 1980, p.3 (news report), where a woman sued successfully under the Defective Premises Act 1972 when injured as a result of rotten floorboards in her sister's council house.

44 *Lambeth L.B.C.* v. *Udechuka* (1980) 79 L.G.R. 1 (but authority bound by statutory requirements as to notice to quit); *Housing Commission of N.S.W.* v. *Allen* (1967) 69 S.R. (N.S.W.) 190. Cf. *Re Humphrey and Ontario Housing Corporation* (1979) 23 O.R. (2d) 583. See also Bradbrook 1976b; Martin 1976.

45 *Bristol D.C.* v. *Clark* [1975] 3 All E.R. 976; [1975] 1 W.L.R. 1443; *Bristol C.C.* v. *Rawlins* (1977) 76 L.G.R. 166; (1977) 34 P. & C.R. 12; *Cannock Chase D.C.* v. *Kelly* [1978] 1 All E.R. 152; [1978] 1 W.L.R. 1; *Sevenoaks D.C.* v. *Emmott* (1979) 78 L.G.R. 346; [1980] J.P.L. 517; *Re Webb and Ontario Housing Corporation* (1979) 93 D.L.R. (3d) 187. Cf. *St Pancras B.C.* v. *Frey* [1963] 2 Q.B. 586.

46 *Escalera* v. *New York City Housing Authority* 425 F. 2d 853 (1970), cert. denied 400 U.S. 853 (1970).
47 *Harrison* v. *Hammersmith and Fulham L.B.C.* [1981] 2 All E.R. 588, 597; [1981] 1 W.L.R. 650, 661.
48 For example, *Woodspring D.C.* v. *Taylor, The Times,* 15 May 1982. See also Andrews 1979: 130–1.
49 Shelter *et al.* 1977. See *Bristol C.C.* v. *Rawlins* (1977) 34 P. & C.R. 12; (1977) 76 L.G.R. 166.
50 Scholfield and Sales 1966: 424. Tenants might possibly argue that a new tenancy has arisen where there is a substantial period between the authority obtaining the possession order and applying for the warrant for possession.
51 See Franey 1980; Harvey 1979; Harbert 1965; National Consumer Council 1976; Newham 1977. That rent arrears are associated with poverty is confirmed by the high level of arrears in areas with substantial unemployment, lower-than-average wages, and a higher-than-average proportion of young tenants (families with young children experience more financial problems).
52 The law in Britain is that public-housing authorities can distrain for rent arrears although private landlords are effectively barred from doing so (Rent Act 1977, s.147). See generally Arden 1978.
53 Moore 1978a.
54 Schifferes 1978.
55 Law of Distress Amendment Act 1888, 51 and 52 Vict., c.21, s.7. See Harvey 1977; Rust 1977.
56 Cf. constitutional claims in the United States. For example, Lineberry 1974.
57 [1925] A.C. 578.
58 Audit (Local Authorities) Act 1927, s.2(6). See also *Woolwich Corp.* v. *Roberts* (1927) 96 L.J.K.B. (n.s.) 757.
59 *In re Decision of Walker* [1944] K.B. 644.
60 *Pickwell* v. *Camden L.B.C.* [1983] 1 All E.R. 602; [1983] 2 W.L.R. 583.
61 [1955] Ch. 210.
62 Public Service Vehicles (Travel Concessions) Act 1955. It is doubtful whether the ratepayer in *Prescott* had standing, but the point was never raised (*Barrs* v. *Bethell* [1982] Ch. 294).
63 *Taylor* v. *Munrow* [1960] 1 All E.R. 455; [1960] 1 W.L.R. 151. See also *Annison* v. *District Auditor for St Pancras B.C.* [1962] 1 Q.B. 489.
64 *Bromley L.B.C.* v. *G.L.C.* [1982] 1 All E.R. 129; [1982] 2 W.L.R. 62. Cf. *R.* v. *Merseyside C.C. ex p. Great Universal Stores Ltd, The Times,* 18 February 1982.
65 See pp.219–20 above; *Anns* v. *Merton L.B.C.* [1978] A.C. 728. An old example of a successful negligence claim is provided by an Australian case, where a social welfare department sent a memorandum to the wife of a pension recipient informing her, inaccurately, that her husband had been committed to a mental hospital. It was held that she had a cause of action (in that case for nervous shock) because the authority had breached its duty of ensuring that that type of

information was accurate (*Barnes* v. *Commonwealth of Australia* (1937) 37 S.R. (N.S.W.) 511).

66 (1978) 76 L.G.R. 727; (1978) 122 Sol. J. 349.
67 (1978) 76 L.G.R. 727, 733.
68 *Pasmore* v. *Oswaldtwistle U.D.C.* [1898] A.C. 387 (a case concerning the Public Health Act 1875); *Southwark L.B.C.* v. *Williams* [1971] Ch. 734 (a homeless person's case).
69 (1979) 123 Sol. J. 436.
70 See generally Griffith 1977; McAuslan 1980.
71 [1979] 2 All E.R. 1016; [1979] 1 W.L.R. 637.
72 Street 1975: 25–32.
73 See Partington 1976; Ganz 1979; D.W. Williams 1979.
74 See Lewis 1979.
75 There is some discussion in Chapter 3.
76 Local Government Finance Act 1982, Part III.
77 *The Times*, 14 April 1980, p.4. See also *Community Action*, No.56, November–December 1981.
78 For some evidence on the complaints to the local government ombudsman, see Lewis 1979: 61.
79 See Widdowson 1975: 16–17. See generally Rhodes 1981.
80 Cf. *Bromley L.B.C.* v. *G.L.C.* [1982] 1 All E.R. 129, 165; [1982] 2 W.L.R. 62, 107.
81 See *Lambeth L.B.C.* v. *Secretary of State for Social Services* (1980) 79 L.G.R. 61, a decision involving the National Health Service.
82 See Jones 1979; Cranston 1979a.
83 *Asher* v. *Lacey* [1973] 3 All E.R. 1008; [1973] 1 W.L.R. 1412; *Asher* v. *Secretary of State for the Environment* [1974] Ch. 208. Cf. *Backhouse* v. *Lambeth L.B.C.* (1972) 116 Sol. J. 802, for Lambeth's attempt to avoid the 1972 Act.
84 Beirne 1977: 175–80; Mitchell 1974; Skinner and Longdon 1975.
85 Cf. Yates 1979: 200.
86 See Selznick 1969: 16; Nonet 1969: 6.
87 For example, Housing Act 1958 (Victoria), s.54AA.
88 *R.* v. *Ealing L.B.C. ex p. Sidhu*, *The Times*, 26 January 1982.
89 See Drake 1977: 464. See also Drake *et al.* 1981: 18–35, 98–100; Greve *et al.* 1971: 109, 176.
90 See Levin 1979: 508; *Attorney-General, ex rel. Tilley* v. *Wandsworth L.B.C.* [1981] 1 All E.R. 1162; [1981] 1 W.L.R. 854.
91 For example, *Cantrell* v. *Windsor Union* (1838) 132 E.R. 822.
92 (1784) Cald. 432.
93 See Glastonbury 1971: 34–5.
94 Halsbury 1912: v.22, 567–8; Poor Law Act 1930, ss.41, 42.
95 S.21(1)(b). There were separate provisions for those who by reason of age, infirmity or any other circumstance were in need of care and attention and for those without a 'settled way of living' – essentially those who would otherwise be sleeping rough (s.21(1)(a); Pt.II).
96 *Roberts* v. *Dorset C.C.*, *The Times*, 2 August 1976. See Pollard 1977: §B 861.

97 See Widdowson 1975; Bailey 1977: 20–1, 32; Bailey and Ruddock
   1972: 67–8.
98 Widdowson 1976: 103.
99 Ss.4(2)-(3). Cf. *Delahaye* v. *Oswestry B.C.*, *The Times*, 29 July 1980.
   Priority need and becoming intentionally homeless are defined in the
   Act (ss.2(1)-(2), 17). There is considerable case-law but see especially
   Dyson v. *Kerrier D.C.* [1980] 3 All E.R. 313; [1980] 1 W.L.R. 1205; *Din*
   v. *Wandsworth L.B.C.* [1981] 3 All E.R. 881; [1981] 3 W.L.R. 918; *R.*
   v. *Hillingdon L.B.C., ex p. Islam (Tafazzul)* [1981] 3 All E.R. 901;
   [1981] 3 W.L.R. 942; *Lambert* v. *Ealing L.B.C.* [1982] 1 W.L.R. 550;
   [1982] 2 All E.R. 394. See generally Hoath 1983.
100 S.5. See *R.* v. *Slough B.C. ex p. Ealing L.B.C.* [1981] Q.B. 801.
101 S.6. See *R.* v. *Bristol C.C. ex p. Brown* [1979] 3 All E.R. 344; [1979] 1
    W.L.R. 1437.
102 S.12; *De Falco* v. *Crawley B.C.* [1980] Q.B. 460.
103 Birkinshaw 1982: 264.
104 The Court of Appeal has said that accommodation must be
    appropriate (*R.* v. *Wyre B.C. ex p. Parr*, *The Times*, 4 February 1982).
    The Code of Guidance recommends that the homeless be placed in
    permanent housing as soon as possible, and favours council housing
    (§§ 4; A2.1).
105 See s.11.
106 Ivatts 1979.
107 General Rate Act 1967, s.17.
108 [1979] Q.B. 626.
109 Robson and Watchman 1981: 78.
110 *De Falco* v. *Crawley B.C.* [1980] Q.B. 460.
111 *Thornton* v. *Kirklees M.B.C.* [1979] Q.B. at p.644.
112 *Cocks* v. *Thanet D.C.* [1982] 3 All E.R. 1135; [1982] 3 W.L.R. 1121.
113 Shelter 1978: 4, 6; Finnis 1978: 139.
114 Graycar and Davis 1979: 94–6.
115 See generally MacPherson 1979; Miller and Kraushaar 1979;
    Pateman 1970: 67–71; Richardson 1979.
116 See Clark and Hopkins 1970: 105, 124; Gittell 1980; Hampton 1970:
    291–2; Hill 1976: 214; Marris and Rein 1974: 224.
117 Moynihan 1970: 182.
118 Nonet and Selznick 1978: 102. Cf. Hill 1976: 228–9; Thursz 1972.
119 See McAuslan 1980; Boaden *et al.* 1979.
120 Darke 1979: 345, 348.
121 For example, Bridges 1979: 241; Roberts 1976: 129.
122 Jacobs 1976: 26–7; English *et al.* 1976: 63, 127ff.
123 Ferris 1972; Hatch *et al.* 1977: 189–93; Levin 1971: 1090.
124 Housing Act 1957, Third Schedule §2(1)(a).
125 McAuslan 1978: 45, 49.
126 Paris and Blackaby 1979: 155; Thornley 1977: 41.
127 Economic Opportunity Act 1964, 42 U.S.C., ss.2781(a)(4), 2791,
    2811. For conflicting views of the programmes, see Bachrach and
    Baratz 1970; Moynihan 1970.

128 Janowitz 1978: 465–77; Marris and Rein 1974: 268.
129 CDP 1977a: 2–16, 49–62; Smith *et al.* 1977: 242, 270.
130 Department of the Environment 1977a: 102. Cf. Ward 1974; Bradbrook 1975: 132–3.
131 See generally Griffiths 1975; Lewis 1977.
132 Andrews 1979: 200–24.
133 For example, Local Government Act 1972, s.102(3). Cf. Lempert and Ikeda 1970.
134 Ss.42–3.
135 See Baron n.d.; Crouch 1980.
136 Compare, e.g., the National Health Service Act 1977 with the National Health Act 1953 (Australia).
137 Royal Commission on the National Health Service 1979: 18–19, 88–92. See also Le Grand 1982: Ch.3; Townsend and Nicholson 1982.
138 See Halsey *et al.* 1980: 88, 189; Rutter *et al.* 1979 on education.
139 For example, Cingranelli 1981.
140 Lawson and Silver 1973: 270.
141 The legislation of four common-law countries is discussed in *Gateshead Union* v. *Durham C.C.* [1918] 1 Ch. 146; *Ex p. Cornford; Re Minister for Education* (1962) 62 S.R. (N.S.W.) 220; *Le Blanc* v. *Board of Education for City of Hamilton* (1962) 35 D.L.R. (2d) 548; *Cardiff* v. *Bismarck Public School District*, 263 N.W. 2d 105 (1978).
142 When Oregon enacted a law to force all children to attend public schools, the United States Supreme Court held that it was an unconstitutional infringement of the rights of parents and those operating the schools (*Pierce* v. *Society of Sisters* 268 U.S. 510 (1925)).
143 Janowitz 1976: 35.
144 *R.* v. *Cockerton* [1901] 1 K.B. 726; *Dyer* v. *London School Board* [1902] 2 Ch. 768. See McBriar 1966: 212.
145 Heidenheimer *et al.* 1976: 153. See also *San Antonio School District* v. *Rodriguez* (1973) 411 U.S. 1.
146 But they were unsuccessful in *Wood* v. *Ealing L.B.C.* [1967] 1 Ch. 364; *Smith* v. *I.L.E.A.* [1978] 1 All E.R. 411.
147 *Bradbury* v. *Enfield L.B.C.* [1967] 3 All E.R. 434; [1967] 1 W.L.R. 1311.
148 *Lee* v. *Enfield L.B.C.* (1967) 66 L.G.R. 195; (1967) 111 Sol. J. 772.
149 *Lee* v. *Secretary of State for Education and Science* (1967) 66 L.G.R. 211; (1967) 111 Sol. J. 756.
150 *Secretary of State for Education and Science* v. *Tameside M.B.C.* [1977] A.C. 1014.
151 Devlin 1976. Cf. *Times Education Supplement*, 19 December 1976, p.8.
152 See *Times Education Supplement*, 20 May 1977, p.5; 9 December 1977, p.4; 9 May 1979, p.1; 9 June 1980, p.6. See also *North Yorkshire C.C.* v. *Department of Education and Science* (1978) 77 L.G.R. 457.
153 See H. Rose 1976a: 264.

CHAPTER 7: Social change and the legal system

1 See Martin 1980: 149, 328.
2 Topping and Smith 1977: 29.
3 Hampton 1970: 276.
4 For example, Beer 1965: 349–50. Cf. Worsley 1973.
5 Comprising groups such as the Child Poverty Action Group (CPAG) and Shelter in Britain and the Australian Council of Social Service. Cf. National Welfare Rights Organization in the United States. See Bradley 1980; Cunningham 1976; Piven and Cloward 1979: ch.5; Rose 1975; Sackville 1981; Seyd 1975, 1976; Whiteley and Winyard 1983.
6 Mogulof 1972: 692.
7 Cf. Corina *et al.* 1979: 14, 37; O'Malley 1977.
8 Zurcher 1970: 22–5. It is doubtful if a sense of efficacy develops when a community group is unsuccessful (as many are).
9 Cf. Marris and Rein 1974: 236.
10 Polmear 1978.
11 Smith *et al.* 1977: 244.
12 Newton 1976: 47.
13 See Wates 1976: 153–6.
14 For example, Cockburn 1977: 85–6.
15 For example, Butcher *et al.* 1979: 232.
16 Law might prove facilitative in this regard. The Swedish Tenants' National Association, with 600,000 members, about a quarter of all flat-dwellers in the country, negotiates collective agreements with landlords regarding rent. A 1978 Act compels landlords to bargain with the Association if they wish to increase the rent. The tenants in a building must agree to any agreement negotiated by the Association before it becomes binding (Victorin 1979).
17 Brager and Purcell 1967: 334.
18 North Islington Housing Rights Project 1976.
19 *Hameed* v. *Hussain* (1977) 242 E.G. 1063. See generally Stewart 1981.
20 Crouch 1977: 10. See also North Tyneside CDP 1978: 25, 60, 64.
21 Clark and Hopkins 1970: 145.
22 Benewick and Smith 1972: 49.
23 Cf. Chamberlain 1977: 187.
24 Alinsky 1971: 59.
25 Hill 1970: 85.
26 Cf. Benington 1975: 238.
27 See Roddewig 1978; Thomas 1978.
28 Cf. Bachrach and Baratz 1970: 76–8.
29 Chambers 1973: 18.
30 The appeal to the House of Lords in *Simmons* v. *Pizzey* [1979] A.C. 37 seems to fall into this category, for although unsuccessful it highlighted the plight of women's refuges.
31 Roberts 1969: 108–9.
32 See Holdsworth 1938: 173; Halévy 1972: 76–8.

33 For judicial review, see *R.* v. *Poor Law Commissioners; In re Newport Union* (1837) 112 E.R. 20; *R.* v. *Poor Law Commissioners; In re Whitechapel Union* (1837) 112 E.R. 13. Cf. *R.* v. *Poor Law Commissioners; In re St Pancras* (1837) 112 E.R. 1.
34 Finer 1952: 88.
35 Freeden 1978: 36, 71.
36 Cf. McBriar 1966.
37 Leat 1975.
38 [1901] A.C. 426.
39 Parl. Deb., Commons, vol.26, 1911, 1022.
40 For example, Hewart 1929.
41 Phillimore 1911: 714.
42 See Abel-Smith and Stevens 1967: 117.
43 See Nye Bevan's remarks: Parl. Deb., Commons, vol. 425, 1946, 1983.
44 D.G.T. Williams 1979.
45 de Tocqueville 1966: 248.
46 Pound 1938: 44–5.
47 Nonet 1969: 16.
48 Hofstadter 1955: 309.
49 Barck and Blake 1949: 564–7.
50 Vose 1967: 36.
51 Isserman 1979; Rabin 1976: 210ff.
52 The response of some groups such as the Nader organization to this situation was to continue using fairly conventional lobbying methods; litigation was seen as ancillary. Marks *et al.* 1972: 159–60; Nader 1976: 247.
53 For example, Handler 1976a.
54 347 U.S. 483 (1954).
55 See text at notes 173–8 of Chapter 3.
56 Shortly after, the Cahns pointed to the deficiencies of the legal system and profession in effecting that change (Cahn 1966, 1970).
57 392 U.S. 309 (1968).
58 394 U.S. 618 (1969).
59 Marris and Rein 1974: 331.
60 See Bellow 1978; Bolner and Eubanks 1978.
61 Cf. Levy 1977.
62 *Wyman* v. *James* 400 U.S. 309 (1971).
63 397 U.S. 471 (1970).
64 *Jefferson* v. *Hackney* 406 U.S. 535 (1972). Not all social welfare cases were unsuccessful: e.g., *U.S. Department of Agriculture* v. *Moreno* 413 U.S. 528 (1973); *Califano* v. *Westcott* 443 U.S. 76 (1979). But there was even retrenchment in the procedural area. Compare *Goldberg* v. *Kelly* 379 U.S. 254 (1970), with *Mathews* v. *Eldridge* 424, U.S. 319 (1976).
65 Buckholz *et al.* 1978.
66 *Gautreaux* v. *Chicago Housing Authority* 296 F.Supp. 907 (1969); 304 F.Supp. 736. See Berney *et al.* 1975: 485–92.
67 See Frug 1978; Brill 1973; Horowitz 1977; Glazer 1978.
68 Chayes 1976.

69 Field 1973.
70 Hodge 1979.
71 Law Centres Working Group 1978: 32–3.
72 [1977] A.C. 239. See also *Community Action*, No.47, Jan.-Feb. 1980, pp.13–14.
73 For example CDP 1977b: 49–50.
74 See Indritz 1971: 16–30; Power 1977.
75 Bailey 1978: 99.
76 Barkun and Levine 1968: 36.
77 Quoted Moorhouse *et al.* 1972: 143.
78 *Kerr* v. *Bryde* [1923] A.C. 16.
79 *Gray* v. *Scanlan* (1924) 41 Sh.Ct.Rep. 3; *Booth* v. *Woods* (1925) 41 Sh.Ct.Rep. 85. Cf. *M'Callum* v. *Currie* (1924) 41 Sh.Ct.Rep. 6.
80 However, as a concession to tenants the legislation provided that they were not liable for arrears before December 1922, when the legislation was announced (Rent Restrictions (Notices of Increase) Act 1923). See Hannington 1977: 70–3.
81 *Guthrie* v. *Stewart* [1926] S.C. 743; *M'Kellar* v. *M'Master* [1926] S.C. 754.
82 For example, Loney 1981: 59–60.
83 [1975] 2 All E.R. 545; [1975] 1 W.L.R. 983.
84 Dec. 1975, p.12.
85 *Adriatic Terrazzo & Foundations Pty Ltd* v. *Robinson* [1972] 4 S.A.S.R. 294. Cf. *Master Builders' Association of N.S.W.* v. *ABCEBLF* (1974) 23 F.L.R. 356.
86 [1976] Q.B. 142.
87 Cf. *Bird* v. *O'Neal* [1960] A.C. 907.
88 *Thornhill* v. *Alabama* 310 U.S. 88 (1940); *Gregory* v. *City of Chicago* 394 U.S. 111 (1969). See Kahn-Freund 1976: 258–62.
89 *Hibbs* v. *Neighbourhood Organization to Rejuvenate Tenant Housing* 252 A. 2d 622 (1969).
90 Examples are provided in Bailey 1973: 28; *Community Action*, No.53, March-April 1981, p.23.
91 *Re 9 Orpen Road, Stoke Newington* [1971] 1 All E.R. 944; [1971] 1 W.L.R. 166; *R.* v. *Wandsworth County Court, ex p. Wandsworth L.B.C.* [1975] 3 All E.R. 390; [1975] 1 W.L.R. 1314.
92 David and Callan 1974.
93 *R.* v. *Beacontree Justices, ex p. Mercer* [1970] Crim.L.R. 103; *The Times*, 3 December 1969.
94 *R.* v. *Robinson* [1971] 1 Q.B. 156; *R.* v. *Mountford* [1972] 1 Q.B. 28. See also Housing Act 1957, s.22(4).
95 Cf. County Court Rules, Ord. 26.
96 *McPhail* v. *Persons Unknown* [1973] Ch. 447; *Westminster C.C.* v. *Chapman* [1975] 2 All E.R. 1103; [1975] 1 W.L.R. 1112; *Burston Finance Ltd* v. *Wilkins* (1975) 240 E.G. 375; *R.* v. *Wandsworth County Court, ex p. Wandsworth L.B.C.* [1975] 3 All E.R. 390; [1975] 1 W.L.R. 1314; *Shah* v. *Givert* (1980) 124 Sol.J. 513; *The Times*, 9 July 1980; *Westminster C.C.* v. *Monahan* [1981] 1 All E.R. 1050; [1981] 1 W.L.R. 698.

97 *Kamara* v. *D.P.P.* [1974] A.C. 104.
98 For example, *R.* v. *Bacon* [1977] 2 N.S.W.L.R. 507. See generally Prichard 1981.
99 Cf. Abbott and Peters 1972: 997n.
100 422 U.S. 490 (1975).
101 *Simon* v. *Eastern Kentucky Welfare Rights Organization* 426 U.S. 26 (1976).
102 372 U.S. 335 (1963).
103 Cf. Hodge 1979: 258.
104 *Murphy* v. *Webbwood Mobile Home Estates Ltd* (1978) 19 O.R. (2d) 300. See Ontario Law Reform Commission 1982: 264–5.
105 *Alden* v. *Gaglardi* (1973) 30 D.L.R. (3d) 760. Cf. *Alden* v. *Gaglardi* (1971) 15 D.L.R. (3d) 380, 381.
106 Fuller 1963.
107 See, e.g., *Duport Steels Ltd* v. *Sirs* [1980] 1 All E.R. 529, 541, 551; [1980] 1 W.L.R. 142, 157, 168.
108 Perhaps the best case in support is *Metzger* v. *Department of Health and Social Security* [1978] 3 All E.R. 753; [1978] 1 W.L.R. 1046. See Lustgarten and Elliott 1976.
109 *R.* v. *Barnsley SBAT, ex p. Atkinson* [1977] 3 All E.R. 1031; [1977] 1 W.L.R. 917; *R.* v. *Bristol SBAT, ex p. Southwell*, (1977) 121 Sol.J. 663, *The Times*, 21 July 1977. The decisions might not disprove the thesis, for when the cases were before the courts it was clear that the government would introduce legislation to negate a successful claim. Knowing this, the judges might not have been apprehensive that their decision would have serious financial repercussions in practice.
110 Wexler 1970: 1061. See *Rosado* v. *Wyman* 397 U.S. 397 (1970); *Dandridge* v. *Williams* 397 U.S. 471 (1970); *Jefferson* v. *Hackney* 406 U.S. 535 (1972).
111 347 U.S. 483 (1954).
112 Krislov 1973: 223–4.
113 *Southwark L.B.C.* v. *Williams* [1971] Ch. 734. See also *R.* v. *Bacon* [1977] 2 N.S.W.L.R. 507.
114 [1973] Ch. 447.
115 Co-ordination of social welfare test cases in the United States has occurred because of the existence of Legal Services Corporation back-up centres and the information network provided through publications such as *Clearinghouse Review* (Garth 1980: 199). In Britain most test cases relating to social welfare benefits have been initiated or assisted by the Child Poverty Action Group. On the other hand, squatting cases have been un-coordinated, one reason being that legal action has been initiated by individual owners and defended by local groups.
116 Cf. Hazard 1970: 249.
117 See Hanks 1980; Pickvance 1976.
118 Bedau 1974.
119 Hall 1974: 237. See also Hazard 1969.
120 Green 1974: 19–20.
121 Small Heath Community Law Centre 1977: 34–5.

122 *Dudley and District Benefit Building Society* v. *Emerson* [1949] Ch. 707.
123 Cf. *Chatsworth Properties Ltd* v. *Effiom* [1971] 1 All E.R. 604; [1971] 1 W.L.R. 144.
124 For example, *Clark* v. *Universal Builders* 501 F. 2d 324 (1974).
125 See Fitzgerald 1975. See also Sullivan 1971: 16–19.
126 CDP 1977b: 14–15. Cf. Wintour 1978: 12; *Roof*, May 1978, 73.
127 For example, Brent Community Law Centre 1979: 10. Contrast the failure recounted in *Law Centres' News*, June 1981: 4.
128 For example, Adamsdown Community Trust 1978: 70–7, 82.
129 Topping and Smith 1977:117.
130 O.E.O. 1968: 323.
131 Newham Rights Centre 1977: 15, 22, 32–3.
132 *Ibid.*, p.323.
133 Piven and Cloward 1979: 24–5.
134 Allen 1971: 338–41.
135 For example, *R.* v. *Bramley* (1947) 11 J.Crim.L. 36. See Dickens 1977; Ward 1976: 13–27.
136 Despite their image as middle-class dropouts etc., large numbers of squatters were working class and many were family groups who were homeless and ineligible for council housing (Kinghan 1977).
137 *Salford C.C.* v. *McNally* [1976] A.C. 379. More radical squatters have criticized licensing and tenancy agreements on the basis that they relieve local authorities of responsibility for homelessness.
138 See *R.* v. *Bacon* [1977] 2 N.S.W.L.R. 507. Apparently one of the continuing tenants in Victoria Street obtained an injunction against the developer to cease harassment. See generally *Australian Financial Review*, 23 November 1973; *Nation Review*, 11–17 January 1974; *Sydney Morning Herald*, 18 April, 2 May and 17 September 1981.
139 Baron 1978; Baron n.d.
140 Burn 1972.
141 *Greater London Council* v. *Connolly* [1970] 2 Q.B. 100.
142 The fate of rent strikes in Ireland has been inextricably linked with political factors. See McAllister 1977: 100–2, on the rent strike in Northern Ireland in the early seventies which, as part of the civil disobedience campaign, extended to about a quarter of all Catholic council households. Cf. *R.* v. *Parnell* (1881) 14 Cox C.C. 508; Boyle *et al.* 1975: 170–1.
143 Lipsky 1970: 86, 158.
144 Baron and Fishman 1970; Glotta 1967.
145 See *Community Action*, No. 53, March–April 1981, pp.16–17.
146 East London Claimants' Union 1974; Rose 1973; Rose and Jakubowicz 1978.
147 Cf. Bailis 1974; Jackson and Johnson 1974.
148 Jordan 1973: 20.
149 Johnson 1974: 189.
150 For example, *Rivera* v. *Division of Industrial Welfare* 71 Cal. Rptr 739 (1968).
151 *King* v. *Smith* 392 U.S. 309 (1968); *Shapiro* v. *Thompson* 394 U.S. 618

(1969).
152 Johnson 1974: 203–4.
153 *Morris* v. *Williams* 433 P. 2d 697 (1967).
154 For example, *Jay* v. *USDA* 308 F.Supp. 100 (1969). Cf. 441 F. 2d 574 (1971).
155 Johnson 1974: 232. See also Champagne 1977.
156 *Goldberg* v. *Kelly* 397 U.S. 254 (1970) is cited by Johnson as apparently bringing benefits of some $100 million a year to the poor, yet as late as the end of 1972 it had not been fully implemented in New York, where the case arose, quite apart from elsewhere in the United States (Berney *et al.* 1975: 854).
157 An example is that New York State complied with a federal judge's decree to improve the standards in a large mental hospital by transferring to it all the funds allocated to the prevention and relief of alcoholism (Cox 1976: 827).
158 347 U.S. 483 (1954).
159 See Rothstein 1974.
160 Rodgers and Bullock 1972: 3; Derfner 1973: 547, 552.
161 [1976] 2 All E.R. 478; [1976] 1 W.L.R. 543.
162 PHAS 1976: 15–17.
163 *The Times*, 2 August 1976.
164 [1974] Q.B. 543 (The case was heard in 1973 but not reported until 1974.)
165 National Insurance and Supplementary Benefit Act 1973, s.6, Schedule 4, para.4.
166 Partington 1974.
167 [1977] 3 All E.R. 1031; [1977] 1 W.L.R. 917.
168 (1977) 121 Sol.J. 663; *The Times*, 21 July 1977. See Prosser 1979: 70–4. Examples of administrative action undermining the effect of favourable test cases are discussed in Partington 1979; *Roof*, March 1977, 60. See generally Prosser 1983: chapter 5.
169 See Capowski 1976: 665–6; (1978) 1 *Low Income Law* 12, 14 (Canada); Barton 1978 (New Zealand).
170 *DeWolf* v. *City of Halifax* (1980) 37 N.S.R. (2d) 259.
171 (1977) 13 A.L.R. 1.
172 Social Security Act 1947, s. 120A (inserted 1977).
173 550 F. 2d 1122, 1132 (1977).
174 See Handler 1978: 18–19. Such factors have been considered in Chapter 4 in relation to the impact of regulation and in Chapter 6 in relation to the legal control of social welfare bureaucracies.
175 For example, Coventry CDP 1975; Pt. 1, 35, 37; Chamberlayne 1978: 64–5; Cousins 1978: 216–17.

CHAPTER 8: Conclusion

1 See generally Bruinsma 1980.
2 See *Green* v. *Daniels* (1977) 51 A.L.J.R. 463. Compare the role of the Code of Guidance under the Housing (Homeless Persons) Act 1977.

3 An area for further study is the extent to which private law ideals such as contracting-out have filtered social welfare legislation.
4 See also Allott 1980: 76–7.
5 For example, Townsend 1979.
6 For example, Le Grand 1982.
7 For example, Pinker 1979.
8 For example, Anderson *et al.* 1981.
9 Quoted Griffith 1977: 173.
10 Devlin 1979: 91.
11 Devlin 1978: 509.
12 de Smith 1980: 526.

REFERENCES

Abbott, C.M. and Peters, D.C. (1972) *Fuentes* v. *Shevin*: a Narrative of Federal Test Litigation in the Legal Services Program. 57 *Iowa Law Review* 955.

Abbott, Grace (1941) *From Relief to Social Security*. Chicago, University of Chicago Press.

Abbott, S.B. (1976) Housing Policy, Housing Codes and Tenant Remedies: an Integration. 56 *Boston University Law Review* 1.

Abel, R.L. (1982a) Introduction *in* Abel, R.L. (ed.), *The Politics of Informal Justice*. New York, Academic.

Abel, R.L. (1982b) The Politics of the Market for Legal Services *in* Thomas, P.A., *Law in the Balance*. Oxford, Martin Robertson.

Abel-Smith, B. and Stevens, R. (1967) *Lawyers and the Courts*. Cambridge, Mass., Harvard University Press.

Abel-Smith, B. and Stevens, R. (1968) *In Search of Justice*. London, Penguin Press.

Abel-Smith, B., Zander, M. and Brooke, R. (1973) *Legal Problems and the Citizen*. London, Heinemann Educational Books.

Ackerman, B. (1971) Regulating Slum Housing Markets on Behalf of the Poor: of Housing Codes, Housing Subsidies and Income Redistribution Policy. 80 *Yale Law Journal* 1093.

Adamsdown Community Trust (1978) *Community Need and Law Centre Practice. An Empirical Assessment*. Cardiff, Adamsdown Community Trust.

Adamsdown Legal Services Group (1976) Legal Services Group Work – the Adamsdown Experience *in* Brooke, R. (ed.), *Advice Services in Welfare Rights*. London, Fabian Society. Fabian Research Series 329.

Adler, M. and Asquith, S. (1981) Discretion and Power *in* Adler, M. and Asquith, S. (eds.), *Discretion and Welfare*. London, Heinemann.

Adler, M. and Bradley, A. (eds.) (1976) *Justice, Discretion and Poverty*. London, Professional Books.

Administrative Review Council (1981) *Social Security Appeals*. Canberra,

Australian Government Publishing Service.

Albrecht, S.L. (1976) The Distribution of Justice *in* Zimmerman, D.H., Wieter, D.L. and Zimmerman, S. (eds.), *Understanding Social Problems*. New York, Praeger.

Alcock, P. and Harris, P. (1982) *Welfare Law and Order*. London, Macmillan.

Alcock, P.C. (1976) Legal Aid: Whose Problem? 3 *British Journal of Law and Society* 151.

Aleshire, R.A. (1972) Power to the People: an Assessment of the Community Action and Model Cities Experience. 32 *Public Administration Review* 428.

Alinsky, S.D. (1971) *Rules for Radicals: a Practical Primer for Realistic Radicals*. New York, Random House.

Allan, G.T. (1978) Observations on the Administration of Cash Benefits. 9 *Victoria University of Wellington Law Review* 201.

Allbeson, J. (1980) *Rent-Stop*. London, Child Poverty Action Group.

Allen, M.S. (1971) A Frontier Challenge to the Urban Landowner: Squatters in New York. 49 *Journal of Urban Law* 323.

Allott, A. (1980) *The Limits of Law*. London, Butterworths.

Almond, G.A. and Verba, S. (1963) *The Civic Culture: Political Attitudes and Democracy in Five Nations*. Princeton, N.J., Princeton University Press.

Altman, B.F. (1976) Disclosure of Paternity of Illegitimate Child. 64 *Georgetown Law Journal* 947.

Anderson, D., *et al.* (1981) *Breaking the Spell of the Welfare State*. London, Social Affairs Unit.

Andrews, L. (1979) *Tenants and Town Hall*. London, HMSO.

Anonymous (1828) On the Custom of Making Allowances out of the Poor-Rate to Able-Bodied Labourers in Increase of their Wages. 1 *Law Magazine* 90.

Anonymous (1829) Poor Laws. 1 *Law Magazine* 599.

Anonymous (1832) Cruelty and Extravagance of a Parish Officer. *Poor Man's Advocate*, No. 29, August 4.

Anonymous (1833) The Poor Laws. 9 *Law Magazine* 276.

Anonymous (1845) Parochial Settlement Bill. 9 *Justice of the Peace* 83; 50.

Anonymous (1865) Poor Law Administration. 9 *Solicitors Journal* 519.

Anonymous (1882) The Jurisdiction of Local Boards under Section 36 of the Public Health Act, 1875. 46 *Justice of the Peace* 675.

Anonymous (1906) The Disqualification of Electors by the Receipt of Relief and Arms. 50 *Solicitors Journal* 523.

Anonymous (1970) AFDC Income Attribution, the Man-in-the-House and Welfare Grant Reductions. 83 *Harvard Law Review* 1373.

Anonymous (1977) The Wages Inspector Cometh. *Department of Employment Gazette*, February, 107.

Anonymous (1978) Legal Aid in Magistrates' Courts – the New Meanness Test. *LAG Bulletin* 226.

Anonymous (1979) 87 *Employment Gazette* 5.

Anonymous (1980) Success Count. *LAG Bulletin* 53.

Archard, P. (1979) *Vagrancy, Alcoholism and Social Control*. London, Macmillan.

Archbold, J.F. (1842) *The New Poor Law Amendment Act*. London, John Richards & Co.

398   REFERENCES

Archbold, J.F. (1858) *An Abridgment of Cases upon Poor Law 1842 to 1858*. London, Shaw.
Arden, A. (1976) What's Left of Illegal Eviction? 126 *New Law Journal* 80.
Arden, A. (1978a) Distress for Rent. *LAG Bulletin* 57.
Arden, A. (1978b) *Housing: Security and Rent Control*. London, Sweet & Maxwell.
Arden, A. (1979a) High Court Guerrillas. 4 *Roof* 78.
Arden, A. (1979b) It's Official – Harassment is Hell! *LAG Bulletin* 114.
Arden, A. (1979c) A Note on Set-Off Against Rent. *LAG Bulletin* 210.
Arden, A. and Partington, M. (1980) *Quiet Enjoyment*. London, Legal Action Group.
Arden, A. and Partington, M. (1983) *Housing Law*. London, Sweet & Maxwell.
Armstrong, S. (1977) Unconvicted Prisoners: the Problem of Bail *in* Armstrong, S., Mossman, M.J. and Sackville, R., *Essays on Law and Poverty*. Canberra, Australian Government Publishing Service.
Arthurs, H.W. (1979) Rethinking Administrative Law: a Slightly Dicey Business. 17 *Osgoode Hall Law Journal* 1.
Ashby, A.W. (1912) *One Hundred Years of Poor Law Administration in a Warwickshire Village*. Oxford, Clarendon Press.
Ashforth, D. (1976) The Urban Poor Law in Fraser, D. (ed.), *The New Poor Law in the Nineteenth Century*. London, Macmillan Press.
Ashworth, A.J. (1979) Protecting the Home through Criminal Law. 1978–79 *Journal of Social Welfare Law* 76.
The Association of Public Health Inspectors (1973) *Environmental Health Report*. London.
Atiyah, P.S. (1979) *The Rise and Fall of Freedom of Contract*. Oxford, Clarendon Press.
Atkinson, A.B. (1970) *Poverty in Britain and the Reform of Social Security*. London, Cambridge University Press.
Aubert, V. (1952) White-Collar Crime and Social Structure. 58 *American Journal of Sociology* 263.
Aubert, V. (1970) Justice as a Problem of Social Psychology. 56 *Archiv fur Rechts und Sozialphilosophie* 465.
Auerbach (1971) *Office of Legal Services. Individual Project Evaluations. Final Report*. Prepared by Auerbach Assoc. Inc., Philadelphia.
Auerbach, J.S. (1976) *Unequal Justice, Lawyers and Social Change in Modern America*. New York, Oxford University Press.
Aydelotte, F. (1967) *Elizabethan Rogues and Vagabonds*. London, Cass.
Baar, K.K. (1977) Rent Control in the 1970s: the Case of the New Jersey Tenants' Movement. 28 *Hastings Law Journal* 631.
Bachrach, P. and Baratz, M.S. (1970) *Power and Poverty: Theory and Practice*. New York, Oxford University Press.
Bailey, R. (1973) *The Squatters*. Harmondsworth, Penguin Books.
Bailey, R. (1977) *The Homeless and the Empty Houses*. Harmondsworth, Penguin Books.
Bailey, R. (1978) Grabbing the Smashers. 3 *Roof* 99.
Bailey, R. and Ruddock, J. (1972) *The Grief Report*. London, Shelter.

Bailey, R. and Brake, M. (1975) *Radical Social Work*. London, Edward Arnold.

Bailis, L.N. (1974) *Bread or Justice: Grassroots Organizing in the Welfare Rights Movement*. Lexington, Mass., Lexington Books.

Baker, J.H. (1979) *An Introduction to English Legal History*, 2nd edn. London, Butterworths.

Balbus, I.D. (1977) Commodity Form and Legal Form: an Essay on the 'Relative Autonomy' of the Law. 11 *Law and Society Review* 571

Baldus, D. (1975) Welfare as a Loan: an Empirical Study of the Recovery of Public Assistance Payments in the United States. 25 *Stanford Law Review* 123.

Baldwin, J. and McConville, M. (1977) *Negotiated Justice*. London, Martin Robertson.

Ball, H.V. (1960) Social Structure and Rent-Control Violations. 65 *American Journal of Sociology* 598.

Bamueller, C.F. (1981) *The National Charity Company*. Berkeley, University of California Press.

Bankowski, Z. and Mungham, G. (1976) *Images of Law*. London, Routledge & Kegan Paul.

Bankowski, Z. and Nelken, D. (1981) Discretion as a Social Problem *in* Adler, M. and Asquith, S. (eds.), *Discretion and Welfare*. London, Heinemann.

Banks, B. (1872) *Compendium of Irish Poor Law*. Dublin, Thom.

Baran, P.A. and Sweezy, P.M. (1966) *Monopoly Capital*. Harmondsworth, Penguin.

Barck, O.T. and Blake, N.M. (1949) *Since 1900: a History of the United States in Our Times*. New York, Macmillan.

Barker, P. (1979) Social Attitudes as we Enter the Eighties. 50 *New Society* 482.

Barkun, M. and Levine, J. (1968) Protest in Suburbia: Case Study of a Direct-Action Movement. 20 *Syracuse Law Review* 21.

Barnes, T.G. (1970) The Prerogative and Environmental Control of London Building in the Early Seventeenth Century: the Lost Opportunity. 58 *California Law Review* 1332.

Barnett, H. (1969) *The Politics of Legislation. The Rent Act 1957*. London, Weidenfeld & Nicolson.

Baron, R.D. (n.d.) *Tenant Management*. St Louis, McCormack, Baron & Associates.

Baron, R.D. (1978) Community Organisations. 21 *St Louis University Law Journal* 634.

Baron, R.D. and Fishman, P.F. (1970) The St Louis Public Housing Rent Strike: a Model for Inducing Community Action. 28 *Legal Aid Briefcase* 111.

Barr, N.A. (1977) Taxation, Benefits and Pay: Action on the Social Division of Welfare *in* Brown, M. and Baldwin, S. (eds.), *The Yearbook of Social Policy in Britain*. London, Routledge & Kegan Paul.

Barrington Baker, W., Eekelaar, J., Gibson, C. and Raikes, S. (1977) *The Matrimonial Jurisdiction of Registrars*. Oxford, Centre for Socio-Legal Studies.

A Barrister (1938) *Justice in England*. London, Gollancz (New Left Books).

Barry, Sir P.R. and Fisher, H.A.P. (eds.) (1952) *Glen's Public Health Act 1936*. London, Eyre & Spottiswoode.

Bartlett, D. and Walker, J. (1978) Inner Circle *in* Baldwin, J. and Bottomley,

A., *Criminal Justice*. London, Martin Robertson.

Barton, G.P. (1978) Law and Orders: a Case Study. 9 *Victoria University of Wellington Law Review* 393.

Barton, J.L. (1957) The Enforcement of Financial Provisions *in* Graveson, R.H. and Crane, F.R. (eds.), *A Century of Family Law, 1857–1957*. London, Sweet & Maxwell.

Basilevsky, A. (1975) Social Class and Delinquency in London Boroughs. 2 *Social Indicators Research* 287.

Bates, E.H. (ed.) (1907) *Quarter Sessions' Records for the County of Somerset*, London.

Baum, D.J. (1974) *The Welfare Family and Mass Administrative Justice*. New York, Praeger.

Bayliss, F.J. (1962) *British Wages Councils*. Oxford, Basil Blackwell.

Bayne, P. (1977) Special Benefits for Migrants: a Fitzroy Legal Service Case-Study. 2 *Legal Service Bulletin* 372.

Beaumont, P.B. (1979) The Limits of Inspection: a Study of the Workings of the Government Wages Inspectorate. 57 *Public Administration* 203.

Beckerman, W. (1979) The Impact of Income Maintenance Payments on Poverty in Britain, 1975. 89 *Economic Journal* 261.

Bedau, H.A. (1974) Our Knowledge of the Law's Effectiveness *in* Pennock, J.R. and Chapman, J.W. (eds.), *The Limits of Law*. New York, Lieber-Atherton. Nomos XV.

Beer, S.H. (1965) *British Politics in the Collectivist Age*. New York, Knopf.

Beirne, P. (1977) *Fair Rent and Legal Fiction*. London, Macmillan Press.

Bell, K. (1975) *Research Study on Supplementary Benefit Appeal Tribunals*. London, HMSO.

Bell, K., Collinson, P., Turner, S. and Webber, S. (1974 and 1975) National Insurance Local Tribunals. 3 & 4 *Journal of Social Policy* 289, 1.

Bellamy, J. (1973) *Crime and Public Order in England in the Later Middle Ages*. London, Routledge & Kegan Paul.

Bellow, G. (1977) The Legal Aid Puzzle: Turning Solutions into Problems. 5 *Working Papers for a New Society* 52.

Bellow, G. (1978) The Trouble with the Burger Court. 6 *Working Papers for a New Society*. Sept./Oct., p.16.

Benenson, P. (1957) *The Future of Legal Aid*. London, Fabian Society, Fabian Research Series 191.

Benewick, R. and Smith, T. (eds.) (1972) *Direct Action and Democratic Politics*. London, Allen & Unwin.

Benington, J. (1975) Gosford Green Residents' Association: a Case Study *in* Leonard, P. (ed.), *The Sociology of Community Action*. University of Keele, Keele, Staffordshire, Sociological Review Monograph 21.

Benn, S.I. and Peters, R.S. (1959) *Social Principles and the Democratic State*. London, Allen & Unwin.

Bennett, T. (1979) The Social Distribution of Criminal Labels. 19 *British Journal of Criminology* 134.

Bentwich, N. (1914) Legal Aid for the Poor. 105 *Contemporary Review* 561.

Benwell CP (Community Project) (1978) *Private Housing and the Working Class*. Final Report Series, No. 3, Newcastle-upon-Tyne.

Bercusson, B. (1978) *Fair Wages Resolutions*. London, Mansell.
Berney, A.L., Goldberg, J., Dooley, J.A. III and Carroll, D.W. (1975) *Legal Problems of the Poor*. Boston, Little, Brown and Co.
Berthoud, R., Brown, J.C. with Cooper, S. (1981) *Poverty and the Development of Anti-Poverty Policy in the United Kingdom*. London, Heinemann.
Best, R. (1980) Remission of Fees in the County Court *Legal Action Group Bulletin* 141.
Birkinshaw, P. (1982) Homelessness and the Law – the Effects and Responses to Legislation. 5 *Urban Law and Policy* 255.
Birmingham CDP (1979) *Leasehold Loopholes*. Final Report, No. 5. Oxford, Birmingham CDP Research Team.
Birtwistle (1972) Presidential Address. 80 *Environmental Health* 373.
Bittner, E. (1967) The Police on Skid Row: a Study of Peace-Keeping. 32 *American Sociological Review* 699.
Black, D.J. (1973) The Mobilization of Law. 2 *Journal of Legal Studies* 125.
Blackstone, Sir W. (1783) *Commentaries on the Laws of England*. London, T. Cadell.
Blankenburg, E. (1976) The Selectivity of Legal Sanctions: an Empirical Investigation of Shoplifting. 11 *Law and Society Review* 109.
Blankenburg, E. and Reifner, V. (1981) Conditions of Legal and Political Culture Limiting the Transferability of Access-in-Law Innovations *in* Cappelletti, M. (ed.), *Access to Justice and the Welfare State*. Alphen aan den Rijn, Sijthoff.
Blau, P.M. and Meyer, M.W. (1971) *Bureaucracy in Modern Society*, 2nd edn. New York, Random House.
Blau, P.M. and Scott, W.R. (1962) *Formal Organisations*. San Francisco, Chandler.
Blaug, M. (1974) The Myth of the Old Poor Law and the Making of the New *in* Flinn, M.W. and Smout, T.C. (eds.), *Essays in Social History*. London, Oxford University Press.
Blom-Cooper, L. and Drewry, G. (1972) *Final Appeal*. Oxford, Clarendon.
Blumberg, A.S. (ed.) (1973) *The Scales of Justice*, 2nd edn. New Brunswick, N.J., Transaction Books.
Blumberg, R.E. and Robbins, B.Q. (1976) Beyond URLTA: a Program for Achieving Real Tenant Goals. 11 *Harvard Civil Rights – Civil Liberties Law Review*. 1.
Boaden, N. *et al.* (1979) Public Participation in Planning Within a Representative Local Democracy. 7 *Policy and Politics* 55.
Boddy, M.J. (1976) The Structure of Mortgage Finance: Building Societies and the British Social Formation. 1 *Institute of British Geographers, Transactions* 58.
Boddy, M. and Gray, F. (1979) Filtering Theory, Housing Policy and the Legitimation of Inequality. 7 *Policy and Politics* 39.
Bodenheimer, E. (1973) *Power, Law and Society*. New York, Crane, Russak & Co.
Bohne, B.H. (1977) *The Public Defender as Advocate: a Study in Administration, Politics, and Criminal Justice*. University of Wisconsin – Madison, Institute for Research on Poverty Discussion Paper 414.

Bolner, J. and Eubanks, C.L. (1978) The Poverty of Justice: The Burger Court and the Poor. 7 *Capital University Law School* 351.

Bond, N. (1975) Knowledge of Rights *in* Butterworth, E. and Holman, R. (eds.), *Social Welfare In Modern Britain*. London, Fontana.

Bone, M. and Mason, V. (1980) *Empty Housing in England*. (A Report on the 1977 Vacant Property Survey carried out on behalf of the Department of the Environment.) Office of Population Censuses and Surveys, Social Survey Division. London, HMSO.

Bonger, W.A. (1967) *Criminality and Economic Conditions*. New York, Agathon Press.

Borrie, G. and Varcoe, J.R. (1970) Criminal Proceedings – A Regional View. 120 *New Law Journal* 997.

Bothmann, S. and Gordon, R. (1979) *Practising Poverty Law*. Melbourne, Fitzroy Legal Services.

Bott, E. (1793a) *Decisions of the Court of King's Bench, Upon the Laws relating to the Poor*, 3rd edn. 2 vols.

Bott, E. (1793b) *Laws Relating to the Poor*, 3rd edn. London, Whieldon & Butterworth.

Bottomley, A.K. (1973) *Decisions in the Penal Process*. London, Martin Robertson.

Bottoms, A.E. and McClean, J.D. (1976) *Defendants in the Criminal Process*. London, Routledge & Kegan Paul.

Boulton, A.H. (1972) *The Law and Practice of Social Security*. Bristol, Jordan.

Bowley, M. (1947) *Housing and the State 1919–1944*. London, George Allen.

Box, S. and Ford, J. (1971) The Facts Don't Fit: On the Relationship Between Social Class and Criminal Behaviour. 19 *Sociological Review* 31.

Boyle, K., Hadden, T. and Hillyard, P. (1975) *Law and the State: The Case of Northern Ireland*. London, Martin Robertson.

Boyson, R. (1971) *Down With the Poor*. London, Churchill.

Bradbrook, A.J. (1975) *Poverty and the Residential Landlord-Tenant Relationship*. Australia. Commission of Inquiry into Poverty. Law and Poverty Series. Canberra, AGPS.

Bradbrook, A.J. (1976a) The Role of the Judiciary in Reforming Landlord and Tenant Law. 10 *Melbourne University Law Review* 459.

Bradbrook, A.J. (1976b) The State Housing Commissions and their Tenants: the Need for Legislative Control. 10 *Melbourne University Law Review* 409.

Bradbrook, A.J. (1977) The Role of State Government Agencies in Securing Repairs to Rented Housing. 11 *Melbourne University Law Review* 145.

Bradley, A.W. (1976) Reform of Supplementary Benefit Tribunals – The Key Issues. 27 *Northern Ireland Legal Quarterly* 96.

Bradley, A.W. (1980) The Role of the Ombudsman in Relation to the Protection of Citizens' Rights. 39 *Cambridge Law Journal* 304.

Bradley, I. (1980) Pressure Groups (2–4). *The Times*. 8–10 April.

Bradshaw, J., Taylor-Gooby, P. and Lees, R. (1974) *The Batley Welfare Rights Project*. Department of Social Administration and Social Work, University of York.

Brager, G.A. and Purcell, F.P. (eds.) (1967) *Community Action Against Poverty: Readings from the Mobilization Experience*. New Haven, Conn., College &

University Press.
Braithwaite, J. (1979) *Inequality, Crime and Public Policy*. London, Routledge & Kegan Paul.
Breger, M.J. (1982) Legal Aid for the Poor. A Conceptual Analysis. 60 *North Carolina L.R.* 281.
Brenner, J.F. (1974) Nuisance Law and the Industrial Revolution. 3 *Journal of Legal Studies* 403.
Brent Community Law Centre (1976) (March) *Report*. London, Brent Community Law Centre.
Brent Community Law Centre (1979) Inspector's Report Means Better Willesden Plan. *Bulletin* No. 11, Autumn.
Brewer, J. and Styles, J. (1980) *An Ungovernable People*. London, Hutchinson.
Bridges, L.T. (1973) The Role of the Harassment Officer in the Provision of Legal Services in Birmingham (Unpublished).
Bridges, L.T. (1979) The Structure Plan Examination in Public as an Instrument of Inter Governmental Decision Making. 2 *Urban Law and Policy* 241.
Bridges, L., Sufrin, B., Whetton, J. and White, R. (1975) *Legal Services in Birmingham*. University of Birmingham, Institute of Judicial Administration.
Briggs, A. (1966) The Welfare State in Historical Perspective *in* Aiyar, S.P. (ed.) *Perspectives on the Welfare State*. Bombay, Manaktalas.
Briggs, E. and Rees, T. (1980) Lost in the Puzzle of Social Security. 51 *New Society* 60.
Brill, H. (1971) *Why Organizers Fail. The Story of a Rent Strike*. Berkeley, University of California Press.
Brill, H. (1973) The Uses and Abuses of Legal Assistance. 31 *The Public Interest* 38.
Brooke, R. (ed.) (1976) *Advice Services in Welfare Rights*. London, Fabian Research Series 329.
Brooke, R. (1977) Legal Services in Canada. 40 *Modern Law Review* 533.
Brooke, R. (1979) *Law, Justice and Social Policy*. London, Croom Helm.
Brown, A.J. (1978) Housing (Homeless Persons) Act 1977: Two Views. I: A Local Government View. 128 *New Law Journal* 971.
Brown, M. (1974) *Sweated Labour. A Study of Homework*. London, Low Pay Unit.
Brown, M. and Madge, N. (1982) *Despite the Welfare State*. London, Heinemann.
Brown, N. (1955) National Assistance and the Liability to Maintain One's Spouse. 18 *Modern Law Review* 110.
Brown, R.G.S. (1975) *The Management of Welfare*. London, Martin Robertson.
Browne, D. (ed.) (1760) *Sessions Cases Adjudged in the Court of King's Bench Chiefly Touching Settlements*. London.
Browne, E.L. (1938) *Lawyers and the Promotion of Justice*. New York, Russell Sage.
Brownell, E.A. (1951) *Legal Aid in the United States*. Rochester N.Y., Lawyers Co-operative Publishing Co.
Bruce, M. (1968) *The Coming of the Welfare State*, 4th edn. London, Batsford.

Bruinsma, F. (1980) The (Non-) Assertion of Welfare Rights: Hirschman's Theory Applied. 15 *Acta Politica* 357.

Bruzelius, A. and Bolding, P.O. (1975) An Introduction to the Swedish Public Legal Aid Reform *in* Cappelletti *et al.*, *Toward Equal Justice*. Dobbs Ferry, N.Y., Oceana.

Bryan, M.W. (1980) The 'Liable Relative' Reviewed. 10 *Family Law* 25.

Bryson, L. and Eastop, L. (1980) Poverty, Welfare and Hegemony, 1973 and 1978. *A.N.Z.J. Sociology*, vol. 16, No. 3, November, p.61.

Buchanan, S. (1981) Support for Single-Parent Families: Whose Responsibility? 6 *Legal Service Bulletin* 76.

Buckholz, R. *et al.* (1978) The Remedial Process in Institutional Reform Litigation. 78 *Columbia Law Review* 784.

Bull, D. (1980) The Anti-Discretion Movement in Britain: Fact or Phantom? *Journal of Social Welfare Law* 65.

Burn, D. (1972) *Rent Strike, St Pancras 1960*. London, Pluto Press.

Burn, R. (1764) *The History of the Poor Laws with Observations*. London, A. Millar.

Burn, W.L. (1964) *The Age of Equipoise*. London, Allen & Unwin.

Burney, E. (1979) *Justice of the Peace: Magistrate, Court and Community*. London, Hutchinson.

Burns, P. and Reid, R.S. (1981) Delivery of Criminal Legal Services in Canada: An Overview of the Continuing 'Judicare versus Public Defender' Debate. 15 *University of British Columbia Law Review* 403.

Butcher, H., Pearce, J., Cole, I. and Glen, A. (1979) *Community Participation and Poverty*. Final Report of Cumbria CDP. York, Department of Social Administration and Social Work, University of York.

Butt, J. (1971) Working-Class Housing in Glasgow, 1851–1914 *in* Chapman, S.D. (ed.), *The History of Working-Class Housing*. Newton Abbot, David & Charles.

Byles, A. and Morris, P. (1977) *Unmet Need*. London, Routledge & Kegan Paul.

Byrne, D. and Beirne, P. (1975) Towards a Political Economy of Housing Rent *in: Political Economy and the Housing Question* (Papers presented at the Housing Workshop of the Conference of Social Economists). London.

CDP (1974) *The National Community Development Project. Inter-Project report*. London.

CDP (1977a) *Gilding the Ghetto: The State and the Poverty Experiments*. London, CDP Inter-Project Editorial Team.

CDP (1977b) *Limits of the Law*. London, CDP Inter-Project Editorial Team.

Cabramatta Tenancy Working Party (1982) *Reforming a Feudal Law*. Sydney, Australian Consumers Association.

Cahn, E.S. and J.C. (1964) The War on Poverty: a Civilian Perspective. 73 *Yale Law Journal* 1317.

Cahn, E.S. and J.C. (1966) What Price Justice: the Civilian Perspective Revisited. 41 *Notre Dame Law Review* 927.

Cahn, E.S. and J.C. (1970) Power to the People or the Profession? – The Public Interest in Public Interest Law. 79 *Yale Law Journal* 1005.

Cain, M. 1973 *Society and the Policeman's Role*. London, Routledge & Kegan Paul.

Cain, M. (1979) The General Practice Lawyer and the Client: Towards a Radical Conception. 7 *International Journal of Sociology of Law* 331.

Cain, M. and Hunt, A. (1979) *Marx and Engels on Law*. London, Academic.

Calvert, H. (1978) *Social Security Law*, 2nd edn. London, Sweet & Maxwell.

Calvert, H. (1980) *Encyclopedia of Social Security Law*. London, Sweet & Maxwell.

Campbell, C.M. and Wilson, R.J. (n.d.) *Public Attitudes to the Legal Profession in Scotland*. Law Society of Scotland.

Campbell, T.D. (1978) Discretionary 'Rights' *in* Timms, N. and Watson, D. (eds.), *Philosophy in Social Work*. London, Routledge & Kegan Paul.

Campbell, T.D. (1980) Counter-Productive Welfare Law. 11 *British Journal of Political Science* 331.

Capowski, J.J. (1976) Introduction to the Welfare Law Issue. 61 *Cornell Law Review* 663.

Cappelletti, M. and Garth, B. (1978) Access to Justice: the Worldwide Movement to Make Rights Effective. A General Report *in* Cappelletti, M. and Garth, B. (eds.), *Access to Justice*. Milan, Giuffre.

Cappelletti, M., Gordley, J. and Johnson, E. (1975) *Toward Equal Justice*. Dobbs Ferry, N.Y., Oceana.

Cappelletti, M. and Weisner, J. (eds.) (1978) *Access to Justice*, vol. II: *Promising Institutions*. Alphen aan den Rijn, Sijthoff and Noordhoff.

Carlen, P. (1976) *Magistrates' Justice*. London, Martin Robertson.

Carlin, J.E., Howard, J. and Messinger, S.L. (1966) Civil Justice and the Poor: Issues for Sociological Research. 1 *Law and Society Review* 9.

Carney, T. (1982) Social Security Reviews and Appeals in Australia: Atrophy or Growth? 1 *Australian Journal of Law and Society* 32.

Carson, W.G. and Wiles, P. (1971) *Crime and Delinquency in Britain*. London, Martin Robertson.

Cashman, P. (1980) Social Security Prosecutions: Are They Too Easy? 5 *Legal Service Bulletin* 183.

Cashman, P. (1981) Legal Representation in Magistrates' Courts *in* Cashman, P. (ed.), *Research and the Delivery of Legal Service*. Sydney, Law Foundation of New South Wales.

Cashman, P. (1982) Representation in Criminal Cases *in* Basten, J. *et al.* (eds.), *The Criminal Injustice System*. Sydney, ALWG & Legal Service Bulletin.

Cass, M. and Sackville, R. (1975) *Legal Needs of the Poor*. Canberra, A.G.P.S.

Cass, M. and Western, J.S. (1980) *Legal Aid and Legal Need*. Canberra, Commonwealth Legal Aid Commission.

Castells, M. (1978) *City, Class and Power*. London, Macmillan.

Catterton, M. (1978) Police in Social Control *in* Baldwin, T. and Bottomley, A., *Criminal Justice*. London, Martin Robertson.

Cawson, Alan (1982) *Corporatism and Welfare*. London, Heinemann.

Centre on Social Welfare Policy and Law (1972) *Materials on Welfare Law*. New York.

Chadwick, E. (1965) *Report on the Sanitary Condition of the Labouring Population of Great Britain*. (1842) Flinn, M.W. (ed.). Edinburgh, Edinburgh University Press.

Chalklin, C.W. (1974) *The Provincial Towns of Georgian England*. London, Edward Arnold.

Chamberlain, C. (1977) Attitudes Towards Direct Political Action in Britain *in* Crouch, C. (ed.), *British Political Sociology Yearbook*, vol. 3: *Participation in Politics*. London, Croom Helm.

Chamberlayne, P. (1978) The Politics of Participation: An Enquiry into Four London Boroughs 1968–74. 4 *London Journal* 47.

Chambers, D.L. (1979) *Making Fathers Pay. The Enforcement of Child Support*. Chicago, University of Chicago Press.

Chambers, J. (1973) Which Way Claimants Unions? 26 *Poverty* 17.

Chamblis, W.J. (1964) A Sociological Analysis of the Law of Vagrancy. 12 *Social Problems* 67.

Chamblis, W.J. and Seidman, R.B. (1971) *Law, Order and Power*. Reading, Mass., Addison-Wesley.

Champagne, A. (1977) *Legal Services: an Exploratory Study of Effectiveness*. Sage Professional Paper, Administrative and Policy Studies Series, vol. 3.

Chayes, A. (1976) The Role of the Judge in Public Law Litigation. 89 *Harvard Law Review* 1281.

Checkland, S.G. and E.O.A. (eds.) (1974) *The Poor Law Report of 1834*. Harmondsworth, Penguin.

Chesterman, M. (1979) *Charities, Trusts and Social Welfare*. London, Weidenfeld & Nicolson.

Chilton, R.J. (1970) Social Control through Welfare Legislation. 5 *Law and Society Review* 205.

Chippindale, P. and Walker, M. (1976) A Growing Right-Wing Pressure Group. *Guardian*, 21 December 1976.

Christensen, B. (1970) *Lawyers for People of Moderate Means*. Chicago, American Bar Foundation.

Cingranelli, D.L. (1981) Race, Politics and Elites: Testing Alternative Models of Municipal Service Distribution. 25 *American Journal of Political Science*. 664.

Clark, K. and Hopkins, J. (1970) *A Relevant War Against Poverty*. New York, Harper & Row.

Clarke, J.J. (1937) *Public Assistance and Unemployment Assistance*, 2nd edn. London, Pitman & Sons.

Clarke, J.J. (1949a) *Introduction to Public Health Law*. London, Cleaver-Hume.

Clarke, J.J. (1949b) *Law of Housing and Planning*, 5th edn. London, Pitman.

Clegg, H.A. (1976) *The System of Industrial Relations in Great Britain*, 3rd edn. Oxford, Basil Blackwell.

Coates, K. (1978) Ashfield – How Participation Turned Sour *in* Coates, K. (ed.), *The Right to Useful Work*. Nottingham, Spokesman Books.

Coates, K. and Silburn, R. (1973) *Poverty: The Forgotten Englishman*. Harmondsworth, Penguin Books.

Cobbett, W. (1977) *The Poor Man's Friend or Essays on the Rights and Duties of the Poor*. Reprint of 1829 edn. Fairfield, New Jersey, Augustus M. Kelley.

Cockburn, C. (1977) *The Local State: Management of Cities and People*. London, Pluto Press.

Cohen, P. (1979) Policing the Working-Class City *in* Fine, B. *et al*. (eds.),

Capitalism and the Rule of the Law. London, Hutchinson.

Coke, Sir E. (1641) *The Compleat Copyholder.*

Coke, Sir E. (1797) *The Institutes of the Laws of England,* 16th edn. London, E. & R. Brooke.

Coleman, J.S. (1974) *Power and the Structure of Society.* New York, Norton and Co.

Coleman, R.J. (1971) *Supplementary Benefits and Administrative Review of Administrative Action.* London, Child Poverty Action Group.

Colenutt, B. (1975) Behind the Property Lobby *in: Political Economy and the Housing Question.* (Papers presented at the Housing Workshop of the Conference of Social Economists.) London.

Commission for Racial Equality (1980) *Local Authorities and the Housing Implications for Section 71 of the Race Relations Act 1976.* London, the Commission.

Commission of the European Communities (1977) *The Perception of Poverty in Europe.* Brussels. Document V/171/77-E.

Committee on Abuse of Social Security Benefits (1973) *Report.* London, HMSO. Cmnd. 5228.

Committee on Administrative Discretions (1973) *Report.* Parliamentary Paper (Australia) No. 316.

Committee on Housing in Greater London (1965) *Report.* London, HMSO. Cmnd. 2605.

Committee on One-Parent Families (1974) *Report.* London, HMSO. Cmnd. 5629.

Committee on the Enforcement of Judgment Debts (1969) *Report.* London, HMSO. Cmnd. 3909.

Committee on the Rent Acts (1971) *Report.* London, HMSO. Cmnd. 4609.

Commons, J.R. (1924) *Legal Foundations of Capitalism.* New York, Macmillan Company.

Community Relations Commission (1976) *Housing in Multi-Racial Areas.* London, the Commission.

The Consumer Council (1970) *Justice Out of Reach. A Case for Small Claims Courts.* London, HMSO.

Cook, T. (ed.) (1979) *Vagrancy: Some New Perspectives.* London, Academic Press.

Cooper, J. (1983) *Public Legal Services.* London, Sweet & Maxwell.

Corina, L. (1976) *Housing Allocation Policy and Its Effects: A Case Study from Oldham CDP.* York, Department of Social Administration and Social Work, University of York.

Corina, L., Collis, P. and Crosby, C. (1979) *Oldham CDP: The Final Report.* York, Department of Social Administration and Social Work, University of York.

Cornish, W.R. (1968) *The Jury.* Harmondsworth, Penguin Books.

Corrigan, P. and Ginsburg, N. (1975) Tenants' Struggle and Class Struggle *in: Political Economy and the Housing Question.* London, Political Economy of Housing Workshop, Conference of Socialist Economists.

Cotler, I. and Marks, H. (eds.) (1977) *The Law and the Poor in Canada.* Montreal, Black Rose Books.

Cottrell, J. (1980) From Rushcliffe to Benson – and Back. 43 *Modern Law Review* 549.

Council for Public Interest Law (1976) *Balancing the Scales of Justice: Financing Public Interest Law in America*. Washington DC.

Cousins, P.F. (1978) Participation and Pluralism in South London. 4 *London Journal* 204.

Coventry CDP (1975) *Final Report: Coventry and Hillfields: Prosperity and the Persistence of Inequality*. Coventry, Coventry CDP.

Cox, A (1976) The New Dimensions of Constitutional Adjudication. 51 *Washington Law Review* 791.

Cox, B. (1975) *Civil Liberties in Britain*. Harmondsworth, Penguin.

Craig, G., Mayo, M. and Sharman, N. (1979) *Jobs and Community Action*. London, Routledge & Kegan Paul.

Cramton, R.C. (1982) Why Legal Services for the Poor. 68 *American Bar Association Journal* 550.

Cranston, R. (1979a) From Co-operative to Coercive Federalism and Back? 10 *Federal Law Review* 121.

Cranston, R. (1979b) *Regulating Business: Law and Consumer Agencies*. London, Macmillan Press.

Cranston, R. (1981) Legal Services and Social Policy *in* Cashman, P. (ed.), *Research and the Delivery of Legal Service*. Sydney, Law Foundation of New South Wales.

Cranston, R. (1984) *Consumers and the Law*, 2nd edn. London, Weidenfeld & Nicolson.

Crine, S. (1980) *Legal Minimum Wages*. London, Workers' Educational Association.

Crine, S. (1981) *The Pay and Conditions of Homeworkers*. London, Low Pay Unit.

Crossman, R.H.S. (1955) *Socialism and the New Despotism*. London, Fabian Society. Fabian Tract No. 298.

Crossman, R. (1975) *The Diaries of a Cabinet Minister*. London, Hamish Hamilton & Jonathan Cape.

Crouch, C. (1977) Introduction: the Place of Participation in Politics *in* Crouch, C. (ed.), *British Political Sociology Yearbook*, vol. 3: *Participation in Politics*. London, Croom Helm.

Crouch, C. (ed.) (1980) *Can Tenants Run Housing?* London, Fabian Society, Fabian Research Series 344.

Cullingworth Committee (1969) *Council Housing Purposes, Procedures and Priorities*. 9th Report of the Housing Management Sub-Committee of the Central Housing Advisory Committee. London, HMSO.

Cunningham, J. (1976) A Birthday Shelter Didn't Want. *Guardian* 1 December 1976, p. 15.

Cunnington, H.J. (1977) Communication between Welfare Agencies and Clients *in: The Delivery of Welfare Services*. Canberra, AGPS.

Curran, B.A. (1977) *The Legal Needs of the Public*. Chicago, American Bar Foundation.

Cutting, M. (1976) Tenants in the County Court. *LAG Bulletin* 101.

Cutting, M. (1977) *Landlord: Private or Public? A Study of the Rent Act 1974*. The Catholic Housing Aid Society Occasional Papers/4.

Dalton, M. (1742) *The Country Justice*. London.

Damer, S. (1974) Wine Alley: the Sociology of a Dreadful Enclosure. 22 *Sociological Review* 221.

Dannefer, D. and Schutt, R.K. (1982) Race and Juvenile Justice Processing in Court and Police Agencies. 87 *American Journal of Sociology* 1113.

Darke, R. (1979) Public Participation and State Power: the Case of South Yorkshire. 7 *Policy and Politics* 337.

David, H. (1976) The Settlement of the Newark Public Housing Rent Strike: the Tenants Take Control. 10 *Clearinghouse Review* 103.

David, H. and Callan, J.M. (1974) Newark's Public Housing Rent Strike: the High-Rise Ghetto Goes to Court. 7 *Clearinghouse Review* 581.

Davies, C. (1971) Pre-Trial Imprisonment: A Liverpool Study. 11 *British Journal of Criminology* 32.

Davies, D.J.L. (1935) The Interpretation of Statutes in the Light of their Policy by the English Courts. 35 *Columbia Law Review* 519.

Davies, J.G. (1972) *The Evangelistic Bureaucrat*. London, Tavistock.

Davies, P. and Freedland, M. (1979) *Labour Law*. London, Weidenfeld & Nicolson.

Davis, A., McIntosh, N. and Williams, J. (1977) *The Management of Deprivation. Final Report of Southwark Community Development Project*. London, Polytechnic of the South Bank.

Davis, K.C. (1978) *Administrative Law Treatise* (vol. 1), 2nd edn. San Diego, K.C. Davis Pub. Co.

Deacon, A. (1976) *In Search of the Scrounger*. London, G. Bell & Sons. Occasional Papers on Social Administration No. 60.

Deacon, A. (1978) The Scrounging Controversy. Public Attitudes Towards the Unemployed in Contemporary Britain. 12 *Social and Economic Administration* 120.

Dean, M. (1975) On the Rights Side of the Law. *The Guardian*, 30 June 1975, p. 11.

Dean, P., Keenan, T. and Kerney, F. (1980) Taxpayers' Attitudes to Income Tax Evasion. *British Tax Review* 28.

Dearlove, J. (1974) The Control of Change and the Regulation of Community Action in Jones, D. and Mayo, M. (eds.), *Community Work One*. London, Routledge & Kegan Paul.

de Friend, R. (1979) Welfare Law, Legal Theory and Legal Education in Partington, M. and Jowell, J. (eds.), *Welfare Law and Policy*. London, Pinter.

Denning, Sir A. (1949) *Freedom under the Law*. London, Stevens.

Denning, Sir A. (1955) *The Road to Justice*. London, Stevens.

Dennis, N. (1970) *People and Planning: the Sociology of Housing in Sunderland*. London, Faber.

Dennis, N. (1972) *Public Participation and Planners' Blight*. London, Faber.

Dennis, N. (1978) Housing Policy Areas: Criteria and Indicators in Principle and Practice. 3 *Institute of British Geographers, Transactions* No. 1 (n.s.) 2.

Department of Employment and Productivity (1969) *A National Minimum Wage: An Inquiry*. London, HMSO.

Department of Employment and Department of Health and Social Security

(1981) *The Payment of Benefits to Unemployed People*. London, HMSO.

Department of the Environment (1977a) *Housing Policy*. London, HMSO. Cmnd. 6851.

Department of the Environment (1977b) *Housing Policy: Technical Volume*. London, HMSO.

Department of the Environment (1977c) *The Review of the Rent Acts: A Consultation Paper*. London, HMSO.

Department of Health and Social Security (1978) *Social Assistance: A Review of the Supplementary Benefits Scheme in Great Britain*. London.

Department of Health and Social Security (1980) *Income During Initial Sickness: A New Strategy*. London, HMSO, Cmnd. 7864.

Derfner, A. (1973) Racial Discrimination and the Right to Vote. 26 *Vanderbilt Law Review* 523.

de Schweinitz, K. (1943) *England's Road to Social Security*. Philadelphia, University of Pennsylvania Press.

de Smith, S.A. (1980) *Judicial Review of Administrative Action*, 4th edn by J.M. Evans. London, Stevens.

de Tocqueville, A.C.H.M.C. (1966) *Democracy in America*, ed. by Mayer, J.P. and Lerner, M.; a new tr. by Lawrence, G. New York, Harper & Row.

Devlin, Lord (1976) The Courts and the Abuse of Power. *The Times*, 27 October 1976, p. 12.

Devlin, P.A. (1978) Judges, Government and Politics. 41 *Modern Law Review* 501.

Devlin, P.A. (1979) *The Judge*. Oxford, Oxford University Press.

Dicey, A.V. (1885) *Lectures Introductory to the Study of the Law of the Constitution*. London, Macmillan & Co.

Dicey, A.V. (1914) *Lectures on the Relation between Law and Public Opinion in England during the Nineteenth Century*, 2nd edn. London, Macmillan.

Dicey, A.V. (1962) *Lectures on the Relation Between Law and Public Opinion in England during the Nineteenth Century*. Reprint of 1914 edn. London, Macmillan.

Dicey, A.V. (1965) *An Introduction to the Study of the Law of the Constitution*, 10th edn. London, Macmillan.

Dickens, B.M. (1970) Discretion in Local Authority Prosecutions. *Criminal Law Review* 618.

Dickens, P. (1977) Squatting and the State. 40 *New Society* 219.

Dickey, B. (1980) *No Charity There. A Short History of Social Welfare in Australia*. Melbourne, Nelson.

Dienes, C.T. (1970) Judges, Legislators, and Social Change. 13 *American Behavioural Scientist* 511.

Diplock, Sir K. (1978) The Courts as Legislators *in* Harvey, B.W. (ed.), *The Lawyer and Justice*. London, Sweet & Maxwell.

Direct Action. London.

Dixon, D. (1980) 'Class Law' – the Street Betting Act of 1906. 8 *International Journal of the Sociology of Law* 101.

Dixon, R.G. (1972) The Welfare State and Mass Justice: A Warning from the Social Security Disability Program. *Duke Law Journal* 681.

Domberger, S. and Sherr, A. (1980) *Economic Efficiency in the Provision of Legal*

Services. Centre for Industrial, Economic and Business Research, University of Warwick, Coventry.

Dorskind, J. (1978) The Concept of 'Availability' in California's Unemployment Insurance Program. 66 *Californian Law Review* 1293.

Dowdell, E.G. (1932) *A Hundred Years of Quarter Sessions: The Government of Middlesex from 1660 to 1760*. Cambridge, Cambridge University Press.

Downes, D. (1979) Praxis Makes Perfect: A Critique of Critical Criminology *in* Downes, D. and Rock, P., *Deviant Interpretations*. London, Martin Robertson.

Drake, M. (1977) Who Are the Homeless? 42 *New Society* 464.

Drake, M., O'Brien, M. and Biebuyck, T. (1981) *Single and Homeless*. London, HMSO.

Dror, Y. (1959) Law and Social Change. 33 *Tulane Law Review* 787.

Dumsday, W.H. (1902) *The Relieving Officers' Handbook*. London, Hadden, Best & Co.

Duniway, B.C. (1966) The Poor Man in the Federal Courts. 18 *Stanford Law Review* 1270.

Dunlop, O.J. and Denman, R.D. (1912) *English Apprenticeship and Child Labour*. London, T. Fisher Unwin.

Dunstan, J. (1850) *A Treatise on the Poor Law of England*. London, Shaw & Sons.

Durcan, J. and McCarthy, W. (1974) The State Subsidy Theory of Strikes: An Examination of Statistical Data for the Period 1956–70. 12 *British Journal of Industrial Relations* 26.

Dworkin, G. (1965) The Progress and Future of Legal Aid in Civil Litigation. 28 *Modern Law Review* 432.

Dworkin, R. (1977) *Taking Rights Seriously*. London, Duckworth.

Dyos, H.J. and Wolff, M. (eds.) (1973) *The Victorian City*. London, Routledge & Kegan Paul.

East London Claimants' Union (1974) East London Claimants' Union and the Concept of Self Management *in* Jones, D. and Mayo, M. (eds.), *Community Work One*. London, Routledge & Kegan Paul.

Edelhertz, H. (1970) *The Nature, Impact and Prosecution of White Collar Crime*. National Institute of Law Enforcement and Criminal Justice. Washington, U.S. Government Printer.

Eden, Sir F.M. (1965) *The State of the Poor*. Facsimile of 1797 edn. New York, A.M. Kelley.

Editorial (1840) State of the Poor, and of Crime, in the Cities and Towns of England. 4 *Justice of the Peace* 39.

Editorial (1973) Welfare Law Practice. 117 *Solicitors' Journal* 153.

Editorial (1978a) Judges and the Rent Acts. *LAG Bulletin* 78.

Editorial (1978b) More Judges and the Rent Acts. *LAG Bulletin* 127.

Edsall, N.C. (1971) *The Anti-Poor Law Movement 1834–1844* Manchester, Manchester University Press.

Edwards, B. (1979) Organizing the Unemployed in the 1920s *in* Craig, C., Mayo, M. and Sharma, N. (eds.), *Jobs and Community Action*. London, Routledge & Kegan Paul.

Edwards, J. and Batley, R. (1978) *The Politics of Positive Discrimination: An Evaluation of the Urban Programme 1967–77*. London, Tavistock Publications.

Eekelaar, J. (1978) *Family Law and Social Policy*. London, Weidenfeld & Nicolson.

Ehrlich, E. (1936) *Fundamental Principles of the Sociology of Law*. Cambridge, Mass., Harvard University Press.

Elks, L. (1974) *The Wage Stop*. London, Child Poverty Action Group.

Elliott, B. and McCrone, D. (1975) Landlords in Edinburgh: Some Preliminary Findings. 23 *Sociological Review* 539.

Ellison, R. (1979) *Occupational Pension Schemes*. London, Oyez.

Elton, G.R. (1955) *England Under the Tudors*. London, Methuen.

Ely, J.H. (1980) *Democracy and Distrust*. Cambridge, Mass., Harvard University Press.

Emmet, T. and Lister, R. (1976) *Under the Safety Net*. London, Child Poverty Action Group.

Engels, F. (1973) *The Condition of the Working-Class in England*. Reprint of 1892 authorised English edn. Moscow, Progress Publishers.

English, J. (1976) Housing Allocation and a Deprived Scottish Estate. 13 *Urban Studies* 319.

English, J. (1979) Access and Deprivation in Local Authority Housing *in* Jones, C. (ed.), *Urban Deprivation and the Inner City*. London, Croom Helm.

English, J. *et al.* (1976) *Slum Clearance: the Social and Administrative Context in England and Wales*. London, Croom Helm.

Environmental Health Officers Association (1975–1983) *Environmental Health Report* (Annual). London.

Ermer, V.B. (1972) *Street-Level Bureaucrats in Baltimore: The Case of House Code Enforcement*. Ph.D. Thesis, John Hopkins University, Baltimore.

Essex, S. and Gore, T. (1979) Time for a New Reform Act? *New Statesman* 968.

Evans, D.L. (1974) *The Law of Landlord and Tenant*. London, Butterworths.

Farrand, J.T. (1978) *The Rent Act 1977. The Protection from Eviction Act 1977*. London, Sweet & Maxwell.

Fassnidge, H. and Robson, P. (1977) Housing Repairs in Context. *LAG Bulletin* 156.

Felstiner, W.L.F. (1975) Avoidance as Dispute Processing: an Elaboration. 9 *Law and Society Review* 695.

Fenn, P. (1980) Sources of Disqualification for Unemployment Benefit 1960–76. 18 *British Journal of Industrial Relations* 240.

Ferris, J. (1972) *Participation in Urban Planning: The Barnsbury Case*. London, Bell.

Feuerstein, B.A. and Shestack, J.J. (1950) Landlord and Tenant – the Statutory Duty to Repair. 45 *Illinois Law Review* 205.

Field, F. (1973) Test Case Strategy. 27 *Poverty* 5.

Field, F. (1979) Poverty and Inequality. 42 *Poverty* 3.

Field, F. (1980) *An Unfair Quota*. Low Pay Paper No. 32. London, Low Pay Unit.

Field, F. (1981) *Inequality in Britain: Freedom, Welfare and the State*. London, Fontana.

Field, F. and Winyard, S. (1977) The Effects of the Trade Boards Act *in* Field, F. (ed.), *Are Low Wages Inevitable?* Nottingham, Spokesman Books.

Fifoot, C.H.S. (1959) *Judges and Jurists in the Reign of Victoria*. London, Stevens & Son.

Finer, S.E. (1952) *The Life and Times of Sir Edwin Chadwick*. London, Methuen.

Finnis, N. (1978) The Heartless and the Homeless. 3 *Roof* 138.

Fishman, R.P. (1978) *Housing for All Under Law*. Cambridge, Ballinger.

Fitzgerald, J.M. (1975) The Contract Buyers League and the Courts: a Case Study of Poverty Litigation. 9 *Law and Society Review* 165.

Fitzgerald, J.M. (1977) *Poverty and the Legal Profession in Victoria*. Canberra, Australian Government Publishing Service.

Flinn, M.W. (1976) Medical Services Under the New Poor Law *in* Fraser, D. (ed.), *The New Poor Law in the Nineteenth Century*. London, Macmillan Press.

Flora, P. (1981) Solution or Source of Crisis? The Welfare State in Historical Perspective *in* Mommsen, W.J. (ed.), *The Emergence of the Welfare State in Britain and Germany 1850–1950*. London, Croom Helm.

Fodden, S.R. (1974) Landlord and Tenant and Law Reform. 12 *Osgoode Hall Law Journal* 441.

Fogelson, F.B. and Freeman, H.E. (1968) Legal Knowledge and Casework with Delinquent Adolescents and their Families *in* Wheeler, S. (ed.), *Controlling Delinquents*. New York, John Wiley & Sons.

Foley, R. (1739) *Laws Relating to the Poor from the Forty-Third of Queen Elizabeth to the Third of King George II*. London, Woodward.

Foote, C. (1956) Vagrancy-Type Law and Administration. 104 *University of Pennsylvania Law Review* 603.

Ford, J. (1975) The Role of the Building Society Manager in the Urban Stratification System. 12 *Urban Studies* 295.

Ford, R. (1926) Imprisonment for Debt. 25 *Michigan Law Review* 24.

Forster, G.C.F. (1973) *The East Riding Justices of the Peace in the Seventeenth Century*. East Yorkshire Local History Society.

Foster, K. (1973) The Location of Solicitors. 36 *Modern Law Review* 153.

Foster, K. (1979) From Status to Contract: Legal Form and Work Relations 1750–1850. *Warwick Law Working Papers*, vol. 3, No. 1. University of Warwick.

Fraenkel, O.K. (1937) Restrictions on Voting in the United States. 1 *National Lawyers' Guild Quarterly* 135.

Francis, R.G. and Stone, R.C. (1956) *Service and Procedure in Bureaucracy*. Minneapolis, University of Minnesota Press.

Franey, R. (1980) Punishment for Rent Arrears. 5 *Roof* 80.

Franey, R. (1983) *Poor Law: The Mass Arrest of Homeless Claimants in Oxford*. London, CHAR.

Fraser, D. (1973) *The Evolution of the British Welfare State*. London, Macmillan Press.

Fraser, D. (ed.) (1976) *The New Poor Law in the Nineteenth Century*. London, Macmillan Press.

Freeden, M. (1978) *The New Liberalism*. Oxford, Clarendon Press.

Freedland, M.R. (1970) *The Application of the General Principles of the Law of Contract to the Termination of the Employment Relationship*. Ph.D. Thesis, Oxford.

Freedland, M.R. (1976) *The Contract of Employment*. Oxford, Clarendon Press.

Freeman, A. (1911) *The Basis of 'Ability to Pay'*. National Conference on the Prevention of Destitution, Report of the Proceedings. London.

Freeman, M.D.A. (1974) *The Legal Structure*. London, Longman.

Freeman, M.D.A. (1980) Rules and Discretion in Local Authority Social Services Departments: The Children and Young Persons Act 1963 in Operation. *Journal of Social Welfare Law* 84.

Friedland, M.L. (1975) *Access to the Law*. Toronto, Carswell.

Friedman, L. (1966) Public Housing and the Poor: An Overview. 54 *Californian Law Review* 642.

Friedman, L. (1967) Legal Rules and the Process of Social Change. 19 *Stanford Law Review* 786.

Friedman, L. (1968) *Government and Slum Housing: A Century of Frustration*. Chicago, Rand McNally.

Friedman, L. (1969) Social Welfare Legislation: An Introduction. 21 *Stanford Law Review* 217.

Friedman, L. (1971) The Idea of Right as a Social and Legal Concept. 27 *Journal of Social Issues* 189.

Friedman, L. (1978) Access to Justice: Social and Historical Context *in* Cappelletti, M. (ed.), *Access to Justice*, vol. 2, bk 1, 3. Milan, Giuffre.

Friedman, L. (1981) Claims, Disputes, Conflicts and the Modern Welfare State *in* Cappelletti, M. (ed.), *Access to Justice and the Welfare State*. Alphen van den Rijn, Sijthoff.

Friedman, L. and Ladinsky, J. (1967) Social Change and the Law of Industrial Accidents. 67 *Columbia Law Review*. 50.

Friedman, M. (1962) *Capitalism and Freedom*. Chicago, University of Chicago Press.

Friedmann, W. (1972) *Law in a Changing Society*, 2nd edn. Harmondsworth, Penguin.

Friend, A. (1978) *Laws that Leak*. London, Garratt Lane Law Centre.

Frost, A. and Howard, C. (1977) *Representation and Administrative Tribunals*. London, Routledge & Kegan Paul.

Frug, G.E. (1978) The Judicial Power of the Purse. 126 *University of Pennsylvania Law Review* 715.

Fryer, B. (1981) State, Redundancy and the Law *in* Fryer, B., Hunt, A., McBarnet, D. and Moorhouse, B. (eds.), *Law, State and Society*. London, Croom Helm.

Fulbrook, J. (1975) *The Appellant and His Case*. London, Child Poverty Action Group.

Fulbrook, J. (1978) *Administrative Justice and the Unemployed*. London, Mansell.

Fuller, L.L. (1963) Collective Bargaining and the Arbitrator. *Wisconsin Law Review* 3.

Furniss, N. and Tilton, T. (1977) *The Case for the Welfare State: From Social Security to Social Equality*. Bloomington, Indiana University Press.

Galanter, M. (1974) Why the 'Haves' Come Out Ahead: Speculations on the Limits of Legal Change. 9 *Law and Society Review* 95.

Galanter, M. (1975) Afterword: Explaining Litigation. 9 *Law and Society Review* 347.

Galanter, M. (1976a) Delivering Legality: Some Proposals for the Direction of Research. 11 *Law and Society Review* 225.

Galanter, M. (1976b) The Duty *Not* to Deliver Legal Services. 30 *University of*

Miami Law Review 929.

Galanter, M. (1983) Mega-Law and Mega-Lawyering in the Contemporary United States *in* Dingwall, R. and Lewis, P. (eds.), *The Sociology of the Professions*. London, Macmillan.

Gallacher, W. (1949) *Revolt on the Clyde*, 3rd edn. London, Lawrence & Wishart.

Galligan, D.J. (1976) The Nature and Function of Policies within Discretionary Power. *Public Law* 332.

Galper, J. (1970) The Speenhamland Scales: Political, Social, or Economic Disaster? 44 *Social Service Review* 54.

Galper, J. (1980) *Social Work Practice: A Radical Perspective*. Englewood Cliffs, N.J., Prentice-Hall.

Gamble, A. (1980) National Insurance Adjudication, *SCOLAG*, No. 42.

Gans, H. (1972) The Positive Functions of Poverty. 78 *American Journal of Sociology* 275.

Ganz, G. (1979) The Role of the Ombudsman in Welfare Law *in* Partington, M. and Jowell, J. (eds.), *Welfare Law and Policy*. London, Frances Pinter.

Garner, R. (1977) *Social Change*. Chicago, Rand McNally.

Garth, B. (1980) *Neighborhood Law Firms for the Poor*. Alphen van den Rijn, Sijthoff & Noordhoff.

Garth, B. (1982) The Movement Toward Procedural Informalism in North America and Western Europe: A Critical Survey *in* Abel, R.L. (ed.), *The Politics of Informal Justice*. New York, Academic.

Gauldie, E. (1974) *Cruel Habitations: A History of Working-Class Housing 1780–1918*. London, Allen & Unwin.

Gee, D. (1974) *Slum Clearance*. Shelter Report. London, Shelter.

Gennard, J. (1977) *Financing Strikers*. London, Macmillan.

Gennard, J. (1979) Do Workers Get Their Strikes on the Cheap? *New Statesman*, 14 September 1979, p. 375.

Gennard, J. and Lasko, R. (1975) The Individual and the Strike. 13 *British Journal of Industrial Relations* 346.

Genovese, E.D. (1972) *Roll, Jordan, Roll. The World the Slaves Made*. New York, Pantheon.

George, V. (1973) *Social Security and Society*. London, Routledge & Kegan Paul.

George, V. and Wilding, P. (1976) *Ideology and Social Welfare*. London, Routledge & Kegan Paul.

George, W.E. (1976) Development of the Legal Services Corporation. 61 *Cornell Law Review* 681.

Gibson, C. (1971) The Effect of Legal Aid on Divorce in England and Wales. (Part 1) 1 *Family Law* 90. (Part II) 1 *Family Law* 122.

Gibson, C.S. (1980) Divorce and the Recourse to Legal Aid. 43 *Modern Law Review* 609.

Giddens, A. (1973) *The Class Structure of the Advanced Societies*. London, Hutchinson University Library.

Gilbert, B.B. (1970) *British Social Policy 1914–1939*. London, Batsford.

Ginsburg, N. (1979) *Class, Capital and Social Policy*. London, Macmillan Press.

Gittell, M. (1980) *Limits to Citizen Participation*. London, Sage.

416 REFERENCES

Glasser, C. (1979) The Royal Commission: the Remuneration of the Profession and Legal Aid. *LAG Bulletin* 201.

Glastonbury, B. (1971) *Homeless Near a Thousand Homes*. London, George Allen.

Glazer, N. (1978) Should Judges Administer Social Services? *The Public Interest*, No. 50, 64.

Gleason, J.H. (1969) *The Justices of the Peace in England, 1558 to 1640*. Oxford, Clarendon.

Glotta, R. (1967) The Radical Lawyer and the Dynamics of a Rent Strike. 26 *National Lawyers Guild Practitioner* 132.

Goffman, E. (1963) *Stigma*. Englewood Cliffs, New Jersey, Prentice-Hall.

Gold, M.E. (1980) Equality before the Law in the Supreme Court of Canada: A Case Study. 18 *Osgoode Hall Law Journal* 336.

Golding, P. and Middleton, S. (1978) Why Is the Press so Obsessed with Scroungers? 46 *New Society* 195.

Golding, P. and Middleton, S. (1982) *Images of Welfare*. Oxford, Martin Robertson.

Goldthorpe, J.H. (1962) The Development of Social Policy in England, 1800–1914. 4 *Transactions of the Fifth World Congress of Sociology* 50.

Goodin, R.E. (1982) Freedom and the Welfare State: Theoretical Foundations. 11 *Social Policy* 149.

Goodman, P.H. (1960) Eighteenth-Century Poor Law Administration in the Parish of Oswestry. 56 *Transactions of the Shropshire Archaeological Society* 328.

Goodwin, L. (1972) *Do the Poor Want to Work?* Washington DC, Brookings.

Gough, I. (1979) *The Political Economy of the Welfare State*. London, Macmillan Press.

Grabosky, P.N. (1978) Theory and Research on Variations in Penal Severity. 5 *British Journal of Law and Society* 103.

Grace, C. and Wilkinson, P. (1978) *Negotiating the Law: Social Workers and Legal Services*. London, Routledge & Kegan Paul.

Grad, F.P. (1968) *Legal Remedies for Housing Code Violations*. National Commission for Urban Problems. Washington DC, US Government Printer.

Grant, M. (1975) Recovery of Overpaid Benefit. *LAG Bulletin* 126.

Graveson, R.H. (1953) *Status in the Common Law*. London, Athlone Press.

Gray, F. (1976) Selection and Allocation in Council Housing. 1 (n.s.) *Institute of British Geographers, Transactions* 34.

Graycar, A. and Davis, J. (1979) *The Australian Assistance Plan Evaluation Report No. 2* (Department of Social Security). Canberra, AGPS.

Green, G. (1974) Towards Community Power *in* Glennerster, H. and Hatch, S. (eds.), *Positive Discrimination and Inequality*. Fabian Research Series 314. London, Fabian Society.

Green, G. and Stewart, A. (1975) Why the Leasehold Reform Act is not Working. 125 *New Law Journal* 400.

Green, S. (1979) *Rachman*. London, Michael Joseph.

Greve, J. (1965) *Private Landlords in England*. Occasional Papers on Social Administration No. 13. London, G. Bell.

Greve, J., Page, D. and Greve, S. (1971) *Homelessness in London*. Edinburgh,

Scottish Academic Press.
Gribetz, J. and Grad, F.P. (1966) Housing Code Enforcement: Sanctions and Remedies. 66 *Columbia Law Review* 1254.
Griffith, J.A.G. (1977) *The Politics of the Judiciary*. London, Fontana/Collins.
Griffiths, J. (1979) Is Law Important? 54 *New York University Law Review* 339.
Griffiths, J. (1980) A Comment on Research into 'Legal Needs' in Blankenburg, E. (ed.), *Innovations in the Legal Services*. Cambridge, Mass., Oelgeschlager, Gunn & Hain.
Griffiths, P. (1975) *Homes Fit for Heroes*. A Shelter Report on Council Housing. London, Shelter.
Gross, H. (1979) *A Theory of Criminal Justice*. New York, Oxford University Press.
Gurney-Champion, F.C.G. (1926) *Justice and the Poor in England*. London, Routledge & Sons.
Haar, C.M. and Liebman, L. (1977) *Property and Law*. Boston, Little, Brown & Co.
Hadden, T. (1976) Public Health and Housing Legislation – Towards an Integrated Code of Procedure. 27 *Northern Ireland Law Quarterly* 245.
Hadden, T. (1978) *Compulsory Repair and Improvement*. Centre for Socio-Legal Studies, Oxford, Research Study No. 1.
Hadden, T. (1979a) Housing Action Areas: an Antiquated Set of Legal Tools. *Journal of Planning and Environmental Law* 725.
Hadden, T. (1979b) *Housing: Repairs and Improvements*. London, Sweet & Maxwell.
Hadley, R. and Hatch, S. (1981) *Social Welfare and the Failure of the State*. London, Allen & Unwin.
Hague, N.T. (1967) *Leasehold Enfranchisement*. London, Sweet & Maxwell.
Hale, Sir M. (1684) *Several Tracts*. London, W. Shrowsbery.
Halévy, E. (1952) *The Rule of Democracy 1905–1914*, 2nd edn. London, Ernest Benn.
Halévy, E. (1972) *The Growth of Philosophic Radicalism*. Reprint of 1928 translated edn. London, Faber & Faber.
Hall, A.S. (1974) *The Point of Entry. A Study of Client Reception in the Social Services*. London, Allen & Unwin.
Hall, J. (1974) Jurisprudential Theories and the Effectiveness of Law in Pennock, J.R. and Chapman, J.W. (eds.), *The Limits of Law*. New York, Lieber-Atherton, Nomos XV.
Hall, S., Critcher, C., Jefferson, T., Clarke, J. and Roberts, B. (1978) *Policing the Crisis*. London, Macmillan.
Halsbury, H.S.G., Earl of. *The Laws of England*. 1907–1917. London, Butterworth.
Halsbury, H.S.G., Earl of (1937) *Halsbury's Laws of England*, 2nd edn. London, Butterworth.
Halsey, A.H., Heath, A.F. and Ridge, J.M. (1980) *Origins and Destinations*. Oxford, Clarendon Press.
Hammer, R.P. and Hartley, J.M. (1978) Procedural Due Process and the Welfare Recipient: A Statistical Study of AFDC Fair Hearing in Wisconsin. *Wisconsin Law Review* 145.

Hammond, J.L. and B. (1913) *The Village Labourer 1760–1832*. London, Longmans, Green & Co.

Hampson, E.M. (1934) *The Treatment of Poverty in Cambridgeshire 1597–1834*. Cambridge, Cambridge University Press.

Hampton, W. (1970) *Democracy and Community: a Study of Politics in Sheffield*. London, Oxford University Press.

Hanbury, H.G. and Maudsley, R.H. (1976) *Modern Equity*, 10th edn. London, Stevens.

Handler, J.F. (1966) Controlling Official Behaviour in Welfare Administration. 54 *California Law Review* 479.

Handler, J.F. (1972) *Reforming the Poor*. New York, Basic Books.

Handler, J.F. (1976a) Public Interest Law: Problems and Prospects *in* the American Assembly, *Law and the American Future*. Englewood Cliffs, N.J., Prentice-Hall.

Handler, J.F. (1976b) *Social Reform Groups and Law Reformers*. Discussion Paper. Institute for Research on Poverty, University of Wisconsin-Madison.

Handler, J.F. (1978) *Social Movements and the Legal System. A Theory of Law Reform and Social Change*. New York, Academic Press.

Handler, J.F. (1979) *Protecting the Social Service Client. Legal and Structural Controls on Official Discretion*. New York, Academic Press.

Handler, J.F. and Goodstein, A.E. (1968) The Legislative Development of Public Assistance. *Wisconsin Law Review* 414.

Handler, J.F. and Hollingsworth, E.J. (1969) Stigma, Privacy, and Other Attitudes of Welfare Recipients. 22 *Stanford Law Review* 1.

Handler, J.F. and Hollingsworth, E.J. (1970) Reforming Welfare: the Constraints of the Bureaucracy and the Clients. 118 *University of Pennsylvania Law Review* 1167.

Handler, J.F. and Hollingsworth, E.J. (1970) Work, Welfare and the Nixon Reform Proposals. 22 *Stanford Law Review* 907.

Handler, J.F., Hollingsworth, E.J. and Erlanger, H.S. (1978) *Lawyers and the Pursuit of Legal Rights*. New York, Academic Press.

Hanks, P. (1979) Cohabitation and Natural Justice. 4 *Legal Service Bulletin* 177.

Hanks, P. (1980) *Evaluating the Effectiveness of Legal Aid Programs*. Canberra, Commonwealth Legal Aid Commission.

Hannington, W. (1977) *Unemployed Struggles 1919–1936. My Life and Struggles Amongst the Unemployed*. Reprint of 1936 edn. London, Lawrence & Wishart.

Hansen, J. (1980) The Poor Cut Off. 51 *New Society* 241.

Harbert, W.B. (1965) Who Owes Rent? 13 *Sociological Review* 149.

Harloe, M., Isaacharoff, R. and Minns, R. (1974) *The Organisation of Housing*. London, Heinemann Educational Books.

Harlow, C. (1976) Administrative Reaction to Judicial Review. *Public Law* 116.

Harlow, C. (1981) Legislation: Discretion, Social Security and Computers. 44 *Modern Law Review* 546.

Harring, S.L. (1977) Class Conflict and the Suppression of Tramps in

Buffalo, 1892–1894. 11 *Law and Society Review* 873.
Harris, B. (1976) Legal Aid: Three Recent Decisions. 126 *New Law Journal* 636.
Harris, N. (1982) The Appointment of Legally Qualified Chairmen for SBATS. 132 *New Law Journal* 495.
Hart, H.L.A. (1961) *The Concept of Law*. Oxford, Clarendon Press.
Hart, J. (1974) Nineteenth-Century Social Reform: A Tory Interpretation of History *in* Flinn, M.W. and Smout, T.C. (eds.), *Essays in Social History*. Oxford, Clarendon.
Hartwell, R.M. *et al.* (1972) *The Long Debate on Poverty*. London, IEA.
Harvey, A. (1964) *Tenants in Danger*. Harmondsworth, Penguin.
Harvey, A. (1977) Dunning It. 42 *New Society* 360.
Harvey, A. (1979) *Remedies for Rent Arrears. A Study in the London Borough of Camden.* London, Shelter.
Hasson, R. (1981) The Cruel War: Social Security Abuse in Canada. 3 *Canadian Taxation* 114.
Hatch, S., Fox, E. and Legg, C. (1977) *Research and Reform. The Case of the Southwark CDP 1969–1972*. London, Hatch, Fox and Legg.
Hay, D. (1977) Poaching and the Game Laws on Cannock Chase *in* Hay, D. *et al.*, *Albion's Fatal Tree*. London, Allen Lane.
Hay, J.R. (1975) *The Origins of the Liberal Welfare Reforms 1906–1914*. London, Macmillan Press.
Hayek, F.A. (1960) *The Constitution of Liberty*. London, Routledge & Kegan Paul.
Hayek, F.A. (1973, 1976, 1979) *Law, Legislation and Liberty*, vols. 1, 2, 3. Chicago, University of Chicago Press.
Hayek, F.A., Friedman, M., Stigler, G.J. *et al.* (1975) *Rent Control. A Popular Paradox*. Vancouver, The Fraser Institute.
Hayes, M. (1978–79) Supplementary Benefit and Financial Provision Orders. *Journal of Social Welfare Law* 216.
Hazard, G.C. Jr. (1969) Social Justice Through Civil Justice. 36 *University of Chicago Law Review* 699.
Hazard, G. (1970) Law Reforming in the Anti-Poverty Effort. 37 *University of Chicago Law Review* 242.
Hazell, R. (1978) Independence and Fusion *in* Hazell, R. (ed.), *The Bar on Trial*. London, Quartet Books.
Heidenheimer, A.T., Heclo, H., and Adams, C.T. (1976) *Comparative Public Policy*. London, Macmillan.
Hennock, E.P. (1973) *Fit and Proper Persons*. London, Edward Arnold.
Henriques, U.R.Q. (1967) Bastardy and the New Poor Law. 37 *Past and Present* 103.
Henriques, U.R.Q. (1979) *Before the Welfare State*. London, Longman.
Herman, M. (1972) *Administrative Justice and Supplementary Benefits*. London, G. Bell & Sons. Occasional Papers on Social Administration No. 47.
Hermann, R., Single, E. and Boston, J. (1977) *Counsel for the Poor: Criminal Defense in Urban America*. Lexington, Mass., Lexington Books.
Hetzel, O. *et al.* (1978) Making Allowances for Housing Costs: A Comparison of British and US Experiences. 1 *Urban Law and Policy* 229.

Hewart, G. (1929) *The New Despotism*. London, Ernest Benn.

Hiestand, F.J. (1970) *The Politics of Poverty Law with Justice for Some: an Indictment of the Law by Young Advocates*. Boston, Beacon Press.

Higgins, J. (1978a) Regulating the Poor Revisited. 7 *Journal of Social Policy* 189.

Higgins, J. (1978b) *The Poverty Business: Britain and America*. Oxford, Blackwell.

Higgins, J. (1980) Social Control Theories of Social Policy. 9 *Journal of Social Policy* 1.

Higgins, W. (1978) State Welfare and Class Warfare *in* Duncan, G. (ed.), *Critical Essays in Australian Politics*. Melbourne, Edward Arnold.

Hill, D.M. (1970) *Participating in Local Affairs*. Harmondsworth, Penguin Books.

Hill, Sir F. (1966) *Georgian England*. Cambridge, Cambridge University Press.

Hill, L.M. (ed.) (1975) *The Ancient State Authoritie, and Proceedings of the Court of Requests*, (selected) by Sir Julius Caesar. London, Cambridge University Press.

Hill, M.J. (1969) The Exercise of Discretion in the National Assistance Board. 47 *Public Administration* 75.

Hill, M. (1974a) *Policies for the Unemployed: Help or Coercion?* London, Child Poverty Action Group. Poverty Pamphlet 15.

Hill, M. (1974b) Some Implications of Legal Approaches to Welfare Rights. 4 *British Journal of Social Work* 187.

Hill, M. (1976) *The State, Administration and the Individual*. London, Fontana/Collins.

Hill, M. (1979) Social Worker and the Delivery of Welfare Benefits *in* Partington, M. and Jowell, J. (eds.), *Welfare Law and Policy*. London, Frances Pinter.

Hill, M. and Laing, P. (1979) *Social Work and Money*. London, Allen & Unwin.

Hill, O. (1883) *Homes of the London Poor*, 2nd edn. London, Macmillan.

Hillman, J. (1980) The Shrinking Pool of Private Rented Housing. 53 *New Society* 17.

Hirsch, W.Z., Hirsch, J.G. and Margolis, S. (1975) Regression Analysis of the Effects of Habitability Laws upon Rent: an Empirical Observation on the Ackerman-Komesar Debate. 63 *California Law Review* 1098.

Hoath, D.C. (1978) Rent Books: the Law, its Uses and Abuses. 1978–79 *Journal of Social Welfare Law* 3.

Hoath, D. (1983) *Homelessness* London, Sweet & Maxwell.

Hobsbawm, E.J. (1968a) *Industry and Empire*. London, Weidenfeld & Nicolson.

Hobsbawm, E.J. (1968b) *Labouring Men*. London, Weidenfeld & Nicolson.

Hobsbawm, E.J. (1977a) *The Age of Capital 1848–1875*. Abacus edn. London, Sphere Books.

Hobsbawm, E.J. (1977b) *The Age of Revolution*. Abacus edn. London, Sphere Books.

Hobsbawm, E.J. and Rudé, G. (1969) *Captain Swing*. London, Lawrence and Wishart.

Hodge, H. (1975) Discretion in Reality *in* Adler, M. and Bradley, A. (eds.),

Justice, Discretion and Poverty. London, Professional Books.

Hodge, H. (1979) A Test Case Strategy *in* Partington, M. and Jowell, J. (eds.), *Welfare Law and Policy*. London, Frances Pinter.

Hofstadter, R. (1955) *The Age of Reform from Bryan to F.D.R.* New York, Knopf.

Holdsworth, Sir W. (1935–1972) *A History of English Law*, 17 vols. London, Methuen & Co.

Holdsworth, Sir W. (1938) *Some Makers of English Law*. Cambridge, Cambridge University Press.

Holingsworth, E.J. (1977) Ten Years of Legal Services for the Poor *in* Haveman, R.H. (ed.), *A Decade of Federal Antipoverty Programs*. New York, Academic Press.

Holman, R. (1978) *Poverty*. London, Martin Robertson.

Home Affairs Committee (1980) *Race Relations and the 'SUS' Law. Second Report. 1979–80 Session*. HC 559. London, HMSO.

Home Affairs Committee, House of Commons (1981) *Vagrancy Offences*. HC 271. London, HMSO.

Home Office 1966 *Report of the Departmental Committee on Legal Aid in Criminal Proceedings*. Cmnd 2934. London, HMSO.

Home Office (1976) *Report of the Working Party on Vagrancy and Street Offences*. London, HMSO.

Honoré, T. (1982) *The Quest for Security: Employees, Tenants and Wives*. London, Stevens.

Hood, R. (1962) *Sentencing in Magistrates' Courts*. London, Stevens.

Hopkins, A. (1977) Is There a Class Bias in Criminal Sentencing? 42 *American Sociological Review* 176.

Horowitz, D. (1977) *The Courts and Social Policy*. Washington, Brookings Institution.

Horwitz, M.J. (1977) *The Transformation of American Law 1780–1860*. Cambridge, Mass., Harvard University Press.

Hosticka, D. (1979) We Don't Care About What Happened, We Only Care about What is Going to Happen: Lawyer-Client Negotiations of Reality. 26 *Social Problems* 599.

House of Representatives Standing Committee on Aboriginal Affairs (1980) *Aboriginal Legal Aid*. Canberra, Australian Government Publishing Service.

Hudson, W. and Tingey, J.C. (eds.) (1910) *The Records of the City of Norwich*. Norwich.

Hughes, D.J. (1976) What is a Nuisance? – The Public Health Act 1936 Revisited. 27 *Northern Ireland Law Quarterly* 131.

Hughes, D.J. (1981) *Public Sector Housing Law*. London, Butterworths.

Hughes, D.J. and Jones, S.R. (1979) Bias in the Allocation and Transfer of Local Authority Housing: a Study of the Reports of the Commission for Local Administration in England. [1978–9] *Journal of Social Welfare Law* 273.

Hughes, G. (1974) Social Justice and the Courts *in* Pennock, J.R. and Chapman, J.W. (eds.), *The Limits of Law*. New York, Lieber-Atherton.

Hughes, J. (1979) Social Welfare – Domestic Purposes Benefit: Lessons from the Furnage Case. *New Zealand Law Journal* 32.

Hughes, S. (1976) *The Development of Statutory Legal Aid and Advice*. Paper given at Research Students' Conference on Socio-Legal Studies, Oxford.

Hunter, L. (1974) The State Subsidy Theory of Strikes: A Reconsideration. 12 *British Journal of Industrial Relations* 438.

Indritz, T. (1971) The Tenants' Rights Movement. 1 *New Mexico Law Review* 1.

Issalys, P. (1979) *The Pension Appeals Board. A Study of Administrative Procedure in Social Security Matters*. Ottawa, Law Reform Commission of Canada.

Issalys, P. and Watkins, G. (1978) *Unemployment Insurance Benefits*. Minister of Supply and Services, Ottawa.

Isserman, A.J. (1979) *CIO* v. *Hague*: The Battle of Jersey City. 36 *Guild Practitioner* 14.

Ivatts, J. (1979) *Homelessness and Legislation*. London, Department of Government, Brunel University.

Jackson, L.R. and Johnson, W.A. (1974) *Protest by the Poor: the Welfare Rights Movement in New York City*. Lexington, Mass. Lexington Books.

Jackson, R.M. (1977) *The Machinery of Justice in England*, 7th edn. Cambridge, Cambridge University Press.

Jacob, I.H. (1978) Access to Justice in England *in* Cappelletti, M. and Garth, B. (eds.), *Access to Justice*, vol. 1. Milan, Giuffre.

Jacobs, B. (1912) *A Manual of Public Health Law*. London, Sweet & Maxwell.

Jacobs, D. (1982) Inequality and Economic Crime. 66 *Sociology and Social Research* 12.

Jacobs, S. (1976) *The Right to a Decent House*. London, Routledge & Kegan Paul.

Jaffe, L.J. and Henderson, E.G. (1956) Judicial Review and the Rule of Law: Historical Origins. 72 *Law Quarterly Review* 345.

James, D.C. (1974) Homelessness: Can the Courts Contribute? 1 *British Journal of Law and Society* 195.

Janowitz, M. (1976) *Social Control of the Welfare State*. Chicago, University of Chicago Press.

Janowitz, M. (1978) *The Last Half-Century*. Chicago, University of Chicago Press.

Jeaffreson, J.C. (1888) *Middlesex County Records*. Clerkenwell.

Jennings, W.I. (1930) Poor Relief in Industrial Disputes. 46 *Law Quarterly Review* 225.

Jennings, W.I. (1936a) Courts and Administrative Law – the Experience of English Housing Legislation. 49 *Harvard Law Review* 426.

Jennings, W.I. (1936b) *The Poor Law Code, and the Law of Unemployment Assistance*, 2nd edn. London, Charles Knight & Co.

Jennings, W.I. (1937) Judicial Process at its Worst. 1 *Modern Law Review* 111.

Jennings, W.I. (1959) *The Law and the Constitution*, 5th edn. London, University of London Press.

John, A. (1975) Race in the Inner City *in* Butterworth, E. and Holman, R. (eds.), *Social Welfare in Modern Britain*. London, Fontana.

Johnson, E. (1974) *Justice and Reform: the Formative Years of the OEO Legal Services Program*. New York, Russell Sage Foundation.

Johnson, E. Jr., Bice, S.H., Bloch, S.A., *et al.* (1978) Access to Justice in the

United States: The Economic Barriers and some Promising Solutions *in* Cappelletti, M. and Garth, B. (eds.), *Access to Justice*, vol. 1, bk. 2. Milan, Giuffre.

Johnson, P. (1978) Green Form Divorce. *LAG Bulletin* 286.

Johnson, T.J. (1972) *Professions and Power*. London, Macmillan.

Joint Select Committee on the Family Law Act (1980) *Family Law in Australia*. Canberra, Australian Government Publishing Service.

Jones, D. (1980) A New Eve in the Organisation and Delivery of Legal Aid in Australia. 54 *Australian Law Journal* 502.

Jones, D. and Mayo, M. (1974) *Community Work 1*. London, Routledge & Kegan Paul.

Jones, G.W. (1979) Central-Local Relations, Finance and the Law. 2 *Urban Law and Policy* 25.

Jones, H.W. (1958) The Rule of Law and the Welfare State. 58 *Columbia Law Review* 143.

Jones, L.A. (1906) *A Treatise on the Law of Landlord and Tenant*. Indianapolis, Bobbs-Merrill.

Jones, W.J. (1967) *The Elizabethan Court of Chancery*. Oxford, Clarendon Press.

Jordan, A. (1975) *Long Term Unemployed People Under Conditions of Full Employment*. Canberra, Australian Government Publishing Service.

Jordan, B. (1973) *Paupers*. London, Routledge & Kegan Paul.

Jordan, B. (1974) *Poor Parents*. London, Routledge & Kegan Paul.

Jordan, D. (1977) *The Wages of Uncertainty*. London, Low Pay Unit.

Jordan, D. (1979) *A New Employment Programme Wanted for Disabled People*. London, Disability Alliance and Low Pay Unit.

Jowell, J. (1973) The Legal Control of Administrative Discretion. *Public Law* 178.

Jowell, J.L. (1975) *Law and Bureaucracy*. New York, Dunellen Publishing Co.

Justice. (1977) *Lawyers and the Legal System*. London, Justice.

Kahn-Freund, O. (1949) Minimum Wages Legislation in Great Britain. 97 *University of Pennsylvania Law Review* 778.

Kahn-Freund, O. (1962) English Law and American Law – Some Comparative Reflections *in* Newman, R.A. (ed.), *Essays in Jurisprudence in Honor of Roscoe Pound*. New York, Bobbs-Merrill.

Kahn-Freund, O. (1965) The Courts and Social Policy *in: Law in Action*. London, British Broadcasting Corporation.

Kahn-Freund, O. (1976) The Impact of Constitutions on Labour Law. *Cambridge L.J.* 240.

Kahn-Freund, O. (1977a) Blackstone's Neglected Child: The Contract of Employment. 93 *Law Quarterly Review* 508.

Kahn-Freund, O. (1977b) *Labour and the Law*, 2nd edn. London, Stevens & Sons.

Kamenka, E. and Tay, A. (1975) Beyond Bourgeois Individualism – The Contemporary Crisis in Law and Legal Ideology *in* Kamenka, E. and Neale, R.S. (eds.), *Feudalism, Capitalism and Beyond*. London, Edward Arnold.

Kanowitz, L. (1969) *Women and the Law*. Albuquerque, University of New Mexico Press.

Karn, V.A. (1979) Low Income Owner-Occupation in the Inner City *in* Jones, C. (ed.), *Urban Deprivation and the Inner City*. London, Croom Helm.

Kay, J. and Morris, N. (1982) No Longer Rich on the Dole? 59 *New Society* 267.

Keating, W.D. and Heskin, A.D. (1972) Rent Withholding: Recent Legislative Developments. 5 *Clearinghouse Review* 728.

Keeler, J. (1980) The Citizen and Welfare *in* Goldring, J. *et al.* (eds.), *Access to Law*. Canberra, Faculty of Law, A.N.U.

Keith-Lucas, B. (1952) *The English Local Government Franchise: A Short History*. Oxford, B. Blackwell.

Keith-Lucas, B. (1962) Poplarism. *Public Law* 52.

Kelly, D. St. L. (1977) *Debt Recovery in Australia*. Australian Government Commission of Inquiry into Poverty. Law and Poverty Series. Canberra, AGPS.

Kelly, P. and Lorber, S. The Medway: Unmet Need for Legal Services. *Praxis No. 4*, University of Kent.

Kennedy, W. (1913) *English Taxation 1640–1799* (new impression 1964). London, Frank Cass & Co.

Kerr, R.W. (1978) Living Together as Husband and Wife. 1 *Low Income Law* (Canada) 29.

Kimball, E.G. (ed.) (1955) *Some Sessions of the Peace in Lincolnshire 1381–1396*. Lincoln Record Society, No. 49.

Kincaid, J.C. (1975) *Poverty and Equality in Britain*. Harmondsworth, Penguin Books.

King, M. (1976) *The Effects of a Duty Solicitor Scheme: an Assessment of the Impact upon a Magistrates' Court*. London, Cobden Trust.

King, M.I. and Lowry, D.R. (1972) The Spouse in the House Case. 1(1) *Bulletin of Canadian Welfare Law* 16.

Kinghan, M. (1977) *Squatters in London*. London, Shelter.

Kirby, D.A. (1979) *Slum Housing and Residential Renewal: the Case in Urban Britain*. London, Longman.

Knowles, C.C. and Pitt, P.H. (1972) *The History of Building Regulation in London 1689–1972*. London, Architectural Press.

Kohler, P.A., Zacher, H.F. and Partington, M. (eds.) (1982) *The Evolution of Social Insurance 1881–1981*. London, Frances Pinter.

Komesar, N.K. (1973) Return to Slumville: a Critique of the Ackerman Analysis of Housing Code Enforcement and the Poor. 82 *Yale Law Journal* 1175.

Komesar, N.K. (1978) Housing, Zoning and the Public Interest *in* Weisbrod, B.A. (ed.), *Public Interest Law*. Berkeley, University of California Press.

Komesar, N.K. and Weisbrod, B.A. (1978) The Public Interest Law Firm: a Behavioural Analysis *in* Weisbrod, B.A. (ed.), *Public Interest Law*. Berkeley, University of California Press.

Krislov, S. (1963) The *Amicus Curiae* Brief: from Friendship to Advocacy. 72 *Yale Law Journal* 694.

Krislov, S. (1973) The OEO Lawyers Fail to Constitutionalise a Right to Welfare: a Study in the Uses and Limits of the Judicial Process. 58 *Minnesota Law Review* 211.

Krohn, R.G. and Tiller, R. (1969) Landlord-Tenant Relations in a Declining Montreal Neighbourhood *in* Halmos, P. (ed.), *Sociological Studies in Economics and Administration*. The Sociological Review Monograph 14.

Ladinsky, J. (1970) *Law, Legal Services and Social Change: a Note on the OEO Legal Services Program*. Discussion Paper, Institute for Research on Poverty, University of Wisconsin-Madison.

LAG (The Legal Action Group) (1977a) *Legal Services in Criminal Cases*. (Memorandum by the Legal Action Group submitted to the Royal Commission on Legal Services). London, LAG.

LAG (1977b) *The Review of the Rent Acts. Submissions to the Department of the Environment*. London, LAG.

LAG (1978) *Life Without Lawyers*. London, LAG.

Lambert, J., Paris, C. and Blackaby, B.(1978) *Housing Policy and the State*. London, Macmillan Press.

Lambeth Community Law Centre (1977) *Annual Report 1976/77*. London, Lambeth Community Law Centre.

Lamond, R.P. (1892) *The Scottish Poor Laws*, 2nd edn. Glasgow, William Hodge & Co.

Law Centres Working Group (1977) *Rent Act 1978?* Submissions to the Department of the Environment's review of the Rent Acts. London, Tottenham Neighbourhood Law Centre.

Law Centres Working Group (1978) *Evidence to the Royal Commission on Legal Services*.

The Law Commission (1972) *Seventh Annual Report 1971–1972*, Law Commission No. 50.

The Law Commission (1973) *Liability for Damage or Injury to Trespassers and Related Questions of Occupiers' Liability*. Working Paper No. 52.

The Law Commission (1975) *Codification of the Law of Landlord and Tenant. Report on Obligations of Landlords and Tenants*. Law Com. No. 67 (HC 377).

The Law Commission (1976) *Report on the Liability for Damage or Injury to Trespassers and Related Questions of Occupiers' Liability*. Law Com. No. 75. Cmnd. 6428.

The Law Commission (1981) *The Financial Consequences of Divorce*. Cmnd. 112. London, HMSO.

The Law Reform Commission (Australia) (1980) *Sentencing of Federal Offenders. Report No. 15 Interim*. Canberra, AGPS.

Law Reform Commission of British Columbia (1973) *Landlord and Tenant Relationships: Residential Tenancies*. Project No. 12. Vancouver.

Law Reform Commission of Canada (1976) *A Report on Dispositions and Sentences in the Criminal Process*. Ottawa, Information Canada.

The Law Society (1972) *Legal Aid and Advice: Report of the Law Society and Comments and Recommendations of the Lord Chancellor's Advisory Committee. 1970–71: 21st Report*. London, HMSO.

The Law Society (1978) Advertising. Statement by the Council of the Law Society on Advertising Restrictions. 97 *Law Notes* 213.

The Law Society (1981) *Legal Aid Handbook. 1981*, 5th edn. London, HMSO.

Lawrence, R. (1978) Representation at National Insurance Tribunals: A Research Note. 5 *British Journal of Law and Society* 246.

Lawson, J. and Silver, H. (1973) *A Social History of Education in England*. London, Methuen.

Lazerson, M.H. (1982) In the Halls of Justice, the Only Justice is in the Halls *in* Abel L. (ed.), *The Politics of Informal Justice*, Vol. 1. New York, Academic.

Leat, D. (1975) The Rise and Role of the Poor Man's Lawyer. 2 *British Journal of Law and Society* 166.

Leevers, M., Nee, P. and Rogers, J. (1977) *A Fair Hearing? – Possession Hearings in the County Court*. London, SHAC (The London Housing Aid Centre).

Lefcourt, R. (1971) Lawyers for the Poor Can't Win *in* Lefcourt, R. (ed.), *Law Against the People*. New York, Vintage.

Leffler, K.B. (1978) Minimum Wages, Welfare, and Wealth Transfers to the Poor. 21 *Journal of Law and Economics* 345.

Legal Aid Annual Reports. London, HMSO.

Legal Services Corporation (1980) *The Delivery Systems Study. A Policy Report to the Congress and the President of the United States*. Washington DC, Legal Services Corporation.

Le Grand, J. (1978) Who Benefits from Public Expenditure? 45 *New Society* 614.

Le Grand, J. (1982) *The Strategy of Equality*. London, Allen & Unwin.

Leibfried, S. (1979) Public Assistance in the Federal Republic of Germany *in* Partington, M. and Jowell, J. (eds.), *Welfare Law and Policy*. London, Frances Pinter.

Leigh, L. (1979) Vagrancy and the Criminal Law *in* Cook, T. (ed.), *Vagrancy*. London, Academic Press.

Lempert, R. and Ikeda, K. (1970) Evictions from Public Housing: Effects of Independent Review. 35 *American Sociological Review* 852.

Levenson, H. (1977) Legal Aid for Mitigation. 40 *Modern Law Review* 523.

Levenson, H. (1979) Legal Aid in Summary Proceedings – London's Magistrates Revisited. 129 *New Law Journal* 375.

Levenson, H. (1982) Legal Aid League Tables. *LAG Bulletin* February 1982, 8.

Levin, J. (1979) Too Much Care. 49 *New Society* 508.

Levin, J. (1981) *A Guide to Supplementary Benefit Law*. London, Legal Action Group.

Levin, P. (1971) Participation: The Planners v. the Public? 17 *New Society* 1090.

Levitan, S.A., Rein, M. and Marwick, D. (1972) *Work and Welfare Go Together*. Baltimore, John Hopkins University Press.

Levy, M. (1977) The Supreme Court in Retreat: Wealth Discrimination and Mr Justice Marshall. 4 *Texas Southern University Law Review* 209.

Lewin, Sir G.A. (1828) *A Summary of the Laws Relating to the Government and Maintenance of the Poor*. London, William Benning.

Lewis, N. (1973) Supplementary Benefits Appeal Tribunals. *Public Law* 257.

Lewis, N. (1976) Council Housing Allocation: Problems of Discretion and Control. 54 *Public Administration* 147.

Lewis, N. (1977) Council House Tenants: Time for Change? *Journal of Planning and Environmental Law* 155.

Lewis, N. (1979) What's the Use of Complaining? A Brief Word on the Local

Ombudsman. *LAG Bulletin* 58.

Lewis, N. and Livock, R. (1979) Council House Allocation Procedures: Some Problems of Discretion and Control. 2 *Urban Law and Policy* 133.

Lewis, P.S.C. (1973) Unmet Legal Needs *in* Morris, P., White, R. and Lewis, P., *Social Needs and Legal Action*. London, Robertson.

Lewis, P.S.C. (1978) *Paper for the Royal Commission on Legal Services*. Unpublished.

Lewis, R.A. (1952) *Edwin Chadwick and the Public Health Movement 1832–1854*. London, Longman.

Lidstone, K.W., Hogg, R. and Sutcliffe, F. (1980) *Prosecutions by Private Individuals and Non-Police Agencies*. Royal Commission on Criminal Procedure, Research Study No. 10. London, HMSO.

Liebman, L. (1976) The Definition of Disability in Social Security and Supplementary Security Income: Drawing the Bounds of Social Welfare Estates. 89 *Harvard Law Review* 833.

Lineberry, R.L. (1974) Mandating Urban Equality: The Distribution of Municipal Public Services. 53 *Texas Law Review* 26.

Lipsky, M. (1970) *Protest in City Politics: Rent Strikes, Housing and the Power of the Poor*. Chicago, Rand McNally.

Lipsky, M. (1980) *Street-Level Bureaucracy*. New York, Russell Sage Foundation.

Lipsky, M. and Neumann, C.A. (1969) Landlord-Tenant Law in the United States and West Germany – A Comparison of Legal Approaches. 44 *Tulane Law Review* 36.

Lister, R. (1973) *As Man and Wife? A Study of the Cohabitation Rule*. London, Child Poverty Action Group.

Lister, R. (1974a) *Justice for the Claimant. A Study of Supplementary Benefit Appeal Tribunals*. London, Child Poverty Action Group.

Lister, R. (1974b) *Take-Up of Means-tested Benefits*. London, Child Poverty Action Group.

Lister, R. (1977) *Patching Up the Safety Net?* London, Child Poverty Action Group.

Lister, R. (1979) *The No-cost No-benefit Review*. London, Child Poverty Action Group.

Lister, R. (1980) Discretion: Getting the Balance Right *in* Coussins, J. (ed.), *Dear SSAC – An Open Letter to the Social Security Advisory Committee*. London, Child Poverty Action Group.

Lister, R. (1981) *Welfare Benefits*. London, Sweet & Maxwell.

Lister, R. and Emmett, T. (1976) *Under the Safety Net*. London, Child Poverty Action Group.

Little, G. (1976) Housing and the Law. Paper presented to SSRC Conference on Socio-Legal Studies, Oxford.

Liverpool Community Development Project (1977) *Government Against Poverty?* Oxford, Social Evaluation Unit.

Logan, B.H. and Sabl, J.J. (1976) The Great *Green* Hope: the Implied Warranty of Habitability in Practice. 28 *Stanford Law Review* 729.

Loney, M. (1981) The British Community Development Projects: Questioning the State. 16 *Community Development Journal* 55.

Longmate, N. (1974) *The Workhouse*. London, Temple Smith.

Lorant, J. (1981) *Poor and Powerless. Fuel Problems and Disconnections*. London, Child Poverty Action Group.

Lumley, W.G. (1842) *A Popular Treatise on the Law of Settlement and Removals*, 2nd edn. London, Shaw & Sons.

Lumley, W.G. (1951) *The Public Health Acts Annotated*, 12th edn. by Simes, E. and Scholefield, C.E. London, Butterworth.

Lumley, W.G. and E. (1876) *The Public Health Act 1876*. London, Shaw & Sons.

Lustgarten, L.S. and Elliott, M.J. (1976) Benefits Uprating: a Problem in Administrative Law. 126 *New Law Journal*.

Lustgarten, L. (1981) The New Legislation. 131 *New Law Journal* 71, 95, 119.

Lynes, T. (1979a) The Relevance of Historical Research *in* Partington, M. and Jowell, J. (eds.), *Welfare Law and Policy*. London, Frances Pinter.

Lynes, T. (1979b) Pensions: Contracted Out. 49 *New Society* 19.

Lynes, T. (1982) At the Tribunal. 59 *New Society* 145.

Macaulay, S. (1963) Non-Contractual Relations in Business: a Preliminary Study. 28 *American Sociological Review* 55.

Macaulay, S. (1979) Lawyers and Consumer Protection Laws. 14 *Law and Society Review* 115.

MacCallum, S.V. and Bradbrook, A.J. (1978) Discrimination Against Families in the Provision of Rented Accommodation. 6 *Adelaide Law Review* 439.

MacCormick, D.N. (1977) Rights in Legislation *in* Hacker, P.M.S. and Raz, J. (eds.), *Law, Morality and Society*. Oxford, Clarendon.

MacDonagh, O. (1958) The Nineteenth-Century Revolution in Government: a Reappraisal. 1 *Hist. Journal* 52.

MacDonagh, O. (1977) *Early Victorian Government*. London, Weidenfeld & Nicolson.

MacDonagh, O. (1980) Pre-transformations: Victorian Britain *in* Kamenka, E. and Tay, A. (eds.), *Law and Social Control*. London, Edward Arnold.

MacDonald, M. (1975) *Why Don't More Eligibles Use Food Stamps?* University of Wisconsin-Madison, Institute for Research on Poverty Discussion Paper 292.

MacGregor, S. (1981) *The Politics of Poverty*. London, Longman.

Mackay, T. (1899) *A History of the English Poor Law*. London, P.S. King & Son.

Maclennan, D. (1978) The 1974 Rent Act – Some Short-Run Supply Effects. 88 *Economic Journal* 331.

Macmorran, A. and Naldrett, E.J. (1905) *Orders issued by the Local Government Board . . . under the Acts relating to the Relief of the Poor*, 2nd edn. London, Shaw.

Macpherson, C.B. (1979) *The Life and Times of Liberal Democracy*. Oxford, Oxford University Press.

McAllister, I. (1977) *The Northern Ireland Social Democratic and Labour Party. Political Opposition in a Divided Society*. London, Macmillan.

McAuslan, P. (1975) *Land, Law and Planning*. London, Weidenfeld & Nicolson.

McAuslan, P. (1978) Administrative Law and Administrative Theory:

the Dismal Performance of Administrative Lawyers. 9 *Cambrian Law Review* 40.

McAuslan, P. (1979) The Ideologies of Planning Law. 2 *Urban Law and Policy* 1.

McAuslan, P. (1980) *The Ideologies of Planning Law*. Oxford, Pergamon Press.

McBarnet, D. (1976) Pre-trial Procedures and the Construction of Conviction *in* Carlen, P. (ed.), *The Sociology of Law*. Keele, Staffordshire, University of Keele.

McBarnet, D.J. (1978) The Police and the State: Arrest, Legality and the Law *in* Littlejohn, G., *et al.*, *Power and the State*. London, Croom Helm.

McBarnet, D.J. (1981) *Conviction, Law, the State and Construction of Justice*. London, Macmillan.

McBriar, A.M. (1966) *Fabian Socialism and English Politics 1884–1918*. Cambridge, Cambridge University Press.

McCarthy, C.P. (1974) *The Consequences of Legal Advocacy: OEO's Lawyers and the Poor*. PhD. Thesis. University of California, Berkeley.

McCrone, D. and Elliott, B. (1979) What Else Does Someone with Capital Do? 48 *New Society* 512.

McDonald, L. (1969) *Social Class and Delinquency*. London, Faber.

McDowell, L. (1978) Competition in the Private-rented Sector: Students and Low-income Families in Brighton, Sussex. 3 *Institute of British Geographers, Transactions* 55.

McGovern, W.M. (1978) Dependent Promises in the History of Leases and Other Contracts. 52 *Tulane Law Review* 659.

McGregor, O.R., Blom-Cooper, L. and Gibson, C. (1970) *Separated Spouses*. London, Duckworth and Co.

McGregor, O.R. (1973) 'Family Breakdown and Social Policy.' 59 *Proceedings of the British Academy* 3.

McNeil, K., *et al.* (1979) Market Discrimination against the Poor and the Impact of Consumer Disclosure Laws: the Used-Car Industry. 13 *Law and Society Review* 695.

Maguire, J.M. (1923) Poverty and Civil Litigation. 36 *Harvard Law Review* 361.

Maine, H.S. (1930) *Ancient Law*. London, John Murray.

Malcolmson, R.W. (1980) A Set of Ungovernable People *in* Brewer, J., and Styles, J. (eds.), *An Ungovernable People*. London, Hutchinson.

Manchester, A.H. (1980) *A Modern Legal History of England and Wales 1750–1950*. London, Butterworths.

Mannheim, H. (1946) *Criminal Justice and Social Reconstruction*. London, Kegan Paul.

Mannheim, H. (1965) *Comparative Criminology*. London, Routledge & Kegan Paul.

Mannheim, H., Spencer, J.C. and Lynch, G. (1957) Magisterial Policy in the London Juvenile Courts. 7 *British Journal of Delinquency* 13.

Markovits, R.S. (1976) The Distributive Impact, Allocative Efficiency, and Overall Desirability of Ideal Housing Codes: Some Theoretical Clarifications. 89 *Harvard Law Review* 1815.

Marks, F.R., Leswing, K. and Fortinsky, B.A. (1972) *The Lawyer, the Public and Professional Responsibility.* Chicago, American Bar Foundation.

Marris, P. and Rein, M. (1974) *Dilemmas of Social Reform.* Harmondsworth, Penguin Books.

Marshall, D. (1926) *The English Poor in the Eighteenth Century.* London, George Routledge & Sons.

Marshall, G. (1971) *Constitutional Theory.* Oxford, Clarendon Press.

Marshall, J.D. (1968) *The Old Poor Law 1795-1834.* London, Macmillan.

Marshall, T.H. (1963) Citizenship and Social Class *in* Marshall, T.H., *Sociology at the Crossroads and Other Essays.* London, Heinemann.

Martin, D.L. (1976) Civil Remedies Available to Residential Tenants in Ontario: the Case for Assertive Action. 14 *Osgoode Hall Law Journal* 65.

Martin, P.W. (1979) Public Assurance of an Adequate Minimum Income in Old Age: the Erratic Partnership Between Social Insurance and Public Assistance. 64 *Cornell Law Review* 437.

Martin, R.M. (1980) *TUC: the Growth of a Pressure Group 1868-1976.* Oxford, Clarendon Press.

Mashaw, J.L., *et al.* (1978) *Social Security Hearings and Appeals.* Lexington, Mass., Heath.

Mason, T. (1979) Politics and Planning of Urban Renewal in the Private Housing Sector *in* Jones, C. (ed.), *Urban Deprivation and the Inner City.* London, Croom Helm.

Massey, G. (1975) Studying Social Class: the Case of Embourgoisement and the Culture of Poverty. 22 *Social Problems* 595.

Matza, D. (1967) The Disreputable Poor *in* Bendix, R. and Lipset, S.M. (eds.), *Class, Status and Power.* London, Routledge and Kegan Paul.

Mawby, R. (1979) *Policing the City.* Westmead, Herts, Saxon House.

Mayhew, L.H. (1968) *Law and Equal Opportunity.* Cambridge, Massachusetts, Harvard University Press.

Mayhew, L.H. (1975) Institutions of Representation: Civil Justice and the Public. 9 *Law and Society Review* 401.

Mayhew, L. and Reiss, A.J. (1969) The Social Organisation of Legal Contacts. 34 *American Sociological Review* 309.

Mayne, A.J.C. (1983) *Fever, Squalor and Vice.* Brisbane, University of Queensland Press.

Meacher, M. (1974) *Scrounging on the Welfare. The Scandal of the Four Week Rule.* London, Arrow.

Meadows, W. (1742) *Cases and Resolutions of Cases Adjudg'd in the Court of King's Bench,* 4th edn. London.

Medcalf, L. (1978) *Law and Identity: Lawyers, Native Americans and Legal Practice.* Beverly Hills, Calif., Sage.

Megarry, R.E. (1967-1970) *The Rent Acts,* 10th edn. London, Stevens. 3 vols.

Megarry, R.E. and Wade, H.W.R. (1975) *The Law of Real Property.* London, Stevens & Sons.

Meltsner, M. and Schrag, P.G. (1974) *Public Interest Advocacy: Materials for Clinical Legal Education.* Boston, Little, Brown & Co.

Merrett, S. (1979) *State Housing in Britain.* London, Routledge & Kegan Paul.

Merricks, W. (1978) Calculating Eligibility and Contributions. [Legal Aid Notes]. *LAG Bulletin* 89.

References   431

Merricks, W. (1979) The Aims and Goals of the Law Centre Movement in
Partington, M. and Jowell, J. (eds.), *Welfare Law and Policy*. London,
Frances Pinter.
Merrifield, L.S. (1980) The Origin of Australian Labour Conciliation and
Arbitration in Gamillsheg, F., *et al.* (eds.), *In Memoriam. Sir Otto Kahn-
Freund*. Munich, C.H. Beck'sche.
Merritt, A. (1981) *Masters and Servants Legislation*. PhD. thesis. Canberra, ANU.
Merton, R.K., *et al.* (1952) *Reader in Bureaucracy*. Glencoe, Ill. The Free
Press.
Mesher, J. (1976a) *Compensation for Unemployment*. London, Sweet & Maxwell.
Mesher, J. (1976b) The Social Security Pensions Act 1975. 39 *Modern Law
Review* 321.
Meyers, C.J. (1975) The Covenant of Habitability and the American Law
Institute. 27 *Stanford Law Review* 879.
Michelman, F.I. (1979) Welfare Rights in a Constitutional Democracy.
Washington University Law Quarterly 659.
Micklethwait, R. (1976) *The National Insurance Commissioners*. London,
Stevens.
Midwinter, E.C. (1969) *Social Administration in Lancashire 1830–1860: Poor Law,
Public Health and Police*. Manchester, Manchester University Press.
Migdal, S.D. (1979) Eviction, Harassment and Exemplary Damages. 129
New Law Journal 849.
Miliband, R. (1974) Politics and Poverty in Wedderburn, D. (ed.), *Poverty,
Inequality and Class Structure*. London, Cambridge University Press.
Miller, S.M., *et al.* (1970) Creaming the Poor. *Transaction*, vol. 7 June 1970, p.
38.
Miller, T. and D., Kraushaar, B. (1979) The Emergence of Participatory
Policies for Community Development – Anglo-American Experiences and
their Influence on Sweden. 22 *Acta Sociologica* 111.
Ministry of Health (1953) *Report of the Working Party on the Recruitment, Training
and Qualification of Sanitary Inspectors*. London, HMSO.
Minns, R. (1980) *Pension Funds and British Capitalism*. London, Heinemann.
Mishra, R. (1977) *Society and Social Policy: Theoretical Perspectives on Welfare*.
London, Macmillan.
Mitchell, A. (1974) Clay Cross. 45 *Political Quarterly* 165.
Moeran, E. (1976) *Practical Legal Aid*, 2nd edn. London, Oyez.
Moeran, E. (1977) Legal Aid and Advice in Pollard, D.W. (ed.), *Social Welfare
Law*. London, Oyez.
Mogulof, M.B. (1972) Advocates and Adversaries: Toward an
Understanding of How Social Planners Function on Behalf of the Black/
Brown/Poor. 49 *Journal of Urban Law* 689.
Moir, E. (1969) *The Justice of the Peace*. Harmondsworth, Penguin.
Monopolies and Mergers Commission (1976) *Services of Solicitors in England
and Wales: a Report on the Supply of Services of Solicitors in England and Wales in
Relation to Restrictions on Advertising*. London, HMSO.
Moore, P. (1978a) In Distress Over Rent. 43 *New Society* 371.
Moore, P. (1978b) People as Lawyers – Lay Advocacy and Self-Help. 5 *British
Journal of Law and Society* 121.

Moore, P. (1980) Counter-Culture in a Social Security Office. 53 *New Society* 68.

Moorhouse, B., Wilson, M. and Chamberlain, C. (1972) Rent Strikes – Direct Action and the Working Class. *The Socialist Register* 133.

Morris, Sir M. (1919) *The Story of English Public Health*. London, Cassell & Co.

Morris, P. (1978) Sociological Research in Legal Services. 2 *Canadian Legal Aid Bulletin* 245.

Morris, P., Cooper, J. and Byles, A. (1973a) Public Attitudes to Problem Definition and Problem Solving: a Pilot Study. 3 *British Journal of Social Work* 301.

Morris, P., White, R. and Lewis, P. (1973b) *Social Needs and Legal Action*. London, Martin Robertson.

Morris, R. (1976) Unfit Housing. 37 *New Society* 499.

Morris, R. (1979) Short-Term Schemes. 47 *New Society* 195.

Morton, J. (1979) Do the Poor Get a Fair Deal? 129 *New Law Journal* 772.

Mosier, M.M. and Soble, R.A. (1973) Modern Legislation, Metropolitan Court, Minuscule Results: a Study of Detroit's Landlord-Tenant Court. 7 *University of Michigan Journal of Law Reform* 8.

Moss, J. (1938) *The Relieving Officers' Handbook*, 7th edn. London, Hadden, Best & Co.

Mossman, M.J. (1977a) Procedures for Making Determinations in Armstrong, S., Mossman, M.J. and Sackville, R. (eds.), *Essays in Law and Poverty*. Canberra, Australian Government Publishing Service.

Mossman, M.J. (1977b) The Baxter Case: De Facto Marriage and Social Welfare Policy. 2 *University of New South Wales Law Journal* 1.

Mossman, M.J. (1979) Decision-Making by Welfare Tribunals: the Australian Experience. 29 *University of Toronto Law Journal* 218.

Moynihan, D.P. (1970) *Maximum Feasible Misunderstanding*. New York, The Free Press.

Moynihan, D.P. (1973) *The Politics of a Guaranteed Income*. New York, Random House.

Muller-Fembeck, L. and Ogus, A.I. (1976) Social Welfare and the One-Parent Family in Germany and Britain. 25 *International and Comparative Law Quarterly* 382.

Murch, M. (1980) *Justice and Welfare in Divorce*. London, Sweet & Maxwell.

Murie, A.V., Niner, P. and Watson, C. (1976) *Housing Policy and the Housing System*. London, Allen & Unwin.

Muther, P.S. (1975) Reform of Legal Aid in Sweden. 9 *The International Lawyer* 475.

Myers, D.M. (1977) *Inquiry into Unemployment Benefit Policy and Administration*. Canberra, Department of Employment and Industrial Relations and Department of Social Security.

Mylan, D. (1979) *Housing Aid and Advice Centres*. Birmingham, The Association of Housing Aid.

Myrdal, G. (1960) *Beyond the Welfare State*. London, Methuen.

NACRO Working Party (1981) *Fine Default*. London.

NCCL (National Council for Civil Liberties) (1976) *Squatting, Trespass and Civil Liberties*. London, NCCL.

Nader, R. (1976) Consumerism and Legal Services: the Merging of Movements. 11 *Law and Society Review* 247.

Nader, R. and Blackwell, K. (1973) *You and Your Pension*. New York, Grossman.

National Association of Pension Funds (1980) *Survey of Occupational Pension Schemes 1979*. London, NAPF.

National Consumer Council (1976a) *Behind with the Rent*. Discussion Paper. London, NCC.

National Consumer Council (1976b) *Tenancy Agreements Between Councils and Their Tenants*. Discussion Paper. London, NCC.

National Consumer Council (1976) *Means-Tested Benefits*. London, NCC.

National Consumer Council (1977) *Access, Allocation and Transfers in Council Housing*. The National Consumer Council's Response to the Department of the Environment. Consultation Paper, unpublished.

National Consumer Council (1977) *The Fourth Right of Citizenship. A Review of Local Advice Services*. Discussion Paper. London, NCC.

National Consumer Council / Welsh Consumer Council (1979) *Simple Justice. A Consumer View of Small Claims Procedures in England and Wales*. London.

NLADA (National Legal Aid and Defender Association) (1976) *Guidelines for Legal Defense Systems in the United States*. Final Report of the National Study Commission on Defense Services. Washington, NLADA.

Neal, D. (1978) Delivery of Legal Services – The Innovative Approach of the Fitzroy Legal Service. 11 *Melbourne University Law Review* 427.

Neligan, D. (1979) *Social Security Case Law. Digest of Commissioners' Decisions*. London, HMSO.

Nelson, W.E. (1975) *Americanization of the Common Law*. Cambridge, Mass., Harvard University Press.

Neumann, F. (1957) The Change in the Function of Law in Modern Society *in* Neumann, F., *The Democratic and the Authoritarian State*. Glencoe, Illinois Free Press.

Neville Brown, L. (1955) National Assistance and the Liability to Maintain One's Family. 18 *Modern Law Review* 113.

Newham Rights Centre (1977) *Two Years' Work 1975–1977. Lousy Houses + Dole Queues = Newham*. London, NRC.

Newnham, R. (1977) *Edinburgh: the Unnecessary Evictions*. Shelter Housing Aid Centre Report. Edinburgh, SHAC.

Newton, K. (1976) *Second City Politics*. Oxford, Clarendon Press.

Nicholls, G. (1898–1900) *A History of the English Poor Law*, vols. 1–3. London, P.S. King.

Nicol, A. (1981) Outflanking Protective Legislation – Shams and Beyond. 44 *Modern Law Review* 21.

Niner, P. (1978) *Homes to Let*. Papers in Community Studies No. 18, University of York, Department of Social Administration and Social Work.

Niskanen, W.A. (1975) Bureaucrats and Politicians. 18 *Journal of Law and Economics* 617.

Nivola, P.S. (1978) Distributing a Municipal Service: a Case Study of Housing Inspection. 40 *Journal of Politics* 59–81.

Noble (1979) The London Homeworkers Campaign *in* Craig, G., Mayo, M. and Sharman, N. (eds.), *Jobs and Community Action*. London, Routledge & Kegan Paul.

Nolan, M. (1825) *A Treatise of the Laws for the Relief and Settlement of the Poor*, vol. 1. London, J. Butterworth & Son.

Nolan, M. (1978) *A Treatise of the Laws for the Relief and Settlement of the Poor*. Reprint of the London 1805 edn. New York, Garland.

Nonet, P. (1969) *Administrative Justice: Advocacy and Change in a Government Agency*. New York, Russell Sage Foundation.

Nonet, P. and Selznick, P. (1978) *Law and Society in Transition; Toward Responsible Law*. New York, Harper & Row.

North Islington Housing Rights Project (1976) *Street by Street – Improvement and Tenant Control in Islington*. London, Shelter.

North Tyneside CDP (1978) *Final Report* (5 vols). Newcastle-upon-Tyne.

OEO (Office of Economic Opportunity) (1968) *Study of OEO Legal Services Programs*, Bay Area, California. Harry P. Stumpf, Project Director. Final Report, vol. 1.

O'Brien, P.J. (1974) The Public Goods Dilemma and the 'Apathy' of the Poor Toward Neighbourhood Organization. 48 *Social Service Review* 229.

Offe, C. (1972) Advanced Capitalism and the Welfare State. 2 *Politics and Society* 479.

Offer, A. (1977) The Origins of the Law of Property Acts 1910–25. 40 *Modern Law Review* 505.

Ogus, A.I. and Barendt, E.M. (1982) *Law of Social Security*, 2nd edn. London, Butterworths.

Olshausen, G.G. (1947) Rich and Poor in Civil Procedure. 11 *Science and Society* 11.

O'Higgins, M. (1981) Aggregate Measures of Tax Evasion: an Assessment. *British Tax Review* 286.

O'Malley, J. (1977) *The Politics of Community Action: a Decade of Struggle in Notting Hill*. Nottingham, Bertrand Russell Peace Foundation for Spokesman Books.

Ontario Law Reform Commission (1968, 1976) *Landlord and Tenant Law*. (1) *Interim Report*. (2) *Report*. Toronto, Ministry of the Attorney-General.

Ontario Law Reform Commission (1982) *Report on Class Actions*. Toronto, Ministry of the Attorney-General.

Osler, J. (1974) *Report of the Task Force on Legal Aid*. Toronto, Ministry of the Attorney-General.

Owen, D. (1976) Rent Controls: Solution or Problem? 41 *Saskatchewan Law Review* 3.

Oxley, G.W. (1974) *Poor Relief in England and Wales 1601–1834*. Newton Abbot, Devon, David & Charles.

Pahl, R.E. (1970) *Whose City? and Other Essays on Sociology and Planning*. London, Longman.

PHAS (Public Health Advisory Service) (1976) *Interim Report*. London, PHAS.

Paley, B. (1978) *Attitudes to Letting in 1976*. Office of Population Censuses and

Surveys, Social Survey Division. London, HMSO.

Paris, C. and Blackaby, B. (1979) *Not Much Improvement: Urban Renewal Policy in Birmingham*. London, Heinemann.

Parker, S. (1981) *Cohabitees*. Chichester, Barry Rose Publishers.

Parkin, F. (1975) *Class Inequality and Political Order*. St Albans, Paladin.

Parry, E.A. (1914) *The Law and the Poor*. London, Smith, Elder & Co.

Partington, M. (1974) Some Thoughts on a 'Test-Case Strategy'. 124 *New Law Journal* 236.

Partington, M. (1975) *Recent Developments in Legal Services for the Poor: Some Reflections on Experience in Coventry*. CDP Occasional Paper. The Home Office and City of Coventry Community Development Project.

Partington, M. (1976) Supplementary Benefits and the Parliamentary Commissioner *in* Adler, M. and Bradley, A. (eds.), *Justice, Discretion and Poverty*. London, Professional Books.

Partington, M. (1978a) *Claim in Time*. London, Frances Pinter.

Partington, M. (1978b) *The Legal Aid Means-Tests*. London, Child Poverty Action Group. Poverty Pamphlet 34.

Partington, M. (1979) Comment. *Public Law* 1.

Partington, M. (1980a) Landlord and Tenant: The British Experience *in* Kamenka, E. and Tay, A. (eds.), *Law and Social Control*. London, Edward Arnold.

Partington, M. (1980b) *Landlord and Tenant*. London, Weidenfeld & Nicolson.

Partington, M. (1980c) Rules and Discretion in British Social Security Law *in* Gamillscheg, F., *et al.* (eds.), *In Memoriam. Sir Otto Kahn-Freund*. Munich, C.H. Beck'sche.

Partington, M. (1981) Supplementary Benefits: Interpretation and Judgment. 131 *New Law Journal* 547.

Pateman, C. (1970) *Participation and Democratic Theory*. Cambridge, Cambridge University Press.

Paterson, A. (1975) Legal Aid as a Social Service *in* Cappelleti, M., Gordley, J. and Johnson, E. (eds.), *Toward Equal Justice*. Dobbs Ferry, N.Y., Oceana.

Pearl, D. and Gray, K. (1981) *Social Welfare Law*. London, Croom Helm.

Pennock, J.R. and Chapman, J.W. (1974) *The Limits of Law*. New York, Lieber-Atherton.

Phegan, C.S. (1977) Public Authorities, Nonfeasance and Breach of Statutory Duty. 11 *University of British Columbia Law Review* 187.

Phillimore, Sir W.G.F. (1911) Presidential Address *in: Report of the Proceedings of the National Conference on the Prevention of Destitution*. London, P.S. King & Son.

Phillips, A. (1979) Social Work and the Delivery of Legal Services. 42 *Modern Law Review* 29.

Phillips, J. and Hawkins, K. (1976) Some Economic Aspects of the Settlement Process: a Study of Personal Injury Claims. 39 *Modern Law Review* 497.

Phillipson, M. (1971) *Sociological Aspects of Crime and Delinquency*. London, Routledge & Kegan Paul.

Pickvance, C.G. (1976) On the Study of Urban Social Movements *in*

Pickvance, C.G. (ed.), *Urban Sociology: Critical Essays*. New York, St Martin's Press.

Pinchbeck, I. and Hewitt, M. (1973) *Children in English Society*. London, Routledge & Kegan Paul.

Pinker, R. (1979) *The Idea of Welfare*. London, Heinemann.

Piven, F.F. and Cloward, R.A. (1979) *Poor People's Movements. Why They Succeed, How They Fail*. New York, Vintage Books.

Podger, A.S., Raymond, J.E. and Jackson, W.S.B. (1980) *The Relationship between the Australian Social Security and Personal Income Taxation Systems – A Practical Examination*. Canberra, Department of Social Security.

Polanyi, K. (1957) *The Great Transformation*. Boston, Deacon.

Pollard, D.W. (ed.) (1977 to date) *Social Welfare Law*. London, Oyez.

Pollock, Sir F. (1929) *A First Book of Jurisprudence*, 6th edn. London, Macmillan.

Pollock, F. (1961) *Jurisprudence and Legal Essays*. A.L. Goodhart (ed.). London, Macmillan.

Pollock, S. (1975) *Legal Aid: the First 25 Years*. London, Oyez.

Polmear, C. (1978) Brown Rice or Rice Pudding: Some Dilemmas in Community Work *in* Curno, P. (ed.), *Political Issues and Community Work*. London, Routledge & Kegan Paul.

Polyviou, P. (1980) *The Equal Protection of the Laws*. London, Duckworth.

Pond, C. (1980) Tax Expenditures and Fiscal Welfare *in* Sandford, C., Pond, C. and Walker, R. (eds.), *Taxation and Social Policy*. London, Heinemann.

Poor Laws and Relief of Distress (Royal Commission) (1909) Cd. 4499, in *Reports from Commissioners, Inspectors and Others*, vol. 37.

Poor Person's Rules Committee (1925) *Report*. Cmd. 2358. London, HMSO.

Popkin, W.D. (1977) The Effect of Representation in Non-Adversary Proceedings. 62 *Cornell Law Review* 989.

Popkin, W.D. (1979) Effect of Representation on a Claimant's Success Rate – Three Study Designs. 31 *Administrative Law Review* 449.

Pound, R. (1938) *The Formative Era of American Law*. Boston, Little, Brown & Co.

Pound, R. (1947) *The Spirit of the Common Law*. Reprint of 1921 edn. Francestown, Marshall Jones.

Power, A. (1977) *Holloway Tenant Co-operative Five Years On*. Holloway Tenant Co-operative and North Islington Housing Rights Project. London.

Poynter, J.R. (1969) *Society and Pauperism*. London, Routledge & Kegan Paul.

Prichard, A.M. (1981) *Squatting*. London, Sweet & Maxwell.

Procacci, G. (1978) Social Economy and the Government of Poverty. *Ideology and Consciousness*. No. 4.

Prosser, T. (1979) Politics and Judicial Review: the Atkinson Case and its Aftermath. *Public Law* 59.

Prosser, T. (1981) The Politics of Discretion *in* Adler, M. and Asquith, S. (eds.), *Discretion and Welfare*. London, Heinemann.

Prosser, T. (1983) *Test Cases for the Poor*. London, Child Poverty Action Group.

Prottas, J.M. (1979) *People-Processing*. Lexington, Mass., Heath.

Rabin, R.L. (1976) Lawyers for Social Change: Perspective on Public

Interest Law. 28 *Stanford Law Review* 207.

Radzinowicz, L. (1956–68) *A History of English Criminal Law*, 4 vols. London, Stevens.

Rank, P.M. (1976) Repairs in Lieu of Rent. 40 *The Conveyancer and Property Lawyer*. 196.

Raz, J. (1973) On the Functions of Law *in* Simpson, A.W.B. (ed.) *Oxford Essays in Jurisprudence*. London, Oxford University Press.

Reddin, M. (1970) Universality versus Selectivity *in* Robson, W.A. and Crick, B. (eds.), *The Future of Social Services*. Harmondsworth, Penguin Books.

Redford, A. (1926) *Labour Migration in England, 1800–1850*. Manchester, Manchester University Press.

Reich, C.A. (1963) Midnight Welfare Searches and the Social Security Act. 72 *Yale Law Journal* 1347.

Reich, C.A. (1964) The New Property. 73 *Yale Law Journal* 733.

Reifner, U. (1980) Types of Legal Needs and Modes of Legalization: the Example of the Berlin Tenants Initiative *in* Blankenburg, E. (ed.), *Innovations in the Legal Services*. Cambridge, Mass., Oelgeschlager, Gunn & Hain.

Rein, M. (1977) Equality and Social Policy. 51 *Social Service Review* 565.

Rein, M. (1981) Private Provision of Welfare *in* Henderson, R.F. (ed.), *The Welfare Stakes*. Melbourne, Institute of Applied Economic and Social Research.

Renner, K. (1949) *The Institutions of Private Law*. London, Routledge & Kegan Paul.

Report on the Poor Law (1834) *see* Checkland, S.G. and E.O.A. (eds.) 1974.

Report of the Committee on Administrative Tribunals and Enquiries (1957) Cmd. 218, London, HMSO.

Rex, J. (1979) Black Militancy and Class Conflict *in* Miles, R. and Phizacklea, A. (eds.), *Racism and Political Action in Britain*. London, Routledge & Kegan Paul.

Rex, J. and Moore, R. (1971) *Race, Community and Conflict: a Study of Sparkbrook*. London, Oxford University Press.

Reynolds, J.I. (1974) Statutory Covenants of Fitness and Repair: Social Legislation and the Judges. 37 *Modern Law Review* 377.

Rhodes, F.W. (1973) *William's Canadian Law of Landlord and Tenant*. 1980 Supplement. Toronto, Carswell.

Rhodes, G. (1981) *Inspectorates in British Government*. Hemel Hempstead, Allen & Unwin.

Richardson, A. (1978a) *Social Security Users – Local Consultative Groups*. Supplementary Benefits Administrative Papers 8. London, HMSO.

Richardson, A. (1978b) *Tenant Participation in Council Housing Management*. Department of Environment, H.D.D. Occasional Paper 2/77, London.

Richardson, A. (1979) Thinking About Participation. 7 *Policy and Politics* 227.

Ringeling, A. (1981) The Passivity of Administration. 9 *Policy and Politics* 295.

Ritchie, J. and Wilson, P. (1979) *Social Security Claimants*. London, Social Survey Division, Office of Population Censuses and Surveys.

Roberts, D. (1969) *Victorian Origins of the British Welfare State*. Reprint of 1960 edn. Hamden, Conn., Archon Books.

Roberts, J.T. (1976) *General Improvement Areas.* Lexington, Mass., Saxon House.

Roberts, K., Duggan, J. and Noble, M. (1981) *Unregistered Youth Unemployment and Outreach Careers Work.* Research Paper No. 31, Department of Employment, London.

Robinson, G.E. (1925) *Public Authorities and Legal Liability.* London, University of London Press.

Robinson, M.J. (1976) Social Legislation and the Judges: a Note by Way of Rejoinder. 39 *Modern Law Review* 43.

Robson, P. (1977) *Public Health and Housing.* PHAS/Canning Town CDP.

Robson, P.W. and Watchman, P. (1981) The Homeless Persons' Obstacle Race. *The Journal of Social Welfare Law* 1, 65.

Robson, P.W. and Watchman, P. (1981) Resisting the Unprivileged *in* Robson, P. and Watchman, P. (eds.), *Justice, Lord Denning and the Constitution.* Westmead, Hants, Gower.

Robson, W.A. (1951) *Justice and Administrative Law.* London, Stevens.

Robson, W.A. (1976a) *Welfare State and Welfare Society.* London, Allen & Unwin.

Robson, W.A. (1976b) What the Crossman Diaries Actually Contain. 47 *Political Quarterly* 276.

Roby, P. (ed.) (1974) *The Poverty Establishment.* Englewood Cliffs, N.J., Prentice-Hall.

Rock, P. (1973) *Deviant Behaviour.* London, Hutchinson.

Roddewig, R.J. (1978) *Green Bans. The Birth of Australian Environmental Politics.* New York, Allanheld, Osmun/Universe.

Rodgers, B. (1969). *The Battle Against Poverty: Volume II.* London, Routledge & Kegan Paul.

Rodgers, H.R., Jr. and Bullock, C.S. III (1972) *Law and Social Change: Civil Rights, Laws and their Consequences.* New York, McGraw-Hill.

Romanyshyn, J.M. (1971) *Social Welfare: Charity to Justice.* New York, Random House.

Romilly, Sir S. (1840) *The Life of Sir Samuel Romilly.* London, John Murray.

Rose, H. (1973) Up Against the Welfare State: the Claimant Unions. *The Socialist Register* 179.

Rose, H. (1975) Bread and Justice: the National Welfare Rights Organization *in* Leonard, P. (ed.), *The Sociology of Community Action.* University of Keele, Sociological Review Monograph 21.

Rose, H. (1976a) Participation: the Icing on the Welfare Cake *in* Jones, K. and Baldwin, S. (eds.), *The Yearbook of Social Policy in Britain 1975.* London, Routledge & Kegan Paul.

Rose, H. (1976b) Who Can De-Label the Claimant *in* Adler, M. and Bradley, A. (eds.), *Justice, Discretion and Poverty.* London, Professional Books.

Rose, H. (1981) Rereading Titmuss: the Sexual Division of Welfare. 10 *Journal of Social Policy* 477.

Rose, H. and Jakubowicz, A. (1978) The Rise and Fall of Welfare Rights. 45 *New Society* 558.

Rose, M.E. (1966) The Allowance System under the New Poor Law. 19 *Economic History Review.* 2nd ser., 607.

Rose, M.E. (1976) Settlement, Removal and the New Poor Law *in* Fraser, D. (ed.), *The New Poor Law in the Nineteenth Century*. London, Macmillan Press.

Rosenthal, D.E. (1977) *Lawyer and Client: Who's in Charge?* New Brunswick, N.J., Transaction Books.

Rothstein, L. (1974) The Myth of Sisyphus: Legal Services Efforts on Behalf of the Poor. 7 *University of Michigan Journal of Law Reform* 493.

Rowland, M. (1976) Postponement of Possession Orders when the Tenant is not Protected under the Rent Acts. *LAG Bulletin* 109.

Royal Commission on Civil Liability and Compensation for Personal Injury (1978) *Report*. Cmnd. 7054. London, HMSO.

Royal Commission on Criminal Procedure (1980) *Prosecutions by Private Individuals and Non-Police Agencies*. Research Study No. 10. London, HMSO.

Royal Commission on the Distribution of Income and Wealth (1978a) *Report No. 6: Lower Incomes*. Cmnd. 7175. London, HMSO.

Royal Commission on the Distribution of Income and Wealth (1978b) [Chairman: Lord Diamond] *Selected Evidence Submitted to the Royal Commission for Report No. 6: Lower Incomes*. London, HMSO.

Royal Commission on Human Relationships (1977) *Final Report*. Canberra, Australian Government Publishing Service.

Royal Commission on Legal Services (1979) [Chairman: Sir H. Benson] *Final Report*, vol. 1 (2 parts); vol. 2 (Surveys and Studies) (2 parts). Cmnd. 7648. London, HMSO.

Royal Commission on Legal Services in Scotland (1980) *Report*. Cmnd. 7846.

Royal Commission on the National Health Service (1979) Cmnd. 7615. London, HMSO.

Royal Commission on Trade Unions and Employers' Associations 1965–1968 (1968) *Report*. Cmnd. 3623. London, HMSO.

Ruggles, T. (1793) *The History of the Poor, Their Rights, Duties and the Laws Respecting Them*. London, J. Deighton.

Runciman, W.G. (1972) *Relative Deprivation and Social Justice*. Harmondsworth, Penguin.

Rust, P.G. (1977) Rent Arrears [letter]. 42 *New Society* 538.

Rutter, M. and Madge, N. (1976) *Cycles of Disadvantage*. London, Heinemann.

Rutter, M., Manghan, M., Mortimore, and Ouston, J. (1979) *Fifteen Thousand Hours*. London, Open University Books.

Ryan, E.F. (1976) *Family Law. Enforcement of Maintenance Obligations*. Ottawa, Law Reform Commission of Canada.

Ryan, P.A. (1978) 'Poplarism' 1894–1930 *in* Thane, P. (ed.), *The Origins of British Social Policy*. London, Croom Helm.

Sackville, R. (Commissioner) (1975a) *Law and Poverty in Australia. Second Main Report, October 1975*. (Australia. Commission of Inquiry into Poverty). Canberra, Australian Government Publishing Service.

Sackville, R. (1975b) *Legal Aid in Australia*. Canberra, AGPS.

Sackville, R. (1977) Cohabitation and Social Security Entitlement *in* Armstrong, S., Mossman, M.J. and Sackville, R. (eds.), *Essays on Law and Poverty*. Canberra, AGPS.

Sackville, R. (1978a) Lawyers, Law Reform and Legal Institutions: Some Reflections *in* Tomasic, R. (ed.), *Understanding Lawyers*. Sydney, Allen & Unwin.

Sackville, R. (1978b) Property Rights and Social Security. 2 *University of New South Wales Law Journal* 246.

Sackville, R. (1978c) Social Security and Family Law in Australia. 27 *International and Comparative Law Quarterly* 127.

Sackville, R. (1981) Residential Tenancies Reform in Victoria: a Study of a Consultation *in: Consultation and Government*. Melbourne, Victorian Council of Social Service.

Sackville, R. and Forbes, K. (1976) *Homeless People and the Law*. (Australia. Commission of Inquiry into Poverty). Canberra, AGPS.

Sadurski, W. (1981) Equality, Law and Non-Discrimination. *Bulletin of the Australian Society of Legal Philosophy*, No. 21, December 1981, p.113.

Sandford, C., Pond, C. and Walker, R. (1980) *Taxation and Social Policy*. London, Heinemann.

Samuels, A. (1971) Rent Control in the Seventies. 68 *Law Society's Gazette* 282.

Sarat, A. (1977) Studying American Legal Culture: an Assessment of Survey Evidence. 11 *Law and Society Review* 427.

Saville, J. (1957–8) The Welfare State: an Historical Approach. *New Reasoner*, vol. 1, No. 3, 5.

Sax, J.L. and Hiestand, F.J. (1967) Slumlordism as a Tort. 65 *Michigan Law Review* 869.

Scarman, Sir L. (1974) *English Law – the New Dimension*. London, Stevens & Sons.

Schafer, R. (1977) Comments on Chapter Six *in* Ingram, G.K. (ed.), *Residential Location and Urban Housing Markets*. National Bureau of Economic Research.

Scheingold, S.A. (1974) *The Politics of Rights*. New Haven, Yale University Press.

Schifferes, S. (1976) Council Tenants and Housing Policy in the 1930s: the Contradictions of State Intervention *in: Housing and Class in Britain*. (Second vol. of Papers presented at the Political Economy of Housing Workshop of the Conference of Socialist Economists).

Schifferes, S. (1978) *In Distress Over Rent*. London, Shelter.

Schofield, A.N. and Sales, H.B. (1966) *Housing Law and Practice*, 4th edn. London, Shaw & Sons.

Schorr, A.L. (1963) *Slums and Social Insecurity*. Washington DC, US Government Printing Office.

Schuck, P. (1980) Suing Our Servants: the Courts, Congress, and the Liability of Public Officials for Damages. *Supreme Court Review* 281.

Schuyt, K., Groenendijk, K. and Sloot, B. (1977) Acces to the Legal System and Legal Services Research *in: European Yearbook in Law and Sociology 1977*. The Hague, Martinus Nijhoff.

Schwartz, G.T. (1981) Tort Law and the Economy in Nineteenth-Century America: a Reinterpretation. 90 *Yale Law Journal* 1717.

Schwarzer, W. (1952) Wages During Temporary Disability. 5 *Stanford Law Review* 30.

Schwartzkoff, J. and Morgan, J. (1982) *Community Justice Centres*. Sydney, Law Foundation of New South Wales.

Scutt, J. (1978) The Fine as a Penal Measure in the United States of America,

Canada and Australia *in* Jescheck, H-H. and Grebing, G. (eds.), *Die Geldstrafe im Deutschen und Auslandischen Recht*. Baden-Baden, Nomos Verlagsgesellschaft.

Secretary of State for the Home Department (1981) *Vagrancy Offences*. Cmnd. 8311. London, HMSO.

Seddon, N. (1978) The Negligence Liability of Statutory Bodies: Dutton Reinterpreted. 9 *Federal Law Review* 326.

Sedley, S. (1973) More on Using the Rent to Pay for Repairs. *LAG Bulletin* 173.

Sells, D. (1939) *British Wages Boards*. Washington DC, Brookings Institution.

Selznick, P. (1969) *Law, Society and Industrial Justice*. New York, Russell Sage Foundation.

Seyd, P. (1975) Shelter: the National Campaign for the Homeless. 46 *Political Quarterly* 418.

Seyd, P. (1976) The Child Poverty Action Group. 47 *Political Quarterly* 189.

Shapiro, D.L. (1980) The Enigma of the Lawyer's Duty to Serve. 55 *New York University Law Review* 735.

Sheilds, G. and Spector, L.S. (1972) Opening up the Suburbs: Notes on a Movement for Social Change. 2 *Yale Review of Law and Social Action* 300.

Shelter (1977) *The Future of Private Rented Housing. Evidence to the Review of the Rent Acts*. London, Shelter.

Shelter *et al.* (1977) *Insult to Injury. Homelessness Policy in South Wales*. Report: Wales. Shelter, Cardiff Housing Action, Shelter Community Action Team *et al.*

Shelter (1978) *Where Homelessness Means Hopelessness*. London, Shelter.

Siegel, S.A. (1975) Is the Modern Lease a Contract or a Conveyance? – An Historical Inquiry. 52 *Journal of Urban Law* 649.

Silburn, R. (1972) The Potential and Limitations of Community Action *in* Bull, D. (ed.), *Family Poverty*, 2nd edn. London, Duckworth & Co.

Simon, D. (1954) Master and Servant *in* Saville, J. (ed.), *Democracy and the Labour Movement*. London, Lawrence & Wishart.

Simon, Sir E.D. (1933) *The Anti-Slum Campaign*. London, Longmans, Green.

Simon, Sir J. (1897) *English Sanitary Institutions*, 2nd edn. London, Smith Elder & Co.

Sinfield, A. (1977) The Social Meaning of Unemployment *in* Jones, K., Brown, M. and Baldwin, S. (eds.), *The Yearbook of Social Policy in Britain*. London, Routledge & Kegan Paul.

Sinfield, A. (1978) Analyses in the Social Division of Welfare. 7 *Journal of Social Policy* 138.

Singer, B. (1974) Welfare Rights – Right of the Department of Social Services to Insist on Deserted Wife's Suing for Maintenance. 38 *Saskatchewan Law Review* 390.

Sjoberg, G., Brymer, R.A. and Farris, B. (1966) Bureaucracy and the Lower Class. *Sociology and Social Research* 325.

Skinner, D. and Longdon, J. (1975) *The Story of Clay Cross*. Nottingham, Spokesman Books.

Skoler, D.L. and Weixel, C.E. (1981) Social Security Adjudication in Five Nations. 33 *Administrative Law Review* 269.

Slack, P.A. (1974) Vagrants and Vagrancy in England, 1598–1664. 27 *Economic History Review* 360.

Slater, G. (1930) *Poverty and the State*. London, Constable.

Sleeman, J.F. (1979) *Resources for the Welfare State*. London, Longman.

Small Heath Community Law Centre (1977) *First Annual Report 1976–77*. Birmingham, SHCLC.

Smigel, E. and Ross, H. (eds.) (1970) *Crimes Against Bureaucracy*. New York, Van Nostrand Reinhold Co.

Smith, A. (1776) *An Inquiry into the Nature and Causes of the Wealth of Nations*. London.

Smith, C.A. (1862) The Law Relating to the Relief and Settlement of the Poor. 7 *Solicitors Journal* 149.

Smith, C. and Hoath, D.C. (1975) *Law and the Underprivileged*. London, Routledge & Kegan Paul.

Smith, F.B. (1979) *The People's Health 1830–1910*. London, Croom Helm.

Smith, G., Lees, R. and Topping, P. (1977) Participation and the Home Office Community Development Project *in* Crouch, C. (ed.), *British Political Sociology Yearbook*, vol. 3, 'Participation in Politics'. London, Croom Helm.

Smith, I. (1980) *Occupational Pensions*. London, Sweet & Maxwell.

Smith, N.J. (1972) *Poverty in England, 1601–1936*. Newton Abbott, Devon, David & Charles.

Smith, P.F. (1980) Remedies of Tenant for Breach of Landlord's Covenant to Repair. 131 *New Law Journal* 330.

Smith, R.H. (1924) *Justice and the Poor*, 3rd edn. New York, Carnegie Foundation.

Snel, B. (1978) Observation in the Courtroom. 14 *Netherlands Journal of Sociology* 173.

Soar, P. (1979) Setting up a Legal Aid Practice, pts. I to VI. 129 *New Law Journal* 911, 935, 979, 1007, 1031, 1055.

Social Insurance and Allied Services. Cmd. 6404. (1942) London, HMSO.

Society of Labour Lawyers (1968) *Justice for All*. London, Fabian Society. Fabian Research Series 273.

Society of Labour Lawyers (1973) *The End of the Private Landlord*. London, Fabian Society. Fabian Research Series 312.

Society of Labour Lawyers (1978) *Legal Services for All*. London, Fabian Tract 454.

Softley, P. (1978) *Fines in Magistrates' Courts*. Home Office, Research Unit. Home Office Research Study No. 46. London, HMSO.

Solomon, H.W. (1966) 'This New Fetish for Indigency': Justice and Poverty in an Affluent Society. 66 *Columbia Law Review* 248.

Sparer, E.V. (1969) 'Materials on Public Assistance Law.' Unpublished, University of Pennsylvania Law School.

Spearrit, P. (1974) Sydney's Slums: Middle-Class Reformers and the Labor Response. *Labor History* No. 26, May 1974.

Spencer, J.R. (1975) The Defective Premises Act 1972 – Defective Law and Defective Law Reform. 34 *Cambridge Law Journal* 48.

Squatters' Handbook (1973, 1975, 1979) London, Advisory Service for Squatters.

Starr, P. (1973) *The Discarded Army: Veterans After Vietnam.* New York, Charterhouse.

Starr, R. (1979) An End to Rental Housing? 57 (Fall) *The Public Interest* 25.

Stedman Jones, G. (1971) *Outcast London.* Oxford, Clarendon Press.

Steele, R.D. (1949) *The National Assistance Act 1948.* London, Butterworth & Co.

Steer, D. (1970) *Police Cautions – a Study in the Exercise of Police Discretion.* Oxford, Basil Blackwell.

Steer, D. (1980) *Uncovering Crime: The Police Role.* (Research Study No. 7, Royal Commission on Criminal Procedure). London, HMSO.

Stein, L.A. (1974) *Urban Legal Problems.* Sydney, Law Book Co.

Stein, P. (1980) *Legal Evolution: the Story of an Idea.* Cambridge, Cambridge University Press.

Stein, P. (1982) Reforming a Feudal Law. 7 *Legal Service Bulletin* 220.

Stephen, Sir J. (1883) *A History of the Criminal Law of England.* London, Macmillan.

Stephens, M. (1980) The Law Centre Movement: Professionalism and Community Control *in* Bankowski, Z. and Mungham, G. (eds.), *Essays in Law and Society.* London, Routledge & Kegan Paul.

Stephens, M. (1982) Law Centres and Citizenship: the Way Forward *in* Thomas, P.A. (ed.), *Law in the Balance.* Oxford, Martin Robertson.

Stevens, D.W. (1974) *Assisted Job Search for the Insured Unemployed.* W.E. Upjohn Institute for Employment Research. Washington DC.

Stevens, R. (1979) *Law and Politics: the House of Lords as a Judicial Body 1800–1976.* London, Weidenfeld & Nicolson.

Stevenson, O. (1973) *Claimant or Client?* London, Allen & Unwin.

Stewart, A. (1981) *Housing Action in an Industrial Suburb.* London, Academic Press.

Stoljar, S.J. (1973) *Groups and Entities: an Inquiry into Corporate Theory.* Canberra, Australian National University Press.

Strauss, A., *et al.* (1971) The Hospital and its Negotiated Order *in* Castles, F.G., Murray, D.J. and Potter, D.C. (eds.), *Decisions, Organizations and Society.* Harmondsworth, Penguin.

Streather, J. and Weir, S. (1974) *Social Insecurity: Single Mothers on Benefit.* London, Child Poverty Action Group.

Street, D., Martin, G.T. and Gordon, L.K. (1979) *The Welfare Industry.* London, Sage.

Street, H. (1975) *Justice in the Welfare State,* 2nd edn. London, Stevens & Sons.

Street, H. (1981) Access to the Legal System and the Modern Welfare State *in* Cappelletti, M. (ed.), *Access to Justice and the Welfare State.* Alphen aan den Rijn, Sijthoff.

Stretton, H. (1980) Social Policy: Has the Welfare State all been a Terrible Mistake? *in* Evans, G. and Reeves, J. (eds.), *Labour Essays 1980.* Melbourne, Drummond.

Stumpf, H.P. and Janowitz, R.J. (1969) Judges and the Poor: Bench Responses to Federally Financial Legal Services. 21 *Stanford Law Review* 1058.

Stumpf, H.P., Turpen, B. and Culver, J.H. (1975) The Impact of OEO Legal

Services in James, D.B. (ed.), *Analyzing Poverty Policy*. Lexington, Mass., Lexington Books.

Styles, P. (1963) The Evolution of the Law of Settlement. 9 *University of Birmingham Historical Journal* 33.

Subrin, S.N. and Sutton, J. (1973) Welfare Class Actions in Federal Court: a Procedural Analysis. 8 *Harvard Civil Rights Civil Liberties Law Review* 21.

Sugden, R. (1982) Hard Luck Stories: The Problem of the Uninsured in a Laissez-Faire Society. 11 *J. Social Policy* 201.

Sullivan, L.A. (1971) Law Reform and the Legal Services Crisis. 59 *California Law Review* 1.

Summers, R.S. (1982) Working Conceptions of 'The Law'. 1 *Law and Philosophy* 263.

Supplementary Benefits Commission (1975, 1976, 1977, 1978, 1979) *Annual Reports*. Cmnd. 6615, 6910, 7392, 7725, 8033. London, HMSO.

Supplementary Benefits Commission (1976) *Living Together as Husband and Wife*. London, HMSO.

Supplementary Benefits Commission (1978) *Take-up of Supplementary Benefits*. London, HMSO.

Supplementary Benefits Commission (1979) *Response to 'Social Assistance: A Review of the Supplementary Benefits Scheme in Great Britain'*. London, HMSO.

Supplementary Benefits Handbooks (1970–1981) London, HMSO.

Sutcliffe, A. (ed.) (1974) *Multi-Storey Living: the British Working-Class Experience*. London, Croom Helm.

Tawney, R.H. (1914) *The Establishment of Minimum Rates in the Chain-Making Industry*. London, Bell & Son.

Tawney, R.H. (1938) *Religion and the Rise of Capitalism*. Harmondsworth, Penguin.

Tawney, R.H. (1979) The Assessment of Wages in England by the Justices of the Peace in Winter, J.M. (ed.), *R.H. Tawney: the American Labour Movement and Other Essays*. Brighton, Sussex, Harvester Press.

Taylor, W., Walton, P. and Young, J. (1975) *Critical Criminology*. London, Routledge & Kegan Paul.

Taylor-Gooby, P. and Lakeman, S. (1977) *Welfare Benefits Advocacy*. Department of Social Administration and Social Work, University of York.

Taylor-Gooby, P. and Dale, J. (1981) *Social Theory and Social Welfare*. London, Edward Arnold.

tenBroek, J. (1964) California's Dual System of Family Law: its Origins, Development and Present Status. 16 *Stanford Law Review* 900.

Thane, P. (1978) Women and the Poor Law in Victorian and Edwardian England. 6 *History Workshop* 29.

Thomas, D.A. (1979) *Principles of Sentencing*. 2nd ed. London, Heinemann.

Thomas, P. (1978) The Green Bans in Australia in Coates, K. (ed.), *The Right to Useful Work*. Nottingham, Spokesman Books.

Thomas, P.A. and Mungham, G. (1977) Duty Solicitor Schemes: in Whose Interest? 127 *New Law Journal* 180.

Thompson, E.P. (1968) *The Making of the English Working Class*. Harmondsworth, Penguin.

Thompson, E.P. (1975) *Whigs and Hunters*. London, Allen Lane.
Thornley, A. (1977) Theoretical Perspectives on Planning Participation. 7 *Progress in Planning*, Pt 1, 1. Oxford, Pergamon Press.
Thursz, D. (1972) Community Participation: Should the Past be Prologue? 15 *American Behavioural Scientist* 733.
Tigar, M.F. and Levy, M.R. (1977) *Law and the Rise of Capitalism*. New York, Monthly Review Press.
Tiley, J. (1978) *Revenue Law*. London, Butterworths.
Tiplady, D. (1981) Recent Developments in the Law of Landlord and Tenant: the American Experience. 44 *Modern Law Review* 129.
Titmuss, R.M. (1968) *Commitment to Welfare*. London, Allen & Unwin.
Titmuss, R.M. (1971) Welfare Rights, Law and Discretion. 42 *Political Quarterly* 113.
Tobias, J.J. (1967) *Crime and Industrial Society in the Nineteenth Century*. London, Batsford.
Tomasic, R., and Feeley, M.M. (1982) *Neighbourhood Justice: an Assessment of an Emerging Idea*. New York, Longman.
Topping, P. and Smith, G. (1977) *Government Against Poverty?* Liverpool Community Development Project, 1970–75. Oxford, Social Evaluation Unit, University of Oxford.
Townsend, J. (1971) *A Dissertation on the Poor Laws*. Reprint of 1786 edn. Berkeley, University of California Press.
Townsend, P. (1979) *Poverty in the United Kingdom*. Harmondsworth, Penguin.
Townsend, P. and Nicholson, D. (1982) *Inequalities in Health: The Black Report*. Harmondsworth, Penguin.
Trattner, W.I. (1974) *From Poor Law to Welfare State: a History of Social Welfare in America*. New York, Free Press.
Trinder, C. (1976) The Social Contract and the Low Paid *in* Willmott, P. (ed.), *Sharing Inflation? Poverty Report 1976*. London, Temple-Smith.
Trubeck, D.M. (1977) Complexity and Contradiction in the Legal Order: Balbus and the Challenge of Critical Social Thought about Law. 11 *Law and Society Review* 529.
Trubeck, D.M., *et al.* (1980) Legal Services and the Administrative State: From Public Interest Law to Public Advocacy *in* Blankenburg, E. (ed.), *Innovations in the Legal Services*. Cambridge, Mass., Oelgeschlager, Gunn & Hain.
Tunnard, J. (1978) *The Trouble With Tax*. London, Child Poverty Action Group.
Tussing, A.D. (1974) The Dual Welfare System. *Society*, vol. II, Jan/Feb. 1974, p. 50.
Unger, R.M. (1976) *Law in Modern Society*. New York, Free Press.
Upex, R. and Morris, A. (1981) Maternity Rights – Illusion or Reality? 10 *Industrial Law Journal* 218.
Utton, A. (1966) The British Legal Aid System. 76 *Yale Law Journal* 371.
Ventantonio, J.B. (1976) Equal Justice Under the Law: the Evolution of a National Commitment to Legal Services for the Poor and a Study of its Impact on New Jersey Landlord-Tenant Law. 7 *Seton Hall Law Review* 233.
Victorin, A. (1979) Landlord and Tenant Relations in Sweden. A Case of

Collective Bargaining. *Scandinavian Studies in Law* 233.

Viner, C. (1741–1753) *A General Abridgment of Law and Equity*. London.

Vinogradoff, P. (1928) *Collected Papers*, vol. II: *Jurisprudence*. Oxford, Clarendon.

Vose, C.E. (1967) *Caucasians Only*. Berkeley, University of California Press.

Walter, J. (1980) Grain Riots and Popular Attitudes to the Law *in* Brewer, J. and Styles, J. (eds.), *An Ungovernable People*. London, Hutchinson.

Wandsworth, M.G.J. (1975) Delinquency in a National Sample of Children. 15 *British Journal of Criminology* 167.

Wandsworth Rights Umbrella Group (1978) *Would the Real Scroungers Stand Up?* London.

Ward, C. (1974) *Tenants Take Over*. London, Architectural Press.

Ward, C. (1976) *Housing: an Anarchist Approach*. London, Freedom Press.

Wasby, S.L. (1975) The Supreme Court as Enunciator of Welfare Policy *in* James, D.B. (ed.), *Analyzing Poverty Policy*. Lexington, Mass., Lexington Books.

Wates, N. (1976) *The Battle for Tolmers Square*. London, Routledge & Kegan Paul.

Wates, N. and Wolmar, C. (1980) *Squatting: the Real Story*. London, Bay Leaf.

Watson, P. (1980) *Social Security Law of the European Communities*. London, Mansell.

Weale, A. (1978) *Equality and Social Policy*. London, Routledge & Kegan Paul.

Webb, S. and B. (1927) *English Local Government. English Poor Law History, Part I: The Old Poor Law*. London, Longmans, Green & Co.

Webb, S. and B. (1929) *English Local Government. English Poor Law History, Part II: The Last Hundred Years*. London, Longmans, Green & Co.

Weber, M. (1954) *On Law in Economy and Society*. New York, Simon & Schuster.

Weiler, P. (1968) Two Models of Judicial Decision-Making. 46 *Canadian Bar Review* 406.

Welch, F. (1974) Minimum Wage Legislation in the United States. 12 *Economic Inquiry* 285.

Welsh Consumer Council (1976) *Council Housing: a Survey of Allocation Policies in Wales*. Cardiff, WCC.

Werner, F.E. and Madway, D.M. (1976) Redlining and Disinvestment: Causes, Consequences and Proposal Remedies. 10 *Clearinghouse Review* 501.

Westen, P. (1982) The Empty Idea of Equality. 95 *Harvard Law Review* 537.

Wexler, S. (1970) Practicing Law For Poor People. 79 *Yale Law Journal* 1049.

Wexler, S. (1971) The Poverty Lawyer as Radical *in* Black, J. (ed.), *Radical Lawyers*. New York, Avon.

White, G. (1979) *The Laws Respecting Masters and Work People*. Reprint of 1824 edn. London, Garland Publishing Co.

White, R. (1973) Lawyers and the Enforcement of Rights *in* Morris, P., White, R. and Lewis, P., *Social Needs and Legal Action*. London, Robertson.

White, R. (1975) The Distasteful Character of Litigation for Poor Persons. *Juridical Review* 233.

Whiteley, P. and Winyard, S. (1983) Influencing Social Policy: the Effectiveness of the Poverty Lobby in Britain. 12 *Journal of Social Policy* 1.

Wicks, M. (1973) *Rented Housing and Social Ownership*. London, Fabian Society. Fabian Tract 421.

Widdowson, B. (1975) *Shelter's Submission to the Department of the Environment. Review of Homelessness*. London, Shelter.

Widdowson, B. (1976) *Blunt Powers – Sharp Practices*. London, Shelter.

Wilcox, A.F. (1972) *The Decision to Prosecute*. London, Butterworths.

Wilcox, S. and Randall, G. (1980) One Simple Housing Court for All Cases. *Roof*, March/April, 42.

Wilensky, H.L. (1975) *The Welfare State and Equality*. Berkeley, University of California Press.

Wilensky, H.L. (1976) *The 'New Corporation', Centralization and the Welfare State*. London, Sage.

Wilkins, J.L. (1975) *Legal Aid in the Criminal Courts*. Toronto, University of Toronto Press.

Williams, B.A.O. (1971) The Idea of Equality *in* Bedau,H.A. (ed.), *Justice and Equality*. Englewood Cliffs, N.J., Prentice-Hall.

Williams, D.G.T. (1979) Judicial Restraint and Judicial Review: the Role of the Courts in Welfare Law *in* Partington, M. and Jowell, J. (eds.), *Welfare Law and Policy*. London, Frances Pinter.

Williams, D.W. (1979) Social Welfare Consumers and their Complaints. *Journal of Social Welfare Law* 257.

Williams, G. (1961) *Criminal Law: the General Part*, 2nd edn. London, Stevens.

Williams, K. (1981) *From Pauperism to Poverty*. London, Routledge & Kegan Paul.

Williams, P. (1976) The Role of Institutions in the Inner London Housing Market: the Case of Islington. 1 *Institute of British Geographers, Transactions* 72.

Williams, W.O. (1956) *Calendar of the Caernarvonshire Quarter Sessions Records 1541–1558*. London.

Williamson, C.R. and Folberg, J. (1971) Legislative Law Reform: a New Challenge. 7 *Clearinghouse Review* 380.

Williamson, J.B. and Hyer, K.M. (1975) The Measurement and Meaning of Poverty. 22 *Social Problems* 652.

Willis, J. (1975) Of Process Servers, Default Summonses and the Judicial Process. 10 *Melbourne University Law Review* 225.

Willis, J.W. (1950) A Short History of Rent Control Laws. 36 *Cornell Law Quarterly* 54.

Wilson, E. (1977) *Women and the Welfare State*. London, Tavistock.

Windschuttle, K. (1979) *Unemployment*. Ringwood, Victoria, Penguin.

Winkler, J.T. (1981) The Political Economy of Administrative Discretion *in* Adler, M. and Asquith, S. (eds.), *Discretion and Welfare*. London, Heinemann.

Wintour, P. (1978) Two-Time Losers. 3 *Roof* 12.

Winyard, S. (1976) *Policing Low Wages*. Low Pay Pamphlet No. 4. London, Low Pay Unit.

Winyard, S. (1978) Points to a Good Policy. 3 *Roof* 106.

Wohl, A.S. (1977) *The Eternal Slum: Housing and Social Policy in Victorian London*. London, Edward Arnold.

Woodward, C. (1962) Reality and Social Reform: the Transition from Laissez-Faire to the Welfare State. 72 *Yale Law Journal* 286.

Worsley, P. (1973) The Distribution of Power in Industrial Society *in* Urry, J. and Wakeford, J. (eds.), *Power in Britain*. London, Heinemann Educational Books.

Wrightson, K. (1980) Two Concepts of Order: Justices, Constables and Jurymen in Seventeenth-Century England *in* Brewer, J. and Styles, J. (eds.), *An Ungovernable People*. London, Hutchinson.

Yates, D. (1979) Rent Allowances – Six Years On. *Journal of Social Welfare Law* 195.

Young, J. (1979) Left Idealism, Reformism and Beyond: from New Criminology to Marxism *in* Fine, B., *et al.*, *Capitalism and the Rule of Law*. London, Hutchinson.

Young, M.D. and Willmott, P. (1957) *Family and Kinship in East London*. London, Routledge & Kegan Paul.

Zald, M.N. (1965) *Social Welfare Institutions: a Sociological Reader*. New York, Wiley.

Zander, M. (1968) The Unused Rent Acts. 311 *New Society* 366.

Zander, M. (1969) The Legal Profession and the Poor. 20 *Northern Ireland Legal Quarterly* 109.

Zander, M. (1977) Waivers – the End of a Long Story? 127 *New Law Journal* 1236.

Zander, M. (1978) *Legal Services for the Community*. London, Temple-Smith.

Zander, M. and Russell, P. (1976) Law Centres Survey. *Law Society's Gazette*, 10 March, 210.

Zemans, F.H. (1978) Legal Aid and Legal Advice in Canada. 16 *Osgoode Hall Law Journal* 663.

Zemans, F.K. (1982) Framework for Analysis of Legal Mobilization: a Decision-Making Model. *American Bar Foundation Research Journal* 989.

Zimmerman, D.H. (1974) Fact as a Practical Accomplishment *in* Turner, R. (ed.), *Ethnomethodology*. Harmondsworth, Penguin.

Zurcher, L.A. Jr. (1970) *Poverty Warriors*. Austin, University of Texas Press.

INDEX

ability to pay, 51
Aboriginal Legal Service, 63
abortion, 51
access to justice, 335
Administrative Appeals Tribunal, 168,
    177, 197, 253
Administrative Review Council, 217
amicus curiae brief, 303
appeals, 33, 173
apprenticeship of children, 21, 343 n.36
armed forces, 38
    liability to maintain family, 39
audit, 253
Australian Commission for Law and
    Poverty, 202

badging the poor, 35
bail, 52
basic wage, 120
bed and breakfast accommodation, 154
begging, 66
benefit administration, passivity of, 210
benefit administration, reform and
    criticism of, 229
benefits, right to, 168
benefits, termination of, 197
Beveridge Report, 16, 191
Birmingham CDP, 282
bias,
    and administration of criminal law,
        49-50
    and access to legal assistance, 50
    and attention to poor, 50
    and disadvantaged groups, 50
breach of statutory duty, 249, 262
burden of proof, 215

Canada Pension Plan, 180
Chartism, 107
Child Poverty Action Group, 187, 294

civil procedure, 53, 54
    Mareva injunction, 53
    for debt imprisonment, 54
Civil Judicial Statistics, 351 n.35
class, status and power, distinguished, 5
Clay Cross, 256
clearance area, 125
cohabitation rule, 194
    reform of, 198
collective action, 19, 143, 230, 280-4
collective agreements, 182
Combination Acts, 40, 118
Commissioner of Consumer Affairs, 78
Committee on the Rent Acts, 365 n.155
common employment, 18
Community Development Projects, 268
community justice centres, 97
community politics, 277, 278, 280
compulsory improvement, 155
Conciliation and Arbitration
        Commission, Australia, 120, 127
Consumer Council, *Justice Out of Reach*,
    84
Contract Buyers' League, 313
controlled tenancies, 116
'creaming the poor', 211
criminal law, 49-50, 225-7, 325

definitions,
    fiscal welfare, 4, 172
    occupational welfare, 4
    poverty, 7
    social control, 191-2
    social rights, 13
    social welfare regulation, 4
    welfare state, 4
demolition order, 124
deposits (bonds), 130
derivative settlement, 345 n.61
direct action, 315, 320

and attitude to legal system, 296
    failure of, 285
    model of social change, 278, 283
disabled, 127, 211
discretion, 50, 68, 166–72, 216, 226, 329
dock brief system, 85
domestic servants, 18
dual system of law, 56
duty-solicitor scheme, 97

education, 270, 271
enclosure of common lands, 20
enforcement agencies, 50, 135, 143, 226
environmental health officers, 136, 140
environmental problems, 55, 122
equality before the law, 1, 46–7, 82, 97,
    98, 143, 193, 213, 324, 325, 326,
    335, 337
estoppel, 219
exceptive hiring, 45
external review, 172–9, 189, 252, 274
eviction, 80, 129–30

Fabianism, 277, 279
Factory Acts, 18
fair rent, 116, 129, 154
family law,
    California, 56
    England, 57
    legal aid, 57
Finer Report, 57
fines, 52, 67
fiscal welfare, 172, 178
Forcible Entry, Statutes of, 300
fraud, 224
free-market economy, 157–9, 332
freedom of contract, 16, 69, 160
freedom of information, 216–17, 264
furnished tenancies, 116

game laws, 20
gleaning, 20
'green bans' campaign in Australia,
    285, 298

habitability laws, US, 157
harassment, 116
Home Affairs Committee, House of
    Commons, 67
homeworkers, 118, 127, 135

homelessness, 67, 258, 259, 285
    appellate procedure, 262
    judicial review, 263
housing, compulsory improvement
    powers, 125
housing standards, 110, 123, 124, 157
    breaches of, 136
    public authority, 137
    public enforcement of, 138
    regulation of, 155
    repair and improvement powers, 138,
    141
housing tribunals, 78, 129

illegitimacy, 37
Independent Labour Party, 108
in forma pauperis, 18, 84, 85
in-kind benefits, 192, 328
incapacity for work, 170
industrial dispute disqualification,
    206–8
inspector of nuisances, 139
insurance, 180
intermediate appellate bodies, 176
internal review, 217

juveniles, 49

labour yards, 43
laissez-faire philosophy, 88, 118
landlord and tenant, 65, 69–81
law centres, 93, 281, 294, 295, 313
lawyers,
    client relationship, 87
    independence of, 87
    involvement in social change, 231,
    291, 295, 313
    motivation re legal aid, 86
leasehold enfranchisement, 51, 94
legal aid, 47, 81–93
legal competence, 54, 325
legal need, defined, 82
legal obligations, evasion of, 113, 153,
    155, 224, 246
legal representation, 59, 63, 64, 70, 81,
    149, 176
legal services commissions, 91
legal services, unequal utilization of, 55,
    58–64
less eligibility, principle of, 32, 43, 44

'lino tenancies', 115
local connection, concept of, 44
lodging houses, 110
London County Court, 63
Low Pay Unit, 127

Macarthur, Mary, 108
maintenance, 37–8, 200
maladministration, 253
management co-operatives, 269
Marxist view of social welfare
    bureaucracies, 234
master and servant legislation, 16–17
maternity leave, 182
means test, 170, 212
miners' strike of 1926, 34
minimum wages, 105, 108, 159, 202,
    248
minimum-wage laws, 127, 140, 156
misrepresentation, 228
Mobilization for Youth Experience
    (New York), 282
Monopolies and Mergers Commission,
    353 n.47
morality and the law, 34, 161, 194, 328
multiple occupation, 122

National Assistance Board, 260
National Consumer Council, 212, 239
National Federation of Claimants
    Unions, 187
National Health Service, 270
natural justice, 147, 174, 178, 218, 337
negligence, 22, 220, 249
neo-conservatism, 332
New poor law, 32
    right to relief under, 32
    punitive nature of, 35
non-exclusive occupation agreement,
    150
North Islington Housing Rights project,
    282
nuisance, 109, 112, 122, 374 n.11
    compensation for, 123, 124
    public authorities' responsibility for,
        146
    remedies for, 114

OEO (Office of Economic
    Opportunities), 268

Ombudsman, 143, 173, 213, 243, 253,
    274
outdoor relief, 42–3
overcrowding, 110, 122

part-time work, 127
participation, 264–74
pension schemes, 5, 182–3
picketing, 208, 284, 298
planning blight, 238
poor,
    historical definition, 6
    test of destitution, 7
Poor Law Commission Report, 107
poor law, Chapter 2 *passim*, 259
    as control of behaviour, 36
    effect of, on courts' decisions, 44
    in England, 14, 15
    in other countries, 342 n.11
poor man's court, 84
Poor Persons Rules Committee, 89
poor rate, relief from, 7
poor relief, 347 n.100
    administrative practices, 30
    curtailment of, 31
    control of, by magistracy, 30
    control of, by superior courts, 31
    liability to maintain, 347 n.100
    repayment by loan, 33
    repayment of, 33
    right to, 29
possession, 62, 115, 240, 300
poverty,
    as cause of criminality, 49
    causes of, 35
    definition, 4–5
    economic dimension of, 6
    lobby, 279
    'poverty advocate', 326
priority need, 260
privacy, 196, 226
property lobby, 374 n.10
property rights, 20, 145, 161, 181, 337
public advocacy, 253
public defender, 87
public health, 105, 109
public health law, 112, 113, 122
public housing, 239
    allocation, 240–3
    repair, 244

security of tenure, 244

Rachmanism, 116
racial bias, 68
recovery of benefits, 228
recovery of wages, 19
refuges, 259
registered rent, 132
regulation, Chapter 4 *passim*, 254–6
regulatory failure, 160
rehabilitation, 125
removal, law of, 23
rent arrears, 245
rent control, 105, 108, 114, 128, 131,
    153, 155, 158, 289
    for public housing, 243
rent premium, 130
rent strike, 79, 80, 297, 315
rent tribunals, 115
repair notice, 125
representative action, 303
residential tenancies tribunals, 70, 78
retaliatory eviction, US, 136
review committees, Canada, 175
right to counsel, US, 89
Royal Commission on Distribution of
    Income and Wealth, 355 n.94
Royal Commission on Legal Services
    (England and Wales), 62, 352 n.42,
    353 n.49, n.54
rule of law, 143, 163, 213, 227

security of tenure, 129
settlement,
    appeals against, 24
    by estate, 23
    by payment of taxes, 23
    by tenement, 23
    development of, 22
    effect in US, 26
    illegitimate child, 25
    law of, 15, 22
    mitigation of harshness of, 25
    operation of, 22
    prevention of, 24
sewerage and drainage, 145
shorthold tenancies, 116
sick pay, 182
'sink' estates, 241
slum clearance, 111, 147, 237, 253, 367
slum dwelling, 110

social change,
    history of, 286
    legal aid and, 83, 96, 292
    role of courts in, 2, 305–7, 335
    role of law in, 2, 286
social control, 191
social rights, Chapter 5 *passim*, 29
social security and social assistance, 5,
    369 n.7
social security commissioners, 177, 179
special benefit, 168
Speenhamland system, 40, 118
squatting, 285, 286, 297, 299, 308, 312,
    315, 316
state subsidy theory, 206–8
status, 36
    in traditional society, 13, 14
    movement from, to equality before
        the law, 13
stigma, 220, 222
strikes, 206
Supplementary Benefits Appeals
    Tribunal, 62
Supplementary Benefits Commission,
    169, 187, 191, 197
suspected person (SUS), 67
sweated labourers, 108

take-up problem, 211, 212, 257, 332
tenancy agreements, 239
tenant self-help, 79
tenants of mortgagors, 311
test-case litigation, 96, 294, 297, 301,
    310
trade boards, 119
trade unions, 107, 156, 176, 183, 193,
    278, 282, 284, 318
Tramp Acts (US), 66
tribunals, 173, 174, 190, 288
trusts law, 183

unemployment, 159, 192, 202
Uniform Commercial Code, 70

vagrancy, 65, 66
    in Australia, 68–9
    punishment for, 66, 67
    in US, 68

wage councils, 156

wage regulation,
  in Australia, 120
  history of, 117
  minimum wage, 117, 127, 137, 154, 159
wage-stop rule, 44
wages inspectorate, 137, 139, 140, 154
Weber, Max, 235
Widgery Committee, 87
widows, 38, 183, 223
women,
  discrimination against, 197
  social control of, 37, 193

work test, 39–40, 203
workhouses, 21, 41, 259
  as condition for poor relief, 41
  control of inmates, 21
  officials of, 22
  power of magistrates over, 21
  relief for children in, 349 n.175
  role of courts, 21
  as test of destitution, 42
Working Party on Vagrancy and Street
  Offences, 66
working to rule, 207
workmen's compensation, 289, 290